Keep this book. You will need it and use it throughout your career.

About the American Hotel & Motel Association (AH&MA)

Founded in 1910, AH&MA is the trade association representing the lodging industry in the United States. AH&MA is a federation of state lodging associations throughout the United States with 11,000 lodging properties worldwide as members. The association offers its members assistance with governmental affairs representation, communications, marketing, hospitality operations, training and education, technology issues, and more. For information, call 202-289-3100.

LODGING, the management magazine of AH&MA, is a "living textbook" for hospitality students that provides timely features, industry news, and vital lodging information. For information on subscriptions and student rates, call 202-289-3113.

About the Educational Institute of AH&MA (EI)

An affiliate of AH&MA, the Educational Institute is the world's largest source of quality training and educational materials for the lodging industry. EI develops textbooks and courses that are used in more than 1,200 colleges and universities worldwide, and also offers courses to individuals through its Distance Learning program. Hotels worldwide rely on EI for training resources that focus on every aspect of lodging operations. Industry-tested videos, CD-ROMs, seminars, and skills guides prepare employees at every skill level. EI also offers professional certification for the industry's top performers. For information about EI's products and services, call 800-349-0299 or 407-999-8100.

About the American Hotel Foundation (AHF)

An affiliate of AH&MA, the American Hotel Foundation provides financial support that enhances the stability, prosperity, and growth of the lodging industry through educational and research programs. AHF has awarded hundreds of thousands of dollars in scholarship funds for students pursuing higher education in hospitality management. AHF has also funded research projects on topics important to the industry, including occupational safety and health, turnover and diversity, and best practices in the U.S. lodging industry. For information, call 202-289-3100.

FOOD and BEVERAGE SERVICE

Educational Institute Courses

Introductory

INTRODUCTION TO THE HOSPITALITY INDUSTRY
Fourth Edition
Gerald W. Lattin

AN INTRODUCTION TO HOSPITALITY TODAY
Third Edition
Rocco M. Angelo, Andrew N. Vladimir

TOURISM AND THE HOSPITALITY INDUSTRY
Joseph D. Fridgen

Rooms Division

FRONT OFFICE PROCEDURES
Fifth Edition
Michael L. Kasavana, Richard M. Brooks

HOUSEKEEPING MANAGEMENT
Second Edition
Margaret M. Kappa, Aleta Nitschke, Patricia B. Schappert

Human Resources

HOSPITALITY SUPERVISION
Second Edition
Raphael R. Kavanaugh, Jack D. Ninemeier

HOSPITALITY INDUSTRY TRAINING
Second Edition
Lewis C. Forrest, Jr.

HUMAN RESOURCES MANAGEMENT
Second Edition
Robert H. Woods

INTERNATIONAL HUMAN RESOURCE MANAGEMENT IN THE HOSPITALITY INDUSTRY
Edited by Sybil M. Hofmann, Colin Johnson, and Michael M. Lefever

Marketing and Sales

MARKETING OF HOSPITALITY SERVICES
William Lazer, Roger Layton

HOSPITALITY SALES AND MARKETING
Third Edition
James R. Abbey

CONVENTION MANAGEMENT AND SERVICE
Fifth Edition
Milton T. Astroff, James R. Abbey

MARKETING IN THE HOSPITALITY INDUSTRY
Third Edition
Ronald A. Nykiel

Accounting

UNDERSTANDING HOSPITALITY ACCOUNTING I
Fourth Edition
Raymond Cote

UNDERSTANDING HOSPITALITY ACCOUNTING II
Third Edition
Raymond Cote

BASIC FINANCIAL ACCOUNTING FOR THE HOSPITALITY INDUSTRY
Second Edition
Raymond S. Schmidgall, James W. Damitio

MANAGERIAL ACCOUNTING FOR THE HOSPITALITY INDUSTRY
Fourth Edition
Raymond S. Schmidgall

Food and Beverage

FOOD AND BEVERAGE MANAGEMENT
Third Edition
Jack D. Ninemeier

QUALITY SANITATION MANAGEMENT
Ronald F. Cichy

FOOD PRODUCTION PRINCIPLES
Jerald W. Chesser

FOOD AND BEVERAGE SERVICE
Second Edition
Ronald F. Cichy, Paul E. Wise

HOSPITALITY PURCHASING MANAGEMENT
William P. Virts

BAR AND BEVERAGE MANAGEMENT
Lendal H. Kotschevar, Mary L. Tanke

FOOD AND BEVERAGE CONTROLS
Fourth Edition
Jack D. Ninemeier

General Hospitality Management

HOTEL/MOTEL SECURITY MANAGEMENT
Second Edition
Raymond C. Ellis, Jr., David M. Stipanuk

HOSPITALITY LAW
Third Edition
Jack P. Jefferies

RESORT MANAGEMENT
Second Edition
Chuck Y. Gee

INTERNATIONAL HOTEL MANAGEMENT
Chuck Y. Gee

HOSPITALITY INDUSTRY COMPUTER SYSTEMS
Third Edition
Michael L. Kasavana, John J. Cahill

MANAGING FOR QUALITY IN THE HOSPITALITY INDUSTRY
Robert H. Woods, Judy Z. King

CONTEMPORARY CLUB MANAGEMENT
Edited by Joe Perdue for the Club Managers Association of America

Engineering and Facilities Management

FACILITIES MANAGEMENT
David M. Stipanuk, Harold Roffman

HOSPITALITY INDUSTRY ENGINEERING SYSTEMS
Michael H. Redlin, David M. Stipanuk

HOSPITALITY ENERGY AND WATER MANAGEMENT
Second Edition
Robert E. Aulbach

FOOD and BEVERAGE SERVICE

Second Edition

Ronald F. Cichy, Ph.D., CHA
Paul E. Wise, CHA

Disclaimer

This publication is designed to provide accurate and authoritative information in regard to the subject matter covered. It is sold with the understanding that the publisher is not engaged in rendering legal, accounting, or other professional service. If legal advice or other expert assistance is required, the services of a competent professional person should be sought.

—*From the Declaration of Principles jointly adopted by the American Bar Association and a Committee of Publishers and Associations*

The authors, Ronald F. Cichy and Paul E. Wise, are solely responsible for the contents of this publication. All views expressed herein are solely those of the authors and do not necessarily reflect the views of the Educational Institute of the American Hotel & Motel Association (the Institute) or the American Hotel & Motel Association (AH&MA).

Nothing contained in this publication shall constitute a standard, an endorsement, or a recommendation of the Institute or AH&MA. The Institute and AH&MA disclaim any liability with respect to the use of any information, procedure, or product, or reliance thereon by any member of the hospitality industry.

2113 N. High Street
Lansing, Michigan 48906

The Educational Institute of the American Hotel & Motel Association is a nonprofit educational foundation.

Printed in the United States of America
6 7 8 9 10 04 03 02 01

ISBN 0-86612-095-5

Project Editors: George Glazer
Jim Purvis

Editors: Thaddeus Balivet
Robert Bittner

Contents

Congratulations. . .

You have a running start on a fast-track career!

Developed through the input of industry and academic experts, this course gives you the know-how hospitality employers demand. Upon course completion, you will earn the respected American Hotel & Motel Association certificate that ensures instant recognition worldwide. It is your link with the global hospitality industry.

You can use your AH&MA certificate to show that your learning experiences have bridged the gap between industry and academia. You will have proof that you have met industry-driven learning objectives and that you know how to apply your knowledge to actual hospitality work situations.

By earning your course certificate, you also take a step toward completing the highly respected learning programs—Certificates of Specialization, the Hospitality Operations Certificate, and the Hospitality Management Diploma—that raise your professional development to a higher level. Certificates from these programs greatly enhance your credentials, and a permanent record of your course and program completion is maintained by the Educational Institute.

We commend you for taking this important step. Turn to the Educational Institute for additional resources that will help you stay ahead of your competition.

Preface

The second edition of *Food and Beverage Service* is designed to show how managers can delight their increasingly sophisticated and demanding guests. In addition to the hard-earned money that guests spend in food service operations, they choose to spend a possession that is even more valuable: their time. The challenge facing food service managers and staff members is to create such a wonderful experience for guests that, even as they are leaving the food service operation, they are already deciding to return in the near future and bring friends. Delighting guests by providing them with excellent service creates guest loyalty and builds repeat business.

The objectives of this book are to show readers how food and beverage professionals can (1) use proven and innovative ways to deliver guest-driven service; (2) enhance value, build guest loyalty, and promote repeat business; and (3) continuously improve the process of providing excellent service to guests. Excellent service is created and delivered by leaders—at all levels of food service operations—who understand guest expectations and work diligently to meet or exceed them.

Part I of the book begins by constructing a framework for providing quality service to guests. Managers can help their organizations achieve success by understanding "moments of truth," training their staffs to deal with every moment of truth appropriately and graciously, and creating organizations that value both guests and staff members.

The menu affects every aspect of a food service operation. In many respects, the menu is an operation's mission statement. An understanding of menu planning, types of menus, menu design, and menu trends is critical to the delivery of guest-driven service. Dining service styles and procedures must be designed to help managers and staff members provide superior guest service. Proven and innovative strategies such as preshift meetings, suggestive selling, service guarantees, and team approaches to service also help operations provide superior service.

Beverage service procedures should be guest-focused. The techniques discussed for selling and serving alcoholic beverages, as well as for providing responsible beverage service, enhance the portfolio of services offered by a food and beverage operation. Service equipment and supplies are resources that must be employed to enhance the guest experience.

Thoughtful facility design produces guest-friendly dining areas, while harmonious decor assists in creating the right environment. Cleaning systems and procedures enhance the dining experience by providing guests with a comfortable environment in which to enjoy the operation's products and services. An understanding of sanitation, safety, security, health, and legal issues is critical for managers, who must prevent guest exposure to unsafe procedures and situations. The fundamental goal is to ensure that guest experiences are both safe and memorable.

Labor control is an important topic for managers, because of the labor-intensive nature of most food service operations. To develop an effective control system, managers must begin by defining or refining the type and quality of service their operations offer, keeping the requirements of guests in mind. Managers must then determine labor standards. Revenue control systems, both manual and computer-based, are designed to help operations maximize revenue.

Various categories of food and beverage operations are presented in Part II of the book, including casual/theme restaurants, banquets and catered events, room service, and on-site operations. Each category's chapter begins with a marketing perspective focused on value. Procedures for getting ready for service are then presented. Next, the delivery of service is discussed, with a clear focus on the unique features of the food service operation under analysis. Finally, the activities that take place after service, including those that help managers evaluate and continuously improve service, are detailed.

Acknowledgments

We would like to acknowledge the contributions of many individuals and organizations who helped us prepare this book. Students and instructors at both two-year and four-year hospitality institutions provided valuable feedback regarding ways to improve the book's first edition, and many of their suggestions are incorporated into this new edition. Scores of industry experts provided useful input as well. We especially would like to acknowledge the industry professionals who helped generate and develop the real-world case studies that appear in the second edition: David Brown, CCM, General Manager, The Heritage Club, Mason, Ohio; Christopher Kibit, C.S.C., Academic Team Leader, Hotel/Motel/Food Management & Tourism Programs, Lansing Community College, Lansing, Michigan; Jack Nye, General Manager, Applebee's of Michigan, Applebee's International, Inc.; Timothy J. Pugh, Regional Manager, Damon's—The Place for Ribs (Steve Montanye Enterprises, East Lansing, Michigan); Lawrence E. Ross, Assistant Professor, Florida Southern College, and owner of Sago Grill, Lakeland, Florida; and Sara J. Shaughnessy, Clubhouse Manager, Somerset Country Club, Mendota Heights, Minnesota.

Research assistants for this book included Robert Emerson, who did a great job of finding reference materials, and Larry Kaplan, who served as a student research assistant. Bridget Swan word-processed the original manuscript, and her contribution is greatly appreciated. We also wish to thank the dedicated members of the editorial and production team at the Educational Institute, and specifically Writer/Editor Jim Purvis, for their perseverance and tenacity in taking this project from manuscript to completed work.

Lastly, we'd like to dedicate *Food and Beverage Service* to our mothers, our wives, and our children. Abraham Lincoln is quoted as saying: "All that I am and all that I hope to be, I owe to my mother." Early in our lives, our mothers taught us the fundamentals of service by meeting our every need. In turn, our mothers, our wives, and our children have given us countless opportunities to serve them in kind and patient ways and attempt to exceed their expectations. Our families have had a tremendous impact on shaping our philosophy of guest-driven service, and for that, we thank them.

Ronald F. Cichy
Okemos, Michigan

Paul E. Wise
Newark, Delaware

About the Authors

Ronald F. Cichy is the Director of and a Professor within *The* School of Hospitality Business at Michigan State University. Previously, he was the Director of Educational Services for the Educational Institute of the American Hotel & Motel Association. Dr. Cichy has also served on the faculties of the University of Denver and Lansing Community College. He has earned a Ph.D. from MSU's Department of Food Science and Human Nutrition, and an MBA and a BA from the university's School of Hotel, Restaurant and Institutional Management.

Dr. Cichy earned the designations of Certified Food and Beverage Executive (CFBE) and Certified Hotel Administrator (CHA) from the Educational Institute in 1983, and the Certified Hospitality Educator (CHE) designation in 1992. In 1996 he was named an Outstanding Alumnus by MSU's College of Human Ecology. His industry experience includes positions in lodging and food service operations as a hotel manager, food and beverage manager, banquet chef, and sales representative.

Dr. Cichy has written more than 125 articles for food service and lodging audiences. In addition to co-authoring *Food and Beverage Service,* he is the author of *The Spirit of Hospitality* and *Quality Sanitation Management,* and is the co-author, with Dr. Lewis J. Minor, of *Foodservice Systems Management.*

Active professionally, Dr. Cichy is Vice Chairman-Academia of the Educational Institute's Board of Trustees, serves on the Institute's Executive Committee, and is a member of the Institute's Presidents Academy Board of Regents. He is a member of the Board of Directors of the Michigan Restaurant Association and the Michigan Hotel, Motel and Resort Association. He has served as a consultant for lodging and food service operations, and has traveled extensively throughout the United States, Australia, Canada, Europe, and Japan to conduct training programs, present seminars, and participate in conferences.

Paul E. Wise is the Founding Director and a Professor of the University of Delaware's Hotel, Restaurant and Institutional Management program and serves as the program's Department Chair. He graduated from Penn State University with a BS degree in Hotel, Restaurant and Institutional Management and later received his MBA from Michigan State University in Food Marketing. Professor Wise has operated restaurants and clubs in Pennsylvania, Panama, and Alaska, and has taught club management for Army and Air Force club managers at Fort Lee, Virginia. During the last ten years of his association with the military, he was responsible for the operation of 670 Army clubs and hotels that produced annual revenues of over $300 million.

Professor Wise is active in numerous hotel and restaurant associations. He currently serves as Vice Chairman of the Greater Wilmington Convention and Visitors Bureau and as a member of the Delaware Restaurant Association's Board of Directors. He is designated by the American Hotel & Motel Association as a Certified Hotel Administrator (CHA) and as a Certified Catering Executive (CCE) by the National Association of Catering Executives. He was chosen as the 1988 Pennsylvania State University Hotel and Restaurant Society Alumnus of the Year and was inducted into the International Military Club Executive Association Hall of Fame. In 1992 he received the Educational Institute's Lamp of Knowledge award, in the "Outstanding Educator—Four-Year School" category, for his efforts to help the Institute better serve the needs of educators. He currently serves on the Certification Commission and Education Committee of the Institute, and is a member of the Institute's Board of Trustees. Professor Wise has also served as a consultant and speaker to numerous corporations and associations.

Study Tips for Users of Educational Institute Courses

Learning is a skill, like many other activities. Although you may be familiar with many of the following study tips, we want to reinforce their usefulness.

Your Attitude Makes a Difference

If you want to learn, you will: it's as simple as that. Your attitude will go a long way in determining whether or not you do well in this course. We want to help you succeed.

Plan and Organize to Learn

- Set up a regular time and place for study. Make sure you won't be disturbed or distracted.
- Decide ahead of time how much you want to accomplish during each study session. Remember to keep your study sessions brief; don't try to do too much at one time.

Read the Course Text to Learn

- *Before* you read each chapter, read the chapter outline and competencies.
- Then, go back to the beginning of the chapter and *carefully* read, focusing on the material included in the competencies and asking yourself such questions as:

  —Do I understand the material?

  —How can I use this information now or in the future?
- Make notes in margins and highlight or underline important sections to help you as you study. Read a section first, then go back over it to mark important points.
- Keep a dictionary handy. If you come across an unfamiliar word that is not included in the "Key Term" section, look it up in the dictionary.
- Read as much as you can. The more you read, the better you read.

Testing Your Knowledge

- Test questions developed by the Educational Institute for this course are designed to measure your knowledge of the material.
- End-of-the-chapter Review Quizzes help you find out how well you have studied the material. They indicate where additional study may be needed. Review Quizzes are also helpful in studying for other tests.

- Prepare for tests by reviewing:

  —competencies

  —notes

  —outlines

  —questions at the end of each assignment

- As you begin to take any test, read the test instructions *carefully* and look over the questions.

We hope your experiences in this course will prompt you to undertake other training and educational activities in a planned, career-long program of professional growth and development.

Part I

Chapter 1 Outline

Guests and Moments of Truth
- The Value of Guests
- The Cost of Guest Dissatisfaction

Managers as Leaders
- Attributes of Leaders

Staff Members: Keys to Success
- The Value of Staff Members
- The Cost of Staff Dissatisfaction
- Staff Members' Perceptions of the Value of Their Work
- Recruiting Staff Members
- Selecting Staff Members
- Orientation of Staff Members
- Training Staff Members

Competencies

1. Define "moment of truth" and explain how this concept affects guests, staff members, and managers; explain the value of guests to a food service organization; and describe the cost of guest dissatisfaction and how it can be calculated.
2. Explain what impact the "moments of truth" concept has had on food service managers, and summarize leadership attributes that food service managers should have in the new service environment of empowered staff members.
3. Explain the value of staff members to a food service organization; describe the cost of staff dissatisfaction and how it can be calculated; explain the concept of "internal moments of truth"; and summarize issues food service managers must face when recruiting, selecting, orienting, and training staff members.

1

Service Management and Leadership

COMPANIES IN THE SERVICE SECTOR of the global economy are changing in response to external as well as internal forces. External forces include the economy (both domestic and international), technology, social changes, demographics, culture, politics, legal changes, and competition. Internal forces include a company's culture, guests or customers, staff members, managers, products, services, markets, technological resources, mission, values, and vision.

Consider that, in the United States, approximately 45 million people (roughly 42 percent of the workforce) are employed in various service industries. These industries provided the majority of U.S. job growth in the 1980s. Yet both external and internal forces are at work to change the ways that service is planned, managed, delivered, and evaluated.

One of the biggest forces driving change in the service sector is the customer. Today's customers are sophisticated, demanding, and vote with their cash, checks, or credit cards for companies that provide service that meets or exceeds expectations. Customers are likely to ignore brand or company loyalty and spend their money for products and services offered by whatever company provides hassle-free, above-average service. In short, today's customers seek *value.* They find value when the products and services they receive consistently meet or exceed their expectations and can be purchased at an acceptable price.

Providing the highest possible quality at acceptable prices is a formula for success for companies in any part of the service sector; certainly food service companies are no exception. On the other hand, low quality at an unacceptable price is a business strategy for failure. In the 1950s and '60s, U.S. automobile companies took advantage of a tide of high demand and low supply and got away with providing low levels of quality at high prices. In the 1970s, however, Japanese automakers introduced cars to U.S. markets that had significantly higher levels of quality and significantly lower prices than U.S. cars. Consumers responded, and in a few short years seeing a Japanese car on American roads went from a very rare to a very common occurrence. It took almost twenty years for U.S. auto manufacturers to begin recovering market share by following suit and providing better value for their customers.

Business *survival* depends on providing value for customers; business *success* depends on increasing your customers' perceptions of the value you are providing to them. How, when, and where can you make your customers aware of the value you provide? By properly handling "moments of truth" with them. For today's food service managers, one of the keys to success is understanding how moments of truth affect service strategies and create new management responsibilities.

We will talk about the importance of moments of truth—"the basic atoms of service"—throughout the chapter. First we will examine the impact moments of truth have on guests. Then we will discuss what impact the necessity to manage for moments of truth has had on food service managers. We will conclude the chapter with a section on staff members, during which the importance of moments of truth with guests and internal moments of truth with co-workers will be discussed, interweaved with other topics such as recruiting, selecting, orienting, and training. As you will see, moments of truth are where the sometimes conflicting needs and goals of guests, managers, and staff members intersect.

Guests and Moments of Truth

Jan Carlzon, president of Scandinavian Airlines System (SAS), reversed an $8 million loss for SAS into a gross profit of $71 million in a little over a year. In explaining how he was able to perform this fantastic turnaround, he coined the term "moments of truth." For Carlzon, a **moment of truth** is "any episode in which a customer comes into contact with any aspect of the company, however remote, and thereby has an opportunity to form an impression." Carlzon went on to say that "we have 50,000 moments of truth out there every day."

While Carlzon coined the term, authors Karl Albrecht and Ron Zemke forged the moments-of-truth concept into a revolutionary approach to service management. They emphasized that the moments of truth a customer experiences with a company form a continuous chain of events that builds the customer's perception of value. In this sense, a moment of truth becomes "the basic atom of service, the smallest indivisible unit of value delivered to the customer."

It is not humanly possible for food service managers to directly influence a positive outcome in the thousands of moments of truth that occur each day in their organizations. However, managers can create a guest-driven organizational culture and provide systems for delivering service that are guest and staff friendly.

For food service staff members to deliver optimum guest service, they must understand the fundamental truths that serving guests is the reason for the existence of their organizations—and the existence of their jobs. In a restaurant, or any other food service organization, if you are not directly serving the needs of a guest, you should be serving the needs of someone who *is* directly serving the guest. Food and beverage servers experience hundreds if not thousands of moments of truth in their one-on-one interactions with guests during a single shift. By contrast, a chef may have little one-on-one contact with guests; however, the chef helps the food servers provide excellent guest service by preparing menu items correctly and on time.

Positive moments of truth result in guests having a delightful experience at a restaurant, which can lead to many repeat guests and an excellent reputation for the restaurant. Negative moments of truth can ruin the service experience of guests. Consider the following story:

A party of eight arrives at a restaurant near closing time on a busy Saturday night. This group of guests had to walk through an inadequately lighted parking lot after parking in the "back forty" near the perimeter of the lot. After being greeted by the hostess, the party's host is informed that there is no record of his reservation and that a table will not be ready for another 20 minutes. The guests are directed to the lounge where, after a 10-minute wait, they are served drinks without cocktail napkins and are informed that they can't run a tab—they have to pay cash for their drinks.

After another 15 minutes, the host's name is announced—but mispronounced—over the public address system. The party of eight is seated at a table with a torn table cover and spotted flatware near the noisy entrance to the kitchen. The menu print is too small for one of the party to read. She asks the server what he recommends and he says that "everything is good here." Another in the party asks about heart-healthy menu items because he is on a restricted diet. The server flippantly replies that "any menu item can be made heart-healthy by the chef—he can wave his 'magic spoon' over the item to remove the 'bad things' before it leaves the kitchen."

While taking their orders, the server rushes the guests and is visibly irritated when he has to repeat items (choice of salad dressings, choice of potatoes) several times, because various members of the party are engaged in a number of side conversations. Before returning his menu to the server, the host notices that there is a statement printed on the menu in bold-face type that reads: "A 15 percent service charge is added to all parties of eight or more."

About five minutes after taking the order, the server returns to the table and announces to three of the guests that the "fresh fish catch of the day" that they ordered is sold out; he recommends that they order the prime rib instead. Two of the guests order a different fish entrée that the server implies is fresh when it is really frozen; the third orders the prime rib, medium rare. The server nods without comment and heads for the kitchen.

By the time the server returns with the salads and the bread, the salads are at room temperature. It is fortunate that the "freshly baked" bread is served with a serrated knife; otherwise, it would be impossible to cut. The butter is so hard that it tears the bread when guests try to spread it on their bread slices. When the entrées arrive, they are all garnished with a spiced apple ring on a lettuce leaf. The fish entrées are also garnished with slices of lemon too thin to squeeze. The prime rib is medium well and, when the person who ordered it questions the server, she is informed that it is late and that is the rarest that the kitchen had available. No offer is made to allow the guest to select an alternative entrée. All who ordered baked potatoes receive them wrapped in aluminum foil without sour cream. When two guests request sour cream, the server informs them there will be an extra charge. The pasta billed as "heart-healthy" arrives swimming in butter. The server simply asks "Does anyone need anything right now?" and leaves the table.

The topic of dinner conversation centers on each guest's dissatisfaction with the meal. One comment fuels another and so it goes throughout dinner. By the end of the entrées, it is clear that no one in the party is satisfied. While clearing the entrée plates, the server communicates with his body language a loud and clear message,

"Okay, I've served you. Now it's time for you to leave so I can clean up and go home." Then one of the guests, followed by several others, has the courage to order decaffeinated coffee. Another asks about the dessert menu and is told by the server that "I'll have to check what's left—it's been a busy night."

When the coffee is delivered, one guest requests cream but none is brought. Three guests order dessert and share the desserts with others at the table. When the check arrives, the host notices the 15 percent service charge and an additional $1 per person charge for those who shared but did not order dessert. By now the host is fuming and asks to see the manager, whom he knows from the local Rotary Club.

When the manager arrives and the host finishes with his long list of complaints, the manager explains away the problems by saying that the server is new, then sends a complimentary round of after-dinner drinks to the party. Just before the drinks are delivered, the dishwasher arrives to mop the floor in the side stand next to the party's table.

Is this story exaggerated? Perhaps, although on any given night in restaurants across the country, each and every one of these moments of truth could happen in exactly the way described. How many negative moments of truth were there in this story? There were at least 33:

1. Inadequately lighted parking lot.
2. Guests had to park far from the restaurant's entrance.
3. No record of the host's reservation.
4. The party is told it will have to wait 20 minutes for a table.
5. There is a 10-minute wait in the lounge before drinks are served.
6. Drinks are served without cocktail napkins.
7. The guests are told that they can't run a tab (which would be the most convenient for them); instead, they have to pay cash.
8. The party has to wait 25 minutes for a table, not the promised 20.
9. The host's name is mispronounced over the public address system.
10. The table cover is torn.
11. The flatware is spotted.
12. The party is seated near the noisy kitchen entrance.
13. The print on the menu is small.
14. "Everything is good here" is not really a recommendation.
15. The server flippantly tells the health-conscious guest that the chef's "magic spoon" can make anything heart-healthy.
16. The server rushes the guests as they are giving their orders.
17. The server lets his irritation about having to repeat some menu selections show to guests.
18. A 15-percent service charge is imposed.

19. The "catch of the day" is sold out.
20. The server implies that the fish entrée is fresh when it is really frozen.
21. The salads are served at room temperature.
22. Both the bread and the butter are unacceptably hard.
23. All of the entrées have the same boring garnishes.
24. The fish entrées also have unusable lemon slices.
25. Medium-well prime rib is served instead of what was ordered—"medium rare"—and no alternative is offered to the guest.
26. Guests are charged extra for sour cream.
27. "Heart-healthy" pasta is swimming in butter.
28. The server provides rude service with a "hurry up and leave" attitude at the end of the meal.
29. The server constantly drops reminders to guests that "it's been a busy night."
30. The server forgets to bring the cream guests requested for their coffee.
31. Guests have to pay an additional charge for sharing desserts, and they were not informed of this fact by the server.
32. The manager blames everything on the "new" server.
33. The floor is mopped in full view of the party.

No one won in this service experience. The guests lost because their expectations were not exceeded or even met; the server lost because his tip was probably small and he was exposed to the displeasure of unhappy guests; the restaurant lost because none of the guests will be eager to return. In addition, these guests are likely to tell others about their bad experience. Given a party of 8 and 33 negative moments of truth, the total number of negative moments of truth personally experienced or witnessed by these guests was 264 (8 × 33). Studies have shown that the average guest who has a complaint tells 8 to 10 people. Translating those averages back to the figures for this scenario, 64 to 80 people may hear about this service fiasco.

It doesn't have to take 33 negative moments of truth to turn off a guest—sometimes it only takes one. Therefore, it's vitally important that each moment of truth be dealt with successfully by staff members. If moments of truth are not handled correctly, guests are not likely to come back, and few restaurants can survive long without a substantial number of repeat guests. Survival and success depend more on retaining guests by providing them with quality service than on continually attracting new guests with costly promotions and sales blitzes.

The Value of Guests

What is the value of a loyal guest? One way of answering this question is to think of the "present value" of a guest as the first-time sale you make to him or her, and the "future value" of the same guest as the revenue potential from that guest over a

Exhibit 1 The Value of a Repeat Dinner Guest

Type of Restaurant	Check Average	Meals per Month	Revenue Potential 1 Month	1 Year	5 Years
Quick Service	$4.50	3	$13.50	$162	$810
Casual/Theme	$12.00	2	$24.00	$288	$1,440
Upscale	$35.00	1	$35.00	$420	$2,100

Note: The check averages and dining frequencies used in this exhibit are for illustrative purposes only and are not meant to reflect local, regional, or national statistics.

specified period of time. Exhibit 1 shows the monthly, one-year, and five-year revenue potential of a dinner guest for three different restaurant segments. The exhibit's calculations drive home the fact that when guests walk through the door of a restaurant, they bring with them the potential for a sizable future revenue stream for the restaurant.

Using a specific dollar amount when communicating the potential value of a guest can help managers emphasize to staff members just how potentially valuable each guest is. Phil Bressler, the co-owner of five Domino's Pizza stores in Montgomery County, Maryland, calculated that regular customers were worth more than $5,000 over the life of a ten-year franchise contract. He made sure that every order taker, delivery person, and store manager knew that number. For him, telling staff members that customers were valuable was not nearly as potent as stating a specific dollar amount: "It's so much more than they think that it really hits home."

The figures in Exhibit 1 actually understate the value of a guest. The revenue potential of a loyal guest also includes the new business that he or she brings to the organization through positive word-of-mouth referrals. In addition, recent research into service-related businesses strongly suggests that revenue and profitability are higher for purchases made by repeat guests than for purchases made by first-time or one-time guests.

The Cost of Guest Dissatisfaction

The potential value of guests demonstrates that when dissatisfied guests walk out the door, they take with them a sizable chunk of future business. Also, the total amount of future business at risk increases in relation to the negative impressions about the business that dissatisfied guests pass on to others. As noted earlier, studies indicate that the average dissatisfied guest tells 8 to 10 people about his or her problems with a business; 1 out of every 5 dissatisfied guests tells 20 people.

Working with these estimates, let's assume that one dissatisfied guest tells ten people about the poor service he or she experienced at a local restaurant. Let's also assume that only three of these ten people have the same dining habits as the dissatisfied guest, and that all four of them (the dissatisfied guest and the three people he or she talked to who have the same dining habits) do not eat at the restaurant for

Exhibit 2 Pattern of Lost Business—100 Dissatisfied Guests

Out of 100 dissatisfied guests:

40 never ask for help.
They tell 8–10 potential guests about their problems.

60 ask for help.
7 out of ten guests will do business with you again if you resolve the problems in their favor.

Of the 60 guests that ask for help:

18 are never helped.
They tell 8–10 potential guests about their problems.

42 are offered assistance.
95% of complaining guests will do business with you again if you resolve their problems immediately.

Of the 42 guests who are offered assistance:

13 remain dissatisfied.
They tell 8–10 potential guests about their problems.

29 become satisfied as their problems are resolved.
They will tell 5 potential guests about how the staff helped to resolve their problems.

The Bottom Line:

71 of 100 dissatisfied guests tell 568–710 potential guests about their problems.

29 of 100 dissatisfied guests tell 145 potential guests that their problems were resolved.

six months. The total lost revenue potential from a single dissatisfied guest for the restaurants shown in Exhibit 1 would be $324 for the quick-service (also referred to as fast-food) operation (4 guests × $13.50 [one month's potential revenue per guest] × 6 months = $324), $576 for the casual/theme restaurant, and $840 for the upscale restaurant. Lost revenue escalates further when you factor in the likelihood that few guests dine alone. Not many restaurants have enough marketing resources to continually drum up enough new business to offset the lost revenue potential from dissatisfied parties of two, three, four, or more.

Research conducted by major hotel chains suggests that one out of every seven guests at a hotel experiences a service-related problem that is serious enough to cause that guest not to return. This is a defection rate of 14%. A **defection rate** captures the percentage of guests lost to competitors because of service-related problems. Based on the same research, Exhibit 2 shows what typically happens to 100 dissatisfied guests. As you can see, hotel employees succeed only 29% of the time in transforming a dissatisfied guest into a satisfied one, and many more people hear about unresolved problems than hear about instances in which the hotel successfully handles a problem. The research also revealed that 4 out of 10 dissatisfied guests never ask for help. In these instances, managers may not even be aware that there are problems that should be addressed!

Exhibit 3 The Point of Guest Contact

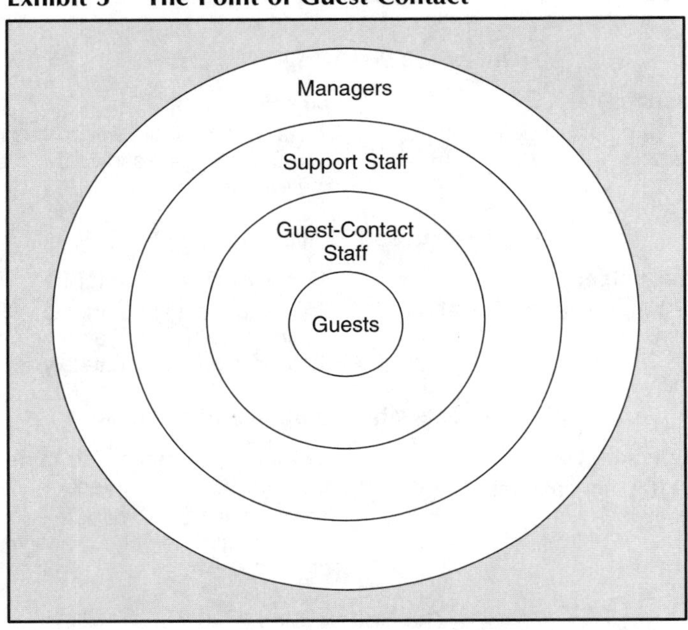

While it may not be possible to resolve the problems of every dissatisfied guest, the value of each guest—and the cost of guest dissatisfaction in lost revenue and negative comments to potential guests—clearly justifies the effort to do just that. Of course, a restaurant should strive to never have dissatisfied guests in the first place.

Managers as Leaders

Since value for guests and profits for the restaurant depend on the restaurant's managers and staff members successfully handling moments of truth, the primary challenge for a restaurant's managers is to create an organizational culture that places a high priority on providing quality service to guests. A hallmark of such a culture is that each manager and staff member realizes the contribution to guest satisfaction that he or she makes at each moment of truth.

Within an organizational culture that emphasizes quality service, the act of managing itself becomes a form of service: managers serve the restaurant's staff members who, in turn, serve guests. (To repeat: If you are not directly serving a customer, you should be serving someone who is.) Exhibit 3 is a diagram that shows the relationships among guests, staff members, and managers during a typical point of guest contact. This diagram illustrates that managers are often absent from many "guest contact" moments or moments of truth. In the face of this reality, managers have two choices: they can attempt to be present at each moment of truth to make sure that it is handled correctly, or they can train and empower staff members to successfully handle these moments.

As mentioned earlier, the sheer number of moments of truth that occur at a typical restaurant make the first option impossible for managers, as any veteran restaurant manager would immediately recognize. For example, let's say that a restaurant's general manager has identified 39 moments of truth in a typical guest's visit to the restaurant. If the restaurant serves an average of 400 guests per meal period, the restaurant averages 15,600 moments of truth per meal period, or 46,800 per day (given three meal periods) and 17,082,000 moments of truth a year! While some restaurants may identify more than 39 moments of truth per guest and others less, the fact remains that the number of moments of truth is enormous for any restaurant. Managers cannot be everywhere at once, peering over the shoulders of staff members, policing procedures, and supervising behaviors. In a service-driven organization, the most important decisions and actions of managers are those that help staff members become more effective at managing moments of truth on their own. The traditional management functions of directing, controlling, and commanding give way to the new management responsibilities of empowering, enabling, and supporting.

The term "empowerment" is a frequently used and abused buzzword. For the purposes of this chapter, we are defining **empowerment** as "the redistribution of power within an organization enabling managers, supervisors, and staff members to perform their jobs more efficiently and effectively." The overall goal of empowerment is to enhance service to guests and increase profits for the organization by releasing decision-making responsibility, authority, and accountability to every level within the organization.

Managers "enable" their staff members by providing the training necessary to help them become competent in performing the fundamental tasks of their jobs. Training is absolutely fundamental to quality service and is most effective when it provides staff members with the "why" behind the "how-to" of their jobs; staff members need to know how they create value for guests.

Managers support their staff members by backing up the good decisions and actions they take on the front lines, serving guests as best they can at each moment of truth. If a staff member makes a truly bad service choice—not just a choice that was effective but happened to be different from what the manager would have done—the manager will have to call the staff member's attention to the mistake, but can still show support by coaching the staff member and providing retraining if necessary.

To carry out their empowering responsibilities, managers must influence individual staff members to accept greater personal responsibility and exercise more control over the way they perform their jobs. However, before exercising more control over their jobs, staff members will want assurances from their manager that the organization values their ideas, has confidence in their judgment, and will support their efforts.

In trying to create a robust service culture in which staff members are empowered to successfully handle moments of truth, many food service managers find themselves lost in a bewildering maze of contradictory functions and roles. Exhibit 4 outlines some of the seemingly contradictory responsibilities that managers need to balance. It's important for managers to continue to do things right, but they

Exhibit 4 Balancing Management and Leadership

The Focus of Management	The Vision of Leadership
Do things right	Do the right things
Direct operations	Monitor guest expectations
Enforce policies and rules	Communicate vision and values
Design procedures and tasks	Manage systems and processes
Control results	Support people
Foster stability	Engage in continuous improvement

must constantly ask themselves whether they are doing the right things. Managers direct operations, but they learn what to direct and how to direct by monitoring guest expectations. Managers must enforce policies and rules, but they must create within their staffs an understanding of "Why these particular policies?" and "Why these particular rules?" by communicating a vision of the organization and the values that drive that vision. Managers must work with their staffs to design procedures and tasks in their areas, but they must also manage the broader systems and processes of which those procedures and tasks are a part. Managers are directly responsible for the results of their operational areas, but they achieve results largely indirectly, by supporting the efforts of staff members. Managers are responsible for fostering stability within their areas, but stability does not necessarily mean preserving the status quo—it can very well mean creating a learning environment by fostering change and engaging in continuous improvement efforts.

While there are no easy answers to the challenges food service managers face, a new direction for managers is emerging from the practices of today's successful food service organizations. These practices encourage managers to find a balance between managing their operations using traditional management tools and leading their staff members using the new management tools of empowerment and coaching.

Attributes of Leaders

A manager's leadership role takes on vital importance in the new service environment of empowered staff members. Today's managers must lead more by example and less by simply commanding and directing. To lead by example, managers must develop qualities within themselves that will help them do a better job of managing and inspire staff members to also perform better at their jobs.

While there has been much written about business leadership in general, substantially less is available specific to the food service industry. Most of the recent leadership studies of the hospitality industry have been conducted by faculty researchers in *The* School of Hospitality Business at Michigan State University. Material in this section is adapted from these studies.

CEOs and presidents of U.S. and Japanese food service organizations that participated in the Michigan State studies indicated that effective leaders:

- Provide a compelling message or vision
- Have a strong personal value or belief system
- Recognize that the ability to adjust is a necessity
- Listen as well as, if not better than, they speak
- Know their strengths and nurture them
- Trust their staff members

These CEOs and presidents indicated that leaders should possess the following characteristics:

- Credibility
- Dependability
- Self-confidence
- Emotional stamina
- Courage

Then the CEOs and presidents were asked the following open-ended question: "If you could give *one* piece of advice to someone who wanted to be a leader like you, what would you say?" In the following sections, their responses are organized into six categories: vision, communication, trust, perseverance, education, and self-awareness.

Vision. A food service manager who wants to be a good leader should develop a clear vision for the organization and base goals, objectives, and plans on that vision. A leader must believe in what he or she is doing and convince others to believe in it, too.

"Dare to be you—set a vision and go after it with all of your energy," advised one CEO. Managers must believe in their goals because commitment is contagious. Current leaders in the food service industry in Japan suggested that vision and humility should be blended: "Keep your vision high, yet keep your head low." A humble, mature-acting manager can do a better job of leading than an arrogant, immature manager. A leader must work to accomplish his or her vision for the organization with passion and persistence.

Communication. Communication is more than simply speaking. First and foremost, communication is listening. "Listen to your people, trust them, and let them take chances," advised one study participant. Leaders should listen and act on what they hear from guests and staff members. It is critical that a manager communicate the big picture, because everyone in the organization wants to know where the organization is going.

Trust. Wise managers develop trust-based relationships with all of their associates. One CEO suggested that "from self-esteem comes trust, from trust comes commitment, and from commitment comes performance. Nothing else will work." Good managers allow people the opportunity to do their jobs and grow in their careers. They let staff members share in the fun, the glory, and the defeats.

Japanese food service leaders stressed that trust is built and reinforced by supporting staff members and encouraging them to make their own decisions. Managers must always be ethical and display understanding and compassion for other human beings—that's how trust is nurtured. An important element of leadership is credibility and honesty. Managers should keep in mind that credibility is much easier kept than recovered. Managers who want to be effective leaders are role models for others in the organization.

Perseverance. Perseverance is a trademark of managers who make a positive difference. To be good leaders, managers must be fully committed to their cause, have a plan, communicate it, and stick with it. Moreover, managers must be honest with themselves and stand by their personal convictions. Good managers are known for digging in, getting involved, being competitive, and working to achieve goals. A manager's commitment to the organization can kindle commitment from others.

The presidents and CEOs surveyed in the studies reminded managers that success is the process of learning to "fail forward." If at first you don't succeed, learn from your mistakes and succeed the second time. Good managers work hard, believe in themselves, create opportunities, and stay after their goals.

Education. Managers who want to be good leaders should never stop learning—a leader can never know enough. New knowledge should be shared with others in the organization. "Look, listen, learn, and communicate" is what one CEO advised. Another challenged managers to enjoy and distribute knowledge, never to waste or hoard it.

Managers who want to be good leaders should learn as much as possible about their business. They should also develop a well-rounded education.

Self-Awareness. Japanese food service leaders were unique in stressing that, to be a good leader, a manager must build self-awareness. They advised managers to be honest with themselves, and stated that leadership in any setting is first, foremost, and always an inner quest. An analysis of self helps a leader to be more effective in achieving an organization's goals. Self-awareness is improved when an individual continuously evaluates inner feelings and motivations.

Many leadership-development programs in Japan foster self-awareness. Mikasa, a leading restaurant in Tokyo, has introduced the Zen meditation system as part of its leadership-development program. The restaurant even has its own meditation room for staff members and managers.

Staff Members: Keys to Success

Staff members are the individuals managers must lead wisely and well if their food service organizations are to be ideally successful. A motivated staff is the key to success in any food service setting.

The Value of Staff Members

Staff members are just as valuable as guests, in the sense that, without them, the restaurant fails: if there is no one to perform the work, no work gets done, nothing of value is produced, no guests come, and the restaurant must close its doors. In a strictly economic sense, the value of staff members is reflected in the wages and benefits managers pay them for their work. But in the context of quality service—that is, in the sense of consistently meeting or exceeding guest expectations—their true value is in their ability to keep guests coming back by providing excellent service during moments of truth.

A staff's performance during moments of truth can be seen as a product of the combination of staff members' personal resources and the organizational resources of the company. The personal resources of a staff member include everything that the individual brings to the task of consistently meeting or exceeding guest expectations. These resources include personality, character, life values, thoughts, feelings, and more. Organizational resources include everything provided by the company for the staff to consistently meet or exceed guest expectations. Typical types of organizational resources include:

- Physical facilities
- Technological systems
- Workplace design
- Training systems

By themselves, these organizational resources do not create value for guests. A food service organization can have the best facilities, state-of-the-art technology, the most efficiently designed work areas, and the most well-intentioned training systems, but it is the performance of staff members that determines whether these resources actually produce value for guests.

To do a good job when handling moments of truth, staff members must merge the organizational resources provided by the company with their unique talents as individuals. Without the contribution of personal resources from staff members, guest expectations are rarely exceeded—in fact, they might not even be met.

For example, consider your own experiences as a restaurant guest when servers begin reciting the "daily specials." The job task is to suggest menu options that might appeal to you and increase revenues for the restaurant. It's all too obvious when a server performs this task with minimal involvement and commitment of personal resources. The presentation becomes a memorized script delivered as fast and as colorlessly as possible by servers who are bored by the monotony of their own performances. Information is communicated to you, but chances are good that the actual message you receive may be something like this: "Reciting daily specials is just part of my job here. It's a necessary evil, a nuisance, an annoyance to everyone. But now it's done. So, what do you want to order?"

You may also have experienced situations in which servers presented the daily specials in an effortless, enthusiastic, and genuinely helpful manner. Sometimes, a server is so talented that letting you know about the daily specials becomes seamlessly woven into the overall welcoming experience you feel at the restaurant. This kind of delivery cannot be drilled into the serving staff during a training session or at a five-minute, pre-shift line-up meeting. It flows from the personal resources of the server, from the individual's talent at blending his or her performance with an organizational resource—daily specials.

Exhibit 5 Direct Costs of Staff Turnover

Termination Costs:

- Severance pay
- Additional FICA and unemployment insurance payments
- Wages and overhead related to recordkeeping and conducting exit interviews
- Overtime pay to cover for open positions

Recruitment and Selection Costs:

- Advertisements for open positions
- Fees paid to employment agencies
- Wages and overhead related to processing employment applications, interviewing job applicants, and checking applicant references

One of the roles of managers as leaders is to encourage their staffs to tap into their current personal resources when performing their jobs. Managers should also encourage staff members to develop new talents that can help them perform their jobs even better. Food service managers maximize the value of their staffs by improving the organizational resources available to staff members and by fostering, encouraging, and rewarding the personal contributions made by staff members in the performance of their jobs.

The Cost of Staff Dissatisfaction

Few food service organizations can succeed without a loyal, satisfied staff. Just as it is much easier for a restaurant to be successful if it retains loyal guests rather than expends the time and energy to replace dissatisfied guests with a constant stream of new ones, so too is it better for a restaurant to develop and retain a committed and productive staff than to manage a revolving door of terminated staff members and new-hires.

The first cost of staff dissatisfaction to consider is lost business. A dissatisfied staff leads to botched moments of truth and other service-related problems for guests, which can lead to guests taking their business elsewhere. A creative way to measure how staff dissatisfaction contributes to lost business is to compare a company's staff **turnover rate** to the company's guest defection rate. This is what Taco Bell did when it examined turnover records for its restaurants. The company found that the 20% of its restaurants with the lowest turnover rates had double the sales and 55% higher profits than the 20% of its restaurants with the company's highest turnover rates. This discovery led Taco Bell to fix the turnover problems at the under-performing restaurants, which not only increased sales but profitability too.

The second area to consider in relation to the cost of staff dissatisfaction is the direct cost of staff turnover, such as termination, recruitment, and selection costs (see Exhibit 5). Additional, indirect costs associated with turnover are not as easily determined, but they exist nevertheless. These costs include the usually low productivity of new staff members and other effects that relate to turnover, such as more waste and more work accidents.

Each restaurant should calculate its own turnover costs. These costs can vary tremendously from restaurant to restaurant and across the various segments of the food service industry. At some restaurants, the cost of turning over a single staff-member position can range from $900 to $4,500. The cost to replace a manager can be three times that amount. Expenses saved by reducing turnover drop these dollars directly to the restaurant's bottom line.

One way of emphasizing the high cost of staff dissatisfaction is to calculate the amount of additional revenue that a business would have to generate in order to compensate for the expenses related to turnover. If the profit margin for the restaurants cited in the previous example is 10%, then it would take between $9,000 and $45,000 in additional sales to make up, on the bottom line, for the loss of a single staff member, and as much as $27,000 to $135,000 in additional sales to compensate for the loss of a manager.

Some turnover can't be avoided—for example, staff members might move out of the area or go back to school. Some terminations are forced—the staff members are fired. So, not every staff termination signals job dissatisfaction, and some turnover must be expected. What a manager wants to do is stop the avoidable turnover.

To tackle the turnover problem, a manager needs information that pinpoints exactly when and where the turnover is occurring. This information can help the manager focus efforts on analyzing why the turnover is occurring and suggesting actions to reduce the turnover. For example, if a manager finds that the majority of turnover occurs within the first 90 days of employment, the manager could focus efforts on reviewing the restaurant's selection and orientation processes, and supervisors could review their training programs for new-hires. Exit interviews with staff members terminating their employment can provide helpful insights. Staff-member satisfaction surveys are also commonly used to determine ways to reduce turnover.

One of the keys to retaining staff members is to increase their level of satisfaction with their positions. Staff members stay with a company longer when they perceive value in the quality of their work environment and feel adequately compensated for the work they perform. For a restaurant to determine what it should do to increase job satisfaction among its staff members, it must begin with learning how they perceive value in relation to their work.

Staff Members' Perceptions of the Value of Their Work

Staff members perceive value and quality in much the same way as guests. A guest's perception of value is based on price and the quality of service received; staff members perceive value in relation to their paychecks and the quality of their work environment. Value is not simply a matter of wages and benefits; staff members expect their pay to be competitive within an industry and commensurate with their skills and abilities. However, in terms of perceived value, compensation is balanced within a context of the quality of the work environment. Staff members evaluate the quality of their work environment by the degree to which their positions, their co-workers, and the resources provided to them by the organization consistently meet or exceed their expectations.

Attracting people to work in the food service industry has long been an uphill battle against the public's perception that the industry offers mainly low-paying, dead-end jobs. To succeed as employers of choice, food service managers must fulfill two important responsibilities. The first is to *enable* new staff members, by providing them with training opportunities through which they can learn how to succeed on the job. The second is to *empower* and *support* new staff members, by providing the coaching and mentoring through which they can grow both personally and professionally.

The same challenges exist in retaining veteran staff members at every level of a food service organization. Managers, supervisors, and staff members all expect to learn and grow professionally and personally through their work. People measure the quality of work offered by a position, company, and industry in part by the degree to which the work meets or exceeds their expectations of personal and professional opportunities for learning and growth.

Staff members also judge a company's value by the quality of their day-to-day work experiences. Just as there are moments of truth throughout a guest's food service experience that form a continuous chain of events and build a perception of value for guests, so too there are internal moments of truth in the day-to-day activities of work that build a perception of value for staff members.

Internal Moments of Truth. Think of **internal moments of truth** as specific events, situations, or interactions in which anyone employed by the company comes into contact with some aspect of the company that contributes to the quality of his or her work life.

Many things contribute to the quality of staff members' work lives. When they arrive at work, do staff members encounter a poorly lit employee parking lot full of potholes and trash, or a well-kept, well-lit place to park? When staff members enter the staff breakroom, is it a welcoming environment or is it a "temporary" storage place cluttered with forgotten odds and ends that are never taken care of? When staff members use equipment to help them perform their jobs, is it the proper equipment, in good working order, or do they have to struggle with inefficient or broken-down tools? All of these situations can be thought of as internal moments of truth.

However, for most staff members, the vast majority of internal moments of truth involve their co-workers. Just as most moments of truth for guests involve encounters with staff members, most internal moments of truth for staff members involve encounters with other staff members—specifically, encounters in which a staff member needs the help of another staff member in order to perform his or her job. Examples include the following:

- A food server discussing a special order with a cook in the kitchen
- A busperson asking another busperson for help with resetting a table
- A banquet manager revising a banquet menu with the restaurant's chef

A primary leadership challenge for managers is to foster an organizational culture that encourages staff members to provide excellent service to each other, so that together they can provide excellent service to guests. In such an organization, staff members are likelier to want to stay with the organization, because they are interacting with cooperative co-workers who are helping them achieve a common goal—providing excellent service to guests. When guests are served well, there are usually fewer problems to deal with, and the workplace tends to be a much happier environment.

Recruiting Staff Members

It is much easier for managers to create a positive service culture, one in which staff members successfully handle moments of truth with guests and internal moments of truth with other staff members, if managers recruit the right people in the first place. Finding positive, service-oriented people is critical if a restaurant wants to build an organization known for its outstanding service.

Unfortunately, the problem of finding qualified people to fill staff vacancies is complicated by the fact that unemployment rates have been extremely low in the United States for some time. However, there are sources of labor that (in some cases) were underutilized in the past which managers should now make special efforts to tap into: people with disabilities, minorities, legal immigrants, and older workers, to name a few. Community colleges and local organizations that work with women in transition can be sources for recruiting women returning to the work force. Teachers needing summer work, dependents of military personnel, and unemployed actors and actresses are additional nontraditional sources of staff members. Of course, students looking for part-time work should not be overlooked.

One strategy managers can use to find good service workers is networking. Managers can network by speaking to student groups in local schools and universities and by contacting community agencies, private industry councils, churches, and other local and state organizations. Food service organizations can promote careers in food service by implementing "Adopt-a-School" programs. Managers can also establish internship programs at local high schools. Current staff members can help by mentioning job openings to acquaintances.

Public relations efforts can also help attract job applicants. Involvement in community-based activities and charity events can help a food service organization maintain a high profile in the local community.

Another strategy to attract applicants is to offer more attractive hiring packages, including higher starting wages, better benefits and retirement plans, college tuition reimbursement, child-care assistance, and training and development programs that help individuals develop the skills and behaviors they need for long-term success in the industry. Some food service organizations are offering year- or season-end bonuses in an attempt to retain staff members.

The federal government and many states offer job training and employment programs that can benefit food service organizations. These programs may provide job training or offer a financial incentive to employers for hiring program

The Signs of Success.

Look closely at the signs of success. You can see them in the cheerful smiles of our managers. Everyday our people carry the signs of success, and while you may not always know their names, you'll see their handiwork in every one of our 1500 Denny's restaurants coast to coast. The more you learn about Denny's -- our generous benefits, our five-day work week, competitive wages, outstanding growth opportunities, exceptional training, including our management entry level STAR advancement program -- the more you'll understand why joining a Denny's restaurant is one of the smartest career moves you'll ever make.

Positions:

General Manager	Managers
Assistant Managers	Supervisors
College Students/Grads	Unit Level

So when you want to enjoy your life AND your career, join Denny's, part of the Flagstar family's 100,000+ employees. It's a sure sign your restaurant career is looking up.

Click here to apply on-line.

or fax your resume to: **(864) 597-7457**

Benefits

Join our top-notch team and you'll receive some of the best benefits in the industry such as:

- Competitive starting salary
- Performance-based bonus
- 5 day work weeks
- Career growth opportunities
- Complete benefits package including Medical/Dental
- Strong advancement potential
- Outstanding training

Click here to apply on-line.

CareerMosaic Home | Employers | JOBS Database | Resume CM | College Connection | Career Resource Center | International Gateway

CareerMosaic Home | Employers | J.O.B.S. Database | ResumeCM
CollegeConnection | Career Resource Center | International Gateway

Sometimes qualified people find *you*—at least that is what food service organizations hope will happen when they invite people to apply for positions over the Internet. Internet sites typically emphasize management opportunities, but some encourage hourly employees to respond as well. This site can be found at http://www.careermosaic.com/cm/dennys/dennys1.html. (Courtesy of Denny's)

participants, such as people with disabilities. The local unemployment office should have information about these programs and how to participate.

Many food service organizations advertise job openings in newspapers, magazines, and trade journals. Some post fliers on bulletin boards in supermarkets and apartment buildings. Creative ads or flier copy can help attract potential applicants. Ads should emphasize the benefits of and reasons for joining the organization from the potential applicant's point of view.

A food service organization should take advantage of whatever works in the local area when recruiting. Whether it be to senior centers, high schools or colleges, churches, or local organizations and agencies, the organization should aggressively market its unique features and benefits. If free meals, transportation to and from work by a company van, or flexible working hours are important to the groups of applicants the organization is attempting to attract, then these benefits should be promoted during recruitment efforts. To some, it might seem that companies are going too far in offering these types of benefits to potential employees. However, these are the kinds of measures more and more companies are having to take in order to compete with other organizations for workers.

Selecting Staff Members

Once a pool of applicants is recruited, selection can take place. **Selection** is the process of screening job applicants in order to identify the right person for the job.

Selecting the right applicants requires patience to find those who are committed and enthusiastic. The selection process should be designed to identify those who are competent, creative, empathetic, enterprising, resilient, and resourceful. These are the kind of people who can successfully handle moments of truth with guests. Leading food service organizations today are paying much more attention to personality and psychology when selecting applicants for positions. These organizations are looking for applicants who can converse with guests, make eye contact with guests, and work under pressure.

Many food service organizations today emphasize the emotional aspects of work. When interviewing applicants for a server position, for example, managers in these organizations ask applicants questions such as "Do you have a bit of actor (or actress) in you?" and "Do you have an uncanny sense for making people feel good?" When an applicant answers affirmatively, these questions are followed up with a request for a personal example from the applicant.

Some food service companies are using outside companies to prescreen applicants. Other food service organizations are exploring the feasibility of using an optically scanned résumé bank that lists the applicant's key skills and presorts the résumé data using whatever criteria the organization chooses.

Interviewing Applicants. Interviewing requires that managers be skilled in both information gathering and information giving. To prepare for an interview, a manager should review the responsibilities and skills needed in the open position; review the applicant's credentials, including the completed application form and the applicant's résumé (if applicable); secure a good location for conducting the interview; and gather the necessary materials for the interview.

Guest Service As a Performance

Walt Disney World has integrated the concept of guest service as a performance into its corporate culture more successfully than other hospitality organizations. Disney staff members are considered to be cast members who play various roles as they engage in a performance in front of a live audience (the guests). Guest-contact staff members are the actors and actresses, while non-guest-contact staff members are the support crew. All of Disney's "players" on "stage" rely on each other, just as actors do in an actual stage production.

At Walt Disney World, managers are considered the directors of the staff's performance. The director's role is to help staff members know their cues, create and deliver delightful service, and improvise when another staff member—or even a guest—changes the planned flow of the performance. The director helps staff members create performances that are memorable to guests.

At the start of an interview, the manager should introduce him- or herself and put the applicant at ease by establishing an atmosphere of cooperative give and take. It is also important to go over the interview format and structure with the applicant so he or she knows what to expect.

During the interview, the manager should find out about the applicant's background and job experiences, compensation expectations, and availability for work. Can the applicant work nights? Weekends? Are there certain times that the applicant cannot work?

Open-ended interview questions are useful because they require more than a simple "Yes" or "No" answer from the applicant and can help the manager get to know the applicant better. Sample open-ended interview questions are listed in Exhibit 6.

The manager should note the applicant's verbal and nonverbal responses to questions. For example, if enthusiasm and good communication skills are important to the position, the interviewer should note not only what is said but also how it is said. Seasoned interviewers use silence effectively and listen actively to responses.

Another phase of the interview is information giving. The manager should tell the applicant about the organization, its compensation and benefits package, and what the manager expects of the person filling the vacant position. It is also essential to leave sufficient time in the interview to answer the applicant's questions.

Some progressive restaurants ask staff members to interview job applicants, too. Not only does this give staff members input into the selection process, it also gives applicants the opportunity to question workers: What is the manager really like? Does the restaurant have a good training program? Are career opportunities really available here?

The interviewer should also pay close attention to the applicant's appearance. Since the food service industry is highly image-conscious and very concerned about sanitation issues, an applicant's sloppy dress or dirty fingernails are indications that the applicant might not be right for a food service job. Some guidelines

Exhibit 6 Sample Open-Ended Interview Questions

Education-Related Questions

1. What subjects did you enjoy the most (or the least) in high school (or college)? Why?
2. What did you learn from your high school (or college) experience that is important today?
3. How did you feel about the importance of grades in high school (or college)?
4. Did you have any part-time jobs while attending high school (or college)? Which jobs were the most interesting? Why?
5. What extracurricular activities did you participate in during high school (or college)?

Employment-Related Questions

1. What job pressures did you experience in previous jobs? Why?
2. What kind of people do you like (or dislike) working with? Why?
3. What were the main advantages (or disadvantages) of your last job?
4. Why are you considering changing jobs?
5. Do you prefer working alone or in groups? Why?
6. Name three food service organizations in which you have worked. Which one would you be proud to own? Why?
7. What do you like most (or least) about working in a guest-service position?
8. What makes you think you are qualified to work in a guest-service position in our organization?

Goal-Related Questions

1. What are your career goals in the next two years? the next ten years?
2. What are your salary goals and objectives?
3. How do you evaluate this organization as a place to help you achieve your career goals?
4. Who (or what) influenced you the most in regard to your career goals?
5. What are your expectations regarding a new job?
6. If you are successful in 1 year (5 years, 10 years), what will be happening?
7. Of all the results that you have achieved in your life, which are you the most proud of? Why?

Self-Awareness-Related Questions

1. Which of your good qualities are most outstanding? Which of your qualities need the most improvement?
2. What qualities do you have that would help you deliver superior guest-service in our organization?
3. Are you a self-motivated individual? Explain why.
4. How do you react to criticism from an employer? a guest? a staff member?
5. Have you engaged in any self-improvement activities recently? What were they?
6. What is your definition of superior guest service?

Exhibit 7 Assessing an Applicant's Professional Image

Personal Appearance

- Is the applicant clean and neat?
- Is the applicant's hair trimmed and in an appropriate style?
- Is the applicant wearing appropriate clothing for the interview?

Overall Personal Presentation

- Does the applicant use good posture when standing or sitting?
- Does the applicant speak clearly?
- Does the applicant speak with confidence?
- Does the applicant avoid chewing gum during the interview?
- Does the applicant smile frequently?
- Does the applicant appear to be extroverted?

Other

- Does the applicant have confidence in him- or herself?
- Does the applicant respond openly and honestly to questions?
- Does the applicant seem to take work seriously?
- Does the applicant appear to have pride in him- or herself, and could that pride be transferred to the organization?
- Does the applicant do his or her best to project a professional image?
- Does the applicant appear to fit the staff member profile in our guest-driven service organization?
- Would I enjoy working with the applicant in creating and delivering superior guest service?

that might help an interviewer assess the applicant's professional image are presented in Exhibit 7.

The manager should close the interview by telling the applicant when the hiring decision will be made and how the applicant will be informed of the decision. After the interview, the applicant's references should be checked.

In some cases, the selection process comes down to a choice between an applicant with the right skills or one with the right personality. Skills can be taught through training, but it is difficult to change an applicant's personality. Therefore, it is often better for a manager to hire someone with the right personality.

Uncovering service personalities. As mentioned earlier, during the interview process, a manager should not only cover the basics of the applicant's work background and skill level; the manager should also assess the applicant's service personality or attitude. For example, the manager might ask the applicant the following questions:

- Do you like to work with people? Provide an example of a work experience that you considered enjoyable.

- Do you like to make decisions and solve problems? Provide an example.
- Do you like to work under pressure? Provide an example of an instance in which you worked well under pressure.
- Do you like to be a contributing member of a team? Provide an example.
- What are some of the service businesses (such as a bank, store, or laundry) that you patronize in a typical week? Give examples of superior and inadequate service that you have received.

Interview questions that include "if ... then" scenarios can be used to gain further insight into an applicant's service attitude. They can also test the applicant's ability to think and act rapidly. Such questions might include the following:

- If a guest is seated in your section at breakfast and demands to be served immediately because he has to attend a meeting within the next half hour, what would you do?
- If a guest is seated at a table outside of your section and calls you over to tell you that her order has been prepared improperly, what would you do?
- If a guest at one of your tables appears tired, irritable, and eager to dine and leave, what would you do?
- If a guest that you are serving appears to have had too much to drink, what would you do?

An appropriate service attitude is the key to guest-driven service, because it directly affects the moments of truth that staff members have with guests.

Testing. In addition to interviewing, some food service organizations use pre-employment testing as part of their selection process. Such testing can help determine an applicant's honesty, reliability, advancement potential, and attitude toward authority. While some experts have raised questions about the ethics, accuracy, and reliability of some pre-employment tests, it is expected that more food service organizations will use pre-employment testing in the future in combination with interviews, application forms, and other selection tools. However, in some cases, courts have ruled that certain pre-employment tests are discriminatory; therefore, managers should check with legal counsel before using a particular test.

A relatively new test to food service organizations is the on-the-job experience or audition test. With this test, the applicant is placed in the actual work environment for several hours or days on a probationary basis before being hired. In this test, the prospective staff member experiences what the job is like, while managers and staff members observe whether the person is right for the position. During this tryout, the prospective staff member has a first-hand opportunity to decide whether the position is right for him or her.

If the organization concludes that the applicant and the position are not suited to each other, it is critical that the organization part company with the applicant on good terms. Applicants who are not selected by the organization will tell friends and acquaintances about their experiences. In addition, the applicant may potentially be—or may already be—an infrequent or a regular guest of the organization.

Orientation of Staff Members

Orientation takes place after an applicant has been selected and reports for work. **Orientation** is the process of introducing a new staff member to the work environment and his or her responsibilities. The objective of orientation is to start the new staff member out correctly. Orientation is designed to reduce the new staff member's anxiety and answer any remaining questions he or she might have. The new staff member's immediate supervisor is typically responsible for providing the orientation.

Orientation helps set expectations for newly hired staff members and also assists them in building work relationships that they can use later when they need information or help. Orientation is also the time to complete any remaining employment paperwork, such as W-4 forms, payroll deduction statements, and benefit enrollment forms. An orientation checklist (see Exhibit 8) can help managers provide a thorough and objective orientation. Checklists can be modified to fit a specific position, the needs of the new staff member, and the individual food service operation.

During orientation, the new staff member should review the company's organization chart, be introduced to co-workers, and be given a tour of the facility. The tour should encompass the exterior and the interior of the facility, including the offices, restrooms (public and private), storerooms, kitchen(s), dishroom(s), dining room(s), banquet room(s) (if applicable), server side stands, and bar(s) (if applicable).

As part of their orientation, new staff members typically are given an employee manual. A manual allows the new staff member to study the information within it later in a more relaxed frame of mind. An organization usually includes its mission, history, service philosophy, and staff member policies in the manual. In order to reinforce the feelings of partnership between management and staff, the manual typically covers both the staff member's and the organization's responsibilities.

Last but not least, the organization's philosophy of guest-driven service should be explained at every opportunity during the orientation process. Each new staff member must clearly understand his or her potential impact on guests, other staff members, and the financial strength of the organization.

After orientation is completed, new staff members should be given the training necessary to help them perform their jobs and provide superior guest service.

Training Staff Members

Ensuring that staff members receive proper training is one of a food service manager's major responsibilities. This does not mean that the manager must perform the training him- or herself. The actual training may be delegated to supervisors or even talented staff members. However, the manager should be responsible for ongoing training programs in the restaurant.

Today's staff members typically do not want to be simply told what to do. The "why's" are also important. Staff members want to understand the reasons for following the organization's policies, procedures, and recommended work methods.

Exhibit 8 Sample Orientation Checklist

1. Outline the new staff member's responsibilities, duties, and expected results.
2. Explain the relationship of the position to the staff member's department, to the organization as a whole, and to the overall outcome of providing superior guest service.
3. Review the staff member's schedule, workdays, work hours, check-in and check-out procedures, and how to use the time clock.
4. Describe acceptable procedures for reporting absences, tardiness, and sick days.
5. Point out staff member break areas, eating areas, restrooms, and first-aid facilities.
6. Describe acceptable methods for requisitioning and receiving supplies needed for the staff member's position.
7. Explain the organization's standards of production and service in detail.
8. Emphasize the organization's sanitation standards and its rules for personal hygiene.
9. Explain safety rules and accident procedures.
10. Review the use of staff member badges, name tags, and uniforms.
11. Indicate areas that are off-limits to staff members.
12. Point out acceptable staff member parking areas.
13. Indicate areas to be used for the storage of the staff member's street clothes (if applicable) and personal property.
14. Show the new staff member where notices are posted on bulletin boards.
15. Review the acceptable reasons for using the organization's telephones for personal and emergency calls.
16. Tell when the staff member gets paid and where the check can be obtained.
17. Explain check-cashing procedures.
18. Introduce the new staff member to co-workers in his or her work area or department.
19. Introduce the new staff member to other personnel important in the successful completion of the job.
20. Answer any questions the new staff member asks.
21. Explain the big picture, including the organization's mission, guest-service philosophies, and how the results achieved by the individual staff member are critical to achieving the organization's overall goals.

These reasons should be spelled out during the applicant's training while he or she is also being taught service techniques and procedures.

Most managers understand that the goal of training is to help staff members develop skills to do their jobs well. Many managers, however, are not sure of the best way to train. Often, they need a framework for training. The four-step training method provides that framework. The four steps in the method are:

- Prepare
- Present

- Practice
- Follow Up

Whether you are training one person or a group, new hires or experienced staff members, the four-step training method will work for you.

Prepare. Preparation is essential for successful training. If you don't prepare, your training may lack a logical sequence and you may omit key details. You may also feel more than normal anxiety regarding the training session. Before you begin training, you should analyze the job you are training someone to do.

Analyze the job. The foundation for training and for preventing performance problems is **job analysis**. Job analysis is determining what knowledge the staff members being trained must have, what tasks they need to perform, and the standards at which they must perform them. Without a complete knowledge of what the staff members are expected to do, you can't train properly.

Job analysis involves three steps: identifying job knowledge, creating a task list for the job, and developing a job breakdown for each task performed. The knowledge, lists, and breakdowns also form an efficient system for evaluating performance.

The "job knowledge" component of a job analysis identifies what a staff member needs to know to perform his or her job. To perform a job well, a staff member needs to know about the food service operation in general, his or her area or department, and the tasks unique to his or her position. For example, restaurant servers need to be given general information that all staff members should know, such as general guest service techniques and information that will help them develop safe work habits. But they also need to know information that all guest-contact food and beverage staff members should know, such as alcoholic beverage terms, sanitation guidelines, and how to operate point-of-sale equipment. Then, restaurant servers need to master knowledge specific to the restaurant server position, such as standard table setup specifications, how to take and serve food and beverage orders, and suggestive selling and upselling techniques.

The tasks on a restaurant server's **task list** should reflect the total job responsibilities of this staff position. Exhibit 9 presents a sample task list for a restaurant server. Note that each line on the sample task list begins with a verb. This stresses action and clearly indicates to a staff member what he or she will be responsible for doing. Whenever possible, tasks should be listed in an order that reflects the logical sequence of a staff member's daily responsibilities.

The format of a job breakdown can vary to suit the needs and requirements of individual food service operations. Exhibit 10 presents a sample job breakdown. The **job breakdown** includes a list of equipment and supplies needed to perform the task, steps in performing the task, how to perform the task, and tips for performing the task.

Develop job breakdowns. If a food service operation does not already have job breakdowns, then they should be developed. If only one person in the operation is assigned the responsibility of writing every job breakdown, the job may never get done, unless the operation is very small with a limited number of tasks. Some of the best job breakdowns are written by those who actually perform the

Exhibit 9 Sample Task List: Server

1. Set up the restaurant for service.
2. Stock and maintain side stations.
3. Fold napkins.
4. Prepare breads and bread baskets or trays.
5. Prepare service trays.
6. Take restaurant reservations.
7. Work efficiently.
8. Greet and seat guests.
9. Approach the table.
10. Provide appropriate service for children.
11. Lift and carry trays, bus tubs, or dish racks.
12. Serve water.
13. Check IDs of guests ordering alcohol.
14. Take beverage orders.
15. Process beverage orders.
16. Prepare and serve coffee.
17. Prepare and serve hot tea.
18. Prepare and serve iced tea.
19. Prepare and serve hot chocolate.
20. Take food orders.
21. Serve bread and butter.
22. Prepare ice buckets.
23. Serve wine and champagne by the bottle.
24. Serve the meal.
25. Check back to the table.
26. Respond quickly to soothe dissatisfied guests.
27. Maintain tables.
28. Sell after-dinner items.
29. Prepare takeout items.
30. Present the guest check.
31. Settle guest checks and thank guests.
32. Clear and reset tables.
33. Handle soiled restaurant linens.
34. Inventory, requisition, and restock restaurant supplies.
35. Perform closing side work.

Source: Adapted from the "Restaurant Server Guide" in the *Hospitality Skills Training Series* (East Lansing, Mich.: Educational Institute of the American Hotel & Motel Association, 1995).

tasks. In organizations with large food service staffs, "standards groups" can be formed to create job breakdowns. Group members should include experienced servers, buspersons, and other staff members as well as managers and supervisors. In very small organizations, experienced staff members might be assigned to write the job breakdowns alone. Exhibit 11 summarizes the process of developing job breakdowns.

The job breakdowns for tasks that involve the use of equipment may already be written in the operating manuals supplied by vendors. Standards groups should not have to write job breakdowns for operating point-of-sale equipment, for example. Instead, a standards group may simply refer to (or even attach) appropriate pages from the operating manual supplied by the vendor to the appropriate job breakdowns.

Within a specified time, standards groups should submit their work to the food service manager, who then can assemble the breakdowns, give them a consistent format (perhaps similar to that shown in Exhibit 10), and provide copies to all of the groups' members. A final meeting can then be held, with the standards groups carefully analyzing the breakdowns for each position. After the job breakdowns have been finalized, they can be used to train the operation's staff.

Exhibit 10 Sample Job Breakdown

Serve Water

Materials needed: *A water pitcher, a tray, and a clean linen napkin.*

STEPS	HOW-TO'S	TIPS
1. If empty water glasses are preset, carry a water pitcher on a tray to each table as soon as guests are seated.		*In some restaurants, servers or buspersons will bring full water glasses to the table.* *In some restaurants, water may only be served by request or may be delayed until after cocktail service.*
2. Pour water.	❑ Pour from the guest's right, using your right hand.	
	❑ Pour to the glass without picking it up from the table.	
	❑ Hold a clean linen napkin in your left hand under the base of the pitcher.	*The napkin will catch drips from the moisture on the pitcher.*
3. Refill water glasses whenever they are less than half-full.		

Source: Adapted from the "Restaurant Server Guide" in the *Hospitality Skills Training Series* (East Lansing, Mich.: Educational Institute of the American Hotel & Motel Association, 1995), p. 32.

Analyze new staff member training needs. The task list is an excellent tool with which to plan your new staff member training. Realistically, new staff members cannot be expected to learn all of the tasks before their first day on the job. Before you begin training, study the task list. Then, rate each task according to whether it should be mastered before working alone on the job (give this a "1" rating), within two weeks on the job (give these tasks a "2" rating), or within two months on the job (give these tasks a "3").

Select several of the tasks that you rated as "1" and cover those in the first training session for the new staff member. After the staff member understands and can perform these, teach the remaining tasks in subsequent training sessions until the new staff member has learned all of the tasks. Appendix A shows a sample training

Exhibit 11 Process for Developing Job Breakdowns

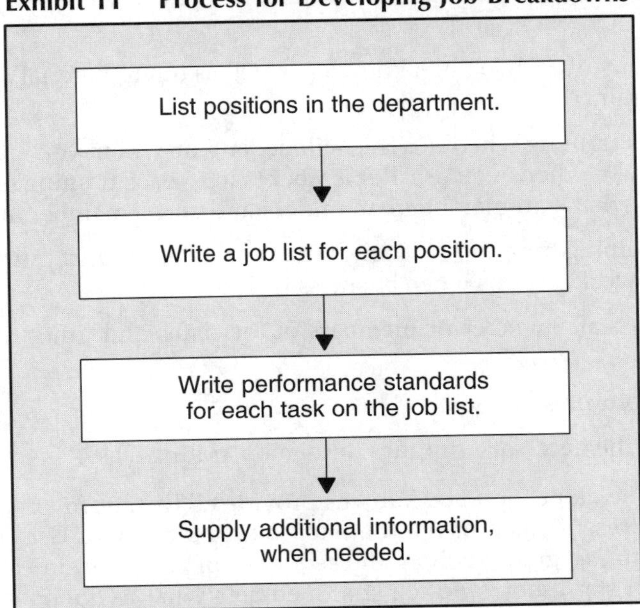

schedule for new employees based on the task list found in Exhibit 9 and a list of "need to know" topics.

Once you've decided which tasks you'll teach in each training session, turn to the job breakdowns. Think of the job breakdown for each task as a lesson plan for training or as a learning guide for self-directed study. Because the job breakdowns list all the steps staff members must perform, they tell exactly what needs to be done during the training. Job breakdowns can direct the instruction and make sure that critical points or steps are not overlooked.

Assign new staff members no more than nine or ten job breakdowns to study at one time. If they try to do more, they might become overwhelmed and probably won't remember enough information to perform the jobs well.

Analyze current staff member training needs. Training is not just for newly hired staff members. Food service managers sometimes feel that there's a problem with a current staff member's work or with several staff members' work, but they're not exactly sure what it is; or they feel that something's not quite right with the staff, but don't know where to start making improvements. A training-needs assessment can help uncover an individual staff member's weaknesses as well as weaknesses in the staff as a whole.

To conduct a needs assessment of a single staff member, observe present performance for two or three days and record it on a form similar to the one in Appendix B. Areas in which the staff member scores poorly are those you'll want to target when you plan refresher training.

Develop your training plan. Follow these steps to prepare for training sessions:

- Carefully review all job breakdowns and other materials that you will use in training.
- Make a copy of each job breakdown (as well as other materials, if applicable) for each trainee.
- Establish a training schedule. This will depend on whom you are training and the training methods you use. Remember to limit each training session's information to what staff members can understand and remember in one session.
- Select a training time and location. When possible, conduct training at the appropriate work stations when business is slow.
- Notify the staff member or members of the dates and times of the training sessions.
- Practice your presentation.
- Gather all the necessary supplies for demonstrating tasks.

Present. Well-developed job breakdowns provide all the information you need to conduct the "present" step of the four-step training method. Use the job breakdowns as a training guide. Follow the sequence of each step in each job breakdown. For each step, show and tell staff members what to do, how to do it, and why the details are important.

Give them a chance to prepare. Let each new staff member study his or her task list to get an overview of all the tasks to be learned. If possible, give the appropriate list to each staff member at least one day before the first training session. At least a day before each training session, let new and current staff members review the job breakdowns that you plan to cover in that session. Then begin each training session by going over what they will do. Let them know how long activities will take and when their breaks will be.

As you explain the steps, demonstrate them. Make sure staff members can see exactly what you are doing. Encourage them to ask questions whenever they need more information.

Be sure to take enough time when presenting your training. Go slowly and carefully. Be patient if staff members don't understand right away. Go over all the steps at least two times. When you show a step a second time, ask questions to assess if staff members understand. Repeat the steps as many times as necessary.

Avoid jargon. Use words that staff members who are new to the food service industry or your property can understand. They can pick up the jargon later.

Practice. When the trainer and trainees agree that the trainees are familiar with the job and able to complete the steps acceptably, trainees should try to perform the tasks alone. Immediate practice results in good work habits. Have each trainee demonstrate each step of the tasks presented during the training session. This tells you whether they really do understand. Resist the urge to do the tasks for staff members who are struggling with them.

Compliment staff members immediately after correct performance. Gently correct them when you observe problems. Bad habits formed now may be very difficult to break later. Be sure that each trainee understands and can explain not only how to perform each step, but also the purpose of each step.

Follow Up. There are a number of things you can do to make it easier for your staff members to carry skills over to the workplace after training. Some of these options include:

- Provide opportunities for staff members to use and demonstrate new skills after training.
- Have staff members discuss the training with their co-workers.
- Provide ongoing, open communication on progress and concerns.

Follow-up activities for trainers also include coaching, giving feedback to, and evaluating staff members.

Continue coaching on the job. While training helps staff members learn new knowledge and develop new skills and attitudes, coaching focuses on the actual on-the-job application of what has been learned in the training sessions. As a coach, you challenge, encourage, correct, and positively reinforce the knowledge, skills, and attitudes learned during the training session.

What follows are some on-the-job coaching tips:

- Observe staff members while they work to ensure that they are performing tasks correctly.
- Make casual suggestions to correct minor problems.
- Tactfully correct staff members when they make major mistakes. Typically the best way to do this is in a quiet location, when neither of you is busy.
- If a staff member is using an unsafe procedure, correct the problem right away.

Give constant feedback. Some tips for giving feedback include the following:

- Let staff members know what they are doing correctly and incorrectly.
- Tell staff members when they perform well. This will help them remember what they learn, and encourage them to continue performing well.
- If staff members are not meeting performance standards, first compliment them for the tasks they are doing correctly. Then, show them how to correct their bad habits, and explain why it's important that they do so.
- Be specific. Describe behavior by stating exactly what the staff member said and did.
- Choose your words carefully; you want to sound helpful, not demanding.

Evaluate staff members. Evaluate the progress staff members make. Use the task list as a checklist to confirm that all tasks have been mastered. Provide further training and practice for tasks that have not been mastered.

Get feedback from staff members. Let them evaluate the training they received. This can help you improve your training efforts for them and other staff members.

A CAHNERS PUBLICATION

Contents
Archive
Recipes
Back Issues
Calendar
Subscribe
E-mail R&I

RESTAURANTS AND INSTITUTIONS™

Go to: Table of Contents

TOP 100

▸ **Top 100 Independents**
Total gross sales at the nation's Top 100 Independent Restaurants hit $1 billion in 1997, a 4% increase over the previous year's $973 million. Learn how the best maintain their leadership positions by catering both to customers and staff.

▸ **Products**
Looking for the latest foodservice products? Check out **R&I Marketplace Online.** We've made it easy for you to request product information via the Web.

▸ **Beyond the Basket**
After a lengthy supporting appearance, bread is out of the basket and easing into a multitude of perfect partnerships. Creative operators are pairing carefully crafted breads with complementary ingredients, slicing up new variations on sandwiches, salads, soups, desserts and more. **With recipes.**

▸ Recent Food Stories
- Entree Salads
- Fried Chicken: The Golden Standard
- Roaming the Southwest
- Dealing Veal
- Asian Elements
- An Italian Renaissance
- Soup Is On

Many food service trade magazines maintain Internet sites. This one is for *Restaurants & Institutions* and can be found at http://www.rimag.com. (Courtesy of *Restaurants & Institutions*)

Keep training records for each person who receives training. Track each staff member's training history and keep a copy of a training log in that staff member's personnel file.

Self-Training. Self-training or self-improvement is an often overlooked aspect of training, yet it is as important, if not more important, when it comes to career development and promotion within a food service organization. Most staff members have an idea about what subjects they can study to help them improve their performance or develop new talents that could help them on the job; if not, they can check with their supervisor for improvement ideas. There are courses available through distance-learning companies; group study in voc-tech, community, or junior colleges is also available in many areas. If there is a university within commuting distance, staff members may find that it offers helpful courses. Some food service organizations reimburse staff members who take and pass courses related to their jobs.

Other sources of self-training material are trade magazines such as *Nation's Restaurant News, Restaurant Business, Restaurants & Institutions,* and *Restaurants USA.* Often, several individuals in a food service organization subscribe to trade publications; they may be willing to let others borrow them. In addition to the articles in these magazines, there are ads from publishers of educational resources. Some trade magazines maintain Internet sites, enabling staff members to access, via computer, past and present magazine articles as well as other trade information.

Self-improvement information can easily be obtained from local and state trade associations. In Michigan, for example, the Michigan Hotel, Motel and Resort Association and the Michigan Restaurant Association both hold an annual meeting as well as regional meetings throughout the year, all with educational seminars designed to improve the skills and knowledge of attendees.

Audio- and videotapes are an additional source of information that may be used for self-training. Home computers offer the opportunity to tap into the Internet for current information to help staff members improve their skills and advance in their careers.

The key to self-training is to decide to spend a specific amount of time and money each year and stick to the plan. The results will pay off both in financial as well as personal rewards associated with career advancement.

Key Terms

defection rate—A measure of guest dissatisfaction, expressed as a percentage of guests lost to competitors because of service-related problems.

empowerment—The redistribution of power within an organization that enables managers, supervisors, and staff members to perform their jobs more efficiently and effectively, with the overall goal of enhancing service to guests and increasing profits for the organization by releasing decision-making responsibility, authority, and accountability to every level within the organization.

internal moment of truth—A specific event, situation, or interaction in which anyone employed by a company comes into contact with some aspect of the company that contributes to the quality of his or her work experience.

job analysis—The process of determining the tasks, behaviors, and characteristics essential to a job.

job breakdown—A document that outlines what a person needs to know to perform a specific job or task; it typically includes a list of equipment and supplies needed to perform the job, the steps a person needs to take to perform the job, and tips to help a person perform the job better.

moment of truth—Any episode in which a customer comes into contact with any aspect of an organization and gets an impression of the quality of its service; considered to be the basic atom of service, the smallest indivisible unit of value delivered to customers.

orientation—The process of introducing a new staff member to the work environment and his or her responsibilities.

selection—The process of screening job applicants in order to identify the right person for the position.

task list—A list of job responsibilities or tasks for a specific position. Whenever possible, tasks should be listed in an order that reflects the logical sequence of a staff member's daily responsibilities.

turnover rate—The rate at which staff members leave a company or work unit.

Review Questions

1. What is a "moment of truth"?
2. What is the "present value" of a guest? the "future value" of a guest?
3. How does guest dissatisfaction cost a food service organization? How can this cost be calculated?
4. What does it mean to "empower" staff members?
5. What are some attributes managers who want to be good leaders should have?
6. What is the value of staff members to a food service organization?
7. How does staff dissatisfaction cost a food service organization? How can this cost be calculated?
8. What are internal moments of truth?
9. What are some ways food service organizations can recruit applicants?
10. What are some techniques managers can use to select new staff members?
11. What is the four-step training method?

Internet Sites

For more information, visit the following Internet sites. Remember that Internet addresses can change without notice.

http://www.amcity.com/journals/retailing_restaurants/

http://www.beverage-retailer.com/

http://www.brinker.com/htm/006_Employment_frame-source_chilis.htm

http://www.careermosaic.com/cm/cm12.html

http://www.careermosaic.com/cm/kfc/kfc1.html

http://www.careermosaic.com/cm/dennys/dennys1.html

http://www.chrie.org/

http://www.ei-ahma.org/

http://www.ei-ahma.org/webs/lodging/index.html

http://www.inndirect.com/inndirect/yp/chrie.html

http://www.nightclub.com/online~1.html

http://www.nrn.com/low/

http://www.nrn.com/low/litebite/linkfest.html

http://www.ranw.com/links.htm

http://www.restaurant.org/index.htm

http://www.restaurant.org/research/research.htm

http://www.restaurant.org/RUSA/index.htm

http://www.restaurantbiz.com/

http://www.restaurantreport.com

http://www.rimag.com/

References

Albrecht, Karl. *At America's Service.* Homewood, Ill.: Dow Jones-Irwin, 1988.

Albrecht, Karl, and Ron Zemke. *Service America!* Homewood, Ill.: Dow Jones-Irwin, 1985.

Anders, K. T. "If Paperwork's a Hassle, Just Call Rent-a-Chef." *Restaurant Business,* March 20, 1993.

Barrow, James W. "Does Total Quality Management Equal Organizational Learning?" *Quality Progress,* July 1993.

Batty, Jennifer. *Women in Food Service: Challenging Issues in a Changing Workplace.* Washington, D.C.: The National Restaurant Association, 1993.

Bell, Alexa. "Searching for Generation X." *Restaurant Business,* October 10, 1993.

Bright, Deborah. "Achiever or Accomplisher?" *Successful Meetings,* August 1994.

Bulkeley, William. "Replaced by Technology: Job Interviews." *Wall Street Journal,* August 22, 1994.

Capezio, Peter, and Debra Morehouse. *Total Quality Management (TQM: The Road to Continuous Improvement.* Shawnee Mission, Kansas: National Press Publications, 1992.

Caudron, Shari. "Keys to Starting a TQM Program." *Personnel Journal,* February 1993.

Chaudhry, Rajan. "Defuse Difficult Diners." *Restaurants & Institutions,* September 15, 1993.

"CHRIE Makes It Easier To Recruit Food Service Workers." *Briefing,* January 1995.

Cichy, Ronald F., and Caroline L. Cook. "Leadership Qualities: The Non-Commercial Food service Industry." *Restaurant Personnel Management,* 1991.

Cichy, Ronald F., Takashige Aoki, Mark E. Patton, and Michael P. Sciarini. "The Five Foundations of Leadership in Japan's Lodging Industry." *FIU Hospitality Review,* 1992.

Cichy, Ronald F., Takashige Aoki, and Mark E. Patton. "Shi-do-sei: Leadership in Japan's Commercial Food-Service Industry." *Cornell Quarterly,* February 1993.

Cichy, Ronald F., Michael P. Sciarini, and Mark E. Patton. "Food-Service Leadership: Could Attila Run a Restaurant?" *Cornell Quarterly,* February 1992.

Cichy, Ronald F., and Michael P. Sciarini. "Do You Fit This Profile of a Hospitality Leader?" *Lodging,* June 1990.

Cichy, Ronald F., Michael P. Sciarini, Caroline L. Cook, and Mark E. Patton. "Leadership in the Lodging and Non-Commercial Food service Industries." *FIU Hospitality Review,* 1991.

Cichy, Ronald F., and Takashige "Teddy" Aoki. "Ira-shai-mase (Welcome)." *Hotels,* June 1992.

Cichy, Ronald F. *Sanitation Management,* Second Edition. East Lansing, Mich.: Educational Institute of the American Hotel & Motel Association, 1993.

Conan, Kerri. "A Kinder, Gentler Kitchen." *Restaurant Business,* April 10, 1994.

DiDomenico, Pat. "Common Complaints ... And How to Avoid Them." *Restaurants USA,* November 1993.

Ettorre, Barbara. "Juran on Quality." *Management Review,* January 1994.

Henkoff, Ronald. "Finding, Training, & Keeping the Best Service Workers." *Fortune,* October 3, 1994.

Heskett, James L., Thomas O. Jones, Gary W. Loveman, W. Earl Sasser, Jr., and Leonard A. Schlesinger. "Putting the Service-Profit Chain to Work." *Harvard Business Review,* March–April 1994.

Iwamuro, Renee. "The Baby-Boomers: Who They Are and How They Spend." *Restaurants USA,* October 1993.

———. "Food service Employment to Top 12 Million by 2005." *Restaurants USA,* February 1994.

———. "Influentials' Drive Word of Mouth." *Restaurants USA,* February 1994.

Jacob, Rahul. "TQM: More Than a Dying Fad?" *Fortune,* October 18, 1993.

Johnson, Richard S. "TQM: Leadership for the Quality Transformation." *Quality Progress,* May 1993.

LeBoeuf, Michael. *How to Win Customers and Keep Them for Life.* New York: Berkley Books, 1987.

Liparulo, Robert. "Server Teams." *Restaurants USA,* February 1993.

Lorenzina, Beth. "Turn Servers Into Menu Masters." *Restaurants & Institutions,* March 1, 1993.

Lorenzina, Beth. "Teach Servers to Sell More." *Restaurants & Institutions,* April 1, 1993.

Mann, Irma S. "Marketing to the Affluent: A Look at Their Expectations and Service Standards." *Cornell Quarterly,* October 1993.

Marvin, Bill. "Exemplary Service Guaranteed." *Restaurants & Institutions,* September 9, 1992.

Massarsky, Alan. "The Benefits of Benefits: Cultivating the Human Factor." *Nation's Restaurant News,* November 15, 1993.

NRA National Restaurant Association, *Food Service Employee Profile—1992.* Washington, D.C.: The National Restaurant Association, 1992.

———. *Food Service Employment 2000: Exemplary Industry Programs.* Washington, D.C.: National Restaurant Association, 1993.

———. *Food Service Manager 2000.* Washington, D.C.: The National Restaurant Association, 1991.

Oleck, Joan. "Why I Hate This Job." *Restaurant Business,* February 10, 1994.

Piskurich, George M. "Service Training Made Simple." *Training & Development Journal,* January 1991.

Prewitt, Milford. "NRA Study Sketches Industry Character." *Nation's Restaurant News,* April 4, 1994.

Reichheld, Frederick F., and W. Earl Sasser, Jr. "Zero Defections: Quality Comes to Services." *Harvard Business Review,* September–October 1990.

"Re-Engineering for Your Customers." *Restaurants USA,* June/July 1994.

Reynolds, Dennis. "Parsimony and Productivity Paying Off." *Nation's Restaurant News,* April 11, 1994.

Rose, Frank. "Now Quality Means Service Too." *Fortune,* April 22, 1991.

Ruggless, Ron. "Bridging the Gap." *Nation's Restaurant News,* March 21, 1994.

Schlesinger, Leonard A., and James L. Heskett. "The Service-Driven Service Company." *Harvard Business Review,* September–October 1991.

Serge, Peter M. *The Fifth Discipline: The Art and Practice of the Learning Organization.* New York: Doubleday Currency, 1990.

Stephenson, Susie. "Get a Clue … Continued." *Restaurants & Institutions,* May 1, 1994.

———. "Who to Hire? How Much to Pay?" *Restaurants & Institutions,* January 1, 1995.

Stevens, William D. "Turn Complaints Into Gold." *Restaurants USA,* May 1989.

Tschohl, John. "Train Yourself for Success in Service." *Nation's Restaurant News,* August 29, 1994.

Wolson, Shelley. "Worker Retention." *Restaurant Business,* May 20, 1991.

Zemke, Ron. "Customer Service as a Performing Art." *Training,* March 1993.

Case Studies

Moments of Truth: A Very Unhappy Birthday

Martin Hagadorn swore under his breath as he pulled into the parking lot of Xavier's, the upscale restaurant his wife, Francine, had chosen for her birthday dinner.

"What did I tell you, Fran. Every kid in town is here tonight for a fancy dinner before the prom," he grumbled. "Are you sure you want to eat here—and tonight? We could always come back next week when it's not so crowded. Besides, I brought Charlie Rogers here for lunch last week, and it wasn't all that great. I haven't been impressed the last few times I've been here with clients."

"But today's my birthday, not next week," Fran protested. "I'm not asking for much, Martin. This is my favorite restaurant, and I've got my heart set on the Maine lobster. I'm sure you'll find a parking spot around back."

The back parking lot was eerily dark; a light was burned out. Fran stepped out of the car, then gave a yelp of surprise and dismay.

"What's wrong?" Martin demanded, hurrying to her side of the car. Fran was shaking her foot.

"I didn't see this can of pop someone left in the parking lot. Now I've ruined my new suede pumps," she explained.

Martin was still grumbling about the lousy lighting as they entered the restaurant. He strode up to the host's station while Fran dashed to the restroom to clean her shoe. He was still waiting when she returned.

"Is our table ready, dear?" she asked hopefully.

"I wouldn't know. There doesn't seem to be anyone working here tonight," he said, craning his neck to try and spot the host, who was seating a large party of teenagers in formal attire. "See, I told you this was a bad idea."

He finally caught the host's eye, and she hurried over to greet them. "Hagadorn, party of two, eight o'clock," Martin barked.

"Oh, yes, Mr. Hagadorn. I see you're here for pleasure rather than business this time," said Monica, the host. "I'm sorry about the wait. I've got your table all ready in the smoking section."

"No-smoking, you mean," said Martin. "I specifically asked for no-smoking. My wife's very sensitive to smoke."

Monica knew there were no available tables in no-smoking, so she suggested that the Hagadorns go to the bar for a 20-minute wait until a table was ready. Martin looked disgruntled, but Fran tried to make the best of it.

"That's a fine idea. I can start my birthday dinner off with a glass of wine," she said as they sat down in the dusky bar. She ordered her favorite, a white zinfandel. When the bartender brought her drink, though, it was not what she had ordered.

"I'm sorry, ma'am, that's my mistake," said the bartender. "Let me bring you another glass—on the house." He returned with her drink as well as the bill for Martin's Rob Roy. "I'll take that whenever you're ready, sir," he said.

Martin looked at the bartender in surprise—usually the bar transferred his bill to the dinner tab. But he paid nonetheless. Nothing's gone right yet, he thought, except for Fran's free drink. He excused himself to check on the status of their table.

"Is the table ready yet?" he asked Monica. "It's my wife's birthday, and I'd really like the rest of her evening to be special, if that's not too much to ask."

"Certainly, sir, I understand. Your table will be ready in a moment," said Monica. She started to jot down "Hagadorn—birthday" on the log to remind herself to tell their server to present them with a complimentary cake, when the phone rang. I wish the other host hadn't called in sick tonight, she thought as she answered the phone. After she hung up, she noticed that a table was free and went to get the Hagadorns.

When Richard Merrill, the manager, glanced over the log a few minutes later, he saw that there was a couple celebrating an anniversary, and an 18th birthday for one of the prom-goers. I'll have to stop by those tables, he thought. Just then, his attention was diverted by a commotion near the kitchen. Monica was attempting to seat an older couple at a table near the swinging doors, and the gentleman looked near apoplexy as he loudly refused the seats.

"Is there anything I can help you with, Mr. Hagadorn?" Richard asked, sizing up the situation and smiling reassuringly at Monica. He spotted a table near the window that had yet to be bussed. "We can have that table ready in a jiffy, sir," he said, striding over and starting to bus the table himself. If only it wasn't prom night, we'd have more bussers on duty to speed things up, he thought.

The Hagadorns stood gamely in the middle of the dining area, abandoned by Monica, who had hurried back to her station to greet more patrons. The manager called a busboy over to help him finish preparing the table, then was called away to deal with a situation in the kitchen. The couple continued to wait, until another busboy, assessing the scene, hurried over to escort them to their table.

"Please let me seat you. I hope you haven't been waiting long," Marco chatted cheerfully. "Here's some water and a basket of bread for you. Andrea will be your server tonight. Can I get you anything else?"

"We're finally getting the attention we expect when we come here," muttered Martin to the busboy as Fran smiled her thanks to him. But Marco forgot one detail—the menus—so the brief bright spot in their evening soon flickered and died as they waited in vain for their server to notice them.

"Andrea, table 26," hissed Marco as he passed her on the way to the kitchen. She sauntered over and smiled pleasantly at Martin and Fran and asked if they were ready to order.

"It's kind of tough to order without any menus, don't you think?" snarled Martin. "Don't bother," he said as she started to fetch some. "We're hungry and we know what we want. Give my wife the Maine lobster special and bring me the veal marsala. French dressing on the salads, and start us off with the stuffed mushrooms."

"Yes, sir," Andrea said. "What a crab," she whispered as she passed Marco on the way to the kitchen, nodding toward the Hagadorn's table. "Wonder what's wrong with them?"

Martin started to cool off as the food began to arrive. The stuffed mushrooms were perfect, and the salads were delicious. He ordered a carafe of wine, and even that was correct—this time. Andrea noticed that "the crab" was smiling as she cleared the salad plates. Well, he seems to have gotten over whatever was bothering him, she observed.

She went to the kitchen to pick up their orders, and saw only the veal marsala. "Where's the Maine lobster for table 26?" she called.

"We've been trying to find you to tell you we're out of lobster," said the chef.

"Someone forgot to mark it on the out-of-stock board," Andrea complained, glancing at the 86 board. But now she saw that someone had hastily scrawled "lobster" on the bottom of the list. She knew it hadn't said that when she had checked it earlier.

"Oh, great," said Andrea. "I'm not dealing with this. Where's Mr. Merrill?"

Richard listened to the server's explanation, then approached the table.

"Excuse me, Mr. and Mrs. Hagadorn. I'm sorry to have to tell you this, but we're all out of the Maine lobster because of our prom crowd. We do have lobster tails, though, and I'd be happy to have the chef prepare our surf and turf special for you—on the house, of course," said Richard.

Fran threw down her napkin. "I can't believe this!" she cried. "All I wanted was a nice lobster dinner and we've had nothing but trouble! I don't know whether I even want to stay here anymore." Seeing the manager's earnest face, she tried to calm down. "Okay, surf and turf. I'd like the filet medium rare."

Richard placed the order, then continued with his other duties, convinced he'd picked up the pieces of what could have been a bad scene. If he'd checked back, he would have learned that the "medium rare" filet came to the table well done. Fran, too hungry to fight about it, ate what she could and left the rest. She was subdued as the meal ended without even a little slice of cake to acknowledge her birthday. Usually her husband made certain the restaurant knew it was a special occasion. Oh well, nothing else had gone right. What did I expect? she thought.

When the server brought the check and asked how everything was, Martin blew his top with a tirade that brought Richard Merrill running from across the restaurant.

"I can't believe you have the audacity to ask that question!" Martin yelled. "I have never had such lousy service in my life, and this has got to be the worst birthday dinner my wife has ever had. This will be the last bill I ever pay in this place, because it's the last time you'll ever see us here! And I'm going to tell my friends and business partners, too. You'll never hear the end of this disaster!"

Richard was astounded. All this because of a bad table and no lobster? What could have gone wrong?

Discussion Questions

1. What went wrong with the Hagadorns' visit to Xavier's? Identify at least 10 (there may be more) service recovery opportunities that were missed by the restaurant's staff. What could have been done at each opportunity to prevent or minimize the problems experienced by the Hagadorns?
2. How should the manager respond on the spot to recover with the Hagadorns?
3. What steps does the manager need to take to develop a strategy for ensuring quality guest service and service recovery?

The following industry experts helped generate and develop this case: Timothy J. Pugh, Regional Manager, Damon's—The Place for Ribs (Steve Montanye Enterprises, East Lansing, Michigan); and Lawrence E. Ross, Assistant Professor, Florida Southern College, and owner of Sago Grill, Lakeland, Florida.

Hobson's Choice: Finding the Best Server for the Job

Bill Hobson, general manager of McFitzhugh's, an independent, casual-dining restaurant, was working late on a Thursday night, reviewing the interview notes he had gathered for a server opening he had to fill right away. On Monday, his assistant manager, Gretchen Jensen, conducted the first round of interviews and eliminated seven of the applicants. This morning he personally interviewed the remaining three candidates and this afternoon he asked the staff who had met them for their own impressions. Bill had told each candidate that he would let them know his decision by three o'clock Friday afternoon.

But the decision was not as easy as he had anticipated. Each candidate had arrived for the interviews well-groomed, well-dressed, and on time. They all had either some restaurant experience or hospitality education. Even so, none was an obvious choice for the job; each person came with his or her own strong points and weak points. Bill hoped that by going over his second-interview notes one more time he would at last be able to make a decision.

Because service skills and availability already seemed a given for these three candidates, Bill had focused on a series of questions designed to find out how well each applicant would fit in with the McFitzhugh's team. How well would they hold up under pressure? Were they able to laugh at themselves? Did they have a guest-friendly, team-friendly personality? To find out, he had developed four specific questions:

1. How well do you think you work with people?

   Although most of the McFitzhugh's team is made up of people under the age of 25, they have various education, family, and lifestyle backgrounds. They don't all share the same work ethic. Yet, when they are on the job, everyone has to work smoothly together if they're going to successfully serve their guests. There's no room for lone rangers or prima donnas.

2. What's the funniest thing that has happened to you in the last week?

   Bill knew that some people scoffed at the importance of a sense of humor, but he had found that a positive and constructive sense of humor can be an invaluable asset when problems or stressful situations arise. And guests enjoy a pleasant, smiling server who can laugh along with them.

3. Can you tell me about a time when you weren't treated fairly? What did you do?

   The answer to this question would help Bill know whether the applicant could be cool under pressure—such as when the kitchen makes a mistake on an order, when two servers are out sick on a busy night, or when guests refuse to be pleasant no matter what you do.

4. Has your personality ever helped you out of a tough situation?

   Over the years, Bill had hired more than his share of job applicants who described themselves as "people persons," but were unable to relate well with people who spoke, dressed, or acted differently than they did. When high-tension situations arose, they were flustered—or worse. McFitzhugh's needed servers who could relate well to a wide variety of guests and co-workers and diffuse even difficult situations comfortably.

Now Bill turned to the notes Gretchen had prepared for him after her initial interviews.

Applicant 1, Preston Clark, had impressed Gretchen with his knowledge of the hospitality industry. "This guy knows more of the terminology than I do!" she wrote on a page in the same folder with his application. He was currently a student in the hospitality program of a local community college, and his professors had nothing but glowing comments about his academic proficiency. He had no previous hospitality experience, although he emphasized his position as a "movie theater clerk" on his application.

Applicant 2, Gwen Farrell, had told Gretchen that she had been a stay-at-home mom since she and her husband moved to town from another state and her son was born. But now she was ready to start earning a second family income again. Previously, she had worked for seven-and-a-half years as a server in a well-known casual-dining franchise in Texas. "Shy and nervous at first," Gretchen had noted, "but soon got comfortable and really opened up."

Applicant 3, Charity Lambert, had graduated from college three years ago and worked as a restaurant server ever since. The details weren't immediately clear on Charity's application, but Gretchen had learned that she had worked at three different restaurants in as many years. "Very bubbly and relaxed," Gretchen penciled in the notes section of the application. "Seems extremely guest-service oriented."

After refreshing his memory about Gretchen's perceptions, Bill shifted his attention to his own interviews from this morning. Studying his notes, he replayed the conversations in his mind.

"Tell me, Preston, how do you think you work with people?"

"Oh, I work great with people," the young man responded. "To be honest, I've never met anyone yet who didn't like working with me."

"Okay," Bill said, taking notes. "If I asked what was the funniest thing that has happened to you in the last week, what would you say?"

"That's easy. It would have to be when Professor Mickelson, who's teaching a seminar on the gaming industry—that's what they call gambling now, you know—anyway, he's telling us something about the win percentage for slot machines, and he got the number wrong! Anyway, I'd been doing some extra reading and looking at sites on the Web, so I knew right away that he had blown it. Everybody else was apparently clueless. So I corrected him in front of the whole class. My friends and I are still laughing about that."

Bill nodded, writing. "Tell me about a time when you weren't treated fairly. What did you do?"

"That's another easy one. Once, I was supposed to work the 4:00 to 10:00 shift at the theater on a Saturday afternoon. I left my house on time, but I ended up getting stopped by a train. So I found a phone, called in, and said I'd be late, and they said 'okay,' but when I finally got there, the manager told me the popcorn machine had to be cleaned. I mean, right! Like nobody else could clean that. I think I got the bum job because I was late, but it wasn't fair."

"So what did you do about it?"

"Well, I cleaned it, of course—but since I was only twenty minutes late, I only worked on it for twenty minutes. It's usually a 45- to 50-minute job, but that's only fair, right?"

Bill went on. "Has your personality ever helped you out of a tough situation?"

"Yes, I believe it has. In one of my classes, we had been divided into teams of seven people each. Well, on my team, three of us seemed to be doing all the work for the whole group. The other four weren't contributing much of anything. So the other two people I was working with were getting really frustrated. They talked about just working on their own thing and letting the other four sink. Since I knew the professor wouldn't go for that, I talked to them, got them to voice their concerns to the other four, and eventually work things out so we could finish the assignment."

Bill turned to his notes on Gwen Farrell, Applicant 2. When he asked how well she worked with people, Gwen noted that she had had some problems working with young people in the past.

"Could you explain?"

She answered that some of her young co-workers had been more concerned about talking with their friends than actually doing their jobs. "I'm sure there are lots of good young people out there, but in my experience they don't always have a good understanding of what it means to deliver great service. Sometimes they just want to be entertained, rather than go the extra mile for excellence."

"What's the funniest thing that happened to you during the last week?" Bill asked next.

"I was waiting in the car to pick up our son from preschool when my husband called on the cell phone. Well, the reception wasn't very good, so he suggested I get out of the car. What I forgot was that I had locked the doors while I was waiting—and locking the doors arms the car alarm. I pulled hard on the door handle and set the alarm off. So, my husband is hollering through the static on the phone, my son is coming out of school wondering why his mother is calling all this attention to herself, and someone inside the school was already on the phone to the police!"

Bill next asked Gwen about being treated unfairly, and she mentioned that she had once offered to switch shifts with another server at the restaurant where she used to work. So Gwen worked the other woman's shift and the woman thanked her profusely for trading. But when it came time for her to work Gwen's shift, she said her child was sick and she couldn't do it. "You know, her child probably was sick," Gwen said, "but I felt that she should have worked something out so she could be there. I ended up working that shift for her, but I decided right then and there that, if I ever had a child to look after, I would make arrangements to ensure I met my work responsibilities."

Finally, Bill asked, "Has your personality ever helped you out of a difficult situation?"

"Once I carded a guest who was actually 42! His wallet was out in his car, and he was pretty indignant—not only because he was going to have to go get his I.D., but because I'd even asked for it in the first place. When he came back, I had to smile when I saw his birth date. 'Well,' I told him, 'you sure seem young at heart to me.' Apparently, that was exactly what he wanted to hear. He was a great guest after that."

Now to Applicant 3, Bill thought. Charity Lambert had not made the best first impression. As they shook hands, Bill could not help noticing that she was wearing too much makeup and perfume. But that could easily be adjusted, he told himself.

("Believe me, Bill, she didn't dress like that when I interviewed her," Gretchen had assured him that afternoon.) She did have good experience, though, a bright smile, and an outgoing personality that seemed tailor-made for a restaurant server.

"How well do you think you work with people?" Bill had asked, settling into his four important questions.

"Well, I think I work great with people," Charity said. "I love meeting all the different guests and making sure their visit is a memorable one. In fact, you should probably be aware that lots of guests seem to move with me from restaurant to restaurant. I think I'm good for business."

"What's the funniest thing that's happened to you in the last week or so?"

Charity bit her bottom lip. "That's a tough one. Well, this was probably a month ago, but I was working at Kilby's downtown, and I had this huge tray loaded with an order for a table of six and there was this spill right by the coffee station and—whoosh—down I went! Oh, but now that I think about it, that probably wasn't all that funny at the time."

"Tell me about a time when you weren't treated fairly, and what did you do about it?"

"Wow, these are great questions. Oh, I know. I had this one job where I was working with about five other servers all the time, and they got mad at me because they said I was spending too much time at guests' tables. I don't know what they thought I should have been doing. I mean, the whole point of the job is guest service, right?"

"So what was your response?"

"I just tried to ignore them."

"Has your personality ever helped you out of a tough situation?"

"Well, I don't want to brag, but I think it has. I've heard that traffic cops really like to pick on people who drive red cars, and that's true because they're constantly harassing me about speeding or something. Anyway, when they pull me over, I'm usually able to be charming enough so that they just let me off with a warning instead of a ticket."

Bill set aside the interview notes and applications, leaned back in his chair, and took a deep breath. "Well," he said to himself, "I think that settles it." Leaning forward, he made a notation in his planner to call his new server tomorrow morning.

Discussion Question

1. Based on the information provided, which applicant do you think Bill Hobson hired, and why?

The following industry experts helped generate and develop this case: Christopher Kibit, C.S.C., Academic Team Leader, Hotel/Motel/Food Management & Tourism Programs, Lansing Community College, Lansing, Michigan; and Jack Nye, General Manager, Applebee's of Michigan, Applebee's International, Inc.

Appendix A

Sample Training Schedule for New Staff Members

A training schedule is only effective if it fits your needs and the needs of the trainee(s). The following is a *suggested* training schedule. Read it carefully and adapt it as necessary to organize your training sessions.

Day 1:

Department Orientation

Knowledge for All Staff Members:

- Quality Guest Service
- Bloodborne Pathogens
- Personal Appearance
- Emergency Situations
- Lost and Found
- Recycling Procedures
- Safe Work Habits
- Manager on Duty
- Your Property's Fact Sheet
- Staff Member Policies
- The Americans with Disabilities Act

The Task List for restaurant servers

Day 2:

Review Day 1 (Plan additional trianing time, if necessary)

Knowledge for All Front-of-House Food and Beverage Staff Members:

- Telephone Courtesy
- Safety and Security
- Kitchen Safety
- Alcoholic Beverage Terms
- House Brands and Call Brands
- Basic Food Preparation Terms and Timing
- OSHA Regulations

Knowledge for Restaurant Servers:

- What Is a Restaurant Server?
- Working as a Team With Co-Workers and Other Departments
- Superior Performance Standards
- Sidework Checklist
- Glassware Types and Use
- Food and Beverage Equipment Terms
- Linens and Napkin Folding
- China

The Job Breakdowns for Tasks 1–4:

Task 1 Set Up the Restaurant for Service
Task 2 Stock and Maintain Side Stations
Task 3 Fold Napkins
Task 4 Prepare Breads and Bread Baskets or Trays

Day 3:

Review Day 2 (Plan additional training time, if necessary)

Knowledge for All Front-of-House Food and Beverage Staff Members: (continued)

- The Restaurant Reservation System
- Restaurant Menus
- Correct Plate Presentation and Garnishes
- Sanitation
- Heimlich Maneuver and First Aid

Knowledge for Restaurant Servers: (continued)

- Suggestive Selling and Upselling
- Silverware
- Standard Table Setup Specifications
- Standard Drink Ingredients and Garnishes
- Calling Order for Drinks
- Anticipating Guests' Needs
- Par Stock System

The Job Breakdowns for Tasks 5–9:

Task 5 Prepare Service Trays
Task 6 Take Restaurant Reservations
Task 7 Work Efficiently
Task 8 Greet and Seat Guests
Task 9 Approach the Table

Day 4:

Review Day 3 (Plan additional training time, if necessary)

Knowledge for All Front-of-House Food and Beverage Staff Members: (continued)

- Liquor Brands and Categories
- Standard Drink Abbreviations
- U.S. Alcoholic Beverage Laws
- Beverage Prices
- Responsible Alcohol Service Procedures
- Tipping Policies
- Health Department Regulations
- Point-of-Sale Equipment
- Community Services

The Job Breakdowns for Tasks 10–16:

Task 10 Provide Appropriate Service for Children
Task 11 Lift and Carry Trays, Bus Tubs, or Dish Racks
Task 12 Serve Water
Task 13 Check IDs of Guests Ordering Alcohol
Task 14 Take Beverage Orders
Task 15 Process Beverage Orders
Task 16 Prepare and Serve Coffee

Day 5:

Review Day 4 (Plan additional training time, if necessary)

The Job Breakdowns for Tasks 17–27:

Task 17 Prepare and Serve Hot Tea
Task 18 Prepare and Serve Iced Tea
Task 19 Prepare and Serve Hot Chocolate
Task 20 Take Food Orders
Task 21 Serve Bread and Butter
Task 22 Prepare Ice Buckets
Task 23 Serve Wine or Champagne by the Bottle
Task 24 Serve the Meal
Task 25 Check Back to the Table
Task 26 Respond to Dissatisfied Guests
Task 27 Maintain Tables

Day 6:

Review Day 5 (Plan additional training time, if necessary)

The Job Breakdowns for Tasks 28–35:

Task 28 Sell After-Dinner Items
Task 29 Prepare Takeout Items
Task 30 Present the Guest Check
Task 31 Settle Guest Checks and Thank Guests
Task 32 Clear and Reset Tables
Task 33 Handle Soiled Restaurant Linens
Task 34 Inventory, Requisition, and Restock Restaurant Supplies
Task 35 Perform Closing Sidework

Review all previous training days and plan additional training time, if necessary

Staff member performs some tasks while the trainer observes

Add more tasks as the staff member progresses

Source: Adapted from the "Restaurant Server Guide" in the *Hospitality Skills Training Series* (East Lansing, Mich.: Educational Institute of the American Hotel & Motel Association, 1995), pp. 19–21.

Appendix B

Sample Training Needs Evaluation Form

How well are your current staff members performing? Use this form to observe and rate their work.

Part I: Job Knowledge

Rate the staff member's knowledge of each of the following topics:	Well Below Standard	Slightly Below Standard	At Standard	Above Standard
Knowledge for All Staff Members				
Quality Guest Service				
Bloodborne Pathogens				
Personal Appearance				
Emergency Situations				
Lost and Found				
Recycling Procedures				
Safe Work Habits				
Manager on Duty				
Your Property's Fact Sheet				
Staff Member Policies				
The Americans with Disabilities Act				
Knowledge for All Front-of-House Food and Beverage Staff Members				
Telephone Courtesy				
Safety and Security				
Kitchen Safety				
Alcoholic Beverage Terms				
House Brands and Call Brands				
Liquor Brands and Categories				
Standard Drink Abbreviations				
U.S. Alcoholic Beverage Laws				
Responsible Alcohol Service Procedures				
OSHA Regulations				

Rate the staff member's knowledge of each of the following topics:	Well Below Standard	Slightly Below Standard	At Standard	Above Standard
Knowledge for All Front-of-House Food and Beverage Staff Members *(continued)*				
Beverage Prices				
Restaurant Menus				
Basic Food Preparation Terms and Timing				
Correct Plate Presentation and Garnishes				
The Restaurant Reservation System				
Tipping Policies				
Heimlich Maneuver and First Aid				
Sanitation				
Health Department Regulations				
Point-of-Sale Equipment				
Community Services				
Knowledge for Restaurant Servers				
What Is a Restaurant Server?				
Working as a Team With Co-Workers and Other Departments				
Superior Performance Standards				
Suggestive Selling and Upselling				
Food and Beverage Equipment Terms				
Glassware Types and Use				
China				
Silverware				
Linens and Napkin Folding				
Standard Drink Ingredients and Garnishes				
Calling Order for Drinks				
Anticipating Guests' Needs				
Standard Table Setup Specifications				
Sidework Checklist				
Par Stock System				

Part 2: Job Skills				
Rate the staff member's knowledge of each of the following tasks:	**Well Below Standard**	**Slightly Below Standard**	**At Standard**	**Above Standard**
Set Up the Restaurant for Service				
Stock and Maintain Side Stations				
Fold Napkins				
Prepare Breads and Bread Baskets or Trays				
Prepare Service Trays				
Take Restaurant Reservations				
Work Efficiently				
Greet and Seat Guests				
Approach the Table				
Provide Appropriate Service for Children				
Lift and Carry Trays, Bus Tubs, or Dish Racks				
Serve Water				
Check IDs of Guests Ordering Alcohol				
Take Beverage Orders				
Process Beverage Orders				
Prepare and Serve Coffee				
Prepare and Serve Hot Tea				
Prepare and Serve Iced Tea				
Prepare and Serve Hot Chocolate				
Take Food Orders				
Serve Bread and Butter				
Prepare Ice Buckets				
Serve Wine or Champagne by the Bottle				
Serve the Meal				
Check Back to the Table				
Respond to Dissatisfied Guests				
Maintain Tables				
Sell After-Dinner Items				

Prepare Takeout Items				
Present the Guest Check				
Settle Guest Checks and Thank Guests				
Clear and Reset Tables				
Handle Soiled Restaurant Linens				
Inventory, Requisition, and Restock Restaurant Supplies				
Perform Closing Sidework				

Source: Adapted from the "Restaurant Server Guide" in the *Hospitality Skills Training Series* (East Lansing, Mich.: Educational Institute of the American Hotel & Motel Association, 1995), pp. 14–16.

REVIEW QUIZ

When you feel you have covered all of the material in this chapter, answer these questions. Choose the *best* answer.

1. A moment of truth is any episode in which:

    a. a customer interacts with a company staff member.
    b. a staff member of a company interacts with another staff member.
    c. a staff member comes into contact with any aspect of a company's management and gets an impression of the quality of its management team.
    d. a customer comes into contact with any aspect of a company and gets an impression of the quality of its service.

2. When staff members are empowered, they are:

    a. given permission by the organization to ignore a manager if they feel that the manager is being unreasonable.
    b. expected to take over the management of the organization.
    c. given greater authority to make decisions and thereby perform their jobs more effectively.
    d. free to ignore internal moments of truth.

3. The OK Restaurant is a 200-seat family restaurant specializing in prime rib. Sarah, one of the restaurant's servers, has decided to quit so she can go back to college in a distant city. The manager has determined that, in direct costs, it costs $800 (in termination, recruitment, and selection costs) to replace a server who leaves the restaurant's employment. If the OK Restaurant has an overall profit margin of 10 percent, it will take ______________ in additional sales to make up, on the bottom line, for the direct costs associated with losing Sarah.

    a. $1.25
    b. $25
    c. $80
    d. $8,000

4. "Do you prefer working alone or in groups?" is an example of a(n):

    a. open-ended question.
    b. close-ended question.
    c. question designed to trip up a job applicant.
    d. question designed to uncover a job applicant's psychological motives for applying for a job in food service.

REVIEW QUIZ *(continued)*

5. The process of determining the tasks, behaviors, and characteristics essential to a job is called a job:

   a. breakdown.
   b. analysis.
   c. preview.
   d. forecast.

Answer Key: 1-d-C1, 2-c-C2, 3-d-C3, 4-a-C3, 5-b-C3

Note: In the answer key, the number of the question is given first, then the letter of the correct answer, then the number of the competency that the question relates to. For example, "1-d-C1" means that for question 1, "d" is the right answer, and the question is drawn from chapter material that relates to Competency 1 (competencies are listed next to the outline on the chapter's first page).

Chapter 2 Outline

Competencies

1. Describe the importance of the menu to food service operations, and explain typical menu-planning objectives.
2. Summarize important menu-planning considerations, including menu pricing and rationalization, and describe how the traditional meal periods (breakfast, lunch, and dinner) influence menu planning.
3. List and describe common types of menus, describe typical food categories on menus, and summarize the recommended menu-planning sequence.
4. Explain the importance of menu design and describe menu design elements.
5. Summarize menu trends, describe some ideas for making promotions successful, and identify external and internal factors that can cause managers to change menus.

2

Menu Development

WHEN YOU DINE AT A RESTAURANT, chances are you don't give a thought to the importance of the menu beyond what selections it offers. But if you take time to think about the menu's importance, you can begin to understand how the menu affects almost every aspect of a food service business. In many respects, a menu is a mission statement; it defines an operation's concept and communicates that concept to guests. Some have described the menu as a restaurant's business card.

A menu is one of the single biggest influences on an operation's development of a loyal guest base and a positive return on its investment of energy, money, time, and other resources. One of the goals of menu development, then, is to influence the behaviors and emotions of the guest reading the menu. From influencing guests to select the most profitable menu items to convincing them to feel good about their menu choices, the menu serves as a statement of the restaurant's theme. As such, a menu should embrace and support the operation's image in addition to describing each appetizer, entrée, or dessert.

As you can see, the menu's role is much larger than just listing the products that are available; the menu serves as a plan for the entire food service system. Just as the menu serves as a plan, the menu has to be planned; it has to be planned with guest needs and expectations in mind.

Today's guests are as sophisticated as any in the history of the food service industry. While many enjoy sampling new menu items that add variety and excitement to their experience, others prefer predictable, familiar products. In any case, today's guests are demanding value. They are building strong and loyal relationships with operations that provide this value. Value, of course, is directly related to price as well as the tangible products and intangible services the operation provides. A guest's perception of value may be based on any combination of factors, such as the selection offered on the menu, the quality of the products, portion sizes, the style and quality of service, and price.

Menu Planning

Any food service operation can be viewed as a system of basic operating activities or **control points,** with menu planning being the initial control point. Each control point is a miniature system with its own identifiable structure and functions (see Exhibit 1).

As Exhibit 1 shows, menu planning is the foundation for the remaining control points: purchasing, receiving, storing, issuing, preparing, cooking, holding,

Exhibit 1 Control Points in a Food and Beverage Operation

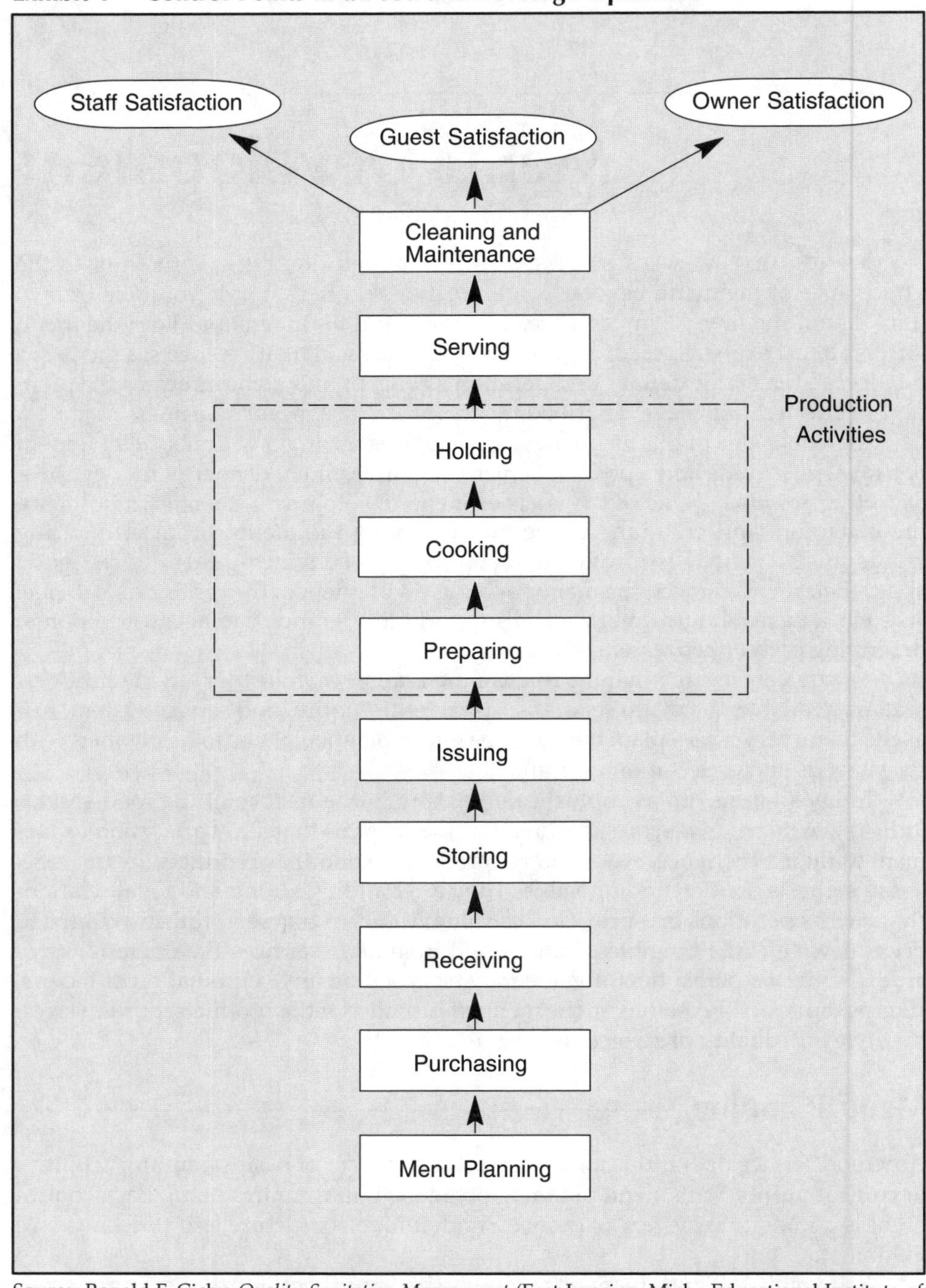

Source: Ronald F. Cichy, *Quality Sanitation Management* (East Lansing, Mich.: Educational Institute of the American Hotel & Motel Association, 1994), p. 3.

serving, and cleaning and maintenance. The end goal is to satisfy guests, staff members, and owners/investors.

Suppliers can help managers plan a menu. Their input and suggestions can help make a restaurant more profitable (or help on-site [noncommercial] food service operations keep costs down) while enhancing guest satisfaction. For example, suppliers can offer preparation and merchandising suggestions for various menu items. Excellent food service operations use their suppliers as sources of market trend information, new promotion ideas, and informal competitive analyses.

In addition to influencing the other control points, menu planning affects, and is affected by, the operation's design and layout, equipment requirements, and labor needs. The success of menu planning determines the success of the other basic operating activities.

Menu-Planning Objectives

To produce a guest-driven menu—one that will please guests and help achieve the goals of the operation itself—there are several objectives that a menu planner must strive to achieve with the menu. These objectives are discussed in the following sections.

The menu must meet or exceed guests' expectations. Because guest satisfaction is the overall goal of food service management, the menu must, above all else, reflect the tastes and preferences of the guests—not those of the chef, the food and beverage director, or the manager. Menu planning is a complex process, but it can be successful when the focus, first and foremost, is on the needs and expectations of guests. All of the factors that go into planning a menu are shown in Exhibit 2. As you can see, guests are listed as the first concern of menu planners.

To plan a menu from the guests' perspective, you must discover exactly what it is that they want. Since the needs and expectations of guests are ever-changing, it is essential that regular input from guests be actively encouraged. Talking with guests, listening to their needs, and acting on this critical input will strengthen an operation's guest-driven reputation. Guests who prefer a casual diner located near a major expressway certainly have different expectations from those having a leisurely dinner in a city hotel's revolving rooftop restaurant.

You can sometimes pinpoint guests' preferences by their ages or socioeconomic status. Whether your operation attracts mostly young families, a singles crowd, or a high percentage of senior citizens, your menu should reflect the kinds of foods and beverages that they enjoy if you wish to continue to attract that particular group.

Another way to identify guest needs and desires is by recognizing what kind of overall appeal your operation has for guests. If your restaurant is part of a "destination" property (a resort, for example) and most of your guests are with you for a week or two, no doubt they would want an interesting, varied diet, and they would be most pleased with either a vast menu or one that changes regularly, even daily.

The menu must attain marketing objectives. While part of marketing is discovering what guests want, another important aspect is providing for guest needs at convenient locations and times and at prices they are willing to pay. In some

Exhibit 2 Factors in Menu Planning

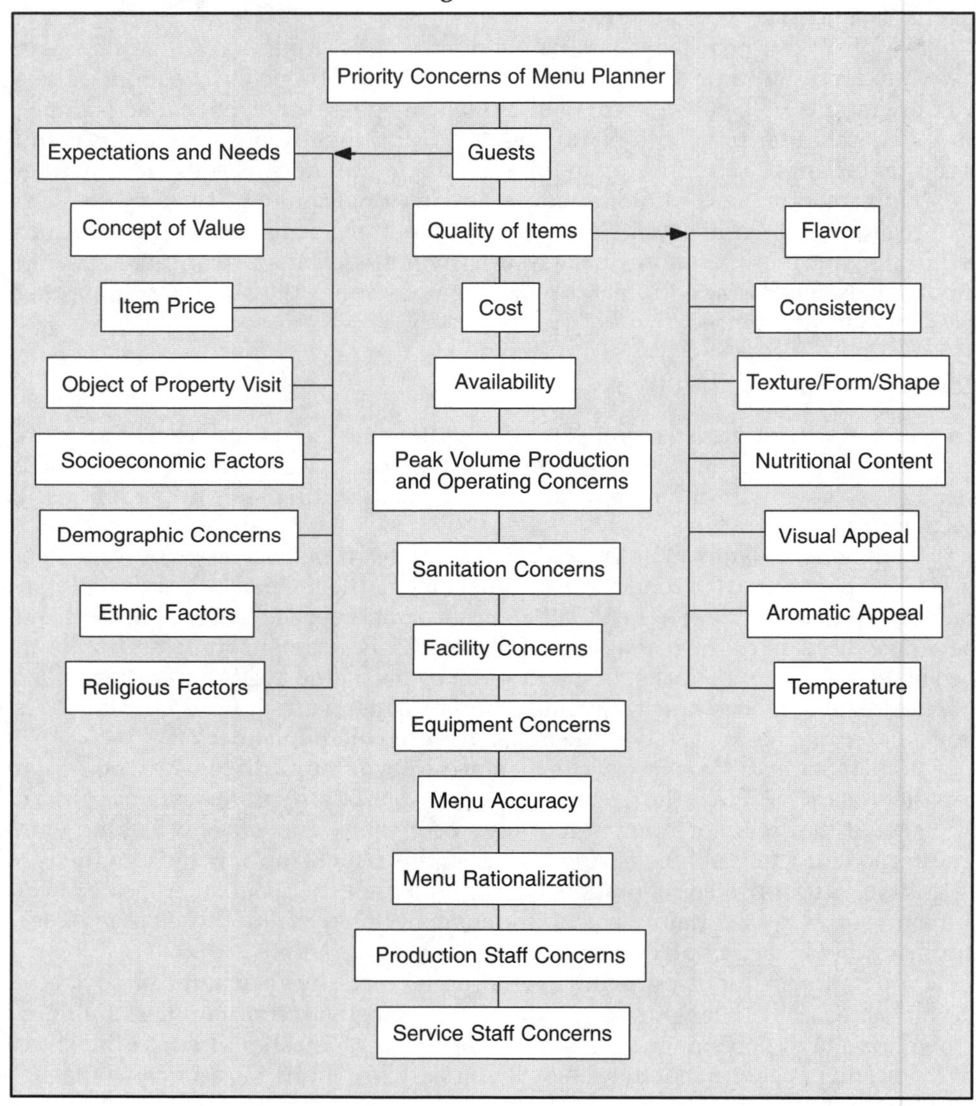

cases, excellent product development, pricing, and promotion will convince guests that you have what they desire—even if they are unaware of what they have been looking for.

Some good examples of specific food items that have been developed and promoted across the United States over the years include pizza, specialty hamburgers, quiche, fish and chips, a vast array of ice cream flavors, fried chicken, variety pancake and crepe dishes, baked potatoes with various toppings, nachos, croissant sandwiches, stuffed potato skins, and pita bread sandwiches. When these items

Nutrition Analysis Tool v1.1

The Nutrition Analysis Tool (NAT) is a web based program that allows anyone to analyze the foods they eat for various different nutrients. This tool is completely free and quite easy to use, just choose one of the options below.

Note to Users: Please be aware that due to heavy usage, there is a certain lag time before the NAT scripts can return computed information back to you and your browser. We are experiencing even greater loads on the server because some users do not seem to realize this and are sending the same request to NAT *over and over again*. Please refrain from hitting a submit button more than once (the server only goes slower the more you hit the button.) Thanks!

- Step by Step with Onscreen Help
- Go Direct to NAT without Onscreen Help

The Step by Step option provides Onscreen Help for beginning users to aid in understanding the steps involved in analyzing different foods. This tutorial also includes pictures to further explain the different functions.

The other option is to go directly to the main NAT page. The same Onscreen Help is available through this option and can be toggled on and off when needed. There are also links to Help screens on every page.

This nutrition-analysis tool found on the Internet (http://www.ag.uiuc.edu/~food-lab/nat/) can help menu planners analyze the nutritional content of menu items. (Courtesy of the Department of Food Science and Human Nutrition, University of Illinois-Urbana/Champaign)

first appeared on menus, marketing objectives may have varied from giving the guests a delicious, nutritious, take-away lunch to introducing the guests to a new gourmet taste treat. Regardless of the marketing techniques used, the menu must help bring guests back for more visits; guests will not return if their perceived expectations are not met or, better yet, exceeded.

The menu must meet quality standards. Quality concerns are closely related to marketing concerns. It is important that you clearly understand all aspects of total quality management requirements and develop menus that incorporate these standards into your food items.

If you are planning a menu for a cafeteria line, buffet, or special banquet, for example, you should know that preparation and holding difficulties preclude the addition of such menu items as omelets, veal marsala, or sole vin blanc.

If you wish to add a number of prepared-to-order food items (broiled steaks and chops, poached fish, and stir-fried vegetables) to your menu—and you have a large dining room that regularly has a high guest count—you must determine whether you have the work space and the production staff members needed to prepare a large volume of high-quality, prepared-to-order dishes. Also, you must decide which items are not practical for your operation.

High quality and good nutrition go hand-in-hand. While food service operations in hospitals, schools, and the military must provide nutritionally well-balanced meals on their menus, restaurants have no such requirement. Yet the expert restaurant manager knows that while people want attractive, good-tasting dishes, most are also interested in the nutritional quality of those foods. Therefore, a menu that met quality objectives would also offer enough choices to the guests so that they could order a nutritionally well-balanced meal. Many menu planners use computer software programs that include nutritional analyses.

Other aspects of food quality include flavor, texture, color, shape, consistency, palatability, flair, and guest appeal. As you plan the menu, remember to balance it so that textures, colors, shapes, and flavors aren't repetitious. Cod in cream sauce, mashed potatoes, and cauliflower—an all-white meal with little variation in texture—is an example of an unbalanced meal. Remember too that some guests cannot eat or do not care for highly spiced or garlic-rich foods, while others cannot get enough of them and would be most unhappy with a menu that offered only bland foods. Because there is a growing trend toward reduced-fat, high-fiber diets, dishes that are both low in fat and high in fiber might attract guests; if these dishes suit vegetarian guests as well, you will add to your potential guest base.

Again, look at your menu from the guests' perspective. What do they want? How can you provide for their needs? Your work is not over until you have produced a menu that not only helps the operation meet quality objectives but also meets the needs of your markets.

The menu must be cost-effective. Noncommercial food service operations as well as restaurants should plan menus that meet financial goals. Generally, restaurants cannot attain their profit objectives unless their product costs, which the menu often dictates, fall within a specific range. Regardless of the type of operation you are planning for, you must select menu items that are within the operation's budget (its estimate of allowable food expenses).

The menu must be accurate. Due to rising consumerism in the United States, **truth-in-menu regulations** are an increasingly important menu-planning consideration. Although such regulations exist primarily at the state and local levels, federal regulations are likely in the future.

Truth-in-menu regulations require accurate descriptions of raw ingredients and finished menu items, in addition to other details. Meat that is described as "choice top butt steak" must be graded "USDA choice," for example. Items billed "fresh" must not be frozen, canned, or preserved in any way. A product's point of origin must also be presented accurately; for example, "fresh Lake Superior whitefish" should indeed be fresh whitefish from Lake Superior. A sample list of common points of origin is presented in Exhibit 3.

The size, weight, and portion advertised on the menu must also be accurate. A bowl of soup should contain more than a cup of soup. Descriptions such as "extra-tall" drinks or "extra-large" salads can lead to guest complaints. "All you can eat" implies that the guest is entitled to exactly that: as much as he or she can eat. For meat items, it is a generally accepted practice to list the precooked weight.

The preparation technique must be accurately described. If there are additional charges for extras (such as substitutions or coffee refills), such charges should be clearly stated on the menu. Any pictures of food products should be accurate. Dietary or nutritional claims, if used, must be precise. "Low-calorie," for example, is vague because it implies that the product is lower in calories but does

Exhibit 3 Common Representations of Points of Origin

Dairy Products

- Danish Bleu Cheese
- Domestic Cheese
- Imported Swiss Cheese
- Roquefort Cheese
- Wisconsin Cheese

Fish and Shellfish

- Cod, Icelandic (North Atlantic)
- Crab
  - Alaskan King Crab
  - Florida Stone Crab
  - North Atlantic Crab
  - Snow Crab
- Frog Legs
  - Domestic Frog Legs
  - Imported Frog Legs
  - Louisiana Frog Legs
- Lobster
  - Australian Lobster
  - Brazilian Lobster
  - Maine Lobster
  - South African Lobster
- Oysters
  - Blue Point Oysters
  - Chesapeake Bay Oysters
  - Olympia Oysters
- Salmon
  - Nova Scotia Salmon
  - Puget Sound Sockeye Salmon
  - Salmon Lox
- Scallops
  - Bay Scallops
  - Sea Scallops
- Scrod, Boston
- Shrimp
  - Bay Shrimp
  - Gulf Shrimp
- Trout
  - Colorado Brook Trout
  - Idaho Brook Trout
- Whitefish, Lake Superior

Meats

- Beef, Colorado
- Ham
  - Country Ham
  - Danish Ham
  - Imported Ham
  - Smithfield Ham
  - Virginia Style Ham
- Pork, Iowa

Poultry

- Long Island Duckling
- Maryland Milk-Fed Chicken

Vegetables and Fruits

- Orange Juice, Florida
- Pineapples
  - Hawaiian Pineapples
  - Mexican Pineapples
- Potatoes
  - Idaho Potatoes
  - Maine Potatoes

Source: Ronald F. Cichy, *Quality Sanitation Management* (East Lansing, Mich.: Educational Institute of the American Hotel & Motel Association, 1994), p. 176.

not specify what the product is being compared to. Servers' descriptions should also accurately portray the menu selections.

The menu should blend the old and the new. Regardless of the type of food service operation, its size, its average check, its guests, or its location, the menu should be a balance between tradition and innovation. The retention of popular and profitable menu items is necessary. Equally important are new additions that give guests something different and a fresh perspective. New menu items can be classified into one of two categories: a creative update of a traditional favorite (Caesar salad with spicy shrimp or filet mignon stuffed with smoked garlic, for example); or a radical departure from traditional menu items (pizza topped with fresh spinach, or fresh pasta served with smoked jalapeño chile peppers, for instance).

Staff members must be able to produce and serve the items on the menu. An operation's staff members are important to the success of its menu. Before management begins menu planning, the skill levels of production and service staff must be assessed. It may be helpful to consider the production staff and service staff separately, although their functions are closely related in practice.

The production staff produces menu items within the confines of the kitchen. In planning the operation's menu, the objective is to avoid overloading any one person or workstation. A well-planned menu features items that the kitchen staff can consistently produce while maintaining the operation's quality, cost, and sanitation standards.

Management should be realistic in determining what can be accomplished with the existing staff. For example, consider a kitchen in a metropolitan hotel where every menu item is prepared from scratch. If all meats are received in the wholesale-cut form (which is less expensive than the retail- or portion-cut form), the staff has to do the additional butchering. If the production staff is not properly trained in butchering wholesale cuts into retail cuts of meat, a lot of time and meat will be wasted, and unnecessary sanitation hazards will probably abound. Rather than saving the business money, this poorly conceived arrangement increases food costs, adds to labor costs, and lowers quality. Such problems can be avoided by organizing the menu-planning function with personnel skills in mind.

The service staff transfers prepared menu items from the production staff to guests. In order to properly serve guests, servers should be ready to answer their questions. Servers should know what items are on the menu, the portion sizes offered, how the items are prepared, and the prices. Even if the menu contains all of this information, a server can provide a personal touch by answering guests' questions directly. Servers should also know the meanings of all terms used on the menu so they can explain them to any guests who are puzzled. This is particularly true if the menu includes ethnic foods.

Again, staff training is critical. In addition to thoroughly training servers, some managers call a five-to-ten-minute meeting with service staff members before each meal period. These brief meetings are informal training sessions. They give the chef and the manager an opportunity to explain daily specials, and they give the servers an opportunity to sample portions of new menu items and ask questions.

Like the skill levels of production staff, the skills of service staff must be considered in menu planning. This is particularly true if management is considering menu items to be prepared in the dining room, such as tossed salads and flambéed desserts. Whether an operation uses tableside preparation methods depends, in part, on the image it seeks. Whatever style of service an operation offers, the service staff must be trained in the skills dictated by the menu.

The menu must be based on the amounts and types of production and service equipment available. Any food service operation must make a large investment in equipment before it can open for business. Naturally, the amounts and types of production and service equipment owned by the business determines what items it can produce and place on the menu. It is imperative to select equipment based on capacity, skill levels of staff members, energy and maintenance costs, and initial purchase price. Equipment should be constructed according to nationally recognized sanitation standards or be listed by accredited testing and listing operations such as Underwriters Laboratories and the National Sanitation Foundation. But above all, it is critical that equipment be easy to clean and sanitize.

Adding a new menu item may require purchasing new production equipment. Such purchases should not be made without an analysis of the flow of products and people through the work area. This analysis helps management anticipate where cross-traffic may create safety and sanitation hazards. Many operations use equipment on wheels or casters so it can be moved easily when necessary. In addition to allowing for adjustments to the product and staff traffic patterns, this mobility facilitates cleaning. Before a new menu item is added, the proper equipment should be available to reduce sanitation hazards. For example, if the proposed menu change involves adding a soup bar to the dining room, the kitchen must have adequate steam-tables, steam-jacketed kettles, or range equipment to reach and maintain safe product temperatures when cooking the soup.

A change in menu may also have implications for the operation's service equipment. Again, sanitation hazards and quality standards must be considered beforehand. In the case of the soup bar, for example, the dining room should be equipped with suitable hot-holding equipment before these new items are added to the menu.

The menu must be appropriate for the operation's facilities. The physical facilities, both indoor and outdoor, affect the image of a food service operation. The layout and design of the physical facilities are also important considerations in menu planning because they establish the physical limits within which food preparation and service take place. The physical facilities must be adequate for the purchasing, receiving, storing, issuing, preparing, cooking, holding, and serving of every item on the menu. Thus, a major change in the menu may necessitate remodeling the physical facilities. By the same token, a change in facilities may force an operation to revise its menu. This mutual influence can be illustrated by the following examples.

Consider a country club food service operation in which 80 percent of the space is allocated to the dining room and 20 percent to the kitchen. Since the kitchen generally prepares menu items from scratch, the production facilities are often pushed to the limit. The kitchen facilities are almost always overtaxed during the summer, when there are more parties and special functions.

Suppose the country club manager decides to expand the dining and banquet facilities by adding a 90-seat patio service area with a clear glass roof. He is convinced that this area will appeal to guests planning parties and banquets because it offers a breathtaking view of the golf course. However, the manager has not considered the production capabilities of the kitchen; to increase the dining facilities without adding to the production area would be a critical error. Such a decision would likely result in lower productivity and morale among production and service staff. A corresponding reduction in guest satisfaction could be expected to follow.

A hotel decides to add room service in an attempt to generate more revenue. Again, the size and layout of the hotel have an impact on the success of the effort.

For example, the kitchen might produce a beautiful and tasty eggs Benedict entrée for breakfast, but by the time room service delivered the order to the farthest wing of the hotel, the product could be cold and unappealing. Room service menus must be limited to those items that can be successfully and safely delivered to guests.

Yet another problem occurs when an overly ambitious restaurant sales force convinces meeting planners that special entrées or desserts will add a touch of elegance to their banquets. These salespeople sometimes fail to consider the limitations of the operation's production and service facilities. Likewise, an outdoor barbecue for 500 people in the hotel's gardens may sound like an exciting affair; but if the kitchen or service staff cannot deliver the products, the guests will not be satisfied.

In all of these examples, the unfortunate results could be prevented. An operation must design its menu around what the physical facilities can realistically handle.

Important Planning Considerations

The complexity of planning a menu varies according to the type of organization. Obviously, table-service restaurants offer menus that differ from cafeteria or buffet menus. Thus, you need to consider the type of operation you are developing the menu for as well as its check average (the typical amount spent by one person on a meal) and overall marketing concerns.

Furthermore, you should consider the items your competitors offer. After all, they are trying to attract the same guests. What are guests purchasing in other restaurants? Why? What can you do to make your products and services special and more attractive to potential guests? If your restaurant has an ethnic theme such as French, Italian, or Mexican, or has an unusual decor such as that of a neighborhood grill and bar or the dining room on a luxury cruise ship, your menu should reflect that theme or atmosphere.

Menu Pricing. Menu pricing is essential to consider as a general planning parameter. Pricing-strategy development requires an understanding of the quality, portion size, and guest service combination as it relates to value. The level of quality has to be based on the requirements of the target markets.

Portion sizes influence the prices charged for menu items; the smaller the portion, the less that needs to be charged for that item. Portion sizes are also tied directly to the value perceived by the guests. It is not advisable to decrease portion sizes across an entire menu; a better strategy is to offer a choice of portion sizes for a menu item when possible.

It is never a good strategy to lower service standards in order to reduce prices. Most guests are willing to pay for good service. Some restaurants are following the strategy of lowering prices or freezing prices at current levels, despite inflationary pressures, to try to build guest loyalty and a base of repeat guests. These operations attempt to make up for the reduced margins by increasing the overall volume and frequency of visits by regular guests. Others are varying their menus with some frequency to build flexibility into menu development.

If an operation has no choice but to raise prices, a number of proven strategies might be used. One is to raise prices at the start of a new accounting period to eliminate problems with accounting. Another is to avoid across-the-board price increases and instead raise them only for menu items that are affected by the higher costs. Guests understand that higher quality requires the purchasing of fresh, and often more expensive, ingredients. A third strategy is to think about implementing new menus each month or quarter to respond more closely to market conditions and prices. Above all, it is essential to keep the focus on value as it is perceived by guests. If menu prices far exceed the perceived value of the menu items, guests are unlikely to return.

Menu Rationalization. The menu directly affects an operation's purchasing, receiving, and storage requirements. The size of storage areas needed for raw ingredients and finished menu items depends on the menu. One of the primary advantages of a limited menu is that it reduces storage area requirements.

In the past, many food service managers attempted to diversify their menus, offering a wide variety of items. Since most items were made on-site, the number and variety of raw ingredients needed increased significantly with each new item. Now, however, there is a trend toward **menu rationalization:** the creation of a simplified menu for the sake of operational efficiency and guest satisfaction. Although this strategy frequently results in a limited menu, the operation can offer several menu items that use the same raw ingredients. The objective of this **cross-utilization** of ingredients is to prepare and serve as many menu items as possible with a limited number of raw ingredients. This helps streamline the purchasing, receiving, and storing functions.

The decision of whether to diversify a menu is driven to a great extent by guest demands. Guests who dine out frequently are looking for diversity in menu choices. Some food service operators reason that, due to increased competition, they must expand business into new meal periods, diversify in order to build guest loyalty and repeat business, and draw on a wider guest base. However, while a constantly changing menu offers variety, it can cause confusion in the operation and result in lowered overall quality standards. An alternative to making frequent changes to the menu is to promote a different item on the existing menu every week, or supplement the existing menu with a few specials each day.

Proponents of menu rationalization say that a food service operation should discover what it does best and continually refine it. Menu diversification requires additional staff training and additional time for taking orders and answering guest questions. Perhaps the best strategy is to create a balanced menu by choosing items from a limited inventory—in other words, create a rational, consolidated menu that maximizes cross-utilization of ingredients and equipment.

Menu Planning and Meal Periods

The traditional meal periods are breakfast, lunch, and dinner. While the focus on all or some of these meal periods in a specific operation varies (some do the majority of their business at breakfast and lunch, others are primarily dinner houses), some generalities can be drawn.

Breakfast. Breakfast is the most profitable meal period, according to many food service operators. Its profitability is the direct result of the relatively low food costs of bakery products and eggs. Often, this relatively high profitability is balanced with fairly low check averages due to relatively low prices.

Some food service organizations offer a limited breakfast menu, with relatively inexpensive prices, that is easy to produce and serve. While traditional breakfast items such as eggs, pancakes, and breakfast meats still appeal to certain guests, other more healthy menu items are making inroads. These healthier options include oatmeal with fresh fruit, multigrain cereals, and breakfast sausage links made from chicken and apples. Food service operators may discover that guests are more judicious in their healthy breakfast choices during the week and more indulgent in their traditional breakfast favorites on the weekends.

Lunch. While lunch menus vary considerably, most have in common at least one objective—speed of service. Lunch items are usually more complex than breakfast items. Healthy choices are a specialty of some operations, although these items are often more costly because of the increased costs of raw ingredients. Many food service operators are searching for a balance between healthy and traditional on lunch menus.

Traditional lunch menu items include hamburgers and variations, soups, salads, steak sandwiches, and fried chicken. Healthier alternatives include grilled fish, turkey burgers, garden vegetable burgers, pasta, grilled boneless chicken breast, and a variety of salads.

Dinner. Dinner is viewed by many people in the United States as the most important meal of the day. People dine out at dinner for many reasons—to reward themselves, save time, conduct business, and celebrate special occasions such as birthdays or anniversaries. Because dinner is generally the most expensive meal, a good strategy to increase dinner business is to promote value from the guests' perspective.

Food service operators are searching for ways to balance dinner menus. Traditional favorites on dinner menus include steak, soup, fish and seafood, pasta, Caesar salad, veal, and chicken entrées. Healthier alternatives are entrées prepared by broiling, entrée salads with reduced-fat dressings, steamed fresh vegetables, and fresh fruits for dessert.

Several fast-food (or, as they prefer to be called, "quick-service") chains that serve primarily burgers are searching for ways to build their dinner business. Although some have tried adding larger burgers, "value meals" (various combinations of a sandwich, fries, and a drink), fried chicken, espresso, pasta, pizza, and even table service during the evening meal, many quick-service burger chains have not been able to successfully build their share of the dinner market.

Types of Menus

Menus can be classified in many ways—by the type of operation in which they appear (coffee shop, room service, casual/theme restaurant, and so on); by meal

NATIONAL RESTAURANT REGISTER'S

MENU-ONLINE

Welcome to Menu-Online, our interactive restaurant information service providing actual menus and other restaurant information.

Restaurant Search
To get started, simply fill out our search form:

Name:
If you know what restaurant you are looking for, enter any part of its name:

Location:
Type in the city below (example: Chicago) and use the pull down menu to select the state.

State: * Choose a State *

☐ Include Fast Food Restaurants
☐ Show Search Icons
(A Table Compatible Browser is suggested)

Price:
In what price range are you looking to find a restaurant?
Any

Food Style:
What kind of food would you like to eat?
Any

Restaurant Search:
Find the restaurants that meet your needs.
Find Restaurants | Clear Form
(To search for a specific food item, use the **Item Search** below).

Food Item Search
To search our extensive database for a specific food item, fill out the following form:

Food Description:
Enter a brief description of the food(s) you wish to find:

☐ Include Fast Food Restaurants
☐ Show Search Icons
(A Table Compatible Browser is suggested)

Location:
Where would you like to dine?
example: northwest washington

State: * Choose a State *

Item Search:
Find the restaurants that serve the item(s).
Find Restaurants | Clear Form

Menu planners can get ideas for their own menus by accessing menus from other restaurants via the Internet. This site can be found at http://www.onlinemenus.com. (Courtesy of On-Line Media Services, Inc.)

period (breakfast, lunch, dinner); by product (dessert menus, beverage menus); and even by age group (children's menus, for example).

Another way to classify menus is to determine whether they are fixed or cyclical. A **fixed menu** does not change from day to day, although it may feature daily specials in addition to regular items. A **cyclical menu,** on the other hand, changes daily for a certain number of days until the menu cycle repeats itself. (This type of menu is usually found in noncommercial food service operations.)

Another popular classification is based on the pricing structures of menus. Many restaurants use an **à la carte menu** that offers and prices each food item on an individual basis. The guests may select from a variety of different salads, entrées, vegetables, desserts, and beverages—all individually priced. In contrast, a **table d'hôte** (fixed-price or *prix-fixe*) **menu** generally provides less choice for guests. This menu usually offers an entire meal with several courses at one price. Guests often have little or no choice regarding individual courses. Some gourmet and other high-check-average organizations use this type of menu; banquets are often served table d'hôte.

Some restaurants feature a basic à la carte menu, then combine selections from it to offer a table d'hôte menu as well. And some restaurants feature a semi-fixed-price menu, selling all the basic meal elements for one price to offer guests value for their money, but then offer desserts and beverages à la carte to increase the check averages.

Food Categories on Menus

Traditionally, food on menus is arranged in the following categories: appetizers, soups, salads, entrées, and desserts. Each category has its own unique features and characteristics.

Appetizers

Appetizers begin the dining experience. Many food service operators have realized the power that appetizers have in making a positive first impression with guests. Winning appetizers are large enough to be shared, give good value for the price, and set the tone for the quality to follow in the rest of the meal. Nutrition is usually not a primary consideration.

Pasta is one of the most popular appetizers nationwide. Shrimp, crabmeat, and fried calamari are extremely popular, as are crab cakes and artichoke and lump-crab fritters. Combinations of pasta and seafood (braised mussels and peppered angel hair pasta served with smoked-tomato fondue, for instance) are also in demand.

Soups

Soups are traditionally the second course in a meal. More often than not, guests choose familiar soups, particularly if they have "homemade" appeal. Soups such as French onion, black bean, and Italian vegetable are popular, as are chili, corn chowder, and potato with cheese soups. A unique garnish can add a signature touch to a basic soup; for example, thinly sliced cooked sirloin on top of black bean soup and diced cooked ham as a garnish for navy bean soup.

Throughout history, soup has served as a comfort food and even as a treatment for the common cold. Soup on a food service menu evokes a nostalgic, old-fashioned mood. Some food service operations report that soup sales are increasing regardless of the season.

Salads

While the leader in the best-selling salad category is still the tossed green salad, sales of Caesar salad have increased in the past few years. Caesar salads are being marketed with cooked protein additions, such as chicken, shrimp, and beef, for both lunch and dinner main courses.

In some operations, salads have surpassed sandwiches as the most popular cold luncheon choice. The key to a top-quality salad is to select only the freshest ingredients and to store and prepare them correctly. Salads as main courses are increasing in popularity, especially those salads that combine grilled chicken, fish, or seafood with fresh salad ingredients.

Many table-service restaurants serve bread just before or just after serving the salad. While, strictly speaking, bread is not a course in a meal, its importance should not be underestimated. Across the country, food service operations are replacing the all-too-familiar dinner roll with unique bread options, such as breads made with jalapeños, sun-dried tomatoes, cheese, or raisins. Bread has been described by some as having "marketing power," since guests are increasingly becoming more choosy and experimental about the breads they eat. The aroma of homemade breads wafting through a restaurant can help differentiate it from competitors.

Entrées

In today's food service operations, menu planners are attempting to balance traditional favorites with innovative items when they are choosing main courses or entrées. New items are being added to regular main course listings in some instances and are being offered as specials in others. In all cases, what differentiates one operation's set of entrées from another are the signature entrées.

Signature entrées are menu items that guests perceive as special and closely associated with the restaurant promoting them. Signature menu items help build repeat business and guest loyalty. Several food service operations are updating traditional beef, chicken, pork, and lamb main courses by serving them with unique accompaniments (lightly cooked fresh vegetables with signature spices, for example). Methods of cooking are also being changed, such as roasting chicken in a wood-fired oven.

Other "signatures" include relatively small protein portions surrounded and garnished by fresh vegetables or fruits. These accompaniments not only add unique textures and flavors, they also appeal to those who are health-conscious. A variety of seafood and fish are being served with unique flavorings such as cilantro, chiles, limes, and olive oil.

Vegetarian entrées have become more popular in recent years. While fruit salad is still a favorite vegetarian item, a variety of vegetable and grain combinations, pasta main courses, and stir-fry entrées are growing in demand. Many of these main courses are adapted from Far Eastern, Indian, and Mediterranean cuisines. Vegetarian entrées provide guests with dining choices that are lower in cholesterol and fat and higher in flavor and fiber. Vegetarian entrées offer the restaurateur favorable food cost percentages and, therefore, higher profits than meat alternatives.

An objective of adding vegetarian menu items is not only to satisfy the needs of guests who are strict vegetarians, but also to appeal to the sometimes-vegetarians who desire a break from their traditional food choices when dining out. Providing main courses that do not include meat helps meet guest demand and satisfy a broad range of appetites.

Vegetarians are categorized based on the amount of animal food or products they eat. **Lacto-ovo-vegetarians** eat eggs and dairy products but no fish. **Lacto-vegetarians** eat dairy products but no eggs or fish. **Pesco-vegetarians** consume dairy products, eggs, and fish. **Vegans** are strict vegetarians and eat no animal products. Each group, and individuals within each group, have unique menu needs.

Desserts

Although guest preferences may have moved toward a more healthy fare in main courses, that is not the case with desserts. Chocolate-based desserts are always popular, and if a dessert is cold and creamy, it usually sells well during hot summer months.

Just as an operation can have signature entrées, so it can have signature desserts. Signature desserts range from simple to complex and tie to the American public's search for unique, value-filled alternatives. Unique desserts that are in demand include fruit cobblers, larger-than-life cinnamon rolls, sawdust pie (named for its ingredients—coconut and pecans), ice cream–filled puffs, deep-fried ice cream balls, mousses, berry desserts, specialty chocolate desserts, red velvet cake, key lime pie, and other desserts that promote regional or local ingredients. Once signature desserts are added to the menu, they should be promoted by servers in ways that paint an irresistible mental picture.

Do-it-yourself sundae bars are popular, and their visual appeal is difficult to match. Toppings—fruit, butterscotch, caramel, chocolate, hot fudge, crushed nuts or cookies, and so on—add to the appeal. For guests who want dessert but with fewer calories, some operations offer fresh fruits and cheeses, served in creative ways. Some top fresh fruits with a light yogurt sauce to create a dessert that is simple, healthy, and refreshing. Frozen yogurt and low-fat, nonfat, and sugar-free frozen desserts are also popular.

Proper handling is critical when storing and serving frozen desserts. Ice cream should not be exposed to temperature changes, since these destroy taste and texture. Frozen items should be stored in a freezer that maintains a temperature of 7°F (−13.9°C) or less. Scoops used to dip frozen desserts must be stored in running tepid water. Before the scoop is used, it should be shaken dry to avoid adding water to the dessert. The person doing the scooping should wear a hair restraint to prevent hair from falling into the product. Additionally, hand contact with the product should be avoided. Frozen desserts should be scooped from the surface to keep the surface level. If scooped this way, the edges of the product will not dry or discolor. As soon as scooping is completed, the scoop should be returned to running tepid water. Frozen desserts that are stored overnight should have surfaces covered with heavy waxed paper to avoid drying.

The Planning Sequence

When planning a menu, begin with the entrées. Keep in mind not only the various types you could offer, but also their cost, their production methods, and, where applicable, their adherence to the theme and atmosphere of your operation.

You can offer a large number of entrées or only a handful. If you feel that you should have something for everyone, keep in mind that you may be faced with some production problems. For instance, you will have to purchase, receive, store, issue, produce, and serve a great number of food items, and you will need sufficient equipment and staff to perform these activities. Your operating costs will probably increase and production and service problems will likely be more numerous than those for operations offering only a limited number of entrées. You should know that the trend in the United States today is toward casual/theme restaurants that offer relatively few entrées. These restaurants not only reduce their marketing costs by focusing on a specific segment of the market (guests who desire seafood dishes, for example, or specialty steaks), but also minimize their production and service problems.

After selecting the entrées, determine the complementary items that will fill each of the remaining categories on the menu. A common procedure is to select appetizers and/or soups, followed by high-starch foods and vegetables (if not part of the entrée), then salads. Finally, you should plan the other menu components such as salads served as entrées, desserts, breads, and beverages. Remember that decisions must be driven by the needs and expectations of guests, both present and potential.

Menu Design

Menu design responsibilities vary according to restaurant types (independent, chain, large, small, full-service, limited-service, and specialty, for example), restaurateurs' preferences, and organizational structures. Some restaurateurs contract with professional menu designers, advertising agencies, and advertising copywriters. Some do it themselves with the help of managers, chefs, other staff members, and a printer. There are computer software programs available that allow restaurateurs to write, format, and print a menu on a personal computer; the software comes complete with templates and clip art.

Regardless of who is assigned the responsibility of menu design, it is advantageous for all menu planners and restaurant managers to be familiar with the process and with the considerations involved. Menu design considerations begin with the needs and expectations of guests. When a menu is presented to a guest, a sales transaction begins. A properly designed menu can stimulate sales and increase the guest-check average. Since a menu presents an image of the operation, its appearance should be in harmony with the image the restaurant wants to project, whether it be elegant, businesslike, fun, ethnic, or casual.

The Ten Commandments of Menu Design

When designing a menu, one of the goals is to create a tool that showcases the personality and virtues of the operation. A well-designed menu communicates the operation's personality and image quickly and effectively. A good menu has been described as a map that encourages easy navigation between hunger and satisfaction. It is also important for the menu to guide guests to both the most profitable and distinctive menu items. What follows are ten commandments of successful menu creation:

1. *Speak plainly.* It is important to use verbiage that is understood by the reader, so carefully select the text to appeal to those who will read it. This is particularly important when the menu features ethnic items.
2. *Say what is important.* This is especially true for menu items that have unique, and perhaps overwhelming, flavors—such as anchovies, chiles, garlic. It is also important (because of diets, allergies, and aversions) that guests know whether a soup is cream-style, or whether an item includes such ingredients as pork, nuts, and shellfish, for example.
3. *Do not be afraid to be descriptive.* The use of appealing adjectives, such as "fresh," "crispy," and "crunchy," paints a mental picture of the item in the guest's mind. These descriptors, if used correctly, will also help sell what you want to sell. Note, however, the cautions that follow.
4. *Say it correctly.* Whenever a description or point of origin or government grade or preparation technique or commonly used term (e.g., "marinated") is used on the menu, it must be accurate.
5. *Describe accompaniments.* It is essential to include a description of all items that accompany the main item so that the guest can have a complete understanding of the full experience.
6. *Remember, "less is more."* It is best to describe only those ingredients that add significantly to flavor and value.
7. *Maintain a sense of perspective.* If you try to recommend everything, you will end up recommending nothing. It is better to recommend signature menu items, and no more than two or three in each menu category.
8. *Spell it properly.* If you wish to create an image of being the expert, be certain that what you say is spelled correctly and utilizes the correct grammar. When spelling or grammatical inconsistencies surface in print on a menu, they may make guests question the authenticity of the overall experience to follow.
9. *Punctuate properly.* It is helpful, for example, to hyphenate compound adjectives—"chile-roasted flank steak." Using a comma between series items and before "and" or "or" in a series—such as "a combination of breadcrumbs, mushrooms, pasta, olive oil, and parsley"—clarifies what could otherwise be a confusing string of words. Remember that an apostrophe is used in contractions (isn't, aren't) and in possessives (chef's); an apostrophe is not used to indicate plurals (except in certain instances with numbers or letters used individually).
10. *Follow rules of good typography.* Select paper color, ink color, and type point sizes that can be read in the dining area in the level of lighting maintained during the meal period. Avoid aligning prices near the right margin, since this makes it too easy for guests to compare prices. Leave sufficient blank space between sections and categories to make category identification by the guests easier.

Source: Adapted from Allen H. Kelson, "The Ten Commandments of Menu Success," *Restaurant Hospitality,* July 1994, pp. 103–105.

Guests are influenced by the menu's visual cues, such as design and layout, artwork, and type styles. As with other communication tools, the way the information is conveyed is as important as the information itself.

For example, quick-service restaurants offer a limited number of menu items but sell these items in large quantities. Since guests are served at a common sales counter, separate menus are not needed. Most guests are familiar with the standardized menu offerings, so elaborate descriptions are unnecessary; they would only slow down the guests' decision-making processes. Quick-service restaurants simply post the names and prices of their products near the sales counter. Enlarged color photographs of menu items show their color and texture and thus may contribute to increased sales. (However, it is important that the items served look like those pictured.) The overall effect is to convey simplicity, speed, and a limited selection of products prepared the same way at every unit.

At the other extreme would be gourmet restaurants catering to affluent, sophisticated guests. These restaurants typically have extensive menus, elegant in design as well as paper and cover. These menus, with detailed descriptions of a wide range of menu items, offer guests a perception of endless possibilities. Since guests in gourmet restaurants usually seek a leisurely and pleasurable dining experience, taking the time to peruse a large menu is usually no problem.

Another element distinguishes the menu of an elegant restaurant from that of a quick-service restaurant: prices. Prices are sometimes omitted from gourmet menus because of seasonal fluctuations in the cost of some items. Some high-check-average restaurants and clubs provide only the guest paying the dining charges with a menu that lists prices. The other guests in the party receive menus that list no prices. A major reason for such a service is to let guests select exactly what they would like without being concerned about what their host must pay for their choices. Another reason is to allow the host the chance to recommend favorites on the menu without causing guests to feel that price is in any way influencing the recommendation.

Most table-service restaurants provide individual menus listing items and prices. Usually, a brief description of major items is included. Some menus have photos of the featured items; some use artwork instead of or in addition to photos.

The information that is printed on the menu is called "menu copy." It is part of the overall menu design. The menu copy is the menu's reason for being; it communicates to guests what the restaurant has to offer. It is imperative, then, that guests be able to understand the names of food items and the words used to describe them. Descriptions of menu items must generate both interest and sales, and they must be in keeping with truth-in-menu regulations. Any general information that the menu provides about the operation must complement the operation's desired image.

Creativity helps make the menu memorable; one creative aspect of any menu is its layout. Exhibit 4 shows examples of menu formats that use different numbers of pages and panels. Once the number of menu items and the sequence the staff members will follow to take guest orders is determined, the menu size, shape, and fold that is most appropriate can be selected. It is especially important that the menu cover be creative and attractive.

Exhibit 4 Menu Formats

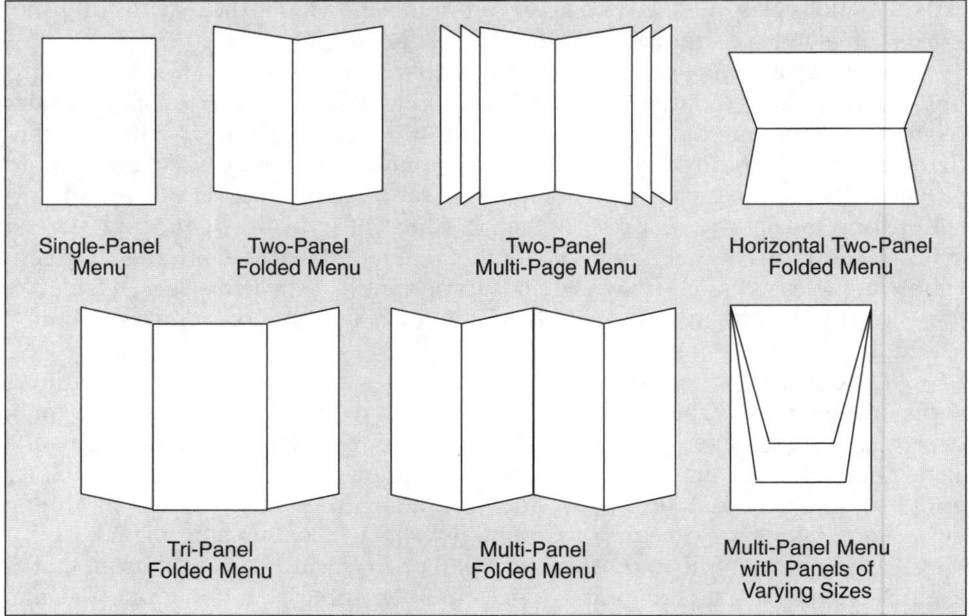

Source: Jack D. Ninemeier, *Management of Food and Beverage Operations,* 2d ed. (East Lansing, Mich.: Educational Institute of the American Hotel & Motel Association, 1995), p. 123.

Above all, a menu must be legible—easy to read. The type style and/or lettering used on the menu, and the size, color, style, and background of a menu affect its legibility. Type that is too small or strange-looking is hard to read. It is usually best to use a combination of upper- and lower-case letters rather than all upper-case letters. Because the lighting in many dining areas is much dimmer than in office areas where menus are designed, the proposed type style, size, and color should be tested in the dining area where the menu will be used by guests.

The type of material on which the menu is printed should be in keeping with the restaurant's image. Generally, inexpensive paper is used if guests use the menu only once (a disposable placemat with the menu printed on it, for example). If a menu will be used longer, higher-quality paper should be selected. Durable menu covers, lamination, and treated papers that resist tears and stains help protect menu pages.

Color gives the menu variety. Since production costs increase as colors are added to the menu, it may be important to try to work with only two or three colors. Usually, dark ink on white or light-colored paper results in an easy-to-read menu.

The menu should not appear crowded. Some designers like to reserve almost half of the menu for white or blank space (side borders and space between menu listings).

Common mistakes on menus include type that is too small, lack of descriptions of food items, spelling errors, and limited use of design techniques to set off items that the restaurant wants guests to notice and order.

A good menu has been described as a map that encourages easy navigation between hunger and satisfaction. It is also important for the menu to guide guests to profitable and distinctive menu items. Profitability of a menu depends to a great degree on its design.

Frequently, the items at the top of a list in a specific menu division are the most popular (the first meat, poultry, or seafood selections; the appetizers or desserts named first). Once you know the items you most wish to sell, place them at the head of the list, put a box around them, or otherwise set them apart. Items on the right-hand page of a two-page, side-by-side menu may sell the best; the middle panel in a three-panel menu is also a good location for food items that you wish to promote. Some operations use clip-ons or inserts in their menus to note daily specials.

If alcoholic beverages are available, say so on the menu. It is possible, but often not practical, to offer separate menus for each meal period. Some restaurants also offer such separate menus as beverage, dessert, children's, or healthy-choices. To make separate menus more practical, you can use a permanent menu cover and simply insert different menus for the changing meal periods or guests.

You can also use a simple menu and lay it out according to meal periods, listing the time periods during the day that such meals are served. If you use a California-style menu, which allows guests to order any item at any time while the operation is open (often 24 hours a day), you should list items according to type (appetizers, salads, entrées, desserts). Many guests prefer to have the traditional menu headings in their natural sequence, beginning with appetizers and ending with desserts. Nonalcoholic beverages (coffee, espresso, tea, milk, soda) are often placed near the end of the menu.

Some restaurants draw attention to daily specials and highlight signature items by boxing the items on the menu. Another way to increase sales of featured items is to write the items on an illuminated board near the restaurant's entrance. Some restaurants specializing in fresh seafood use a chalkboard to list the flight arrival times of the jet-fresh catch of the day. While this approach sacrifices a degree of elegance, it provides convincing evidence of the freshness and variety of the operation's offerings.

The restaurant's address, telephone number, and hours of operation should appear on the menu. Some guests may want to take their menus home, which some restaurants allow or even encourage, especially if the menus are inexpensive. Restaurants using expensive menus might consider making smaller, take-home versions for guests who request them.

It is better to replace menus than to scratch out old prices and insert new, higher prices. To resolve this problem, menu designers may indicate "market price" on items with fluctuating costs.

No matter how well menus are designed, they must be kept in good condition. Dirty, worn, out-of-date, or unattractive menus indicate management's lack of concern for the restaurant's image. Because they create a negative first impression, such menus should be discarded. Someone should be responsible for checking the condition of the menus before each meal period begins.

This Internet site (http://www.yumyum.com) can help menu planners come up with ideas for new recipes. (Courtesy of YumYum.Com)

Menu Trends

In recent years, several menu trends have had a dramatic impact on the menu-planning control points of all food service operations. These trends—smaller portions; regionalized menus; lighter, healthier foods; and ethnic and exotic foods—are the result of restaurant managers' responses to changing consumer preferences throughout the country. (More information on menu trends can usually be found on *Restaurants & Institutions* magazine's Web page at www.rimag.com.)

Smaller Portions

Many guests are interested in sampling a variety of foods in smaller portions, as part of the more casual approach to dining that emerged in the 1980s. (Spanish *tapas* and Oriental *dim sum* are examples of this concept.) This approach calls for mini-meals that can be shared and offers guests a great deal of flexibility. Some restaurants feature expanded appetizer and finger food selections, half portions, and a variety of smaller desserts in response to this trend. Known variously as "grazing" or "modular cuisine," interchangeable courses appeal to many of today's guests.

However, this menu strategy has its disadvantages. It can overwork a kitchen at peak times, slow table turnover (since it takes longer to serve guests), and raise labor costs because of the small, hand-prepared food items and elaborate plate presentations. Food handling may increase and present more potential for contamination and loss of temperature and quality control.

Regionalized Menus

Building on a trend that started in the 1980s, many chain operations are regionalizing their menus to appeal to a larger number of local guests. Regional foods include Cajun cuisine with its blackened entrées, Southwestern cuisine with its liberal use of chiles, and California cuisine with its fresh vegetables and goat cheese. "Nostalgic cuisine," also known as "comfort food," features foods such as pot roast, meat loaf, and mashed potatoes with real lumps, as well as grilled burgers and blue plate specials. Regional cuisine enables food service operations to feature fresh, high-quality local produce that often costs less than imported items. As the number of fresh items on the menu increases, procedures at the various control points change.

The strategy of regionalizing menus is often driven solely by competition from local independent restaurants. Some national food service chains today dictate only half of the items that must be offered on the menu; the region or locality determines the other half. The goal is to attempt to position the operation as a neighborhood or community eating and drinking establishment. Some chain operations keep their menus the same, but add regional or local ingredients or seasonings to recipes. Examples of the first strategy include the Olive Garden's menus in New Jersey with more veal dishes and in Chicago with more sub sandwiches. McDonald's has added crab cakes in the Chesapeake Bay area, Burger King features tacos in California and grits in Kentucky, and Country Kitchen has added

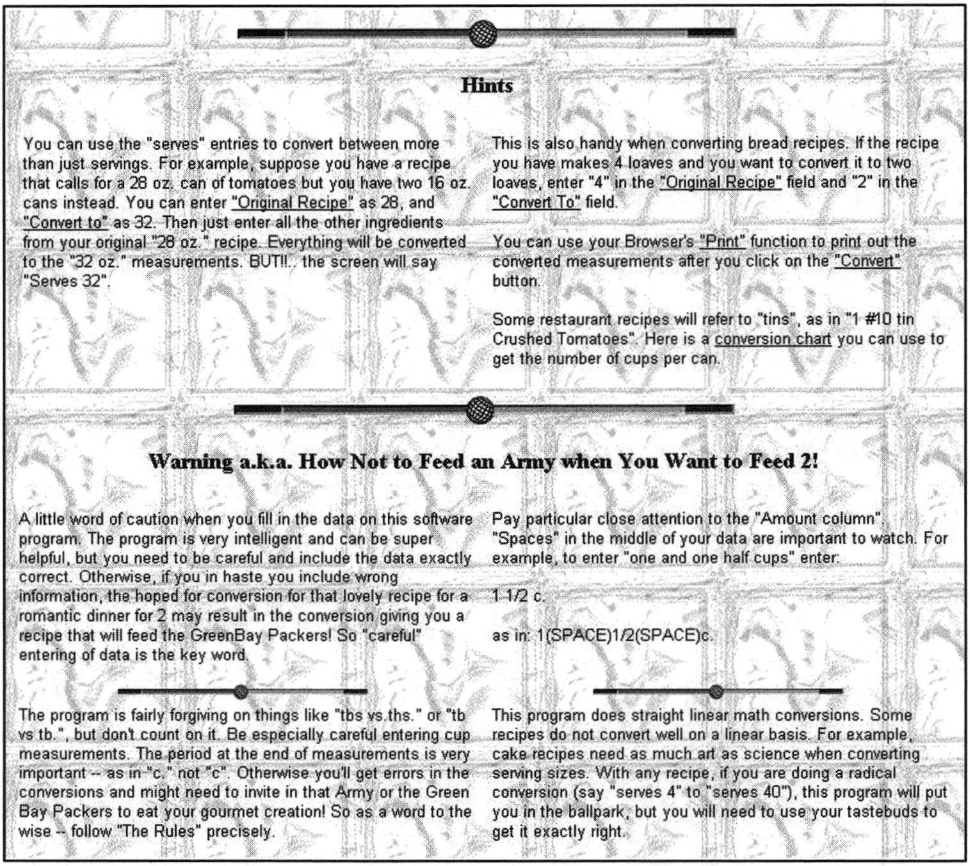

Hints

You can use the "serves" entries to convert between more than just servings. For example, suppose you have a recipe that calls for a 28 oz. can of tomatoes but you have two 16 oz. cans instead. You can enter "Original Recipe" as 28, and "Convert to" as 32. Then just enter all the other ingredients from your original "28 oz." recipe. Everything will be converted to the "32 oz." measurements. BUT!!.. the screen will say "Serves 32".

This is also handy when converting bread recipes. If the recipe you have makes 4 loaves and you want to convert it to two loaves, enter "4" in the "Original Recipe" field and "2" in the "Convert To" field.

You can use your Browser's "Print" function to print out the converted measurements after you click on the "Convert" button.

Some restaurant recipes will refer to "tins", as in "1 #10 tin Crushed Tomatoes". Here is a conversion chart you can use to get the number of cups per can.

Warning a.k.a. How Not to Feed an Army when You Want to Feed 2!

A little word of caution when you fill in the data on this software program. The program is very intelligent and can be super helpful, but you need to be careful and include the data exactly correct. Otherwise, if you in haste you include wrong information, the hoped for conversion for that lovely recipe for a romantic dinner for 2 may result in the conversion giving you a recipe that will feed the GreenBay Packers! So "careful" entering of data is the key word.

Pay particular close attention to the "Amount column". "Spaces" in the middle of your data are important to watch. For example, to enter "one and one half cups" enter:

1 1/2 c.

as in: 1(SPACE)1/2(SPACE)c.

The program is fairly forgiving on things like "tbs vs.ths." or "tb vs tb.", but don't count on it. Be especially careful entering cup measurements. The period at the end of measurements is very important -- as in "c." not "c". Otherwise you'll get errors in the conversions and might need to invite in that Army or the Green Bay Packers to eat your gourmet creation! So as a word to the wise -- follow "The Rules" precisely.

This program does straight linear math conversions. Some recipes do not convert well on a linear basis. For example, cake recipes need as much art as science when converting serving sizes. With any recipe, if you are doing a radical conversion (say "serves 4" to "serves 40"), this program will put you in the ballpark, but you will need to use your tastebuds to get it exactly right.

This Internet site (http://www.tpeaks.com/converter/metric.html) can help menu planners convert the serving sizes of recipes. This portion of the site gives helpful hints to successfully using the site's conversion program. (Courtesy of Twin Peaks Trading Company)

buffalo burgers in South Dakota. Examples of changed ingredients or seasonings include Olive Garden's addition of cumin or chili powder to some of its dishes in areas with large Hispanic populations, and its use of some local cheeses in Wisconsin.

Regionalizing or localizing a menu should not be done without exploring several questions. Will the menu change affect the organization's equipment needs? Some regionalized menus require more griddle space, others demand more refrigerated storage. How does producing (preparing, cooking, and holding) the new menu items affect the flow of other products in the kitchen? A localized menu, for example, may require more preparation staff members and space if it uses more fresh ingredients. Will the sales of the regionalized or localized products take away sales from other traditional menu items? How will the regionalized menu affect the service staff and quality of service? Staff members may need additional training to properly serve the new menu items.

Lighter, Healthier Foods

Perhaps no other trend has so dramatically affected menu planning as the consumer demand for lighter, fresher, more healthful food choices. Many people in the United States are ordering smaller portions of fresh and light food, such as meatless entrées and grilled rather than fried items. Healthier alternatives to beef burgers include turkey, garden vegetable, and black bean burgers. Foods prepared with olive oil are perceived to be healthier. Salads, pasta, chicken, and seafood are gaining popularity, as are new ways to offer them: for example, northern Italian cuisine is a lighter version of America's favorite ethnic food. Appetizing foods with reduced sodium, cholesterol, fat, and calories are much in demand.

Some operators present nutritional information on their menus, and some use the American Heart Association symbol to highlight items with controlled fat and cholesterol. Others emphasize fresh, seasonal, wholesome food choices. Fresh menu items call for adjustments in purchasing frequencies, receiving schedules, storage procedures, and production techniques. As preparation and cooking methods change, the skill levels of staff members and managers must also change.

Some food service operations are coupling their healthy cuisine with an increased emphasis on ecology. Using more recyclable products, rewarding guests who return reusable to-go containers, and even replacing matchbooks with small packets of flower seeds are examples of this healthy cuisine–ecology partnership.

Ethnic and Exotic Foods

The menus of most food service operations, both commercial and noncommercial, offer ethnic items from more than one ethnic cuisine. Besides Mexican and Italian, popular cuisines on U.S. menus include Chinese, Japanese, and Thai.

Mexican food served most often in the United States is a blend of the flavors of the southwestern United States and northern Mexico. Often featured at quick-service and table-service chain and independent restaurants, Mexican cuisine in the United States is variously labeled Gringo Mexican, New Wave Ameri-Mex, Southwestern, or Tex-Mex. While these variations appeal to mass markets, other food service operations have decided to promote authentic, regional Mexican cooking. Authentic Mexican cuisine, by comparison to Gringo Mexican, is lower in fat due to reduced amounts of cheese and preparation with less frying. Chile varieties used in this cuisine vary. Chiles and other spices are often incorporated into sauces that are served as optional accompaniments to flavorful, fresh, and not overly hot foods.

Italian cuisine is known for its versatility as well as its popularity. Today, some operations are creating new types of pizzas, including four-cheese pizzas or pizzas topped with pesto, fresh spinach, apricots, grilled vegetables, jalapeños, or just plain mozzarella cheese and basil. Pastas are surfacing as pumpkin-stuffed ravioli, *pasta e fagioli* (pasta and beans), pasta with steamed fresh vegetables, and old-fashioned spaghetti and meatballs.

Because they often have exotic flavors or unusual ingredient combinations and may require unique preparation techniques, ethnic and exotic foods should be added to a menu with care. Caution must be exercised whenever ingredients or

Exhibit 5 Promotion Ideas

Promotion	Components
Culinary History	Tie history of cuisine (such as pasta) to the history of an appropriate wine.
Decorations	Offer posters, T-shirts, or sweatshirts as prizes.
Special Events	In addition to cuisine and service, build a promotion around a party, craft show, musical, play, or other special event that fits with the theme.
Free Items	Offer prospective guests a free menu item (appetizer, dessert) to encourage repeat business.
Fruit Extravaganza	Feature fresh in-season fruits such as blueberries, cherries, or strawberries. Provide giveaways such as T-shirts or sweatshirts that fit with the theme.
Local and Regional	Showcase foods native to the state or locality; feature those from local farms.
Olive Lovers	Offer menu items that use olives. Tie the theme into giveaways such as photographs, recipe books, and other merchandise.
Pasta	Offer a combination of imported and domestic pasta menu items, served with freshly baked bread.
Seafood	Add unique seafoods from around the world to build seafood sales.
Specialty Foods	In partnership with suppliers, offer unique specialty foods ranging from regional cuisines to specific menu item ingredients.
Wines and Food	Combine cuisine with wines that are appropriate for new taste sensations.

Source: Adapted from Cecile Lamalle, "Profitable Promotions," *Restaurant Hospitality,* November 1993, pp. 103–104.

preparation and cooking processes are altered and staff members are not familiar with them. Adding new menu items can result in sanitation and quality problems if staff members are not properly trained.

Promotions

As part of the overall marketing strategy for all categories of menu items and all types of menus, **promotions** are designed to build value for guests, excitement for staff members, and profits for owners and investors. Exhibit 5 lists a number of promotion ideas that represent only a sampling of the endless variety of promotions available—limited only by one's creativity and the needs of guests.

The key to successful promotions is communication to staff members as well as to guests. Rather than simply announcing a promotion to staff members, managers should get them involved from the start. By soliciting their ideas regarding what to promote, what sorts of decorations to use, what kind of advertising approach might work best, what changes to current service procedures might help enhance the promotion, and so on, staff members will take "ownership" of the promotion. If a new menu item is being promoted, managers should give staff members an opportunity to taste it. With this first-hand knowledge, staff members will do a better job of selling the promoted item to guests.

All staff members, both guest-contact and support, should be given the opportunity to be involved with the promotion. If staff members spend time after-hours decorating the restaurant to fit the promotion's theme, managers should create a festive atmosphere so that staff members can have some fun while putting in the extra work. If the promotion includes giveaways for guests, then managers—rather than giving the prizes away themselves—should let staff members have the fun of giving them away. These strategies can help build staff member enthusiasm for promotions.

And, last but not least, successful promotions have specific goals—a set sales figure or a targeted percentage increase, for example. Staff members should know these goals in advance.

Changing the Menu

Because conditions change, a food service operation's menu must also change. Menu changes are influenced by both external and internal factors.

External factors include guest demands, economic factors, the competition, supply levels, and industry trends. Guest demands are the most important factor to consider in changing a menu. Management should first decide which potential markets it wants to attract with a modified menu. The proposed menu change should then be evaluated in light of its potential impact on the current markets. Economic factors include the cost of ingredients and the potential profitability of new menu items. The competition's menu offerings can also influence menu decisions. For example, a hotel food service operation located next door to a restaurant offering "the best Mexican food in town" might elect not to serve Mexican cuisine. Supply levels affect the price and the quality and quantity of the proposed menu items. Supply levels are highly variable for some seasonal raw ingredients, such as fresh fruits and vegetables. Industry trends affect menus as menu planners try to keep current with what's popular with guests. Regionalization of menus and putting more healthy menu items on menus are two trends mentioned earlier in the chapter.

Internal factors that may result in a proposed menu change are the facility's meal pattern, concept and theme, operational system, and menu mix. The typical meal pattern is breakfast, lunch, and dinner. Management must decide if existing meal periods should be continued or altered. The target markets' expectations directly influence this decision. Any menu change must also be compatible with the operation's concept and theme; a restaurant that is known as the best steakhouse in the city may do itself a disservice by offering fewer steak selections in order to add fresh fish and shellfish to the menu. An operation's image may also rule out foods that do not match its theme and decor.

Menu changes are also modified by the organization's operational system. For example, a menu change may raise both food and labor costs to unacceptable levels. Production and service staff members may lack the necessary skills to produce and present the new menu item. If extensive new equipment is crucial to the successful production and service of a new item, the change may be too costly. Many operations deal with this factor by designing flexible kitchens with multipurpose equipment. For example, a combination convection oven/steamer can bake, roast, and steam. Tilt skillets can be used for baking, braising, frying, griddling, or steaming.

An operation's existing menu has a certain overall combination or mix of items. This menu mix will be affected by any change in individual items. All of these factors should be evaluated before menu changes are finalized.

The dual goal of any menu should be to satisfy guests and to meet the financial objectives of the organization. First and foremost, it is important to know the guests and their requirements. The more you know about your guests, the more likely it is that you will build a menu that will satisfy and delight them. It is equally important to keep up with trendy foods that should be considered for possible addition to the menu. You should keep in mind the availability of ingredients used to produce the menu items, and remember that variety can be added to the same raw ingredients through the use of additional spices, herbs, and textures. Remember too that it is important for menu items to fit with the production equipment and staff capabilities, the service equipment and staff capabilities, and the operation's concept and theme.

In many respects, menu development is never finished; it is an ongoing process.

Key Terms

à la carte menu—A menu that offers and prices each food item on an individual basis. Guests may select from a variety of different salads, entrées, vegetables, desserts, and beverages—all individually priced.

control points—A system of basic operating activities common to all types of food service operations. Each control point is a miniature system with its own identifiable structure and functions. The control points are menu planning, purchasing, receiving, storing, issuing, preparing, cooking, holding, serving, and cleaning and maintenance.

cross-utilization—In food service operations, a menu-planning strategy that calls for preparing and serving as many menu items as possible from a limited number of raw ingredients. It is a part of menu rationalization.

cyclical menu—A menu that changes daily for a certain number of days, then repeats the sequence.

fixed menu—A menu that does not change from day to day.

lacto-ovo-vegetarian—An individual who does not eat meat but eats eggs and dairy products (but no fish) in addition to vegetables, fruits, grains, and nuts.

lacto-vegetarian—An individual who does not eat meat but eats dairy products (but no eggs or fish) in addition to vegetables, fruits, grains, and nuts.

menu rationalization—The creation of a simplified, balanced menu for the sake of operational efficiency and guest satisfaction. This approach frequently results in a limited menu, but through cross-utilization an operation can offer several items using the same ingredients.

pesco-vegetarian—An individual who does not eat meat but eats dairy products, eggs, and fish in addition to vegetables, fruits, grains, and nuts.

promotion—All the ways in which a business tries to persuade people to buy its products and services.

signature entrée—A menu item that guests perceive as special and closely associated with the restaurant promoting it. Signature menu items help build repeat business and guest loyalty.

table d'hôte menu—A menu that offers a complete meal with several courses at one price. Also called a fixed-price (or *prix-fixe*) menu. Guests generally have little or no choice regarding individual courses, but there may be two or more complete meals to choose from.

truth-in-menu regulations—Truth-in-menu regulations require accurate descriptions of raw ingredients and finished menu items, in addition to other details.

vegan—A strict vegetarian who eats no animal products whatsoever.

Review Questions

1. What are some common objectives that menu planners should keep in mind when planning a menu?
2. What is "menu rationalization"?
3. What are some considerations menu planners should keep in mind when planning menu items for the breakfast meal period? lunch meal period? dinner meal period?
4. What are some typical menu classifications?
5. What are typical food categories on menus?
6. What are some menu design elements and considerations that menu planners should be aware of when planning menus?
7. What are some examples of menu trends?
8. What are some keys to successful promotions?
9. What are some typical external factors that lead managers to change menus? What are some typical internal factors?

Internet Sites

For more information, visit the following Internet sites. Remember that Internet addresses can change without notice.

http://www.byte2eat.com

http://www.cyber-kitchen.com

http://www.cybermenus.com/brochure

http://www.dinefind.com

http://www.dinenet.com

http://www.exit109.com/~mstevens/menulink.shtml

http://www.foodwine.com/digest

http://www.kitchenlink.com/comm.html

http://www.menudesigns.com

http://www.menupro/menus.html

http://www.moorebp.com/cafe

http://www.onlinemenus.com

http://www.ranw.com/links.htm

http://www.restaurant-pages.com

http://www.rimag.com

References

Brooks, Steve. "McFumble." *Restaurant Business,* January 20, 1994.

Cichy, Ronald F. "Developing a Winning Menu." *Michigan Restaurateur,* March/April 1990.

———. *Quality Sanitation Management.* East Lansing, Mich.: Educational Institute of the American Hotel & Motel Association, 1994.

Cloutier, M. M. "All Over the Map." *Restaurant Business,* November 20, 1993.

"Creating Menus That Sell." *Menus Today,* Winter 1995.

"Ethnic Foods Shine as Menus." *Restaurants & Institutions,* April 1, 1994.

Kelson, Allen H. "The Ten Commandments of Menu Success." *Restaurant Hospitality,* July 1994.

Liberson, Judy. "Developing Profitable Menus." *Lodging,* January 1998.

Lorenzini, Beth. "Promotion Success Depends on Employees' Enthusiasm." *Restaurants & Institutions,* February 12, 1992.

Nabisco Food Group, *Profit Workbook,* an advertising supplement to Restaurant Business, Inc. Publications, undated.

National Restaurant Association, "1995 Foodservice Industry Forecast." *Restaurants USA,* December 1994

Ryan, Nancy Ross. "Balancing the Menu." *Restaurants & Institutions,* March 1, 1993.

———. "Pizza and Pasta: Two Too Good to Be True?" *Restaurants & Institutions,* March 1, 1994.

———. "Entrées: Where Signature Is King." *Restaurants & Institutions,* March 1, 1994.

Schechter, Mitchell. "Brave New Foods." *Restaurant Hospitality,* February 1993.

"Specialty Sweets." *Menus Today,* Winter 1995.

Straus, Karen. "Authentic Ethnics: Mexican." *Restaurants & Institutions,* March 15, 1994.

Swanson, Elizabeth. "Customers Want More Than a Guilt-Free Meal When Dining Out." *Inn Touch,* February 1994.

Weiss, Steve. "Salads Make a Play for Mass Appeal." *Restaurants & Institutions,* March 1, 1994.

———. "Appetizers: Don't Ditch the Deep-Fat Just Yet." *Restaurants & Institutions,* March 1, 1994.

———. "Customers Look for the Familiar in Soup Bowls." *Restaurants & Institutions,* March 1, 1994.

Winchester, Sarah Hart. "Making Sure the Price Is Right." *Restaurants USA,* December 1994.

Case Studies

Anatomy of a Restaurant Promo, or How Seymour Learned to Love Seafood

Schultzie's is a 30-unit casual-dining chain in the heart of the Midwest. Seymour Tidwell, who manages a Schultzie's, likes his job. His unit is clean and attractive, he has lots of regular guests, and he is located in a college town where the pool of workers is relatively large.

Today, however, Seymour is attending a managers' meeting at corporate headquarters, and he's not very happy about it. "I hate these promo roll-outs," Seymour whispers to the manager next to him. The promos are part of the chain's new policy of "freshening" its menu with several new items each quarter.

He leans closer to the manager's ear. "My guests come to my restaurant because they like the tried-and-true items. This promo stuff corporate comes up with is just too exotic for them. Like those Tongue-Burner Fajitas—they were just too spicy for this part of the country."

"I don't agree," the manager whispers back. "My guests have been asking for more interesting items. I'm glad corporate headquarters is finally responding."

"Well," Seymour murmurs grudgingly, "I guess everyone has different tastes." But he decides to try to keep an open mind about the new items.

Meanwhile, a corporate vice president is telling the managers, "Our theme for this promo is 'Bounty from the Sea.' Market research indicates that Midwesterners are eating seafood more often. And with Lent coming up, we think these items will be very popular. They're also higher-priced items—something you and your servers might appreciate. We've got three new items you'll be sampling at lunch. The first item is 'Brandied Shrimp from the Barbie,' an appetizer. We've also got a 'King of the Sea' salad and the 'Seafood Puff,' a seafood paté wrapped in a puff pastry with a lemon sauce."

Seymour, who dislikes fish and seafood to begin with, isn't looking forward to sampling the items. But the shrimp isn't bad, he thinks. He reminds himself that he's going to keep an open mind and makes a note to tell his servers that their check averages—and tips—will increase if they are successful at selling the promo items.

As usual, the corporate VP provides a package of training items for managers to use back at their units. There is an introductory videotape and some quizzes for servers. "We're also sending you back to your units with these special guest comment cards," the VP says. "Please make sure each guest who orders one of the promo items receives a comment card, and send the cards you collect each week back to us. Make sure servers understand that they should not give cards to guests who order substitutions on the promo items."

The next day, Seymour meets with Jennifer, Steve, and Rollo, members of the service staff, to discuss the new menu items. Seymour is running late and decides he doesn't have time to use all of the training materials corporate headquarters provided. He decides to just show the videotape and have the kitchen make up some sample items. "I don't happen to like seafood myself," Seymour tells the servers, "but these are higher-priced items, so pushing them will help you increase your check averages. The kitchen is making up some sample batches so you can taste them. Oh, and please make sure that guests who order these get one of these comment cards—I have a supply for each of you. If you run out, let me know. Who knows? Maybe the guests will really like this stuff."

Back in the kitchen, the cooks are learning to prepare the new items. "Hey," Mike, the head cook, says to Seymour, "H-Q didn't send any lemon sauce for the puff pastry."

"Well, just put some white sauce on it," Seymour says. "Tell the servers to pretend it's lemon sauce. I'll call and make sure we have the lemon sauce on hand when we roll out the new items to guests tomorrow."

"And we only have two burners for this shrimp, you know," Mike says. "Orders are going to get backed up, and shrimp is so fussy. We've got to turn it right on time or it'll get rubbery. This is going to be a problem if this item is popular."

"Let's not worry about it now. I don't think our guests are going to go for this stuff in a big way," Seymour says.

But Seymour is wrong. When the promos hit the menu at lunchtime the following day, Seymour is surprised to hear guests say, "Oooh, that brandied shrimp sounds good," and, "I'm going to try the 'King of the Sea' salad," and, "I love puff pastry. I'm going to try the 'Seafood Puff.'"

Unfortunately, the servers don't quite understand how to maintain the guests' initial enthusiasm for the new items:

> "Is there shrimp in the 'Seafood Puff'? I'm very allergic to it," a guest asks Jennifer.
>
> "Um, I forgot," Jennifer replies. "I tried it this morning and it didn't taste like there was shrimp in it. Want me to ask?"
>
> "No, I'm on my lunch hour and I've only got 45 minutes. Just bring me a burger," the guest says.

> "Is the lemon sauce on the 'Seafood Puff' made with cream?" another guest asks Steve.
>
> "I don't know," says Steve. "When I had it, they put white sauce on it."
>
> "Could I have that instead of the lemon sauce?" asks the guest.
>
> "It's not supposed to be served that way," says Steve. "Could I get you something else? Maybe the salad?"
>
> "No, that's okay," says the guest. "Just bring me a burger."

"What kind of dressing do you recommend on the seafood salad?" another guest asks Rollo.

"Gee, I don't know, I really don't like seafood," Rollo says. "We have French, Thousand Island, Bleu Cheese, Ranch, and Italian. Want to try any of those?"

"No, I guess not," says the guest. "I'll have a burger."

Seymour is surprised by the small number of guest comment cards the servers turn in at the end of their shift. "I was afraid these promos wouldn't go over," Seymour says to Rollo.

"Well, I think I could have sold more," Rollo volunteers, "but I just didn't know enough about them. Why didn't we get any fact sheets and quizzes to help us?"

Seymour says nothing, but he decides perhaps he should use more of the training materials for the evening servers. Before the evening shift begins, he not only shows them the videotape and gives them meal samples, but he goes over the frequently-asked-question cards and quizzes servers about the ingredients. "Gee, it didn't take that long," Seymour says when the training is over. "I should have done this at lunchtime."

Seymour watches the service staff carefully and notices that all of the new items are moving faster than at lunchtime—especially the "Brandied Shrimp from the Barbie." "I wonder if Mike's able to keep up with the orders?" Seymour worries. He goes to the kitchen to find out.

Mike is having problems. "Seymour, I've had to throw out four of these shrimp orders because they got really rubbery, and this stuff isn't cheap. We're doing our best, but we don't have time to watch them like we should. I think we might run out before the night's over. We're also getting behind on some of our other orders because we're backed up with shrimp orders on these burners. The servers are getting cranky with us, and the kitchen staff is really frustrated. This shrimp is nothing but trouble."

"Do what you can for now," says Seymour, "and I'll try to come up with something for tomorrow."

At the end of the evening, Seymour is glad to see many more guest comment cards. Most of the reviews are glowing, especially about the "Brandied Shrimp from the Barbie." "Great stuff! I loved the cocktail sauce." "Cocktail sauce?" wonders Seymour. "The servers must be substituting. Oh well, whatever the guests want. Maybe these promo items aren't so bad after all."

Discussion Questions

1. What did corporate headquarters do right in its introduction of the new menu items? What could it have done to improve the chances for the promo's success?

2. What did Seymour do right with regard to the promo? What did he do wrong or fail to do to help the promo succeed?

3. How could the servers have helped make the promo more successful?
4. What can Seymour do in the next week to make the promo more successful?

The following industry experts helped generate and develop this case: Christopher Kibit, C.S.C., Academic Team Leader, Hotel/Motel/Food Management & Tourism Programs, Lansing Community College, Lansing, Michigan; and Jack Nye, General Manager, Applebee's of Michigan, Applebee's International, Inc.

REVIEW QUIZ

When you feel you have covered all of the material in this chapter, answer these questions. Choose the *best* answer.

1. Which of the following statements about a food service operation's menu is *true?*

   a. The menu affects almost every aspect of the food service operation.
   b. The menu is a relatively unimportant part of the food service operation.
   c. The menu seeks to influence the behaviors and emotions of the guest reading the menu.
   d. a and c.

2. Truth-in-menu regulations require that:

   a. descriptions of menu items be accurate.
   b. restaurant managers hit certain financial goals.
   c. restaurateurs provide healthy menu items on their menus.
   d. all taxes on the sale of menu items be paid in full each year.

3. What is "menu rationalization"?

   a. Menu rationalization refers to the excuses restaurant managers typically give for failing to follow truth-in-menu laws.
   b. It is the creation of a simplified menu for the sake of operational efficiency and guest satisfaction.
   c. Menu rationalization refers to the process restaurant managers go through to reach "rational" (i.e., market-driven) prices for menu items.
   d. It is a name for the research menu planners go through when they plan menus; specifically, it refers to the activity of studying scores—sometimes hundreds—of menus from competitors in order to help the planners gather ideas for the menu they are designing.

4. An à la carte menu:

   a. lists entrées only.
   b. is not used in chain restaurants.
   c. offers and prices each menu item on an individual basis.
   d. is exempt from truth-in-menu regulations in most states.

REVIEW QUIZ *(continued)*

5. In order to compete with a popular independent restaurant down the street, Chris's chain restaurant has added locally popular ingredients and seasonings to recipes. Chris also was given the authority to add items to the menu that are favorite dishes of the locals. This illustrates which of the following menu trends?

   a. smaller portions
   b. regionalized menus
   c. lighter, healthier foods
   d. exotic ingredients

Answer Key: 1-d-C1, 2-a-C1, 3-b-C2, 4-c-C3, 5-b-C5

Each question is linked to a competency. Competencies are listed on the first page of the chapter. An answer reading 3-b-C4 translates to:

3: the question number
b: the correct answer
C4: the competency number

Chapter 3 Outline

Dining Service Staff Positions
- Server
- Busperson
- Host
- Cashier
- Dining Room Manager

Styles and Procedures
- Plate Service
- Cart Service
- Platter Service
- Family-Style Service
- Buffet Service

Providing Superior Service
- Preshift Meetings
- Suggestive Selling
- Service Guarantees
- Resolving Guest Complaints
- The Team Approach to Service
- Serving Guests Who Have Disabilities

Competencies

1. List and describe typical dining service staff positions, and distinguish among the most common styles of dining room service.
2. Describe the following strategies and procedures related to providing superior service to guests: preshift meetings, suggestive selling, service guarantees, resolving guest complaints, the team approach to service, and serving guests who have disabilities.

3

Dining Service: Styles and Procedures

IN A TABLE-SERVICE RESTAURANT, a guest's full enjoyment of the food and beverages depends in large part on the quality and style of service. The menu items may be prepared faultlessly and the decor may be interesting and attractive, but if staff members display no courtesy, personality, or interest in serving guests—or if the restaurant doesn't offer the quality and style of service the guest desires—the dining experience will be unsatisfactory and the guest probably won't return. Poorly prepared menu items can produce the same result; excellent service can do a lot to soften the disappointment of a below-standard meal, but the guest will not totally enjoy the experience. All aspects of the dining experience must be excellent in themselves to add up to total enjoyment and excellent value for guests. Everything the guest encounters or perceives should be guest-driven—designed or performed with the guest's interests in mind. Production and service as well as design and decor must be planned, implemented, and maintained to delight guests.

Food service managers should choose the service style and level of service that is appropriate for their types of food service operations and their guests. This chapter discusses service staff positions, table-service styles and procedures, buffet service, and strategies that food service operations can use to provide superior service to guests.

Dining Service Staff Positions

Different table-service styles require different types of service staff positions. The position descriptions in the following sections are meant to introduce readers to the types of positions that are commonly found in most food service operations. (When we cover specific service styles later in the chapter, we will identify staff positions and responsibilities that are unique to each style.)

Standard titles for dining service staff positions do not exist. Which titles are used depends on the food service operation's type of service and degree of formality, as well as management's preferences. In the following sections we will discuss the most common dining service staff positions under their most common titles: server, busperson, host, cashier, and dining room manager.

Server

In many restaurants, servers perform the bulk of the food and beverage serving duties, assisted by buspersons. Depending on the food service operation, servers may greet and seat guests, take their food and beverage orders, bring the ordered items to the table, check back with guests to make sure everything is satisfactory, present the guest check for payment, take the check to a cashier, return change to the guest, thank the guest, and clear tables. Managers sometimes require servers to also help with such minor food preparation tasks as adding dressings to salads, portioning soups, and dishing up desserts from service equipment located behind counters or in **side stations.** (Side stations are service stands in the dining room that hold equipment such as coffee makers and ice machines, and service supplies such as tableware and condiments for easy access by servers and other staff members).

Servers must also perform **sidework**—service-related but non-guest-contact tasks such as making coffee, refilling condiment containers, and restocking side stations with service supplies. Since servers earn tips only when directly serving guests, they frequently view these types of tasks with disfavor. However, sidework is an extremely important part of a server's responsibilities.

Servers must work quickly yet carefully. They must be able to do several things during one trip through the dining area, such as carry food to one table, present a guest check to another, and remove used dishes from a third. Exhibit 1 is a typical job description for a server in an operation that uses plate service (plate service will be discussed later in the chapter).

Busperson

Buspersons perform a wide array of tasks designed to help servers provide better service to guests (see Exhibit 2). The primary duty of a busperson is to clear tables and deliver soiled dishware, glassware, and flatware to the dishwashing room. It is also common for buspersons to perform some or all of the following tasks:

- Clean tables and chairs (including highchairs and booster chairs).
- Reset tables with fresh linens, clean serviceware, and glasses.
- Pour water and refill coffee and tea cups.
- Take bread and butter, chips, or popcorn to tables.
- Serve food and beverages during busy periods.
- Perform preopening duties such as setting tables, filling ice bins with ice, and moving tables.

A busperson's closing responsibilities might include the following:

- Cleaning side stations and stocking and replenishing side station supplies
- Emptying and cleaning food preparation carts
- Cleaning the coffee urn and the bread warmer
- Returning soiled linens to the laundry

If a restaurant offers tableside food preparation, buspersons may restock the food carts used for this purpose.

Exhibit 1 Sample Position Description: Server

Position Title: Server

Reports to: Dining Room Manager

Tasks:

1. Greets guests and presents them with the menu; informs guests of specials and menu changes; makes suggestions and answers questions regarding food, beverages, and service.
2. Takes food and beverage orders from guests (by either writing them down or memorizing them) and relays orders to kitchen staff and the bartender as appropriate.
3. Ensures that all food and beverage items are prepared properly and on a timely basis; communicates with the host, buspersons, kitchen staff, and the bartender; and coordinates his or her assigned station to ensure guest satisfaction with the food and beverage products and service.
4. Serves courses from kitchen and service areas promptly, garnishes menu items prior to serving them, and properly presents them.
5. Observes guests to ensure their satisfaction with the food and service, to respond to any additional requests, and to determine when the meal has been completed.
6. Totals guest bills and accepts payments or refers guests to the cashier or host as appropriate.
7. Assists buspersons with stocking side stations, removing soiled dishes and flatware from tables at the conclusion of each course, transporting soiled items to the dishwashing area, and cleaning and resetting vacated tables.

Prerequisites:

Education: High school graduate or equivalent; must be able to speak, read, write, and understand the primary language(s) of the work location; must be able to speak and understand the primary language(s) of the guests who typically visit the restaurant; must be able to perform simple mathematical calculations.

Experience: Should have first-hand knowledge of the sequence of service and basic dining room procedures; experience as a busperson helpful; must be guest-sensitive and possess a sense of timing to serve different courses at the proper time.

Physical: Must be able to move quickly and stand for periods of up to four (4) hours; must have a good sense of balance and be able to lift and carry trays and bus tubs that frequently weigh up to 25 pounds.

Exhibit 2 Sample Position Description: Busperson

Position Title: Busperson

Reports to: Dining Room Manager

Tasks:

1. Maintains the cleanliness and sanitation of the dining area, including all tables, chairs, floors, windows, and restrooms.
2. Restocks the dining room with tableware, flatware, utensils, condiments, and linen; maintains adequate supplies in the side stations when the dining room is open; prepares beverages required for service, including coffee, iced tea, and hot water; prepares ice buckets for wine and champagne service.
3. Greets guests as appropriate after they are seated; serves water, bread, rolls, and butter to guests and replenishes these items as needed.
4. Communicates with the host, dishwashing personnel, managers, and servers to maintain service efficiency and ensure guest satisfaction.
5. Assists servers during rush periods by serving hot beverages such as coffee and tea; assists servers in serving wine and champagne.
6. Removes dirty tableware and flatware from tables between courses and after guests leave; sets clean dishes and flatware for the next course and resets vacated tables; restocks condiments as needed; returns dirty tableware and flatware to the dishwashing area, sorting and placing the items in the prescribed areas.

Prerequisites:

Education: Some high school; must be able to speak and understand the primary language(s) of the work location.

Experience: None required.

Physical: Must be able to move quickly and stand for periods of up to four (4) hours; must be able to lift and carry trays, bus tubs, and other objects that may weigh 25 pounds or more.

Host

The person who first greets guests when they arrive may be called a "receptionist," "host," "greeter," "captain," or "dining room manager," depending on the extent of his or her responsibilities. (Some restaurants use the term "hostess" for a female host, but "host" is acceptable for both men and women.) If the food service operation also has a dining room manager, the host's responsibilities usually are limited to welcoming guests, confirming the number of guests in a party, leading guests to the appropriate section of the restaurant, and providing menus. (If the operation does not have a dining room manager, the host usually will perform many of the duties described in the "dining room manager" section coming up.) Hosts may ask guests if they have seating preferences before choosing tables for them. The host is usually responsible for thanking departing guests and inviting them to return.

Cashier

A cashier collects payments of guest checks from servers or guests. Cashiers must follow income control procedures at all times and must accurately account for all transactions, collections, and disbursements. Cashiers who have guest-contact duties should be friendly and courteous. A cashier's responsibilities may overlap with those of a host, particularly the responsibility for thanking departing guests.

Dining Room Manager

The manager in charge of dining room service has a wide variety of responsibilities and tasks that differ according to the type and size of the operation. For example, in small restaurants, the dining room manager may perform the responsibilities of host and manage the entire restaurant as well as the dining room. In large restaurants, dining room managers may have one or more hosts who report to them, and these managers in turn may report to a general manager or owner/manager who manages the restaurant as a whole—in which case the dining room manager's responsibilities are more narrowly defined and consist mainly of managing the dining room and its staff. (See Exhibit 3 for a sample job description for a dining room manager.)

Typically, dining room managers have had many years of training and experience and have held several dining room positions before becoming managers. While some operations do not use the "manager" designation, they always employ one or more people who perform managerial tasks.

Before the dining room opens for guest service, the dining room manager inspects the entire room and checks side stations to see that they are adequately stocked. The manager may check the number and condition of menus or may assign this duty to the host. Dining room managers also look for safety problems such as loose tabletops and wobbly chairs.

Supervising dining service staff members is a major responsibility of the dining room manager. Dining room managers assign tables or dining room sections to servers and conduct preshift meetings to inform the staff about daily specials, menu changes, and other matters of interest. During the meal period, dining room managers make certain that service flows smoothly. They must know sanitation and safety procedures and ensure that staff members follow them. After the dining room closes, dining room managers supervise staff members as they set up the room for the next day.

Styles and Procedures

There are many variations in the procedures and techniques food service operations use to serve food to guests, but most can be categorized under one of four

Exhibit 3 Sample Position Description: Dining Room Manager

Position Title: Dining Room Manager

Reports to: General Manager

Tasks:

1. Oversees dining area; supervises food and beverage service staff in accordance with operating policies that he or she may help establish.
2. Maintains records of staff performance and operating costs; maintains payroll and bookkeeping records.
3. Works with food and beverage staff to ensure proper food presentation and proper food-handling procedures.
4. Checks function sheets against room setup and staff member scheduling; may help design, set up for, or service functions.
5. Schedules periodic food and beverage service staff meetings to ensure correct interpretation of policies and obtain feedback from staff members.
6. Trains service staff to deliver the various types of food service.
7. Handles guest complaints.
8. Assists in planning regular and special-event menus.
9. Establishes standards, such as the amount of linen to be used in dining areas, and sets labor cost goals.
10. Reviews financial transactions and ensures that expenditures stay within budget limitations; maintains a system of cost controls while managing service and purchasing items and services.

Prerequisites:

Education: College degree in restaurant or hotel field or equivalent experience; must be able to speak, read, write, and understand the primary language(s) of the work location.

Experience: Requires experience in various phases of guest service; must possess a general knowledge of food and beverage procedures and service; must understand and possess a strong sense of cost control.

Physical: Must have the ability to lift up to 25 pounds occasionally and up to 10 pounds frequently; requires good communication skills, both oral and written.

main styles of table service: plate service, cart service, platter service, and family-style service. Some operations offer a combination of styles.

In addition to table-service styles, buffet service is being used by an increasing number of operations, often in combination with a table-service style. Some operations give guests a choice between eating at a buffet or selecting items from the menu. Others offer a special buffet only at certain times, such as on weekends or holidays (Mother's Day, Easter, or Thanksgiving, for example). In the United States, the Sunday buffet is very popular and can represent a significant percentage of business. Buffet service is also used for some banquets.

Plate Service

Plate service (also called American service) is the most common style of table service in the United States; most U.S. restaurants use variations of this style. Some managers borrow elements of other service styles to supplement their plate service in order to fulfill the requirements and preferences of their guests. Managers may combine plate service with some tableside food preparation, for example, or—in less formal establishments—with self-serve soup and salad bars.

Plate service follows these basic procedures:

1. Servers take guests' orders in the dining area.
2. Kitchen staff members produce food orders, portion them, and place them on plates in the kitchen.
3. Servers place the orders on trays, sometimes using plate covers to keep foods warm and facilitate stacking, and take them to the guests. They may use tray stands to hold the trays while they place the orders in front of guests.
4. Buspersons assist servers and clear tables.

There are variations, however. In some restaurants, servers plate some menu items and add garnishes to the plates in the kitchen before taking orders to guests; and in some operations, servers take trolleys of desserts out to guests and, after guests have made their selections, plate the desserts at tableside in front of the guests.

Before guests arrive, staff members usually set tables with all but the plates required for the entrée, so that bread and butter plates, water and wine glasses, napkins and flatware, and other items are already on the table when guests are first seated. Some restaurants, especially high-check-average and gourmet restaurants, also preset tables with a **show plate** or **base plate**. Often ornately designed with the organization's logo or made of fine china, pewter, or another attractive material, this plate enhances the table presentation.

In most operations that use plate service, guests are served all food items from the left and beverages from the right. In others, especially those that have booths, staff members are instructed to serve in the way that causes the least inconvenience to guests. After a guest is finished eating, the server typically removes everything from the right. (For a matrix showing the techniques used in various service styles, see Appendix A at the end of the chapter.)

Servers generally serve several tables simultaneously. The actual number depends upon how much experience the server has, the distance from his or her side station to the food pickup area, the menu itself, and the number of guests that can be seated at each of the tables in the server's assigned section (generally, for example, it is easier to serve three tables that can each seat four guests than six tables that each seat two guests, even though both sections seat 12 guests). Many other factors affect the number of tables that one server can adequately serve. For example, the number of tables a server can properly serve decreases under any of the following conditions:

- When the server is responsible for some tableside food preparation
- When the server must serve drinks as well as food (alcoholic beverage service in some restaurants is provided by a wine steward or cocktail servers)
- When no busperson is available to help clear and set tables

Well-designed, well-stocked side stations for food servers are a must for plate service. The dining area must be designed so that staff members have convenient access to the side stations. At the same time, these stations should not be a cause of disturbance to guests seated near them—there should be no excessive noise or traffic jams caused by service staff, for example, or unattractive views of service supplies and equipment. Partitions and other devices can help keep side stations out of guests' view.

In many operations featuring plate service, the server who takes the orders is also responsible for picking up the orders and delivering them to guests' tables. Some operations delegate these tasks to others by using team service. One team-service variation is to assign **"runners"** to take food from the kitchen to tray-stands, from which servers serve guests; this cuts down on the number of trips servers must make to the kitchen and allows them to spend more time with their guests. (Team service will be discussed in more detail later in the chapter.)

Plate service requires that servers clear each course's emptied plates and used flatware before serving the next course (unless the guest prefers otherwise). For example, if a guest has soup or salad as a first course, the server should remove the dishes and soup spoons or salad forks before serving the entrée.

It is unacceptable to scrape or stack plates in front of guests. If this is done on the server's tray away from the sight of guests, the tray should be temporarily covered with a clean napkin before being promptly removed. Beverage glasses should not be cleared unless the guest is first asked or the glasses are completely empty. These procedures not only show consideration for guests but also reduce the need for a large inventory of tableware, because soiled tableware can be cleaned and put back into service more quickly. These procedures also minimize the chance that guests will take home as souvenirs such items as flatware and glassware that is imprinted with the operation's logo.

With the plate-service system, food quality is solely controlled by the chef and the production staff. The policy in many restaurants is that the chef has sole responsibility for food quality during its presentation in dining areas as well as during its production in the kitchen. Plate service easily accommodates this policy, since production staff members prepare and plate food products under the chef's direction.

[SUPPLIER SEARCH] [FOODSERVICE JOBS] [TALENT AVAILABLE] [TRADE SHOWS] [INDUSTRY NEWS] [FOOD FORUMS] [EXPERT ADVICE] [ONLINE DIRECTORY] [DESIGN CENTER] [WEB SITE DESIGN RATES] [HOSTING RATES] [ADVERTISING RATES]

[Find a Job] [Find an Employee] [Buy & Sell Stuff]

Foodservice.com Wins Dow Jones "Select Site" Award!

Foodservice.com has been chosen as a "Select Site" by the editors of the Dow Jones Business Directory, sister publication to the **Wall Street Journal** and the definitive guide to high-quality, business Web sites! Click here to read the review!

^^^ CLICK BANNER TO LEARN MORE - Banner will open new window ^^^

Please visit our sponsors. Without them, Foodservice.com wouldn't be possible.

Hospitality students and professionals alike will find a wealth of information about food service on the Internet. This site (at http://www.foodservice.com) allows viewers to post or search for job openings, search for suppliers, learn about trade shows, and much more. (Courtesy of NationsWeb)

While it is never proper to rush guests, those who desire fast service are more likely to receive it with plate service than with some of the other table-service styles. Another advantage of plate service is that it does not require servers to have as much experience and training as staff members who provide cart or platter service. Finally, plate service has low equipment costs, since it does not require elaborate serving trays, carts, or other expensive service equipment. However, plate service does not offer the flair and elegance that cart and platter service offer. Except when menus state that different portion sizes are available, plate service also makes it difficult to modify portions to meet the specific needs of guests.

Tips for Providing Plate Service. What follows are a few tips to help staff members at plate-service operations provide good service to guests. (These tips may apply to other operations as well.)

Greeting guests. Servers should acknowledge each guest with eye contact and a warm smile. Servers should use "Sir" and "Ma'am" when greeting guests; if they know the guests, they should use the guests' titles (Doctor, Mister, or Ms.) and their surnames.

Seating guests. In seating guests, the objective is to make the guests feel welcome—not as if they were part of a perfunctory exercise. When seating two guests at a table for four, the two additional place settings should be removed. This both reduces soiled tableware and provides guests with more room to enjoy the dining experience.

Unfortunately, dining areas usually have some tables that are not as desirable as others. Seats in high-traffic aisles, next to side stations, and close to the dishwashing and kitchen areas are examples. Servers or hosts should seat guests at these tables only after all others are full. They should also know which seats are best for privacy or for a good view of the surrounding grounds. If the best seats are occupied, servers or hosts should give guests the choice of sitting at a less desirable table or waiting until a better one becomes available.

Making introductions. If the server did not seat the guests, the server should give the guests a prompt and friendly greeting once they are seated. After this initial contact, servers should introduce themselves in a friendly manner, using creativity when appropriate (writing their names on placemats for hearing-impaired guests, for example), then proceed with attentive listening and helpful suggestions.

It should be noted that the managers of some food service operations discourage servers from introducing themselves by name; they think that this can be a distraction to both guests and servers. These managers feel strongly that the focus should not be on the server; rather, it should always be kept on the guests and the task of providing them with quality food and beverage products and services. Obviously, servers should follow whatever policy is in place at their operation.

Presenting menus. Servers or hosts should present menus open, first to women, then to men, moving around the table clockwise. Daily specials should also be discussed at this time as briefly as possible without leaving out essential information. Service staff might use this opportunity to suggest menu items to guests. (Suggestive-selling techniques are covered in more detail later in the chapter.)

Treating children appropriately. Servers should treat children as courteously as they treat adult guests. A smile and a promise to quickly bring a complimentary appetizer to the table go a long way toward beginning the dining experience well. If the operation does not offer crackers, bread, or some other complimentary snack items for a party that has children, the server might ask the adults at the table whether it would be acceptable to serve the children first. If they welcome this idea, the server should try to expedite the production and service of the children's orders. Servers should also attempt to involve the children in the conversation. When children feel welcome and satisfied, so do their parents and other family members.

Checking quality. Because they perform the final quality control check of menu items before they are served, servers should be trained to recognize acceptable quality. Food quality can be judged by appearance; the appearance of foods should always match the pictures and descriptions of the items on the menu. The sizes and shapes of foods also contribute to their appearance. Broken, misshapen, or ragged vegetables, for example, can destroy the appearance of an entire plate of food.

The neatness of the food presentation also makes a statement about the food service operation's standards. Food items should not be crowded on the plate or hanging over the edge. Liquid foods should not spill or run over the edges of tableware. If two foods with sauces are to be served at the same time, one should be served in a side dish. If a menu item is served with a thin sauce, the sauce should be served in a side dish.

The textures and consistencies of food products are also important components of quality. Dried-out bakery products, broken bread sticks and crackers, wilted salads, lumpy gravies and puddings, and runny custards are examples of foods of poor quality. Some operations display photographs of standard food presentations in the pickup area of the kitchen so servers can easily compare their finished orders to the photos before taking the orders out to guests.

Product temperature contributes to the overall quality of food products as well. Hot foods should be served on heated tableware, cold foods on chilled tableware. When assembling orders, servers should gather room temperature products first, then chilled foods, then hot foods.

Knowing who gets what. When presenting and serving the guests' orders, servers should make sure they know who ordered what. Many guests are irritated when a server asks, for example, "Who gets the salmon?" After the food is served, servers should make such comments as "Your prime rib looks delicious," or "The spinach pizza has a wonderful aroma," in addition to asking "May I bring you anything else right now?"

Checking in. After giving guests a chance to taste their food, the server should go back to the table and check in. Instead of asking if everything is okay, servers should ask specific questions, such as "Is the entrée cooked exactly as you like it?" Servers should be empowered to remove unacceptable menu items and return them to the kitchen for a replacement or "repair" (for example, cooking a steak a little longer for a guest who ordered a "medium" steak and received a "rare" one). When an order is returned to the kitchen for replacement, the fresh order should always be brought back to the guest's table on a fresh plate.

Anticipating guest needs. Anticipating guest needs is a hallmark of superior service. Staff members can anticipate guest needs by offering something before it is requested and filling a water glass before it is empty. Removing used water glasses when guests have finished their entrées and providing fresh water glasses with ice water is a special touch. Servers should always check for the presence of proper eating utensils and other tableware as each course is served.

Handling the guest's payment. It is a good idea for servers to stay close to the guest's table once the check has been presented, to avoid unnecessary delays in processing the check and payment. If a guest pays with a credit card, the server should refer to the guest by name when the credit card charge is returned to the table.

Ending on a positive note. Ensuring that guests leave the restaurant on a positive note is one of the fundamentals of superior service. Guests should be thanked and invited to return. Guests also are likely to remember it if a staff member opens the door for them as they are leaving. Exhibit 4 lists other ways in which service staff can provide superior service; Exhibit 5 lists service practices to avoid.

Cart Service

Cart service (also called French service) is popular internationally, but used less frequently in the United States. Cart service is an elaborate service style in which menu items are prepared on a cart beside guest tables by specially trained staff members; menu items are cooked—sometimes flambéed—in front of the guests. In the United States, restaurants that use cart service are generally gourmet, high-check-average operations. Restaurant managers who are considering using this high-priced and labor-intensive service style should undertake detailed feasibility studies to confirm the existence of a guest base sophisticated enough to support it.

Cart service costs are high for several reasons. First, service staff need enough dining area space (with wide aisles) to move preparation carts through the dining area and prepare food alongside guest tables; this reduces the number of tables and seats in the dining area, which reduces the operation's gross sales potential. Cart service incurs higher capital costs than other kinds of service because of the extensive amount of serving and preparation equipment required. Typically, serviceware for cart service is very elegant; ornate service pieces such as silver platters are often used. Operating costs are also higher; a large number of staff members are required to serve relatively few guests, and the table turnover rate is much lower than those of other service styles. To generate enough income to cover labor and other costs, food and beverage prices in operations that use cart service must reflect those costs.

It is difficult to find professionally trained service staff who understand and can follow all of the procedures required for effective tableside food preparation; cart service requires highly skilled and experienced service staff who have been formally trained.

In hotel dining rooms that offer cart service, a **maître d'hôtel** who knows the intricacies of cart service is required to seat guests, supervise the dining room, and perform other duties. A sommelier typically helps guests select wines and then serves them, adhering to the many rituals of formal wine service. In a very large and busy dining room, it may be difficult for one sommelier to approach each table to suggest, sell, and serve wine. In this instance, there may also be a head wine server with a staff of several assistants.

Exhibit 4 More Ways to Provide Superior Service

1. Serve soup hot at tableside to allow guests at the table to enjoy the aromas and to encourage guests at other tables to order soup.
2. When possible, encourage undecided guests to taste a food item or beverage before they order.
3. Offer and feature daily specials that appeal to loyal, regular guests.
4. Distinctively indicate which items are vegetarian on the menu.
5. Serve bakery products at tableside that are fresh out of the oven.
6. Clearly indicate by the color of the cup or coaster who is drinking regular or decaffeinated coffee at a table. That way, whoever provides refill service will know which cup to fill with what.
7. Warm desserts (as appropriate) prior to serving them to guests.
8. Briefly meet as a service team each day to review the menu, taste menu items, and review service standards and techniques.
9. Divide and plate in the kitchen those items that guests ordered to be shared.
10. When guests are asked to wait for excessive periods for a table, issue them personal electronic pagers.
11. Offer guests complimentary beverages if waiting periods are excessive.
12. Give guests something that they do not expect (e.g., a complimentary side dish, a cookie with their ice cream) to exceed expectations.
13. Offer cordless phones for use by those who need them in the dining room. (But be certain that this does not disturb other guests.)
14. When guests request the recipe for a signature menu item, give it to them on a preprinted card that has the operation's logo on it.
15. When servers are not serving, have them check tableware, ashtrays, water glasses and coffee cups, and other items on other servers' tables that might need attention.
16. Encourage staff members and reward them for learning guests' names and preferences.
17. Train staff members in telephone-answering skills.
18. Empower staff members to delete from guest bills the charges for food or beverage items that are unacceptable to guests.
19. Tailor menu suggestions to guests' unique needs.
20. Provide the kind of service that you enjoy receiving.

Source: Adapted from "55 Ways to Super Service," *Restaurants & Institutions*, November 15, 1993.

At least two food service staff members are needed in each dining area station for cart service: the *chef du rang* and the *commis du rang*. The ***chef du rang*** is generally responsible for taking orders, serving drinks, preparing food at the table, and collecting guest payments. He or she must be very experienced and versatile; in the

Exhibit 5 Unacceptable Service Practices

- Greeting guests with a single-word question, such as "Two?" or "Smoking?"
- Not acknowledging waiting guests.
- Seating guests at a table with a gratuity on it.
- Answering "I'll have to find out" in response to questions about the soup or specials of the day.
- "Auctioning off" food by saying such things as, "Who ordered this lasagna?"
- Talking to guests while holding dirty plates.
- Pouring coffee from a stained pot.

Source: Adapted from Gail Bellamy, David Farkas, and John Soeder, "Sensational Service," *Restaurant Hospitality,* July 1994, pp. 63, 64, 65, 70, 72.

absence of a sommelier, for example, the *chef du rang* also may serve dinner wines. Normally, production staff partially prepare the food in the kitchen, then the *chef du rang* finishes it at tableside. He or she must be able to cook or flame a wide variety of menu items at tableside, carve meat, and bone fish and poultry. The *chef du rang* also must know how to use a fork and spoon to transfer prepared food to plates and know how to garnish food attractively.

The ***commis du rang*** assists the *chef du rang*. He or she is responsible for taking food orders to the kitchen, placing the orders, picking up food in the kitchen, and bringing it to the tableside carts, often on silver trays. When the *chef du rang* is busy with preparation duties, the *commis du rang* also delivers drink orders and serves food to guests. The *commis du rang* also acts as a busperson.

Cart service requires a cart or ***guéridon*** that holds a portable heating unit (***réchaud***). To serve soup, for instance, the *commis du rang* brings it into the dining room in a service bowl and places it on the cart's *réchaud.* He or she then places an empty, hot soup bowl on a service plate or underliner. The *chef du rang* portions the item, and the *commis du rang* serves it.

In cart service, food is nearly always served with the right hand to the guest's right side. The only exceptions are when the *commis du rang* is left-handed and when there are side plates that are placed to the left of the guest, such as those for salad or bread and butter.

Many special rules of courtesy, etiquette, and tradition are components of cart service, but they are beyond the scope of this chapter. It should be noted, however, that the impact that cart service has on facility design, staffing, and guest satisfaction is profound. For example, as mentioned earlier, cart service requires a well-designed environment; it is impossible to implement cart service in a poorly planned dining room, and the furniture, fixtures, and equipment in the room must be compatible with the elegant service style offered. The use of cart service requires a configuration of the food preparation area that differs from the configurations other service styles require. Production personnel do not handle finished, plated foods; food preparation is finished at guest tables. The service staff required for cart service usually cannot be assigned to other tasks; they must be available to use their highly specialized skills whenever guests want them. Finally, the guests who desire and pay for cart service are unlikely to accept mistakes.

Some hotels that want to offer cart service have found it more profitable, because of the many special challenges associated with this detailed and demanding style of service, to lease space to an independent operator of a cart-service restaurant.

Platter Service

Platter service (also called Russian service) requires servers to deliver platters of fully cooked food to the dining room, present the platters to guests for approval, and then serve the food. This type of service is featured in many of the best international restaurants and hotels; some food service operations in the United States, particularly banquet operations, also use it.

The food is prepared (and sometimes precut) by food production staff in the kitchen. They arrange the food attractively on the service platters for food servers to deliver to the dining room. Generally, service staff members use a team approach; one server carries the entrée and a second carries the accompaniments. Servers line up in the kitchen and, at the appropriate time, parade into the dining area. After presenting (showing) the food to the guests, they place the platters on side stands to keep foods warm while they position a very hot, empty dinner plate in front of each guest. Holding the platter in the left hand, the server transfers the food to guest plates by artfully manipulating a fork and spoon held in the right hand. Service proceeds in this way around the table counterclockwise.

Soup service is as follows: the server places a hot soup bowl on a service or base plate and positions it in front of the guest. The server then brings a service bowl of soup to the table and ladles the soup into guests' soup bowls.

Platter service typically calls for servers to use their discretion in portioning food for guests; the platter must retain its attractiveness until the last guest is served, and the last guest served must receive an adequate portion. In many operations, the servers circle tables twice, serving each guest each time; any food remaining on the platter must be discarded. When guests order a wide variety of items, food servers may need to bring several different platters to the table concurrently, which can cause service problems. For this reason, some operations use platter service only at banquets where all guests receive the same menu items.

Platter service can be as elegant as cart service, but it is much more practical because it is faster and less expensive. Platter service can provide a special touch and still allow managers to control labor and product costs closely. Like cart service, platter service incorporates many traditions that mean superior service for guests; it also requires professionally trained—and highly skilled—staff members. Managers who are considering adopting platter service should recognize that they will have to make a sizeable capital investment in service platters and plate and bowl warmers.

Family-Style Service

Family-style service (also called English service) requires food to be placed on large platters or in large bowls that are delivered to the guests' tables by servers. Guests at each table then pass the food around their table and serve themselves.

Family-style service is relatively easy to implement, for service staff members do not need to be highly skilled. In fact, with family-style service, they generally put more effort into clearing tables than into presenting and serving the food. In effect, each of the disadvantages of cart service can be countered with the advantages of family-style service. Family-style service requires relatively little dining area space or special equipment (except serving bowls and platters); table turnover rates and service time can also be rapid, which makes it easy to serve foods at their proper temperatures. Additionally, operations need not charge exceptionally high prices for family-style service, since there are reduced equipment and labor costs. This service style is sometimes used for banquets.

One possible disadvantage of family-style service is that it is difficult to implement portion-control procedures. The last guests served may not receive as much of an item as they would like if the first guests served take too much. This problem can be reduced if the initial amount of food placed in the bowl or on the platter is generous.

The informal atmosphere of family-style service can be a major disadvantage if guests expect a more formal atmosphere or expect special attention from servers. If guests are seeking elegance or a great deal of contact with servers in their dining experience, they may not find family-style service acceptable.

Buffet Service

Buffets display food on counters or tables, and guests help themselves to as many and as much of the items as they wish to eat. Buffets can range from a simple offering of several food items to elaborate presentations that appeal to guests with sophisticated, gourmet tastes. Buffet service is sometimes used in combination with (rather than in place of) table service; for example, servers may serve drinks and desserts using plate service while allowing guests to serve themselves at a buffet for the main course.

Typically the chef plans the buffet menu, since his or her responsibility for the food extends into the dining area. However, concerns such as the placement of the buffet, the flow of guests as they pass through the buffet line, and related service details are generally the responsibility of the dining room manager. As the manager plans the buffet line, he or she should pay a great deal of attention to the presentation of the food. For instance, ice or tallow (fat) sculptures, fresh flowers, or edible vegetable or fruit centerpieces can be attractive focal points on the buffet line. Decorative service platters or bowls also can enhance the food presentation. Because almost any food item is more appealing when decorated with such garnishes as radish roses, accordion pickles, carrot curls, or turnip lilies, close attention to the placement of garnishes is necessary.

Foods usually are placed on buffets in the following order: salads and other chilled meal accompaniments, hot vegetables, meats, poultry, fish, and other hot entrées. Some buffets feature "steamship" rounds of beef, large hams, and other roasts that servers or production staff carve as guests request a portion. Such items as crepes and omelets are sometimes cooked to order on a buffet line. Sauces, dressings, and relishes should be placed close to the menu items that they accompany.

Desserts may be placed in a display area separate from the rest of the buffet to facilitate traffic flow.

Many variables affect the speed of buffet line traffic. Among them are the variety of available menu items, whether items are prepared to order, and even the beauty of the buffet presentation (guests may pass through the line slowly to maximize their view of centerpieces and other visual attractions). Therefore, it is difficult to develop statistics about the average serving line speed. Experience is often the best guide for managers.

Planning the layout for a buffet requires special attention to the number of guests expected, the size and shape of the room, and the amount of time available for service. Some managers say that 75 is the maximum number of guests that one buffet line in a banquet setting can serve; an event for 150 guests would therefore require two buffet lines.

There are many popular layouts for buffet service that can be used in place of the traditional straight-line setup (see Exhibit 6). Some organizations use a **scramble system** for their buffets. The term "scramble system" was first used to describe cafeterias in which guests could go to separate stations to be served, rather than waiting in a single line. For example, hot foods might be at one station, beverages at another, and desserts and salads at still others. Using this plan for buffets simply involves making each station a small buffet. While requiring more setup space than other buffet-service styles, the scramble system lessens bottlenecks because it doesn't force guests into a single line.

Guest tables in operations that use buffet service must receive special attention. The manager must select appropriate centerpieces, for instance, and make decisions regarding such details as the following:

- Will tables be preset with tableware and napkins or will guests pick up these items on the buffet line?
- Will crackers, breads, or other snack items be placed on the tables so that guests who do not go through the buffet line immediately will have some food available to them?
- What provisions should be made for guests who do not want to go through a buffet line or, for some physical or other reason, cannot?

Buffet service requires a system to maintain cleanliness and order. Staff members must consistently keep buffet containers full, quickly attend to food spills on and around the buffet line, properly attend to guest tables in dining areas, and efficiently remove soiled serviceware from the room. Staff members should display only small batches of food to maintain proper temperatures and encourage frequent replenishing. Efforts to create an attractive buffet are often defeated if the buffet is left unattended during service. Spills, serving utensils that have been dropped into food products, almost-empty food containers, and unsightly, burned food left in hot chafing dishes can easily ruin a buffet's visual appeal.

The required serviceware must be constantly available during the buffet period. When flatware and plates are not available, guests have a right to complain. Guests also have a right to complain if they are given hot plates (just out of the dishwashing machine) for their chilled foods. These examples help illustrate

Exhibit 6 Buffet Setup Variations

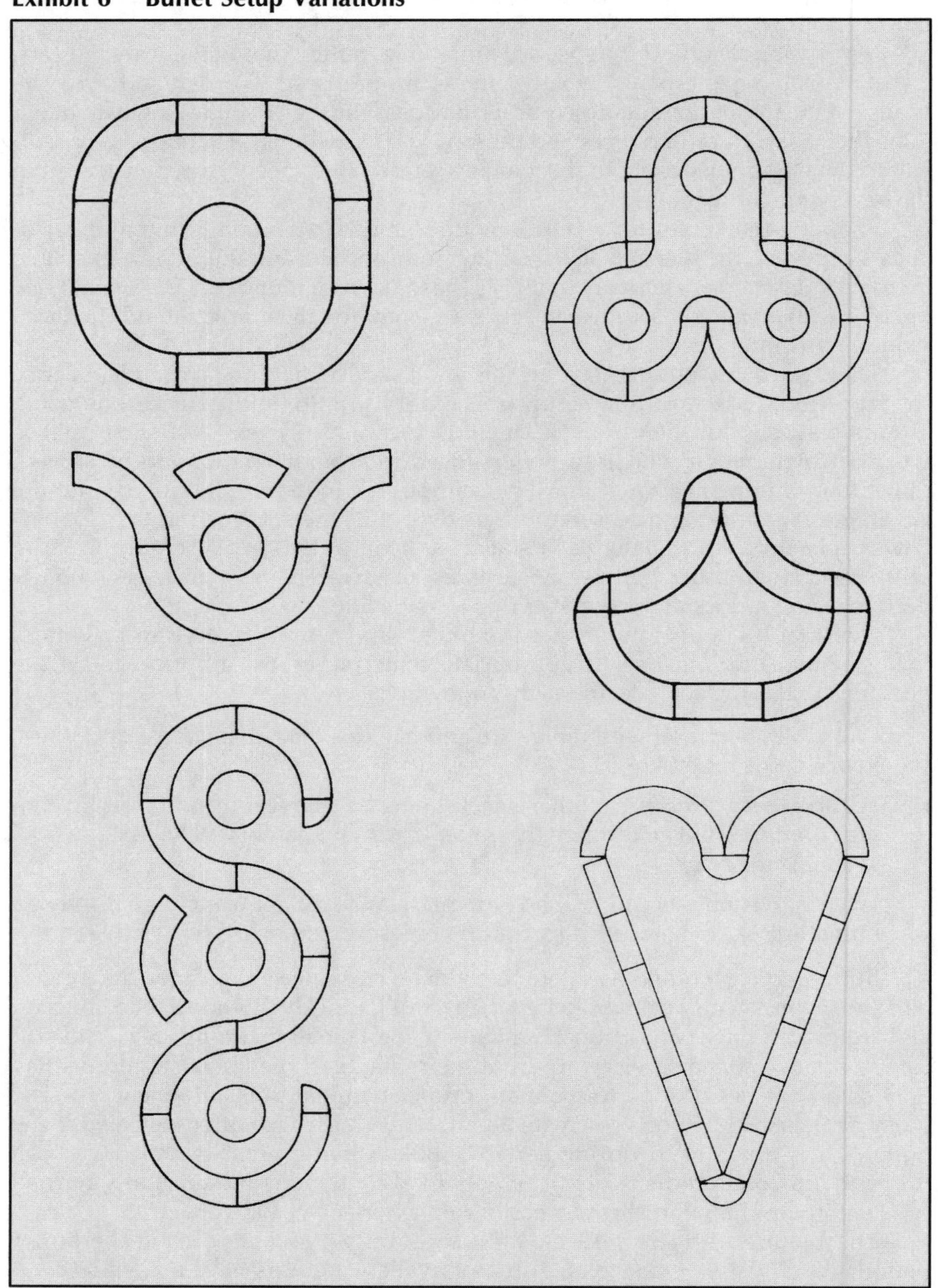

Source: Gerhard M. Peter, *Function Room Set-Up Manual* (Hospitality Sales and Marketing Association International).

why staff members must pay constant attention to buffet lines to ensure that they meet the quality standards expected by guests.

The fact that the work of servers is limited in buffets lowers labor costs. (Servers typically just remove soiled dishes, reset tables, provide beverage and sometimes dessert service, and perform related tasks.) Also, since food can be produced over a longer period of time and items do not need to be portioned, production labor costs may be reduced slightly. However, additional kitchen staff may be required to prepare such items as centerpieces and the large quantities and varieties of buffet food.

Banquet planners should be informed about the potential advantages of buffet service because, for many occasions, buffets are an excellent alternative to table service. Buffets allow guests to obtain food at their leisure and in the quantities they desire, all for what is usually a reasonable price.

Many buffets have themes that are suggested by holidays and other special occasions. When managers plan buffets for special groups or to emphasize special foods, they often select a theme that provides consistency among the elements of food, service, and atmosphere. For instance, a group's logo or insignia could be used as a design theme for its buffet. Foods themselves can also serve as the unifying feature.

Managers must consider several potential difficulties when planning buffets. The proper service equipment (serviceware, centerpieces, and food presentation trays) must be available in adequate quantities in order for service to flow smoothly. Carpet wear can be a problem when large numbers of guests frequently travel through the same area of a room. Grease can soil dining room furnishings (this is especially true for buffets that feature some cooking on the buffet line).

Providing Superior Service

Once managers have decided which style or combination of styles their operation will use, they must provide their service staff with the skills, procedures, supplies, and equipment necessary to do their jobs properly and delight guests.

The sections that follow discuss general strategies and procedures managers from many different food service operations might use to help their staffs provide excellent service to guests. The rest of the chapter will cover:

- Preshift meetings
- Suggestive selling
- Service guarantees
- Resolving guest complaints
- The team approach to service
- Serving guests who have disabilities

Preshift Meetings

Many food service operations use "line-up" or **preshift meetings** to facilitate staff communication and as an ongoing, daily method of training. Typically, a preshift meeting takes place just before the start of a shift and lasts 15 to 20 minutes. Preshift meetings should always begin on time and include all the appropriate staff members. Preshift meetings give dining room managers opportunities to gather information from the staff members as well as give information to them.

Managers should listen closely to the concerns and ideas staff members express during preshift meetings. For example, staff members might suggest a change that would improve service to guests. The way for managers to encourage such suggestions is to listen to them and adopt or at least try out the best of them.

Information given to service staff during a preshift meeting might include any of the following:

General Information:

- Planned special events or promotions
- Events in the local community that could make the upcoming shift busier than usual
- Special arrangements for guests celebrating birthday parties, anniversaries, and other occasions.
- Special arrangements for upcoming holidays

Product or Service Information:

- Daily food and beverage specials (this may include taste tests)
- Strategies for or changes to food and beverage service
- Tips or in-depth instruction for handling equipment and supplies
- Readings of comment cards that guests have turned in

Sales Information:

- Merchandising and upselling techniques
- Goals for food and beverage sales, either in general or for particular items
- Reports of ancillary income brought in by special-function business

Staff Information:

- Introductions of new staff members
- Recognition of staff member achievements

Preshift meetings are ideal times for managers to emphasize teamwork and develop common goals with staff members. Preshift meetings should also give staff members an opportunity to ask questions and have them answered.

Suggestive Selling

Food and beverage operations have integrated the sales function into service position descriptions for so long that **suggestive selling** is viewed as a natural part of food and beverage service at many operations. Service staff often appreciate the opportunity to practice suggestive selling, because it is an area in which they are usually allowed to let their individual judgment and personal style shine. Staff members do not give in-depth sales presentations or use high-pressure tactics on guests. Rather, suggestive selling is a way service staff can enhance a guest's dining experience by making sure the guest orders all that he or she really wants. Food and beverage sales must always be based on the needs and expectations of the guests, not the operation. If servers understand what the operation offers and can communicate it to guests, they will be better able to match the requirements and expectations of guests with the operation's products and services.

There are three components to suggestive selling: knowing your guests, knowing your products and services, and matching guest needs and desires with your products and services.

Know Your Guests. Being able to "read" guests and identify their requirements gives servers clues about what to sell. Guests who arrive as a family will often want quick service, including snacks or appetizers for the children and something to occupy them (activity books, games, or crayons and placemats to color) while they wait for orders to arrive. This gives servers the opportunity to sell appetizers appropriate for children. Guests who are primarily interested in conducting business over a meal have different requirements. Rapid, attentive, unobtrusive service will allow them to discuss their business without major interruptions. These guests may not be interested in hearing a long list of food and beverage alternatives, and servers should tone down their suggestive-selling efforts accordingly.

Know Your Products and Services. The second component of effective suggestive selling is a thorough knowledge of the products and services the operation provides. Servers should thoroughly know the menu, including menu item ingredients, the origins of unique menu items or ingredients, the correct pronunciation of menu item names, menu item production methods and times, and how products taste and are presented (servers should know this for both regular and special menu items). Some organizations use flash cards with pictures when training servers, to enhance their retention of menu information. Some restaurant chains forbid new servers from serving guests until they can pass a test that measures their knowledge of the menu (and other subjects of importance to guests).

Servers should taste every item on the menu during their initial training. Specials of the day should be tasted each day during preshift meetings. Organizations that do not hold tastings can use discounts and gift certificates to encourage service staff members to "dine in." Initial and follow-up training, coupled with regular taste tests, can enhance the product knowledge of servers and therefore make them better salespeople. Additional information that enhances a server's ability to sell includes a knowledge of the garnishes for each menu item, allowable substitutions, allowable portioning options (such as half portions or extra-large portions), and the plate presentation of each menu item. With a thorough knowledge of products, servers are better able to identify and describe items that truly match the needs of guests.

Match Guest Needs with Your Products and Services. The basic strategy of suggestive selling is to show guests how they can enhance their dining experience by ordering one of the server's suggestions. Some suggestive-selling techniques

Basic Food Preparation Terms and Timing

One of the best suggestive-selling techniques that servers can use is to describe how food is prepared. Servers should use the following terms accurately when describing menu items:

baked—Cooked by dry heat in an oven.

boiled—Cooked in boiling or rapidly simmering liquid.

braised—Browned in a small amount of fat, then cooked slowly in a small amount of liquid.

broiled—Cooked by direct heat from above or below.

fried—Cooked in fat or oil.

deep-fried—Cooked in enough fat or oil to cover the food.

grilled—Cooked on a grid over direct heat (usually hot coals).

poached—Cooked in enough simmering liquid to cover the food. A liquid is simmering when it is just below the boiling point.

roasted—Cooked uncovered without water added, usually in an oven, by dry heat.

sautéed—Browned or cooked in a small amount of hot fat or oil.

steamed—Cooked in steam with or without pressure.

stewed—Simmered slowly in enough liquid to cover the food.

Source: Adapted from the "Banquet Server Guide" in the *Hospitality Skills Training Series* (East Lansing, Mich.: Educational Institute of the American Hotel & Motel Association, 1995), p. 22.

and strategies are listed in Exhibit 7. These should be adapted to the unique needs of the operation's guests.

Sometimes guests are unsure of what to order and may simply ask their server, "What's good here?" In such cases, servers should not answer, "Everything is good"; this approach will only frustrate guests. Rather, servers should take their cue to make suggestions. Appealing descriptions of the operation's signature specialties are particularly appropriate when guests are undecided about what to order. Servers could also suggest dishes they themselves enjoy. However, they must never discourage a guest from ordering any item and must not let a guest know if they personally dislike the item he or she has ordered. It is the preferences of the guest, not those of the server, that must drive the process.

Many operations offer incentives to help motivate servers to reach sales goals. While servers should be enthusiastic when making recommendations to guests, they should never be pushy; servers should merely guide guests' decision-making by highlighting options that fit guests' needs and desires. Guests who know what they want may be irritated by a lot of suggestions from their server, so servers should learn to recognize when guests know what they want and tailor their service accordingly.

Today's flexible menus require a flexible selling style. Multiple preparation methods are available for many menu items, and guests sometimes request half-

Exhibit 7 Suggestive-Selling Techniques and Strategies

1. Evaluate the moods of guests and make recommendations based on your observations.
2. Very early in the ordering process, mention that the guest may want to save room for tonight's featured signature dessert.
3. When guests order drinks (e.g., vodka on the rocks), suggest a premium brand (e.g., Absolut Citron on the rocks).
4. Talk about menu items that the operation is famous for and take every opportunity to suggest these items to guests.
5. When describing menu items, mention brand-name ingredients that the chef uses; this creates an image of quality.
6. Recommend appetizers immediately after serving the first round of drinks.
7. Promote wine, either by the glass or in bottles, to enhance guest enjoyment and to increase server tips.
8. Instead of asking a question that can simply be answered "no," such as, "Would you like an appetizer?" ask a question that gives the guest a choice, such as, "Would you prefer our nachos or our fried mozzarella sticks as an appetizer tonight?"
9. Paint a creative picture of the food you are trying to sell, using descriptive images and stories. A brief history of how a dish became popular can add appeal. Also, by creating mental images through a unique story, servers can make menu items more memorable.
10. Present desserts on a tray or cart to enhance visual appeal. At no extra charge, offer extra dishware and flatware to guests who want to share their desserts with others.
11. Practice suggestive-selling techniques and strategies at every opportunity. The odds are that you will sell more.

portions or want to combine appetizers as a replacement for a full meal. Servers may suggest splitting large portions or ordering several small-portion items rather than one large-portion item.

Some servers are reluctant to mention the price of a menu item, particularly when its cost is higher than the average for other menu items. Chalkboards or easels that list specials and their prices, and menu inserts with prices are some solutions to this problem.

Service Guarantees

Borrowing from strategies in other, unrelated service businesses, some food service operations now offer **service guarantees**—unconditional commitments to complete guest satisfaction. With a service guarantee, guests who are not satisfied with their menu items or the service they received do not have to pay for their meals. Some operations have time-related service guarantees for time-sensitive meal periods such as breakfast and lunch; guests who do not receive their orders within 15 minutes of ordering are not charged, for example. Service guarantees work well when a food service operation and its management and staff are focused on the same desired outcome: satisfied guests.

Service guarantees help an operation identify where and when it has (and has not) satisfied its guests. Information gleaned from failures in service delivery can be used to improve the operation. To be effective, service guarantees must be clearly understood by guests as well as staff members, must be part of each staff member's training program, and must be easy to use.

Resolving Guest Complaints

Guests complain because their needs or expectations are not met. Few dissatisfied guests actually voice their complaints to service staff; most suffer in silence. Some guests will not complain directly, but will show by their actions that they are displeased. Some of the warning signs of guest dissatisfaction include asking a server to remove a beverage or menu item from the table soon after it is served, not eating or drinking the item or simply moving food around on their plate, covering the plate with their napkin, being rude for no apparent reason, or looking around for their server. It is critical for the server to investigate if he or she observes any of these behaviors, since the guest will leave dissatisfied if the server fails to turn the situation around.

The process of resolving guest complaints begins with an understanding of why guests complain. A sample list of reasons for guest complaints is presented in Exhibit 8. This list is not exhaustive, nor is it in any particular order; it's merely a sampling of the variety of reasons for which guests complain.

Fundamental to successfully resolving guest complaints is having the right attitude. With the right attitude, staff members can usually resolve complaints quickly. But if a staff member ignores a guest's dissatisfaction, retreats behind company policies, takes the complaint personally, blames the guest or other staff members, argues with or belittles the guest, makes the guest feel as if he or she was wrong to complain, or discusses the complaint so that other guests or servers can hear, the staff member will only further upset the guest. A fundamental rule staff members must remember is that "The guest is always right." While some operations have modified this rule to say "The guest may not always be right, but the guest is always the guest," the message is the same.

Guests want their complaints to be handled rapidly, fairly, and professionally. A complaint should never be ignored or allowed to fester. Rapid resolution of a complaint is in everyone's best interest: the guest wants someone to salvage his or her dining experience as soon as possible, and the operation wants to make sure the guest does not leave dissatisfied, because a dissatisfied guest will likely tell others about the problem and may never return.

Approaches to dealing with guest complaints should include four steps:

1. Calmly and patiently listen and empathize.

Exhibit 8 Why Guests Complain

- Unfriendly staff or lack of a warm greeting
- Pushy servers
- Excuses by the server
- Lack of courtesy by servers
- Unhelpful attitudes of servers
- Overly friendly servers
- Inattentive service
- Inadequate response to guest complaints
- "Vanishing" servers who are unavailable to take care of needs
- Excessive waiting times
- High prices
- Unacceptable food quality or methods of preparation
- Unclean facilities, equipment, or servers
- Unacceptable noise levels
- Policies that are not guest friendly, such as charges for splitting or sharing items, automatic service charges, and a prohibition on substitutions
- Crowded parking lots, lobbies, or bathrooms
- Cramped dining area
- Unavailability of management
- Unequal treatment of guests, or "playing favorites"
- Unacceptable no-smoking sections—sections that are smoky or have a poor view or poor furniture
- Failure to thank guests for coming or to invite them to return

2. Apologize and commit yourself to solving the problem and satisfying the guest.
3. Identify a mutually acceptable solution.
4. Check back to determine if the complaint truly has been resolved.

Listen and Empathize. By calmly and patiently listening and empathizing, staff members can show courtesy and respect to complaining guests and prevent situations from spiraling out of control. Treating an agitated or angry guest with calmness and patience can be difficult, but it often quiets the guest, which is a necessary first step if the server is to learn about the reason for the complaint in detail.

Listening is the most important—and most frequently ignored—component of the communication process. When a staff member listens with sensitivity, the guest's feelings and concerns usually will surface in such a way that a solution can be identified. Servers should attempt to maintain eye contact with the guest while listening and refrain from interrupting. To be certain that he or she understands the causes of the complaint, it is a good idea for the server to repeat or rephrase the complaint back to the guest calmly and professionally. For example, a staff member could begin by saying, "What I'm hearing from you is that...." The goal of listening is to learn about the events or circumstances that upset the guest and allow the guest to vent his or her frustration in a way that does not disturb other guests.

Servers and other staff members should not make the mistake of becoming defensive. They should remember that it is impossible to please everyone all of the time and that different guests arrive with different ideals for their dining experience. When listening to complaints, staff members should avoid taking them personally; rather, they should concentrate on trying to understand the guest's perspective and the reason for the complaint. The best way to view complaining guests is as consultants to the operation; their complaints offer an opportunity for the operation to identify weaknesses and areas for improvement.

Having empathy is being aware of and sensitive to the emotions of others. In short, empathy is knowing where someone is "coming from"—in this case, seeing the world through the guest's eyes. Empathetic responses include "I think I know how you feel," "I understand what is upsetting you and I'm glad that you told me," and "I can see why this is important to you and I want to resolve it right now." When coupled with a sincere apology, an empathetic response will go a long way toward soothing a guest and beginning the process of resolving the complaint.

Apologize and Commit Yourself to Solving the Problem. Apologizing is not necessarily the same as accepting blame or passing the blame to another staff member—though when blame clearly belongs to the operation, the staff member should acknowledge that. A staff member can be sorry that an event occurred or that circumstances are what they are, even if the staff member had nothing to do with the event or the circumstances. An apology simply is an agreement that the guest's complaint or feelings have merit, and it helps to reduce the guest's feelings of frustration and anger. But a staff member should never assume that an apology by itself will satisfy a guest. After apologizing, the staff member should accept responsibility for the problem's resolution, regardless of who is at fault; the staff member must become the guest's advocate in fixing the problem.

Accepting responsibility means giving complete and undivided attention to resolving the complaint. This sense of urgency will communicate to the complaining guest that the problem is going to be taken care of—quickly. Many operations empower their servers to resolve complaints on the spot (and give guests compensation for their trouble, such as a complimentary meal or a free beverage or dessert); other operations still require managers to become involved. When guests become extremely angry or violent, managers should *always* intervene directly, but most complaints can be solved by empowered service staff. Managers must train staff members in how to handle the responsibility for complaint resolution if they assign it to them.

Identify a Mutually Acceptable Solution. Once the staff member has listened to the complaint and apologized for the problem, the staff member and guest must identify a mutually acceptable solution. Some managers train staff members to simply ask the guest to suggest a way to resolve the complaint. Most guests respond reasonably. Other managers train staff members to offer guests alternatives or options. In any case, it is essential that the solution be mutually acceptable, one in which everyone wins. When a complaint is handled to the satisfaction of all involved, the complainer may be transformed into a loyal guest.

This brings us to some logistics for resolving guest complaints. If food items or beverages are unacceptable, the staff member should immediately remove them and quickly offer to bring a replacement. If the new item is one that requires preparation or cooking, the staff member should immediately inform the person in charge of production of the need to quickly provide the item. If the staff member must continue serving other guests, he or she should tell the manager about the situation so the manager can go to the guest's table, apologize again, and explain to the guest what is being done to solve the problem. It may be necessary to void or alter the guest check if the guest does not desire a replacement.

What about complaints that have nothing to do with the food or beverages served? Some guests might complain that the restaurant is too cold, for example, or might complain about a smoker sitting at a nearby table. If a guest is too cold, a server might suggest a move to a table farther away from air-conditioning ducts or to a table next to a window (if it's sunny outside). In the case of a guest who complains about another guest's smoking, it is best to quietly move the guest who complains, not the guest who smokes.

Check Back and Follow Up. The final step in resolving a guest complaint is to check back to determine whether the complaint has truly been resolved. Depending on the situation, another apology might be in order, if for no other reason than to acknowledge the operation's failure to meet the guest's expectations on the first try. Some operations also follow up a day or so later with a letter or telephone call. This strongly demonstrates that the operation and its staff are genuinely committed to continuous quality improvement.

Additional intervention may be necessary with difficult guests—those who are grouchy, unruly, or just plain rude. When it becomes clear that the server cannot resolve a guest's complaint, the dining room manager should step in and try to handle the situation. This is particularly true when a difficult guest's behavior disturbs other guests or staff members. Managers should isolate the difficult guest by moving him or her to an area away from other guests and staff members. By moving difficult guests away from the scene, managers can often calm them, as long as they treat them politely. In a group that has one difficult guest, the manager may be able to appeal to the common sense of others in the group. (This strategy also may work well when one guest in a group becomes intoxicated.)

The Team Approach to Service

The team approach to guest service helps all staff members view guest service as an activity to which everyone in the operation must be committed. It involves cross-training each staff member to perform a variety of service functions, including taking orders, using suggestive-selling techniques, delivering orders, resolving guest complaints, and busing and resetting tables. Team members may or may not retain traditional titles such as "server" and "busperson." For the team concept to reach its full potential, it takes motivated and enthusiastic staff members. Appendix B is a tool managers can use to select new or evaluate current team members.

Server teams can have one of three structures: small teams, loose stations, or all-inclusive server teams. *Small teams* are responsible for one dining room area and are structured so that some team members focus on service in the dining room and others are responsible for delivering products from the kitchen and bar, clearing tables, and performing other general service tasks. In *loose stations,* servers are discouraged from thinking in terms of territories, a mind-set that is evident in statements like "It's not my station" (or "table" or "responsibility"). Instead, staff members are encouraged to focus on exceeding guests' expectations, regardless of the station or table location. The first-available-server system (guest orders are served as soon as they are ready by whichever server is readily available) is an example of this kind of team approach. In an *all-inclusive server team,* not only do service staff and managers dress the same, but all perform guest service duties, respond to guest inquiries, and handle complaints.

Managers who use team service systems must develop very detailed order-taking procedures so that service staff who are unfamiliar with the guests' orders will be able to match orders with the guests who ordered them. Hand-held point-of-sale devices are one possible solution to confusing or illegible handwritten orders.

Members of server teams usually have more authority than servers in traditional structures. This empowerment can lead to increased motivation and enthusiasm on the part of team members. If structured properly, the team approach to service can lead to fewer mistakes and fewer negative guest encounters than are experienced in traditional service systems. This, of course, results in reduced guest complaints. If team service results in more team-member interaction and interaction with guests, communication will be enhanced both among team members and between team members and guests. Improved communication can result in an operation that is invigorated, attentive, and confident in providing guest service.

Server teams provide continuous service and attention to guests, and they are more likely to deliver food to guests when the food is ready (and fresh), not when the server who took the order is ready. Service teams may also be able to serve more guests in less time than team members could do as individuals. Unexpected staff member absences are less likely to dramatically affect guest service if an operation uses a team-service system, since team members are trained to perform each other's functions.

While those who oppose the team approach to service point out disadvantages that include extensive training, possible guest confusion, challenges with distributing tips, and possible over-service, in most circumstances—when correctly implemented with properly trained staff—team service is a dramatic leap forward in improving guest service.

Serving Guests Who Have Disabilities

Food service operations should be committed to giving the best possible service to everyone. In the case of guests with disabilities, this commitment is reinforced by the Americans with Disabilities Act (ADA), a law that gives people with disabilities the right to equal access to the goods and services enjoyed by the rest of the public.

Courtesy is the key to giving excellent service to all guests—including guests with disabilities. Staff members should offer to help, but should not insist on helping. Rather than assume they know what a disabled guest needs, staff members should ask the expert—the guest who has the disability. Staff members should be flexible about meeting the guest's needs; the guest can often help the staff member find a creative way to deal with an obstacle or some other problem.

Managers should inform all staff members about the operation's services for guests with disabilities. Knowledgeable staff members can help these guests feel welcome and wanted. Managers should train staff members to notify them of the presence and locations of guests with disabilities whenever an emergency arises.

Guests with disabilities have various needs that are related to their disabilities. What follow are some general guidelines only; as just mentioned, staff members should communicate with disabled guests in order to determine exactly how they want to be helped—if they want help at all.

Mobility Impairments. People with mobility impairments have difficulty walking or cannot walk; they may or may not use a wheelchair. If the guest is in a wheelchair, staff members should put themselves at eye level with the guest whenever they can. This puts the guest and the staff member on equal ground and helps the guest avoid neck or back strain. Staff members should not touch or lean on wheelchairs, and should only push a wheelchair if asked to do so. When pushing wheelchairs, staff members should push the chair at a normal pace, be careful around corners, and tilt the chair slightly back when going down ramps or over curbs.

To best serve people with mobility impairments, an operation should have wide entrance and restroom doorways (minimum widths are mandated by ADA law), and place wheelchair-accessible tables near the entrance.

Speech Impairments. Guests with speech impairments have difficulty speaking clearly or easily. When speaking to a guest who has a speech impairment, staff members should be patient and ask the guest to repeat what they do not understand. It's okay if staff members don't understand, but they shouldn't pretend that they understand if they really don't. If necessary, staff members can ask the guest to show them what he or she is trying to say.

When talking with a guest who has a speech impairment, it's helpful for staff members to make eye contact with the guest and speak clearly and at a normal pace. Staff members do not have to talk loudly or slowly.

Visual Impairments. Guests with visual impairments are blind, have poor vision, or have certain eye diseases. When guests with visual impairments ask for directions, staff members should give the directions in specific and descriptive terms. If a staff member offers to lead the way and the offer is accepted, the staff member should offer his or her left elbow to the guest and let the guest follow close behind. As they move forward, the staff member should tell the guest about stairs, doorways, large plants, and other obstacles.

When giving change to visually impaired guests after they have paid their guest checks, staff members should identify each bill and coin separately. If braille menus and signs are not available, staff members should be trained in how to graciously read menus aloud to guests when asked. Lastly, if guests have guide dogs, staff members should help the dogs concentrate on their jobs by not petting them while they are working.

Hearing Impairments. Guests with hearing impairments cannot hear at all or cannot hear very well. When attempting to speak to a guest who has a hearing impairment, staff members might have to use visual signals or gestures to get the guest's attention. Staff members should let the guest decide how to communicate (through lipreading or writing things down, for example). If the guest has an interpreter, staff members should speak directly to the guest, not the interpreter. If the guest reads lips, staff members should speak at a moderate pace and use facial expressions that give visual clues about what they are saying. (However, staff members should not overly exaggerate their expressions.) Obviously, for lipreading to take place, there must be enough light for the guest to see faces and lips (this can be a problem in dimly lit dining rooms).

Mental Retardation. Guests who are mentally retarded might have any of a variety of mental disabilities. When serving adult guests who are mentally retarded, staff members must remember to treat them as adults, not children. Usually the best approach is to use simple, direct language and short sentences. Above all, staff members must be patient, take their time, and be positive and encouraging.

Key Terms

buffet service—A typically large assortment of foods attractively arranged for self-service by guests.

cart service—A table-service style in which specially trained staff members prepare menu items beside the guests' tables using a cart; the food is prepared and plated on the cart, then served to the guest. Also called French service.

chef du rang—In cart service, the person generally responsible for taking orders, serving drinks, preparing food at the table, and collecting the guests' payments. In the absence of a sommelier, he or she may serve dinner wines.

commis du rang—In cart service, the person who assists the *chef du rang*. He or she is responsible for taking food orders to the kitchen, placing the orders, picking up food in the kitchen, and bringing it to the tableside cart, often on silver trays. The *commis du rang* also delivers drink orders, serves food to the guests, and acts as a busperson.

family-style service—A table-service style in which servers take food on large platters or in large bowls from the kitchen and deliver it to guest tables; the guests at each table then pass the food around their table, serving themselves. Also called English service.

guéridon—A cart or rectangular table mounted on wheels with workspace, shelves, and a heating unit (*réchaud*); used for tableside food preparation in cart service.

maître d'hôtel—In fine hotel dining rooms, especially those with cart service, the person who supervises the dining room, seats guests, and performs other duties.

plate service—A table-service style in which fully cooked menu items are individually produced, portioned, plated, and garnished in the kitchen, then carried to each guest directly. Also called American service.

platter service—A table-service style in which servers carry platters of fully cooked food to the dining room and present them to guests for approval. Servers then set hot plates in front of each guest and place food from the platters onto the plates. Also called Russian service.

preshift meeting—A meeting held just before a dining service shift that managers use to exchange pertinent information (daily specials, menu changes, table assignments) with staff members. Preshift meetings may also be used to train staff members and give them opportunities to taste menu items.

réchaud—A portable heating unit used for food preparation on the *guéridon* in cart service.

runner—A staff member who delivers guests' orders from the kitchen to tray stands or tables in the dining room so that servers are able to spend more time with guests.

scramble system—A system used for cafeterias or buffets in which guests go to separate stations rather than wait in a single line. For example, hot foods are at one station, beverages at another, and desserts and salads at others.

service guarantee—An unconditional commitment to complete guest satisfaction. Guests who are not satisfied with the products or services they receive do not pay for them.

show plate—Often ornately designed with the organization's logo or made of fine china, pewter, or another attractive material, this plate enhances the table presentation when guests first arrive. Also called a base plate.

side station—A service stand in the dining area that holds equipment (such as a coffee maker) and service supplies (such as tableware and condiments) for easy access by servers and other staff members. Also called a server station, sidestand, or workstation.

sidework—Service-related but non-guest-contact tasks such as making coffee, folding napkins, refilling condiment containers, and end-of-shift activities.

suggestive selling—The practice of influencing a guest's purchase decision through the use of sales phrases.

Review Questions

1. What staff positions are commonly found in food and beverage service operations, and what are their typical functions?
2. How does plate service work?

3. What is cart service, and what types of service positions and procedures does it entail?
4. How does platter service differ from family-style service?
5. What are the advantages and disadvantages of buffet service?
6. What are some general strategies and procedures that food service managers might use to help their staffs deliver superior guest service?
7. What information do servers need to adequately practice suggestive-selling techniques?
8. What strategies should service staff use to resolve guest complaints?
9. What is team service, and how do operations use it in serving guests?
10. What are some general service guidelines for serving guests who have disabilities?

Internet Sites

For more information, visit the following Internet sites. Remember that Internet addresses can change without notice.

American Culinary Federation
http://www.acfchefs.org

American Dietetic Association
http://www.eatright.org

American Hotel & Motel Association
http://www.ahma.com

American School Food Service Association
http://www.asfsa.org

Bon Appetit Restaurants around the Globe
http://www.yellow-net.com/APPETITE.HTM

Club Managers Association of America
http://www.cmaa.org

The Educational Foundation of NRA
http://www.edfound.org

The Educational Institute of AH&MA
http://www.ei-ahma.org

Electronic Gourmet Guide
http://www.foodwine.com

The Food Institute
http://www.foodinstitute.com

Food Management
http://www.penton.com/corp/mags/fm.html

FoodWeb
http://www.foodweb.com

Hospitality Financial and Technology Professionals
http://www.hftp.org

International Hotel & Restaurant Association
http://www.ih-ra.com

Internet Food Channel
http://www.foodchannel.com

National Association of College and University Food Services
http://www.nacufs.org

National Restaurant Association
http://www.restaurant.org

On the Rail—News for Food Professionals
http://www.ontherail.com

Restaurant Hospitality
http://www.penton.com/corp/mags/rh.html

Restaurant Report Online
http://www.restaurantreport.com

Restaurants and Institutions
http://www.rimag.com

References

"Banquet Server Guide" in the *Hospitality Skills Training Series.* East Lansing, Mich.: Educational Institute of the American Hotel & Motel Association, 1995.

Bellamy, Gail, David Farkas, and John Soeder. "Sensational Service." *Restaurant Hospitality,* July 1994.

"55 Ways to Super Service." *Restaurants & Institutions,* November 15, 1993.

Liberson, Judy. "Courting the Community." *Lodging,* July 1998.

National Restaurant Association. *Foodservice Employment 2000: Exemplary Industry Programs.*

Peter, Gerhard M. *Function Room Set-Up Manual.* Hospitality Sales and Marketing Association International, n.d.

Stephenson, Susie. "Who to Hire? How Much to Pay?" *Restaurants & Institutions,* January 1, 1995.

Case Study

Adrift in a Sea of Apathy: Putting Dining Room Service Back on Course

Owen O'Brien, a general manager for CJ's, a casual, family-dining restaurant chain, had a reputation as a troubleshooter with a knack for turning around under-performing units within the chain. That's why corporate headquarters was sending him to the CJ's in Westmont, Illinois, a Chicago suburb. While other Chicago-area CJ's were thriving, the Westmont restaurant posted merely average operational results, and was below standards in a number of areas, particularly service. Given the restaurant's size and location, the company felt the operation should have been performing better than it was. Owen's assignment was to uncover problem areas and implement solutions that would bring the operation up to speed.

Owen decided to spend his first week at the restaurant simply observing staff members and guests and gathering information about the operation, rather than trying to jump in with quick-fix solutions. What he saw was certainly at odds with the glowing staff member and supervisor performance evaluations he had read in preparation for his move. Where was the teamwork, the attention to detail that CJ's stressed in its training? Everyone seemed to be doing just enough to get by.

The Thursday dinner shift was typical of what Owen had witnessed during his first week in Westmont. It wasn't that service was really bad, but the lackluster attitude of the servers contrasted with the upbeat, friendly image called for in CJ's server training manual. One of the more experienced servers, Laura, started out the evening with what Owen considered the best attitude, but as the night wore on, Laura seemed to lose her sparkle. He saw her arguing with another server over by the kitchen, and when the shift supervisor ignored the altercation, Owen walked over to intervene.

"What seems to be the trouble, ladies?" he asked in a calm voice.

"Well, Erin here delivered entrées to my table, but she mixed up everyone's order," said Laura. "If she can't do her job right, she should leave my tables alone."

"But we're supposed to help each other, aren't we?" asked Erin. "I thought we weren't supposed to let orders sit. I've seen you take orders to other servers' tables. Why are you on my case?"

"The problem," snapped Laura, "is that you didn't get the orders right, and that makes me look bad."

"Wait a minute," Owen cut in. "Don't you use the company's pivot point system for taking and delivering orders?"

Erin looked confused, then explained that Ned, her supervisor, had said something about training the newer servers to use that system, but had never gotten around to it. She had been on the job for three months, and figured that it must not be a big deal since it never came up.

Owen commended Erin for her willingness to pitch in with getting orders to tables in a timely fashion, but suggested that she concentrate on her own tables until she and the other newer servers were more fully trained.

Owen learned that Laura had been delayed in picking up the food order because she was explaining to guests at another table that their meal would take longer than expected. Apparently John, the head cook, had taken an order of chicken fajitas meant for Laura's table and had given it to Grace, who had forgotten to place the order for a guest at one of her tables.

"Then shouldn't Grace have been the one to wait?" asked Owen. This was definitely not standard procedure for CJ's, or any other restaurant he knew of, for that matter.

"Oh, John and Grace are an 'item,' so of course she can do no wrong," grumbled Laura. "You'll see what kind of favoritism goes on after you've been here a few more weeks."

Later that evening, as Owen visited at tables and poured coffee for guests, he caught snatches of conversations about mixed-up orders, servers who didn't know—and didn't care—about the specials, and about the futility of having free refills on soft drinks if the servers never seemed to notice when the glasses became empty.

Owen saw Carl, a veteran server, carrying a soda pitcher past a table of diners who were conspicuously rattling the ice cubes in their empty glasses. Thinking Carl just hadn't noticed them, Owen pointed them out. Carl returned to the table and filled the glasses.

"Thanks, Carl," said Owen. "I know that's not your table, and I appreciate your help. At CJ's, it's everyone's job to see that our guests don't go thirsty."

Carl sighed. "Yeah, I know the routine. But I got tired of being the only one doing it. None of the other servers, except maybe Laura, even knows that 'ever-full' soft drinks are a CJ's tradition. I finally decided that if they're not going to do it, then neither am I."

"I can understand your frustration," said Owen. "But perhaps you can be a role model for the others. We need experienced servers like you to show the newer staff members what it means to be a CJ's server."

Carl smiled at the implied compliment. "You know," he told Owen, "it used to be really fun to work here. That's why I came to CJ's. But now, nobody seems to care. Poor Ned is so busy finding new servers to replace the ones who split after two or three months that he barely has time to train them on the basics, much less on the standards I learned when I started here. Confidentially," he whispered, "I think Ned's getting burned out, especially since he's had to be acting manager, until you showed up."

The next day, Owen learned that Ned was not the only one dropping the ball. It was evident during the line check before the 4 P.M. shift that Jeanette, the kitchen manager, was passing on the same slipshod attitude in the kitchen that Ned was conveying to the dining room staff.

Owen watched as Jeanette checked off items on her list with barely a glance at the coolers. She lifted the lids on the steam table as she passed by, stirred the sauces, but neglected temperature and quality checks, including tasting the sauces. He followed behind, tasting as he went, and made a horrible face as he tried the sweet-and-sour sauce.

After the line check was completed, Owen motioned Jeanette away from the kitchen and told her in a low voice that the sweet-and-sour sauce tasted like it was made with salt instead of sugar.

"Oh, no, not again. Julie must be working today," said Jeanette. "It looked fine to me."

"That just emphasizes how important it is to taste the sauces," said Owen. "And what do you mean, 'not again'?"

She explained that at least twice before, Julie had mistaken salt for sugar in that sauce. When Owen commented that he hadn't seen any mention of that on Julie's performance evaluation, Jeanette just shrugged.

"It's tough enough keeping cooks who'll work well with John. I find it's easier to overlook minor things like this than risk losing them over a poor evaluation," she said.

"But we risk losing guests if we serve them inedible food," Owen replied. "And it's not fair to Julie to let her think she's doing a good job if she's not. Please have her prepare a new batch of sweet-and-sour sauce—I don't want this going out to guests."

Owen left the kitchen and joined Ned and the servers at their preshift meeting. Ned was reading off the evening's specials and Owen heard him say, "It's that chicken pasta thing corporate's trying to push on us. Try to make a big deal about it, if you want to." Two of the servers were talking throughout Ned's description of the dish, and Owen doubted they'd be able to "make a big deal" about the special to their guests, if they even bothered to try after Ned's less-than-enthusiastic presentation.

As Ned assigned workstations for the night, Owen saw another storm brewing as Erin complained that Ned was once again giving Laura the best section.

"She always gets the best tables, so she always gets the best tips," Erin whined.

Laura retorted, "Did you ever think that maybe it's because I give the best service?"

"Well, that's not my fault," said Erin. "Maybe if I'd had the training you got, I'd be as good as you. I'm doing the best job I know how."

Owen stepped in. "An argument is not the best way to start a shift. Let's all do the best jobs you can at the stations you've been assigned tonight. After the weekend, I'd like to sit down and hear your ideas for how we might do things better. You know I've called an all-staff-member meeting for Monday, and I'd like everyone to bring at least one idea to share, or you can write down your suggestions if you can't make it. I've got some ideas of my own, but I'd like to know what you think needs to be done, too."

Owen asked Ned if he could meet with him privately before the meeting, then returned to the kitchen to remind Jeanette about Monday's brainstorming session.

Discussion Questions

1. What are some of the problem areas at the Westmont CJ's restaurant?
2. What are some possible causes of these problems?
3. What steps can Owen take immediately to start to turn around operations at CJ's?
4. What long-term strategies could be implemented to turn around operations at CJ's?

The following industry experts helped generate and develop this case: Christopher Kibit, C.S.C., Academic Team Leader, Hotel/Motel/Food Management & Tourism Programs, Lansing Community College, Lansing, Michigan; and Jack Nye, General Manager, Applebee's of Michigan, Applebee's International, Inc.

Appendix A

Service Techniques	American System					European System			
	Plate	Platter	Cart	Family-Style	Butler	Plate	Platter	French or Butler	Side Table
Service to the left of the guest									
• Platters presented to guest/host		•			•		•	•	
• Plates held with left hand, served with left hand	•								
• Platters carried on left forearm		•			•		•	•	
• Move counterclockwise	•	•	•	•	•	•	•	•	•
• Fingerbowl (placed above dinner fork)	•	•	•	•	•	•	•	•	•
• Food served with spoon and fork in right hand of servers		•					•		
• Guest serves self with spoon and fork					•			•	
• Serve bread and butter	•	•	•		•	•	•	•	•
• Serve salad (as side dish)	•	•	•		•	•	•	•	
• Crumb table	•	•	•	•	•	•	•	•	•
• Clear salad plate	•	•	•	•	•	•	•	•	•
• Clear B & B plate	•	•	•	•	•	•	•	•	•
• Food plated on guerdon			•						
• Soup	•								
Service to the right of the guest									
• Set hot or cold plates (movement clockwise			•			•		•	•
• Clear plates	•	•	•	•	•	•	•	•	•
• Change flatware	•	•	•	•	•	•	•	•	•
• Move clockwise	•	•	•	•	•	•	•	•	•
• Pour beverages	•	•	•	•	•	•	•	•	•
• Present wine bottles	•	•	•	•	•	•	•	•	•
• Soup						•	•	•	•
• Food plates held and served with right hand			•			•			

(continued)

Appendix A *(continued)*

	American System					European System			
Service Techniques *(continued)*	Plate	Platter	Cart	Family-Style	Butler	Plate	Platter	French or Butler	Side Table
Service performed near table									
• Food is cooked in kitchen and finished at tableside			•						
• Food is carved/boned for plating			•						•
• Food is finished on rechaud (stove)			•						•
• Food is plated from silver platter			•						•
• Two hands (fork and spoon) used to plate food			•						•
Service performed by guests									
• Side dishes, sauces, and vegetable on table to pass				•				•	
• Meat carved and plated by host and served by butler or passed by guest				•					

Appendix B

Team Behavioral Skills Index

Team Behavioral Skills	An Individual Who Is:
Anticipative	Able to provide guest needs without a request
Appearance	Able to take care and pride in his/her appearance
Appreciative	Capable of expressing gratitude
Assertive	Capable of selling and suggesting
Commitment	Dedicated to serving the guest and others
Confident	Marked by assurance
Cooperative	Willing to engage in joint activity—a team player
Diversity	Sensitive to the culture of others
Emotionally Stable	Predictable in his/her attitudes; positive outlook
Empathy	Understanding of another's situation or feelings
Flexible	Able to respond positively to change
Friendly	Able to make guests feel welcome with visual cues
Helpful	Useful and assisting to others
Honest	Able to demonstrate truthfulness and integrity
Informative	Source of information for guest
Innovative	Creative in the workplace
Observant	Watches attentively for guest needs/expressions
Passionate	Enthusiastic in a desire to serve
Persuasive	Able to convince someone to change/buy products
Physically Capable	Able to perform specific work requirements
Polite	Marked by consideration for guests and others
Positive	Able to act with certainty and acceptance
Probing	Able to inquire into the needs of guests/others
Professional Knowledge	Competent in technical/service skills
Recognition	Remembers and uses guests' names
Reliable	Someone you can depend on
Respectful	Willing to demonstrate acceptable forms of etiquette
Responsible	Answerable for his/her own behavior
Self Esteem	Values his/her worth
Sense of Humor	Able to enjoy or express what is humorous
Sensitive	Capable of perceiving diverse feelings of others
Service Planning	Able to sequence work effort efficiently
Smiling	Able to express visual warmth and friendship

(continued)

Appendix B *(continued)*

Standards	Meets corporate and unit performance standards
Tactful	Says and does the right thing
Zero Defects	Works for perfect service
Communication	
Listener	Actively listens to guests
Presentation	Able to express ideas clearly in speech and/or visually
Technical	Able to perform correct procedures repeatedly
Writing	Able to express ideas clearly
Thinking Skills	
Judgement	Able to select or make the right decision
Problem Solver	Able to resolve complex problems

Task Breakdowns: Dining Service

The procedures presented in this section are for illustrative purposes only and should not be construed as recommendations or standards. While these procedures are typical, readers should keep in mind that each food service facility has its own procedures, equipment specifications, and safety policies.

RESTAURANT SERVER: *Stock and Maintain Side Stations*

Materials needed: *A sidework checklist, glasses, silverware, dishes, ashtrays, napkins, condiments, garnishes, cleaning cloths, a bar towel, sanitizing solution, and gloves.*

STEPS	HOW-TO'S
1. Stock the side stations.	❑ The items that need to be stocked vary among properties. Items should be stocked at par levels. A "par" is the number of supplies you will need to get through one workshift. ❑ If you used items from your side stations when you checked your tables, replace these items so that the side stations are fully stocked for service. ❑ Side stations should be completely stocked with items such as glasses, silverware, dishes, and ashtrays before a new shift begins. ❑ Bring clean glasses, silverware, dishes, and ashtrays from the dish room to replace the used ones. ❑ Fold extra napkins. ❑ Make sure there is always a fresh supply of condiments at the side stations. ❑ Make sure there is a bucket of sanitizing solution and a clean cloth at each side station.
2. Maintain the stations throughout your shift.	❑ Check the sidework checklist to see which tasks you are responsible for. A sidework checklist lists sidework and the restaurant server who is assigned to complete each task. Common sidework tasks include folding napkins and wiping service trays. ❑ Perform your assigned sidework duties throughout your shift. Sidework tasks are a very important part of keeping your restaurant running well.

RESTAURANT SERVER: *Stock and Maintain Side Stations* *(continued)*

STEPS	HOW-TO'S
	❑ Wipe up spills, bread crumbs, etc., as soon as possible.
	❑ Pick up broken glass with a linen napkin or gloves to prevent cuts. Throw away broken glass in the proper container.
	❑ Throw away wilted or discolored garnishes. Wash and dry the garnish container. Refill the container with fresh garnishes as needed.
	❑ Empty used ice buckets and wipe them out with a bar towel. Store them until they are needed.
	❑ Ask buspersons or stewards to empty full trash cans for you.
	❑ Check the side stations throughout the meal period. Work with the busperson assigned to each station to restock the area as needed.
	❑ Keep side-station supplies and equipment orderly.
3. Clean the side stations.	❑ Take soiled items to the dish room. Wipe the shelves and countertop with a clean, damp cloth and a sanitizing solution.
	❑ Keep the cleaning cloth in the sanitizing solution when you are not using it.
	❑ Change the sanitizing solution periodically throughout your shift.
	❑ Throughout service, clean side stations as needed and as your time permits.
	❑ Do not overlook the needs of guests while maintaining the side stations.
	❑ Work as a team with buspersons to complete all tasks.

RESTAURANT SERVER: *Greet and Seat Guests*

Materials needed: *Menus, special supplies (such as booster seats, highchairs, braille menus, etc.), snacks, and a wine list.*

STEPS	HOW-TO'S
1. Approach guests who are waiting to be seated.	❑ Smile and give a warm greeting, such as "Good morning!" or "Welcome to (name of the restaurant)." ❑ Be positive when greeting guests. Your manner will affect guest satisfaction.
2. Direct guests to the coatroom if your restaurant has one.	❑ Do not take responsibility for guests' coats, packages, or other articles.
3. Ask guests if you are holding a reservation for them.	❑ The steps to mark in the reservations book that a party has arrived vary among properties. ❑ If guests do not have a reservation, ask them if anyone else will be joining them. Then check available seating to see if you can accommodate them.
4. Ask if guests prefer to be seated in a smoking or nonsmoking section.	
5. Accommodate special guest needs.	❑ Ask guest with visual impairments if they would like braille menus, if they are available. ❑ Ask guests with disabilities if they have special seating needs. A guest in a wheelchair may prefer to sit in a chair. ❑ Ask guests with small children if they would like a highchair or a booster seat. ❑ Ask the busperson to rearrange tables or to set up special equipment if necessary. ❑ If necessary, ask the party to wait while you meet their needs.

RESTAURANT SERVER: *Greet and Seat Guests*

(continued)

STEPS	HOW-TO'S
6. Look at the seating chart and decide where you are going to seat the party, according to your restaurant's seating policies.	❑ Overloading one section will make good service difficult. However, if a party requests a certain table and it is available, you should seat them at that table, even if it overloads a section. Then tell the dining room manager so he or she can adjust the server's workload. Also, let the server for that section know about the guests.
7. Direct guests to their table.	❑ Pick up enough menus for each guest, plus one wine list, if appropriate. ❑ Ask the party to follow you, and lead the way to the table at a reasonable pace. ❑ Hold the menus high on your arm, not down by your side. ❑ Stand up straight and give your full attention to the party you are seating. Do not stop along the way to talk to co-workers unless it relates to seating the party you are leading. ❑ Move service equipment to one side to clear a path for the guests. Make sure the party is following. ❑ As you walk, describe restaurant highlights, such as a salad bar, buffets, or house specials.
8. Help the guests with seating.	❑ Help children get into booster seats. Pull highchairs away from tables so that guests can place small children into them. Never touch a child—or any other guest—unless you have permission ❑ Help guests with disabilities as appropriate. If you're not sure how to help, ask guests what you can do for them.

(continued)

RESTAURANT SERVER: *Greet and Seat Guests*

(continued)

STEPS	HOW-TO'S
	❑ Pull out a chair for a guest and adjust the chair as the guest sits. Help others with seating as appropriate. Let the guests decide who will sit in the chair you pull out.
9. Present the menus.	❑ Give a closed menu, right-side-up, to each guest in the following order: • Children (children's menu when available) • Women • Men ❑ Present the menu from the guest's right side, using your right hand. ❑ The procedures for when and how to present menus vary among properties. ❑ Hand the wine list to the host of the party if there is one. If not, place the wine list on the table. ❑ Introduce yourself and tell guests who their server will be. ❑ Serve water (if appropriate) and items such as crackers, bread sticks, or other snacks (if appropriate).
10. Remove extra place settings.	

RESTAURANT SERVER: *Take Food Orders*

Materials needed: *An order pad or guest checks and a pen.*

STEPS	HOW-TO'S
1. Tell guests about specials.	❑ Know the daily specials. If appropriate at your restaurant, try to taste each one. ❑ Always describe specials and chef's choice items, such as the soup of the day, before guests ask. ❑ Describe the ingredients and the preparation of specials in an appealing way. Always give the price of specials.
2. Ask for the food order.	❑ Offer to help guests with menu selections. Answer any questions about the menu. ❑ Ask if they are ready to order.
3. Follow an order-taking system.	❑ Know the numbering system for the chairs at each table. Chair #1 at each table is typically the chair closest to the door or some other landmark in your restaurant. By taking orders in a standard clockwise fashion, you make it possible for someone else to serve your guests without having to ask who ordered what. ❑ When writing orders on your order pad or guest check, write the order for the guest in chair #1 on the first line of the order form. Remember that the chair numbers identify each seat at the table. They don't stand for the order in which you'll write things down. ❑ Take the orders of children first, then women, and then men. Write their orders in the corresponding places on the order pad. For instance, if the guest in chair #2 is the only woman at at the table, take her order first and write it on line #2 on the order pad.

(continued)

RESTAURANT SERVER: *Take Food Orders* *(continued)*

STEPS	HOW-TO'S
	❑ Your supervisor will show you abbreviations and other tips for writing food orders that will be understood by everyone who works at the restaurant. ❑ Continue to take food orders in a clockwise pattern around the table.
4. Stand in the correct position to take orders.	❑ The place where you stand to take orders may be one of the following: • In different positions around the table so you can speak one-on-one to each guest. • In one position to get the attention of the entire table so that everyone can hear your suggestive selling. • It depends on the table and the guests. ❑ Always stand up straight as you take orders. Do not rest the order pad on the table. ❑ Look at each guest when he or she is ordering. Watch for hesitation in making a decision. This provides you an opening to offer a suggestion.
5. Ask the appropriate questions.	❑ Pay attention to details and know your menu thoroughly. Try not to sound mechanical when describing choices. Make every item sound good. ❑ Know what questions to ask for each item to determine the guests' choices. For instance, know if a guest must choose soup or salad. If you don't ask the right questions when taking the order, you will have to interrupt your guests to find out necessary preparation and service information. This is embarrassing to you and annoying to your guest. ❑ Repeat each completed order to the guest, especially if there are special details or requests regarding preparation or service.

RESTAURANT SERVER: *Take Food Orders* *(continued)*

STEPS	HOW-TO'S
6. Suggest additional courses.	❑ Suggest additional courses such as appetizers, soups, and salads when you take the food order. By suggesting additional items, you can enhance the dining experience, increase revenue for the restaurant, and increase your tips. ❑ Think about what the guest has selected and suggest items that will go well with the entree.
7. Suggest a bottle of wine.	❑ Try to sell a bottle of wine after taking the food order. If guests are celebrating a special occasion such as a birthday, anniversary, or other celebration, they may want to have wine or champagne with their meal. ❑ Know which wines will go well with certain foods. ❑ Always know how much alcohol your guests are drinking. Don't suggest wine or other alcoholic beverages if your guests are intoxicated or are close to becoming intoxicated.
8. Try to meet special requests.	❑ Some guests may request that an item be prepared in a way not listed on the menu. ❑ Write all special requests on your order pad and tell the kitchen staff about the requests when you place the order. ❑ You may need to check with the chef or your supervisor before making a promise to a guest.

(continued)

RESTAURANT SERVER: *Take Food Orders* *(continued)*

STEPS	HOW-TO'S
9. Ask if guests would like another beverage.	❑ Check on drink levels. Suggest another drink if a beverage is one-half to three-fourths empty and guests are not nearing intoxication. ❑ If guests are drinking alcoholic beverages but do not want another, suggest a nonalcoholic beverage. ❑ Clear empty glasses before serving new beverages.
10. Collect the menus and wine list, if you haven't already done so.	
11. Change ashtrays as needed, and tidy the table to keep it as fresh as possible.	
12. Pre-ring the food order.	❑ The steps to pre-ring orders vary among restaurants. ❑ Food checks must be rung into the point-of-sale unit before the kitchen will prepare any food.
13. Place food orders with the kitchen.	❑ The steps to place an order with the kitchen vary among restaurants. ❑ Special orders may require speaking with the chef. Always be polite and limit conversations to a minimum when possible.

RESTAURANT SERVER: *Serve the Meal*

Materials needed: *An order pad or guest check, a service tray, condiments, and ashtrays.*

STEPS	HOW-TO'S
1. Time the preparation of the food.	❑ The timing of food preparation is important to a smooth dining experience. Each guest in a party should be served at the same time. ❑ Turn in the order for each course when guests are about three-fourths finished with the previous one. If the kitchen is busy, turn in the orders sooner. ❑ Serve courses in the following order, unless guests request a different order: • Appetizers • Soup • Salads • Entrees • Dessert • Cordials • Coffee ❑ Check with the cook or your supervisor if you are concerned that an order is not being prepared in a reasonable amount of time. Don't make guests wait without an explanation from you or your supervisor. If there is a problem with a guest's order, do not avoid the table. Guests appreciate knowing what's going on. ❑ If you are too busy to pick up an order as soon as it is ready, ask another restaurant server for help.
2. Prepare the table for each course before serving it.	❑ Clear any empty plates or glasses from the guest's right with your right hand. Always ask guests if they are finished. ❑ Wait to clear glasses or plates until more than one guest at a table is finished so guests who are still eating or drinking do not feel rushed.

(continued)

RESTAURANT SERVER: *Serve the Meal* *(continued)*

STEPS	HOW-TO'S
	❑ Never stack dirty plates in front of guests. Pick them up separately and stack them away from guests. ❑ Bring all condiments and accompaniments to the table before serving the order. You shouldn't have to set food under a heat lamp or on your tray while you collect condiments. ❑ Only bring full—not partially full—condiment bottles to guests. ❑ If you will be serving an item that guests will share, bring a plate for each guest.
3. Pick up the food order.	❑ The steps to pick up food orders may vary among restaurants. ❑ Planning and organization will make it possible for you to serve all of your guests quickly. ❑ Check the food before you take it out of the kitchen: • Does the food look fresh and appealing? • Have all preparation instructions been followed? • Is the presentation garnished? • Have all special requests been met? • Is the plate clean? • Is hot food hot and cold food cold? ❑ Ask the cook to make any corrections necessary to meet the restaurant's high standards. ❑ Notify your supervisor immediately of any problem in the food preparation so that he or she can speak to the guests and correct the situation. ❑ If you are having trouble meeting guest needs, ask your supervisor or another server for help until you can catch up.

RESTAURANT SERVER: *Serve the Meal* *(continued)*

STEPS	HOW-TO'S
	❑ Don't let the guests suffer because you're busy. ❑ Thank the kitchen staff for their cooperation.
4. Deliver food.	❑ The way food is delivered may be by: • Using a tray draped with a napkin • Using a tray without a napkin ❑ Use your order pad or guest check to help remember who ordered what. You shouldn't have to ask the guests. Good service is so smooth that the guests are hardly aware of you. When you are able to serve each course without asking questions, guests are not interrupted. ❑ Serve the children first, women next, then men, and the host last. ❑ Serve food from the guest's left side with your left hand whenever possible. Don't reach in front of guests. ❑ Place the plate with the first course on top of the base plate, if a base plate is included in your restaurant's table setting. ❑ Place the entree plate so that the main item is closest to the guest. ❑ Place side dishes to the left of the entree plate. ❑ If a guest asks for something extra, deliver it as quickly as possible so that the meal does not get cold. ❑ Ask if guests would like you to bring or do anything else for them at this time. ❑ Remove empty beverage glasses and exchange ashtrays as needed.

RESTAURANT SERVER: *Settle Guest Checks and Thank Guests*

Materials needed: *A guest check, a guest check folder, a credit card voucher, a credit card imprint machine, and a pen.*

STEPS	HOW-TO'S
1. Settle guest checks paid by cash.	❑ The steps to settle guest checks paid by cash vary among restaurants. ❑ Present change in the guest check folder. Do not claim a tip until guests leave. If the guest leaves while you are settling the check, the change is your tip. ❑ Always provide a receipt with the change.
2. Settle guest checks paid by traveler's check.	❑ Ask the guest to sign the traveler's check in your presence. ❑ Ask to see a driver's license if the guest signed the check when you were not present. ❑ If the signatures do not match, calmly report the problem to your supervisor. ❑ The steps to keep a record of traveler's checks vary among restaurants. ❑ Always put the receipt and any change in the guest check folder and give it to the guest.
3. Settle guest checks paid by credit card.	❑ Get an approval code. ❑ If a credit card is declined, politely ask the guest for another card or form of payment. If necessary, ask the guest to step away from his or her group so that he or she will not be embarrassed. ❑ Imprint the card on the back of the guest check and on a credit card voucher. ❑ Underline the account number and the expiration date on the imprint. If the card has expired, return it and ask for another form of payment.

RESTAURANT SERVER: *Settle Guest Checks and Thank Guests* *(continued)*

STEPS	HOW-TO'S
	❑ Complete the voucher. Enter the date, your name, the guest check number, which credit card is being used, the approval code, and the amount of the purchase. ❑ Present the voucher and a pen to the guest in a guest check folder. Ask the guest to total and sign the voucher. ❑ Make sure the voucher is totaled and signed. ❑ Return the card along with the guest's copy of the credit card voucher.
4. Settle guest checks charged to house accounts (for food service operations in hotels).	❑ Ask guests to print their names and room numbers on the guest checks and to sign them. Guests who are staying at the property with approved credit accounts may charge restaurant meals and drinks to their room. This is called a "house account." ❑ Ask guests to present their room keys as identification, unless the point-of-sale unit verifies occupancy.
5. Settle guest checks charged to city ledger accounts (for food service operations in hotels).	❑ Ask guests to print the company name or group name on the check. Some local customers may have charge accounts. This allows them to be directly billed each month. Such local accounts are called "city ledger accounts." ❑ Ask guests to provide the city ledger account number. ❑ Ask guests to sign the guest check. ❑ Verify with the front desk that guests who don't know the account number are authorized. Get the account number from the front desk. ❑ Give guests a receipt showing the charge.

(continued)

RESTAURANT SERVER: *Settle Guest Checks and Thank Guests* *(continued)*

STEPS	HOW-TO'S
6. Settle guest checks paid by personal check.	
7. Settle checks paid by coupon, voucher, or gift certificate.	❑ Read the document carefully to determine if it is valid and unexpired. Find out what charges are covered. Many restaurants do not give change for gift certificates and coupons. However, guests may receive smaller gift certificates in place of change. ❑ Make sure your restaurant accepts the coupon or other documents presented. Know your restaurant's policy for each type of coupon, voucher, or gift certificate. ❑ Treat the document as cash if it is valid. Collect the balance of the account if the document doesn't cover the full amount. ❑ Always put the receipt and any change or gift certificates in the guest check folder and give it to the guest.
8. Thank the guest when you return the change and receipt, and invite the guest to return.	
9. Inform security and your manager immediately if a guest leaves without settling the bill.	

RESTAURANT SERVER: *Perform Closing Sidework*

Materials needed: *A closing duty checklist, a clean kitchen funnel, cleaning cloths, a condiment requisition, clean silverware, water pitchers, and a bar towel.*

STEPS	HOW-TO'S
1. Consult your closing duty checklist.	
2. Remove soiled linens.	❑ Check side stations and the entire dining room for scattered soiled linens.
3. Store condiments.	❑ Remove condiments from the side stations and return them to the kitchen pantry. Combining condiments reduces costs and improves the appearance of the condiment containers. But only combine condiments if your local health department allows it. ❑ Use a clean kitchen funnel to combine each type of condiment. Wipe the containers with a damp cleaning cloth before storing them. ❑ Complete a condiment requisition for the next day. Order enough condiments to bring stock back to par levels.
4. Store bread and butter.	❑ Return unused butter and unserved rolls or bread to the kitchen. The chef will decide if the bread will be saved for future use or thrown away. Unserved bread is sometimes used for making other items, such as croutons or stuffing. ❑ Follow sanitation rules in judging what to save and what to throw out. ❑ Place unserved butter in the proper kitchen cooler.
5. Restock silverware.	❑ Take soiled silverware to the dish room. Follow dish room procedures for unloading soiled silverware. ❑ Pick up clean silverware from the dish room and restock the side station.

(continued)

RESTAURANT SERVER: *Perform Closing Sidework*

(continued)

STEPS	HOW-TO'S
6. Break down the coffee station.	❑ Empty all coffeepots into an approved sink. ❑ Throw away coffee grounds. Rinse the grounds holder and return it to the coffee maker. ❑ Take coffeepots to the dish room for washing. ❑ Throw away open cream or cream that has been out of the refrigerator too long. ❑ Return all other cream to the correct kitchen cooler. ❑ Store all unused coffee filter packs. ❑ Wipe the coffee maker and the surrounding area with a clean, damp cloth. ❑ Clean the nozzle head on the grounds holder, and clean the area around the nozzle head.
7. Break down ice buckets.	❑ Remove corks, foil scraps, labels, and other debris from buckets to avoid plugging drains. ❑ Empty ice and water into the appropriate sink. ❑ Return empty wine and champagne bottles to the bar for inventory. ❑ Dry the ice buckets with a bar towel. ❑ Store buckets in the designated side station.
8. Break down water pitchers.	❑ Empty ice and water into an appropriate sink. ❑ Take pitchers to the dish room for washing. Pitchers should be washed and sanitized between meal periods. ❑ Restock the side stations with clean pitchers.

RESTAURANT SERVER: *Perform Closing Sidework*

(continued)

STEPS	HOW-TO'S
9. Reset all tables.	❑ Follow table setup polices for the next meal period. ❑ In a restaurant with tablecloth dinner service and place mat breakfast service, do not strip and reset tables for breakfast while guests are still seated in the area. ❑ Clear the table down to the tablecloth and centerpiece, and wait to reset the table until the guests leave. ❑ Turn glasses upside-down so they will not collect dust. ❑ Check the appearance of each table to be sure it is complete.
10. Straighten, clean, and restock all side stations.	❑ Restock side stations after the rest of the area has been cleared. ❑ Remove all soiled equipment and restock with clean dishes, silverware, and glassware. Leave everything in spotless condition at the end of your shift.

BUSPERSON: *Set Up the Restaurant for Service*

Materials needed: *A pen, an opening duty checklist, a vacuum cleaner, caution signs, cleaning cloths, brass polish, and a blinds duster.*

STEPS	HOW-TO'S
1. Pick up and store restaurant linens.	
2. Dust wine displays.	❑ Carefully remove each wine bottle and wipe it with a clean, dry cloth. Do not use a wet cloth. Dusty wine racks and bottles ruin the effect of the wine display. A wet cloth will damage the label. ❑ Return each bottle to its original location.
3. Polish brass.	❑ Use approved brass polish, and a soft cloth. ❑ Apply polish and rub the brass to remove tarnish and spots. Buff with a soft, dry cloth. ❑ Never use steel wool or other abrasive materials on brass.
4. Adjust drapes and blinds.	❑ Check drapes to be sure they are hanging neatly. Adjust them to give the best appearance. ❑ Set blinds based on the angle of the sun to ensure guest comfort. ❑ Use a special blinds duster to clean blinds as needed. This helps maintain the restaurant's image. ❑ Report any food residue or stains on drapes or blinds to the restaurant manager so that cleaning can be scheduled with the housekeeping department.
5. Vacuum carpeted areas.	❑ Place caution signs. ❑ Empty the vacuum cleaner bag if necessary.

BUSPERSON: *Set Up the Restaurant for Service*

(continued)

STEPS	HOW-TO'S
	❑ Use a damp cloth followed by a dry cloth to remove spills before vacuuming. Do not use a linen napkin to clean up spills. Use only designated cloths or cleaning towels. ❑ Report stained or damaged upholstery or carpeting to your supervisor. ❑ Unwind the cord and plug the vacuum cleaner into an outlet near the door. Make sure the cord is out of the way so that no one trips. To avoid being shocked, do not stand in water when plugging in the vacuum cleaner. ❑ Begin vacuuming at the far side of the room and work toward the main entrance. ❑ Move tables and chairs as needed. ❑ Pay special attention to room corners, carpet edges, high-traffic areas, and areas under booths or banquettes. Careful vacuuming improves the restaurant's appearance and reduces problems with pests and rodents. ❑ Vacuum booth seats and upholstered chairs if necessary. ❑ Unplug the vacuum and carefully wind the cord. ❑ Empty the vacuum cleaner bag if needed. ❑ Store the vacuum cleaner as soon as you finish vacuuming to prevent accidents. ❑ Report carpet or equipment problems to your supervisor.
6. Adjust the environmental controls in the room.	❑ Adjust heat, ventilation, air conditioning, lighting, music, and other environmental controls if assigned to do so.

(continued)

BUSPERSON: *Set Up the Restaurant for Service*

(continued)

STEPS	HOW-TO'S
	❑ If controls are automatic, do not adjust them unless instructed to do so by a manager.
7. Check off this task on your opening duty checklist.	

BUSPERSON: *Prepare Tables for Service*

Materials needed: *Tablecloths or place mats, cleaning cloths, sanitizing solution, foodservice film, packets of crackers, a broom, a dustpan, a service tray, a tray jack, a dish dolly or cart, napkins, cream, butter, and flowers.*

STEPS	HOW-TO'S
1. Clean tables and chairs.	❑ Clean all tables and chairs before setting up the side station, even if they were cleaned at the end of the previous meal period. ❑ Wipe tabletops with a damp cloth and sanitizing solution followed by a dry cloth. Clean tabletops before wiping table legs and chairs. ❑ Wipe the legs, rungs, and bases of the tables. Rinse the cloth as needed. ❑ Wipe chair seats, backs, legs, and rungs. Wipe booths, banquettes, and any other seats. If possible, pull out seating cushions and wipe up crumbs. ❑ Check under tables and chairs for gum, and remove any gum you find.
2. Clean children's seating.	❑ Wipe highchair trays with a damp cloth and sanitizing solution and let them air-dry. Children may eat directly from the tray, and parents will appreciate the cleanliness. ❑ After trays have dried, place two packets of crackers on each tray and wrap each tray with foodservice film. ❑ Wipe the seats, backs, and legs of highchairs and all children's booster chairs. ❑ Check that the safety straps on highchairs are clean and in working order. Replace any missing or broken straps.
3. Check floors.	❑ Check under tables for crumbs, food spills, or stains. Sweep up crumbs. ❑ Use a damp cloth followed by a dry cloth to wipe up spills.

(continued)

BUSPERSON: *Prepare Tables for Service* *(continued)*

STEPS	HOW-TO'S
	❑ Report stubborn stains to your supervisor before setting up the station for service.
4. Place tablecloths or placemats.	❑ Setting and resetting tables is a very important duty of the busperson. The guest's first impression of the table is important in setting the tone for a pleasing dining experience. ❑ Check each new tablecloth or placemat for: • Correct size • Stains • Tears or holes • Unsightly wrinkles ❑ If placemats are used, make sure the pattern is right-side-up and facing the guest so words on the place mat can be read. ❑ Line up placemats with the table edge and with the placemats on the opposite side of the table. ❑ Place the tablecloths on the tables. Make sure they are right-side-up and centered on the tables.
5. Position tabletop items.	❑ Pick up tabletop items from your side station. Get enough of each of the following items to set all tables: • Centerpieces • Salt and pepper shakers and grinders • Sugar bowls • Condiments and cracker baskets • Ashtrays and matches ❑ Check the condition and appearance of each item. Clean or replace any items if necessary.

BUSPERSON: *Prepare Tables for Service* (continued)

STEPS	HOW-TO'S
	❑ Place the items on a service tray. Do not overload the tray. Make as many trips as necessary to safely carry items.
	❑ Carry the tray to the dining room and place it on a tray jack.
	❑ Place each item neatly in the center of the table according to standard table setup specifications.
	❑ If you are setting booths or tables that are against the wall, place the items at the end of the tabletop, near the wall.
5. Place base plates (if called for by the meal).	❑ Get a rack of clean plates from your side station or the dish room. In fine-dining restaurants, the base plate enhances the appearance of the table and acts as an underliner for cocktails and starter courses.
	❑ Carry the rack into the dining room. At some restaurants, you will need to empty items from the rack onto a service tray lined with linen napkins before carrying items into the dining room.
	❑ Place the rack on a tray jack. Most dish racks will fit on a tray jack.
	❑ Only use a dish dolly or cart to transport dishes when the restaurant is closed.
	❑ Check each base plate to be sure it is clean and free of water spots, chips, and cracks.
	❑ Return soiled or spotted plates to the dish room. Give chipped or cracked plates to your supervisor.
	❑ Place a base plate directly in front of each chair about two inches from the table edge.
	❑ If the plate has a logo, place the plate so that the guest can read the logo.
	❑ Return empty dish racks, dollies, or carts to the dish room.

(continued)

BUSPERSON: *Prepare Tables for Service* (continued)

STEPS	HOW-TO'S
7. Place silverware.	❑ Get a rack of clean silverware from your side station or the dish room. ❑ Carry the rack to the dining room and set it on a tray jack. ❑ Check each knife, fork, and spoon for cleanliness. ❑ Return spotted or soiled silverware to the dish room. ❑ Use a linen napkin to place silverware on the table. Touch the silverware only by the handle. ❑ If no base plates are called for by the meal, leave a 12-inch space directly in front of each seat. ❑ Place forks to the left of the base plate or space. ❑ Place knives to the right of the base plate or space, with the cutting edge of the knife toward the plate or space. ❑ Place spoons to the right of the knives. ❑ Leave small spaces between pieces of silverware. ❑ Line up all silverware handles about two inches from the table edge.
8. Place bread and butter plates.	❑ Get a rack of clean bread and butter plates from your side station or the dish room. ❑ Carry the rack to the dining room and place it on a tray jack. ❑ Check each bread and butter plate to be sure it is clean and free of chips or cracks. Return soiled plates to the dish room. Throw away chipped or cracked plates. ❑ Place bread and butter plates to the left of or above the forks at each place setting. ❑ Return the empty rack to the dish room.

BUSPERSON: *Prepare Tables for Service* *(continued)*

STEPS	HOW-TO'S
9. Place glassware.	❑ Get racks of clean glasses from your side station or the dish room. ❑ Carry one rack at a time to the dining room. ❑ Place the glassware rack on a tray jack. ❑ Make sure glasses are clean and free of water spots, lipstick, food residue, chips, or cracks. ❑ Return soiled glasses to the dish room. Throw away chipped or cracked glasses. ❑ Place a water glass one-half inch above the tip of the knife blade at each place setting. ❑ Place wine glasses (if appropriate) to the right of and slightly below the water glass. ❑ Return empty racks to the dish room.
10. Fold and place napkins.	❑ Napkins may be folded earlier as an opening sidework duty. ❑ Place one napkin at each place setting.
11. Place cream, butter, flowers, and other perishable items.	
12. Check the overall appearance of the table.	❑ Place each chair so the edge of the seat is even with the table edge. ❑ Step away from the table and view the results. ❑ Make sure place settings are lined up. ❑ Adjust tables and chairs as needed.

BUSPERSON: *Clear and Reset Tables*

Materials needed: *A bus tub, a service tray, a tray jack, clean tablecloths and napkins, clean serviceware, cleaning cloths, sanitizing solution, candles or lamp fuel, clean ashtrays, and matches.*

STEPS	HOW-TO'S
1. Gather items needed to reset the table.	❑ Place the correct number of place settings, napkins, etc., needed to reset the table on a service tray. Get a clean tablecloth if necessary. ❑ Carry the tray to the table and place it on a nearby tray jack. ❑ Always carry a clean, damp cloth when clearing and resetting tables. ❑ Get an empty bus tub.
2. Clear used dishes, silverware, glasses, and linens after guests leave the table.	❑ Clear tables within five minutes of guest departure. It is important that tables are cleared and reset promptly. This makes it possible to seat waiting guests quickly, and it adds to the neat appearance of the dining room. ❑ You may work with the server to clear and reset tables, but if he or she is busy, you should clear and reset the tables yourself. Teamwork is important to the success of the restaurant. ❑ Scrape food and debris from dishes into a bus tub. ❑ Do not scrape plates in view of guests. Work with your back to nearby guests to shield them from seeing the clearing process. ❑ Place soiled dishes in the bus tub. Carefully stacking dishes will help prevent breakage. ❑ Stack like items together. ❑ Clear tables as quietly as possible. ❑ Sort used linens. Place the soiled linens in the bus tub.

BUSPERSON: *Clear and Reset Tables* *(continued)*

STEPS	HOW-TO'S
	❑ Remove any silverware, small dishes, or glasses from the liners and place them in the bus tubs.
3. Clean the table.	❑ If tables don't have tablecloths, clean and sanitize the tabletops. There should be sanitizing solution at each side station. ❑ Always use a clean, damp cloth to wipe tabletops and condiment containers. ❑ Wipe under condiment containers and the centerpiece. ❑ Wipe the condiment containers that will be left on the table.
4. Replace tablecloths if necessary.	❑ Remove the top cloth from a double-clothed table. Replace only the top cloth if the base cloth is not soiled. ❑ If there are stains on the base cloth that will show, change both cloths, and clean and sanitize the table. ❑ To change tablecloths, move flowers, condiments, etc., to the edge of the table away from the side where you are standing. ❑ On your side of the table, fold the edge of the soiled cloth to the top of the table. ❑ As you fold the soiled tablecloth up, unfold the new tablecloth on the part of the table you are uncovering. Do not shake out or completely unfold the clean cloth before spreading it onto the table. In a formal dining area, a table should never be stripped in view of guests. Guests should not be able to see the table surface when you change a tablecloth. ❑ Check to make sure the new tablecloth's seam is facing down.

(continued)

BUSPERSON: *Clear and Reset Tables* *(continued)*

STEPS	HOW-TO'S
	❑ Spread the new cloth halfway across the tabletop, moving the dirty cloth out of the way as you spread the new cloth. Arrange the new cloth on your side of the table so it is centered and hangs evenly. ❑ Move to the opposite side of the table. Move flowers, condiments, etc., to the clean cloth to keep it in place. ❑ As you pull the new cloth toward you, remove the soiled cloth in the same motion. ❑ Roll up the soiled cloth so crumbs are caught in the middle of the cloth. Do not dump crumbs onto the chairs or floor. ❑ Place rolled-up soiled linens on a chair until you have completely reset the table. Do not place soiled linens on the floor. ❑ Make sure the new cloth is centered and hangs evenly with no wrinkles. ❑ Wipe the condiment containers and centerpieces with a clean, damp cloth and move them back to the correct spot on the table.
5. Reset the table.	❑ Make sure all glassware, silverware, and dishes are clean, polished (if appropriate), and free from spots, chips, and cracks. ❑ Place the serviceware on the table. Set all tables the same way to give the restaurant a neat and appealing appearance. ❑ Handle glassware by the base—never near the lip. Never put your fingers inside glasses. ❑ Handle plates by the edges. Never place your fingers on the food surface of the plates. ❑ Handle silverware by the handles.

BUSPERSON: *Clear and Reset Tables* *(continued)*

	HOW-TO'S
	❑ Place a clean ashtray and a fresh pack of matches on the table, if appropriate. Leave the matches closed. ❑ Relight table lamps that have gone out. Replace candles or fuel as needed. ❑ Wipe clean and replace promotional table tents as needed.
6. Clean chairs.	❑ Remove soiled linens from the chair and place them in a bus tub. ❑ Wipe crumbs from chairs into your cleaning cloth. ❑ Brush crumbs into the bus tub, and not onto the floor. ❑ Push chairs to the table so the front edge of the seat is even with the edge of the table.
7. Check tables.	❑ Adjust anything that is not lined up properly. ❑ Check the centerpiece to make sure it is still attractive.
8. Take soiled dishes and linens to the correct area.	❑ Use safe lifting techniques.

BUSPERSON: *Bus Soiled Dishes to the Dish Room*

Materials needed: *A clean cloth and a bus tub or a service tray.*

STEPS	HOW-TO'S
1. Carry soiled dishes to the dish room.	❑ Bussing soiled dishes to the dish room will occur: • Throughout meal service as new courses are served and old courses are cleared • When clearing and resetting tables • When cleaning side stations at the end of the meal period • Whenever requested by a server
2. Unload soiled dishes.	❑ In the dish room, sort the items according to the decoy system set up by the stewards. Scrape dishes (if you haven't already scraped them) and stack them by type. ❑ A decoy system consists of bus tubs and dish racks with one dirty dish, glass, etc., in them to show you where to place dirty items. ❑ Put broken glass in the proper trash can, not in the soiled linen bin. ❑ Place glasses upside-down in the correct washing racks. ❑ Place silverware in the silverware-soaking solution.
3. Rinse the bus tub or tray and wipe it dry with a clean cloth before returning it to its proper place.	

Sources: Adapted from the "Restaurant Server Guide" and "Busperson Guide" in the *Hospitality Skills Training Series* (East Lansing, Mich.: Educational Institute of the American Hotel & Motel Association, 1995).

REVIEW QUIZ

When you feel you have covered all of the material in this chapter, answer these questions. Choose the *best* answer.

1. Two service staff members are circling a guest table and serving food from large platters. They are delivering __________ service.

   a. cart
   b. plate
   c. family-style
   d. platter

2. All of the following styles of service require special containers or platters from which to serve food *except* __________ service.

   a. cart
   b. plate
   c. family-style
   d. platter

3. Which of the following is designed to avoid the bottlenecks that sometimes occur with straight buffet lines?

   a. a scramble system
   b. a guéridon
   c. cart service
   d. the team approach to service

4. Mark and Sheila have a drink in the lounge while they wait for a table to open up in the dining room. After a few minutes the host is able to seat them at their table. Jennifer approaches the table with a smile and says: "Hello, my name is Jennifer; I'll be your server this evening. How are you doing tonight?" Mark looks at her angrily and says: "I was doing fine until I ran into your bartender. He messed up my drink order twice, Sheila's sea breeze was so strong she couldn't drink it, and then he wouldn't let me run a tab—he said I had to pay for the drinks before we left the bar! He was kind of rude about it, too." Which of the following possible responses by Jennifer is the *best* response?

   a. "He shouldn't have been rude, but the bartender was only following restaurant policy."
   b. "I'm sorry that happened. Would you like to hear about tonight's specials?"
   c. "I'm sorry, sir. Ma'am, can I get you another sea breeze? This time we'll make sure it isn't too strong. And sir, I'll deduct the price of your lounge drinks from your bill. Sorry for the inconvenience."
   d. "You know, I'm sure that's because it's Ted's first night; he should get better with a little experience. Now, how about an appetizer this evening? The chicken quesadillas are delicious!"

REVIEW QUIZ *(continued)*

5. When serving a guest with a speech impairment, staff members should:

   a. pretend they know what the guest is saying, even if they don't.
   b. talk loudly and slowly.
   c. ask the guest to show them what he or she is trying to say, if necessary.
   d. avoid eye contact with the guest.

Answer Key: 1-d-C1, 2-b-C1, 3-a-C1, 4-c-C2, 5-c-C2

Each question is linked to a competency. Competencies are listed on the first page of the chapter. An answer reading 3-b-C4 translates to:

3: the question number
b: the correct answer
C4: the competency number

Chapter 4 Outline

Competencies

1. Distinguish between public and service bars; describe the duties and responsibilities of a beverage server, bartender, and beverage manager; and describe techniques and procedures for selling and serving cocktails and beer.
2. Describe techniques and procedures for selling and serving wine; summarize procedures for serving alcoholic beverages responsibly; and describe nonalcoholic specialty beverages.

4

Beverage Service: Styles and Procedures

THIS CHAPTER discusses beverage service, which, for many guests, is the first part of their dining experience. While the main focus of the chapter is on the service of alcoholic beverages, nonalcoholic specialty beverages will also be discussed, since they are increasing in popularity and are a significant part of the beverage service of many food service operations.

Beverage Service

Many people know that the United States' Declaration of Independence was adopted in 1776, but fewer people know that 1776 may also have heralded the birth of the cocktail. As one version of the story goes, that was the year Betsy Flanagan, a New York tavern barmaid, served a guest a mixed drink that was decorated with a tail feather from a rooster. As a result, the drink was dubbed a "cocktail." Although feathers as a garnish have since fallen out of favor, cocktails themselves have become a staple of beverage service.

The tavern itself was a major part of early American life and was a forerunner of today's hotels and motels. In fact, taverns were so important to the Massachusetts colonists of the mid-1600s that they fined any town in the colony that didn't have one. Later, as Americans began moving west, their eating and drinking establishments went with them. Those establishments that did not provide lodging were generally called taverns or saloons; the more spectacular inns started calling themselves hotels.

Alcoholic beverages were prohibited by a constitutional amendment in 1920. Prohibition lasted nearly 14 years in the United States and forced some famous restaurants (such as Delmonico's in New York City) and a number of grand hotel barrooms and dining rooms to close due to lost business. At the same time, it led to the opening of some very famous freestanding restaurants after Prohibition was repealed, including Club "21," Lindy's, and El Morocco—all of which were former speakeasies.

Today, beverage service is an integral part of the overall operating philosophy and standards of many food service operations. Many restaurants offer beverage service both in the dining room and in separate lounge areas; hotels might serve drinks in their lobbies and guestrooms as well as their lounges and food and beverage outlets. Beverages are an important part of private club operations as well.

Types of Bars

There are two types of bars in food service operations: **public bars** (often known simply as bars or lounges), in which guests are served by a bartender or a beverage server; and **service bars,** at which bartenders prepare drinks only for servers, who then take the drinks to guests. Many bars are a combination of the two.

The public-bar category encompasses a variety of operations that differ in decor, size, entertainment options, level of service, theme, price, and products served. Some bars or lounges specialize in one product, such as wine or beer. Some serve only beverages, some serve snacks and a limited number of other foods, while still others offer complete food and beverage service. Appetizers are often featured at bars or lounges that function as holding areas for guests awaiting service in dining areas.

Staff Members

The number of beverage service staff members needed and the kinds of tasks they perform depend on the size and organization of the operation. The following sections discuss three positions usually involved with beverage service: beverage server, bartender, and beverage manager.

Beverage Server. Beverage servers are important guest-contact staff members whose responsibilities are many-faceted and demanding. They are salespeople as well as greeters and monitors. As salespeople, they must know the correct terminology for and ingredients of the various beverages offered (Exhibit 1 lists a selection of terms related to liquors). They must know suggestive-selling techniques; provide proper, friendly, and efficient service; graciously deal with difficult guests; cash checks and accept credit cards; and perform a number of opening and closing tasks.

Beverage servers require special training to responsibly serve alcoholic beverages. Servers must know how to identify guests who are underage and diplomatically refuse them service. They also must know how to monitor guests' alcohol consumption and "cut off" guests who are in danger of becoming intoxicated.

Bartender. Like servers, the **bartender** (also called a "mixologist") has many roles to play and holds a demanding position. In addition to preparing drinks, a bartender interacts with guests while selling and serving drinks, unless he or she works only in a service bar. Bartenders often are perceived as part entertainers, part amateur psychologists; they can make a lounge or bar famous and draw guests back repeatedly. Good bartenders are not only willing to listen to guests, they also are able to occasionally lighten the conversation with a new joke, bring about a deft change of subject, or defuse an argument in the making. A bartender's memory should be good enough so that when a regular guest who always orders the same drink returns to the bar, the bartender can ask simply (and impressively), "The usual?"

Professional bartenders make certain that no one waiting to be served is ignored, even when one guest tries to monopolize their attention. Bartenders often have to do several tasks at once, yet they must be able to prepare each guest's drink

Exhibit 1 Beverage Terms: Liquor

Liquor, also called "spirits," has the highest alcohol content of the three types of alcoholic beverages (liquor, beer, and wine). Some types of liquor are brandy, gin, rum, vodka, and whiskey. Liquors differ depending on what they are distilled from and what flavorings are added. For example, brandy is made from fruit (usually grapes); rum is made from sugar cane or molasses; and gin is made from grain, juniper berries, and various botanicals.

Others liquors include:

- Bitters—liquors flavored with herbs, bark, and/or roots; usually used as a cocktail flavoring ingredient
- Cognac—grape brandy produced in France's Cognac region; considered the most prestigious brandy
- Liqueur or cordial—usually sweet spirits made with redistilled fruits or botanicals (or their juices or extracts); alcohol content ranges from relatively moderate (Amaretto di Saronna, Kahlúa) to relatively high (Chartreuse, Grand Marnier)
- Schnapps—in Europe, an herb-flavored dry spirit; in the United States, a sweet liqueur usually flavored with fruits or herbs
- Tequila—a liquor distilled from the juice of the century plant; the main liquor used in the popular margarita cocktail

efficiently, expertly, and seemingly effortlessly. They may invent new drinks or think of new ways to market traditional ones.

Some bartenders, like the nineteenth century's Professor Jerry Thomas (inventor of the Tom and Jerry and other cocktails), are akin to actors. Thomas concocted a drink called the "blue blazer" that amazed his guests. It consisted of whiskey, which he ignited and, lifting the glass high, poured into a glass of hot water, making a stream of flame. He continued to pour the drink back and forth, to the astonishment and peril of all who gathered to watch.

Bartenders must be knowledgeable about the products they prepare. They must know how alcoholic beverages should taste, the ingredients necessary to make them, and their standard recipes. While experienced bartenders know that fashions in mixed drinks come and go, they generally have in their repertoire methods for making and garnishing the traditionally popular drinks: the martini, manhattan, daiquiri, scotch and soda, Rob Roy, Bloody Mary, gimlet, old-fashioned, margarita, whiskey sour, screwdriver, gin and tonic, and Tom Collins.

Bartenders must be very conscientious about their personal appearance and hygiene. They must know the proper procedures for beverage service, so they typically participate in many of the same training sessions that beverage servers attend. Bartenders also perform opening and closing procedures related to income control, beverage production, and cleanup duties.

Finally, bartenders must be trustworthy. Opportunities for theft abound behind the bar, such as under-reporting drink sales (and pocketing the difference),

Suggestive Selling and Upselling

"Suggestive selling" means encouraging guests to buy additional food and beverages. An example of suggestive selling is asking, "Would you like a glass of bordeaux or merlot with your steak this evening?" "Upselling" means suggesting more expensive and possibly better-quality items. Instead of simply bringing a guest the house brand of scotch, for example, servers can upsell by asking, "Would you prefer Dewars or Johnnie Walker Black?" when a guest orders scotch. Tips for suggestive selling and upselling include the following:

- Be enthusiastic. It's easier to sell something you are excited about.
- Make beverages sound appealing. Use words like "fruity," "icy," and "thirst-quenching" when describing them.
- Ask questions. Find out if guests are unhurried or only have time for a quick drink; whether they like sweet or tart beverages; if they feel like having something hot or cold.
- Suggest your favorites. Try as many beverages as you can, and tell guests you've tried them: "You'll like the rum punch; it's one of my favorites here." But be honest—don't say that something is your favorite if it isn't.
- Offer a choice: "Would you like Smirnoff's or Absolut in your vodka and tonic?"
- Suggest the unusual. People go to bars and lounges to get away from their routines, and most guests don't know what they want to order when they arrive.
- Suggest beverages and foods that naturally go together—beer and pizza, wine and cheese, margaritas and nachos.
- Always ask for the sale. After you suggest and describe a beverage, ask if the guest would like to try it.

pouring free drinks for friends, and pouring drinks from private bottles (the bartenders then pocket the money guests pay for these drinks). Managers who regularly monitor liquor use and cash register procedures behind the bar can help keep bartenders honest.

Beverage Manager. Hotels and large restaurants may employ a **beverage manager** who is responsible for beverage service in the total operation. He or she generally reports to the food and beverage director or the director's assistant (in hotels) or to the general manager (in large restaurants). In small operations, the beverage manager's tasks might be performed by a head bartender.

When functioning as a department head or section supervisor, the beverage manager is involved in selecting, orienting, training, supervising, scheduling, and evaluating staff members. Because he or she frequently plans the beverage service for banquets and other special functions, the beverage manager is often on the banquet-planning team.

Many of the beverage manager's duties involve day-to-day management activities—for example, purchasing supplies, controlling inventory, standardizing recipes (especially for new promotions), and designing and constantly improving income control systems. Working with the food and beverage controller or the food and beverage director, the beverage manager of a hotel frequently determines standard beverage costs and develops a departmental operating budget. Issues related to the design of beverage service areas and the purchase of beverage supplies and equipment are also important to the beverage manager.

Beverage managers must develop procedures to minimize operating problems that can occur, especially during peak business times. They must also ensure that staff members consistently follow those procedures. Because the beverage manager's job involves supervising and controlling the production and service of beverages throughout the operation, the beverage manager and the operation's general manager or dining room manager must develop a close working relationship. In the same way that the chef is responsible for food production and food-related concerns in the dining area, the beverage manager is responsible for beverage production and beverage-related concerns in dining and bar areas—including service. The quality and presentation of beverages, the speed of beverage production, and the appearance and conduct of beverage staff all have an impact on how guests experience the food service operation.

Beverage Service Procedures

The beverage manager and other managers within the operation should work together to develop the best procedures for ordering, preparing, and providing drinks to guests, keeping in mind guest requirements and such factors as the operation's design, equipment, and staff size.

Many beverage service procedures directly relate to income control. Some operations, for example, require beverage servers to take drink orders and pay for drinks received from the bartender out of their own cash banks, then replenish their banks with payments from guests. In others, beverage servers have to present to the bartender both the guest's payment and a guest check that they may have previously rung through a precheck register. No matter what system is used, managers must develop—and see that staff members consistently use—a process that minimizes the possibility that dishonest beverage servers or bartenders will pocket money that is rightfully the operation's or guest's.

In some operations, servers can run tabs for guests (serve several rounds of drinks and not collect payment until just before the guests leave) or can transfer charges for beverage service in the lounge area to the dining area for later payment by guests; in other operations, they cannot. An operation's beverage service procedures and policies must be communicated to staff members, who in turn must know how to convey the policies appropriately to guests.

In some dining areas, food servers take and serve beverage orders. Frequently, these servers use the backs of guest checks to record beverage orders. In many operations, a beverage order must go through a precheck register to record sales information for later use by management. Some operations connect a remote printer to the precheck register; as servers record sales information in the precheck register, the remote printer automatically transfers the information to the

Exhibit 2 Sample Calling Order

Because some drinks take longer to make than others, and some drinks don't hold up as well as others, most food service operations require servers to order drinks in a specific sequence, such as this one:

1. Frozen drinks
2. Highballs
3. Straight spirits
4. Liqueurs or cordials
5. Mixed drinks
6. Blended drinks
7. Cream drinks
8. Plain sodas and juices
9. Wine by the glass
10. Beer

bartender, who prepares the drinks that appear on the printed slip. There are several variations of such procedures, and changing technology is constantly creating new options.

Cocktail Service

The following cocktail-service procedures for servers are common in restaurants and lounges:

- Greet guests with a smile, and ask if they are ready to place a drink order. If there are daily drink specials, this is the time to tell guests.
- When taking the guests' drink orders, number guest checks to indicate who ordered what and note the exact specifications of each order, including choice of garnish and whether the drink should be "straight up" or "neat" (without ice) or "on the rocks" (with ice). When the guest requests a specific brand—a **call brand**—be certain to write it down (for example, Maker's Mark rather than house bourbon, Chivas Regal rather than house scotch). When writing checks, stand straight and rest guest checks in one hand, never on the guests' table.
- Order the drinks from the bartender, using the correct calling order for your operation (see Exhibit 2 for a sample calling order).
- Add the correct garnishes (unless this step is performed by the bartender), stirrers, or straws (if appropriate for the drinks).
- Place the drinks and an appropriate number of cocktail napkins on a cocktail tray and carry the tray to the table.
- Rest the cocktail tray in one hand and serve drinks with the other; the tray should never rest on the table.

- Serve drinks from the right when possible. For booths and other settings where service from the right is impossible, serve with the least inconvenience to the guests.
- Clear cocktail glasses as soon as they are empty; ask if guests would like a refill when glasses are approximately one-quarter full.
- Change ashtrays as often as necessary. To avoid scattering ashes, cover the soiled ashtray with the clean one when removing it from the table, then put the clean one on the table.

Trends in cocktail service point to the increasing popularity of **premium brands**—high-quality, usually high-priced call brands. Premium-brand promotions, often sponsored by suppliers offering discounts, can help an operation exceed guest expectations while adding to the operation's profitability from beverage service. Suppliers can often be counted on for training programs and other support as well.

Beer Service

Today there are more than 1,250 breweries and brewpubs operating in the United States. On average, imported beer sales are increasing approximately 11 percent each year. Beer now comprises 88 percent of total U.S. beverage alcohol consumption. According to Bob Weinberg, one of the leading analysts on the U.S. malt beverage industry, the public demand for beer is expected to grow more than 6.5 percent annually between 2005 and 2010.

Good beer service requires that servers know the basic beer terms shown in Exhibit 3. In addition, operations offering specialty beers must make sure that servers know their style, origin, and unique characteristics, along with which foods they best complement. Beer suppliers are a good source of information for training programs. Training programs often include information about a beer's production and its various flavor nuances. Some suppliers sponsor staff tastings. Beer sales usually increase when servers are well trained and are given incentives to sell more beer.

Beer promotions that feature specific brands can also stimulate sales. Glassware with the featured beer's logo adds value when guests are encouraged to take the emptied glassware home as a souvenir. Frequent reminders are the key to selling more beer. By recommending high-quality specialty beers, servers can build guest check averages (and their tips).

Regular tastings by staff members, including blind tastings to check the staff's knowledge, are important components of a comprehensive beer sales program. To reinforce the initial training, regular refresher sessions should be scheduled.

Wine Service

Wine sales in the United States are increasing at a fast pace. Some guests already know a great deal about wine; many are interested in knowing more. Therefore, it is important for dining service staff and beverage servers in the lounge to know the basics of wine service, including the terms shown in Exhibit 4.

Exhibit 3 Beverage Terms: Beer

Beer is made from fermented grain and hops. It has the lowest alcohol content, the highest food value, and the shortest life span of the three types of alcoholic beverages (liquor, beer, and wine). There are two classes of beer: ale, which is top-fermented at warmer temperatures and requires a longer time to age, and lager, which is bottom-fermented and aged at colder temperatures. Other beer terms include:

- Bock beer—darker, richer, higher in alcohol content, and sweeter than regular 3.2 percent beer; typically brewed in the winter for spring consumption
- Draft beer—beer drawn from a keg or a cask to a glass
- Dry beer—beer that is less sweet
- Light beer—beer with lower alcohol content and one-third to one-half fewer calories than regular beer
- Malt liquor—a lager-type brew that is darker than regular beer and usually higher in alcohol content; in the United States, any beer with more than five percent alcohol can be labeled "malt liquor"
- Nonalcoholic beer—beer with less than 0.5 percent alcohol; once dismissed as "near beer," it is now an increasingly popular choice
- Head—foam that forms at the top of a glass when beer is poured; ideally, one-half to one inch thick
- Keg—aluminum or wooden container for storing beer
- Pilsener—a style of lager that is light-bodied, dry, and fairly high in carbonation; most mass-produced U.S. beers are brewed in a light Pilsener style
- Porter—a dark-brown, heavy-bodied, malt-flavored beverage
- Stout—a dark, almost black, rich, malty brew with a bitter hop taste and high alcohol content; made from roasted barley
- Tap—beer faucet used to pour beer from a keg; or the process used to set up a beer keg for service

When managers select wines to be served in their operations, they should focus first on their guests. Because many guests recognize the most popular wines, managers must decide whether to offer them. Experienced managers realize that sophisticated guests in a high-check-average operation might find it inconsistent to be offered an unfamiliar label or an inexpensive product. Similarly, serving a very expensive product to guests in a low-check-average operation would be inconsistent and, ultimately, unsuccessful.

Selling house or "jug" wine by the glass or carafe is gaining popularity in many restaurants, and it is often an excellent merchandising method. However, in some cases it may reduce the sale of bottled wines. Therefore, managers must make sure that guests desire the sale of wine by the glass or carafe and that such an alternative will increase wine sales beyond the level of income lost from declining bottle sales. Some restaurants offer relatively expensive bottled wines by the glass

Exhibit 4 Beverage Terms: Wine

Wine is made from fermented grapes or other fruits or botanicals, and is usually classified according to color. Red wines are dark red to purple in color and are served at a cool room temperature. White wines have a pale yellow color ranging from straw to gold and are served chilled. Blush or rosé wines are pink and are served chilled. These three types of wines are known as table wines. The following terms apply to wine-making, tasting, and drinking:

- Aging—storing wines in wooden (typically oak) or stainless-steel barrels before bottling
- Aroma—the odor of a young wine, usually fruity or flowery
- Bouquet—the complex smell of a mature wine
- Body—the feel and weight of a wine in the mouth
- Dry—not sweet
- Vintage—the year a wine's grapes were harvested and wine-making was begun

Types of wine include:

- Aperitif wine—wine with spirits added, and sometimes flavored with herbs and spices (sherry or vermouth, for example)
- Bordeaux—wine from the Bordeaux region of France; traditionally sold in high-shouldered bottles
- Burgundy—wine from the Burgundy region of France; Burgundy bottles are known for their low, sloping shoulders
- Claret—a generic name for a red Bordeaux wine
- Dessert wine—sweet wines suitable for drinking with or after dessert; includes table wines as well as fortified wines (wines with added spirits) such as port and madeira
- Port—a dessert wine fortified with brandy; traditionally produced in Oporto, Portugal
- Sparkling wine—wine containing carbon dioxide, which produces bubbles when the wine is poured (Champagne, for example)
- Still wine—wine with no carbon dioxide or bubbles

as a signature item to enhance their reputation. This practice can be very profitable, because the operation usually receives more revenue selling the wine by the glass than by the bottle. Clearly, restaurant managers must consider marketing and guest-related concerns as well as profit objectives as they make decisions about purchasing and selling wines.

Pairing wine with food has always been a matter of taste. While, in general, lighter wines complement lighter foods and heavier wines complement heavier foods, many restaurants now recognize that whatever the guest desires is appropriate. Dining service staff should be trained not to react negatively to any

Wine Tastings

Servers whose training includes wine tastings are better able to sell wine than those whose training is limited to procedures. When servers have personally tasted the wines, they can make informed recommendations to guests.

Tastings do not have to be complex. Managers should eliminate wine snobbery from training programs. It is important to present wine simply, without using overly technical terminology.

At tastings, managers should encourage servers to taste a variety of wines from the menu and experiment with food and wine combinations. Servers should make comparisons and discover which characteristics they like about each wine. They should also be taught that although they can suggest traditional food and wine combinations to guests seeking guidance, guests can choose whatever wine and food combinations they like best. Servers should not raise their eyebrows or express surprise or disapproval if guests order white wine with red meats or red wine with white meats and seafood.

Facts about the moderate consumption of wine should be presented from a medical standpoint. It is also a good idea to familiarize servers with wine publications and, if appropriate, to offer them an opportunity to attend a wine seminar.

wine orders that guests place. To help guests unfamiliar with wine, some restaurants develop wine lists with specific food recommendations or make wine suggestions on the food menu.

Wine tasting should be part of server training so that servers can make informed suggestions to guests. A question or comment about wine by the server can provide a strong incentive for guests to order the product ("What wine did you wish to be served tonight?" or "We're featuring the new Beaujolais this week—would you like to try it?"). Because the names of foreign wines intimidate some guests, some restaurants include a bin number on the menu so guests can order wine by number rather than name.

Some restaurants, especially high-check-average operations, employ a **wine steward** or sommelier as an in-house expert to suggest and serve wines to guests. Wine stewards also help train servers in the proper serving temperatures for wine as well as in wine terminology and service procedures.

Managers usually develop guidelines for servers to follow when opening and serving wine from corked bottles. The following are typical and can be adapted as necessary:

- The server should bring the bottle of wine to the table before opening it. (Older red wines should be carried carefully to avoid disturbing the sediment that forms at the bottom.) The server should present the bottle to whomever ordered the wine by holding it in a food service towel or napkin and showing the label so that the guest can confirm that it is the correct wine.

- After the guest has approved the wine, the server may open it. This is done by holding the bottle firmly, cutting the foil below the top bulge on the bottleneck, and peeling the foil off. The server then wipes the cork and exposed glass rim with the food service towel and twists a corkscrew into the center of the cork until it is well-seated. Then, hooking the corkscrew's lever on the bottle's rim, the server should press down and draw the cork out; it may be necessary to slightly wiggle the cork for the last inch. The server should then remove the cork from the corkscrew and place it on the right side of the host, who may wish to examine it to see if the cork is moist, which would indicate that the wine has been properly stored.

- After the cork is removed, the server should wipe the bottle's rim again with the service towel.
- The server should allow the host to sample a small amount of the wine. (Servers should allow uncorked vintage red wines to "rest" or "breathe" before they offer them to guests.) After the host approves, the server may fill the wine glasses of all the guests. Wine service typically is counterclockwise, starting with the guest on the host's right. As a courtesy to guests, many operations train their servers to serve women first.
- The server should fill the glass according to the operation's specifications; usually a "full" glass is no more than two-thirds full. (Wine connoisseurs may request the server to fill the glass no more than one-third full. The added space allows room for the wine's bouquet to develop.) Some restaurants like to use very large wine glasses for presentation purposes.

If red wine is served, the server should place the bottle to the right of the host's wine glass, with the label facing the host. If white wine is served, the remaining wine should be placed in an ice bucket or chilled holder to the host's right. Sometimes a freestanding wine-bucket stand is used, in which case the bucket is draped with a clean food service napkin and the server refills glasses as needed.

The basic procedures for serving sparkling wine are similar to those for serving still wine. However, the process for opening the bottle differs. First, the server must cut and remove the foil cover. Then, while placing a thumb on the cork, the server can loosen the wire harness and the hood. The server should remove the cork, harness, and hood at the same time while twisting the *bottle* to loosen the cork. While doing this, he or she should hold the bottle at a 45-degree angle and point it away from all guests and other service staff. The secret to opening sparkling wine is to hold the cork and twist the bottle—not the reverse. When service is done correctly, the cork is not forcibly expelled from the bottle; the server always has the cork in hand so that no damage or injury results from a flying cork. After the cork is removed, the server should wipe the rim of the bottle and pour the wine carefully so that effervescence is not lost.

Staff members must know what to do if the host rejects the wine after he or she has tasted it. In some operations, servers simply return inexpensive wines to the bar, and production staff members use it later for cooking. Expensive wines, however, call for more exacting procedures. If an expensive wine is rejected by the guest and found unacceptable by the wine steward or beverage manager, it can probably be returned to the supplier for credit. If, in the judgment of the wine steward or beverage manager, the rejected wine is acceptable, it might be offered for sale (by the glass) to other guests as a "special." Unusually expensive wines on the wine list may have a note indicating that guests are obligated to make at least partial payment if they return a wine that is deemed to be of acceptable quality by the wine steward. This policy has many negative marketing and guest service implications, however, and managers should carefully consider the consequences of such a policy before they implement it.

Responsible Beverage Service

The careful service of alcoholic beverages is a responsibility of all who work in a food service operation. Alcohol is a factor in many of the driving fatalities in the United States every year. It also plays a contributing role in many fights, drowning accidents, and suicides. In states that have dram shop laws, servers, bartenders, and owners can be held liable if an intoxicated guest causes injury to another person.

There are proven techniques for serving alcoholic beverages responsibly, and these must be communicated to service staff members during their initial training as well as during follow-up training sessions. It is an obvious advantage that the public's awareness has increased when it comes to the responsible consumption of alcohol. Most guests understand that alcohol-service rules are not simply house rules, but apply at whatever operation they choose to visit.

Verifying Legal Drinking Age. It is illegal to serve alcohol to minors. Since it can be difficult to tell whether someone is a minor, servers should always ask for identification when they are uncertain. Examples of a valid ID include a driver's license, a state-issued ID, an international driver's license, and a U.S. passport or military ID. When checking ID, servers should:

- Check the birth date on the ID. It should show that the person is of legal drinking age. (Servers should make sure the person looks to be the age indicated by the birth date.)
- Check the photo. Obviously, it should look like the person, but servers should keep in mind that the guest's weight or hairstyle may have changed. Many state IDs have a different-colored background for pictures of minors.
- Know how to spot fake IDs. They may have cuts, erasures, changes, different styles of type, or odd-sized seals. They may feel odd or be badly wrinkled or damaged.
- If a server suspects that an ID is false, he or she should ask for a second ID, or ask the guest to give his or her address, middle name, or height, and compare the guest's answer with the information on the ID.
- If a server still has doubts about an ID, he or she should refuse to serve alcohol to the guest, or should ask for assistance from a manager. Servers must remember that it is better to lose a guest than to lose a lawsuit or the operation's liquor license.

Welcome to the Fun and Exciting World Of Bordeaux!

Come join us for a tour of the Bordeaux countryside and learn how the best wine in the world is made. We'll give you tips on how to enjoy Bordeaux wine and even show you how to have your own wine tasting party! You'll learn how the wine is made, what restaurants are "Bordeaux-friendly" and how to read a Bordeaux wine label.

Have fun, mon ami, and remember... Bordeaux is always à propos!

A variety of Internet sites offer a wealth of information about alcoholic beverages (including "virtual tours" of wineries!) and responsible alcohol service. This site can be found at http://www.bordeaux.com. (Courtesy of Food and Wine from France, July 22, 1998)

Monitoring Alcohol Intake. Servers should keep track of the number of drinks guests have had; the size, type, and proof (alcohol content) of the drinks; and how quickly guests have consumed them. Managers should provide servers with a form they can use to easily tally drinks. Servers should know how much alcohol is in each drink they serve; alcohol content changes with the recipe, the glass size, and the amount of ice used. A 12-ounce beer, a 5-ounce glass of wine, a cocktail with 1.25 ounces of 80-proof liquor, and a cocktail with 1 ounce of 100-proof all contain approximately the same amount of alcohol.

Servers should look for the following signs of intoxication as they monitor guests:

- *Unusual conduct.* Depending on a guest's personality, he or she may become outspoken, noisy or rowdy, overly friendly, withdrawn, sleepy, antisocial, or obnoxious. He or she may use foul language.
- *Impaired judgment.* Guests may become careless with their money, make foolish statements, or drink faster.
- *Slowed reaction time.* Guests may have glassy eyes, dilated pupils, or slurred speech.
- *Decreased coordination.* Guests may become clumsy, spill drinks, or lose their balance.

Some operations have adopted the so-called "traffic light" system for recognizing and rating a guest's level of intoxication. In this system, "green" means the guest is sober, "yellow" means the guest is becoming intoxicated, and "red" means the guest is intoxicated. Servers should adjust their service as a guest's status changes. For example, if a guest moves from "green" to "yellow," a server might suggest that the guest order an appetizer or a meal; the server should also wait for the guest to re-order an alcoholic beverage, rather than recommending additional drinks. Once the guest moves from "yellow" to "red," servers must be prepared to deal with the ensuing situation. Usually, that means stopping alcohol service altogether.

Cutting Off Alcohol Service. From time to time, beverage servers must face the prospect of telling a guest that he or she will not be served any more alcoholic beverages. Although this may initially seem daunting, the operation's managers—not to mention the law—will likely support such actions. In fact, when guests are at risk of becoming a danger to themselves or others, it may be the only responsible action to take.

Servers should keep these general guidelines in mind when denying or stopping alcohol service:

- If possible, ask a co-worker to accompany you when you refuse to serve alcohol to a guest. You may need the co-worker's help.
- Talk with the guest away from other guests.
- Calmly and firmly state your operation's policy: "I'm sorry, but I've served you all the alcohol that my manager will allow."
- Do not judge the guest, make accusations, or argue. Don't say, "You're drunk" or "You've had too much to drink."
- Repeat your operation's rules: "We care about your safety, and I can't serve you any more alcohol."

- Remove all alcohol from the guest's reach—even if it is his or her drink.
- When possible, offer the guest something to eat; food will absorb alcohol and help slow the rate of intoxication.
- Get a manager to help you if necessary, or if this is the policy at your operation.
- Offer to phone for a taxi, if one is needed. Try not to let an intoxicated guest drive away or even walk away—even if that means calling the police. It is better to risk making a guest angry than to risk lives.
- Make sure the guest has all of his or her personal belongings when he or she leaves.
- Fill out an incident report to describe the situation and record all actions taken; this will help protect the operation against lawsuits.

It is every staff member's responsibility to provide safe alcohol service. Managers and staff members should always be alert for situations that might bring harm to a guest or bystander.

Nonalcoholic Specialty Beverages

Specialty teas, mixed juices, alcohol-free cocktails, and coffee drinks are becoming increasingly popular as alternatives to alcoholic beverages.

Specialty teas include premium blended teas as well as teas flavored with botanicals and spices. Herbal teas are infusions of a variety of flowers, herbs, and spices; they are a popular alternative for guests wishing to limit their caffeine. In addition to these more traditional offerings, a number of coffee bars now offer specialty tea drinks—including *chai,* a spiced and sweetened milk-tea beverage that originated in India.

As an increasing number of people in the United States seek out healthier foods and beverages, juice bars have filled an important niche. Currently, more than 500 juice bars across the United States offer custom-blended juice cocktails made from freshly squeezed fruits and vegetables. Juice bars have given rise to "smoothie bars," which sell shakes made from blended fruits, juices, yogurt, and other ingredients. Some food service operations catering to health-conscious guests are adding an extensive variety of mixed juices to their beverage menus.

For guests who desire the look and taste of a traditional bar drink, but without the alcohol, food service operations may offer alcohol-free cocktails sometimes known as "virgin" cocktails or "mocktails" (for example, a Virgin Mary is a drink made of Bloody Mary mix without vodka). Proper ingredients and mixing techniques—as well as attention to presentation and garnishing—are critical to successfully merchandising these beverages.

Specialty coffee drinks range from espresso to cappuccino to café latte (a glossary of coffee-drink terminology is presented in Exhibit 5). For servers to sell and serve specialty coffee successfully, they must know the specialty coffees' ingredients and how the coffees are made. Espresso, for example, usually is made with dark French-roast coffee beans and an espresso machine. The machine

Exhibit 5 Beverage Terms: Specialty Coffees

Term	Definition
Americano	A shot of espresso with four to five ounces of hot water
Breve	A café latte with half-and-half substituted for milk
Café au lait	A 50/50 mix of strong coffee and heated milk
Café latte	A shot of espresso in seven to eight ounces of steamed milk
Café mocha	A shot of espresso in seven to eight ounces of hot chocolate and steamed milk
Cappuccino	Approximately one-third espresso, one-third steamed milk, and one-third froth
Espresso con panna	Espresso with whipped cream
Luongo	A two-ounce portion of espresso made with seven grams of coffee
Ristretto	A one-ounce, more flavorfully intense portion of espresso
Skinny	Any espresso drink made with skim milk

produces a "shot" of espresso by forcing hot (approximately 194°F [90°C]) water through seven grams of finely ground coffee at high pressure. A single shot typically takes about 18 seconds to produce. A quality grind is slightly gritty. "Tamping" is the process of flattening the grounds to ensure an even flow of water. The standard yield is an ounce to an ounce and a quarter per espresso shot. Servers should be able to answer guests' questions about any of their operation's specialty coffee drinks.

Key Terms

bartender—A staff member who mixes and serves drinks at a bar. Generally, the bartender serves guests seated at the bar and prepares drinks for servers to take to guests seated at lounge tables or in the dining room. Also called a mixologist.

beverage manager—The person responsible for general day-to-day management activities in the beverage department.

call brand—A specific liquor that guests request by brand name.

premium brands—Expensive call brands specified by guests when they order cocktails (an Absolut vodka and tonic, for example).

public bars—Often known simply as bars or lounges, these are establishments in which guests are served by a bartender or a beverage server.

service bars—Bars at which bartenders prepare drinks only for servers, who then take the drinks to guests.

wine steward—A staff member who helps guests select wines, serves wines, and resolves any operating or serving problems connected with wine service. He or she may also manage the wine inventory, make purchasing decisions, and provide wine-related training for other staff members. Also called a sommelier.

Review Questions

1. How does a service bar differ from a public bar?
2. What are the major responsibilities of a beverage server, bartender, and beverage manager in a typical food service operation?
3. How does wine service differ from cocktail service?
4. Why is knowing the right terminology important in beer and coffee service?
5. What differences arise in uncorking and serving sparkling wines and still wines?
6. What are some signs that a guest may be intoxicated?
7. How should a server cut off alcohol service to an intoxicated guest?

Internet Sites

For more information, visit the following Internet sites. Remember that Internet addresses can change without notice.

Publications

Ale Street News On-line
http://www.alestreetnews.com

Bartender Magazine
http://www.bartender.com

Beverage Digest
http://www.beverage-digest.com

Beverage Retailer
http://www.beverage-retailer.com

Coffee & Cuisine Magazine Online
http://www.coffeetalk.com

Food & Wine
http://www.foodwinemag.com

Fresh Cup Magazine
http://www.freshcup.com

Modern Brewery Age
http://www.breweryage.com

Restaurants & Institutions
http://www.rimag.com

Smart Wine
http://smartwine.com

Tea & Coffee Trade Journal
http://teacofmag.com

Wine Spectator
http://www.winespectator.com

Organizations

American Vintners Association/ National Association of American Wineries
http://www.americanwineries.org

Distilled Spirits Council of the United States
http://www.discus.health.org

Educational Institute of the American Hotel & Motel Association
http://www.ei-ahma.org

Napa Valley Vintners Association
http://www.napavintners.com

National Restaurant Association
http://www.restaurant.org

Specialty Coffee Association of America
http://www.scaa.org

Tea Council of Canada
http://www.tea.ca

Wine Tasting Association (Washington, D.C.)
http://www.winetasting.org

Additional Resources

BevNET: The Beverage Network
http://www.bevnet.com

Chai!
http://www.sni.net/chai

Coffee Universe
http://www.coffeeuniverse.com

Stash Tea
http://www.stashtea.com

The Tea Review Archive
http://www.best.com/~smurman/tea

Wines on the Internet
http://www.wines.com

Wine Today
http://www.winetoday.com

The World of Bordeaux
http://www.bordeaux.com

World Wine
http://www.eno-worldwine.com/index_e.htm

References

Bellamy, Gail, David Farkas, and John Soeder. "Sensational Service." *Restaurant Hospitality,* July 1994.

Castagna, Nicole G. "Smoothing Out the Juice Bar." *Restaurants & Institutions,* September 15, 1997.

Crecca, Donna Hood. "Microbrew Mania." *Restaurants & Institutions,* February 15, 1997.

"Drinking Responsibility." *Lodging,* February 1998.

Educational Institute of the American Hotel & Motel Association. *Controlling Alcohol Risks Effectively.* East Lansing, Mich.: Educational Institute of the American Hotel & Motel Association, 1993.

Farkas, David. "How to Make Coffee That Tastes Great." *Restaurant Hospitality,* May 1994.

Hinkle, Richard. "Wine Tasting for the Server." *F&B Business,* July/August 1994.

Kotschevar, Lendal H., and Mary L. Tanke. *Managing Bar and Beverage Operations.* East Lansing, Mich.: Educational Institute of the American Hotel & Motel Association, 1991.

Lawler, Edmund O. "Going for the Gold." *F&B Business,* September/October 1993.

Liberson, Judy. "The Great Taste of Coffee Profits." *Lodging,* June 1997.

———. "Tending to Their Business." *Lodging,* November 1997.

Maloney, Patrick. "The Specialty Beer Craze." *F&B Business,* July/August 1994.

Marvin, Bill. "Exemplary Service Guaranteed." *Restaurants & Institutions,* September 9, 1992.

Moomaw, Paul. "Service Strategies." *F&B Business,* November/December 1994.

Straus, Karen. "Cappuccino on Every Corner." *Restaurants & Institutions,* March 1, 1994.

Case Studies

Responsible Alcohol Service: A Rose Between Two Thorny Situations

It was just after 9:00 P.M., at the end of a long Saturday shift, when Rose Wheaton, a server at Vic's Restaurant, noticed a group settling into one of her tables by the bar. Although she had only been at Vic's less than a month—and had yet to receive all of her server training—she recognized four of them as some of the restaurant's best guests. There were six people in the group: two older couples that were Saturday-night regulars whom she called by name, and a younger man and woman she did not know.

"Hey, Rose!" one of the men called out. "Sure looks busy tonight."

"Never too busy for you and your friends, Mr. Grove," Rose said, smiling as she reached their table. "How are you all doing?"

"We're fine. Just waiting for a table." Mr. Grove reached over and put his arm around the young man beside him. "This here's my son, Tommy. He's been away at college, but he's finally going to graduate next weekend. And this is Gwen, his fiancée. We're out for a kind of two-for-one celebration—graduation and engagement."

"That's great!" Rose said. "What can I get for you while you wait for your table?"

"I think champagne is in order," Mr. Grove said. "And six glasses."

Rose glanced up from her pad at Tommy and Gwen. She quickly remembered that she had been 22 years old when she graduated from college. And Tommy and Gwen looked young. Were they even able to drink legally?

"I'll bring your champagne right out," she said. She moved around the table toward the younger couple. "Could I please see your driver's licenses?" she asked the couple.

"You've got to be kidding," Tommy said.

"We card everybody who looks really young."

Tommy's face flushed a deep crimson as he turned to Gwen. "Do you have yours?"

"I left my purse at your parents' house," she said.

"Along with my wallet," Tommy said, staring back at Rose. "What about a passport? I've got mine out in the car."

Rose shook her head. "It's got to be a driver's license."

"That's crazy. What if we didn't drive a car?"

"Look, I don't make the—"

"I swear, we're both 22. We're getting married, for Pete's sake. Trust us."

"I do trust you, but, you know, it's not up to me. It's my boss's rule. He says that unless you have a driver's license, you can't drink alcohol here. The last thing we need to deal with is a bunch of drunk teenagers!" she said with a laugh.

"What? I—"

"It's okay, son," Mr. Grove interrupted, looking up at her with a smile. "You just bring us four glasses, Rose, and we'll be fine here."

"But, Dad—"

"It's okay," he said with a wink.

Ten minutes later, Rose was picking up a round of beers for a group in bowling-league shirts having a shouting match at table 7 when Gary Hammond, the bartender, called her over. "Did you card those two at table 5?" he asked, nodding toward the Grove party.

"Of course," she said. "They didn't have their I.D.s, but it's okay. They're not drinking."

"You could have fooled me," Gary said. "See for yourself." She looked over in time to see Mr. Grove refill four champagne glasses—and two "water" glasses sitting in front of the engaged couple.

Rose shook her head. The bowlers were hollering for their beer. "Gary, I don't have time to play games with these people. Where's Vic?" she asked, referring to the restaurant's owner/manager. When she found Vic overseeing the dinner production in the kitchen, she quickly explained the situation and asked him to go out and talk to the Grove party.

When Vic approached the table, he immediately greeted the four adult regulars by name and asked how they were doing. Everyone seemed to be in especially fine spirits, though he noticed that the young man and woman suddenly weren't drinking their "water."

"May I talk with you for a moment, Ted?" he asked Mr. Grove. The two stepped over to the bar for a private conversation. "Ted," Vic began quietly, "people without a valid photo I.D. cannot be served alcohol here."

"They weren't," Mr. Grove said, his smile starting to fade. "Well, not really, anyway. Rose said you wouldn't allow it, but I didn't see why you couldn't do us a little favor."

"It isn't a matter of favors, Ted, it's a legal requirement for running a restaurant in this state. You know that we trust and respect you and your guests, but this isn't about that. It's simply a matter of obeying the law. Now, I understand you're out for a celebration tonight, and I certainly don't want to ruin that. But, to avoid any further embarrassment, I do have to take the champagne away from your son and his fiancée. I also need to ask that you not give them any more."

"Is that all?" Mr. Grove asked glumly.

"Well, no. Because this is a special night for your family and friends, I want to offer you a complimentary appetizer platter. Your table in the dining room should be ready in about five minutes, and I'll have the appetizer delivered hot from the kitchen the minute you all sit down."

"Really? Well, thanks, Vic. I appreciate that." As the two men headed back to table 5, Mr. Grove approached Tommy and Gwen, relayed what Vic had said, and asked for their glasses. He handed them over to Vic, along with an apology and another "thank you" for the offer of the appetizer platter. Vic took the glasses back to the bar, where Gary was loading a service tray with five 23-ounce beers.

"Nice work, boss," Gary said. "I wish you could handle every problem that comes up like that."

"What do you mean?"

"Look at table 7. Or maybe I should say, listen to table 7. It's the Bolingbrook Bowling League again. They must start drinking at the bowling alley. And for some reason they always come in with their volume stuck on 10."

"How long have they been here?"

Gary checked his watch. "Forty minutes. And this is round two of large beers."

That meant the five bowlers had each consumed the equivalent of four beers within forty minutes. And who could know how much they may have had to drink before they arrived? "Who's serving table 7?"

"It's Rose's table, but I told her I'd cover during her break. I could be wrong, but I'd say there are a couple people there moving straight into the yellow," he said, referring to the cautionary zone between sobriety (green) and inebriation (red). "Even though they started loud, they seem to be getting even rowdier. And for a while they were telling everyone around them that we're watering down the beer. Unless I'm misreading the signs or they start slowing down, this round will turn the whole table yellow."

"All right. Take five waters along with these beers. You might also ask if anyone would care for coffee. Keep a close eye on them and fill Rose in when she comes off break. I don't think she's ever had to deal with a situation like this before."

"So I'm not cutting them off?"

Vic shook his head. "They're obviously feeling good—and loud—but they still seem to be under control to me."

Fifteen minutes later, Rose was back at the bar with an order for another round of beer for table 7. "That's some wild group," she said, rubbing her temples. "Another round of these and they'll be bowling me across the restaurant."

"That's it, then," Gary said. "You need to cut them off. Offer them coffee, soda, sparkling juice, whatever—but let them know that you can't serve them any more alcohol."

"Are you serious?"

"Absolutely."

Rose nervously approached the table, but instead of finding five bowlers, she now discovered eight people squeezed around the table.

"Come over here, little lady, and meet some of our new friends!" one of the bowlers said, grabbing her arm and yanking her toward the table.

"Hey," another one spoke up, "where's our brewskies? I s-s-succinctly remember ordering another brewskie."

"You did," Rose said, "but it's obvious that you've all had enough. In fact, I'd say it's obvious to every other person in the restaurant. I'm cutting you off. Now, if you'd like something else to drink, or something to eat, I'd be happy—"

"But what about us?" one of the newcomers asked. "We just got here, and we want something to drink."

"'Course you do, buddy," chimed in one of the original five, slapping the man hard across the back. "You got catching up to do. Lots. Nobody's cutting anything off as long as I'm here."

"Are you saying we have to sit here nursing a soda pop or something while our friends are drinking real drinks? You gotta be kiddin'!"

"Look, missy, you're new here, so you probably don't have any idea how much money we spend in this place," another added.

Rose looked up helplessly at Gary behind the bar. Where's Vic now? she wondered.

Discussion Questions

1. What mistakes did Rose make in her handling of the Grove party? the Bolingbrook Bowling League?
2. What steps can a server take to effectively manage someone in the yellow zone?
3. What could Vic have done to better prepare his staff for responsible alcohol service?

The following industry experts helped generate and develop this case: Christopher Kibit, C.S.C., Academic Team Leader, Hotel/Motel/Food Management & Tourism Programs, Lansing Community College, Lansing, Michigan; and Jack Nye, General Manager, Applebee's of Michigan, Applebee's International, Inc.

Task Breakdowns: Beverage Service

The procedures presented in this section are for illustrative purposes only and should not be construed as recommendations or standards. While these procedures are typical, readers should keep in mind that each food sevice facility has its own procedures, equipment specifications, and safety policies.

BARTENDER: *Inventory and Requisition Bar Stock*

Materials needed: *An inventory form, a beverage requisition, a food requisition, a par stock list, a banquet event order, and a pen.*

STEPS	HOW-TO'S
1. Inventory alcohol.	❑ Count the full bottles of each type of liquor, wine, and beer. Record the amounts on an inventory form. ❑ Estimate in tenths ($^1/_{10}$ = 0.1) how much alcohol is left in each open bottle of liquor and wine. Record the amount on the inventory form as 0.1, 0.2, 0.3, etc.
2. Prepare a beverage requisition.	❑ Consult your par stock list to determine how much of each item should be on hand. Par stock lists provide consistent setup and control of the bar operation. ❑ Consult your inventory form to determine how much of each item you already have. ❑ Find out how much to order by subtracting the amounts on the inventory form from the total amounts on the par stock list. Write these amounts on the beverage requisition.
3. Inventory food.	❑ Count whole fruits, vegetables, unopened containers of juice, and dairy products (such as whipped cream) used in drinks. Juice is usually counted as food. ❑ Do not count fruits or vegetables that are already cut, or juices and mixes that are open. ❑ Record the amounts of food on an inventory form.
4. Prepare a food requisition.	❑ Consult your par stock list to determine how much of each item should be on hand. ❑ Consult your inventory form to determine how much of each item you already have. ❑ Find out how much to order by subtracting the amounts on the inventory form from the total amounts on the par stock list. Write these amounts on the food requisition.

BARTENDER: *Prepare Alcoholic Beverages*

Materials needed: *Standard recipes, mixes, ice, measuring cups, an ice scoop, a jigger, a bar spoon, shakers, a mixing glass, garnishes, swizzle sticks, straws, service glasses, a blender, and mugs.*

STEPS	HOW-TO'S
1. Follow standard recipes.	❑ Standard recipes keep drinks consistent. Make it your goal to memorize standard recipes at your property. ❑ Some bartenders think they are doing guests a favor by overpouring. A strong drink is not necessarily a quality drink. ❑ Read all recipes twice before preparing drinks if you have not memorized the recipes. ❑ Gather all ingredients and needed equipment. Do not use a mix or garnish that has spoiled or lost its freshness. ❑ Measure all ingredients every time you prepare a drink. If you use an automated liquor gun for pouring well-brand liquors, the gun will pour a standard shot of alcohol.
2. Select the glass specified by the recipe.	
3. Make sure glasses are free from water spots, lipstick, and chips or cracks.	
4. Use clean ice when preparing and serving drinks.	❑ Clean the ice bin before adding ice each day. ❑ Handle ice with a clean ice scoop. Do not scoop ice with a glass or with your hands. ❑ Use cubed or cracked ice for stirred or shaken drinks. Use crushed ice for mists. ❑ If glass breaks in the ice bin, or anything spills into the ice bin, empty all ice, clean the bin, and refill it with fresh, clean ice.
5. Prepare stirred drinks.	❑ Put ingredients in a mixing glass.

(continued)

BARTENDER: ***Prepare Alcoholic Beverages*** *(continued)*	
STEPS	**HOW-TO'S**
	❑ If several guests order the same stirred drink, prepare the drinks in a batch. ❑ Stir with a spoon if the beverage is mixed with fruit juices or aromatic. Add a scoop of ice. ❑ Stir the drink about three to four times to mix and chill it. ❑ Do not overstir; the alcohol will be watered down by the melting ice. ❑ Strain the ingredients from the mixing glass into the correct serving glass. ❑ Strain drinks made in a batch into glasses, filling each glass to the midpoint. Then evenly divide the remainder. ❑ Garnish appropriately as directed by the recipe.
6. Prepare shaken or blended drinks.	❑ If several guests order the same shaken or blended drink, prepare the drinks in a batch. ❑ Preparing drinks in a shaker is an opportunity to add flair to your work. ❑ Place ice in the mixing glass. Add nonalcoholic ingredients first. Add the alcohol last. ❑ Place a metal shaker firmly upside-down on top of the mixing glass. Hold the mixing glass and shaker securely together. ❑ Shake the items hard and fast. ❑ Some bartenders hold the mixing glass and shaker over their head and shake them vigorously to put on a show for guests. This type of showiness works well in a noisy "action" bar, but would be in poor taste in a quiet, intimate bar and lounge. ❑ After shaking the mixing glass and shaker, strain the drink into the correct glass. Garnish as directed by the recipe.

BARTENDER: *Prepare Alcoholic Beverages* *(continued)*

STEPS	HOW-TO'S
7. Prepare frozen drinks.	❑ Place a scoop of ice in a blender cup and add other ingredients. ❑ Place the mixture on an electric blender and blend until the ice is crushed and the ingredients are pureed. Pureeing is the process of reducing to a pulp and then rubbing through a strainer. ❑ Do not over-blend frozen drinks. Pour the drink from the blender cup into the correct glass. ❑ Garnish as directed by the recipe.
8. Prepare drinks using the build method.	❑ Place ice in the correct serving glass. Add the liquor. ❑ Add the correct amount of mixer, the garnish, and a swizzle (stir) stick. ❑ Serve the drink without mixing, stirring, or shaking.
9. Prepare layered drinks by the "float" method.	❑ A layered drink involves pouring each beverage on top of the previous one in layers to form multicolored stripes in the glass. ❑ Do not use ice. ❑ Pour heavier ingredients first so that the lighter ingredient will "float" on top of the heavier layer. Some layered drinks have only one alcoholic beverage, and sweet cream (whole cream, not whipped) is "floated" on top. ❑ If the recipe calls for milk or cream, be sure it is fresh. If in doubt, smell or taste it to be certain. ❑ If a recipe asks you to float an ingredient off the back of a spoon, pour the ingredient over the rounded part of a spoon into the glass. The spoon method reduces the chance of disturbing the layer below.

(continued)

BARTENDER: *Prepare Alcoholic Beverages* *(continued)*

STEPS	HOW-TO'S
10. Prepare coffee drinks.	❑ Pour fresh hot coffee into the correct glass or mug. ❑ Add the other ingredients called for in the recipe. ❑ Gently stir the ingredients with a bar spoon. ❑ Add whipped cream as called for by the recipe. ❑ Add garnish (such as nutmeg) as called for by the recipe. ❑ Insert the correct-size straw.

BARTENDER: *Draw Draft Beer and Pour Wine by the Glass*

Materials needed: *Glassware, a bar tap, and a corkscrew.*

STEPS	HOW-TO'S
1. Choose the correct glasses.	❑ Always examine beer and wine glasses before pouring to be sure they are clean. Glasses with starch or detergent residue can cause a flat beer taste. ❑ Make sure glasses have no spots, lipstick, chips, or cracks. ❑ A glass froster is sometimes used to frost beer glasses or mugs. Make sure glasses are sparkling clean before placing them in the froster.
2. Draw draft beer.	❑ Hold the glass near its base. ❑ Tilt the glass slightly (about 30°) under the tap so the first few ounces of beer will pour down the side of the glass. Do not pour all of the beer down the side of the glass. A direct pour down the center releases carbon dioxide and will result in a smoother tasting beer. ❑ Open the beer tap dispenser quickly and completely. If you try to hold the tap in a half-open position, you will draw too much air. This creates too much head and changes the taste of the beer. ❑ Tilt the glass to an upright position as it fills. Pour the beer directly into the center of the glass to form a head about one-half to one inch thick. ❑ If the beer doesn't develop a head, change the keg before serving any beer. Beer that will not develop a head may have gone bad in the keg. Age or a leaking keg can result in a loss of carbon dioxide and in flat beer. Check that the carbon dioxide tank is full. ❑ Close the tap quickly and completely.

(continued)

BARTENDER: *Draw Draft Beer and Pour Wine by the Glass* *(continued)*

STEPS	HOW-TO'S
3. Pour wine by the glass.	❑ Uncork the bottle, using a corkscrew. ❑ Pour the glass two-thirds full. ❑ White wine is normally served in a smaller glass than red wine. However, in bar operations, one standard size may be used for all house wine service. ❑ Recork the bottle to slow the rate at which the wine goes bad. ❑ If your restaurant uses a special vacuum system to reduce spoilage, ask your supervisor to show you how it works.

BARTENDER: *Clean Bartop and Lounge During Service*

Materials needed: *Clean ashtrays and a service tray.*

STEPS	HOW-TO'S
1. Change ashtrays often using the "capping" method.	❑ Turn a clean ashtray upside-down and place it over the dirty ashtray on the bar or table. ❑ Pick both ashtrays up and place the dirty on your tray or behind the bar. The "capping" method will prevent ashes from falling on guests, the bartop, or the table as you remove ashtrays. ❑ Place the clean ashtray back on the table or bar.
2. Keep the bartop and lounge neat at all times.	❑ Remove glasses, napkins, food plates, and silverware that are not being used. ❑ Clear empty plates from the guest's right with your right hand. ❑ Wait to clear glasses and plates until more than one guest at a table is finished, so guests who are still eating or drinking do not feel rushed. ❑ If a guest appears to be finished with an item, but the glass or plate is not empty, ask the guest if you may remove it. ❑ Put used glasses and plates onto your service tray. ❑ Never stack dirty plates in front of guests. Pick them up separately and stack them away from guests. ❑ Pick up any popcorn or snacks on the floor.

BARTENDER: *Process Drink Reorders*

Materials needed: *An order pad or guest checks, a pen, a service tray, and beverage napkins.*

STEPS	HOW-TO'S
1. Ask guests if they would like another beverage.	❑ Suggest another beverage when the guest's glass is one-half to three-quarters empty. ❑ Always count the number of alcoholic beverages each guest has. Remember that a glass of wine, a beer, and a typical mixed drink all have about one ounce of alcohol apiece. ❑ Provide nuts or other high-fat snacks to slow absorption of alcohol into the bloodstream.
2. Write the second order on your pad or on the guest check.	❑ Draw a line under the first order and write the new orders below the line. ❑ Write "Repeat" on your order pad or guest check if all guests in a party order the same thing for the next round.
3. Serve additional beverages.	❑ Clear any empty glasses when you serve or before you serve another drink. ❑ Always bring a fresh glass with a fresh bottle of beer. ❑ Never put your fingers inside glasses when you are removing them from the bar or lounge tables. ❑ Put used glasses onto your service tray. ❑ Place a new beverage napkin in front of the guest. ❑ Place the new drink on the beverage napkin.
4. Monitor guests closely for signs of intoxication.	
5. Stop alcohol service to intoxicated guests.	❑ Ask a co-worker or manager to watch or help as you refuse to serve alcohol to a guest.

BARTENDER: *Process Drink Reorders* *(continued)*

STEPS	HOW-TO'S
	❑ Move the guest away from others, if possible. ❑ Remove all alcohol from the person's reach—even if it is his or her drink. ❑ Calmly and firmly state your property's policy: "I'm sorry, but I've served you all of the alcohol that I legally can." ❑ Do not make accusations, judge the guest, or argue. ❑ Suggest nonalcoholic drinks and food instead.

COCKTAIL SERVER: *Set Up the Lounge for Service*

Materials needed: *An opening duty checklist, a vacuum cleaner, caution signs, cleaning cloths, sanitizing solution, candles or lamp fuel, polish, vases, flowers, table tents, ashtrays, matches, standard tabletop items, guest checks, and a cash bank.*

STEPS	HOW-TO'S
1. Vacuum carpeted areas.	❑ Place caution signs. ❑ Empty the vacuum cleaner bag if necessary. ❑ The steps to empty a vacuum cleaner bag vary depending on the vacuum cleaner model. Housekeeping may vacuum and perform cleaning duties in the lounge. Careful vacuuming improves the lounge's appearance and reduces problems with pests and rodents. ❑ Clean up spills with a damp cloth, followed by a dry cloth. Do not use a linen napkin to clean up spills. Use only designated cloths or cleaning towels. ❑ Report stained or damaged upholstery or carpeting to your supervisor. ❑ Unwind the cord and plug the vacuum cleaner into an outlet near the door. Make sure the cord is out of the way so no one trips. To avoid being shocked, do not stand in water when plugging in the vacuum cleaner. ❑ Begin vacuuming at the far side of the room and work toward the main entrance. ❑ Move tables and chairs as needed. ❑ Pay special attention to room corners, carpet edges, high-traffic areas, and areas under booths or banquettes. ❑ Vacuum booth seats and upholstered chairs if necessary. (Crevices in chair upholstery may collect crumbs. ❑ Unplug the vacuum cleaner and carefully wind the cord. ❑ Empty the vacuum cleaner bag if needed.

COCKTAIL SERVER: *Set Up the Lounge for Service*
(continued)

STEPS	HOW-TO'S
	❑ Store the vacuum cleaner to prevent accidents. ❑ Report carpet or equipment problems to your supervisor.
2. Clean tables and chairs.	❑ Wipe all tabletops with a damp cloth and sanitizing solution followed by a dry cloth. ❑ Use a second damp cloth to wipe all chairs and stools. You may use one cloth if you wipe all tables before you wipe chairs and stools.
3. Check, clean, and refuel table lamps.	❑ Place a new candle in each candle lamp as needed, or refill lamps using liquid fuel. Make sure that wicks are in good condition. ❑ Be careful refueling lamps. Clean up all spills. Make sure there are no open flames near you when you are filling lamps. ❑ Make sure lamps are clean and free of chips and cracks. Clean or replace lamps as needed. ❑ If lamps have brass or silver trim, make sure the trim is free from spots and tarnish. Polish brass or silver trim if necessary.
4. Check flower arrangements.	❑ Check vases for cracks, chips, and fingerprints. Clean or replace vases as needed. Make sure vases are full of fresh water. ❑ Make sure flowers and greenery are fresh and neatly arranged. Replace wilting flowers. ❑ Make sure artificial arrangements are free from dust. Use a soft, dry cloth to gently wipe the leaves and petals of artificial flowers and plants. A wet cloth can damage and wrinkle leaves and petals on silk flowers.

(continued)

COCKTAIL SERVER: *Set Up the Lounge for Service*
(continued)

STEPS	HOW-TO'S
5. Adjust drapes and blinds.	❑ Check drapes to be sure they are hanging neatly. Adjust them to give the best appearance. Keeping the blinds adjusted will present a good appearance to guests. ❑ Set blinds based on the angle of the sun to ensure guest comfort. ❑ Report to your manager any food residue or stains on drapes or blinds so cleaning can be scheduled with the housekeeping department.
6. Supply lounge tables with appropriate items.	❑ Put fresh, clean table tents and promotional items on each lounge table. Table tents and displays are sometimes used to promote food and beverage items. ❑ Follow your tabletop specifications for determining what else to place on each table. ❑ Place clean ashtrays on tables in the smoking section. Place a fresh, closed book of matches in each ashtray.
7. Get guest checks.	❑ Get guest checks from the host, bartender, or whomever is assigned to issue checks. The point-of-sale equipment may produce a sales check from a tape. If so, no guest checks will be issued. ❑ Sign for enough checks to last throughout your shift, unless your point-of-sale unit produces guest checks. Guest checks help the lounge track its sales and control its income. ❑ Always double-check that you have the correct number of checks. Make sure they are in the correct sequence. You are responsible for every check signed out to you. Some lodging properties do not distribute guest checks for service. ❑ Keep track of every check. Follow your restaurant's check-control procedure.

COCKTAIL SERVER: *Set Up the Lounge for Service*

(continued)

STEPS	HOW-TO'S
8. Set up your cash bank if you are responsible for settling guest checks yourself.	❑ The steps to set up your cash bank vary among properties. ❑ Set up your bank in a secure, back-of-house area away from the public.
9. Complete other tasks according to your opening duty checklist.	

COCKTAIL SERVER: *Greet Guests, Take Orders, and Serve Complimentary Food*

Materials needed: *Restaurant menus, guest checks or an order pad, a pen, complimentary items, silverware, dinner napkins, beverage napkins, and plates.*

STEPS	HOW-TO'S
1. Greet guests as soon as they are seated.	❑ Smile and give a warm greeting. Introduce yourself by name. For example: "Welcome to (name of property). I'm Juan, your cocktail server." ❑ If you are unable to greet your guests within your property's standard greeting time, stop by the table and let them know you'll be back soon. Apologize for the wait when you return. Many properties have a standard greeting time of two minutes or less. Some have only a 60- or 30-second greeting time. ❑ Tell guests about the specials. ❑ Try to "read" your guests right away. "Reading" guests means determining what type of service they need. Be alert to guests who have been drinking and who may become intoxicated quickly.
2. Verify the legal drinking age of guests who order alcoholic beverages.	
3. Follow an order-taking system.	❑ Place a beverage napkin in front of every guest as you ask for his or her order. This will help you keep track of who has ordered. If guests are not ready to order, leaving a beverage napkin at the table will let other servers know you've checked with the guests. This is another way to use teamwork to provide excellent guest service. ❑ If the beverage napkins have a logo, place each napkin so the logo faces the guest.

COCKTAIL SERVER: *Greet Guests, Take Orders, and Serve Complimentary Food* *(continued)*

STEPS	HOW-TO'S
	❑ Take orders from women first, then men. When you use a standard order-taking system, anyone can serve your guests without having to annoy them by asking who ordered which item. ❑ Write orders on the guest check or order pad according to how the guests are seated. Follow a clockwise direction. You may be told to write the orders on the back of a guest check, and the point-of-sale equipment will print the orders neatly on the front side. ❑ Assign a number to each chair at a table. Chair number one at each table is typically the one closest to the door or some other landmark in the lounge. All cocktail servers should use the same reference point as a starting point. ❑ Write the order for the guest in chair number one on the first line of the guest check or order pad. ❑ Write the order for the guest in chair number two on the second line of the guest check or order pad, and so forth. ❑ Use standard drink and food abbreviations. ❑ Listen carefully to each guest's order, and repeat the order and details. ❑ Note special requests on the guest check or order pad. ❑ Find out the guest's preference for service, such as "on the rocks" or "straight up." ❑ Suggest the most popular call brands when a guest does not specify the brand. ❑ Suggest a specialty drink if a guest is not sure what to order.

(continued)

COCKTAIL SERVER: *Greet Guests, Take Orders, and Serve Complimentary Food* *(continued)*

STEPS	HOW-TO'S
	❑ When offering cocktails, ask guests who don't want a cocktail if they would like a glass of wine or a nonalcoholic drink. ❑ Always suggest specific alcoholic and non-alcoholic drinks, such as a Beefeater gin and tonic, a sparkling water, or a strawberry daiquiri.
4. Bring complimentary food to guests.	❑ Bring popcorn, nuts, bar snacks, or other food provided by the lounge or bar for each group of guests. Some types of food, such as pasta or pretzels, increase the absorption of alcohol into the bloodstream. Foods high in fat, such as fried cheese, slow the absorption of alcohol into the bloodstream. ❑ Bring two or three service dishes for large parties. ❑ If complimentary food is offered on an hors d'oeuvres table: • Offer to bring items to the guests. • Select four to six items from the hors d'oeuvres table and place them on a small service plate for each guest. • Bring the appropriate silverware and present it to each guest on a dinner napkin. For serving food in the bar or lounge, silverware may be wrapped in linen napkins in advance These are typically called "roll-ups."
5. Suggest menu items.	❑ If complimentary food is not offered, try to sell appetizers, such as shrimp cocktails or nachos, along with each drink order. ❑ Offer restaurant menus to help guests make selections. ❑ Provide appropriate silverware for the items ordered.
6. Sell reorders.	

COCKTAIL SERVER: *Place Beverage and Food Orders*

Materials needed: *An order pad or guest checks, glasses, a beverage tray, an ice scoop, ice, garnishes, beverage napkins, stirrers or straws, and point-of-sale equipment.*

STEPS	HOW-TO'S
1. Pre-ring drink orders using your restaurant's point-of-sale equipment.	❑ The steps to pre-ring drink orders vary among properties. Point-of-sale (POS) equipment varies by restaurant. You will learn to use the equipment at your restaurant. ❑ Some POS units require you to insert a guest check into the unit's printer. Others print guest checks on a tape that comes out of the unit.
2. Set up glasses for drink orders.	❑ Know which drinks go in which glasses. ❑ If you follow a calling sequence when ordering drinks, set up the glasses in the order you will call the drinks. Place glasses near the edge of the bartender's side of the service bar. ❑ Fill glasses with ice for drinks that require it. ❑ Always use a scoop when putting ice in glasses. ❑ If drinks are for pool guests, do not use glassware. Use only plastic glasses to avoid injuries.
3. Place drink orders.	❑ In a clear voice, say "Ordering," and then tell the bartender your drink orders, including any special instructions. At your lounge, you may not need to call drink orders. ❑ The reason for following a calling order is that some drinks take more time to prepare than other drinks, or they do not hold up as well as other drinks. ❑ Call drink orders for all tables at the same time.

(continued)

COCKTAIL SERVER: *Place Beverage and Food Orders*

(continued)

STEPS	HOW-TO'S
	❑ Make sure you've written each order clearly and correctly on a guest check or order pad. You may need to hand in the written order instead of or in addition to calling out the orders. ❑ Place written orders in the proper location so the bartender can refer to them.
4. Garnish drinks.	❑ Select garnishes according to the drink recipe or the guest's preference. Garnishes will usually be prepared and placed in the drinks by the bartender. However, you may be asked to help. ❑ Make sure each garnish is fresh and attractive. ❑ To prevent splatters, place garnishes after drinks have been poured. Garnishing a drink before it is poured blocks the bartender's sight and causes liquor to splash out of the glass.
5. Set up beverage napkins and stirrers or straws.	❑ Place one beverage napkin on your beverage tray for each glass. ❑ Make sure napkins are clean and free from tears, folds, and wrinkles. ❑ Insert stirrers or straws in drinks if needed.
6. Pre-ring and place food orders.	❑ The steps to pre-ring food orders vary among properties. ❑ Food checks must be rung into the point-of-sale unit before the kitchen will prepare any food. ❑ These steps to place appetizer orders and entree orders vary among properties.

COCKTAIL SERVER: *Pick Up and Serve Beverages*

Materials needed: *A pen, an order pad or guest checks, beverage napkins, beverages, a linen napkin, and a beverage tray.*

STEPS	HOW-TO'S
1. Make sure beverages are complete as ordered.	❑ Mixing, pouring, garnishing, and serving drinks the same way every time is the mark of a quality operation. ❑ Check each beverage: • Is it the correct beverage? • Is it in the correct glass? • Is the garnish correct? • Have special instructions been followed? • Has anything spilled over the side? • Should it have a chaser? ❑ Take care of any problems right away.
2. Place drinks on the beverage tray.	❑ Line the tray with a linen napkin to improve the look of the tray and to avoid spills and moisture. ❑ Keep an extra pen and extra beverage napkins on the tray. ❑ Center glasses so the tray will be balanced. If possible, put heavy or tall glasses in the center of the tray. ❑ Keep in mind the order in which you will serve the drinks so your tray will be balanced until the last drink is removed.
3. Carry the tray to the table.	❑ Bend at the knees so that your shoulder is below the tray. ❑ Pull the tray with one hand onto the palm of the other hand. ❑ Balance the tray at shoulder level on your fingertips, not on your forearm. If the tray is carried on your forearm, it may tip over.

(continued)

COCKTAIL SERVER: *Pick Up and Serve Beverages*

(continued)

STEPS	HOW-TO'S
	❑ Keep your back straight as you stand up. ❑ Steady the tray with your free hand.
4. Serve beverages to guests.	❑ Always serve women first, and the host of the group last. In a "no-host" situation, simply serve women first and men last. ❑ Place a beverage napkin on the table in front of the guest, unless you've already placed one. ❑ If the beverage napkins at your property have a logo, place the napkins so that the logo faces the guest. ❑ Avoid reaching across guests. Move around the table and serve every guest from his or her right side with your right hand when possible . ❑ Handle glasses away from their rims or lips. Handle stemmed glasses by the stem or base. Your hands will warm the drink if you touch the outside of a glass. However, you should never put your fingers inside a glass. ❑ Place the glass on the center of the beverage napkin. ❑ Follow the guest check or order pad to serve the correct drink to each guest. Do not ask who ordered which drink. ❑ Repeat the name of the drink and any special requests as you serve each drink to ensure that it is correct.
5. Serve bottled beer to guests.	❑ The steps to serve bottled beer vary among properties. At some lounges, cocktail servers pour bottled beer into a glass at the table, while at other lounges, guests pour their own beer from the bottle.

COCKTAIL SERVER: *Pick Up and Serve Beverages*

(continued)

STEPS	HOW-TO'S
6. Serve cordials and ports to guests.	❑ The steps to serve cordials and ports vary among properties.
7. Deny alcohols service to guests who are intoxicated, swimming, or engaging in horseplay.	❑ Tactfully tell guests that you care about their safety and can't serve them alcohol. Alcohol impairs judgment and can lead to serious accidents around the pool. It is better to upset a few rowdy guests than to endanger bystanders or be sued for an accident. ❑ Do not make accusations, judge the guest, or argue. ❑ Suggest nonalcoholic drinks and food instead. ❑ Tell your supervisor whenever you deny someone alcohol service.

COCKTAIL SERVER: *Clean and Secure the Lounge for Closing*

Materials needed: *A closing duty checklist, cleaning cloths, beverage napkins, a bar towel, lemon wedges, a brush, sanitizing solution, a marker, food containers, and trash can liners.*

STEPS	HOW-TO'S
1. Clean throughout your shift to reduce the amount of work that has to be done at closing.	❑ Closing duties are different in different lounges. Your closing duty checklist lists your responsibilities for the end of your shift. ❑ If you are ending your shift but it is not closing time for the lounge, know your responsibilities for turning the shift over to your "relief" person.
2. Clean tables and chairs.	❑ Wipe crumbs from chairs and tables into beverage napkins and throw them away. ❑ Wipe tables and chairs with a clean damp cloth, followed by a dry cloth. Never use linen napkins for cleaning. ❑ Arrange tables and chairs neatly as guests leave. Pick up paper or debris whenever you see it.
3. Take soiled tableware to the dish room.	❑ Follow standard dish-room procedures for scraping and stacking soiled dishes. ❑ Help the bartender put away items and wash glasses.
4. Empty ashtrays, and clean them with a damp beverage napkin followed by a dry beverage napkin.	
5. Clean out and store ice buckets.	❑ Remove corks, foil scraps, labels, and other debris from buckets to avoid plugging drains. ❑ Empty ice and water into the appropriate sink. ❑ Return empty wine and champagne bottles to the bar for inventory.

COCKTAIL SERVER: *Clean and Secure the Lounge for Closing* *(continued)*

STEPS	HOW-TO'S
	❑ Dry the ice buckets with a bar towel. ❑ Store buckets in the designated side station.
6. Clean service trays.	❑ Wash trays in the kitchen at the end of the meal period. ❑ If the trays are cork-lined, rub the cork with lemon wedges to remove odors. Then let the trays stand for a few minutes before washing. ❑ Spray trays with hot water to remove food residue. ❑ If the trays are cork-lined, use a brush to scrub the cork. Then rinse the trays. ❑ Spray the trays with an approved sanitizing solution. Then stack them upside-down at right angles to allow them to air-dry.
7. Store food.	❑ Date and store food, such as condiments and garnishes, that has not been exposed to contamination. ❑ Throw away food that has been in the Temperature Danger Zone too long.
8. Remove flowers from tables.	❑ Throw away wilted flowers. ❑ Store fresh flowers in a refrigerator.
9. Clean the side station.	
10. Vacuum carpets.	
11. Turn in guest checks at the end of your shift.	❑ Account for all guest checks assigned to you. ❑ Turn in all voided, used, and unused checks.
12. Complete all other duties on your closing duty checklist.	

(continued)

COCKTAIL SERVER: *Clean and Secure the Lounge for Closing* *(continued)*

STEPS	HOW-TO'S
13. Remove all trash and reline trash cans.	
14. Help the bartender close and secure the bar.	❏ The steps to help close and secure the bar and lounge vary among properties.

RESTAURANT SERVER: *Check IDs of Guests Ordering Alcohol*

Materials needed: *A pen and a pad of paper.*

STEPS	HOW-TO'S
1. Ask for IDs from all guests who look like they are under age 30.	❑ Smile, look directly at the person, and greet him or her. ❑ Politely ask to see the person's ID: "May I please see your ID?" ❑ If the person does not remove the ID from his or her wallet, politely ask the person to do so: "Could you please remove the ID from your wallet?" Never remove an ID from a guest's wallet or purse yourself.
2. Examine the ID.	❑ Look at the birth date on the ID. Check to see if the person is of legal drinking age. ❑ Check whether the photograph appears to be that of the person handing you the ID. Look at the physical description on the ID, especially the height and weight. Do they match the person with the ID? Some states may use different-color backgrounds on pictures of minors. ❑ Check the expiration date on the ID to make sure it is valid. If it is not valid, ask for another piece of identification. All driver's licenses have an expiration date. ❑ Check the state seal to ensure that it is the right size and in the proper location.
3. Respond to possible false IDs.	❑ Feel the surface to make sure a new layer of lamination has not been added. ❑ See whether the type has been tampered with. ❑ Examine the official information, such as the state seal, number of digits in the driver's license number, border, and colors.

(continued)

RESTAURANT SERVER: *Check IDs of Guests Ordering Alcohol* *(continued)*

STEPS	HOW-TO'S
	❑ If you have any doubts about the validity of the ID, ask the owner questions he or she should be able to answer immediately, such as, "What is your birth date?" or "What is your middle name?" ❑ If the guest is slow to answer questions, or answers them incorrectly, ask the person to sign his or her name, and compare the signature to the signature on the ID to see if they match. ❑ Be firm and polite when telling a minor you cannot serve alcohol to him or her. Say something such as, "I'm sorry, but it's against the law for me to serve you alcohol," or "I'd be happy to bring you something else, but I can't serve you alcohol."

RESTAURANT SERVER: *Take Beverage Orders*

Materials needed: *A pen and an order pad or guest checks.*

STEPS	HOW-TO'S
1. Offer beverages.	❑ Always know how much alcohol your guests are drinking. ❑ Don't suggest alcohol if your guests are intoxicated or close to becoming intoxicated. ❑ At lunch and dinner, suggest that guests start their meal with a cocktail and an appetizer. Cocktail and appetizer sales can make the difference between a profitable and an unprofitable restaurant. The added sales will also increase your tip, as most guests figure their tips based on a percentage of the total bill. ❑ Take the wine order after the food order, unless guests choose otherwise. ❑ During the breakfast period, offer coffee and orange juice immediately after seating the guest. ❑ Know the drinks available and the customary ways of serving them.
2. Verify legal drinking age.	
3. Follow an order-taking system.	❑ Take orders from women first and then from men. All servers should use the same order-taking system to help remember who ordered what. ❑ Write orders on the order pad or guest check according to how the guests are seated. Follow a clockwise direction. ❑ Use standard food and drink abbreviations. ❑ Listen carefully to each guest's order. Repeat the order. ❑ Note special requests on the order pad or guest check. ❑ Find out the guest's preference for service such as "on the rocks" or "straight up."

(continued)

RESTAURANT SERVER: *Take Beverage Orders* (continued)	
STEPS	**HOW-TO'S**
	❑ Suggest the most popular call brands when a guest does not specify the brand. ❑ Suggest a specialty drink if a guest is not sure what to order. ❑ When offering cocktails, ask guests who don't want a cocktail if they would like a glass of wine or a nonalcoholic drink. ❑ Always suggest specific alcoholic and nonalcoholic drinks, such as a Beefeater gin and tonic, sparkling water, or a strawberry daiquiri.

RESTAURANT SERVER: *Process Beverage Orders*

Materials needed: *An order pad or guest checks, a pen, glasses, ice, an ice scoop, garnishes, beverage napkins, linen napkins, stirrers or straws, and a beverage tray.*

STEPS	HOW-TO'S
1. Pre-ring drink orders using your restaurant's point-of-sale equipment.	❑ At some restaurants, the bartender may pre-ring drink orders for the server. ❑ Point-of-sale (POS) equipment varies by lodging property. You will learn to use the equipment at your restaurant. ❑ Some POS units require you to insert a guest check into the unit's printer. Others print guest checks on a tape that comes out of the unit.
2. Set up glass for drink orders.	❑ Know which drinks go in which glasses. ❑ If you follow a calling sequence when ordering drinks, set up the glasses in the order you will call the drinks. Place glasses near the edge of the bartender's side of the service bar. ❑ You may need to fill glasses with ice for drinks that require it. ❑ Always use a scoop when putting ice in glasses.
3. Place drink orders.	❑ If you need to call orders, say in a clear voice, "Ordering," and then tell the bartender your drink orders, including any special instructions. ❑ Follow your restaurant's calling order. Some drinks take more time to prepare than other drinks, or they do not hold up as well as other drinks. ❑ Call drink orders for all tables at the same time.

(continued)

RESTAURANT SERVER: *Process Beverage Orders*

(continued)

STEPS	HOW-TO'S
	❑ Make sure you've written each order clearly and correctly on a guest check or order pad. You may need to hand in the written order instead of or in addition to calling out the orders. ❑ Place written orders in the proper location so the bartender can refer to them.
4. Garnish drinks.	❑ Select garnishes according to the drink recipe or the guest's preference. ❑ Make sure each garnish is fresh and attractive. ❑ To prevent splatters, place garnishes after drinks have been poured. Garnishing a drink before it is poured blocks the bartender's sight and causes liquor to splash out of the glass.
5. Set up beverage napkins and stirrers or straws.	❑ Put one beverage napkin on your tray for each drink. ❑ Make sure napkins are clean and free from tears, folds, and wrinkles. ❑ Put stirrers or straws in drinks if needed.
6. Check your beverage order.	❑ Check each beverage: • Is it the correct beverage? • Is it in the correct glass? • Is the garnish correct? • Have special instructions been followed? • Has anything spilled over the side? • Should it have a chaser? ❑ Mixing, pouring, garnishing, and serving drinks the same way every time is the mark of a quality operation. ❑ Take care of any problems right away.

RESTAURANT SERVER: *Process Beverage Orders*

(continued)

STEPS	HOW-TO'S
7. Place drinks on the beverage tray.	❑ Line the tray with a linen napkin to improve the look of the tray and to absorb spills and moisture. Many restaurants use a cork-lined tray so glasses don't slip. ❑ Keep an extra pen and an extra beverage napkin on the tray. ❑ Center glasses so the tray will be well-balanced. If possible, put heavy or tall glasses in the center of the tray. ❑ Keep in mind the order in which you will serve drinks so your tray will be balanced until the last drink is removed.
8. Carry the tray to the table.	
9. Serve beverages to guests.	❑ Always serve women first, and the host of the group last. ❑ In a no-host situation, simply serve women first and men last. ❑ Place the beverage napkin first, in the center of the base plate or in the center of the plate space, with the logo facing the guest. If tables have linen tablecloths, you may not need to use beverage napkins. ❑ Avoid reaching across guests. Move around the table and serve each guest from his or her right side with your right hand. ❑ Handle glasses away from their rims or lips. Handle stemmed glasses by the stem or base. Your hands will warm the drink if you touch the outside of the glass. However, you should never put your fingers inside a glass. ❑ Place the drink glass on the center of the beverage napkin. ❑ Follow your order pad or guest check to serve the correct drink to each guest.

(continued)

RESTAURANT SERVER: *Process Beverage Orders*

(continued)

STEPS	HOW-TO'S
	❑ As you serve each drink, repeat the name of the drink and any special requests to be sure that it is correct. Do not ask who ordered the drink.
10. Serve bottled beer to guests.	❑ At some restaurants, servers pour bottled beer into a glass at the table, while at other restaurants, guests pour their own beer from the bottle.
11. Serve cordials and ports to guests.	
12. Suggest another drink when the guest's glass is one-half to three-quarters empty.	❑ Pay attention to how much alcohol your guests are drinking. Count the drinks each guest has had. Remember that the amount of alcohol in a mixed drink with one ounce of alcohol is about equal to that in one beer or in one glass of wine. ❑ Only suggest another drink to guests who are not intoxicated or close to becoming intoxicated. ❑ Only serve drinks to guests who want them. Do not simply bring "another round" for everyone if some guests do not want another drink.
13. Deny alcohol service to intoxicated guests.	❑ Tactfully tell guests that you care about their safety and can't serve them alcohol. ❑ Do not make accusations, judge the guest, or argue. ❑ Suggest nonalcoholic drinks and food instead. ❑ Tell your supervisor whenever you deny someone alcohol service.

RESTAURANT SERVER: *Process Beverage Orders*

(continued)

STEPS	HOW-TO'S
14. Pick up napkins and empty glasses and replace them when serving additional drinks.	❑ If a guest has not finished the first drink, ask if he or she wishes to have the glass removed. ❑ Never put your fingers inside glasses when you are removing them from the table. ❑ Carry used glasses on a beverage tray to the dish room.

Sources: Adapted from the "Bartender Guide," "Cocktail Server Guide," and "Restaurant Server Guide" in the *Hospitality Skills Training Series* (East Lansing, Mich.: Educational Institute of the American Hotel & Motel Association, 1995).

REVIEW QUIZ

When you feel you have covered all of the material in this chapter, answer these questions. Choose the *best* answer.

1. Which of the following is *not* a primary responsibility of a beverage manager?

   a. standardizing recipes
   b. purchasing supplies
   c. controlling inventory
   d. mixing drinks

2. When a server is serving cocktails at a guest table, the server should rest the cocktail tray:

   a. on a guest's head.
   b. between the slats on the back of a guest's chair (for greater stability).
   c. in one hand.
   d. on the table.

3. In wine terminology, "__________" refers to the complex smell of a mature wine.

   a. body
   b. bouquet
   c. claret
   d. aroma

4. What do a 12-ounce beer, a 5-ounce glass of wine, and a cocktail with 1.25 ounces of liquor have in common?

   a. They all contain approximately the same amount of alcohol.
   b. They will all affect every person in the same way.
   c. They all contain enough alcohol to intoxicate a person.
   d. They all have little effect on a person's blood alcohol level.

REVIEW QUIZ *(continued)*

5. Which of the following statements is *not* appropriate when cutting off alcohol service to an intoxicated guest?

   a. "We care about your safety, and I cannot serve you any more alcohol."
   b. "I'm sorry, but I've served you all the alcohol my manager will allow."
   c. "I can't serve you any more alcohol, but I would be happy to bring you coffee or a soft drink."
   d. "I'm sorry, but you've clearly had too much to drink."

Answer Key: 1-d-C1, 2-c-C1, 3-b-C2, 4-a-C2, 5-d-C2

Each question is linked to a competency. Competencies are listed on the first page of the chapter. An answer reading 3-b-C4 translates to:

3: the question number
b: the correct answer
C4: the competency number

Chapter 5 Outline

Purchasing
- Establishing Quality and Other Specifications
- Establishing Par Inventory Levels

Receiving and Storing

Issuing

Controlling
- Misuse
- Waste
- Breakage
- Theft

Supplies and Equipment
- China
- Glassware
- Flatware
- Disposables
- Uniforms
- Napery
- Furniture
- Equipment
- High-Tech Equipment

Competencies

1. Describe procedures and issues involved with purchasing, receiving, storing, issuing, and controlling food service operation supplies and equipment.
2. Summarize purchasing criteria for and characteristics of china, glassware, flatware, disposables, uniforms, napery, furniture, and common equipment items used by food service personnel.

5

Food Service Supplies and Equipment

FOOD SERVICE OPERATIONS of all types require a wide variety of supplies and equipment in order to serve guests properly. This chapter will focus on basic principles that managers should practice when purchasing, receiving, storing, issuing, and controlling supplies and equipment. The chapter also provides an overview of the kinds of supplies and equipment that food service personnel typically use, and discusses factors managers should consider when selecting supplies and equipment.

Purchasing

Purchasing is more than just placing an order. It is very important to purchase the *right* product at the *right* time from the *right* supplier for the *right* price. Planning for the purchase of supplies and equipment begins long before a new operation opens its doors. Before any supplies and equipment are purchased, managers must determine what their guests will want and assess how the operation can best provide for those requirements. The types and quality of supplies and equipment that are used will affect the quality of dining service. Just as you would not use expensive china in a quick-service operation such as Taco Bell, you would not use plastic flatware and paper plates in an upscale gourmet restaurant. Beyond these obvious points, how should managers plan the purchase of service supplies and equipment?

Establishing Quality and Other Specifications

It is crucial for managers to consider the requirements and expectations of their guests, as well as applicable operating criteria, as they set quality requirements for supplies and equipment. At large operations, purchasing department staff can help the general manager and other managers by obtaining information from suppliers, discussing alternatives with the suppliers, and bringing samples to user departments for further analysis and consideration. Ideas and suggestions from the guests themselves, as well as guest-contact and other staff members, can also help managers establish the right quality requirements for these items.

After managers have a general idea about the level of quality required, they must do a great deal of research. Studying brochures, talking with sales representatives, and reviewing sample products are techniques they can use to help formulate quality requirements. Examining the competition's supplies can also provide them with insight about the practicality of the items they are considering.

Price and the Purchase Decision

Wise purchasers want to buy products at the lowest possible price. They also know that product quality is a primary factor in determining price. Therefore, they use purchase specifications to make sure that suppliers quote prices for products of similar quality. Purchase specifications ensure that price differences between vendors are not likely to be caused by differences in product quality.

Wise purchasers also know that more than just the products themselves are purchased from suppliers. Along with dining service supplies and equipment, suppliers also provide intangibles such as helping purchasers solve problems or always coming through with timely deliveries. A supplier may give a manager a low price, but if the supplies are not delivered on time, it can cause a lot of problems for the food service operation.

Credit provisions can also cause a manager to choose one supplier over another; having an extended period of time to pay for products might be worth a higher price to a manager. Some suppliers offer discounts for volume purchases or timely payments. If a supplier offers a two percent discount for timely payment on a bill of $5,000, the $100 bottom-line savings is substantial when you consider that a restaurant with a profit margin of 10 percent must generate $1,000 in sales to put $100 on the bottom line.

Wise purchasers consider all of these factors—price, quality, supplier intangibles, and flexible payment plans—when choosing a supplier. Although low prices are desirable, the supplier with the lowest price is not always the best supplier to choose.

Whenever possible, managers should consider manufacturers' brands that are available from more than one supplier. **Open-stock items** are much easier to replace than **custom-made items** produced by a single supplier. If managers decide to purchase a brand carried by only one supplier or a custom-designed item manufactured by only one supplier, they have less leverage to negotiate prices.

When managers are developing a new independent restaurant, it is critical that they consider china and other tabletop items early in the development process so that these items can be matched with the menu, uniforms, and other features of the restaurant's decor. Managers should think about how tabletops that are completely set will appear to guests as they enter the room and as they are seated at their tables. Tabletop items should comfortably fit the size of the tables that will be used in the dining area. Whenever possible, managers should ask suppliers to furnish them with samples of tabletop items that they can try out before making a purchase decision. By taking tableware for a "test drive," managers will have a better feel for how each type of ware will fit their needs. The same is true for dining area chairs; managers should sit in a variety of them to determine which chair best meets their needs.

As managers make decisions about quality requirements, they should write the details down in a format similar to the one shown in Exhibit 1. In large operations, information about quality requirements is often sent to a purchasing department. In smaller operations, the general manager him- or herself might use the

Exhibit 1 Sample Standard Purchase Specification

Standard Purchase Specification

Royale Room
(Name of food and beverage outlet)

1. *Product name:* Tablecloths
2. *Product used for:* Tables in our gourmet restaurant, the Royale Room
3. *Product general description:*
   (Provide general quality information about desired product.)
   To be made of cotton damask, weighing 6 1/4 oz. per square yard.
4. *Detailed description:*
   (Purchaser should state all factors that help to clearly identify desired product. Examples of specific factors, which vary by product being described, include brand name, color, materials composed of, and style.)
   Material to have approximately 170 threads per square inch; thread count should be 91 (warp) and 79 (weft). Cloth should be 72" x 72" and shrink less than 10% (warp) and 5% (weft). Color to be white, non-fading (see attached sample for color/sheen).
5. *Product test procedures:*
   (Test procedures occur at time product is received and as/after product is used.)
   Sample cloth will be laundered by laundry manager immediately upon receipt to check shrinkage and durability.
6. *Special instructions and requirements:*
   (Any additional information needed to clearly indicate quality expectations can be included here. Examples include bidding procedures, if applicable, labeling and/or packaging requirements and delivery and service requirements.)
   Bids should include price for 150 tablecloths, a sample cloth, and estimated delivery date. (Delivery date to be within 4 months of order.) All bids to be returned in 30 days; chosen bidder to be notified by phone.

details to fill out a **standard purchase specification form.** After the form is completed, it should be sent with a cover letter to all eligible suppliers. Since the purchase specification form outlines the quality requirements for the products requested, chances are good that all suppliers will quote prices for the same quality of product, thus making it easier for the manager to make a selection based on price.

Managers can consult a checklist of food and beverage service accessories similar to the one shown in Exhibit 2 for suggestions for supplies and equipment their operations might need. To help make good purchasing decisions, managers should study advertising brochures available from suppliers, review products at trade shows, and draw on their own experiences and those of their staffs.

Exhibit 2 Checklist of Food and Beverage Service Accessories

- ❑ Menu boards
- ❑ Cutting boards
- ❑ Ashtrays
- ❑ Flower vases
- ❑ Bottle openers
- ❑ Condiment holders
- ❑ Coffee creamers
- ❑ Sugar bowls
- ❑ Napkin holders
- ❑ Butter dishes
- ❑ Candles
- ❑ Salt and pepper shakers
- ❑ Teapots
- ❑ Coffee warmers
- ❑ Water pitchers
- ❑ Plate covers
- ❑ Serving ladles
- ❑ Pie servers
- ❑ Napkin dispensers
- ❑ Silverware bins
- ❑ Food server trays
- ❑ Cocktail server trays
- ❑ Tray stands
- ❑ Baby chairs
- ❑ Chafing dishes
- ❑ Corkscrews
- ❑ Flashlights
- ❑ Pens
- ❑ Mobile transport carts
- ❑ Bus carts
- ❑ Utility carts
- ❑ Bus boxes
- ❑ Dish storage carts
- ❑ Ice tongs
- ❑ Table numbers
- ❑ Coffee servers
- ❑ Oil and vinegar cruets
- ❑ Relish dishes
- ❑ Wine cooler stands
- ❑ Side stands
- ❑ Cheese trays
- ❑ Tip trays
- ❑ Pastry carts
- ❑ Wine carts
- ❑ Salad carts
- ❑ Pepper mills
- ❑ Service plates
- ❑ Wine decanters
- ❑ Food service towels
- ❑ Menus
- ❑ Utility buckets
- ❑ Side towels
- ❑ Serving utensils

Questions a manager should consider before purchasing a supply or equipment item include the following:

- Does the operation need the item at this time?
- Will it serve the purpose for which I need it?
- Does it satisfy the unique needs of the operation and its guests?
- Does the item's quality justify the cost?
- Is the item easy to clean (if applicable)?
- Is its appearance and design appropriate to the operation?

Exhibit 3 Purchase Record Form for Small Operations

Date: ______________ Supplier: ______________

Delivery Date: ______________ Order Taken By: ______________

Freight charge confirmation: ______________
(e.g., prepaid, COD, truck shipment)

Item	Purchase Unit	Cost per Purchase Unit	Amount	Total Cost

And, for equipment:

- Is it safe?
- Will it fit through aisles, doorways, and other areas through which it may routinely be moved?

After receiving bids and making a purchase decision, managers should record the appropriate information on a **purchase record** (see Exhibit 3). Food service managers are very busy; they may not be able to recall the brand, quoted purchase price, and quantity they ordered of an item when it is delivered, sometimes weeks or even months after they purchased it. The purchase record documents this information and is useful to the receiving personnel who actually receive the products. (Large operations may also use **purchase orders** as control documents that authorize purchases and detail exactly what is being purchased.) Purchase records and purchase orders are computerized at many properties.

Establishing Par Inventory Levels

Some of the major purchases for any food service operation are such common supply items as china, flatware, glasses and other beverage containers, and napkins. These supplies are maintained at what are known as **par inventory levels** or stock levels. When an independent food service operation uses the par inventory method, its managers must set the par levels and decide the minimum level that each item can be allowed to reach before an order must be placed to build the item's inventory back up to its established par level; this minimum level is called the **re-order point.** (Restaurant chains either mandate or strongly recommend par levels and re-order points for franchisees.) If par levels are set too high and supplies are overstocked, problems with cash flow, theft and pilferage, or wasted storage space can occur. In contrast, if par levels are set too low and there aren't enough supplies on hand, guest and staff member frustration and dissatisfaction can result.

There are so many different kinds of food service operations that it is extremely difficult to generalize about the specific par inventory levels that should be maintained for a given supply item. The general manager in each independent operation must identify the operation's specific needs, based on the type of operation, the number of seats, the hours of operation, the availability of supplies, the frequency and style of dishwashing, the availability of an on-site laundry (for large on-site [institutional] food service operations or food service operations that are part of a lodging property), and—first and foremost—the requirements and expectations of guests.

Once the manager of an independent operation has set par inventory levels for the operation, he or she should re-evaluate them frequently to accommodate any changes in business conditions. There are some rules of thumb in the following sections that can help managers of independent operations establish their own par levels for various supplies. (As mentioned earlier, chain operations often have their par levels set by corporate headquarters.)

Par Inventory Levels for China. Ideally speaking, an operation's china inventory should permit one complete setup in the dining room, one complete setup in process (in the dish room or in transit), and one complete setup in reserve (storage).

When managers open a new food service operation, the following guidelines can help them establish order quantities for china:

1. Dinner plates—3 times the number of seats
2. Salad plates—3 to 4 times the number of seats
3. Bread and butter plates—3 to 4 times the number of seats
4. Cups—3 to 4 times the number of seats
5. Saucers—3 to 4 times the number of seats
6. Fruit dishes or bowls—2 to 3 times the number of seats
7. Sugar containers—$^1/_2$ to 1 times the number of seats

The cost of each place setting (the items needed for a complete setting at each seat) can vary from $2.95 per three-piece place setting to $200 or more per place setting. As you can see, a tableware purchase can be a significant expense.

Specially made or high-quality china may take extra time to produce and deliver. However, some managers feel that the unique atmosphere and food presentation experiences that can result from the use of such china justifies its high purchase price, as well as the long wait for it. The lead time needed for custom-designed china can be as long as 90 to 120 days.

Par Inventory Levels for Glassware and Flatware. The rule of thumb for flatware is one-and-one-half to three place settings per seat. For glassware, managers should maintain a par of three per seat for each of the most frequently used kinds of glasses, such as water glasses and wine glasses. Obviously, many factors affect the choice of actual pars. For example, if an operation has high breakage (glassware) or

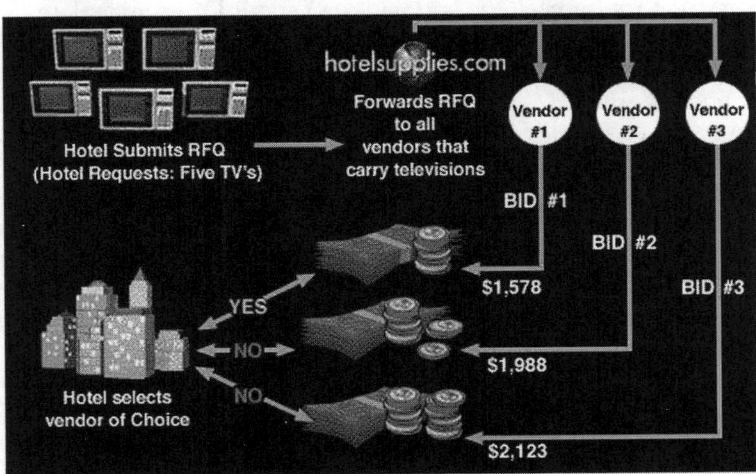

I. Hotels/Motels/B&Bs nationwide log on to hotelsupplies.com and submit their RFQs (Request For Quotes).

II. hotelsupplies.com forwards that RFQ to all our vendors that are registered in related categories.

III. Vendors can see all the details needed to make a accurate bid but don't have the hotel's direct contact information. (They may fax the hotel if more information is needed)

IV. The vendor's bid is sent directly to the hotel's personal mailbox.

V. Hotels review the bids and the vendor's details (price, service, trade references etc.) and select the vendor that they want to do business with.

VI. At this stage a hotel can:
- choose to contact the vendor directly,
- have the vendor contact them, or
- e-mail the purchase order directly to the vendor.

iBO$™ *(Internet Bidding Operating System)* **Software**
iBO$, inc. 1996/1997

Internet Bidding Operating System (iBO$) software enables food service managers to request quotes for supplies and equipment from every supplier who has registered with the Internet company—all with a single submission (see http://www.hotelsupplies.com). The manager selects items, provides specifications, quantities, and other information, then waits for bids from suppliers, to whom his or her request has automatically been emailed. (Courtesy of hotelsupplies.com, LLC, 25 June 1998)

losses (flatware), the operation will need higher inventory levels. Par levels also are influenced by how quickly soiled items can be cleaned and side stations restocked.

Par Inventory Levels for Uniforms and Napery. The service staff's uniforms and the operation's **napery** (tablecloths and napkins) should be immaculately clean at all times. Many food service operations make three complete uniforms available to each service staff member. With this plan, the staff member can store one, launder another, and wear the third. Managers must make some provision for staff members whose uniforms become soiled during a shift; they may require a uniform change in order to maintain the sanitation and quality requirements of the operation.

Par inventory levels for napery are frequently set higher than those for uniforms. Many operations use a par level of four times the number of tablecloths and napkins used during a busy shift. With this system, one set is in use, a second set is in the laundry, and the third and fourth sets are on the shelf, "resting." Linens need to "rest" or "breathe" between uses in order to maintain their quality and prolong their useful life.

Receiving and Storing

The processes involved in **receiving** and storing food service supplies can be summarized as follows:

1. Check incoming products against the purchase record (Exhibit 3). This document reminds whomever is receiving the shipment of the commitments made at the time of purchase. If, for example, a manager ordered five dozen tea saucers of the Staffordshire style from the Syracuse China Company at a specific price, the purchase record would help the receiving clerk (or other staff member) check that the proper quantity of these saucers was delivered at the agreed-upon price. (Receivers should carefully count costly items.)

2. Check incoming products against the standard purchase specification form (Exhibit 1). If managers have put quality requirements in writing and given them to suppliers, receiving personnel can review incoming products against these quality requirements to ensure that the operation receives the correct type of product.

3. Check incoming products against the delivery **invoice.** The supplier provides a delivery invoice that a representative of the food service operation must sign. Since this document is the basis for the charges from the supplier, it is important that the type and quantity of products the operation receives match those for which the supplier is billing the operation.

4. Record in writing any variances between what has been received and what was ordered. Also record any errors in price. Write credit memorandums for price corrections and unsatisfactory or damaged goods that are returned to the supplier.

5. Remove items to secure storage areas. Items should not be left unattended in receiving areas. Rather, they should be brought under strict storeroom control

as quickly as possible to prevent damage, staff member or guest theft, or other problems.

In large operations, it is usually wise to split the responsibilities for product purchasing and product receiving. For example, personnel in the purchasing department can purchase the products, and personnel in the accounting department can receive and store the products. Dividing these duties reduces the possibilities of theft.

Small operations may not be able to assign different staff members to purchase and receive supplies. Frequently, the owner/manager of a small operation will handle both duties. Alternatively, whoever is closest to the back door may do product receiving, as long as they have been trained in the operation's receiving procedures. The complexity of the receiving procedures just outlined suggests that staff members need training to properly receive orders, whatever the size of the operation.

Typically, service supplies are purchased less frequently and in smaller quantities than food and beverage products; service supplies are generally purchased only to restore inventory to par stock levels. Therefore, it may be possible, even in the smallest operations, to keep service supplies in a locked area.

Of course, there is no point to locked storage facilities unless the operation uses key control procedures. Simply stated, only those staff members with a need to use storeroom keys should have access to the keys. Managers do need to ensure, however, that enough staff members are authorized to access keys so that there is always someone available to unlock the storeroom(s). The manager responsible for the storage area should have the keys on his or her person for the entire shift. When he or she is off duty, the operation should keep the keys under lock. Some operations keep keys under lock at all times and use a control form to keep track of who issues the keys and at what times. Locks should be changed when staff members who have had access to the keys leave the employ of the operation. Likewise, keys should not be labeled to identify the locks that they open. Should unauthorized staff members find such keys, the labels would make it easier for them to misuse the keys.

Many food service operations use the "precious room" or "vault" concept for storing expensive service supplies such as china and flatware. This plan entails the use of a locked storage area *within* the locked storeroom, which doubly protects these expensive items from theft.

Entering the quantity of incoming products into a **perpetual inventory** record (Exhibit 4) gives managers a running balance of supplies in stock. This plan is especially important for controlling supplies when managers use par inventory levels and re-order points. A perpetual inventory record shows the quantity of supplies in inventory at any given moment. It also helps determine usage rates by indicating when supplies are withdrawn (issued) from inventory and in what quantity.

Periodically, managers must verify that the quantity of each item listed in the perpetual inventory records is the amount that is actually available. A **physical inventory**—that is, an actual count of the items on hand—serves a dual purpose: it verifies the perpetual inventory figures, and managers can use it to assess the inventory's value. This information is important to producing the balance sheet, which lists the value of an operation's assets, including its service supplies.

Exhibit 4 Sample Perpetual Inventory Record Form

Item: ______________________

Par Levels

Minimum	Maximum

Specification Number: ______________

Balance Carried Forward: ______________ Balance Carried Forward: ______________

Date	In	Out	Balance	Date	In	Out	Balance

Issuing

Service supplies are transferred from storage areas to dining areas as they are needed. This process is called **issuing,** and operations should have specific control procedures for managing this process.

Exhibit 5 illustrates an issue **requisition** that staff members can use during the issuing process. Staff members list the items they need on the form, recording the unit size (for example, a box of 50 candles) and the quantity they need (such as two boxes). Depending on the operation, the issue requisition might be completed by the general manager, an assistant manager, a host or hostess, or another staff member. In large operations, a staff member might complete it and then need authorization from a manager to receive the products from storage.

The use of par inventory levels in the dining area can help staff members assess the quantity of supplies that should be issued to the dining area. For example, managers might determine that, at the beginning of each shift, there should be five boxes of paper goods, one box of sugar packets, a gross of matches, and one box of novelties for children available in the dining area. The issuing plan would involve restocking these products in the dining area to the required par levels before each shift begins.

Space for the storage of supplies in dining areas is often scarce. Therefore, managers must ensure that the proper quantities of service supplies—and no more—are available in these areas. Excessive quantities of service supplies waste valuable dining space; service supplies also become more susceptible to pilferage when they are not in central storage areas. When greater-than-needed quantities are readily available, some staff members may have the attitude, "There's plenty; we can waste (or take) a little."

Exhibit 5 Sample Issue Requisition Form

Date: ______________ Dept.: ______________

Item	Unit Size	Quantity	Cost per Unit	Total Cost

Authorized By: ______________

Issued By: ______________

On the other hand, it is not good to have insufficient quantities of supplies on hand. Running out of service supplies will adversely affect service speed and guest satisfaction. The term *mise en place,* which literally means "put in place," applies well to service supplies. While this term is commonly used to refer to the process of setting up tools and assembling raw ingredients for cooking, the concept of *mise en place* is applicable to stocking dining areas with service supplies before the start of service. Maintaining the correct par is a responsibility that should never be ignored.

Controlling

Service supplies are costly; therefore, managers must properly control them. Unlike food and beverage products, which can deteriorate in quality, primary control problems with service supplies revolve around misuse, waste, breakage, and theft.

Misuse. There are countless ways that service supplies can be misused. Service staff members who use napkins as pot holders or food service towels, for example, or who use sugar packets to level wobbly tables are misusing supplies.

Staff members should always have the supplies and equipment available to them that they need to do their jobs. Often, creative staff members improvise when they do not have the materials they need to do their work effectively. To help prevent misuse of supplies in dining areas, managers should purchase the proper supplies and equipment, develop procedures to make sure they are available when and where needed, and train and supervise staff members effectively.

Waste. Waste is a serious control problem with service supplies. Giving guests handfuls of matches, throwing away unopened prepackaged condiments such as jelly or mustard, discarding washable supplies because it is easier than sorting them, and accidentally discarding flatware into garbage receptacles or folding it into dirty linen to be sent to the laundry are all wasteful practices. Some staff members may think that the costs of some of these items are so low that wasting them makes no difference; other staff members simply may not care. Regardless of the reason, managers should not tolerate the waste of supplies. Training and supervision can help reduce the problem. Useful techniques to reduce supply waste include developing procedures to improve staff attitudes, motivating staff members to pursue higher standards, and building a team of staff members whose goals are compatible with those of the operation.

Breakage. Breakage of china, glassware, and other service supplies is another potentially serious problem. Managers must train staff members to properly handle breakable items. In most food service operations, 75 to 80 percent of all breakage occurs in the soiled-dish area, so good supervision in this area is essential. Proper stacking of soiled china on trays and clean china in storage areas or on dish carts helps reduce breakage, as does properly handling stemmed glassware and properly dropping off dishes in dishwashing areas. For example, dishwashers can set up a decoy system with dishes of each type; managers can train service staff to stack similar dishes on top of these decoys to help prevent staff members from building unstable stacks of unsorted dishes that often topple and cause breakage.

Theft. Some guests like to take home items that have the operation's logo for souvenirs; some staff members also like imprinted items or just feel that the operation owes them something. Whatever the reason, the result is the same: these stolen items must be replaced, and costs of service supplies increase.

Some food service operations implement inspection programs in which managers inspect all packages that staff members bring into or take out of the facility; such programs help detect staff member theft of service supplies and other items. Managers should check with attorneys to make sure such programs are legal in their localities before implementing them. Managers should also be aware that such programs may create an atmosphere of distrust between managers and staff members.

To help reduce guest theft, managers should train food and beverage servers to remove empty glassware and other tableware items when they serve a second drink or an additional course. This practice not only helps prevent theft, it gives guests more room and gets tableware to the dishroom faster. A number of food service managers have reduced guest theft by offering service supplies for sale. With this approach, guests who desire these items have a legitimate opportunity to obtain them.

Problems with the control of supplies are especially prevalent in bar and lounge areas. Not only are the beverage products themselves susceptible to theft or misuse, but bar supplies, garnishes, and cash might also be stolen. Many of the same principles discussed earlier in the chapter (creating operating procedures, training staff members, and supervising to ensure that staff members follow required procedures) help minimize these problems. However, because of the increased possibilities of theft in bar and lounge areas, management must give special attention to them.

Supplies and Equipment

There are a number of issues managers must address as they develop purchase specifications for service supplies and equipment. These range from whether to use disposable napkins to how to select the most suitable chairs for the dining room. Above all, managers should seek value from any purchase. Value relates to not only durability and affordability, but attractiveness and functionality as well; supply and equipment items should enhance the operation's concept/theme, interior design, and menu. In the following sections we will discuss supply and equipment items commonly used in food service operations.

China

It can cost many thousands of dollars to purchase an initial china inventory and to replace items as breakage and theft occur. Therefore, it is very important for managers to analyze all factors before making purchase decisions. The pattern they choose will likely "lock in" their operations for years to come, because the high cost of china makes pattern switching impractical, even if managers later find other products that better meet the operation's quality requirements or harmonize more closely with the decor. Managers who want to change the china in their operations must consider a great deal more than the direct cost:

1. Many orders for new china require a long lead time (typically, three to four months or more).
2. Managers must not discontinue re-ordering replacement items for current stock too soon; if they do, they may face shortages until the new china arrives and can be readied for use.
3. The sizes of the new china items must be compatible with the operation's self-leveling plate-dispensing equipment, storage units (such as side stations), dishwashing machines, service trays, and plate covers. (Made of either plastic or metal, plate covers keep foods warm and facilitate the stacking of plates for transport to service areas. Obviously, covers need to be the correct size for the china with which they are used.)
4. Food presentation procedures and the placement of garnishes may be affected by new china.
5. New china items frequently become "collectibles," and managers can expect an increased amount of pilferage or theft after the new china arrives, especially when a logo or other identifying mark is imprinted on it.

Many managers prefer to use open-stock, multipurpose china (e.g., a single plate that can be used to serve an appetizer, side dish, or dessert), because by doing so they pay less and have products that are more versatile than special-purpose china.

Know the Definitions of Tableware Alternatives

Pottery

The term "pottery" properly applies to the clay products of primitive people or to decorated art products made by unsophisticated methods with unrefined clays. As a generic name, "pottery" includes all fired clayware. As a specific name, "pottery" describes the low-fired porous clayware that is generally colored.

Ceramic products acquire strength through the application of heat. The chemical compositions of the materials used to make a product determine, after heat is applied, the strength, porosity, and amount of glazing of the fired product. Primitive pottery, often baked in the sun and composed of one or more unrefined clays, has little strength and is quite porous.

Earthenware

A porous type of ceramic product fired at comparatively low temperatures, producing an opaque product that is not as strong as stoneware or china and lacks the resonance of those products when struck. The product may be glazed or unglazed.

Crockery

A term, often synonymous with earthenware, used to describe a porous opaque product for domestic use. Because of its permeability, it is normally glazed.

Stoneware

A nonporous ceramic product made of unprocessed clays, or clay and flux additives, fired at elevated temperatures. It is quite durable but lacks the translucence and whiteness of china. It is resistant to chipping and rings clearly when struck. It differs from porcelain chiefly in that it comes in colors other than white. These result from the iron or other impurities in the clay.

Ironstone Ware

A historic term for durable English stoneware. The composition and properties of this product are similar to porcelain, except that the body is not translucent and is off-white. In more recent times, this term has been used to describe a number of other products.

Cooking Ware

A broad term applied to earthenware, stoneware, porcelain, and china designed for cooking or baking as well as serving. It has a smooth, glazed surface and is strong and resistant to thermal shock.

Fine China

A term applied to a thin, translucent, vitrified (fired to produce a nonporous glaze) product, generally fired at a relatively high temperature twice: first, to mature the purest of flint, clay, and flux materials; second, to develop the high gloss of the beautiful glaze. It is the highest-quality tableware made for domestic or retail trade.

Porcelain

A term used frequently in Europe for china. European porcelain, like china, is fired twice. In the United States, porcelain may be fired in a one- or two-fire process. Porcelain has a hard, nonabsorbent, strong body that is white and translucent. European porcelain is made primarily for the retail market.

Bone China

A specific type of fine china manufactured primarily in England. The body contains a high proportion of bone ash to produce greater translucency, whiteness, and strength. Like fine china, it is made primarily for the retail trade.

Restaurant China

A uniquely American blend of fine china and porcelain, designed and engineered specifically for use in commercial operations. The body was developed in the United States to give it great impact strength and durability, as well as extremely low absorption, which is required of china used in public eating places. Decorations are applied between the body and the glaze, to protect the decorations during commercial use. Most of this tableware is subject to a high temperature during its first firing and a lower temperature during its second. However, some of it is fired in a one-fire operation during which the body and glaze mature at the same time. Like fine china, American restaurant china is vitrified (fired to produce a nonporous glaze).

Source: *Questions and Answers,* American Restaurant China Council, Inc., n.d.

Since china is expensive, durability is an important selection factor. China of strong construction will last longer than china of lower quality. Commercial-quality china is available that is resistant to breaking, chipping, and scratching. Most food service operations do not use bone china because it is very expensive and very fragile. China with a rolled edge is better reinforced than china without this edge and does not chip as easily. A rolled edge distributes the force of an impact over a larger area than an unrolled edge, so it can absorb more shock than an unrolled edge.

When selecting coffee cups, managers often select thick mugs for low-check-average outlets and graceful cups with comfortable-to-hold handles and matching saucers for upscale operations. Heavy or thick china, which is most often used in fast-service operations, will hold heat more efficiently, but it is not necessarily more durable than other products. It may also make service awkward (because of its weight) and may require extra storage space.

China should be glazed, with its pattern (if any) under the glaze. To assess the durability of the china's design, managers should test samples of the china they are thinking of buying. Wise managers wash sample pieces of china many times and observe the ability of the samples to withstand standard dishwashing procedures. This helps assure managers that the china's design will not fade or become scratched easily. It can also tell them whether the china itself breaks, chips, or scratches easily.

The color and pattern of china should complement the decor and uniforms in the dining area. When colors are selected for china, managers should accent the secondary (not dominant) colors of the dining area's carpet, walls, and window treatments. Pastel colors (especially peach and mint) complement lighter, healthier foods; deep, rich, warm earth tones complement hearty ethnic cuisine.

China patterns should also complement the food that is served on the plate. Simple, clean lines are preferred in china as well as in glassware, flatware, and linens. Sometimes china is ordered with lines or bands that provide simple framing for foods. China with floral patterns can provide a soft, warm, elegant feeling. Geometric shapes on china present a bold, dramatic image. However, if an operation wants to focus maximum attention on the food served, the center of the plate should be pattern-free. Trends in china patterns include embossed rims on dinnerware; fruit motifs; and hand-painted plates.

While a pattern or logo may look fine on menus or signs, it might lose its appeal on plates or pieces of flatware. However, some managers believe that having the operation's logo or other special imprint on the china enhances the operation's image, and they are willing to pay the typically higher prices for custom-designed products. The type of design (spray-on, print, decal, or hand-decorated) also affects costs.

While the longevity of a china design's production cannot be guaranteed, managers should check with suppliers to make certain that the pattern they are considering is not on the verge of being discontinued. Even with the best storage and handling practices, breakage is likely. Because food service operations typically do not mix china patterns (use two or more patterns) in the same dining area, they must be certain that their chosen design will be available for at least the near future.

Additional purchasing considerations for china include how easy it is to clean, how well it holds heat, whether it can be used in microwave ovens, and its rim sizes. Rim sizes on china affect guest perceptions of portion size, value, and the overall presentation. China with wide rims provides maximum framing for the food served on it. Wide rims create an open, spacious feeling, since they put the greatest distance between the food and other tabletop items. Wide rims also make smaller portions appear to be larger, since they focus the guests' eyes on the food presentation. Medium-sized rims provide maximum versatility—they can be used for a formal as well as an informal food presentation. Narrow rims are ideal for larger portions. Rimless plates present foods in the plainest way; however, foods with sauces may not look as appealing on them. Additionally, when servers handle rimless china, they have little material to grip.

Managers can purchase china of almost any quality from domestic or international sources. As a result, an additional selection factor—national pride—may be important in the purchase decisions made at some operations. Although it may have only very subtle image implications for outlets in some areas, overt theft or breakage problems can arise in other areas when certain brands (or patterns) of china stir the emotions of guests or staff members.

Some upscale restaurants use service plates (base plates) to heighten the elegance of their tabletop appointments and their service. These plates frequently are works of art that are custom-designed for each operation. Generally, managers must special-order them, and they require a great deal of care and control to ensure that they are not damaged, broken, or stolen. Typically, staff members wash service plates by hand in the dining or pantry area—rarely in the kitchen's dishwashing machine.

Some restaurants purchase special china specifically for the presentation of one or two signature items from the menu. This strategy is designed to set signature menu items apart from other menu items. By the addition of a different piece of china, managers can create an illusion of serving more food more elegantly. This approach can exceed guests' expectations for food presentation. Some hotel dining rooms, searching for ways to compete with freestanding restaurants, are adding specialty salad, entrée, and dessert china in an effort to set themselves apart. When used with classic white china, a specialty china piece in a bright geometric or flowered design can highlight a signature item.

The quality of china that managers select must be compatible with that of the other service items they use. It is inconsistent and jarring to use high-quality china with low-quality glassware and flatware (or vice versa). In addition to the need for supplies of similar quality, the total presentation of serviceware, decor, staff, and food must be harmonious; china has an obvious impact on the total appearance of the dining area and must be in step with the area's other elements. Experienced managers know that the appealing presentation of food on the correct china is as important to some guests as the flavor of the food, so the size, shape, thickness, pattern, and color of an operation's china must harmonize with the dining area's atmosphere and theme.

Glassware

Many of the factors important to making purchase decisions about china also apply to the purchase of glassware. Open-stock glassware is less expensive than custom-made glassware; however, just as with china, many operations want their logos or other unique imprints on their glasses, which means the glassware must be custom-made. As is true with china, the selection of glassware has marketing implications, so the glassware must be compatible with the theme and atmosphere of the operation. As with china, breakage occurs with glassware; therefore, managers should consider replacement as well as initial purchase costs. Glassware suppliers typically offer a wide range of glassware styles (see Exhibit 6).

The type of glass in which a drink is served greatly affects its presentation. Some operations have begun to use the same style of glassware for several different beverages. This practice reduces the number of kinds of glassware that they must maintain in inventory. However, other operations like the presentation and marketing implications of fancy, special-purpose glassware and use a wide variety of styles.

Some food service operations are using creative alternatives to traditional glassware. For example, rather than serving a margarita in a traditional margarita glass, some operations are using a heavy glass mug. Other operations are using glassware as ways to feature salads, side dishes, desserts, and hot beverages. Oven-safe glassware is gaining in popularity, because it is ideal for baked custards, bread puddings, individual cobblers, and soufflés. This efficient choice uses the

Exhibit 6 Types of Glasses Available in One Family of Glassware

Courtesy of Libbey Glass

same container for preparation and service, reducing the number of dishes needed and the amount of storage space needed.

Mass-produced glassware is generally thick and may have imperfections not found in fine, expensive products. However, this type of glassware is quite acceptable in the vast majority of food service operations that consider value important. Rolled edges and rims on glasses reduce problems with chipping and cracking. Selecting glassware with thick glass and certain shapes can also reduce breakage.

Stemmed glassware is very susceptible to breakage, although some designs are harder to tip over than others. Despite its fragility, stemmed glassware should be used if operations serve certain types of beverages. A good wine glass, for example, should have a stem for guests to hold so that the heat of their hands does not affect the wine's temperature.

Some operations are choosing nontraditional wine glasses. Bowl-shaped wine glasses are popular, particularly when they are oversized and made of clear glass. Another trend is the use of colored stemmed glassware, particularly in mid-priced food service operations (this type of glassware may not be acceptable in fine-dining outlets). If managers choose colored glassware, they should make sure the stem has a color that accents the colors of plates and other tabletop items.

Many operations have begun to use shatterproof glassware. While shatterproof glasses are initially more expensive than other glasses, their long life usually results in cost savings over the long term. Shatterproof glassware helps prevent glass particles from contaminating food and beverage products and is very useful in many kitchen and bar areas.

The size of glassware is also important. Some food service operations like to use oversized glasses because they enhance the presentation possibilities and the perception of value. Consider, for example, a colorful cordial in an oversized brandy snifter, or an exotic specialty drink in a large hurricane glass. Some banquet operations use small wine glasses so that one bottle of wine will serve eight guests.

Food service operations that stress quality use crystal. To minimize breakage of expensive crystal, these operations use a racking system; staff members take crystal to and from dishwashing areas in racks to prevent crystal items from coming in contact with each other or with anything else that could cause them to break. When practical, managers should use a racking system for other types of glassware as well.

It is important for managers to think about function as well as form when purchasing glassware. Glassware must not only highlight the beverages served in it, but also withstand the rigors of handling and the dishwashing or glass-washing machine.

Flatware

Washable flatware items such as forks, knives, and spoons are typically made of stainless steel. Genuine silverware is prohibitively expensive for almost all food service operations; however, some elegant food service operations use "hotel plate" (silver-plated) flatware. Most operations prefer to use stainless steel eating utensils of good quality rather than silver-plated flatware, however, because the plating on the latter can chip and peel. In addition, commercial-grade stainless steel flatware is less expensive and more durable than silver plate; stainless steel is difficult to bend, dent, scratch, or stain; does not tarnish or rust; and does not require replating.

Managers can buy flatware in a wide range of prices and styles to suit almost any requirement. Plain flatware is more popular than patterned because it is less expensive and easier to clean. High-priced flatware generally incorporates alloys of various metals that provide greater durability, grain, and luster than low-priced flatware. A finish can be highly polished, dull, or matte. In addition to the traditional knife, fork, and spoon, a vast array of specialty flatware is available to use with such food items as butter, grapefruit, asparagus, oysters, corn on the cob, lobster, and grapes. To reduce theft, managers must carefully control flatware, especially flatware with logos or small flatware items such as demitasse spoons and corn-on-the-cob holders.

Managers should choose flatware that is balanced, has good weight, has a simple pattern (or is plain), matches their operation's style of service, and enhances guests' dining experiences. The most popular flatware today has clean, simple lines and a composition of eight percent nickel and 18 percent chrome. Flatware must be kept clean and shiny. The larger fork that is widely used in Europe is also becoming popular in the United States, because well-traveled guests expect operations to have it available.

Disposables

Some food service operations use disposable dinnerware items in their quick-service, takeout, catering, delicatessen, and other high-volume operations. **Disposables** are a useful alternative in these operations, since they cost less, are consistent with the quality of service guests desire, and allow guests to consume products off-site. They also reduce the cost of labor needed to clean dinnerware. (However, in some areas of the United States, the cost of sending used disposables to a landfill is about as much as the cost of their initial purchase.)

Because environmental degradation affects all of us and because guests and staff members are increasingly concerned about the environment, managers must also consider the ecological implications of using disposables. Managers must be certain that no environmental problems will arise and that no bad publicity or legal or other problems governing the disposal of these products will create difficulties for their operations.

In deciding whether to use disposables, managers need to calculate the different costs associated with permanent ware and disposables. But before calculating these costs, managers should ask themselves this important question: "What types of tableware do guests expect in our food service operation?" If the operation's guests clearly expect permanent ware, managers need not perform a cost analysis on using disposables; managers should only take the time and trouble to do a cost analysis when it appears that disposables are potentially appropriate or acceptable to their guests.

Of course, a wide variety of quality levels are available in disposable products. Managers should select a type of disposable plate that has minimal ink coverage and a predominantly white background; this combination reassures guests that the plate is a clean and sanitary product. If managers want disposables with a design, they might decide to choose a design that features blades of grass, birds, the sun, trees, waves, or other natural elements in order to encourage guests to not litter when they are finished with the disposables. Two-color contemporary designs with colors that complement the operation's decor add interest and brightness to food service operations. Additionally, disposables offer a fairly inexpensive way to display a logo or other distinctive design.

Uniforms

Uniforms for service staff members are an important part of the atmosphere and image of a food service operation. The range of uniform styles, designs, colors, and fabrics is almost endless. Appearance and style are important, but so are such factors as comfort, practicality, durability, and ease of maintenance.

When managers purchase uniforms, they always make trade-offs between aesthetic and practical concerns. Comfort is important because staff members must reach, lift, and stretch to do their work. Because uniform pockets are frequently used to carry pencils, guest checks, and related dining-area necessities, inside pockets are often best; they also present a more "crisp" appearance. Zippers and Velcro strips are more convenient than snaps or buttons. Belts may add to a uniform's appearance, but they are easily lost unless they are attached to the uniform in some fashion. Shoes are seldom if ever part of the uniform; however, managers should give some thought to setting basic footwear guidelines covering such variables as colors, laces, and the toes of the shoes (many operations ban open-toed shoes, for example).

Should uniforms have short or long sleeves? This question raises another criterion for selecting uniforms: safety. Short sleeves can contribute to burn and splash problems. Conversely, long sleeves can get in the way as servers use their arms and can also brush serviceware, food, or heating units, causing sanitation and safety problems. There is no clear-cut answer to the short-sleeves-versus-long-sleeves dilemma that will apply to all operations.

When selecting uniforms, managers should get samples from suppliers and ask staff members of all shapes and sizes to try them on. A uniform can look very attractive on some staff members and most unattractive on others; managers should try to find a uniform that makes *all* staff members look good. Managers should also try to find uniforms that staff members can wear year-round. With air conditioning, year-round uniforms are seldom a problem. Managers should involve staff members in the process of selecting uniforms; they are more likely to accept uniforms that they helped select. If staff members like their uniforms and are comfortable in them, they are likelier to have a positive attitude about their work. If they do not like their uniforms, their feelings can have a negative effect on their attitudes and work habits.

Custom-designed uniforms can reflect a unique image that a food service operation wishes to portray; however, the cost of such uniforms can be excessive. Custom designs take a great deal of time to produce for both initial orders and reorders. On the other hand, customized accessories such as special belts, hats, or scarves and neckties can make open-stock uniforms "special" and create the illusion that they have been customized.

High personnel turnover rates in food service operations generally require the ready availability of a wide range of uniform sizes. Therefore, operations often purchase a large number of uniforms of the most common sizes.

The initial purchase price of uniforms can be significant. Managers should also consider maintenance and replacement costs as they make their selection. Proper laundering is important to the longevity and appearance of uniforms. Uniforms made of permanent-press or other synthetic fabrics should last for a long time if they receive the proper care.

Managers should carefully keep track of uniforms during their distribution, use, and storage. Some food service managers in operations that take care of laundering staff member uniforms suggest that the most satisfactory method of controlling uniforms is to require staff members to turn in a soiled uniform in exchange for a clean one. While further control details are beyond the scope of this chapter, managers should keep in mind that they will incur excessive costs if they do not maintain strict control over uniforms.

Napery

Fabric tablecloths and napkins (napery) must be compatible with the operation's design and atmosphere. When managers select napery, they must consider quality requirements. Seasoned managers recommend maintaining a wide selection of colored napery to accommodate the varied decor requirements of banquet guests.

Many managers who undertake cost studies find that on-site laundry facilities would reduce their operating costs. However, managers must be sure to maintain the proper quality of finished linens in the dining area. Sometimes special procedures and specialized cleaning compounds are needed to remove food and beverage stains. Using linens that contain stains is unacceptable. Some napkin folds require very heavy starch that on-site laundries often find difficult to process.

Many operations today choose striped or plaid linens. Above all, managers should select appropriate colors for linens (see Exhibit 7). Linens should also feel good to the user. Cotton and cotton blends are less scratchy and have less of a tendency to slide off guests' laps than synthetics; they are preferred for napkins. Half-polyester tablecloths are becoming more popular. A trend in napkin colors is toward deep yellow, cobalt blue, and dark red, presented on a simple white tablecloth. These colors complement ethnic cuisine well.

Furniture

Dining area furniture can help create almost any atmosphere the designer wishes the area to have. However, dining area furniture can be very expensive. Managers must purchase furniture in a price range that fits their operation's budget, while keeping in mind guest expectations, the operation's image, and the need for quality.

When selecting furniture, managers should remember that the comfort of guests is one of the most important factors to consider. (This statement does not apply to quick-service operations such as McDonald's, which use uncomfortable seats to encourage fast guest turnover.) The elbow room at tables and the amount of space between tables and chairs are important concerns. When some interior designers select the furniture for a dining area, they allow concerns about the ambiance and decor of the facility to have precedence over guest preferences. This should never happen; compatibility with the decor should always take second place to guest comfort. Other factors to consider when selecting furniture include available space and the aisle widths required by fire codes.

Wood is perhaps the most commonly used material in dining area furniture. Wood is strong, rigid, and able to resist wear and stains. Metals, including aluminum, steel, and brass, are also becoming popular in dining areas, as are plastics,

Exhibit 7 Color Choices for Linens

Colors have meanings, according to Bibb Hospitality and Leatrice Eiseman, a color specialist the firm hired to select appropriate colors for its line of linens. Here's what they mean:

Brown: The number one association is the deliciousness of chocolate, followed by earthy, rich-warm, woodsy, durable, and rugged connotations.

Beige and Taupe: These are among the most classic of neutrals; they are thought of as soft, warm, earthy, sophisticated basic colors that withstand time and trends.

Pink and Dusty Rose: The ultimate colors of romance; in the lighter tints, associated with sweet scents and sweet tastes. They are seen as soft, soothing, cozy, subtle, classic, and romantic.

Red: Red is always the most stimulating, dramatic, high-energy and happy color. In bright reds and fuchsias, it is often associated with ethnic themes. Berries and burgundies are always associated with wine and are seen as elegant, rich, refined, and classic.

Blue: Shades of blue vary in mood, depending on their intensity. Light to medium blues are calming, restful, fresh, and cool; deep blues are seen as traditional, service-oriented, credible, and classic. Brighter electric blues are as exciting and energetic as red. Teal is seen as the most upscale blue, uniquely pleasing and rich.

Orange: Orange is the hottest of all hues. In the deeper terra cotta shades, orange tones are closely associated with earth or ethnic themes—welcoming, wholesome, country looks. In the lighter values of peach or apricot, it is perceived as sweet, delicious, luscious, inviting, and appealing. The brighter values are happy and playful.

Yellow: Light yellows are seen as mellow, appetizing, lemony, soft, sunny, warm, happy, and sweet, while bright yellows are more luminous and create a cheerful atmosphere. Golden amber yellows and ochers are more closely associated with earth.

Purple: Lavenders are associated with flowers and sweet tastes—soft, delicate, and nostalgic; orchid is more exotic and tropical. Bright purple is flamboyant, sensual, and exciting, while deep-plum purples are seen as expensive, regal, powerful, spiritual, and artistic.

Gray: Gray is the timeless color—a cool classic, always thought of as a quality look. The deeper values are viewed as sophisticated.

White: The essence of purity, white is pristine, airy, cool, and clean. The human eye sees white as brilliant. Cream is a much warmer version of white; it is associated with sweet, smooth, rich tastes—a classic neutral.

Black: Black is the quintessential expression of elegance—basic, bold, dramatic, sophisticated, and, at the same time, magical and mysterious.

Green: Green is the color of leafy, healthy growth; light to medium greens are cool, rich, traditional, and classic. The green to avoid for food service is bright chartreuse—the color of nausea. Blue-greens are the most pleasant, both aesthetically and emotionally—refreshing, cooling, and soothing.

Source: Adapted from John Sanger, "Setting the Course," *Club Management*, July–August 1993, p. 45.

fiberglass, and vinyl. Wood and glass tabletops with metal bases are examples of how manufacturers can use different materials to make attractive, functional furniture. If an operation uses placemats or runners rather than tablecloths, its managers must give careful attention to the tabletops they select. Materials used for tabletops should be easy to clean and long-wearing.

Managers must also make decisions about table size and shape. In general, the table sizes managers are choosing are getting smaller. Tables must match the chairs and provide the proper height between the tabletop and the seat base (usually 30 inches [76 centimeters]). When selecting tables, managers should keep in mind that guests are often more comfortable seated at tables with pedestals rather than legs.

Choosing a variety of table shapes and sizes enhances the dining area's appearance and helps the staff accommodate various group sizes—as long as the shapes and sizes are compatible with each other. For example, if the operation's two-top tables (the term **"top"** is used in the industry to represent a guest; a "two-top" table seats two guests) were the same width as its four-top tables, staff members could combine a two-top and a four-top to accommodate a party of six guests. Of course, when staff members put tables together in this manner, they must ensure the tables are stable. Staff members also need to be certain that no "valley" is created between the two tables when they are placed together, forming an uneven surface where glasses might tip or plates rock.

Round tables frequently have drop sides that make the tables square when the sides are down. Staff members can put the sides up to accommodate large groups when necessary.

Folding tables are essential for banquets and meetings, and they can be purchased in many shapes and sizes. These tables should be easily movable and stackable for convenient storage. Folding tables often have padded tops so that tablecloths can be placed directly on them. However, improper handling during setup and breakdown can damage these pads.

All chairs should be durable, easy to clean, and appropriate for the existing decor. If managers select chairs that contain fabric, they should be aware of potential fire hazards. Some furniture is made of fabrics that burn more quickly than others; some fabrics resist burning but will smolder and give off dangerous fumes. Also, some fabrics wear more slowly and resist stains better than others. When selecting fabric-covered chairs, managers should check to see whether the fabric has been treated with a fire retardant and a stain-resistant or waterproof solution. Because synthetic fabrics can cause perspiration and discomfort, operations with low guest turnover (that is, at which guests spend a relatively long period of time seated at their tables) should not use chairs made with synthetic fabrics.

Some chairs are designed more for fashion than for safety or comfort. Therefore, managers should be careful when selecting chairs and avoid choosing chairs, for example, with chair backs and legs that stick too far out into traffic aisles and might trip guests and staff members. Also, managers should select rigidly constructed chairs with bracing; this can prevent breakage and possible injury to guests. These suggestions apply no matter what type of chair managers select, including stackable or lightweight chairs.

While chairs with arms may be the most comfortable from the guest's perspective, they are likely to take up more space than chairs without arms. At round tables, many operations use chairs with arms. Typically, tables and chairs used for banquets must withstand a great deal of wear and tear; therefore, strength and durability should be central concerns when managers develop purchase specifications for them.

Equipment

Food service personnel must use a wide range of equipment items that perform such specialized jobs as making ice or holding food at its proper temperature until it is served.[1] In the following sections we will mention just a few of the most commonly used items:

- Holding tables
- Coffee urns and makers
- Refrigerators and freezers
- Ice machines
- Dishwashing machines

Holding Tables. Holding tables (also called "food warmers" or "steam tables") keep food hot until it is served. They should never be used as a substitute for fast and efficient service, since food that is kept hot for excessive periods of time generally deteriorates in quality and guest appeal. Holding tables are particularly important in operations serving banquets, buffets, and catering functions. While many models are manufactured and available for purchase, four main categories of holding tables exist: cabinet food warmers, hot-food tables, pot warmers, and radiant warmers.

Cabinet food warmers include mobile food-warming carts and food-warming drawers. In many models, either moist heat or dry heat can be used. Some cabinet food warmers are used to display foods for merchandising purposes, particularly if they contain Ferris wheels, rotisseries, or turntables to keep the food items within them in motion. Lighting is frequently added to further enhance the visual appeal of the food display. Portable cabinet food warmers are either hand-carried or moved on casters. They may be heated by electricity or simply keep food hot through insulation or by canned, gel-type fuel. These warmers are ideal for banquets and off-site catering.

Hot-food tables are popular choices for buffets and use either moist heat (steam tables with *bains marie* or water baths) or dry heat (dry-well hot-food tables). Some dry-well hot-food tables can also be used to produce moist heat by placing water in the wells and then placing containers of food in the water.

Some of the following sections on food service equipment were adapted (without citations) from David M. Stipanuk and Harold Roffmann's *Hospitality Facilities Management and Design* (East Lansing, Mich.: Educational Institute of the American Hotel & Motel Association, 1992), pp. 247–259.

InterTrade (http://www.itrade.net) provides an electronic commerce system designed specifically for food service operations and their suppliers. InterTrade's site includes a broad range of business-to-business resources and some suppliers' online catalogs; many suppliers also have their own Internet sites. (Courtesy of InterTrade Systems Corporation, 26 June 1998)

Pot warmers heat by conduction and can be pot-shaped (hence the name) or rectangular or square in shape. They are used to keep chili, soups, sauces, and certain ice cream toppings hot. A feature many operations prefer is a removable stainless steel insert that allows easy access and cleaning. Pot warmers are ideal for displays of hot foods at self-service buffets and may be recessed into tabletops to prevent them from being bumped and tipped over.

Radiant warmers heat food by radiation, using infrared energy provided by alloy, ceramic, or quartz strips or infrared bulbs. These warmers are used for food pickup stations in the kitchen, for buffets in the dining area, or for plating stations. Adjustable radiant warmers, often on tracks, can be focused where the heat is needed most.

Coffee Urns and Makers. A **coffee urn** is a non-pressure-vented water tank heated by electric immersion heaters, gas burners, or steam coils and controlled by a thermostat and relay. Coffee urns range in capacity from 2 to 125 gallons (8 to 473 liters) and have faucets for easy pouring.

Coffee makers are automatic or semiautomatic units that make coffee and dispense it into a coffeepot or into individual cups. Coffee makers are often used when relatively small quantities of coffee are needed, because the quantity and quality of the coffee can be more effectively controlled.

Refrigerators and Freezers. Refrigerators and freezers are used to maintain the quality of stored food. They preserve the color, texture, flavor, and nutritional value of food items by keeping them chilled or frozen. Refrigerators and freezers range from cabinet models and reach-in units to large walk-in units.

Cabinet models are small refrigerators or freezers that are located on or under countertops right at a kitchen workstation or dining room side station to keep food handy for food preparers or servers.

Pass-through and reach-in refrigerators with glass doors are used in some food service operations to store prepared food such as salads and desserts. Staff members can then take food items from the refrigerators and serve them as guests order them, or the guests may serve themselves (in cafeterias, for example). To reduce staff member trips to walk-in refrigerators (which are usually outside the kitchen area), operations use reach-ins in kitchens to store some food.

Typical upright reach-ins are 78 to 84 inches (198 to 213 centimeters) high and 32 inches (81 centimeters) deep. They commonly come with one, two, or three doors. A one-door unit would be about 28 inches (71 centimeters) wide; a three-door, 84 inches (213 centimeters). Doors are usually self-closing.

Walk-in refrigerators and freezers provide food storage away from the production areas of a kitchen and allow managers to buy food in large quantities, keeping costly deliveries to a minimum. Walk-ins should be installed to make the delivery of food and the movement of food from the walk-ins to production areas as convenient as possible.

Walk-ins are typically built from prefabricated modular panels. Panel sizes vary, and walk-ins can be custom-built. A typical unit measures 8 feet by 12 feet (2.4 meters by 3.7 meters).

A walk-in can be an integral part of a building or a prefabricated room installed in sections within a larger room. Walk-ins can be built outside the building as well. In some cases, outdoor units are installed right next to the main building with a connecting door between them; a door on a different wall is used for deliveries. This saves interior space and allows deliveries to be made easily, without disrupting the normal staff member traffic flow.

Since the ideal storage temperatures for food items vary, an operation may have more than one walk-in. For example, a large operation may have a walk-in refrigerator for vegetables, one for meats, and one for dairy items, as well as a walk-in freezer for frozen items.

Ice Machines. Ice machines make cubed, crushed, or flaked ice. They can be floor models or mounted on a wall. Capacities range from 20 to 800 pounds (9 to 360 kilograms) of ice per day. Machines that allow the first ice made to be the first ice dispensed are desirable. So are machines designed to allow staff members to run cleaning solutions through them during periodic maintenance.

For very large operations, there are machines that make ice in block or bulk form; the ice must then be chipped or crushed. The capacities in these machines run from 40 to 4,000 pounds (18 to 1,800 kilograms) of ice per day.

Dishwashing Machines. Although service personnel do not operate dishwashing machines, they are involved in returning tableware to dishwashing areas and depend on dishwashing machines for clean tableware. There are other types of warewashing machines besides dishwashers—pot and pan, glass, tray, and silverware washers to name a few. But dishwashers are the most commonly used, and we will focus our discussion on them.

When managers must purchase a dishwashing machine, they should take the following factors into account:

- How well the machine cleans and sanitizes ware
- The average and maximum volumes of ware to be washed
- The number of staff members management wants to dedicate to warewashing
- The cost of detergents and other chemicals
- The amount and shape of available floor space
- Budgetary considerations

A dishwashing machine is a long-term investment. Managers should look at the machine they are considering in light of the operation's business volume forecasts and marketing plan. If the operation plans on significant growth and the budget permits it, managers may want to choose a machine that can handle more volume than the operation is now generating. That way, as the operation grows, managers will not need to purchase a new machine too soon.

In the following sections we will briefly discuss door-type, conveyor, flight-type, and energy-saving dishwashers.

Door-type. A **door-type dishwasher**—also called a "single-tank" or "stationary-rack" dishwasher—has a tank holding a solution of heated wash water and detergent. This solution is circulated through spray nozzles above and below the dishes. As with most dishwashers, water for washing is at 140°F to 160°F (60°C to 71°C). Rinse water is circulated through the same spray nozzles. To kill bacteria, rinse water is heated to 180°F (82°C) with a booster heater (most tap water only reaches 140°F to 160°F [60°C to 71°C]). Dishes are placed on racks for cleaning; these racks remain stationary throughout the washing process. Doors may be on one or more sides.

Conveyor. With **conveyor dishwashers,** racks of dishes are placed on a conveyor belt that carries the dishes through the machine. These dishwashers have curtains rather than doors. At one end, a staff member loads the racks of soiled dishes into the machine; after going through the cleaning cycle, the dishes are automatically pushed out onto the clean-dish table at the other end, eliminating the need for a staff member to open a door and manually remove the racks.

The simplest conveyor dishwasher has one tank of hot wash water. After the dishes are washed, they remain in place for the final rinse. In a two-tank machine, the dishes are washed, then moved down the line to a second tank to be rinsed. A

Exhibit 8 Diagram of a Flight-Type Dishwasher

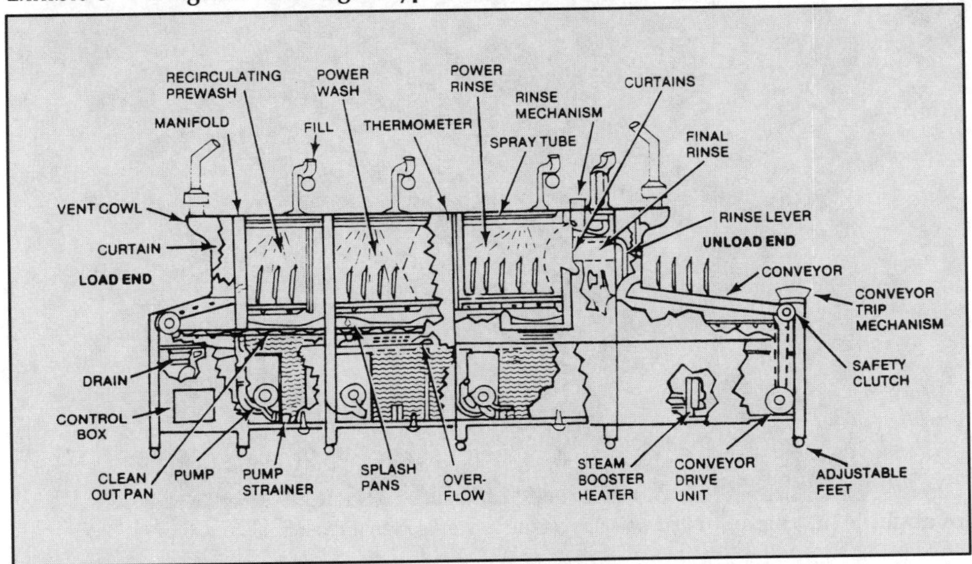

Source: Robert A. Modlin, ed., *Commercial Kitchens*, 7th ed. (Arlington, Virginia: American Gas Association, 1989), p. 259.

three-tank machine has a tank for rinsing off food remaining on the dishes before they are moved to the wash tank and then to the rinse tank. Obviously, the more tanks a conveyor dishwasher has, the longer and more expensive it is.

Flight-type. In **flight-type dishwashers,** the conveyor is not a belt upon which dish racks are placed; the conveyor itself acts as one continuous rack because it is made up of pegs on stainless steel bars (see Exhibit 8). Plates, pans, and trays are placed between the pegs; cups, glasses, and flatware still have to be racked, however. Flight-type dishwashers are built to handle very large dishwashing demands. They are typically used in large commercial or institutional operations that serve more than 1,000 guests per meal.

Energy-saving. In the early 1970s a new type of dishwasher was developed—the low-temperature or **energy-saving dishwasher.** These dishwashers come in door-type and single-tank conveyor models. Whereas conventional dishwashers sanitize dishes by heating rinse water to 180°F (82°C), energy-saving dishwashers use water heated to 120°F to 140°F (49°C to 60°C) and sanitize dishes with a chemical (usually chlorine).

High-Tech Equipment

Advances in technology have helped food service operations become more productive and improve service to guests. Three "high-tech" pieces of equipment used by many food service operations are **point-of-sale (POS) systems,** hand-held terminals, and pagers.

An example of a menu board overlay. (Courtesy of National Cash Register Corporation)

POS Systems. POS systems help food service operations take guest orders and process sales transactions more efficiently. Guest check totals, including taxes and service charges where applicable, are calculated automatically, and payments by credit, debit, or "smart" card can be processed quickly. (A "smart card" is similar to a credit card and is used in much the same way; however, unlike a credit card, a smart card contains a microprocessor that can read, store, and transfer information.) In addition, POS terminals throughout an operation can be interfaced with food production areas (especially printers in these areas) and managerial and accounting programs to allow quick, accurate transfer of data.

A **cashier terminal** is a POS device that is connected to a cash drawer. A POS terminal without a cash drawer is commonly called a **precheck terminal.** Precheck terminals are used to enter orders, not to settle accounts. For example, a server can use a precheck terminal located in a dining room side station to relay guest orders to the appropriate kitchen and bar production areas, but cannot use the terminal to settle guest checks. Cashier terminals can be used both for check settlement and for order entry.

POS order-entry devices consist of keyboards and monitors. The two primary types of keyboard surfaces are micro-motion and reed style. The micro-motion keyboard design has a flat, waterproof surface, while the reed keyboard design has waterproof keys raised above the surface of the keyboard. More important than the physical design of the keyboard is the number of hard and soft keys the keyboard provides. **Hard keys** are dedicated to specific functions programmed by the manufacturer. **Soft keys** can be programmed by managers to meet their operations' specific needs.

Both keyboard design types can usually support interchangeable menu boards. A **menu board** overlays the keyboard surface and identifies the function performed by each key during the specified meal period. Managers can work with manufacturers to develop the menu boards that will be most useful for their operations.

Touch-screen technology, light pens, card readers, and computer mouse input devices are increasingly popular as input devices for POS systems. With touch-screen terminals, a microprocessor inside a monitor displays "buttons" or graphical representations of functions on the screen. Touching one of the sensitized screen areas produces an electronic impulse that is translated into digital signals that activate programs or make an entry. Staff members can also use a light pen to activate programs or make entries.

Some quick-service operations have installed countertop-recessed touch-screen terminals that guests can use to place orders without interacting with staff members. This new self-service option may improve the accuracy with which guests' special requests and substitutions are transmitted to production staff. It can also reduce labor costs and speed up service, and guests may enjoy the interactivity these systems afford. Overall service may improve as service staff members are freed to focus on guest service.

The digital capture of signatures is also becoming common on precheck POS terminals. Guests sign for payment, whether for checks or credit cards, on a pressure-sensitive pad that "captures" the signature as a digital image that can be stored on disk or verified. Exhibit 9 shows the screen of one signature capture program. Some operations maintain databases of digitized guest photographs to verify guest identities for payment purposes. Such applications can help reduce fraud and problems with overdrawn checks.

Hand-Held Terminals. Hand-held terminals reduce unproductive time spent by service staff, particularly during busy meal periods. These terminals help make POS systems mobile. As soon as a server takes an order with a hand-held terminal at a guest's table, the order can be transmitted to the kitchen. Hand-held terminals avoid the wait associated with having servers walk handwritten guest checks to the kitchen (in operations with manual systems) or input orders from an insufficient number of fixed terminal workstations. Hand-held terminals can also free servers to spend more time with guests.

Hand-held terminals may weigh less than one pound (0.45 kilograms) and are battery powered. Some models use buttons; others are activated by using a pen or fingers to touch their screens. Hand-held terminals permit two-way communication between servers and production staff, making it easier for production staff to inform servers when a menu item has been "86'd" (**86** in food service jargon means the kitchen has run out of a menu item). These terminals work very well with food service operations that have heavy rush periods, long distances between the dining area and kitchen or bar, or reduced server staffs (since the terminals improve productivity). Some hand-held terminals have been improved by adding built-in credit card readers and signature capture features.

Electronic Pocket Pagers. First introduced to inform servers when their orders were ready for pickup in the kitchen, **electronic pocket pagers** are now also being used to inform guests when their tables are ready in the dining area. When guests arrive at an operation and their table is not yet ready, they can be given a pocket

Exhibit 9 Sample Screen of a Signature Capture Program

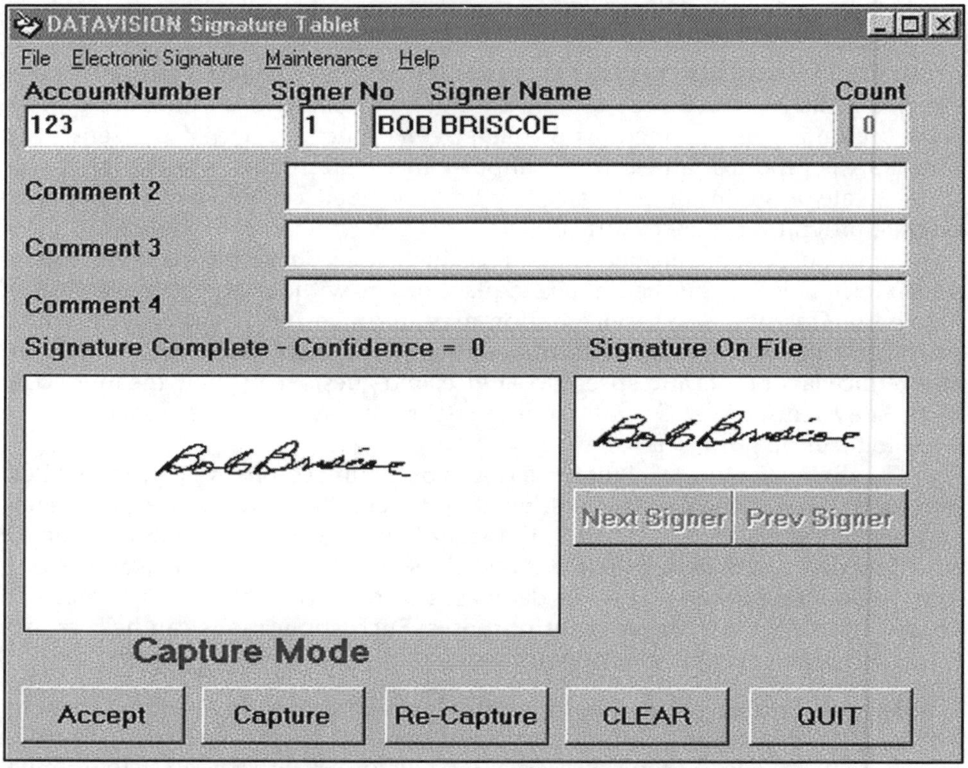

Courtesy of DATAVISION Corporation (http://www.datavisionimage.com), 29 June 1998

pager. When the table is ready, the manager, host, or hostess telephones the guest's pager number. The pager alerts the guest with a beeping sound or a vibration.

Pocket pagers eliminate the confusion caused by difficult-to-hear public address (PA) systems in crowded operations. By reducing the time it takes to seat guests, pagers speed guest turnover. Pagers also eliminate the need to search for guests when tables are ready, and avoid inaccurate pronunciations of guests' names over a PA system. Guests are free to visit the bar or lounge area and even shop nearby or walk around the grounds of the operation while waiting for their table. Some operations report that once guests register with the host or hostess and are given a pager, they are less likely to leave and go to another operation for their dining. To avoid losing pagers, some operations ask guests to leave a credit card, deposit, or driver's license as security when they are issued a pager. The name and address of the operation should be written on the pager so that if guests accidentally take the pagers home, they can return them in person or by mail.

Pager signals have ranges of 100 feet to two miles; the strength of the signal can be adjusted on some models. Pagers that vibrate are a great way to communicate with guests who have hearing impairments. Some pagers are waterproof and come with reinforced clips. Pagers operate with batteries that need to be recharged or replaced, depending on the model. Managers should learn about and evaluate any model's features before purchasing pagers of that model in quantity.

Key Terms

cashier terminal—An electronic point-of-sale device that is connected to a cash drawer.

coffee maker—An automatic or semiautomatic machine that makes coffee and dispenses it into a coffee pot or into individual cups.

coffee urn—A non-pressure-vented water tank heated by electric immersion heaters, gas burners, or steam coils, and controlled by a thermostat and relay.

conveyor dishwasher—A dishwashing machine in which racks of dishes are placed on a conveyor belt that moves the dishes through the machine.

custom-made items—Supply items (such as china) that are designed specifically for one food service operation and are available only from the supplier that designed them.

disposables—Disposable dishes, cups, flatware, and other supply items; usually made of paper or plastic.

door-type dishwasher—A dishwashing machine in which a rack or racks of dishes remain stationary while heated wash and rinse water is sprayed from nozzles above and below the dishes. Also called a single-tank or stationary-rack dishwasher.

86—A food service code that indicates that the kitchen has run out of a menu item.

electronic pocket pager—A pocket-sized electronic device used to page people or to send them short messages.

energy-saving dishwasher—A dishwashing machine that uses a chemical (usually chlorine) to sanitize dishes, thereby saving the energy other dishwashing machines require to heat rinse water to 180°F (82°C) for sanitization.

flight-type dishwasher—A dishwashing machine in which dishes are placed on a conveyor made of pegs or bars and are moved through several washing and rinsing chambers.

hand-held terminal—Wireless server terminal, also called a "portable server terminal"; performs most of the functions of a precheck terminal and sometimes some account settlement functions; enables servers to enter orders at tableside.

hard keys—Keys on an electronic point-of-sale device that are dedicated to specific functions programmed by the manufacturer.

holding table—An appliance that keeps food hot until it is served. Also called a "food warmer" or "steam table."

invoice—A supplier's transaction statement containing the names and addresses of both the buyer and the seller, the date of the transaction, the terms, the methods of shipment, quantities, descriptions, and prices of the goods.

issuing—The control point at which food products are released from storage; issuing controls ensure that products are only released to authorized staff members in proper quantities.

menu board—A keyboard overlay for an electronic point-of-sale device that identifies the function performed by each key during a specific meal period.

napery—Table linens such as tablecloths and napkins.

open-stock items—Supply items (such as china) that are of manufacturer brands that are available from more than one supplier.

par inventory (stock) level—The standard number of a particular inventory item that must be on hand to support daily operations.

perpetual inventory—A system of tracking inventory that records all additions to and subtractions from stock as they occur and provides a running balance of the quantity and cost of merchandise in inventory.

physical inventory—A count of items in storage.

point-of-sale (POS) system—A network of electronic cash registers and order-entry devices capable of capturing data at point-of-sale locations.

precheck terminal—An electronic point-of-sale device without a cash drawer, used to enter orders and transfer them to food and beverage production areas, but not to settle accounts.

purchase order—A form used for maintaining purchasing control. It contains the details of an order for food or other supplies that is prepared by an operation's purchasing staff and submitted to suppliers. A copy is retained to facilitate in-house recordkeeping.

purchase record—A detailed record of all incoming shipments from suppliers.

receiving—A critical control point at which ownership of products is transferred from the supplier to the operation. The receiving function involves checking the quality, quantity, and price of the incoming purchased products.

re-order point—The inventory level at which a particular item must be re-ordered to bring supplies back to par.

requisition—A written order identifying the type, amount, and value of items needed from storage.

soft keys—Keys on an electronic point-of-sale device that can be programmed by users to meet the specific needs of their operations.

standard purchase specification form—A form staff members can use to record purchasing guidelines that precisely define the quality, quantity, and other characteristics desired for particular supply and equipment items.

top—A term used in the food service industry (when referring to tables) to represent a guest; a "six-top" table is a table that seats six guests.

Review Questions

1. What are some important considerations when purchasing supplies and equipment?
2. What types of forms are involved in the processes of purchasing, receiving, and issuing items, and what is the function of each?
3. What role do par inventory levels and re-order points play in an inventory maintenance system?
4. What are the primary control concerns for food service supplies and equipment, and how do operations typically address them?
5. What do purchasers look for when selecting china, glassware, flatware, and disposables for a food service operation?
6. What do purchasers look for when selecting uniforms, napery, furniture, and equipment for a food service operation?
7. What "high-tech" devices are particularly useful in food service operations, and what are their capabilities?

Internet Sites

For more information, visit the following Internet sites. Remember that Internet addresses can change without notice.

Ann Arbor Dinnerware Exchange and Oneida Ltd.
http://www.aadinex.com

The Chef's Store
http://www.AveryKitchenSupply.com/chef

Commercial Food Equipment Service Association (CFESA)
http://www.cfesa.com

DATAVISION Corporation (signature capture technology)
http://www.datavisionimage.com

The Delfield Company (equipment manufacturer)
http://www.delfield.com

Gasser Chair Company, Inc.
http://www.gasserchair.com

Grant Madison (serviceware supplier)
http://www.eden.com/~gmadison/index.htm

Hospitality Financial & Technology Professionals
http://www.hftp.org

Hospitality Industry Technology Exposition and Conference (HITEC)
http://www.hitecshow.org

Hospitality Info Technology Association
http://www.hita.co.uk

Hospitality News
http://bizpubs.corp.com

Hotelier Magazine
http://www.foodservice.ca/hotelier/hotel.htm

HotelsWeb Interactive (searchable database of suppliers)
http://www.hotelsweb.com

International Food Service Executives Association (IFSEA)
http://www.ifsea.org

InterTrade Systems Corporation
http://www.itrade.net

Jet-Tech (warewasher manufacturer)
http://www.jet-tech.com

Micros (POS systems)
http://www.micros.com

National Restaurant Association
http://www.restaurant.org

NRN (*Nation's Restaurant News*) Online
http://www.nrn.com

Restaurants.com (links to yellow pages for international suppliers)
http://www.restaurants.com

Room Service Depot
http://www.valflo.com/roomservice.html

Server Products
http://www.server-products.com

Servolift Eastern Corporation
http://www.servolift.com

Smart Card Forum
http://www.smartcrd.com

Society of American Silversmiths
http://www.silversmithing.com

Supply and Equipment Foodservice Alliance
http://www.itrade.net/company/pub/sefa/buscntr.htm

References

Burke, Brenda. "Shopping for POS." *Lodging,* November 1997.

Carper, James. "Products for a More Productive Waitstaff." *HOTELS,* September 1993.

Cheney, Karen. "Set a Sensational Tabletop." *Restaurants & Institutions,* October 15, 1993.

Durocher, Joseph. "Flatware." *Restaurant Business,* October 10, 1992.

———. "Intimate Details." *Restaurant Business,* June 10, 1993.

Kasavana, Michael L., and John J. Cahill. *Managing Computers in the Hospitality Industry.* East Lansing, Mich.: Educational Institute of the American Hotel & Motel Association, 1997.

Liberson, Judy. "Cooking in Style." *Lodging,* October 1997.

———. "Form and Function." *Lodging,* April 1997.

———. "Functional Multi-Purpose Equipment." *Lodging,* November 1997.

———. "More with Less." *Lodging,* April 1998.

———. "Serving Up Technology." *Lodging,* June 1998.

Lorenzini, Beth. "High-Tech Touches Make Service Shine." *Restaurants & Institutions,* May 6, 1992.

Mannix, Margaret. "Checkout Tech." *U.S. News and World Report,* February 27, 1995.

National Restaurant Association. "1995 Foodservice Industry Forecast." *Restaurants USA,* December 1994.

Ninemeier, Jack D. *Planning and Control for Food and Beverage Operations.* Lansing, Mich.: Educational Institute of the American Hotel & Motel Association, 1998.

Patterson, Patt. "Turn Up the Heat on Your Food Warmer Search." *Nation's Restaurant News,* December 13, 1993.

"The Perfect Pager." Promotional brochure by Signologies.

Rogers, Monica. "Cashless Operations Get Smart." *Restaurants & Institutions,* November 1, 1993.

Sanger, John. "Setting the Course." *Club Management,* July–August 1993.

Stipanuk, David M., and Harold Roffmann. *Hospitality Facilities Management and Design.* East Lansing, Mich.: Educational Institute of the American Hotel & Motel Association, 1996.

"Take a New Look at Your Tabletop." *SYSCO's Menus Today,* July 1994.

Thompson, Pamela Kleibrink. "A New Page in Customer Service." *Restaurants USA,* September 1993.

Case Studies

Supplies Surprise

"Waitress! Waitress!"

"Yes, sir, may I help you?" Sara asked.

"Take a look at the streaks on my glass. You expect me to drink out of this?"

"No, sir, of course not. I'm very sorry, I'll get you a new one as soon as I can," Sara assured the guest. As soon as I get one from the dishroom that isn't stained with lipstick, broken, or too hot to handle, she thought to herself as she hurried away.

• • •

Leroy Rader had been the general manager of Pete's Eats, an independent, mid-scale family restaurant, for a little over a year. The restaurant had recently doubled the size of its banquet facility and had purchased divider walls so smaller parties could be accommodated for banquets simultaneously.

The new banquet room had been open about a month. Leroy had purchased as many new place settings for the banquet room as the owner would allow—which was not enough, in Leroy's opinion. But the owner had told him that the expansion itself had been over budget and that money for new tableware would be limited. Purchases would also have to be minimized for both the dining room and the banquet room for the next few months. Leroy and his assistant manager Eric told each other, "It will just have to do." They consoled themselves with the fact that the tableware would be the same for both facilities, so there would be no danger of mismatching them. They would be able to use reserves from one to cover shortfalls in the other, if necessary.

So far, operations had run fairly smoothly. The dining room had been full for hours on the evening of Valentine's Day, but with only modest banquet bookings that night, Pete's Eats had handled the volume adequately. Tonight, though, the first large banquet was scheduled: a 100-person awards banquet. But the dining room was drawing some attention of its own.

• • •

Leroy looked out across the dining room. It was only 6:15 P.M., and the operation was much busier than anyone had expected. That's weird, thought Leroy. Forecasts called for only an average night. A waiting line was forming and the lounge was filling up.

"Mr. Rader, we're bussing tables as quickly as possible," said Zeke, the senior busperson in the dining room, "but we're not getting clean dishes soon enough."

"What are you running out of the most?"

"Glasses," answered Zeke. "And the ones we're getting are—well, I'm telling the other bussers to look them over carefully before they set them."

"Good," said Leroy. "I'll go talk to Stan in the dishroom." Leroy popped in the dishroom and asked Stan how he was doing. Then he asked Stan to put the glasses through the dishwashing machine a little faster than usual.

"I usually send racks through only three-quarters full," said Stan, "but I'll start sending them through half full. If we had the right kind of racks, the glasses wouldn't break as much."

"See what you can do to send glasses through faster without breaking any. We're short on those tonight. How are the dishes coming through?"

Stan said, "Okay, I guess. I know that some have been coming through dirty, but bussers have been bugging me for more and more, so I haven't had time to look at them as closely as I usually do."

Leroy thanked Stan for the hard work. Why are we so short on settings? he thought. And so early in the evening? Even with a full banquet room, we shouldn't be so short. Leroy thought about how the chef had approached him earlier that week and asked about renting supplies for tonight because of the large banquet. Leroy and Eric had talked about it and decided it wouldn't be necessary; with only an average night in the dining room, theyshould be able to handle a large banquet. Better see how the banquet room captain is doing, thought Leroy.

His conversation with the banquet room captain turned up part of the explanation. The full-house banquet had started on schedule with 60 settings to spare—due to a little bit of hoarding by banquet servers—and those were vanishing fast as dining room buspersons brought them to the dining room. Still, 60 settings is not that much extra, thought Leroy.

"Mr. Rader, I've got two guests who would like to speak with you," Sara said out of the corner of her mouth as she moved past Leroy, carrying a platter to a lone diner. "Ooo, please be careful, that plate is hot, ma'am," she told her guest. She turned back to Leroy. "The two guests are over here, Mr. Rader." Sara nodded toward a nearby table.

"Hi, I'm Leroy, the general manager. How can I help you folks tonight?"

"It's like this," growled the male guest. "I was just eating my chicken parmigiana and I found a piece of something fishy stuck to my plate underneath the noodles."

"Something fishy, sir?"

"Yeah, I can't tell what it is, but it smells like fish. What are you trying to push on us?"

"I'm very sorry, sir. I'll see to it that you get a new meal as soon as possible, and this one's on the house."

"Excuse me, Mr. Rader?" Mike, a server, was at Leroy's elbow.

"Please excuse me," Leroy told the guests. "What is it, Mike?" he asked.

"The group at 14 is complaining about chipped plates and dirty glasses. I brought them new ones, but those weren't much better."

"Don't worry, I'll handle it, Mike," Leroy said as he started to head for that table.

"Leroy?"

Leroy turned and found himself face-to-face with Eric. "I need to talk to you, *now,*" Eric said. Eric was obviously upset.

Leroy told Eric he'd be with him in a minute. He talked with the guests at table 14, then returned to Eric. "What's up?"

"The dirty dishes are showing up because Stan is having to push racks through faster than the machine normally pulls them through. Dishes are wet because we're out of drying agents for the dishwashing machine. Bussers are short on everything, even though they're practically pulling plates out from under guests, and servers are sometimes bringing guests' food before their drinks, we're so low on glasses. Even the bar is falling short. If we had known the dining room would be so busy, we could have rented more supplies. What do we do now?"

"We'll make it work. I know things aren't perfect, Eric.We've been caught a little off guard. It's times like these when managers have a chance to shine."

"Mr. Rader?" Leroy turned to face a middle-aged woman. "I understand you're the general manager here," she continued. "I'm Mrs. Carey. One of your servers gave me a cracked glass. I didn't notice until I was done with my drink. How does one know if one is bleeding internally?"

Leroy inspected the glass and found a hairline crack. "There are no splinters missing. Are you feeling all right? I'm very sorry this happened to you. I'll correct the problem right away. In the meantime, let me get you a free drink. Would you excuse me a moment?" He pulled Eric aside. "Eric, I'm going to help Mrs. Carey. Go talk to Stan about this, please."

Eric agreed and went to the dishroom. As Leroy was serving Mrs. Carey, he heard some sharp voices coming from the dishroom. Sara was over there with Eric, and both were speaking heatedly to Stan through the window. Moments later, Eric and Sara rushed up to Leroy.

"Leroy, Stan's walking out!" Sara said breathlessly. "We've got to do something quick! We can't make it tonight without him."

"I know, I know! Where is he?" Leroy asked.

"This way, hurry!" Eric led Leroy to the back of the restaurant.

Discussion Questions

1. How can Leroy and Eric handle the crisis with Stan? What are their options?

2. How can the managers handle the crisis of a shortage of supplies for the rest of the shift?
3. What can be done to prevent this kind of crisis from happening in the future?

The following industry experts helped generate and develop this case: Christopher Kibit, C.S.C., Academic Team Leader, Hotel/Motel/Food Management & Tourism Programs, Lansing Community College, Lansing, Michigan; and Jack Nye, General Manager, Applebee's of Michigan, Applebee's International, Inc.

REVIEW QUIZ

When you feel you have covered all of the material in this chapter, answer these questions. Choose the *best* answer.

1. Leroy is a food service manager who wants to tell suppliers he wants lemons for his operation that have been picked within 30 days of the time they arrive at his outlet. To do this, he would use a:

   a. requisition checklist.
   b. standard purchase specification.
   c. perpetual inventory record.
   d. par inventory record.

2. Carol is starting a new restaurant in a building that is still under construction. Opening day is six months away. She wants her outlet's decor, uniforms, and china to match, and she knows she wants custom-made china. The best time for her to order her custom-made china would be:

   a. a week before she opens the restaurant, once she has actually seen the decor.
   b. two months after she opens the restaurant.
   c. a month before she opens the restaurant.
   d. as soon as possible.

3. Which of the following statements about custom-designed glassware and open-stock glassware is *true?*

   a. Custom-designed glassware is more expensive than open-stock glassware.
   b. Open-stock glassware is more susceptible to theft than custom-designed glassware.
   c. Open-stock glassware typically has fewer imperfections than custom-designed glassware.
   d. Open-stock glassware is glassware that is left in racks for guests to take as needed, while custom-designed glassware is glassware that is available only to guests who request them from servers.

4. Which of the following types of dishwashing machines uses chemicals to sanitize dishes?

   a. an energy-saving dishwasher
   b. a flight-type dishwasher
   c. a conveyor dishwasher
   d. a door-type dishwasher

REVIEW QUIZ *(continued)*

5. A POS (point-of-sale) device that is connected to a cash drawer is called a(n):

   a. precheck terminal.
   b. menu board.
   c. cashier terminal.
   d. electronic pocket pager.

Answer Key: 1-b-C1, 2-d-C1, 3-a-C2, 4-a-C2, 5-c-C2

Each question is linked to a competency. Competencies are listed on the first page of the chapter. An answer reading 3-b-C4 translates to:

3: the question number
b: the correct answer
C4: the competency number

Chapter 6 Outline

Competencies

1. Explain the process necessary to plan an effective design for a food service operation, including the role of a planning team and a market analysis; describe trends in food service design; and describe how space requirements and traffic-flow patterns affect an operation's overall layout.
2. Describe the importance of decor—specifically, color, decorations, lighting, ventilation, sound, and furniture—for a successful food service operation.
3. Summarize cleaning issues for food service facilities, including exterior and interior inspections, dining area cleaning programs, and cleaning schedules and procedures.

6

Facility Design, Decor, and Cleaning

A TOTAL DINING EXPERIENCE consists of not only food and beverages but also the food service facility's design and decor. The design and decor must harmonize with the cuisine and the service. Of course, even the most attractive design and nicest decor is negated if the food service facility is not kept clean. Not only is cleanliness an issue of meeting guest expectations, it is also a legal issue; food service facilities must comply with state and local sanitation laws with regard to facility cleanliness. In this chapter we will discuss the importance of facility design, decor, and cleaning to a food service operation's success.

Design

As designers of food service facilities develop design plans from a guest's perspective, they must consider such elements as noise, lighting, color coordination, and use of space. They also must be aware of government regulations concerning safety. These laws govern such factors as emergency lighting, emergency exits, and the maximum number of occupants that public areas may accommodate.

Design also affects service. In a dining area that is laid out properly, guests are comfortable and service staff members are able to do their work efficiently.

The proper design can even help assure guests that they have chosen the right place to dine. Not only is appropriate decor important, but also the way the dining-area space is configured. One factor that experienced designers take into account is that dining areas should usually appear comfortably full; few things are worse than having just 30 or so guests dining in a large open dining room designed for 200 people. In this situation, the guests start to wonder if choosing to eat at this restaurant was a wise decision, since it appears nearly empty. Once this doubt enters their minds, they tend to start finding fault with the food and service, since (their reasoning goes) if the restaurant was any good, more people would be eating there. To avoid this problem, many food service operations divide their dining area into sections or rooms; they sit guests in one section and fill it up before opening up a second section or room.

In many food service operations, the physical environment where service is created and delivered has shifted from a severely cost-efficient, staid appearance to a high-quality, lifestyle-oriented, comfortable environment. More food service operations are coordinating design elements (e.g., lighting, furnishings) with their menus and uniforms. In addition, guests expect flexibility in the physical environment, for privacy, socialization, quick service, or other desires. The physical environment has a fundamental and dramatic impact on a guest's feeling of comfort.

Planning an Effective Dining Area

Properly designed dining areas require an organized planning process to ensure that:

1. Guest needs and expectations are considered foremost.
2. Dining areas are flexible, to allow changes as guest needs and expectations evolve.
3. Dining areas have the proper appeal and ambiance.
4. A maximum return on the investment in space is realized.
5. A practical layout ensures an efficient flow of staff members and guests within dining areas.
6. Simplified procedures for performing required tasks are possible.
7. Dining areas provide safe work space for staff members and public access space for guests.
8. Dining areas adhere to the sanitation standards the organization requires.
9. Dining areas lend themselves to low maintenance costs.
10. Dining areas are energy-efficient and ecologically sound.
11. Dining areas are designed to support the service staff and efficient operations.

Effective dining area design takes time, and it generally requires the specialized knowledge of several people as the process progresses. These people should form a **dining area planning team.** The owner/manager and the dining area manager should be on the team to help make decisions that affect guest-contact areas. In many instances, an architect is part of the team. The team may also require a food service facility consultant, interior decorator, and other specialized designers. People with backgrounds and experiences ranging from managing operations to designing them are needed to develop the best plan for a dining area.

One of the first steps in the planning process is to determine just what the completed design must accomplish and who it is intended to attract. A high-check-average dining area requires a luxurious ambiance, which includes a generous allocation of floor space per guest; the costs of this ambiance are included in the prices guests pay. While the atmosphere of a low-check-average dining area must be comfortable and pleasant in order to enhance the dining experience, it does not require elegance or spaciousness. The key is for the design to meet the needs of the guests that the food service operation is seeking to attract. One method the planning team can use to understand the needs of guests is **market analysis**—a detailed study of potential guests and their wants, needs, and expectations.

WELCOME TO..

Virtual Seating

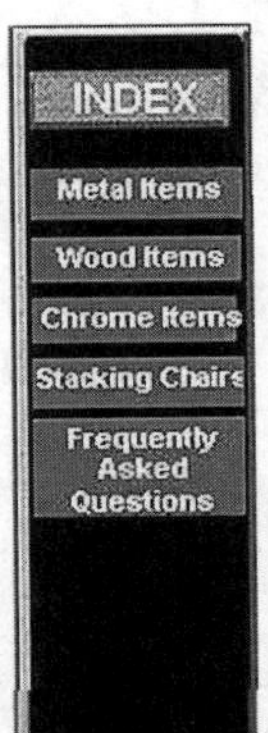

Chairs and Stools for bar, restaurant and catering use. Styles for any restaurant decor and a quality that will stand (actually, sit) the test of time.

See Below for the 'DEAL OF THE MILLENIUM'**

At virtual seating we carry a large assortment of chairs, stools, stacking chairs, dinette sets and assorted other furnishings. Whether you are furnishing a restaurant or banquet hall, we have what you are looking for.

Virtual Seating (www.virtualseating.com) offers an online catalog to restaurateurs and others interested in purchasing chairs or stools for their food service facility. (Courtesy of Virtual Seating, Brooklyn, New York)

Guests do care about design, according to a *Restaurants & Institutions* magazine survey of 1,000 restaurant guests. When asked what they would change about the layouts of their favorite restaurants, these guests said, among other things:

- "I'd change the layout of the tables."
- "The smoking area should be bigger."
- "Put the bar in a more discreet location."
- "More restrooms."
- "Make it bigger, so there's not such a long wait when I go."

Managers contemplating a change to their operation's design should ask their guests for suggestions, then listen carefully to what they say.

In commercial food service organizations, economic viability depends on profit. A feasibility study is needed to ensure that an organization's design is cost-effective and has the potential to help the organization be profitable. For example, commercial food service organizations base their estimated income on the anticipated turnover of guests and the expected check average. Seating capacities in dining areas affect the number of guests that can be served—and, therefore, affect potential income.

The planning team must also assess cost estimates for dining area plans. Not only is the dining area space itself expensive, but the furniture, fixtures, and equipment necessary to furnish it properly also add to the expense.

Members of the dining area planning team should identify the activities that must be performed to meet the guests' and the operation's objectives, then determine the space and equipment required to perform those activities. In part, this task involves an analysis of the flow of guests and staff through the operation.

Preliminary layout and equipment plans will help the team allocate available space. Preliminary plans show the proposed arrangement of equipment, traffic-flow aisles, and the relationship of each area to the other. When the team is at the point of examining preliminary floor plans, members can assemble basic cost estimates and make any adjustments needed to bring the project in line with the funds that have been budgeted for it.

When members of the planning team have reviewed, modified, and approved all preliminary plans, they can produce final blueprints for the dining area and prepare specifications for the necessary equipment. They will use these documents to request price quotations and select contractors and suppliers for the project. Construction and installation tasks follow according to a mutually agreed upon schedule.

The planning process involves many steps and many people. Since a design and construction project usually requires a large commitment of capital funds, a great deal of planning is required to ensure that the project's goals are met without unwelcome financial surprises.

Selecting a Designer

When selecting a designer, managers should allow ample time to review the credentials of several individuals representing a number of design firms. Managers should use the following criteria when selecting a designer:

- *Membership in the American Society of Interior Designers (ASID).* Ideally, the designer should be a member of ASID. Each ASID member has a formal, accredited education and professional experience, and has successfully completed a comprehensive two-day examination. This association stresses high standards of ethical conduct.

- *Education.* Managers should inquire about the degrees that a designer holds, the institutions that granted them, and the designer's major field of study.

- *Experience.* Does the designer have experience in food service design? Is he or she knowledgeable about food service systems? With which food service organizations has he or she worked? Managers should ask for references and contact them.

- *Portfolio.* Professional designers generally have many photographs, drawings, and other information illustrating their creative skills. Managers should examine a designer's portfolio to see if they like what the designer has done in the past.
- *First impressions.* Does the designer seem to be professional? Is he or she a good communicator? Does it appear that the designer understands what the managers want? Do the managers believe the designer can do the job?
- *Contacts.* With which suppliers does the designer work? What services will the designer provide and what additional work will others need to do? Do the managers have any problems using the suppliers suggested by the designer?
- *Design Fees.* What will the designer charge? What additional fees will the managers need to pay to others as a result of the designer's contacts?
- *Budget.* Does the designer think he or she can deliver the design within budget?

These criteria can be modified to address the unique characteristics of any food service organization.

A professional designer will provide a number of ideas for consideration by the design team, but to help a designer come up with good designs, managers must be candid about all details of the organization. Who are its guests and potential guests? What are the organization's menu and marketing concepts? What are its economic concerns? What are the elements that the owner/manager does and does not like in food service design? Effective communication is important.

Trends in Design

Although design trends are numerous and ever-changing, we will consider seven trends that will likely have a lasting effect on various types of food service establishments.

Homelike Atmosphere. The designers of many food service operations are attempting to create a homelike atmosphere to attract potential guests away from the comforts of their own homes. They do this by using natural colors and materials to achieve a casual and inviting atmosphere.

Entertainment. Today, dining out often means entertainment. Some theme restaurants use animatronics, antiques, or movie or music memorabilia to entertain, create emotional connections with guests, and build a link between other popular guest interests and dining.

Coupled Areas. A third design trend is the movement toward **coupled areas**—that is, areas that combine the dining area with a distinct bar section and a service space to handle guest overflow. Large dining spaces are being divided into smaller spaces, such as a bar that is more intimate and enclosed, an informal primary dining area, and a flexible atrium space that can be used for breakfast, light lunches, after-dinner business, and overflow from the bar or dining area. The coupling concept provides guests with the opportunity for pre-dinner cocktails in the bar, dinner in the dining room, and after-dinner drinks with entertainment in the atrium. It furnishes a food service organization and its guests with flexibility.

Small Operations. Small food service operations succeed by developing unique identities as intimate gathering places that appeal to very targeted markets. Usually they are also more profitable for their owners/investors. "Small" sometimes also means having more integration between the kitchen and dining area. Exhibition kitchens featuring guest-contact-area pantries, open grills, and rotisseries are designed to appeal to all of the guests' senses, as well as to add interest.

As kitchen areas shrink, mobile and multiuse food preparation equipment become more popular. Easily moved equipment creates flexibility in kitchen layouts, increasing efficiencies. Multiuse equipment is flexible enough to meet changing demands. For example, a single deck oven can be used for baking, pizza making, and roasting. Many designers favor multiuse equipment over single-use equipment.

A kitchen workstation analysis prior to final design is recommended. Such an analysis identifies the tasks to be performed in each workstation and details what support is needed from other kitchen areas/workstations. Ideally, the person or people working in a workstation should not have to leave it to accomplish their tasks. Therefore, workstations are being designed to include storage space for tools, tableware, and food supplies.

Accommodating Solo Guests. Designers are coming up with unique solutions to meet the needs of solo guests. Some food service operations feature a special table—known as a "chef's table," "singles' table," or "family table"—that typically seats 8 to 12 single guests, who may or may not know one another. An operation can draw single guests to such a table by serving chef specialties at the table before they make it onto the standard menu or by providing a higher level of service. Some chef's tables feature special themes or tabletop grills that make the dining experience entertaining and unique.

Robotic Food Delivery. Robotic food delivery is being used as a high-tech design strategy to improve service in hospitals. Robots on wheels deliver food trays from the dietary department to nursing stations; nurses then deliver the trays to patients. Thanks to a variety of built-in sensors, these robots can travel the halls, call and board elevators, open automatic doors, and find nursing stations without help. Although robots have worked successfully in hospitals, it will probably be some time before they are used for service in commercial food service organizations.

***Liaison-Froid* System.** Another design innovation in hospital food service is the ***liaison-froid* (cold-link) system**. Used in many hospitals in Europe, the system is based on the principle of *marché en avant*, a French phrase meaning "continually moving forward." In this system, food products are considered either "dirty" or "clean."

Food that is received from suppliers is considered dirty, as are areas used to store food just received. Dirty food cannot be handled or stored near or with clean food. In a "deconditioning room," food items needed for production are removed from delivery containers (e.g., cans, boxes) and placed into clean, stainless-steel containers before being issued to production staff members. Produce is received daily and preliminarily stored in a cold production room at 50°F (10°C), where it is washed and cut. Separate rooms are maintained for fish and meat products. In an ideal *liaison-froid* design, foods move through a production line and become progressively "cleaner." The system is based on fundamentals of time and temperature control, as well as proper handling and storage to minimize sanitation risks.

Space Requirements

Determining space needs for dining service is always challenging, since such requirements depend on many factors that are unique to each organization: the number of meals planned, the exact tasks the staff members must perform in dining areas, the equipment staff will use, and the amount of dining space needed for guests. The facility must also have space for storing service supplies, exercising sales income controls, and carrying out various guest-contact activities.

When estimating the total size of a facility, planners often start with the number of seats. Income and profit levels—both of which relate to the number of meals that will be served—determine the feasibility of the organization's design.

Food service managers in the academic market and the business and industry market are able to estimate the number of meals they will serve with relative ease. They base their estimates on past history or, if they are dealing with new facilities, on a percentage that similar facilities have calculated as their averages. The number of dining periods that the organization will offer will also affect the dining area's seating capacity. For example, if a school has an enrollment of 1,000 students, 80 percent of whom eat three meals a day, and it offers four specific dining periods for each meal, then it must design a seating capacity of 200 for the dining area (80 percent of 1,000 students = 800 per meal; 800 students divided by 4 meal periods per meal = 200 seats per period).

Lodging property managers plan the size of their dining areas according to estimates of room occupancy, the extent to which the local community will use their dining facilities, and the number of banquet functions they expect to schedule.

To determine the dining space required for any type of organization, managers must consider the number of guests that will be seated at one time and the total square feet allowed per seat. Exhibit 1 is a base from which specific calculations can be made. Today, designers generally recommend 15 or 16 square feet (1.4 to 1.5 square meters) per seat for casual restaurants or coffee shops. Fine dining is generally designed at 20 square feet (1.9 square meters) per seat. For fine dining with a great deal of tableside service, the recommendation is 22 to 24 square feet (2 to 2.2 square meters) per seat. For bars, the recommendation is 20 square feet (1.9 square meters) per seat. The actual space that must be allowed is determined by the amount of comfort guests desire and by any applicable government regulations that dictate aisle width and space requirements (such as the amount of unobstructed space in front of emergency exits). Design and placement of cashier stations, host stands, side stations, and salad bars also affect the amount of space a specific facility needs.

Exhibit 1 Range of Estimated Square Feet for Dining Area Space

Facility	Dining Area Space (Per Person)	
	(Square Feet)	(Square Meters)
Table service	12–18	1.1–1.7
Counter service	16–20	1.5–1.9
Booth service	12–16	1.1–1.5
Cafeteria service	12–16	1.1–1.5
Banquet service	10–12	.9–1.1

Traffic Flow

Traffic flow refers to the movement of staff members, guests, products, supplies, and refuse through a facility. Managers must address issues related to the movement of people and items through support areas as well as through guest-contact areas.

Exhibit 2 is an example of a preliminary drawing developed during the early planning stages of a food service facility. It is not drawn to scale. Instead, it is the kind of drawing that planners make to help them decide how to locate various spaces relative to each other. In the design represented in this exhibit, guests would typically enter the organization through the main entrance (#1). (The organization may find a separate entrance—#2—helpful for banquet guests only.) The location of the emergency exit (#3) will be dictated by local ordinances. Parking areas should be situated on the side of the building where the entrances are located.

As Exhibit 2 shows, when guests use the main entrance to the facility, they can either go to the lounge or register with the host for service. Some people do not like to go through a lounge to get to the dining room; therefore, a separate entrance to the lounge area is useful. Managers might even design an outside lounge entrance; however, such an entrance might cause problems with sales income control. To avoid the potential problem of guests who "drink and dash," the facility can be designed so that guests must enter and exit the lounge through a public foyer. Upon entering the facility, guests may have access to coat racks, telephones, and restrooms.

In Exhibit 2's drawing, the designer placed the salad bar so that dining room guests and, when practical, small groups of guests in the banquet rooms could use it. Likewise, the restrooms are placed so that guests in the banquet rooms as well as the dining room can use them. (If this plan complies with local municipal codes, it can significantly reduce non-revenue-producing space.)

A service corridor provides service staff quick access to banquet rooms. The service bar is in an area that facilitates service to dining room and banquet guests. (Portable bars also are an option.) Side stations are in areas designed to reduce the distance that servers must walk to get supplies.

As you study Exhibit 2, you may be able to suggest improvements to the design. This is part of the value of a preliminary drawing. A preliminary drawing

Exhibit 2 Example of a Preliminary Drawing

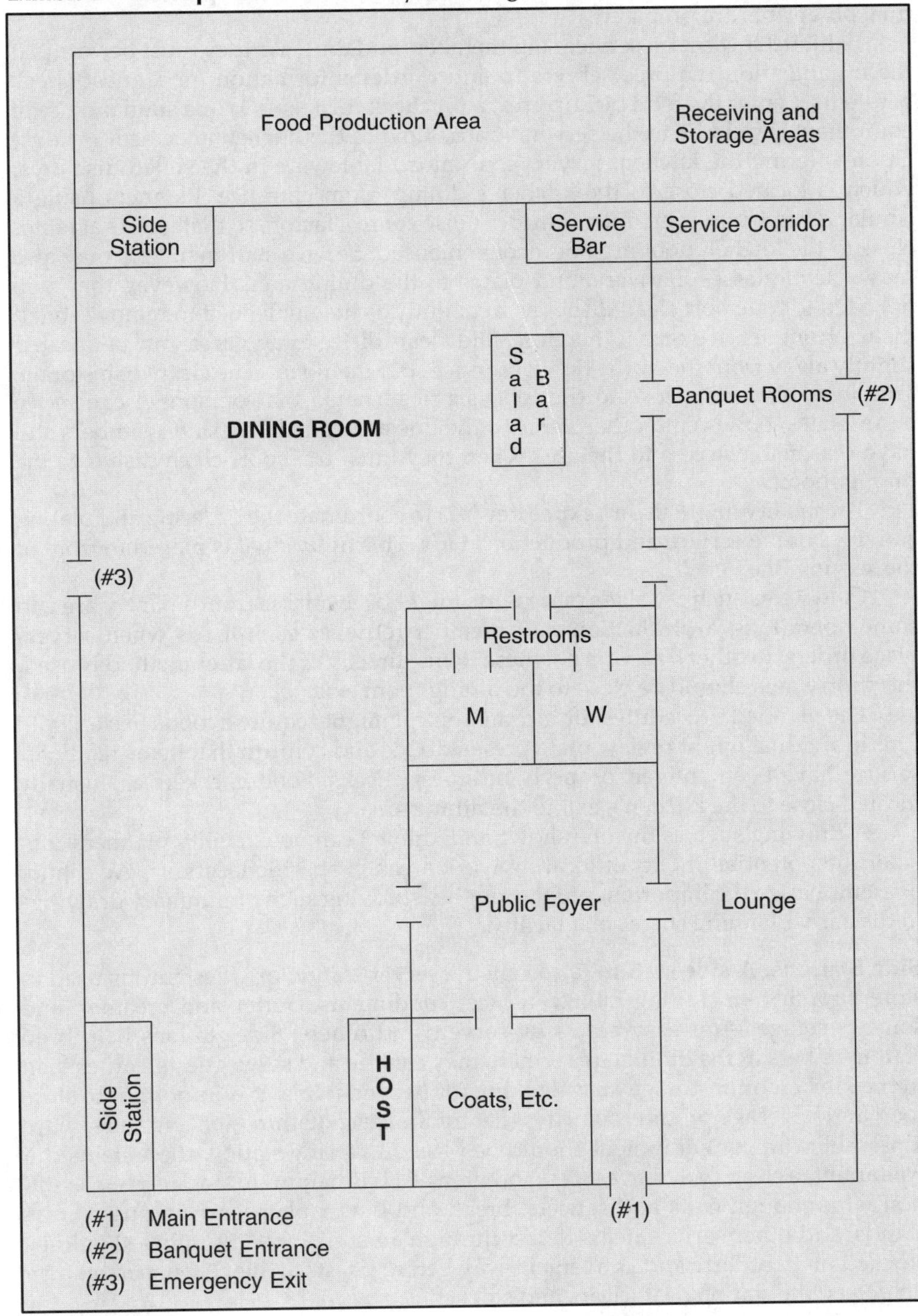

allows members of the design team to react to it and make improvements before final blueprints are prepared.

Exhibit 3 focuses on service staff members and the tasks they must perform. (If the organization requires servers to enter order information on a guest check before they enter the food pickup area, a precheck register (#1) or a similar piece of equipment should be in the servers' traffic flow to the kitchen area, as it is here.) Upon entering the kitchen, servers can unload tableware in the soiled dish area, which is located close to the kitchen's dining room entrance. Planners using a similar design, however, must consider noise control factors so that guests at tables close to the kitchen door are not inconvenienced. Service staff members may also move clean glasses, flatware, and plates to the dining area. However, they will not need to transport clean dishes as frequently as they will need to remove soiled dishes from service areas; therefore, the clean dish storage area can be located slightly away from the traffic flow of service staff members. The clean dish storage area in Exhibit 3 is close to the food service line so that personnel can move clean plates, bowls, and other items to the line as needed, but staff members still have reasonable access to the area when they must transport clean dishes to the dining room.

The facility might use an **expediter** (#2) to coordinate the ordering and plating activities of the service and production staffs. This individual is placed in front of the serving line.

Cold items such as salads or desserts might be available from a pantry area. In some operations, a production staff member retrieves such foods when servers place orders; in others, servers get these items directly. If the latter method is used, the pantry area should be close to the dining room exit.

The planned procedures for income control might require a food checker (#3). This individual might review plate presentations and confirm that items ready for service have been entered properly on guest checks. Food checkers are usually located close to the kitchen's exit to the dining area.

A drawing such as the one shown in Exhibit 3 can help facility planners consider the potential impact of locating work areas in specific locations. We cannot overemphasize the importance of thoroughly studying such preliminary drawings in the early planning stages of a facility.

Side Stations. A **side station** (also called a server station or sidestand) is used to store supplies—including tableware, ice, condiments, butter and creamer, and some beverages—for easy access by servers and others. Side stations help keep staff members in the dining area, where they can see and serve guests, rather than in the kitchen or in storage areas looking for needed items. It is important to store food and beverage products in ways that minimize contamination. No soiled napkins, tableware, or equipment should be placed in a side station; these items can contaminate clean food, beverages, and utensils. It is helpful to stock each side station with enough cups and saucers, bread and butter plates, serving trays, tray stands, and other service items to last through an entire shift. Supplies should be stocked in an orderly and convenient way before guests arrive. A busperson may help keep the station neat, clean, and stocked.

Exhibit 3 Traffic Flow Patterns in Support Areas

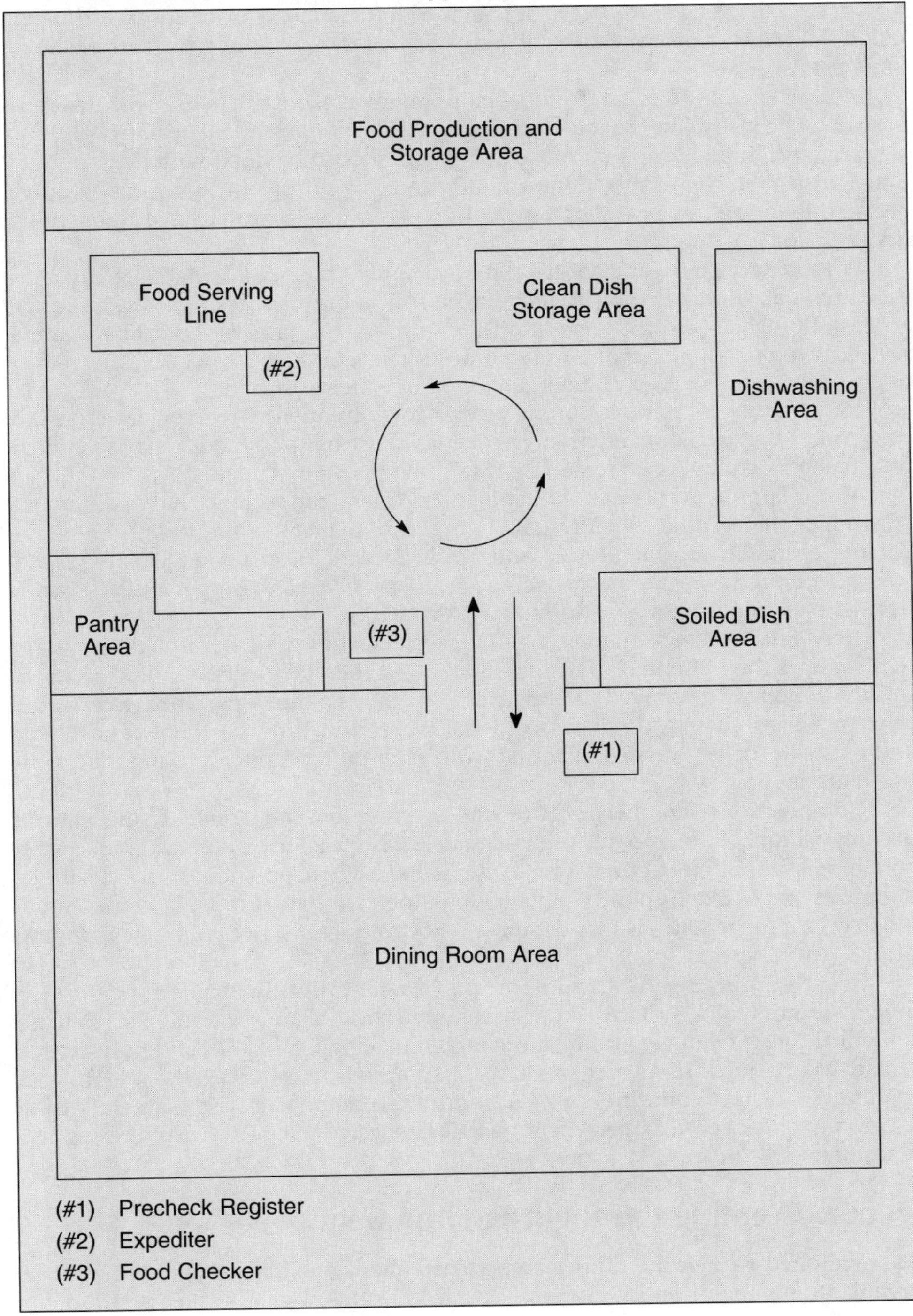

Refuse. One additional traffic-flow consideration must not be overlooked: the storage and disposal of refuse. People in the United States throw out an estimated 180 million tons of garbage annually; approximately 135 million tons are destined for landfills.

Refuse is often stored outdoors before removal. Containers used for this purpose must be insect- and rodent-resistant, durable, nonabsorbent, leakproof, easily cleaned, and in good repair. Refuse containers should be lined with wet-strength paper or plastic bags. Bags alone should not be used for outdoor refuse storage because they are not pest-resistant. Outdoor receptacles must have tight-fitting doors or lids.

A food service organization's refuse facilities must be of adequate capacity. Refuse containers not in use should be stored outdoors on a rack or in a storage box at least 18 inches (46 centimeters) off the ground. Containers should be cleaned regularly to prevent insect and rodent infestation. Containers can be cleaned effectively with a combination of detergent and hot water or steam.

Refuse must be removed from service areas frequently to prevent odor and pest problems. Outdoor refuse storage areas must have a smooth, nonabsorbent base (such as asphalt or concrete) that is sloped to drain.

Many large food service operations use trash compactors. Such equipment can reduce the volume of solid waste by up to 75 percent. In addition, some compactors automatically deodorize and apply insecticides to solid waste. Liquid waste generated by a compactor should be disposed of as sewage. Suitable facilities with hot water are also required for compactors.

New developments on the compactor scene include a waste-reduction system that reduces the volume of refuse by 8 to 1 and then produces a moist, compact pulp. All food waste as well as paper refuse is thrown into a partially water-filled tank in which cutting devices grind the waste into fine particles. The water and waste particles form a slurry that is dewatered to produce a damp, popcorn-like material.

Composting is another form of refuse reduction and re-use. Using natural decomposition, biodegradable organic material is transformed into humus, a soil-enriching compound. Composting systems have great potential in food service organizations, which typically have 60 to 80 percent biodegradable waste. Some food service organizations that compost report reductions in landfill fees ranging from 33 to 50 percent.

Recycling has become an important consideration for some food service organizations. Quick-service establishments such as McDonald's and Taco Bell are sometimes accused of generating large amounts of paper, plastic, and polystyrene refuse. Many quick-service chains have responded by reducing the weight and thickness of their containers or by completely changing the materials they use. Many quick-service operations are using recycled paper for cash receipts and placemats.

Decor: Creating the Right Environment

As mentioned earlier, the dining area environment must be compatible with an organization's menu and service style. All too often, owners think yesterday's steak house can become today's pizzeria by simply hanging up a few pictures of the Italian landscape, or believe their Olde English pub can become an 1880s frontier saloon just by changing the uniforms the staff wears. While extreme, these examples point to the tendency on the part of many managers to pay scant attention to the atmosphere created in a dining area. Successful managers do not overlook the fact that details such as fixtures and equipment make their own contributions to dining area decor and ambiance. For example, stainless steel and glass no more fit into an Early American theme than heavy wooden furniture fits into a twenty-first century motif.

Service staff members themselves contribute to a dining room's atmosphere. Guests in a gourmet dining room find it appropriate, for instance, for the manager to wear a tuxedo; the ambiance of a dining room with a Mexican or other ethnic theme is enhanced when servers wear national costumes.

When trying to create the perfect dining environment, managers should not neglect proper function. Furniture, fixtures, and equipment must be easy to clean and durable. Concerns about costs and whether replacement products will be available in the future must be addressed. Managers should purchase products of commercial quality that can withstand the wear and tear to which guests and staff will expose them. Very delicate or rare decorative items should not be used unless they are out of reach and well-anchored. (Unfortunately, it is a fact of life that guests and staff alike may take such decorations for souvenirs if they are not vandal-proofed.) Many people do not treat furnishings in public areas the same way that they do in their own homes; furnishings must be able to withstand misuse or mischief.

Color. The colors used in dining areas profoundly affect the atmosphere of those areas. The important consideration for managers is, "What do our guests want?" The answer to that question may be far different from the feelings that an operation's managers or owner has about specific colors and color combinations. For this and many other reasons, it is wise to involve a professional interior decorator in the design of dining areas and to depend on him or her for color-coordination ideas.

Violets, blues, and light greens are cool colors that tend to make guests feel relaxed; facilities emphasizing leisurely dining may want to use these colors. In contrast, warm colors such as reds, yellows, and oranges are stimulating; they encourage activity. Therefore, these colors subtly encourage fast table turnover.

Rooms that receive little sunlight should have light and warm colors, while those receiving a lot of sunlight should balance that by using cool, dark colors. Colors also have an impact on perceived room size. Light colors make a room appear large; dark colors tend to make a room look small. Dark colors also make ceilings look lower than they are. When one wall is a very bright color, the adjoining wall should be more neutral, perhaps in the same shade or tint.

Decorations. Small pictures, wall hangings, and other decorations should be used in small rooms. Large items should be used with care, even in large rooms. When decorations from various periods or with differing styles are selected, a unified effect can be created if their colors are coordinated. Such decorations should be

The Psychology of Lighting

More than any other design element, lighting creates the mood of a space. Lighting can also reduce or enhance the effectiveness of all other design elements. Here are some guidelines for lighting:

- Sparkle enhances appetite and encourages conversation. Chandeliers, candles, and multiple pin lights can achieve sparkle. Light bouncing off mirrored surfaces, wet-looking finishes, and shiny tableware also create sparkle.
- Dark shadows appear hostile; small patterns of light appear friendly.
- Brightly lit architectural surfaces tend to move people along and are therefore good for high-volume facilities.
- Light should always flatter people. If lighting makes flesh tones look good, it also tends to make food look good.
- Design lighting in transition zones so guests entering or leaving a facility on a sunny day can still see.
- Use a dimmer switch to permit mood changes:
  - Brightness and cheer for breakfast
  - Restfulness for lunch
  - Animation for early evening
  - Romance for dinner

selected carefully if they are to help portray a theme. For example, a nautical theme might include anchors, oars, buoys, fishing nets, seashells, and models of ships. Such items as copper cooking utensils, saloon signs, whiskey barrels, and branding irons might be appropriate for an Old West theme. Of course, a number of popular restaurants have made a theme out of combining mismatched and eclectic decorations. Yet even these apparently haphazard collections of items are chosen with care to appeal to specific, targeted markets. Whatever the theme or style, careful thought and often considerable expense are necessary to decorate dining areas effectively.

Lighting. Like color, the effects that can be created with lighting are endless. Adequate lighting is essential for tasks such as reading the menu. Adequate lighting also improves safety by lessening the chance of an accident for guests as well as staff members.

Light intensity is measured in units called **footcandles**. A footcandle equals one lumen per square foot. (A *lumen* is equal to 0.0015 watts.) Footcandles are measured with a light meter. Most lighting engineers and occupational safety and health inspectors recommend 50 to 70 footcandles of light for dining areas.

While too much light can negatively impact a dining area's ambiance and atmosphere, too little may be undesirable at certain meal periods. Guests can get annoyed when there is insufficient lighting in dining areas. One solution is to add track lighting or use dimmer switches to achieve flexibility.

Ventilation. Ventilation equipment is designed to remove smoke, fumes, condensation, steam, heat, and unpleasant odors from kitchens and dining areas. Sufficient ventilation also helps to maintain comfortable temperatures and minimizes dust buildup on walls, ceilings, and floors. When ventilation fails or underperforms, the entire dining experience may be spoiled. State and local building codes and, in some jurisdictions, public health officials dictate specific ventilation requirements for each area of a food service operation.

The major ventilation problem is the transfer of unpleasant odors and fumes from the kitchen to public areas such as dining, meeting, and banquet rooms. This problem usually occurs when the kitchen ventilation system is improperly designed. To avoid ventilation problems, air from the kitchen must be exhausted to the outside and replaced with an equal amount of "tempered" (fresh outside) air.

Sound. While some designers use sound to create a feeling of excitement, some guests are annoyed when the dining area is too noisy. Sound problems can be alleviated by decor changes as well as design modifications. Acoustical panels, carpeting, and draperies can be added to service areas to dampen noise. Items such as padded furniture and fabric wall hangings can be included in the decor to further reduce unwanted noise. Noisy kitchen activities (dishwashing, for example) can be placed in locations farthest from the dining room. This may be particularly important to establishments with many older guests, who may wear hearing aids that amplify background sounds.

Furniture. In most food service operations, furniture—chairs in particular—must be comfortable to guests. (Some quick-service operations use hard chairs to discourage guests from lingering after their meals.) Dining area chairs should have a slightly more upright back than lounge chairs. While high-backed chairs can be designed to be upright, low-backed chairs should recline a bit. Chair arms should be low enough to easily slide under tables.

Tables must be balanced so that they do not teeter and rock when used. While booths may be part of the decor because they take less space, guests may not like the inability to move their seats closer to the table. Some recommended standards for furniture are presented in Exhibit 4.

Many guests view today's food service organizations as works of art. To these guests, the size, flow of people and products, space, equipment, furniture, decorative items, sound, lighting, colors, tabletops, and materials used in all areas blend to attract attention and communicate an overall image to guests. Decor must be based on who the guests are and what they find attractive. The goal of a food service establishment is to turn guests into loyal repeat guests who tell their friends and associates about the establishment.

Cleaning

In the following sections we will discuss cleaning issues for food service facilities, including exterior and interior inspections, dining area cleaning programs, and cleaning schedules and procedures.

Exhibit 4 Recommended Standards for Furniture

Chairs

Armrest height: 25 inches (64 centimeters) or less
Seat back angle: 100 to 110 degrees
Seat depth: 20 inches (51 centimeters)
Seat height: 18 inches (46 centimeters)
Seat width: 20 inches (51 centimeters)

Place-Setting Allowances

Minimum width (average): 24 inches (61 centimeters)
Minimum width (fine dining): 27 inches (69 centimeters)
Minimum width (self-service): 21 inches (53 centimeters)

Tables

Minimum depth allowed for each place setting: 14 inches (36 centimeters)
(Measure from the edge of the table in front of the guest toward the middle.)

Diameters of round tables for comfortable seating:

- 3 guests: 32 inches (81 centimeters)
- 4 guests: 40 inches (102 centimeters)
- 6 guests: 50 inches (127 centimeters)
- 8 guests: 60 inches (152 centimeters)

Height—29 to 31 inches (74 to 79 centimeters)

Exterior

Exterior masonry surfaces are typically brick, concrete block, stucco, stone, or a combination of these materials. These surfaces are porous and attract water, dirt, and scale. Cleaning such surfaces is difficult, but cleaning them is important if an operation is to make an excellent first impression. Cleaning methods vary according to the climate, the type and condition of the masonry, and the design of the building.

Exterior masonry cleaning solutions are frequently applied with spray guns and hoses. During cleaning operations, glass and aluminum exterior surfaces, as well as plants and shrubs, must be protected. Damaged masonry surfaces can be repaired and waterproofed with special chemical compounds. These applications not only enhance the building's appearance, but also prolong its life and increase its value.

Clean parking lots and sidewalks contribute to a positive first impression as guests approach a facility. Ideally, they should be easy to maintain and should not cause dust problems. The type of outdoor cleaning equipment used on parking lots and sidewalks depends on the area to be cleaned, surface characteristics, the type of debris to be removed, the frequency of cleaning, and the financial resources available. There are a number of different types of sweeping machines.

Air-recycling machines create an air blast to loosen debris; the debris is then pulled up through a hose and deposited in a collection tank. Broom-vacuum machines loosen debris with a rotating broom and deposit it into a hopper. Push-vacuum machines are used primarily to clean large, outdoor surfaces. They function much like standard vacuum cleaners.

Managers deciding when to clean the exterior of a building should begin with a walk-around inspection. This is particularly important for establishments in locations with long, cold, and wet winter seasons. The sides of the building should be inspected for dirt and grease buildup from the kitchen's exhaust system. If the exterior façade needs repainting, timing is critical. In wet climates, for example, damp wood must first be allowed to dry before repainting.

Cobwebs, dead bugs, and other debris should be removed from windowsills. Outside windows can be cleaned with a squeegee dipped in a bucket of water with a drop of dish soap.

Plants and shrubbery should be inspected; damaged parts should be pruned and dead plants replaced. Shrubs can be washed with a mild soap-and-water solution. Spring and summer perennials can add freshness to building exteriors.

Interior

The manager should inspect the interior of the building at the same time as the exterior. In addition to highlighting specific areas in need of cleaning, the manager should make a safety check as well. Problems can occur when:

1. Entryways are slippery on rainy or snowy days.
2. Rug edges are exposed (they can trip staff members and guests).
3. Furniture and equipment are highly flammable.
4. Wooden furniture has splinters or metal furniture has sharp edges.
5. Glass doors and windows are neither covered nor marked to prevent people from walking into them.
6. Steps are not lighted and there are no railings.
7. Public areas are so dark that people cannot see as they move about.
8. Furniture is unstable and tips easily.
9. Fixtures or hanging decorations are too low for tall people.
10. The emergency-exit traffic-flow pattern is obstructed.

The list of examples could continue and will vary from organization to organization. However, the point is that when staff members are performing cleaning activities, they should be alert for potential safety problems as well.

Dining Area Cleaning Program

Managers know that dining areas should be cleaned routinely to meet sanitation standards. Furthermore, cleanliness is of paramount importance to guests. Against this need for cleanliness must be balanced the costs involved. For example, the frequency and method of routine cleaning affect how much money must be spent on service supplies.

Managers must develop an effective **cleaning program** and monitor the routine cleaning and maintenance of furniture, fixtures, and equipment in dining areas. They should establish written cleaning procedures for each area and piece of equipment in the organization. The procedures should briefly describe the cleaning task, list the steps in the task, and indicate the materials and tools necessary. Each manager should monitor cleaning procedures in his or her department. This follow-up demonstrates to staff members that management cares about maintaining a clean environment.

Staff members are more likely to follow cleaning procedures if they understand their importance. Training in cleaning procedures must be systematic to be effective. Proper training reduces the risks associated with cleaning. Training should cover cleanliness standards and recommend methods, products, and equipment. Only after proper training should staff members be assigned regular cleaning duties.

Cleaning Schedule

A written **cleaning schedule** further systematizes a cleaning program by indicating who is responsible for each cleaning task and how often the task should be performed. The schedule should be based on a survey of an organization's cleaning needs. If a survey has never been done, managers and staff members should work together to identify cleaning needs for each area in the facility. Include such questions as:

- What is to be cleaned/maintained?
- Who is responsible for the cleaning/maintenance?
- When is the area or equipment to be cleaned/maintained?
- What safety and sanitation precautions must be observed?
- How should the cleaned item be stored to prevent resoiling?
- Who is responsible for supervising and checking the work?
- What must be done to reduce risks?

Once the survey is completed, a cleaning schedule can be developed.

Cleaning Procedures

Who should perform cleaning activities? Typically, service staff should clean tabletops, the interiors of side station refrigerators, and the side stations themselves. But what about vacuuming floors, washing table bases, cleaning window ledges, and other jobs? The general manager, working closely with other managers who help oversee the cleaning of the facility, should make these decisions. Job descriptions should indicate the specific tasks that staff members in each position are to perform, and cleaning/maintenance schedules should be developed with these activities in mind. It is a good general policy to require all staff members, regardless of position, to clean when they are otherwise unoccupied with guest service activities.

Because differences of opinion often occur over which cleaning procedures are best, organizations should obtain specific advice from experts. Some general guidelines are provided in Exhibit 5. Managers should also consult with manufacturers and suppliers of cleaning equipment and supplies for their recommended cleaning procedures.

Curtains, Draperies, and Upholstered Furniture. Careful vacuuming will prolong the lives of curtains, draperies, and upholstered furniture. Some fabrics may be hand-washed when soiled, while other fabrics must be dry-cleaned. Because of the variety of fabrics used for these items, it is best to follow the manufacturer's cleaning recommendations.

Use hot-solvent cleaning for silks, crushed velvet, and other fine fabrics. This method minimizes color bleeding and shrinkage. Portable equipment can be used for in-place cleaning.

A dry-foam soil extractor may be used to shampoo and remove spills from upholstery. An extractor can also be used to clean carpeted stairs. Some upholstery fabrics can be made soil-resistant by applying a protective coating after cleaning.

Blinds and Shades. Blinds and shades should be vacuumed or dusted frequently. Some metal and plastic surfaces can be washed with a mild detergent solution and rinsed with clean water. Cloth or fabric materials may require specialized cleaning chemicals and procedures.

Glass. Glass is easy to clean and maintain, and the necessary equipment and supplies are relatively inexpensive. Squeegees come in a variety of sizes; brass models with hardwood handles are more durable than aluminum versions. An ammonia-and-water solution cleans glass effectively. Alcohol may be added to the water as an antifreeze when cleaning windows at temperatures below freezing. Commercial glass cleaners are also effective.

Periodic, scheduled cleaning of glass surfaces is necessary to prevent excessive soil buildup. Some organizations contract their outdoor window cleaning to professional companies. This reduces the safety risks for the organization's own staff members.

Floor Coverings. Use floor mats and runners at entrances and in heavy traffic areas to keep carpets clean. They also prevent wear, help control noise, and reduce the risk of slip-and-fall accidents. Routine care includes daily light vacuuming, thorough weekly vacuuming, periodic shampooing, and regular deep-cleaning with steam or some other method.

Carpeted heavy-traffic areas and dining spaces where spills often occur may require vacuuming after each meal and shampooing with a dry-foam chemical each night. As is true with hard floors, a wide variety of supplies and equipment is available to clean carpets. Contact experts in carpet cleaning to obtain specific information about the best products and procedures to use.

Lighting Fixtures. Lighting fixtures, including lamps and shades in dining areas, should be cleaned routinely by dusting or vacuuming, as dust is the primary cause

Exhibit 5 How to Care for Materials in Your Establishment

Acoustical Tile

Remove loose dirt or dust with a vacuum or soft brush. A gum eraser will remove most smudges. Soft chalk can cover many small stains. More thorough cleaning can be accomplished with wallpaper cleaners or mild soap cleaners.Excessive water and abrasive rubbing actions should be avoided; using a soft sponge is best.

Aluminum

Wash with a mild detergent solution; avoid common alkalis, which dull the finish. A fine abrasive may be used periodically; rub in one direction, not in a circle.

Bamboo, Cane, Rattan, Wicker

Wash with a mild soap or detergent solution. Rinse with clear water, and dry. Periodic shellacking maintains a natural finish.

Brass

Acidic brass cleaners and polishes are used for unfinished brass. Wash lacquered brass with a mild detergent solution, rinse, and wipe dry.

Carpets

All types of carpets must be vacuumed regularly to extend their useful life. Deep cleaning can be accomplished with impregnated granular cleaners, shampoos, or extraction chemicals with a dry residue to prevent rapid resoiling.

Ceramic Tile

Use a neutral soap or detergent. Remove excess cleaning solution, rinse, and dry thoroughly. Avoid alkalis, salts, acids, and abrasive cleaners. Some soap cleaners may result in a soap-film buildup.

Glass

Wash with a special window-cleaning concentrate dissolved in water. Use a squeegee or chamois to dry glass.

Leather Furniture

Wash with a neutral soap or saddle soap.

Linoleum

Wash with a mild detergent solution; rinse with clear water. Remove water and dry as rapidly as possible. Avoid alkaline solutions.

Painted Surfaces

Immediately remove spots with a cloth wrung from a detergent solution.

Wood Floors

Wood floors must be sealed if they are to be maintained properly. Dust-mopping and damp-mopping sealed floors are usually all that is necessary if a regular maintenance program is followed. Polishing with a floor wax may be required. Some soft woods can be seriously damaged by strong solutions of soap or detergent and water. Oils, grease, and strong alkalis are also harmful. Avoid using excessive water, and always remove water as rapidly as possible.

of reduced light intensity. Bulbs or lamps must be replaced promptly when necessary. Small glass fixtures can be removed for cleaning. Large fixtures, including chandeliers, are usually cleaned in place. This difficult job is sometimes turned over to an outside contractor.

Wall Coverings. Because walls in dining areas can be covered with paint, tile, wallpaper, wood, foil, cork, or other materials, managers must be aware of the various methods used to clean them.

It is wise to dry-dust walls before washing them. When it is time for washing, use the cleaning solution recommended by the manufacturer of the wall covering. Staff members should apply a weak solution to a small, hidden part of the wall as a test before cleaning the entire wall. Generally, a water-based cleaning solution—strong enough to be effective without damaging the wall covering in any way—should be used.

Badly soiled areas may need to be saturated with the proper solution. Heavily soiled areas should be rinsed and wiped immediately. Washing marble, ceramic, plastic, metal, acoustic, and papered walls requires special procedures. Seeking advice from an expert is best in these cases.

Key Terms

cleaning program—Formalized cleaning procedures for each area and piece of equipment in a food service organization. The procedures should briefly describe the task, list the steps in the task, and indicate the materials and tools necessary.

cleaning schedule—A written schedule indicating who is responsible for each cleaning task and how often the task should be performed.

composting—Recycling that transforms biodegradable organic material into humus, a soil-enriching compound.

coupled areas—A design trend toward combining the dining area with a distinct bar section and a service space to handle guest overflow.

dining area planning team—A specially selected group brought together to develop an efficient and practical design for a food service interior. The team typically includes the owner/manager and the dining area manager, an architect, a food service facility consultant, an interior decorator, and other specialized designers.

expediter—A staff member who acts as a communication link between kitchen personnel and servers. The expediter must know cooking times, coordinate them to sequentially deliver cooked foods for pickup, and provide leadership during rush periods.

footcandle—A unit of illumination; it is the intensity of light on a surface that is one foot away from a standard candle.

***liaison-froid* (cold-link) system**—A food service delivery system based on the principle of *marché en avant* ("continually moving forward"), in which food products are considered either "dirty" or "clean." Once placed into the highly controlled system, dirty food is on a strictly supervised path toward becoming clean food.

market analysis—A survey or study that depicts the demographic characteristics of the market area to be served by a proposed food service operation. If used in an existing establishment, such a study may report on menu or design changes guests desire.

side station—A service stand in the dining area that holds equipment (such as a coffee maker) and service supplies (such as tableware and condiments) for easy access by servers and other staff members. Also called a server station, sidestand, or workstation.

traffic flow—The movement of staff members, guests, products, and supplies through an organization.

Review Questions

1. Why are design and decor issues important for food service establishments?
2. What criteria can help managers select a facility designer?
3. What design trends are affecting food service operations?
4. What is the idea behind the *liaison-froid* food service delivery system?
5. How does color affect guests?
6. How does lighting affect guests?
7. What questions might appear on a cleaning needs survey?
8. How should cleaning responsibilities be assigned and monitored?

Internet Sites

For more information, visit the following Internet sites. Remember that Internet addresses can change without notice.

American Society of Interior Designers
http://www.asid.org

FHG International Inc.
http://www.fhgi.com

Foodservice and Hospitality
http://www.foodservice.ca/fsh/fsh.htm

Foodservice World
http://www.foodserviceworld.com

Green Bee Designs, Inc.
http://www.gbd.com

Hospitality Design
http://www.billcom.com/hdmag

Nation's Restaurant News
http://www.nrn.com

Restaurant Business
http://www.restaurantbiz.com

Restaurant Report
http://www.restaurantreport.com

Restaurants & Institutions
http://www.rimag.com

Virtual Seating
http://www.virtualseating.com

Whitman Lane Associates
http://www.whitmanlane.com

References

Caro, Margaret Rose. "Lighten Up." *Lodging,* March 1997.

Cichy, Ronald F. *Quality Sanitation Management*. East Lansing, Mich.: Educational Institute of the American Hotel & Motel Association, 1994.

"Customers Are Talking About...Space." *Restaurants & Institutions,* March 15, 1994.

Doocey, Paul. "Restaurants Become Leaner and Meaner." *Hotel Business,* May 7–20, 1993.

"Global Resources Bring Innovations in Patient Feeding." *Restaurants & Institutions,* March 1, 1994.

Hertneky, Paul. "The Comfort Zone." *Restaurant Hospitality,* April 1993.

Hysen, Paul, *et al.* "Anticipating Paradigm Shifts in Foodservice." *Food Management,* January 1993.

Kooser, Ron. "10 Tips for Putting Productivity on the Front Burner." *Restaurant Hospitality,* June 1993.

Murray, Charles J. "From the Lab to the Kitchen." *Restaurants & Institutions,* October 15, 1993.

Patterson, Patt. "It Could Be a Loooong Way from the Kitchen." *Nation's Restaurant News,* November 29, 1993.

Weinstein, Jeff. "Sensory Designs Entice Customers." *Restaurants & Institutions,* January 1, 1994.

———. "Spruce Up for Spring." *Restaurants & Institutions,* February 12, 1992.

Case Study

Clean With an In-House Crew or Outsource to a Contract Cleaning Service?

Francesca Almanza was riding a wave of exhilaration after a meeting with her staff members about cleaning the restaurant themselves. For years, Emma's Family Restaurant, a 200-seat independent casual-dining operation, had been cleaned by an outside cleaning company, but Francesca had sold Emma, the owner, on the idea of cleaning with an in-house crew. Emma had asked Francesca to look for ways to cut costs. Francesca told Emma that with the current high level of staff member loyalty at the restaurant, the staff members would care about their cleaning work more than any outside crew would. Perhaps if the cleaning were done in-house, the occasional, mysterious thefts of liquor, food, and dishware would end. Cooks would no longer arrive to find detergents splattered on their prep areas and floors still wet. Tips would increase as guest satisfaction with the restaurant rose, and the predicted savings of $400 per month would eventually have an effect on paychecks, if all went well.

At the meeting with her staff members, Francesca had sold them on the idea, too. Francesca had asked for volunteers for the first work crew, and so many staff members had volunteered that she easily filled the crews for the first two weeks. Staff members had left the room talking about what they would do with their extra pay and how much better the restaurant would look when they had cleaned it.

Even some of those who hadn't volunteered talked about the higher tips they'd get from impressed guests.

On the first night of in-house cleaning, Francesca explained in detail the crew's responsibilities. "The kitchen and dishroom floors should be swept, soaped down, scrubbed with these deck brushes, and squeegeed dry. The mats should be cleaned with these detergents and brushes, then hosed down. Let me show you how to use these detergent dispensers." Francesca demonstrated their use. "When you're cleaning these areas, make sure you get behind the equipment, down around the legs of tables and machines. All the walls will need to be washed like this." She showed them the methods and materials. "Now, the bar area is going to need at least three of you. Some spills can be pretty stubborn. If you let them soak a while in this detergent, they should come up easier. While you're waiting for those to soak, you can vacuum the carpets and polish the brass in the front of the house. Two of you will work on the bathrooms...." Francesca spent many of the first few nights training and coaching crews on all their tasks.

The first couple of weeks saw success overall in the in-house cleaning program. Francesca, other staff members, and guests all saw a noticeable difference in the appearance of the facility. Francesca even invited Emma in for an extra inspection, and Emma was pleased with what she saw. Emma did notice that the inventory of cleaning chemicals was much lower than it should have been for that time of month. Francesca assured her that she would talk to cleaning crews about how much detergent to use. When Emma asked about thefts, Francesca reported that nothing had been missing since the switch to in-house crews. "That settles that question," said Emma. "If we ever do go back to a contract crew, we won't use that company again."

In the beginning of the third week of the in-house cleaning program, some servers who had not worked on cleaning crews came to Francesca with a complaint. They said that those servers who were on the cleaning crew were not cleaning up their side stations before they started their night cleaning duties. That Monday, one of the cleaning-crew members called and said he'd be late for work. Two others were late reporting for morning shifts that week, and they also called in sick two nights apiece. The quality of cleaning began to show signs of slipping. When Francesca urged the cleaning crews to be more thorough, she found that some began neglecting their regular duties in the last hour of the regular shifts so they could start cleaning early. And service quality began to sag.

One night Francesca noticed some cleaning crew members using a certain chemical without wearing goggles. She reminded them that goggles were required while that chemical was being used. "I know the goggles can be annoying, but they're for your own safety," she told them.

On Saturday morning of the third week of the program, a cook reported to Francesca that someone had taken two bites out of a dessert in the line cooler, and the bartender reported two bottles of beer missing. Francesca made a mental note to start keeping an eye on the cleaning crews. She was beginning to feel the fatigue of the 15- to 17-hour days she'd been working since the new program began. Cleaning in-house may save money, but it sure doesn't save time and effort in supervision, she thought to herself.

Francesca performed her regular monthly inspection the next week. She noticed that the vents, light fixtures, and blinds that were supposed to be cleaned weekly were not very thoroughly cleaned. At least that's about the same as what the contract crew did, she thought. She asked some staff members how they were feeling about the in-house cleaning program. One server said, "I don't know, I was all excited about it at first, but it's really hard work. And I wonder whether guests will really notice some of the stuff I'm cleaning." Overall, Francesca found that staff members were less enthusiastic about the program than they had been before, but several still thought it was worthwhile. Francesca noted that while crews were using less detergent than they had used initially, they were still using more than they should.

That night Francesca happened to overhear a conversation between two of the cleaning-crew members who were working on the floor of the bar. "Wow, the pay for this cleaning is great. Now I just wish I had time to spend it."

"Yeah, I'm worried that it'll come out equal to my old wages—I'm having to spend more on food, laundry, clothes—"

"Hey, why are you working so hard on those spills? Don't you remember what Francesca said about letting the detergents soak them?"

"Yeah, but—"

"'Yeah, but' nothing. With your back hurting you like it is, you should let the soaking do the work."

"This floor is always disgusting. Sweet-and-sour mix, strawberry daiquiri mix, ice cream, ashes—it just seems like no matter how long you let this stuff soak, you still have to scrub."

"You and I are pluggers: we plug away at this, and we're not afraid of hard work. But one of the cooks was complaining that he's a culinary something-or-other and that it's demeaning for him to scrub walls. I said to him, 'If you don't like it, why did you sign up?' He said, 'I didn't think I'd have to do this kind of stuff.' I don't know what he was thinking, when this is a cleaning crew."

"Well, I'm not afraid of hard work, but just the same, I think I hear my bed calling."

Francesca walked away and thought to herself, This schedule is taking a toll on all of us. I'll go figure out how much we're saving, and I'll tell the staff and Emma about it tomorrow—that will get our spirits up again. Francesca figured out the savings and was shocked to see that, in the first four weeks of the program, they had saved only $50—far less than the $400 she had hoped for. Okay, so the savings haven't hit the target, but what about tips and guest satisfaction? She tallied the month's reported tips and guest satisfaction ratings and found both about the same as what they had been with the contract cleaning crew. Francesca sat back and took a deep breath. Maybe it was time to review the situation.

First, Francesca identified the reasons that savings weren't what they should have been. Then she thoroughly evaluated the in-house cleaning program, examining all the facts at her disposal. Finally, she thought back to the pros and cons of the old contract cleaning arrangement. A couple of hours later, she began preparing a formal report for Emma on the in-house cleaning program.

Discussion Questions

1. What did Francesca learn from the experience of switching from contract cleaners to in-house cleaners?
2. Should Francesca continue the in-house cleaning program or should she recommend to Emma that the restaurant go back to a contract cleaning company? Why?
3. If Francesca decides to recommend contract cleaning, what information should she include in her presentation to Emma to back her position?

The following industry experts helped generate and develop this case: Christopher Kibit, C.S.C., Academic Team Leader, Hotel/Motel/Food Management & Tourism Programs, Lansing Community College, Lansing, Michigan; and Jack Nye, General Manager, Applebee's of Michigan, Applebee's International, Inc.

REVIEW QUIZ

When you feel you have covered all of the material in this chapter, answer these questions. Choose the *best* answer.

1. Whose needs and expectations should be considered the most when a dining area is being designed?

   a. guests'
   b. staff members'
   c. managers'
   d. those of the owner of the food service facility

2. When estimating the total size of a facility, planners often start with the number of __________ in the facility.

   a. workstations
   b. kitchens
   c. seats
   d. tables

3. A restaurant that seeks to subtly promote leisurely dining should choose a color scheme consisting of:

   a. warm colors.
   b. peach and teal.
   c. violets, blues, or light greens.
   d. reds, yellows, or deep oranges.

4. Light intensity is measured in units called:

   a. wattages.
   b. footcandles.
   c. light lumens.
   d. bulbs.

REVIEW QUIZ *(continued)*

5. The lives of curtains, draperies, and upholstered furniture can be prolonged by:

   a. careful vacuuming.
   b. washing these items with a pressure sprayer.
   c. shampooing these items with a dry-foam chemical once a week.
   d. painstaking saturation with a mild soap-and-water solution.

Answer Key: 1-a-C1, 2-c-C1, 3-c-C2, 4-b-C2, 5-a-C3

Each question is linked to a competency. Competencies are listed on the first page of the chapter. An answer reading 3-b-C4 translates to:

3: the question number
b: the correct answer
C4: the competency number

Chapter 7 Outline

Sanitation Issues
- Sanitation Risk Management Programs
- Hazard Analysis Critical Control Point System
- Service Staff Training
- Guidelines for Serving Food
- Guidelines for Servers
- Equipment, Furniture, and Supply Guidelines
- Guidelines for Facilities

Safety Issues
- The Importance of Training
- Fire Safety

Security Issues
- Robberies
- Bomb Threats

Health Issues
- Nutrition
- Smoking

Legal Issues
- Risk Management
- Sexual Harassment
- Americans with Disabilities Act
- Minimum Wage and Immigration Reform
- Health Care Reform
- AIDS and Herpes

Competencies

1. Describe the critical role of food sanitation in food and beverage operations, explain the HACCP concept of food safety, and describe the role of staff members in ensuring food safety in relation to food handling, personal hygiene, equipment use, and facility cleanliness.
2. Outline preventive steps for workplace safety and the appropriate follow-up and investigation procedures when accidents occur; identify the three common types of fires and how to extinguish them; and list recommendations for handling robberies and bomb threats.
3. Describe the fundamentals of sound nutrition, how food and beverage operations are addressing guest requests for healthier food options, and the changing guest attitudes toward smoking.
4. Summarize the following legal issues as they apply to food service operations: risk management, sexual harassment, the Americans with Disabilities Act, minimum wage and immigration reform, health care reform, and AIDS and herpes.

7

Sanitation, Safety, Security, Health, and Legal Issues

ALL SERVICE STAFF must pay close attention to sanitation, safety, security, health, and legal issues. While local, state, and federal laws require service organizations to protect food and beverage products from contamination, prevent guests from being exposed to unsafe procedures and situations, provide no-smoking sections in dining areas, and accommodate guests who have physical disabilities, these and other legal mandates are only the beginning. Professional food service staff members must do everything in their power to ensure that guests' experiences are enjoyable and safe. That obligation goes far beyond the dictates of laws.

In more practical terms, food service managers, staff members, and owners do not want headlines about a food-related illness traced to their operations. Experienced managers know that a kitchen or dining room emergency can adversely affect business, so they ensure that safety and security training is a major part of their standard operating procedures for all service staff. Today's food service operations must find ways to please guests who want nutritious and "heart-healthy" menu items when dining out. And legal issues such as serving alcohol responsibly cannot be ignored by food service managers and staff. In the following sections we will discuss these and other sanitation, safety, security, health, and legal issues as they affect food service operations.

Sanitation Issues

Imagine a newspaper headline or radio or TV lead story that starts out by stating: "Guest dies from eating contaminated oysters" or "Guests wretch uncontrollably after noticing worms in their rice." Each of these situations actually happened, and both resulted in media coverage as well as lawsuits against the food and beverage operations that served the food. Large-scale, nationwide recalls of food have made headlines in recent years as well. When more than 1,000 people became ill after eating raspberries from Guatemala, Guatemala's 1998 crop of raspberries was banned from the United States. A wholesale food supplier recalled 25 million pounds of ground beef because of food safety concerns. And in 1993, a bacteria outbreak almost forced the Jack in the Box quick-service chain out of business after a number of guests died or became seriously ill after eating hamburgers infected with *E. coli* at its restaurants. As you can see, food sanitation issues are high on the list of concerns for guests and owners of food service businesses.

The U.S. Centers for Disease Control and Prevention report that millions of people in the United States are stricken with **foodborne illnesses** each year; thousands die from them. Yet the dining public is not fully aware of the scope of potential food dangers.

The source of many foodborne diseases is infectious microorganisms, or pathogens. A foodborne illness also results when food containing toxic or toxigenic (toxin-producing) agents is eaten. The potential problems are getting worse as a result of emerging new pathogens, the increase in imported foods grown and processed under loosely monitored conditions, and the rising number of food service staff members whose training does not impart a basic understanding of personal hygiene and sanitation. Add to these risks hot, humid kitchen production areas, language barriers among food service staff, and high turnover, and you have the formula for dramatic increases in foodborne illnesses. Food service businesses must develop risk management programs to help control sanitation risks.

Sanitation Risk Management Programs

A **sanitation risk management (SRM) program** focuses on reducing overall sanitation risks by identifying the risks at each control point in a food service operation. In an SRM program, standards and procedures for each control point are presented as they relate to the four resources under a manager's control: inventory, people, equipment, and facilities. A resource evaluation is necessary at each control point. The result is a systematic approach to managing risks. Exhibit 1 presents an SRM diagram for baked chicken. The right side of the diagram indicates the appropriate SRM actions that reduce risks at each control point.

Inventory is an essential management resource because it is converted into revenue and, ultimately, into profits. Inventory in a food service operation normally consists of food products, beverages, and nonfood items such as table linens and cleaning chemicals. Inventory control is a vital link in an operation's cost and quality control systems; inventory items are assets that must be protected from spoilage, contamination, pilferage, and waste.

Because the hospitality industry is labor-intensive, people are an especially important resource. It is management's responsibility to train staff members in proper sanitation practices. Failing to properly train staff members undermines an operation's SRM program and jeopardizes the organization's bottom line.

Equipment selection is important to an SRM program, as are the proper cleaning and maintenance of each piece of equipment. In addition, facility design and layout have a great impact on the success of an SRM program. At an SRM program's core, however, is the FDA *Food Code.*

The 1993 ***Food Code,*** published by the Food and Drug Administration (FDA), represents the FDA's best advice for a uniform system of regulations to ensure that food prepared at retail establishments is safe and properly protected and presented. The *Code* provides guidelines designed to minimize foodborne illness and promote staff member health, manager knowledge, safe food, nontoxic and clean equipment, and acceptable levels of sanitation where food is served. It also promotes fair dealing with guests.

Exhibit 1 Sample SRM Diagram for Baked Chicken

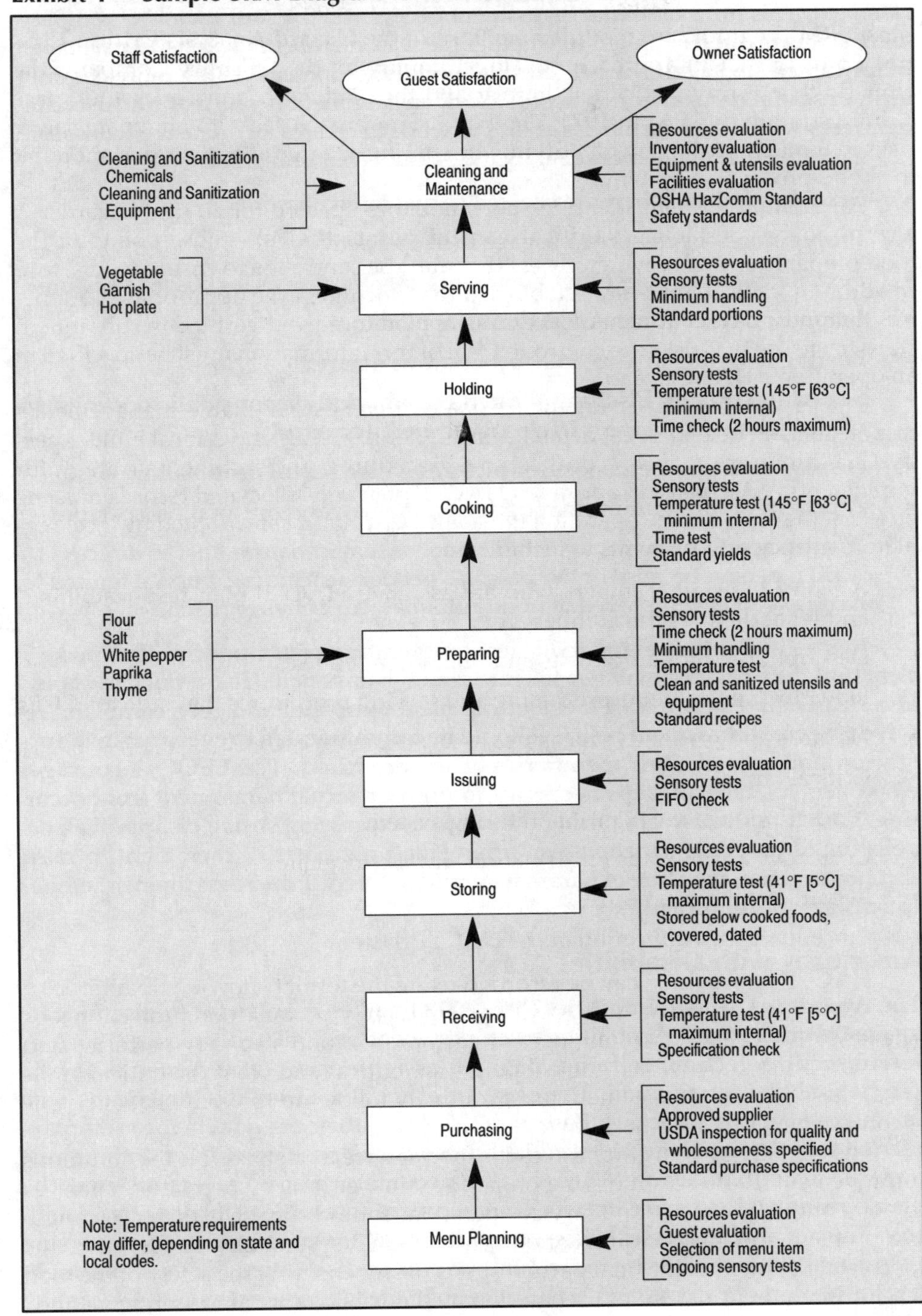

Hazard Analysis Critical Control Point System

Most SRM programs are modified versions of the **Hazard Analysis Critical Control Point (HACCP)** approach developed jointly by the Pillsbury Company, the United States Army Natick Laboratory, and the National Aeronautics and Space Administration (NASA) in 1974. The HACCP approach seeks to eliminate safety risks in food processing by identifying the specific hazards at each important point in a food production system.

An HACCP system identifies and monitors specific foodborne hazards. A hazard analysis establishes **critical control points (CCPs)**—those points in the food preparation and serving process that must be controlled to ensure food safety. In addition, critical limits are established that document the appropriate parameters that must be met at each CCP. CCPs are monitored and verified in subsequent steps to ensure that risks are controlled. All of this information must be specified in an operation's **HACCP plan**.

The preparation and maintenance of a written HACCP plan is management's responsibility. The plan must detail hazards, identify CCPs and critical limits, specify CCP monitoring and recordkeeping procedures, and outline a strategy for implementing the plan. An approved HACCP plan and associated records must be on file at the food service operation if the *Food Code* has been adopted by local regulatory agencies. Documents to include are:

- A list of the staff members who are assigned HACCP plan responsibilities, and what their responsibilities are
- Descriptions of food products and their intended uses
- Flow diagrams of food-processing and serving procedures that indicate CCPs
- Hazards and preventive measures associated with each CCP
- Critical limits
- A description of the plan's monitoring system
- Corrective action plans for deviations from critical limits
- Recordkeeping procedures
- Procedures for verification of the HACCP system

HACCP information can be recorded using the format shown in Exhibit 2.

When used properly, the HACCP system is an important food protection tool. The key to success is staff training. For each preparation step they perform, staff members must know which control points are critical and what the critical limits are at these points. Management must routinely follow up to verify that everyone is complying with the critical limits.

The HACCP system emphasizes the food service industry's role in continuous improvement. Rather than relying on periodic inspections by regulatory agencies to point out deficiencies, food service operations should engage in their own ongoing problem solving and prevention. The HACCP system clearly identifies the food establishment as the final party responsible for ensuring the safety of the food it sells. It requires analysis of preparation methods in a rational, scientific manner.

Exhibit 2 Sample HACCP Information Reporting Form

Process Step	CCP	Chemical/ Physical/ Biological Hazards	Critical Limit	Monitoring Procedures/ Frequency/ Person(s) Responsible	Corrective Action(s)/ Person(s) Responsible	HACCP Records	Verification Procedures/ Person(s) Responsible

Source: Adapted from the FDA 1993 *Food Code.*

Management is responsible for maintaining records that document adherence to the critical limits that relate to the identified critical control points. This results in continuous self-inspection. The HACCP system also helps managers and staff determine the establishment's level of compliance with the *Food Code.*

An operation's HACCP plan must be shared with local regulatory agencies, which must have access to the CCP monitoring records and other data necessary to verify that the HACCP plan is working. With conventional inspection techniques, a regulatory agency can only determine conditions that exist during the time of the inspection. However, both past and current conditions can be reviewed when an HACCP approach is used. Therefore, regulatory agencies can more effectively ensure that food production processes are under control. Traditional approaches to inspection are reactive; HACCP is preventive.

The Seven HACCP Steps. The National Advisory Committee on Microbiological Criteria for Foods (NACMCF) has developed seven widely accepted HACCP steps.

Step #1: Hazard analysis. Hazard analysis identifies significant sanitation hazards, estimates the likelihood of their occurrence and severity, and develops preventive measures to improve food safety. Hazards can be categorized as biological, chemical, and physical. Biological hazards include bacteria, viruses, and parasites. Chemical hazards may be naturally occurring or may be introduced during food processing. Physical hazards are foreign objects found in food.

In the hazard analysis process step, management must ask and answer a series of questions for each control point in its flow diagrams of food-processing and serving procedures (see Exhibit 3). Once these questions are answered, preventive measures (which may be physical or chemical) can be taken to control hazards. For example, cooking sufficiently to kill pathogens is a physical preventive measure.

Step #2: Identify the CCPs in the food process. A critical control point is a step or procedure at which control must be applied to prevent, eliminate, or reduce to acceptable levels a food safety hazard. Some safety measures used at CCPs are cooking, chilling, recipe control, prevention of cross-contamination, and certain staff hygiene procedures (handwashing, for example). While there may be many control points in a food preparation and serving process (as shown in Exhibit 1), few may be *critical* control points. CCPs differ with the layout of a facility as well as with the equipment, ingredients, and processes used to prepare and serve a particular menu item.

Step #3: Establish critical limits for preventive measures associated with each identified CCP. A critical limit is a boundary of safety. Some preventive measures have upper and lower critical limits. For example, the **temperature danger zone** has a lower critical limit of 41°F (5°C) and an upper critical limit of 140°F (60°C); potentially hazardous foods should not be held within this range—41°F–140°F (5°C–60°C)—of temperatures.

Consider the cooking of freshly ground beef patties. Critical limit criteria in this instance would include temperature, time, and patty thickness. Each patty should be cooked to a minimum internal temperature of 155°F (68°C) for a minimum of 15 seconds if using a broiler set at 400°F (207°C). Patty thickness should not exceed one-half inch (2.6 centimeters). These three critical limit criteria must be evaluated and monitored regularly. There are other critical limit criteria for cooking freshly ground beef patties as well, including humidity, preservatives, and salt concentration.

Step #4: Establish procedures to monitor CCPs. Monitoring comprises a planned sequence of measurements or observations taken to ascertain whether a CCP is under control. Monitoring procedures should (1) track the HACCP system's operation so that a trend toward a loss of control can be identified and corrective action taken to bring the process back into control before a deviation occurs; (2) indicate when a loss of control and a deviation have actually occurred; and (3) provide written documentation for use in verifying that the HACCP plan is working. Examples of measurements for monitoring include sensory observations (such as with sight, smell, touch), temperature, and time.

Monitoring procedures must be effective to avoid unsafe food. When feasible, continuous monitoring is always preferable. Instruments used for measuring critical limits must be carefully calibrated and used accurately, and calibration records must be maintained as part of an operation's HACCP plan documentation. When it is not possible to monitor continuously, sampling systems or statistically designed data collection should be used. The most appropriate staff member should be assigned responsibility for monitoring each CCP and must be trained to be accurate. If an operation or product does not meet critical limits, immediate corrective action should be taken. All records used for monitoring should be initialed or signed and dated by the person doing the monitoring.

Exhibit 3 Hazard Analysis Food Process Questions

1. **Ingredients**
   - Does the food contain any sensitive ingredients that are likely to present microbiological hazards (e.g., *Salmonella, Staphylococcus aureus*), chemical hazards (e.g., aflatoxin, antibiotic, or pesticide residues), or physical hazards (stones, glass, bone, metal)?

2. **Intrinsic factors of food**

   Physical characteristics and composition (e.g., pH, types of acids, fermentable carbohydrate, a_w, preservatives) of the food during and after the process can cause or prevent a hazard.

   - Which intrinsic factors of the food must be controlled to ensure food safety?
   - Does the food allow survival or multiplication of pathogens and/or toxin formation before or during the process?
   - Will the food allow survival or multiplication of pathogens and/or toxin formation during subsequent control points, including storage or consumer possession?
   - Are there similar products in the marketplace? What has been the safety record for these products?

3. **Procedures used for the process**
   - Does the procedure or process include a controllable step that destroys pathogens or their toxins? Consider both vegetative cells and spores.
   - Is the product subject to recontamination between production (e.g., cooking) and packaging?

4. **Microbial content of the food**
   - Is the food commercially sterile (as is low-acid canned food)?
   - Is it likely that the food will contain viable sporeforming or nonsporeforming pathogens?
   - What is the normal microbial content of the food stored under proper conditions?
   - Does the microbial population change during the time the food is stored before consumption?
   - Does that change in microbial population alter the safety of the food?

5. **Facility design**
   - Does the layout of the facility provide an adequate separation of raw materials from ready-to-eat foods?
   - Is positive air pressure maintained in product packaging areas? Is this essential for product safety?
   - Is the traffic pattern for people and moving equipment a potentially significant source of contamination?

6. **Equipment design**
   - Will the equipment provide the time/temperature control that is necessary for safe food?
   - Is the equipment properly sized for the volume of food that will be prepared?
   - Can the equipment be sufficiently controlled so that the variation in performance will be within the tolerances required to produce a safe food?
   - Is the equipment reliable or is it prone to frequent breakdowns?
   - Is the equipment designed so that it can be cleaned and sanitized?
   - Is there a chance for product contamination with hazardous substances, e.g., glass?
   - What product safety devices such as time/temperature integrators are used to enhance consumer safety?

(continued)

Exhibit 3 *(continued)*

7. **Packaging**
   - Does the method of packaging affect the multiplication of microbial pathogens and/or the formation of toxins?
   - Is the packaging material resistant to damage, thereby preventing the entrance of microbial contamination?
   - Is the package clearly labeled "Keep Refrigerated" if this is required for safety?
   - Does the package include instructions for the safe handling and preparation of the food by the consumer?
   - Are tamper-evident packaging features used?
   - Is each package legibly and accurately coded to indicate production lot?
   - Does each package contain the proper label?
8. **Sanitation**
   - Can the sanitation practices that are employed adversely affect the safety of the food that is being produced?
   - Can the facility be cleaned and sanitized to permit the safe handling of food?
   - Is it possible to provide sanitary conditions consistently and adequately to ensure safe foods?
9. **Staff member health, hygiene, and education**
   - Can staff member health or personal hygiene practices adversely affect the safety of the food being produced?
   - Does the staff understand the food production process and the factors they must control to ensure safe foods?
   - Will the staff inform management of a problem that could negatively affect food safety?
10. **Conditions of storage between packaging and the consumer**
    - What is the likelihood that the food will be improperly stored at the wrong temperature?
    - Would storage at improper temperatures lead to a microbiologically unsafe food?
11. **Intended use**
    - Will the food be heated by the consumer?
    - Will there likely be leftovers?
12. **Intended consumer**
    - Is the food intended for the general public, a population that does not have an increased risk of becoming ill?
    - Is the food intended for consumption by a population with increased susceptibility to illness (e.g., infants, the elderly, the infirm, and immunocompromised individuals)?

Source: Adapted from the FDA 1993 *Food Code.*

Step #5: Establish the corrective action to be taken when monitoring shows that a critical limit has been exceeded. Although food and beverage operations aim at perfection every time they prepare and serve food, problems or deviations from plan procedures sometimes occur. A corrective action plan determines the disposition of any food produced while a deviation was occurring, corrects the cause of the deviation, ensures that the CCP is back under control, and maintains records of the corrective actions taken.

Specific corrective action plans are required for each CCP. Corrective action procedures should be well documented in the HACCP plan. When a deviation occurs, more frequent monitoring may be required temporarily to ensure that the CCP is under control again.

Step #6: Establish effective recordkeeping systems that document the HACCP system. Recordkeeping is a very important part of the HACCP system. The level of sophistication of recordkeeping depends on the complexity of the food service operation. The simplest effective recordkeeping system is the best.

Step #7: Establish procedures to verify that the HACCP system is working. Typically, there are four phases of verification. The first phase is scientific or technical verification that critical limits at CCPs are satisfactory. (This may be complex and may require expert assistance.) The second phase ensures that the HACCP plan is functioning effectively. It involves frequent reviews of the HACCP plan, review of CCP records, and verification that appropriate risk management decisions and product dispositions are made when production deviations occur. The third phase comprises documented periodic revalidations performed by staff members with HACCP plan responsibilities. The fourth phase is verification by the regulatory authority or authorities that have jurisdiction over the food service operation.

HACCP plan verification procedures may include the following:

- Review of deviations and their resolutions, including the disposition of food
- Visual inspections of operations to observe if CCPs are under control
- Random sample collection and analysis
- Review of critical limits to verify that they can adequately control hazards
- Review of modifications to the HACCP plan

Managers should conduct HACCP verification inspections:

- Routinely or on an unannounced basis
- When it is determined that intensive scrutiny of a specific food is necessary because of new information concerning food safety
- When foods prepared at the establishment have been implicated as vehicles of foodborne disease
- When consultants request them and resources allow the operation to accommodate the request
- When established criteria have not been met

Staff training is an important element in the success of a food establishment's HACCP system. An HACCP system works best when it is integrated into each staff member's duties and not seen as an "add-on." The fundamental training goal should be to make managers and staff members proficient in the specific tasks required by the HACCP plan. In addition, the training plan should be specific to the establishment.

Options for training include the American Hotel & Motel Association's *Fast Track Food Safety* program, which provides video-based training for food receiving and storage, food production, food service, and warewashing; HACCP training videos; reminders about HACCP critical limits such as "Handwashing Pays Big Dividends" printed on time cards or checks; and workstation reminders such as posters on how and when to take food temperatures. The HACCP plan should include a "feedback loop" so that staff members may suggest what additional training is required.

Service Staff Training

Service staff training is the key to reducing sanitation risks and increasing management, staff member, guest, and owner satisfaction. Food establishments should begin with a well-defined training process—focusing on inventory, people, equipment, and facilities—and use the resources of local, state, and national regulatory agencies.

The first phase of staff training should provide information on the history and structure of the operation's sanitation risk management program and emphasize specific sanitation goals and objectives. The study of the epidemiology of foodborne illness—including organisms, foods, contributing factors, and all aspects of basic microbiology—is critical. The second phase of training is on-site training conducted by trainers familiar with HACCP inspecting. Trainees should demonstrate expertise in data gathering and analysis before moving to the third phase of training: standardization. In this phase, points of violation are fully discussed and differentiated from similar conditions that are not violations. The final phase of training—lifelong or continuing education—is ongoing. Managers and staff members must remain current in this rapidly changing world, through seminars and workshops offered by colleges and universities, professional associations, regulatory agencies, and private companies. Food service training programs offer excellent opportunities for acquiring and reinforcing food safety knowledge.

Guidelines for Serving Food

The *Food Code's* specific requirements for safe food display and service apply not only to food served from the kitchen but also to items set up for guest self-service at soup and salad bars, buffet tables, and sandwich and dessert bars. The following sanitation guidelines can help an operation control its investment in inventory and reduce its risks at the serving control point.

Potentially hazardous foods must be kept out of the temperature danger zone (TDZ) at the serving control point. A **potentially hazardous food** is any food or ingredient capable of supporting the rapid growth of infectious or toxigenic microorganisms, or the slower growth of *Clostridium botulinum*. The TDZ is the temperature range defined by the U.S. Public Health Service as the range in which most pathogenic activity takes place and food spoilage can occur. It is typically 41°F–140°F (5°C–60°C), although the TDZ may vary from locality to locality; managers should check with their state and local regulatory agencies. Hot food should be served on heated plates, cold food on chilled plates. This practice helps to keep product temperatures outside the TDZ and enhances product quality.

Milk and milk products served as beverages should be served in unopened, commercially filled packages of one pint (.47 liter) or less or drawn from a com-

The Centers for Disease Control and Prevention (http://www.cdc.gov) offer an Internet site with numerous food service sanitation and safety resources. (Courtesy of the Centers for Disease Control and Prevention, Atlanta, Georgia)

mercial milk dispenser into a cleaned and sanitized glass. Dairy and non-dairy coffee creamers should be individually packaged, drawn from a refrigerated dispenser, or poured from a covered pitcher. If stored at a sidestand, milk or cream must be refrigerated. Individually portioned coffee creamer that has been ultra-high-temperature pasteurized, aseptically filled, and hermetically sealed is the only liquid dairy or non-dairy coffee creamer exempted from refrigeration requirements. It has a shelf life of 120 days at room temperature.

Dressings, seasonings, and condiments such as chutney, mustard, and relish that are placed on tables or self-service stands must be presented in covered containers, dispensers, or single-serving packages. Ketchup and other sauces may be served in their original containers or in pour-type dispensers. Generally, the refilling of original containers is prohibited. Sugar on tables should be in either individual packets or pour-type dispensers.

Ice for guest consumption should be handled with ice-dispensing scoops or tongs or dispensed by an automatic ice machine. Guests should serve themselves only from automatic dispensers. Utensils for dispensing ice should be stored in a sanitary manner between uses.

Staff members should use utensils or gloves when dispensing food to guests. In-use dispensing utensils can be stored in the food with the handles extended, or under running water, or clean and dry. Production staff or servers should never dispense food (biscuits or rolls in a buffet line, for example) with their hands unless wearing single-use gloves; likewise, guests should use utensils and not their hands for serving themselves.

Leftover food returned to the kitchen must not be re-served. For example, crocks of cheese or butter should be served only once. The exception to this rule is packaged, non-hazardous food in sound condition. Self-service guests should not reuse tableware when they return to the service area for additional food; however, they may reuse beverage glasses and cups. Unpackaged food on display should be protected from guest contamination by easily cleaned food shields (sneeze guards).

Guidelines for Servers

The term *server* may be used to refer to any person directly involved in the service of food and beverages. The image and size of the operation generally determine whether other positions are included in the serving function. At many operations, a host greets and seats guests and supervises the dining room staff, for example. In some large or formal dining rooms, a maître d'hôtel may supervise service and be assisted by a captain. Buspersons assist servers by clearing and setting up tables. Frequently, a cashier is assigned the responsibility of handling all guest payments. In some operations, certain positions are combined. For example, one staff member serves as cashier and host. Servers sometimes clear and set tables.

Servers, like all food service staff members, must practice good personal hygiene and cleanliness. Standards of personal hygiene should be adapted to the individual operation and presented to all staff members during orientation and training.

Proper handwashing is extremely important. Servers should wash their hands before starting work and frequently throughout the shift. It is also important that they wash their hands immediately after touching hair or skin, sneezing, coughing, using a handkerchief, smoking, visiting the restroom, handling raw food products, or handling soiled containers or tableware.

In addition to proper handwashing, the following sanitation standards apply to all servers:

- Do not smoke, chew gum, or eat in the dining area or kitchen.
- Never serve food that has left the plate or fallen to the floor.
- Replace dropped tableware with clean items.

- Use recommended utensils and store them in a sanitary manner when they are not in use.
- Avoid touching food with your hands. Dishes, cups, glasses, and flatware should only be handled in places that will not come into contact with food or with the guest's mouth. Dishes should be held with four fingers on the bottom and the thumb on the edge, not touching the food. Cups and flatware should be touched only on the handles. A glass should be grasped at the base and placed on the table without touching the rim.
- Never carry a service towel or napkin over your shoulder or under your arm.
- Be certain the bottom of a piece of tableware is clean before placing it on the table. Remove all soiled tableware and return it to the dirty-dish station to prevent its reuse.
- Keep the tops, bottoms, and sides of serving trays clean to prevent unnecessary soiling of uniforms, tableware, and tablecloths.
- Maintain a clean and professional appearance.
- Work carefully and always keep standards of cleanliness in mind.

Guests expect their dining experiences to be pleasant and safe. If servers violate the standards of personal hygiene or cleanliness with unsanitary practices, disease agents may be transmitted to guests. In addition, physical foodborne contaminants, such as hair or glass fragments, can result in an unpleasant dining experience or even guest injury.

When placing orders in the kitchen, the server's timing is critical to the rapid flow of products to the dining area. Properly timed orders are plated and served almost simultaneously, thus maintaining product temperatures and reducing sanitation risks. In some operations, an expediter acts as a communication link between the kitchen staff and servers. Servers give their orders to the expediter, who calls the orders to the appropriate kitchen stations. The expediter must know cooking times, coordinate them to sequentially deliver cooked foods for pickup, and provide leadership during hectic rush periods. He or she should be a member of the management team.

In some operations, servers are responsible for a few production and portioning tasks, such as portioning beverages, soups, or desserts; adding dressings to salads; garnishing plates; and obtaining food accompaniments such as sauces. In all cases, servers must follow the organization's sanitation and portioning standards.

Servers should load serving trays carefully to reduce the likelihood of accidents. Once food is served, servers should return frequently to the table to remove dirty dishes, refill water glasses, and empty ashtrays. After guests leave, the table should be cleared and reset with clean items. Whoever performs this duty—a server or a busperson—should wash his or her hands after handling soiled tableware and before resetting the table with clean items.

Servers need not wash their hands every time they handle money. Although money is often thought of as "dirty," the FDA has determined that currency does not support enough microorganisms to be a source of contamination. However, guests generally do not like to see servers handle money and then serve food.

Equipment, Furniture, and Supply Guidelines

Serving equipment must be cleaned, sanitized, stored, and handled in a manner that prevents subsequent contamination.

Preset tableware must be wrapped or set no sooner than one meal period before use. Presetting should not be a substitute for proper utensil storage. Extra settings of tableware should be removed from the table when guests are seated. This not only helps protect the sanitary quality of tableware, but also prevents needless washing, rinsing, and sanitizing of clean tableware. Sneeze guards and proper serving utensils are required on self-service food bars in the dining area.

Self-service food bars, if not properly maintained, can be perceived as messy and unsanitary. Some outbreaks of foodborne illness have been traced to salad bars. However, certain procedures can help reduce risks. The conditions and temperatures of the food and the salad bar should be checked every 10 to 15 minutes. Spills should be wiped up and utensils replaced when necessary. To ensure freshness and quality, food in salad bars should be placed in relatively small containers, replaced frequently, displayed on crushed ice or in cold inserts, and protected by properly designed sneeze guards. These safety devices should extend the length and width of the bar and be positioned 10 to 12 inches (25.4 to 30.5 centimeters) above the food. Display stands for unwrapped food must be effectively shielded to intercept the direct line between the average guest's mouth and the food being displayed.

Soup and dessert bars call for similar procedures. Equipment should be capable of properly maintaining food temperatures. Covers, but not food shields, are required for self-service soup containers. The covers do not have to be hinged or self-closing. It is a good idea to display small amounts of each food item and replenish items frequently. Constant supervision of all types of food bars is crucial to risk reduction and should be part of every server's responsibilities.

Tables and chairs should be dusted or wiped to remove food debris before the organization opens each day. Servers should inspect them frequently throughout their shifts for cleanliness and proper setup.

Items placed on tables must be kept clean. This is often a part of the server's sidework. Sugar dispensers and salt and pepper shakers should be wiped clean at least once a day. If glass dispensers or shakers are used, they should be periodically emptied, washed, rinsed, dried, and refilled. The volume of business affects the amount of sugar, salt, and pepper used at each table and, therefore, the frequency of refilling. Some operations use disposable dispensers and shakers to reduce the labor costs associated with maintaining these items.

If syrup or condiments are placed on tables, the exteriors of the containers should be cleaned regularly. They can be wiped with a damp cloth to remove fingerprints and drips. Original condiment containers designed for dispensing (like ketchup bottles) should not be washed and refilled. Wide-mouth condiment or syrup bottles can easily become contaminated and should not be used in the dining area.

Napkins are usually folded before service. They should be stored so as to prevent soiling. Paper napkins should be discarded from tables after service, even if they look clean. Cloth napkins must be properly laundered after each use and should never be used to wipe flatware, glasses, cups, or ashtrays. Ashtrays should be clean and stocked with matches. Servers should check their service trays before beginning work to make sure the bottoms, tops, and sides of the trays are free from grease, food, and other debris.

One item frequently neglected during sidework is flatware. Soiled, spotted eating utensils are both unsightly and unsanitary. Soiled flatware may require soaking before being washed in the dishwashing machine. After washing, it should be checked to ensure that it is clean.

Plate and platter covers allow servers to carry more orders on each tray. They also help maintain a menu item's serving temperature if the item is placed on a heated or chilled plate in the kitchen. Covers also help guard against contamination during transportation from the kitchen to the guest. Plate and platter covers must be regularly cleaned, sanitized, and stored in such a manner as to prevent contamination before their next use.

Takeout service requires additional equipment to hold hot and cold packaged foods. Some holding units have clear covers or doors to display the selection of hot and cold items to guests. Equipment selection is based on the menu items offered for take-out. Holding equipment should be able to maintain the proper temperatures and relative humidities. It should be cleaned and sanitized regularly.

Care should be exercised in handling all equipment and supplies used for serving. Waste and breakage can be costly to the organization. Each time a server carelessly soils linen, wastes supplies, or throws away or breaks tableware, the operation's costs increase. If fragments of glass find their way into guests' food and beverages, safety is sacrificed and the organization's reputation and revenues will suffer.

Guidelines for Facilities

The cleaning, repair, and maintenance of the operation's facilities are essential at all control points. These activities are particularly important at the serving control point, because the dining area environment directly affects guest satisfaction. A clean and pleasant dining area enhances the organization's image and makes a positive first impression on guests.

The dining area supervisor should inspect the facilities with all the lights turned on before service begins. This daily inspection is part of the overall preparation for service. The supervisor should check floors, walls, and ceilings to see if they need to be cleaned or if any maintenance or repairs are necessary. In addition, tables, chairs, and booths should be inspected for cleanliness. If the dining area has windows, the ledges should be dusted. Menus should be inspected to ensure that daily specials are attached. Dirty or damaged menus should be removed from circulation. The inspection should include food displays and sidestands. If there are pieces of equipment in sidestands (coffee makers or small coolers, for example) they should be checked to make sure they are functioning properly.

After the inspection, the dining area supervisor should adjust the lighting levels to create the proper ambiance. The ventilation system should be designed so that the dining area does not become stuffy or smoky while guests are dining.

While wood is sometimes used to create a cozy dining atmosphere, untreated wood is subject to decay caused by bacteria and fungi. This process is accelerated by alternating periods of moisture and dryness. Wood for holding and displaying fresh fruits, fresh vegetables, and nuts in the shell may be treated with a preservative approved for such use.

One additional sanitation consideration is important for serving facilities: animals. Although there are some exceptions, animals are not generally allowed in food service operations in the United States. One notable exception is guide dogs; they are permitted in dining areas to accompany guests with visual impairments.

Safety Issues

According to the Federal Bureau of Labor Statistics, the food service industry recently had an annual injury rate of approximately 6 injuries per 100 workers. One-third of these injuries were serious and resulted in an average work loss of 35 days. However, most food service accidents and injuries are preventable.

The National Safety Council notes that the most frequent accident in a food service establishment is a fall in either the kitchen or service area. (The Occupational Safety and Health Administration is another agency that closely monitors food service safety and safety violations.) These accidents cost employers an estimated $200 million each year in workers' compensation payments to injured staff members. Slippery floors, often the result of unattended spills, cause most of these falls. A well-designed safety training program can reduce such accidents.

The Importance of Training

Safety training should be a part of every staff member's regular job training. In food service organizations, learning solely by experience may be dangerous. In addition to a lack of training, accidents and injuries may also be caused by unsafe equipment or conditions. It is management's responsibility to periodically conduct in-house safety inspections to identify and correct hazards.

Successful safety training involves a combination of defining precise techniques and operating procedures, teaching staff those techniques and procedures, assigning specific jobs, carefully supervising staff, and properly maintaining the facilities and equipment. Staff members will show an interest in safety if management emphasizes its importance during initial training and then regularly reminds them about safety. Posters, displays, and other visual aids can help remind staff members to take safety precautions every day.

Preventive Measures. Food service injuries include burns, cuts, and injuries caused by lifting improperly or falling. Exhibit 4 presents some safety rules designed to prevent common food service accidents.

Staff members should know how to operate equipment safely before they use it. Malfunctioning equipment should be reported to the department supervisor, who should then contact the maintenance department so repairs can be completed as soon as possible. Staff should wear the appropriate protective gear when using potentially dangerous machinery or chemicals.

Floors should be kept clean and dry. Spills should be wiped up immediately. Aisles and passageways should be kept clean, uncluttered, and unobstructed.

Exhibit 4 Safety Rules for Food Service Operations

Burn Prevention

1. Maintain traffic and workflow patterns in production and service areas.
2. Maintain adequate working space around hot holding and cooking equipment.
3. Use a clean, dry cloth or pot holder when handling hot dishes, pans, and equipment.
4. Follow the manufacturer's recommendations when operating equipment.
5. Use coffee urns with care. Do not talk or turn away while filling coffeepots or cups. Look before turning with coffeepots in your hand.
6. Do not leave empty coffeepots on heating units.
7. Carry only as many cups of coffee at one time as you can manage safely.
8. Turn off all electrical equipment immediately after you are finished using it.
9. Keep the range and surrounding areas grease-free to prevent fires and burns.
10. When lifting covers from pots and pans on the range, tilt the covers away from you, not toward you, to allow steam to safely dissipate.
11. Keep pot holders and towels away from open flames.
12. Maintain safety and sanitation precautions at all times.

Cut Prevention

1. Do not use any cutting, slicing, or grinding equipment without learning how to operate it properly.
2. Be sure all safety devices are in place before using dangerous machinery such as slicers and grinders.
3. Use the right tool for each kitchen job. For example, do not use knives to open bottles or cans.
4. Keep knives and cutting tools sharp and in good condition.
5. Do not turn away from your work while handling knives.
6. Do not pick up a knife by the blade. Never try to catch a falling knife.
7. Handle glass with care to avoid breaking it.
8. Discard all chipped glasses and dishes promptly and safely.
9. Wear protective gloves and be careful when putting your hands in water containing knives or glassware.
10. Use a broom and dustpan to pick up all broken china and glass. Do not use your hands.
11. When using steel wool, protect your hand with a cloth or glove.
12. Remove or bend down nails and pieces of metal protruding from barrels and boxes.
13. Clean and sanitize knives after use and store them away from other utensils.
14. Do not use your fingers to push the end of an item through a moving slicer blade.

(continued)

Exhibit 4 *(continued)*

Fall Prevention

1. Keep all floors dry around workstations.
2. Wipe up spilled food, water, oil, and grease immediately.
3. Keep all aisles and work areas clear and free of obstructions. Do not leave drawers or doors open.
4. Do not leave debris or boxes where other staff members might fall over them.
5. When you drop something on the floor, pick it up as soon as possible.
6. Avoid blocking passageways when bending down. Make sure no one is coming along with hot food.
7. Do not stand in a doorway or otherwise block the flow of traffic.
8. When you walk, place your feet firmly on the floor. Do not run.
9. Wear shoes with good soles and heels. Wear full-leather shoes with anti-skid soles in the kitchen.
10. Load trays carefully and distribute the weight evenly.
11. Pass to the right of others when carrying trays.
12. Say "Passing on the right" when carrying trays through congested traffic areas.
13. Allow others the right of way when they are carrying trays.
14. Set trays, dishes, pots, and pans away from the edges of surfaces. Do not allow serving spoons or pot handles to stick out into aisles.
15. Do not use chairs or boxes to reach high shelves; use a solid ladder.
16. Use grates or anti-skid mats on floors in areas where spills are likely.

Lifting Injury Prevention

1. Before lifting, get a firm grasp on the object.
2. When lifting, keep your back straight and bend only your knees. Use your leg muscles—not your back—to lift heavy objects.
3. Lift with a smooth action, keeping the object close to your body. Never jerk a load.
4. If necessary, shift your footing, but do not twist your body while lifting.
5. Exercise caution to prevent fingers and hands from getting pinched.
6. Obtain help when lifting bulky or heavy objects. Never try to lift a load you know is too much for you. The probability of injury increases as the weight of the object approaches 40 pounds (18.16 kg). When in doubt, ask for assistance.
7. Use available lifting and moving equipment (such as dollies and hand trucks).
8. Maintain clean, dry, and uncluttered floors in areas such as storerooms where lifting is necessary.

Hot pans or utensils should be handled only with dry cloths, mitts, pot holders, or towels. Staff members should know how to avoid steam burns (for example, when lifting the lid from a pot of boiling soup or some other hot liquid, tilt the lid away from you, not toward you).

Glass breaks easily if handled carelessly. Broken glass should only be picked up with a broom and a dustpan—never with bare hands. Staff members must be trained to be very cautious when handling glass, especially during dishwashing. Trays or racks of glass items must be handled carefully. Personal drinking glasses should not be allowed in food service areas.

Sharp objects such as knives must also be handled with care. Several manufacturers are marketing cut-resistant, lightweight, seamless knitted gloves for food service staff members to use when cleaning slicers and knives.

As alluded to earlier, improper lifting can cause injuries. Staff members must be trained to assess the weights, sizes, and shapes of objects before lifting them. They should also be trained to lift properly—keeping a straight back and lifting with their legs. They should know when and how to use mechanical lifting devices. Heavy objects should be stored at least 12 inches (30.5 centimeters) off the floor to avoid causing strains when lifted.

Strains or falls may occur when staff members stretch or over-reach to obtain objects overhead. Staff members should always use a ladder to reach items on high shelves; chairs, boxes, or containers are not safe substitutes for ladders. Carried boxes should be stacked squarely so they will not fall and should not be stacked higher than eye level; staff members must be able to see where they are going. Caution should be exercised to avoid collisions when moving around corners and through congested areas. When carts or other types of equipment on wheels need to be moved, they should be pushed, not pulled.

For obvious reasons, staff and supervisors should not work under the influence of alcohol or illegal drugs. Staff members should be informed when they are hired that any person working under the influence of alcohol or illegal drugs is subject to immediate disciplinary action.

Handling Accidents and Injuries. Every food service organization should have a clearly stated policy on how to handle emergencies such as injuries to staff members or guests. If an accident occurs, staff members should notify their supervisors immediately. After appropriate medical attention has been secured, management is responsible for investigating the incident. Once the causes of an accident are identified, corrective action can help eliminate further accidents. Managers can use an accident reporting form (see Exhibit 5) to record and analyze accidents.

Any staff member may provide first aid *if properly trained.* Immediate first aid treatment could mean the difference between life and death to a severely injured person. At least one staff member trained in first aid techniques should always be on duty.

Every organization should have at least one conveniently located first aid kit. First aid kits are available in three basic types: unit, bulk, and combination. Unit first aid kits are compact and contain compresses, splints, tourniquets, and triangular bandages. Bulk first aid kits usually contain adhesive tape, bulk cotton, and elastic and plastic bandages. Combination first aid kits contain a mixture of both

Exhibit 5 Accident Reporting Form

Establishment: Address:

Supervisor: Name of injured:

Department: Position:

Date of accident: Time of accident:

Place of accident:

Nature of injury:

Type of treatment received:

None First aid Medical doctor Ambulance
Hospital Other (specify):

Medical attention necessary:

Action of injured at time of accident:

Conditions in the environment contributing to the accident:

Corrective action necessary to prevent further accidents:

Date corrective action taken:

Staff member's signature: Supervisor's signature:

Date: Date:

Accident Investigation and Prevention

When an accident occurs, investigation should occur immediately and focus on determining the accident's cause in order to prevent future accidents. The following steps will help general managers make the most of their investigations.

1. Be objective. Resist the temptation to speculate on what caused an accident.
2. Consult with managers and supervisors responsible for the area where the accident occurred.
3. Investigate immediately after the accident is reported. This is particularly important in incidents involving guests. Conditions and opinions change with time and discussion. Only delay an interview if the subject needs time to regain composure or is undergoing medical treatment. Take photographs of the accident scene whenever possible.
4. Interview all witnesses. Establish a relaxed, nonthreatening atmosphere. Don't ask leading questions (for example, "Did John seem distracted today?"). Ask open-ended questions, such as "What exactly did you see?"
5. Record all significant information. Detailed notes can suffice as a permanent record of an interview. Collect information first; edit and review your notes later. Be sure the facts collected and recorded are pertinent to the investigation.
6. Provide a definite recommendation and schedule of corrective action.
7. Be aware of state reporting requirements. Each state sets requirements for adequate and timely reporting of accidents. Fines for violating these requirements can total $1,000 in some states.

unit and bulk kit supplies. In addition, combination kits usually contain antiseptic sprays, antacids, aspirin, burn sprays, cold treatments, eye solutions, and special bandages. A supervisor should be responsible for checking first aid supplies each month and restocking them when necessary. Refills can be obtained from manufacturers, suppliers, or drugstores.

When an accident involves a guest, staff members should avoid discussing similar accidents with the injured guest. Regardless of who might be at fault, staff members should never be discourteous or argue with a guest. On the other hand, staff members should not admit that the organization is at fault when an accident occurs; there should be no discussion of insurance claims or settlements. Guest injuries must be recorded on an accident report; the form shown in Exhibit 5 can be adapted to this purpose.

Staff members and supervisors should notify top management of a guest injury as soon as possible. The supervisor should attempt to get as much information as possible about how and why the accident occurred. It is a good idea to have emergency numbers (ambulance, doctor, hospital, fire, police) posted so calls for assistance can be made quickly. When in doubt about an injured person's condition, it is best to leave treatment to a trained professional.

Because of the nature of the business, food service staff members must be prepared to handle incidents involving choking. Choking is a leading cause of

Exhibit 6 Procedures for Aiding Choking Victims

1. Send someone for help, but don't wait for it to arrive.
2. Ask the victim if he or she can talk. If the victim is conscious but unable to make a sound, you can be reasonably sure he or she is choking.
3. Using a napkin to get a firm grip, pull the victim's tongue forward as far as possible. This should lift the obstruction into view.
4. Using the index and middle fingers like tweezers, grasp the obstruction and pull it out.
5. If this fails, use the Heimlich maneuver. Stand behind the victim and wrap your arms around his or her waist, allowing the head and arms to hang forward.
6. Make a fist with one hand and clasp it with the other hand. Place your hands against the victim's abdomen just above the navel and below the rib cage.
7. Press in forcefully with a quick upward thrust. Repeat several times. This pushes the diaphragm up, compressing the lungs, and may force the object out of the windpipe. (Measures 5–7 may be used on children and adults. Infants and toddlers should be held upside down over the arm of the rescuer and struck between the shoulder blades.)
8. After the obstruction is removed, restore breathing by artificial respiration if necessary. Keep the victim warm and quiet. Seek medical help.

accidental death in the United States, responsible for more than 3,000 deaths each year, many of which could be prevented. Food service staff members must be trained to recognize choking symptoms and respond rapidly with acceptable techniques.

If the victim is able to talk or cough, he or she is not choking and staff members should not intervene. A person who is choking is unable to breathe or make a sound but may look very alarmed. The victim may attempt to stand up and may clutch at his or her throat. With no intervention, the victim will eventually turn blue and lose consciousness. Death may occur in a matter of minutes. Therefore, fast action is necessary.

There are two generally accepted techniques for saving a choking victim (see Exhibit 6). Some rescuers attempt to remove the obstruction directly, usually with their fingers or with plastic tongs. The other technique is called the **Heimlich maneuver**, an action that forces trapped air out of the victim's lungs and often expels the obstruction from the throat. Regardless of which method is used, treatment must begin immediately if the victim is to survive.

Artificial respiration is necessary when a person's heart or lungs have stopped functioning. In most cases, a fatality can be avoided if prompt action is taken. **Cardiopulmonary resuscitation (CPR)** is a technique used to provide artificial circulation and breathing to the victim. The American Red Cross regularly conducts CPR courses consisting of lectures, demonstrations, and student practice. This valuable training usually takes only eight hours and could save a person's life. It is a good idea to have at least one person certified in CPR on duty at all times.

Fire Safety

A fire can destroy a food service organization's property and, more tragically, injure or kill its staff members and guests. A comprehensive fire safety program can help managers reduce this tremendous risk.

Some fires in food service operations are ignited intentionally. Cases of arson have been traced to owners attempting to collect insurance money, angry or recently terminated staff members, vandals, guests with unsatisfied complaints, and mentally unbalanced individuals. Good security—locked doors, proper key control, bright outdoor lighting, and burglar alarms—can help prevent arson.

Faulty electrical wiring also causes many fires; managers should have the operation's wiring periodically checked. Proper grounding is essential, as is strict adherence to all codes. Faulty electrical appliances also cause fires. Equipment should always be used according to the manufacturer's recommendations.

Most cooking fires are caused by grease or fat on hot surfaces or in equipment. To prevent these fires, equipment and exhaust hoods and filters must be kept clean. Appliances must be cleaned daily to prevent bonded dust (a potentially flammable film of grease and dust) from accumulating on their surfaces. Grease drippings from broiler and griddle drip pans should be emptied daily. Spills of fats, oils, sugar sauces, and other flammable foods should be wiped up immediately.

Exhaust-duct fires can be prevented with regular maintenance. The ducts should be cleaned and inspected at least quarterly (more frequently, if necessary) by a qualified service contractor. An exhaust-duct fire is very dangerous because it can smolder unnoticed for hours and then rapidly burn out of control.

Heating and air conditioning equipment also must be regularly inspected and maintained. Inspections should include chimneys, flues, filters, and air ducts. Whenever replacement parts are necessary, the correct sizes and types should be installed. This is particularly important for fuses and circuit breakers.

Flaming drinks, desserts, and entrées are forbidden in some parts of the United States because of the fire risk. Accidents with flaming foods occasionally occur that cause property damage as well as personal injury to guests and staff. Municipal codes may regulate whether a food service establishment can flame foods, or they may specify the type and maximum amount of fuel that can be used. If a restaurant does flame food items, staff members must know what they are doing, and fire safety concerns must be reflected in procedures. For example, because carrying flaming items from the kitchen to guest tables is especially dangerous, some operations have rules forbidding this in crowded dining areas. When flaming is allowed, the proper types of fire extinguishers should be readily available.

Smoking should be restricted to certain areas. Dry storage areas, for example, are particularly vulnerable to fires because of the dry foods they contain. Powdery substances such as flour are susceptible to spontaneous combustion. Smokers should never discard smoking materials in receptacles containing paper trash. Signs to this effect should be posted in all smoking areas.

Types of Fires and Extinguishers. According to the National Fire Protection Association, there are three major classifications of fires (see Exhibit 7). **Class A fires** involve ordinary combustibles such as wood, paper, and cloth. These fires can be

Exhibit 7 Fire Classifications

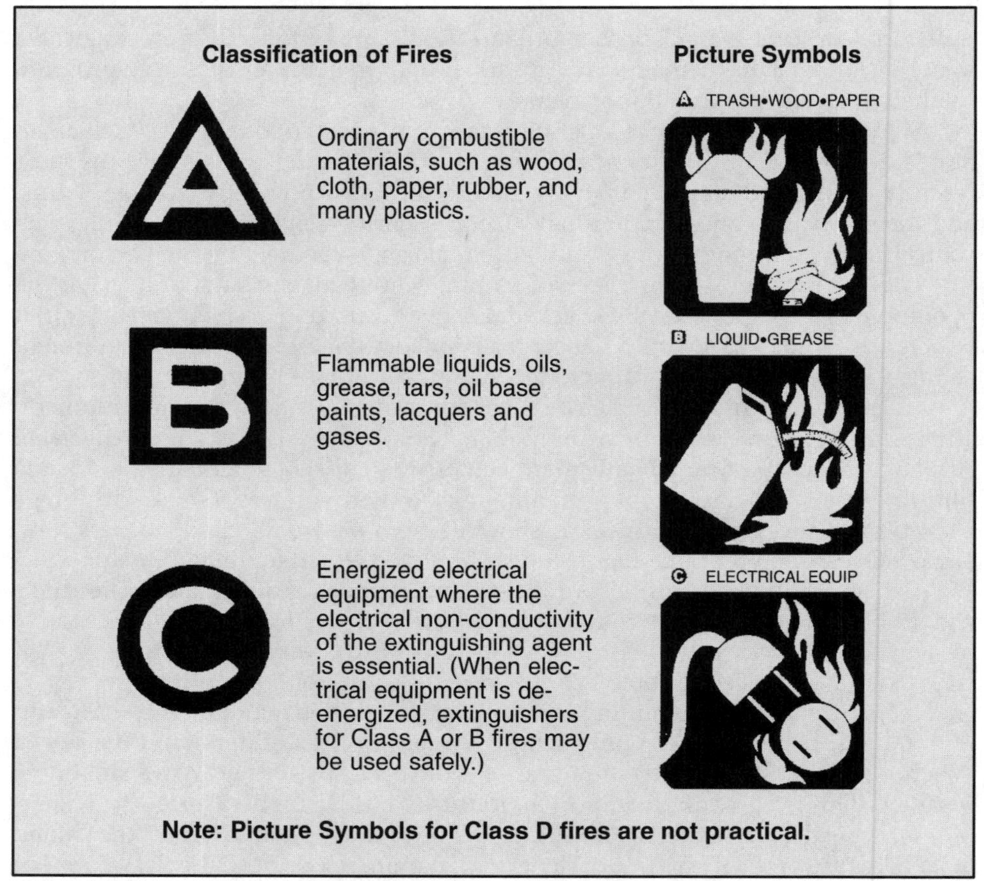

Source: The National Association of Fire Equipment Distributors.

extinguished by water or the cooling action of water-based or general-purpose fire-extinguishing chemicals. **Class B fires** involve flammable liquids such as grease, gasoline, paints, and other oils. They are extinguished by eliminating the air supply and smothering the fire. **Class C fires** are electrical and usually involve motors, switches, and wiring. They are extinguished with chemicals that do not conduct electricity. (Fires classified as Class D, caused by combustible metals, are rare.)

Never use water on a Class B or C fire. A grease fire may be smothered by simply covering it with a tight-fitting lid. Salt may also put out a small grease fire. In the United States, all state fire codes require both hand-held portable fire extinguishers and fixed automatic fire suppression systems in food service organizations. Automatic systems must be installed in exhaust hoods and duct work, and over charbroilers, upright broilers, fryers, and griddles. Portable extinguishers and automatic fire suppression systems should be checked regularly by an expert. The local fire department usually provides this service.

The Fire Safety Program. Staff training is the key to fire safety. Initial orientation and training should stress fire prevention. Additional training should cover specific staff duties in the event of a fire. Without proper training, staff members are likely to panic if a fire breaks out. Fire safety should also be reviewed periodically at staff meetings. Fire departments, hotel/motel associations, and restaurant associations may offer in-house training sessions.

Advance planning is necessary to control a fire emergency. Staff members and managers should know what to do if a fire is discovered. They should call the fire department immediately and then calmly evacuate the guests. Attempting to be secretive about a fire could endanger everyone in the building. Each server should be responsible for the guests in his or her station. The dining area manager or host should check other public areas to ensure that everyone has been evacuated. Kitchen workers should also have an evacuation plan. It is more important to protect human lives than to stay and fight an overwhelming fire.

A fire safety checklist can be used during regular inspections of the property. A team approach to fire safety inspections (involving both supervisors and staff members) is beneficial because it raises the fire safety consciousness of the entire staff. Most fires are preventable if management and staff members are aware of fire hazards, exercise caution, and use common sense.

Security Issues

Food service managers must be prepared for anything. Only intensive preparation can help ensure that they will handle emergencies in a professional manner with a minimal threat to both staff members and guests. In this section we will talk about two security issues that food service operations might experience: robberies and bomb threats.

Robberies

Food service organizations can be targets for robberies. A thief may confront a staff member or a guest and demand money or other valuables.

Managers need to carefully think about and develop procedures to follow during robberies. As an organization considers robbery precautions, its paramount concern should be the safety of staff members and guests. While sales income is obviously important, concern for everyone's personal safety has a much higher priority.

When a robbery attempt is made, staff members can benefit by following procedures such as the following:

1. Cooperate in every respect with all requests made by the criminal. Do not say or do anything that would jeopardize your safety.
2. Give the robber cash, food, beverages, or anything else he or she demands.
3. Do not attempt to deceive, lie, resist, or be uncooperative in any way.
4. Do not volunteer unsolicited information.

5. Attempt to observe everything possible about the criminal, if you can do so without provoking him or her, including:
   - Gender.
   - Height. One easy way to gauge relative height is to note whether the criminal's eyes are above or below your line of vision.
   - Skin color.
   - Eye color.
   - Hair. Note the length and color of the criminal's hair. Also, is there any facial hair?
   - Facial characteristics, such as size of nose, scars, and so on.
   - Weight.
   - Voice. Is it high- or low-pitched? Does the criminal talk fast or slow? Is there an accent?
   - Right- or left-handedness: In which hand is the weapon?
   - Weapon. What kind is it?
   - Clothing. Is the clothing new or old? What is the color, type, and style of each item? Is the criminal wearing any unusual item, such as a special belt buckle or designer's logo?
   - Miscellaneous items. Any distinctive personal characteristics, such as earrings, elaborate rings, or other jewelry? Tattoos? Piercings?
6. Do not follow the criminal out of the building. If the business has a window or other safe viewing place, you may be able to note the criminal's mode of transportation. If possible, note the license plate number, the color and type of the vehicle, and any rust, dents, or other special characteristics of the vehicle.
7. Try to determine the direction the robber took when he or she left.
8. As soon as the criminal leaves, notify the police, then notify the general manager (if he or she is not already on the scene). Even before the police arrive, staff members should begin to write down all that they can recall about the criminal and his or her personal characteristics. Each staff member should make notes without talking to other staff members. Items that were touched by the robber should not be moved or handled.
9. Encourage guests who were witnesses to remain until the police arrive.
10. Give police officers your full cooperation as they attempt to obtain relevant information about the robbery.

There are several procedures a food and beverage service organization can use to reduce the impact of robberies. For example, the manager can remove large sums of money from the cash register(s) during each shift and place them in a safe or other secure place. This procedure reduces the amount of sales income that someone can take during a robbery, since most robbers would not know how to open a safe on the premises. Making frequent bank deposits can help reduce the amount of cash on the premises. Some operations employ such anti-theft measures as silent alarms, bullet-proof cashier cages, and on-site guards. Finally, closed-circuit television can be used to monitor cashier areas; the obvious presence of a camera may deter some robbers.

Additional precautions are necessary to protect sales income that is in transit to a bank for deposit. Organizations with large amounts of sales income should consider the use of an armored car or bonded messenger service. Managers who make bank deposits should avoid routines when making them—for example, they should leave for the bank at varying times and should not always use the same exit when leaving the building. A few trusted staff members can take turns making deposits. If staff members use their own cars to make bank deposits, they should park them as close as possible to the door they will use to exit the building. If a manager makes a night deposit after the facility closes, the manager should exit through doors within the public's view rather than through back doors that may not be visible to passing cars or pedestrians. Managers can contact local police for additional, specific suggestions that can help reduce the possibility and magnitude of losses from theft.

Bomb Threats

Unfortunately, the possibility of bomb threats is real for just about every type of food service organization. Managers have the responsibility to develop written procedures for handling these threats and training staff members in these procedures. The number of bombs or other potentially dangerous devices that are found as a result of threats is much lower than the actual number of threats. Nevertheless, experienced managers treat bomb threats as real announcements of potential death, injury, and extensive damage.

If threats are received by mail (regular, e-mail, or fax), they should immediately be referred to the local police. In addition, when the United States mail service is involved, postal inspectors and the Federal Bureau of Investigation (FBI) should be notified.

Many bomb threats are communicated by telephone. Therefore, management must train staff members in advance to solicit as much information as possible from the caller. For example, if it is the policy of the organization, the staff member who receives the bomb threat should:

1. Attempt to keep the caller talking. If possible, alert another staff member who can listen on another telephone.
2. Attempt to discover when the bomb will explode, where it is located, what type of device it is, and what it looks like.
3. Listen to the voice. Is the person male or female, sober or intoxicated, rational or irrational? Is it someone you know? Does the speaker have an accent or speech impediment? Is the voice that of a child, teenager, or older person?
4. Listen for any identifiable noises in the background (e.g., factory, nightclub, or street sounds).
5. Note any additional information, such as an explanation of why the caller placed the bomb and if the caller has any demands.

6. Note the time the call was received and the time the caller hung up.
7. Attempt to recall the exact words the caller used.
8. Notify local police immediately.

Frequently, if a caller is serious, he or she will provide information helpful in finding the bomb. If the caller is incoherent, obviously intoxicated, or sounds as though he or she thinks the telephone call is a joke, the call is probably a hoax. Even so, the staff member who calls the police should carefully follow any advice they provide.

If the top manager on duty did not take the call, he or she should be notified. If the operation has an internal security department, its staff members should also be notified, according to company guidelines.

Time cannot be wasted when an organization receives a bomb threat. Yet, managers and staff members must not panic; advance training in security procedures can help keep everyone calm.

Police and other personnel who are looking for the bomb may request the aid of staff members who know the work areas being searched and who would more readily notice anything out of the ordinary. Staff members should call attention to anything out of place or unusual, such as a bag, box, case, or package that should not be in the area. Police may allow staff members to make a preliminary search before officers arrive. If anyone notices an unusual package or other item whose presence cannot be explained, no one should attempt to move, touch, examine, or in any other way disturb it. Rather, all staff members should leave the area, and the police should be notified about the suspicious object's exact location.

While the factors surrounding every situation are unique, many authorities suggest that it is generally unwise to evacuate a facility before a search confirms that a bomb or suspicious device is present. However, if you have a strong feeling that the threat is real, an immediate, calm evacuation is in order. Again, closely follow the advice of police officials regarding the need to evacuate the premises.

Generally, guests evacuating a building during a bomb threat should leave through the fire exits. Staff members should exit according to plans that enable the organization's management to account for them. All evacuation plans should ensure that absolutely no one remains in the building.

If an evacuation is in order but no imminent danger exists, managers should lock all equipment containing cash. Doors should remain unlocked in order to facilitate the search for the bomb. If police do not object, equipment can be turned off and other precautions taken to protect the facilities.

After an evacuation is complete, no one should return to the building and grounds until the police declare the areas safe. Staff members should then return to their assigned work areas to await instructions from their managers.

Health Issues

Health issues discussed in this chapter cover two broad areas: nutrition and smoking. With the trend toward more healthy menu items and food and beverage service concepts, a basic knowledge of nutrition is valuable for all managers and staff members in a guest-driven service organization. Similarly, the move toward elimination of smoking from public areas in buildings requires a fundamental knowledge of smoking issues on the part of all individuals who work in food service organizations.

Nutrition

Americans are increasingly making lifestyle choices and changes that contribute to healthier living. Food service organizations are selling less alcohol today than a decade ago. Guests are choosing smaller portion sizes and demanding more foods that are low in fat, sodium, cholesterol, and sugar than in years past. Vegetarian menu items are appealing to a growing number of those who consume meals away from home. Nutrition and health issues are not fads, but trends that are expected to grow in importance with the graying of America.

Nutrition Basics. An understanding of the fundamentals of nutrition is a foundation for exceeding guests' expectations. Food consists of its building blocks: nutrients. The kinds and qualities of nutrients, along with their order and arrangement, determine the characteristics of a food product.

Much of the nutrient content of the raw materials used in food service kitchens is determined by the genetic makeup of the plant or animal. Nutrient quality is also influenced by the kind of fertilizer or feed. Once the food is harvested, however, its nutrient profile changes. Some changes are out of an operation's control. Others can be managed, to an extent. For example, the organization controls:

- How foods are received
- Storage conditions—including light, temperature, time, and relative humidity
- Handling conditions—whether the product is thawed, frozen, or canned
- How the food is prepared and served

The objective should be to avoid losing any more nutrients than necessary.

The six nutrient classes are:

- Proteins
- Carbohydrates
- Lipids (fats and oils)
- Vitamins
- Minerals
- Water

Of these six, four are organic—proteins, carbohydrates, lipids, and vitamins; minerals and water are inorganic. An organic compound contains the element carbon, which can chemically bond with many other elements. The word *organic* is often misunderstood. Some believe that "organic" signifies quality. For example, some believe that organic vitamin C taken from oranges is better than synthetic vitamin C manufactured in the laboratory. The truth is that the nutrient profile of both vitamins is exactly the same. While the vitamin C in both cases is the same, additional nutrients (vitamin A, potassium) present in the orange would not be found in the pure vitamin C from the laboratory. *Inorganic* simply means that the nutrient does not contain carbon.

The three nutrients that provide energy to the human body are proteins, carbohydrates, and lipids. Weight for weight, both proteins and carbohydrates have equal energy values (4 kilocalories per gram), while lipids have over twice as much energy (9 kilocalories per gram).

Proteins. Proteins are large molecules that consist of approximately 500 amino acids chemically linked together. Proteins serve several critical roles. They function as enzymes to speed up the rate of chemical reactions in the body. They are used for transportation and storage of other components of the body; for example, oxygen is transported in the blood by the protein hemoglobin and is stored in muscles in myoglobin, another protein. Proteins help produce antibodies, which recognize and control foreign substances such as viruses and bacteria. Proteins generate and transmit nerve impulses in the body. Finally, proteins can be used as a source of energy. However, using protein for energy is like using expensive, handmade furniture for kindling wood. Since proteins have so many more important functions in the human body, carbohydrates and lipids are preferred for energy sources.

The recommended daily intake of proteins varies based on a person's age. Relative to body weight, children need a higher amount of protein than adults. This is reasonable, since children are growing and need the extra protein for building body tissues. Protein requirements increase during the last six months of pregnancy for women and during lactation. The daily intake of protein is also affected by a person's activity; active people require more protein than sedentary individuals.

Important sources of protein include meat, poultry, fish, seafood, milk and milk products, legumes (e.g., dried beans and peas), soybeans, and nuts. The quantity and quality of protein found in each of these foods will vary, based on the amounts and kinds of amino acids present in the foods. Most U.S. adults are in little danger of getting an inadequate amount of protein in their diets.

Carbohydrates. Carbohydrates are classified into three broad categories: monosaccharides, disaccharides, and polysaccharides. Both monosaccharides and disaccharides are known as sugars.

Monosaccharides are the simplest of the three categories and include glucose, fructose, and galactose. Glucose is the primary source of energy within the human body. It is found in some fruits and vegetables (e.g., grapes, young peas, and carrots). Fructose, the sweetest of all sugars, is present with glucose in many fruits; it also is found in honey and is used as a sweetener in some processed foods. Galactose is normally only found linked to glucose.

When two monosaccharides bond together, they form a disaccharide. Disaccharides include sucrose, lactose, and maltose. Sucrose is common sugar, and it also gives fruits their characteristic sweet taste. Lactose is the only carbohydrate found in milk. Maltose is produced in malted grains and is important in the production of alcoholic beverages.

Polysaccharides are the most complex carbohydrates. They include starches, cellulose, glycogen, pectin, agar, and alginate. These carbohydrates are useful in cooking, improve the "mouth feel" of certain foods, and help the digestive process.

There are no recommended daily allowances (RDAs) for carbohydrates, although the average adult human needs about 100 grams (roughly 3.5 ounces) per day. This amount is less than one-third of the amount consumed daily by most adult Americans, although the kinds of carbohydrates consumed in the average American diet could be changed for the better. A healthy diet emphasizes complex carbohydrates that are high in fiber (e.g., vegetables, fruits, and whole grains) rather than sugary foods.

Lipids. Fats and oils are collectively known as "lipids" and are made up of fatty acids and glycerol.

Although we group them together, there are differences between fats and oils. Fats are usually found in animal products, while oils are usually extracted from vegetable sources. Fats are solid at room temperature and contain a large amount of saturated fatty acids. Oils, on the other hand, are liquid at room temperature and contain more unsaturated fatty acids.

Fats or oils and water generally do not mix. However, when a substance known as an emulsifying agent is added, the mixture stabilizes and does not separate, because an emulsion is created. Milk and ice cream are examples of fat-in water emulsions, butter is an example of a water-in-fat emulsion, and margarine is a water-in-oil emulsion. Some other important food emulsions include mayonnaise, hollandaise sauce, cream soups, salad dressings, and sauces. Some of these foods contain egg yolks, which are natural emulsifiers.

Nearly all meats contain considerable fat. You can reduce your intake of fat by trimming away all of the visible fat, but the resulting meat may be far from fat-free. There can remain a considerable amount of fat within the tissue of the meat, a characteristic known as "marbling." The one common food of animal origin that can be made virtually fat-free is milk; skim milk has less than 1.6 percent fat, allowing it to qualify for "fat-free" labeling.

Fats and oils are concentrated sources of energy, so they take longer to burn once consumed. Fats and oils contain nine kilocalories per gram, more than double the energy value of equal weights of proteins or carbohydrates. Excessive calories (whether in the form of lipids, carbohydrates, or proteins) are converted into fat by the body and stored in adipose tissue cells. The adipose tissue acts as an energy reserve and helps protect vital organs of the body, such as the kidneys. Fats and oils are also a source of the fat-soluble vitamins A, D, E, and K.

There are a number of sources of fat in the diet. The fat content of meat can vary from animal to animal and from one part of the animal to another. Some fish, particularly salmon and trout, are relatively high in fat content compared to other fish. Butter can contain as much as 80 percent fat, while margarine may have just as much oil. Unless they are specially produced, products made from milk and milk products—including yogurt, sour cream, and cheese—contain fat. Fat typically plays an important role in the preparation of pastries and breads.

Most foods of plant origin, such as grains, fruits, and vegetables, are low in fat when harvested. (One notable exception is the avocado, which contains a high percentage of fat.) For example, only one-thousandth of the weight of a potato is fat. But when a potato is prepared by frying or by adding sour cream, butter, margarine, and/or cheese, the fat content can easily be one hundred times the original. Potatoes are not "fattening," but the extra ingredients add considerable calories and fat.

There is no recommended daily allowance for fat, since the average adult American is in little danger of consuming too little. In fact, the situation is just the opposite. One estimate states that adult Americans consume, on average, 40 percent of their total energy needs in the form of fats and oils.

Vitamins. Vitamins are complex organic compounds required by the body to maintain health. These essential nutrients are found in foods in very small amounts, but their importance is great. Vitamins help speed the release of energy from proteins, carbohydrates, and lipids. (By themselves, vitamins are not nutrients, since they cannot be used by the body for energy.)

Vitamins are either water-soluble or fat-soluble. Water-soluble vitamins dissolve in water and include the vitamin B complex of vitamins and vitamin C. Excessive amounts of water-soluble vitamins are eliminated by the body through urination. Fat-soluble vitamins, on the other hand, dissolve in fats or oils. They include vitamins A, D, E, and K. Excess amounts are stored in the body.

The vitamin content of food changes as it is harvested, processed, shipped, stored, prepared, cooked, and held for service. For example, when wheat is refined into flour, many of the B vitamins present in the original bran are lost. In addition, heat, light, and oxygen can have devastating effects on the vitamin content of food. Water-soluble vitamins are lost when food is soaked or cooked in excessive amounts of water for long periods of time.

Minerals and Water. Minerals and water are similar in that they are both inorganic yet are critically important to human nutrition.

Minerals are chemical elements other than carbon, oxygen, hydrogen, and nitrogen. In general, they make up between four to six percent of total body weight. Compared to other nutrients, minerals are incompletely absorbed. Therefore, the amount required in your diet is greater than what is actually needed by your body. Excess minerals exit the body through urine, perspiration, and blood. Minerals are lost from food when they dissolve in the water used to soak or cook food products. However, they are generally much more stable than vitamins when exposed to heat, light, or oxygen. Minerals important to the human body include calcium, iron, sodium, chlorine, potassium, phosphorus, iodine, and magnesium.

The remaining nutrient is *water.* Water is essential to life, and all living organisms contain it. It is the vehicle in which chemical reactions take place. It also transports nutrients to cells and carries waste products away from cells and out of the body.

Water is available from three sources: liquids, solid foods, and—internally—through oxidation. (Oxidation forms water inside cells as a by-product of chemical reactions.) Soda, beer, and fruit juices contain a large percentage of water. Fruits and vegetables are largely water; melons are as much as 94 percent water, while cabbage contains roughly 90 percent water.

The average adult eliminates about two quarts of water per day. This amount increases when an individual exercises—or works in a hot environment—and loses water in the form of perspiration. This lost water must be replaced for metabolism to continue. The amount of water taken into the body is influenced by habit and social custom as well as by thirst. It is a good idea to consume at least eight glasses of water per day.

Dietary Guidelines. A healthy diet can be sustained by following these guidelines:

- Eat a variety of foods.
- Choose foods low in fat and cholesterol.
- Include foods with adequate starch and fiber.
- Limit high-sugar foods.
- Avoid foods high in sodium.
- If you drink alcoholic beverages, do so in moderation.

Debates continue to escalate over which foods are "good" for you and which foods are "bad." Whether the subject is fats, calories, antioxidants, vegetarian or vegan diets, or various ethnic cuisines, mountains of conflicting data usually do little more than confuse the public. When in doubt regarding the soundness of nutrition advice, it may be best to consult a registered dietitian.

Marketing and Merchandising Nutrition. Marketing and merchandising nutrition is paying large dividends for many food service organizations. While strategies differ, the key to improving business is to focus on nutritious menu items, perceived quality, and value.

Whether promoting more nutritious menu items makes sense is a decision that depends on an establishment's guests and potential guests. As with any guest-driven service organization, it is important to correctly identify guests' needs, preferences, and expectations. Many guests have growing preferences for foods that are lower in calories, fat, salt, and sugar. These same guests want information to help them identify nutritious items on the menu and sort out menu options. Of course, guests' needs can differ by age, meal time, regional location, or special dietary considerations.

Guest feedback is absolutely essential when it comes to evaluating and planning ongoing and future nutrition programs. Surveys might precede the addition of new menu items; a good strategy is to use daily specials to test items for possible addition to a menu. Tasting parties can be held to evaluate new recipes. Nutritious or healthy options should be presented in every menu category—from appetizers, soups, and salads to entrées and desserts. Condiments and side dishes that are lower in calories, fat, salt, and sugar should also be presented.

On the menu, boxed sections or graphic indicators (for example, a heart logo) can draw guest attention to healthy choices. Guests should also be invited to request nutrition information from service staff. Some menus clearly state: "Ask your server how we can prepare this menu item without salt or fat." Cooking procedures should be described to convey healthy preparation and cooking methods ("broiled without butter," "garnished with lemon and herbs"). As an alternative, a separate menu or menu insert can be used to feature nutrition information.

Many food and beverage organizations are already offering more nutritious fare; these items should be clearly promoted on the menu. Other items may need only slight modifications to meet guests' needs. When menus are rewritten, a larger number of nutritious options can be added.

The entire staff should be included in promoting nutrition. Fact sheets, food tastings, and staff discussions can help prepare staff members to match nutrition-minded guests with the meals they would most appreciate and enjoy.

Smoking

A decade or so ago, restaurant seating was divided 75 percent smoking and 25 percent no-smoking. Today, that ratio is reversed. People in the United States have changed their attitudes about the acceptability of smoking in public places, including the dining areas of food service operations.

One of the turning points came in 1993, when the Environmental Protection Agency (EPA) classified secondhand smoke as a Class A carcinogen. As such, it was linked to lung cancer and other respiratory diseases, and it was put in the same category as such cancer-causing substances as asbestos, benzene, and radon.

Based on the EPA's report, the Working Group on Tobacco (an organization of 18 state attorneys general) recommended that all quick-service chains voluntarily ban smoking in their restaurants. McDonald's was one of the first to do so, issuing a no-smoking policy for its 1,400 corporate restaurants. The National Council of Chain Restaurants (NCCR), representing 40 of the nation's largest chain restaurant companies, went on to support the Smoke-Free Environment Act of 1993. Many other food service organizations have banned or severely restricted smoking.

In the spring of 1993, Vermont became the first state to outlaw smoking in public places. In 1995, California banned smoking in most indoor workplaces, including the nonbar areas of restaurants; in 1998, however, the 35,000 previously exempt bars, casinos, and restaurants in the state became legally smoke-free. But the fight isn't over; food service owners and managers on both sides of the issue are pressing for legislative changes.

The economic effects of no-smoking laws on food service operations are still undetermined and vary based on the type of operation, its location, and its guests. The situation is not black-and-white. Guests who frequent upscale food and beverage organizations are reportedly less likely to smoke whether it is prohibited or not. Yet, a number of upscale restaurants in major urban areas are adding special cigar and pipe rooms and hosting all-smoking "steak and cigar" nights. In addition, negative attitudes in the United States toward smoking are not necessarily shared by the rest of the world; food service establishments serving international guests must be prepared to accommodate large numbers of smoking customers.

Some organizations that have voluntarily become smoke-free report increased business from former guests and new guests who had been avoiding smoky environments. On the other hand, some food service businesses that banned smoking as a result of local ordinances report that the ban has meant lost guests, lost revenues, and staff cutbacks. Each food service establishment will have to decide for itself how best to meet the needs of its guests and staff members and comply with existing laws and ordinances.

Legal Issues

Several issues that affect the legal responsibilities of a food and beverage business have already been presented. Additional legal issues in this section include risk management, sexual harassment, the Americans with Disabilities Act, minimum wage and immigration reform, health care reform, and AIDS and herpes. Each has a real or potential impact on food service organizations.

Risk Management

Earlier in this chapter, the fundamentals of a sanitation risk management (SRM) program were presented. Recall that the goal of an SRM program is to reduce sanitation risks, as well as address key quality and cost control issues. Risk management, as it relates to legal liability, has surfaced as an area of acute concern in the food service industry. Often, liability issues are raised because service to guests did not meet guest expectations.

Alcohol service is an area of particular concern when managing risk. Some states have modified their dram shop laws to make drinkers of alcoholic beverages more responsible for their actions. These states have outlined in detail the procedures that organizations should follow to provide responsible alcohol service. When an intoxicated guest leaves the premises and is involved in someone's injury or death (and a subsequent lawsuit), some states now require proof that the provider or seller of alcoholic beverages knew the guest was intoxicated when the guest was served and that the intoxication was the direct cause of the injury or death. It is essential for food service managers to stay current on the laws that affect them, their staffs, and their operations in the areas of alcohol service and liability.

The goal of food service organizations is to move toward an ideal level of service. As service moves toward this level, the sales potential (as well as tip income and guest loyalty) increases, while the liability potential is reduced. By lowering legal exposure and liability while meeting or exceeding guests' expectations, managers of an operation can create a win-win situation for guests, staff members, and the operation.

Sexual Harassment

Sexual harassment has no place in any food service operation. It is illegal, immoral, and potentially devastating to the lives of everyone involved. In more practical terms, sexual harassment interferes with an operation's efficiency, and sexual harassment complaints have the potential to cost an operation a great deal of money. It's been estimated that legal fees for defending a civil case in court average $250,000, and judgments in sexual harassment cases routinely exceed $1 million. Even food service operations that are never taken to court are affected. The U.S. Department of Labor estimates that U.S. businesses lose about $1 billion annually due to workplace problems caused by sexual harassment.

Title VII of the Civil Rights Act of 1964 protects staff members from sexual harassment. However, until 1991, victims who had lost their jobs were allowed only to collect back pay and lost wages and be reinstated. In 1991, Congress amended the Civil Rights Act to allow sexual harassment victims to receive compensatory and punitive damages.

The Equal Employment Opportunity Commission (EEOC) guidelines define sexual harassment as "unwelcome sexual advances, requests for sexual favors, and other verbal or physical conduct of a sexual nature." Title VII defines two forms of sexual harassment that might occur in the workplace. The first is *quid pro quo* harassment. This form of sexual harassment occurs when a staff member's employment status is directly linked to whether the staff member is willing to participate in unwanted sexual activity. A "hostile work environment" is the more common form of sexual harassment. A hostile work environment is one that unreasonably interferes with a staff member's ability to work or creates an offensive workplace.

Prohibited sexual harassment includes, but is not limited to:

- Sexual assault or otherwise coerced sexual intercourse
- Propositions or pressure to engage in sexual activity
- Sexual innuendo, suggestive comments, insults, threats, or obscene gestures
- Inappropriate comments concerning appearance
- Leering or ogling in a sexually provocative manner
- Sexual or sexually insulting written communications or public postings, including those that appear in electronic media or email
- Display of magazines, books, or pictures with a sexual connotation
- A pattern of hiring or promoting sex partners over more qualified persons
- Any harassing behavior, whether or not sexual in nature, that is directed toward a person because of the person's gender—including, but not limited to, hazing workers employed in nontraditional work environments

It is essential that every food service operation create policies that make it clear that the operation will not tolerate sexual harassment. These policies should also clearly state how a staff member can file a complaint and get a complaint resolved. Sexual harassment policies should be communicated to everyone in the operation and to new staff members as they are hired. The EEOC encourages employers to "take all steps necessary to prevent sexual harassment from occurring, such as affirmatively raising the subject; expressing strong disapproval; developing appropriate sanctions; informing staff members of their right to raise, and how to raise, the issue of harassment under Title VII; and developing methods to sensitize all concerned."

Americans with Disabilities Act

The **Americans with Disabilities Act (ADA)** makes it unlawful to discriminate against workers with disabilities in employment and related practices, such as recruitment, selection, training, pay, job assignments, leave, benefits, layoff, promotion, and termination. There are an estimated 43 million Americans who have some type of disability. Based on the ADA, they are qualified for employment if they can perform the essential functions of a position with or without reasonable accommodation. "Reasonable accommodation" refers to what the employer must do to make the work environment accessible to those with disabilities. The act also addresses design considerations for public areas, to make sure these areas are accessible by individuals who have disabilities. For example, high-contrast colors for doors and walks in public areas can assist guests in locating doorways. Doors must be fitted with push or levered handles. Textural differences on floors not only are appealing, but allow those with visual impairments to sense when they are moving from one kind of space to another. Deep pile carpeting and uneven floors should be eliminated.

Wheelchair accessibility presents additional challenges. Steps should be removed between lobbies and dining areas and replaced with ramps. Dining area seating should be spaced wide enough to permit wheelchair access. Buffets, salad bars, and other bar setups can be constructed to be low enough for people who use wheelchairs to access, yet still be comfortable for other guests. Restrooms may need to be remodeled to accommodate everyone's needs. Where steps are present in addition to ramps, they should be equipped with lighted strips to indicate level changes. Elevator doors must operate with slow timers so that guests with disabilities who are entering or exiting are not rushed. Gift shops and other public areas can be designed with access in mind by providing T-shaped corners and other areas where wheelchairs can maneuver. Vending machines should be accessible to all guests. Tax incentives in the form of deductions may help offset the costs associated with ADA compliance.

Thorough staff training is a key to complying with the ADA and making all guests feel comfortable. Information can be adapted from existing sources or developed using input from people with disabilities or advocacy groups for the disabled.

Minimum Wage and Immigration Reform

The minimum wage was implemented in 1934 because Congress believed that paying less than "decent" wages was illegal. In recent years, however, there has been increasing debate among business owners, workers, and legislators over what constitutes a "decent" minimum wage. As the figure rises every few years, each increase directly affects food service businesses, which typically rely on large numbers of entry-level, minimum-wage-earning staff members.

Minimum wage opponents firmly believe that food service organizations cannot simply pass wage increases on to guests through higher prices. Guests have alternatives; they can dine at home or purchase takeout food from a supermarket, for example. In addition, opponents cite more than two dozen studies that indicate higher minimum wages may shrink the number of entry-level jobs by as much as 2.5 percent for every 10 percent rise in the minimum wage. Yet minimum-wage positions can provide staff members with basic job skills that are transferable to other positions in other industries. The Employment Policies Institute has reported that:

- 93 percent of current and former food service staff members said they were glad to have had the experience of working in a hospitality job for tips.
- 80 percent said the experience helped them develop important work skills useful for future employment.
- 79 percent would recommend such work to others.

Because of an acute shortage of qualified hospitality workers, due to record low unemployment in many areas of the United States, many food service operations are already paying entry-level workers more than the minimum wage. However, if minimum wages continue to rise, they may negatively affect the employment opportunities for entry-level food service workers, since operations may have to cut staff or hire fewer workers.

The **Immigration Reform and Control Act (IRCA)** of 1986 was passed to control the hiring of illegal aliens in the United States and to prohibit discriminatory hiring practices. Fines for violations range from $100 to $10,000 and may include back pay, legal fees, and reinstatement of staff members.

Compliance with IRCA is not simply a matter of checking for correct documentation and completing the government's I-9 Employment Eligibility Verification Form. Discrimination can take the form of "citizenship status discrimination," "document abuse," and "national origin discrimination." While employers must verify that potential staff members are legally authorized to work in the United States, employers should not ask for additional information (e.g., work-status documentation) unless they ask everyone for such information. Otherwise, they might be accused of discrimination.

Several community-based organizations are educating immigrants regarding their workplace rights. Others are encouraging immigrants to fight discrimination in hiring. For these and other reasons, food service managers should be fully aware of IRCA and its ramifications for their businesses. Enforcement of IRCA provisions is expected to increase.

Health Care Reform

Food and beverage service organizations have joined other service and manufacturing businesses in their concern over proposed health care reform mandates. The Business Roundtable, an association of 200 chief executive officers representing some of the largest U.S. companies, has spoken out against specific legislation that would determine the scope of employer-provided health care.

"Employers are working to improve the quality of health care we provide because it's good for our employees, and it's good business," says Tony Burns, CEO of Ryder System, Inc., and chair of the Roundtable's Health and Retirement Task Force. "While government plays an important role in encouraging health care quality, especially in the publicly financed health care programs, it should not erect regulatory barriers that make it more difficult for us."

The National Restaurant Association (NRA) also is opposed to health care as an employer-paid option. According to their promotional material, "The National Restaurant Association will fight against employer mandates and for medical malpractice reform, increased deductibility for the self-insured, voluntary employer purchasing groups, and medical savings accounts." Food service managers should track proposed health care legislation and stay well informed on health care reform issues.

AIDS and Herpes

Although AIDS and herpes simplex are *not* foodborne according to current scientific information, they are topics of growing concern on the part of food service owners, managers, staff members, and guests.

AIDS—**acquired immune deficiency syndrome**—is caused by HIV, a virus that attacks a person's immune system. As the virus reproduces in the body, it reduces the body's natural ability to resist infections. The virus can survive in the human body for years before actual symptoms appear. AIDS is transmitted in the following four ways:

- Sexual contact with a person infected with the AIDS virus
- Sharing drug needles and syringes with a person infected with the AIDS virus
- Blood-to-blood contact involving infected fluids
- Perinatal transmission from mother to child during pregnancy or through breast-feeding

There is no medical evidence that proves the AIDS virus can be transmitted through saliva, tears, perspiration, or mosquito bites, or by using drinking fountains, toilet seats, toothbrushes, or other items used by someone with AIDS. The Centers for Disease Control and Prevention (CDC) have stated: "All epidemiologic and laboratory evidence indicates that bloodborne and sexually transmitted infections are not transmitted during the preparation or serving of food and beverages." The CDC guidelines on AIDS in the workplace state, "Food service workers known to be infected [with the AIDS virus] need not be restricted from work unless they have evidence of other infection or illness for which any food service worker should be restricted." Perhaps the best way to handle AIDS is to initiate an educational campaign that clearly presents the facts to staff members.

The U.S. Supreme Court ruled in 1985 that someone infected with the AIDS virus must be classified as having a disability. The court held that persons impaired by contagious diseases are entitled to protection from discrimination.

In 1993, a jury ordered one of San Francisco's most well-known and respected restaurant owners to pay a dismissed staff member with AIDS $30,000 in damages. The attorney for Rolando Iglesias convinced a majority of jurors that his client was fired because his medical condition represented a health insurance liability. Restaurateur Jeremiah Tower said the server was fired because he lied to the restaurant's guests about the availability of cappuccino soufflés. Such a case clearly demonstrates the legal ramifications of AIDS for the food service industry. (Managers who need answers to specific questions about AIDS in the workplace should consult legal counsel.)

Although it has been overshadowed by the AIDS virus, **herpes simplex virus (HSV)** is also receiving attention because of its increasing incidence. HSV consists of two different but closely related viruses: HSV-type 1, which causes approximately 90 percent of ocular and oral (fever blisters and cold sores) herpes infections; and HSV-type 2, which causes about 85 percent of genital herpes infections.

HSV can be transmitted when any part of a person's body directly touches active HSV or sores containing active HSV. Mucous membranes and broken or damaged skin are easy points of entry into the body. Even though HSV cannot survive very long outside of the human body, recent data suggest that HSV might be able to survive in warm, damp towels.

HSV is not known to be transmitted by food or drinking water, through the air, by water in hot tubs and swimming pools, or by toilet seats. HSV is not transmitted by food-contact surfaces or equipment. Nevertheless, it is critical for all staff members to practice good personal hygiene and personal cleanliness procedures, including proper handwashing.

Key Terms

acquired immune deficiency syndrome (AIDS)—A disease affecting the immune system, caused by a virus that can be transmitted through bodily fluids.

Americans with Disabilities Act (ADA)—Legislation passed by the U.S. Congress in 1990. This act requires commercial operations to remove barriers to persons with disabilities in the workplace and to provide facilities for customers with disabilities.

cardiopulmonary resuscitation (CPR)—A technique used to provide circulation and breathing to a victim whose heart or lungs have stopped functioning.

Class A fire—The burning of ordinary combustibles such as wood, paper, and cloth. A Class A fire can be extinguished with water and water-based or general-purpose fire-extinguishing chemicals.

Class B fire—A fire involving flammable liquids such as grease, gasoline, paint, and other oils. It can be extinguished by eliminating the air supply and smothering the fire.

Class C fire—An electrical fire, usually involving motors, switches, and wiring. It can be extinguished with chemicals that do not conduct electricity.

critical control point (CCP)—A point or procedure in a food preparation or serving process where loss of control may result in an unacceptable health risk.

Food Code—A model code published by the U.S. Food and Drug Administration (FDA) in 1993. It represents the FDA's best advice for a uniform system of regulations to ensure that food sold at retail establishments is safe and properly protected and presented.

foodborne illness—An illness caused either by germs in food (known as "food infection") or by germ-produced poisons in food (known as "food poisoning").

HACCP plan—A written document that delineates formal procedures for following the Hazard Analysis Critical Control Point principles.

Hazard Analysis Critical Control Point (HACCP) system—A system that identifies and monitors specific foodborne hazards. The hazard analysis identifies critical control points (CCPs), those points in the food preparation or serving process that must be controlled to ensure food safety. CCPs are monitored and verified in subsequent steps to ensure that risks are controlled. All of this information is specified in an operation's HACCP plan.

Heimlich maneuver—A generally accepted technique for saving a choking victim by squeezing the trapped air out of the victim's lungs, forcing the obstruction out.

herpes simplex virus (HSV)—A term used for two different but closely related viruses: HSV-type 1 causes the majority of oral and ocular herpes infections; HSV-type 2 causes the majority of genital herpes infections. HSV can be transmitted when any part of a person's body directly touches active HSV or sores containing active HSV. It is not known to be transmitted by food or drinking water or by food-contact surfaces or equipment.

Immigration Reform and Control Act (IRCA)—Legislation passed in 1986 to regulate the employment of aliens in the United States and to protect staff members from discrimination on the basis of citizenship or nationality.

potentially hazardous foods—Any foods or ingredients in a form capable of supporting (a) the rapid and progressive growth of infectious or toxigenic microorganisms, or (b) the slower growth of *Clostridium botulinum*. Includes any food of animal origin, either raw or heat treated, and any food of plant origin that has been treated or that is raw seed sprouts.

sanitation risk management (SRM) program—A program that identifies food-safety risks and implements procedures for reducing those risks.

temperature danger zone (TDZ)—The temperature range of 41°F–140°F (5°C–60°C), defined by the U.S. Public Health Service as the range in which most pathogenic activity takes place and food spoilage can occur.

Review Questions

1. What does "HACCP" mean?
2. What role do servers play in ensuring food safety?
3. What preventive measures can be taken to help reduce workplace accidents?
4. What are the differences between Class A, B, and C fires?
5. What steps can be taken in the event of a robbery? a bomb threat?
6. What nutritional information is increasingly important to guests?
7. What does the Americans with Disabilities Act mean for food and beverage operations?
8. What effects might minimum wage and health care legislation have on food service businesses?

Internet Sites

For more information, visit the following Internet sites. Remember that Internet addresses can change without notice.

Americans with Disabilities Act (U.S. Department of Justice)
www.usdoj.gov/crt/ada/adahom1.htm

Centers for Disease Control and Prevention (CDC)
www.cdc.gov

FDA Center for Food Safety and Applied Nutrition
http://vm.cfsan.fda.gov/list.html

Food Regulation Weekly
www.foodregulation.com

International Food Information Council Foundation (IFIC)
www.ificinfo.health.org

International Meat & Poultry HACCP Alliance
http://ifse.tamu.edu/HACCPALL.HTML

National Food Safety Database
www.foodsafety.org

National Restaurant Association (NRA)
www.restaurant.org

Nation's Restaurant News
www.nrn.com/index.htm

NRN-Online Food Safety, Science, and Nutrition Links
www.nrn.com/links/ssn.htm

Nutrition Navigator
www.navigator.tufts.edu/index.html

OSHA
www.osha.gov

Restaurants & Institutions
www.rimag.com

References

Allen, Robin Lee. "Congress Moves to Extinguish Smoking Debate." *Nation's Restaurant News,* November 15, 1993.

———. "Fast Feeders Boycott Smoking Hearing." *Nation's Restaurant News,* February 7, 1994.

———. "Food Safety High on List for Operators, Patrons." *Nation's Restaurant News,* March 21, 1994.

———. "Industry Airs Health Gripes in Washington." *Nation's Restaurant News,* February 21, 1994.

———. "NCCR Backs Nationwide Bill to Stamp Out Public Smoking." *Nation's Restaurant News,* March 7, 1994.

American Hotel & Motel Association. *Risk Management Bulletin,* September 1994.

Barsban, Regina S. "Designing for the ADA." *Restaurant Hospitality,* January 1994.

Brooks, Steve. "Can Video Cameras Stop a Crime Spree?" *Restaurant Business,* February 10, 1995.

Brumback, Nancy. "Rising to the Challenged." *Restaurant Business,* May 1, 1994.

Bruns, Richard. "When the Biggest Barrier Falls." *Lodging,* February 1998.

Cichy, Ronald F., editor. *ACFEI Nutrition Certification Course,* 2d Edition. St. Augustine, Fla.: American Culinary Federation Educational Institute, 1991.

———. *Quality Sanitation Management.* East Lansing, Mich.: Educational Institute of the American Hotel & Motel Association, 1994.

Davis, Ronald. "Gut-Wrenching Food Causes Legal Upheaval." *Restaurant Hospitality,* December 1993.

"Employers Walk Immigration, Discrimination Tightrope." *Nation's Restaurant News,* November 1, 1993.

Estrin, Stephen. "Take Precautions: Restaurant Accidents Happen." *Nation's Restaurant News,* March 27, 1989.

Frumkin, Paul. "All Fired Up: NYC Smoking Bill Raises New Concerns." *Nation's Restaurant News,* May 16, 1994.

Gerlin, Andrew. "A Matter of Degree." *The Wall Street Journal,* September 1, 1994.

Gottlieb, L. "Protection Measures in the Event of a Robbery." *Restaurant Business,* June 1, 1980.

Hayes, Jack. "North Carolina County OKs Restaurant Smoking Ban." *Nation's Restaurant News,* October 11, 1993.

Howard, Theresa. "Company-Owned McD Units Adopt Non-Smoking Policy." *Nation's Restaurant News,* March 7, 1994.

Kochak, Jacque. "Preventive Maintenance." *Restaurant Business,* May 20, 1989.

Liberson, Judy. "The Year of Cooking Safely." *Lodging,* February 1998.

Liddle, Alan. "Tower to Appeal AIDS Discrimination Suit." *Nation's Restaurant News,* December 13, 1993.

Lorenzini, Beth. "Here Comes HACCP." *Restaurants & Institutions,* January 1, 1995.

Lohman, Jack E. "Breathe Easy: Going Smoke-Free Can Be Painless." *Nation's Restaurant News,* November 22, 1993.

Marshall, Anthony. "Choking Risk Demands First-Aid Training for Employees." *Hotel & Motel Management,* April 17, 1989.

Ohlin, Jane Boyd. "Creative Approaches to the Americans with Disabilities Act." *Cornell Quarterly,* October 1993.

Oleck, Joan. "Who's Afraid of OSHA?" *Restaurant Business,* February 10, 1995.

Papit, Ted. "Congressional 'Love' Hurts Minimum Wage-Earners." *Nation's Restaurant News,* February 14, 1994.

Peters, James. "Risk Management." *Restaurant Business,* May 1, 1991.

"Rival Health Plans Jockey for Position." *Restaurants USA,* January 1994.

Ruggiero, Tina. "The War on Fat: An Update from the Frying Front." *Restaurants USA,* February 1995.

Walter, Kate. "Separate But Equal." *Restaurant Business,* January 1, 1994.

Woods, Robert H. *Managing Hospitality Human Resources,* 2d Edition. Lansing, Mich.: Educational Institute of the American Hotel & Motel Association, 1997.

REVIEW QUIZ

When you feel you have covered all of the material in this chapter, answer these questions. Choose the *best* answer.

1. Which of the following sanitation guidelines does *not* apply to servers?

   a. Servers should not smoke while on duty.
   b. Servers should keep the tops, bottoms, and sides of serving trays clean.
   c. Servers should wash their hands after they handle money.
   d. Servers should not carry a service towel over their shoulders or under their arms.

2. The Heimlich maneuver can help save someone who is:

   a. having a heart attack.
   b. choking.
   c. intoxicated.
   d. on fire.

3. Class B fires may involve:

   a. grease and paint.
   b. oils and electrical wiring.
   c. wood, paper, and cloth.
   d. combustible metals.

4. A nutrient that does not contain carbon is a(n) __________ nutrient.

   a. protein
   b. organic
   c. lipid
   d. inorganic

5. According to the ADA, people with disabilities are qualified for employment if they can:

   a. perform their specific job functions as quickly as any other staff member.
   b. do their jobs without requiring special accommodations of any kind.
   c. perform the essential functions of a job with or without reasonable accommodation.
   d. a and b.

Answer Key: 1-c-C1, 2-b-C2, 3-a-C2, 4-d-C3, 5-c-C4

Each question is linked to a competency. Competencies are listed on the first page of the chapter. An answer reading 3-b-C4 translates to:

3: the question number
b: the correct answer
C4: the competency number

Chapter 8 Outline

Establishing Labor Standards
- Developing a Staffing Guide

Forecasting Sales
- Moving Average Method
- Weighted Time Series Method
- Forecasting for Lodging Properties

Preparing Work Schedules

Analyzing Labor Costs

Revenue Control Systems
- Manual Guest Check Systems
- Point-of-Sale Guest Check Systems
- Accepting Personal Checks
- Processing Credit Cards
- Point-of-Sale Settlement Devices

Revenue Collection
- Server Banking System
- Cashier Banking System
- Protecting Cash after Collection

Competencies

1. Explain how food and beverage managers develop labor standards for service positions.
2. Identify factors food and beverage managers consider when constructing a staffing guide.
3. Distinguish between fixed and variable labor in relation to food and beverage service positions.
4. Forecast food and beverage sales using the moving average and the weighted time series methods.
5. Explain how food and beverage managers use staffing guides to prepare work schedules and analyze labor costs.
6. Describe revenue control procedures for manual guest check systems and for computer-based guest check systems.
7. Distinguish the server banking system from the cashier banking system and explain how managers determine revenue standards for separate meal periods.

8

Labor and Revenue Control

EVERY DOLLAR in excessive labor costs represents a dollar subtracted from the bottom line. Consider a restaurant operation that consistently exceeds its standard labor costs by $100 a week. During the course of a year, this would drop $5,200 off the bottom line. How much revenue would the restaurant have to generate to restore that amount to the bottom line? Much more than $5,200! If the restaurant's profit margin is 12 percent (.12), the restaurant would have to generate $43,333 in gross sales to make $5,200 in profit ($43,333 × .12 = $5,200 [rounded]). Clearly, when actual labor hours exceed standard labor hours, the restaurant must pull in a substantial amount of additional revenue to make up for the additional labor costs.

This chapter presents a systematic approach to labor cost control. The system begins with defining the quality of service offered by an operation and then determining labor standards. Labor standards indicate the number of labor hours required to deliver quality service at various volumes of business. Using a labor staffing guide and sales forecasts for various meal periods, managers are able to match up the required labor hours to the forecasted volume of business. Labor hours are then scheduled on the basis of labor standards and sales forecasts. Variances between actual labor hours and standard labor hours are analyzed and plans for corrective action are implemented to complete the cycle of labor cost control.

This chapter also addresses revenue control procedures. Obviously, a dollar of lost revenue also has an impact on the bottom line. Revenue control begins with establishing standards—the amount of revenue the operation expects to collect for specific meal periods. This chapter demonstrates how revenue standards are established by operations with manual guest check systems and by those with computer-based, point-of-sale guest check systems. In addition, sections of the chapter present procedures designed to help ensure that the actual revenue collected corresponds with established revenue standards.

Establishing Labor Standards

All work should have a standard against which actual performance can be measured. Managers develop **labor standards** by determining the amount of time required to perform assigned tasks. Some managers know how long it should take to perform a particular task in a manner that meets the operation's service quality requirements. In this case, it is only necessary to formalize the knowledge by putting it in writing. However, in many operations, managers do not have this detailed knowledge. Perhaps no one has analyzed the job recently, perhaps work

Exhibit 1 Position Performance Analysis Form

Position Performance Analysis

Position: *Service* Name of Employee: *Joyce*

Shift: *A.M.—Lunch*

	4/14	4/15	4/16	4/17	4/18
No. of Guests Served	*38*	*60*	*25*	*45*	*50*
No. of Hours Worked	*4*	*4*	*4*	*4*	*3.5*
No. of Guests/Labor Hour	*9.5*	*15*	*6.3*	*11.3*	*14.3*
Review Comments	*Even workflow; no problems*	*Was really rushed; could not provide adequate service*	*Too much "standing around"; very inefficient*	*No problems; handled everything well*	*Worked fast whole shift; better with fewer guests*

General Comments

Joyce is a better than average server; with all the tasks that service personnel must do in our restaurant, approximately 10 guests per labor hour can be served by one server. When the number of guests goes up, service quality decreases. When Joyce really had to rush, some guests waited longer than they should have had to. When the number of guests per labor hour dropped and Joyce was not busy, there was a lot of unproductive time.

Suggested Guests/Labor Hour (for this position): *10*

Performance Review by: *W. Brown*
Restaurant Manager

procedures have been changed since the last **job analysis**, or perhaps the management team is new to the unit.

Exhibit 1 suggests how to develop labor standards that incorporate service quality requirements. Let's assume that the manager (working with the host as well as with selected servers and other staff members) has established quality guest service levels in the dining area for the lunch period. This would entail defining the tasks performed by servers and outlining those tasks in a sequence of activities such as greeting the guests; approaching the table; providing beverages, salad, entrée, and dessert; and so on. An observation period is then set up during which the service staff follows all policies and procedures. The manager supervises the service staff during this period and assesses job performances by closely observing better-than-average servers. During the assessment, the manager answers such questions as:

- Is the server providing the required level of service?
- Does the server seem rushed or overworked?
- Could the server do more work and still maintain the required level of service quality?

- How many guests are served?
- How many more guests could be served, or how many fewer guests should be served in order to meet the required level of service quality?
- Are there any changes that can be made to improve the efficiency and effectiveness of the server?
- How long should it take for a new server to perform at the same skill level as an experienced server?

In the case of Exhibit 1, the manager observed a server over five lunch shifts. For each shift, the manager recorded the number of guests served and hours worked. For example, 38 guests were served during a four-hour work period on April 14. That means 9.5 guests were served per labor hour (38 guests divided by 4 hours of work).

Before calculating a labor standard for this position, the manager would have completed worksheets for several trained servers who worked similar lunch shifts. In our example, the manager determined a labor standard of 10 guests per labor hour. That is, in the manager's view, trained servers should be able to serve 10 guests for each hour worked without sacrificing quality requirements.

With slight alterations, Exhibit 1's format can be used to determine labor standards for other positions in the operation. A performance analysis should be completed for each position and meal period. This is because labor standards for positions are often different for each meal period due to the different tasks required by the various menus and service styles. Also, if a business (such as a hotel, for example) has more than one food and beverage outlet, separate studies should be conducted for each outlet.

A labor standard functions as a productivity rate. Determining productivity rates by position and shift yields more useful information than determining an overall productivity rate for the entire operation. For example, suppose that, after carefully studying the operation, a manager determines that a productivity rate of 15 meals per labor hour is a desired efficiency level. Let's assume that productivity rates for cooks, dishwashers, and service staff were not considered separately. After a given meal period, the manager discovers that the actual productivity rate was only 13 meals per labor hour. Since the productivity rate was established without considering positions separately, the manager cannot pinpoint the cause of the lower overall productivity. If, however, the manager had known that the labor performance standard for servers was 10 guests per labor hour, while the actual productivity rate during the meal period was only 8, then at least part of the problem could have been immediately traced to the service staff.

Developing a Staffing Guide

A staffing guide answers the question, "How many labor hours are needed for each position and shift to produce and serve a given number of meals while meeting minimum quality requirements?" The **staffing guide** incorporates labor standards and tells managers the number of labor hours needed for each position according to the volume of business forecasted for any given meal period. By converting the labor hour information into labor dollars, the manager can also establish standard labor costs. The staffing guide serves as a tool for both planning work schedules and controlling labor costs. When the number of actual labor hours significantly exceeds the standard labor hours identified by the staffing guide, managers should analyze the variance and take corrective action.

A staffing guide can be developed either for each department within the food and beverage operation or for each position within each department. If the staffing guide is developed for a department as a whole, first analyze and summarize each position within the department (such as cook, assistant cook, and kitchen helper in the food production department). Then, average the required labor hours. Developing a staffing guide for each position within each department provides more useful labor control information because it enables the schedule-maker to plan the number of labor hours needed for each position. If actual labor hours exceeded standard labor hours, it becomes obvious which position incurred the additional hours.

When constructing staffing guides, managers should keep in mind the following points:

- Each operation must set specific labor standards. Standards developed by another operation are generally meaningless, unless both operations are part of a chain offering uniform products and services.
- Labor standards should reflect the productivity rates of better-than-average staff members.
- As staff members become more efficient through experience, work simplification, or other efficiency measures, managers should change the staffing guide to reflect the higher productivity rates.
- The standard labor hours of a staffing guide need to be converted to labor dollars to ensure consistency with labor costs permitted by the operating budget.

Fixed and Variable Labor. Fixed labor refers to the minimum labor required to operate a food service facility regardless of the volume of business. This minimum amount of labor must be considered and incorporated into the staffing guide as the minimum staffing level. For example, if the dining area is open from 6:00 A.M. to 11:00 A.M. for breakfast, there must be at least one server on duty no matter how slow the period may be. One server may work the entire five-hour shift or may work until 9:30 A.M., at which time another server takes over until 11:00 A.M. Regardless of the schedule pattern, in this example there is a fixed labor requirement of five labor hours for the server position during the breakfast shift. Up to a certain volume of business (a point determined by management), no additional servers are necessary. Above this defined level, however, additional labor is needed. This additional labor is referred to as **variable labor**, which varies according to the volume of business activity. As more guests are served or as more meals are produced, additional service and production labor is needed.

Exhibit 2 provides a sample staffing guide format for positions in a food service operation. The hours noted in the staffing guide include the fixed hours required regardless of business volume. Examine the position of food server. When

Exhibit 2 Sample Staffing Guide

Standard Labor Hour Staffing Guide: Dinner

	Number of Meals				
	50	**75**	**100**	**125**	**150**
Position Food Server	8.5 5:00–9:30 7:00–11:00	9.5 5:00–9:30 6:30–11:30	16.0 5:00–9:30 6:30–10:00 7:00–10:00 7:30–12:30	16.0 5:00–9:30 6:30–10:00 7:00–10:00 7:30–12:30	19.0 5:00–10:00 6:00–11:00 6:00–11:00 7:30–11:30
Bartender	9.0 4:00–1:00	9.0 4:00–1:00	9.0 4:00–1:00	9.0 4:00–1:00	9.0 4:00–1:00
Cocktail Server	6.5 4:30–11:00	6.5 4:30–11:00	6.5 4:30–11:00	6.5 4:30–11:00	6.5 4:30–11:00
Cook	7 4:00–11:00	14 3:00–10:00 5:00–12:00	14 3:00–10:00 5:00–12:00	14 3:00–10:00 5:00–12:00	16 3:00–11:00 4:00–12:00
Steward	6.5 5:00–11:30	6.5 5:00–11:30	9.0 3:00–12:00	9.5 3:00–12:30	9.5 3:00–12:30
Busperson	—	2 7:30–9:30	4 7:30–9:30 7:30–9:30	5 7:00–9:30 7:30–10:00	7 7:00–9:30 7:30–10:00 7:30–9:30
Host (Manager serves as host on slow evenings)	—	3 6:00–9:00	3.5 6:00–9:30	4.0 6:00–10:00	4.0 6:00–10:00

NOTE: Labor hour standards are used for illustrative purposes only. Information must be developed for a specific operation based upon factors that influence worker efficiency within that food service operation.

50 dinners are forecasted, 8.5 food server labor hours should be scheduled. The 8.5 labor hours represent this operation's standard of meals served per labor hour, based upon its analysis of the food server position. That is, the labor standard (8.5 labor hours) equals the total hours this operation allows to serve 50 meals. The boxes also indicate the recommended number of servers to schedule (2 when 50 to 75 meals are forecasted, 4 when 100 to 150 meals are forecasted). The manager must decide which food servers to schedule, based on their abilities and availability.

The shifts listed in each box represent a staff schedule that takes into account typical peaks and valleys in business volume for each shift during the dinner period. In the first box, for example, the first server works a 5:00 P.M. to 9:30 P.M. shift, the second works a 7:00 P.M. to 11:00 P.M. shift, so that both servers are working during the peak dinner hours of 7:00 P.M. to 9:30 P.M. These shift times are based on patterns of business volume, reservation records, and other information suggesting times during which a specific number of servers are needed during the meal period. Also, note that the staffing guide in Exhibit 2 incorporates economies of scale. That is, the efficiency per unit of output increases as business volume increases. The exhibit shows that 16 server labor hours are scheduled when 100 or 125 meals are expected to be served.

Because the amount of fixed labor significantly affects the labor control program, if a business has more than one food and beverage outlet (a hotel or resort, for example), fixed labor requirements should be established for each outlet. While a manager designates the amount of fixed labor judged necessary, the assessment is always open for review. Factors such as changes in service quality requirements, menus, service styles, operating procedures, and guests' expectations influence the amount of fixed labor required. Careful analysis of work performance ensures that staff members are as productive as their situation permits. For example, on an average slow shift (when most labor is fixed), how much of the staff members' time is spent on work normally expected of the position? As the amount of idle time increases, it is important for managers to reconsider the hours of operation. Perhaps the outlet can open later or close earlier. Or managers might consider adding tasks for the fixed-labor staff members to perform. Servers performing additional duties during slow times could reduce the amount of labor needed during subsequent shifts.

Salaried labor costs do not increase or decrease according to the number of guests served. One manager, paid at a predetermined salary rate, represents a fixed labor cost. Normally, salaried personnel should be scheduled to perform only the work their job descriptions require. Managerial tasks should be scheduled during slow times during the day. During busy times, managers must be available to perform supervisory and operational duties. However, during slow periods, salaried staff could be assigned duties normally performed by hourly staff members. For example, an assistant restaurant manager might be stationed at the host stand, seating guests and taking reservations. However, salaried staff should not be used indiscriminately to reduce hourly labor costs. It is often wise to develop responsibilities, tasks, and the volume of work for salaried staff first; then schedule variable-labor staff to perform the remaining tasks. Although managers should know how to perform all the tasks in the operation, salaried staff should not be the first chosen to replace hourly staff members who fail to report to work. Efficiency, attitude, and ability all decrease as the length of the workweek increases. Turnover in management positions can often be traced to overwork.

Operations with unionized work forces must incorporate a wide range of other restrictions into the staffing guide. It is not uncommon, for example, for a labor contract to stipulate the minimum and maximum hours that a server can work per shift. Some unionized operations have a specific ratio of seats or guests that one staff member can serve. Overtime restrictions for unscheduled labor hours and the number and timing of work breaks may also need to be considered. Another basic part of many union contracts is the exact definition of tasks that union members in each position can and cannot perform. For example, if food and beverage servers cannot clear tables, the variable staffing guide should exclude the time required to perform this task from the server's labor hours and include it only under the labor hours required for buspersons.

Forecasting Sales

Sound sales forecasts are crucial to many areas of a food and beverage operation. Production staff use sales forecasts to purchase, receive, store, issue, and produce menu items in sufficient quantities to serve the estimated number of guests. Forecasting sales involves more than just predicting sales volumes in terms of dollars. To schedule the right number of production and service staff, managers must know approximately how many guests to expect, what they are likely to order, and when they are likely to arrive. This is all part of forecasting sales as well.

Reliable forecasting helps managers ensure that staff members and workstations are ready for guest service at the start of each service period. The number of guests that is forecasted helps managers know how many supplies to stock in service areas, for example. In many operations, food servers perform some preparation duties, such as filling portion containers with condiments, preparing butter chips, slicing bread, portioning sour cream, preparing iced tea, and wrapping flatware in napkins. The forecasted number of guests obviously affects the quantity of these items that service staff must make ready for service. Some restaurants find a correlation between the total number of guests they expect to serve and the number of two-person, four-person, and other-sized groups. Forecasts help them determine how to set up dining area tables to accommodate these different groups.

When guests typically arrive is important information for managers to know when scheduling staff. Electronic **point-of-sale (POS) systems** can provide useful historical data for forecasting guests and labor needs. Exhibit 3 presents a sample report itemizing the revenue, number of guests, number of guest checks opened in the system, and number of labor hours and dollars, as well as the labor/revenue ratio for each hour of operation during a single day. By analyzing a number of these hourly sales reports for the same day over several weeks, managers can identify the hours during a meal period that require the greatest number of servers and determine the best beginning and ending times for shifts during breakfast, lunch, and dinner periods.

Forecasting techniques vary from relatively simple intuitive methods to extremely complex mathematical formulas. For our purposes we will look at two commonly used methods: the moving average approach and the weighted time series method. These approaches to forecasting are based on historical data and mathematical formulas and their projections must be tempered by a variety of other factors, such as holidays, the weather, and community activities, as well as ongoing and special advertising and promotional activities of the food and beverage operation.

Moving Average Method

The **moving average method** of forecasting is based on averaging historical sales data and is expressed mathematically as follows:

$$\text{Moving Average} = \frac{\text{Activity in Previous } n \text{ Periods}}{n}$$

Exhibit 3 Hourly Revenue Report

Through Time	Revenue	Guests	Checks	Labor Hrs	Labor $$	Lbr/Rev
8:00 AM	0.00	0	0	0.00	0.00	0.00%
9:00 AM	0.00	0	0	0.13	0.70	0.00%
10:00 AM	0.00	0	0	5.52	27.46	0.00%
11:00 AM	0.00	1	1	10.28	47.68	0.00%
12:00 PM	100.45	12	5	16.30	65.98	65.68%
1:00 PM	93.40	7	8	17.78	67.81	72.60%
2:00 PM	139.05	14	13	18.00	67.81	48.77%
3:00 PM	76.80	6	10	18.00	67.81	88.29%
4:00 PM	615.89	86	56	17.67	64.42	10.46%
5:00 PM	240.55	7	12	25.17	85.85	35.69%
6:00 PM	609.85	48	28	39.73	137.82	22.60%
7:00 PM	1,319.29	141	89	45.42	160.94	12.20%
8:00 PM	1,573.40	167	131	52.70	190.49	12.11%
9:00 PM	1,815.77	92	169	56.95	213.66	11.77%
10:00 PM	1,376.40	67	213	57.50	229.18	16.65%
11:00 PM	1,317.80	159	237	51.53	203.61	15.45%
12.00 AM	1,281.95	34	237	47.18	181.08	14.13%
1:00 AM	1,220.30	22	231	38.62	152.32	12.48%
2:00 AM	791.30	122	161	32.97	128.98	16.30%
3:00 AM	2,575.50	3	3	20.90	78.13	3.03%
4:00 AM	0.00	0	0	6.73	11.67	0.00%
5:00 AM	0.00	0	0	0.00	0.00	0.00%
6:00 AM	0.00	0	0	0.00	0.00	0.00%
7:00 AM	0.00	0	0	0.00	0.00	0.00%
Total	15,147.70	988	1604	579.08	2,183.40	14.41%

Source: Ibatech, Inc., Aloha Hospitality Software, Hurst, Texas.

where n is the number of periods in the moving average. Exhibit 4 lists the number of Tuesday dinners sold over a 10-week period. Using a 3-week moving average, the estimated number of dinners for the coming Tuesday would be 272, determined as follows:

$$\text{3-Week Moving Average} = \frac{285 + 270 + 260}{3} = 272 \text{ (rounded)}$$

As new weekly results become available, they are used in calculating the average by adding the most recent week and dropping the oldest week. In this way, the calculated average is a "moving" one because it is continually updated to include only the most recent data for the specified number of time periods.

More than 3 weeks could be used to determine the forecast for the upcoming Tuesday. For example, a 10-week moving average of the data in Exhibit 4—"dinners served on Tuesdays"—would forecast 283 meals, determined as follows:

$$\text{10-Week Moving Average} = \frac{285 + 270 + 260 + 290 + 280 + 290 + 300 + 275 + 285 + 295}{10} = 283$$

Exhibit 4 Dinners Served on Tuesdays

Previous Weeks	Dinners Served
1 (most recent)	285
2	270
3	260
4	290
5	280
6	290
7	300
8	275
9	285
10	295
	2,830

The more periods averaged, the less effect random variations will have on the forecast. However, a serious limitation to the moving average method is that it gives equal weight to each of the data gathered over the specified number of time periods. Many managers would agree that data from the most recent time periods contain more information about what might happen in the future and, therefore, should be given more weight than older data used to calculate the moving average. A forecasting method that counts recent data more heavily than older data is the weighted time series method.

Weighted Time Series Method

The **weighted time series method** of forecasting allows for placing greater value on the most recent historical data when forecasting sales. For example, if we are forecasting the number of next Tuesday's dinners, we could base our projection on data from the five most recent Tuesday dinners shown in Exhibit 4 (Weeks 1, 2, 3, 4 and 5). For purposes of this example, assume weights of 5, 4, 3, 2, and 1 for the prior Tuesdays, with 5 assigned to the most recent Tuesday, 4 to the next most recent Tuesday, and so on. To forecast the number of dinners for the upcoming Tuesday using the weighted time series method, the following steps are taken:

1. Multiply each week's number of dinners sold by its respective weight and total the values:

   $(285)(5) + (270)(4) + (260)(3) + (290)(2) + (280)(1) = 4{,}145$

2. Divide the computed total by the sum of its weights. This will yield the weighted forecast:

$$\frac{4{,}145}{5 + 4 + 3 + 2 + 1} = \frac{4{,}145}{15} = 276 \text{ (rounded)}$$

Electronic point-of-sale systems and hospitality computer software provide forecasting programs that quickly analyze data and make mathematically correct projections. These programs forecast on the basis of stored data, manually inputted data, or data transferred from point-of-sale systems within the operation. The forecasts help managers plan production and purchase supplies, as well as schedule labor hours.

Forecasting for Lodging Properties

Additional factors affect food and beverage sales forecasts in lodging operations. Since the number of guests staying at a lodging property affects its level of food and beverage business, the occupancy forecast developed by the property's rooms department influences forecasts developed in the food and beverage outlets. Food and beverage outlets within a hotel or resort also depend on timely and accurate information from the sales and catering departments. For example, food and beverage managers need to know what events the banquet or catering department has scheduled and whether the events are for local attendees or for hotel guests. A hotel's restaurant and room service operation would expect less business than normally anticipated at a certain occupancy level if the banquet department is serving breakfast, lunch, and/or dinner to group of guests staying at the property.

Preparing Work Schedules

The staffing guide and sales forecasts are the tools managers use to schedule staff members. For example, if 150 meals are expected to be served during the evening shift on Thursday, and the staffing guide indicates that 19 food server labor hours are needed to handle this volume of business, then 19 food server hours are scheduled. If less than 19 hours are scheduled, the quality of service is likely to suffer, since the staff probably will be rushed. If more than 19 hours are scheduled, the staff will not work efficiently, labor costs will increase, and productivity will be lower than labor standards permit.

In most food service operations, the work flow is rarely constant throughout a shift. There is usually a mixture of rush, normal, and slow periods. Therefore, it is generally not a good idea to have all staff members begin and end workshifts at the same time. By staggering and overlapping workshifts, managers can ensure that the greatest number of staff members is working during peak business hours. For example, one server might begin work an hour before the dining room opens. The server can use this time to check or set up tables and perform other miscellaneous tasks. A second server could be scheduled to arrive one-half hour before opening to perform other preopening duties. Both staff members can begin serving when needed. Staggered ending times are also encouraged to ensure maximum worker efficiency. The first staff member to check in might be the first to leave. Of course, it is necessary to comply with the operation's policies as scheduling decisions are made.

Two of the most useful scheduling tools are the manager's past experience in putting together work schedules and the manager's knowledge of the staff's capabilities. In many food and beverage operations, the pattern of business volume stabilizes, creating a recognizable pattern of labor requirements. The more experience the manager acquires in relation to a specific operation, the easier it becomes to stagger work schedules, balance full-time and part-time staff members, and effectively use temporary workers. Similarly, the better the manager understands the capabilities of the staff, the easier it becomes to schedule the right staff members for particular times and shifts. For example, some servers may work best when they are scheduled for the late dinner shift. These factors can be taken into account when planning work schedules.

Some managers find it convenient to schedule required labor hours during the midweek for the next workweek (Monday through Sunday). Others may develop work schedules for longer or shorter time periods. In any case, the important point is to establish a routine scheduling procedure. Whenever possible, managers should consider staff members' preferences. Staff members can be given schedule request forms to indicate which days or shifts they want off. These requests should be submitted by staff members several weeks in advance and honored by management to the maximum extent possible. Once the working hours for each staff member are established, they should be combined in a schedule and posted for staff member review and use. The posted schedule attempts to provide staff members with the best possible advance notice of their work hours.

Of course, schedule plans do not always work. Staff members might call in sick or fail to show up without warning. Also, the number of actual guests and the volume of meals might be lower or higher than expected. Therefore, it is often necessary to revise posted work schedules. Having staff members who are willing to come in on short notice helps protect the operation when personal problems of staff members result in a reduced number of workers on a given shift.

Analyzing Labor Costs

Using the department's staffing guide and a reliable sales forecast to develop work schedules does not guarantee that the hours staff members actually work will equal the number of hours for which they were scheduled to work. Managers must monitor and evaluate the scheduling process by comparing, on a daily and weekly basis, the actual hours each staff member works with the number of hours for which the staff member was scheduled to work. Automated time-clock systems and electronic point-of-sale systems enable managers to monitor and verify the number of hours each staff member actually works.

Many operations use a **computerized time-clock system** that records time in and time out for staff members. Exhibit 5 shows a sample time card from one of these systems. When the time-clock system is interfaced to a host computer system, data may be transferred each day to the back office payroll system and the previous day's pay calculated for each staff member. Many of these systems can be programmed to handle several job codes for a single staff member. This is an important feature for food and beverage managers, because a single staff member could work at different jobs (each with different pay rates) over a number of workshifts.

When time clocks are used, it is important for managers to clearly communicate to staff members the operation's policies regarding punching in and out. For example, many operations have policies requiring staff members to get approval from their managers before they punch in prior to their scheduled shifts or remain

Exhibit 5 Sample Electronic Time Card

TIMEKEEPER 35 FEATURES

- Employee Classification
- Department #
- Employee name
- Column headings
- Day or date (01–31)
- Automatic meal deduction
- Daily total
- Separation of hours into categories
- 9-digit employee number
- Pay period ending
- Automatic timecard preparation
- Automatic rounding of punches
- Weekly total breakout
- Hours/minutes or Hours/hundredths of hours

BROOKS, JACK 1234 1 230145687 04/08

NAME PERIOD ENDING

SIGNATURE FORM NO. TK-572

DAY	IN	OUT	DAILY	REG	OT
MO	7:30A	12:00P	4:30	4.50	0.00
MO	12:30P	4:00P	8:00	8.00	0.00
TU	7:23A	12:00P	4:30	12.50	0.00
TU	12:30P	4:05P	8:00	16.00	0.00
WE	7:30A	4:00P	8:00	24.00	0.00
TH	7:24A	4:07P	8:00	32.00	0.00
FR	7:30A	12:00P	4:30	36.50	0.00
FR	12:30P	6:00P	10:00	40.00	2.00

R= 40.00 OT= 2.00 P= 0.00 M= 0.00

PAT. 4,270,043; 4,361,092 & FOR. PRINTED IN U.S.A. ©1981–84, KRONOS

KRONOS INCORPORATED TIMEKEEPER

Source: Kronos Inc., Waltham, Mass. Visit this company's Internet site at: http://www.kronos.com.

"on-the-clock" after their scheduled shifts end. Also, most operations clearly define the disciplinary action that will be taken against anyone who punches in or out for another staff member.

Automated point-of-sale systems generally include a labor management module that incorporates a time-clock function. Staff members are issued pass codes or staff member numbers and, as they log into terminals, their time and attendance records are developed. The **labor master file** of a POS system contains one record for each staff member and typically maintains the following data:

- Staff member name
- Staff member number

- Social Security number
- Authorized job codes and corresponding hourly wage rates

This file may also contain data required to produce labor reports for management. Each record in the labor master file may accumulate:

- Hours worked
- Total hourly wages
- Tips
- Credits for staff member meals
- Number of guests served
- Gross sales

Data accumulated by the labor master file can be accessed to produce a number of reports. A labor master report contains general data maintained by the labor master file. Managers generally use this report to verify a staff member's hourly rate(s), job code(s), or Social Security number. A daily labor report, such as the one shown in Exhibit 6, typically lists the staff member numbers, hours worked, wages earned, and wages declared for each staff member on a given workday. A weekly labor report contains similar information and may be used to determine which staff members are approaching hour totals beyond which they must be paid for overtime.

A weekly labor hour and cost report, such as the one shown in Exhibit 7, enables managers to identify variances between standard labor hours (dictated by the staffing guide) and actual hours worked by the staff. Since variances will almost always exist, management generally specifies either dollar or percentage amounts to define significant variances that warrant explanations and may trigger corrective action.

When budgeted labor costs are based on the same labor standards as the staffing guide, it is relatively easy for managers to keep labor costs in line with budgeted goals. When this is not the case, managers must ensure that labor hours permitted by the staffing guide remain within budgeted labor costs. To ensure consistency with budgeted labor costs, the standard labor hours of a staffing guide must be converted to labor dollars and forecasts of guest counts must be expanded to include revenue forecasts for meal periods. These conversions allow a direct comparison because labor costs are generally expressed as dollars and budgeted as a percentage of revenue. If the comparison shows that the staffing guide yields higher labor costs than were budgeted, then several courses of action could be taken. One would be to revise the budget accordingly. If costs could not be reduced in other expense areas, or if revenue could not be increased, profit expectations would have to be lowered. Another course of action would be to revise the quality requirements and increase the productivity rates on which the staffing guide is based.

If managers can explain the variances that occur, there is generally little or no need for corrective action. For example, recent turnover in the dining room may

Exhibit 6 Sample Daily Labor Report

SMITH'S RESTAURANT 1050 ← User-specified name

18:25 ← Date and time

DAILY LABOR REPORT ← Report title

JOB CODE: 10 ← User-specified job code

EMP	IN	OUT	HOURS	WAGES	D WAGE
210	09:34	15:05	5:31	10.58	8.90
•					
•					
224	13:05	18:08	6:03	13.57	7.73
		SUBTOTAL	11:34	24.15	16.63

← Staff member line for this job code (D WAGE means declared wages)

← Totals for this job code

JOB CODE: 16

EMP	IN	OUT	HOURS	WAGES	D WAGE
321	06:00	14:18	8:18	42.95	0.00
•					
•					
387	08:26	14:07	5:41	40.76	0.00
		SUBTOTAL	13:59	83.71	0.00
		TOTAL	25:33	107.86	16.63

← Totals for all job codes

18:26

Source: International Business Machines Corporation, White Plains, New York.

have resulted in several new servers who are at various stages of training and not yet performing to standard. Since these servers would handle fewer tables, additional servers would have to be scheduled. Therefore, actual labor hours would exceed standard labor hours until the new servers are fully trained. Also, a sales forecast could significantly differ from the number of meals actually served for a given meal period. A forecast that was too high would help explain some overstaffing; a forecast that was too low would help explain some understaffing.

On the other hand, a problem exists if actual labor hours vary from standard labor hours and managers cannot explain or defend the variance. The next step would be to discuss possible causes and potential solutions with other managers, the immediate supervisor, and affected staff members. Managers must then identify where the problem is actually occurring, assess the options, and select a course of action from the alternatives to resolve the problem. When developing a corrective action plan, managers should consider the following:

- *Probability of success.* How successful will a particular alternative be in reducing the variance?

Exhibit 7 Sample Weekly Labor Hour and Cost Report

Week of: 7/14/00

Department: Food Service **Supervisor:** Sandra

Shift: P.M.

Actual Labor Hours Worked

Position/ Staff Member	Mon 7/14	Tues 7/15	Wed 7/16	Thurs 7/17	Fri 7/18	Sat 7/19	Sun 7/20	Total Labor Hours		Hourly Rate	Total Labor Costs	
								Actual	Standard		Actual	Standard
1	2	3	4	5	6	7	8	9	10	11	12	13
DINING ROOM												
Jennifer	7	—	7	6.5	7	6	—	33.5	31.0	$5.00	$167.50	$155.00
Brenda	—	7	6.5	7	6.5	6.5	5	38.5	38.5	5.15	198.28	198.28
Sally	—	5	8	7	8	10	—	38.0	36.0	5.25	199.50	189.00
Patty	8	6	6	4.5	—	—	6	30.5	31.0	5.10	155.55	158.10
Anna	4	4	6.5	—	4.5	—	5	24.0	22.0	5.10	122.40	112.20
Thelma	6	5	5	5	5	—	—	26.0	24.0	5.40	140.40	129.60
Elsie	6	—	—	6	6	8	8	34.0	34.0	5.05	171.70	171.70
								224.5	216.5		$1,155.33	$1,113.88
COOK												
Peggy	4	4	4	4	4	—	—	20.0	20.0	11.00	220.00	220.00
Kathy	4	4	4	—	—	4	4	20.0	20.0	11.15	223.00	223.00
Tilly	4	—	—	4	4	4	4	20.0	18.0	11.50	230.00	207.00
Carlos	—	4	4	4	4	4	—	20.0	20.0	11.00	220.00	220.00
Sam	4	4	—	—	—	—	4	12.0	12.0	11.10	133.20	133.20
								92.0	90.0		$1,026.20	$1,003.20
DISHWASHING												
Terry	—	—	6	6	6	—	—	18.0	18.0	6.50	117.00	117.00
Andrew	6	6	—	—	8	5	5	30.0	30.0	6.25	187.50	187.50
Robert	8	8	8	8	—	—	6	38.0	38.0	6.55	248.90	248.90
Carl	5	—	5	5	5	6	—	26.0	26.0	6.50	169.00	169.00
								112.0	112.0		$722.40	$722.40
											$2,903.93	$2,839.48

- *Cost.* What costs are involved in implementing an alternative? Do the benefits of an alternative outweigh the costs of implementing it?
- *Guest impact.* How will guests be affected by the corrective action plan? Guests' needs and expectations must be evaluated in relation to the proposed action.
- *Past experience.* What actions were taken in the past to address similar problems?
- *Feasibility.* Is it really possible to successfully implement the chosen alternative? While this may seem obvious, some managers waste time wishing things were different instead of accepting the situation as it is and working within its constraints.
- *Compromise.* The best plan to resolve a labor control problem is often a compromise between two or more possible solutions.

- *Experimentation.* Sometimes it is best to test a solution before fully implementing it throughout a department or operation. For example, one staff member or one shift could evaluate proposed revisions to procedures.
- *Learning from others.* A study of similar food and beverage operations, a review of hospitality literature, and conversations with managers with similar responsibilities may help identify ways to reduce labor costs.

The success of labor control efforts is often dependent on the reactions of staff members to corrective actions. Managers must carefully and regularly communicate with staff members so that everyone clearly understands what is expected. When corrective action entails new work procedures, managers must implement additional training, reinforcement, and on-the-job coaching. Some staff members may resist changes and defend the status quo. Managers can best address these situations by clearly explaining the need for change and, when possible, detailing how staff members will benefit from the change. After implementing corrective action, managers must evaluate the results to ensure that the variance between actual labor hours and standard labor hours has been appropriately reduced and to ensure that revised procedures have not created spin-off problems in other areas.

Revenue Control Systems

Guest check systems are designed to ensure that food production areas produce only items actually ordered and that revenue is collected for all items served. As electronic point-of-sale technology becomes more affordable, fewer food service operations use manual guest check systems. However, when automated systems crash, the manager who knows how to implement a backup, manual guest check system can save the day. The following sections describe fundamental features of both manual and computer-based guest check systems.

Manual Guest Check Systems

A basic revenue control procedure for manual systems requires that servers neatly write all food and beverage orders on guest checks. Servers generally use pens, not pencils, and mistakes must be crossed out rather than erased. In many operations, the server must have a supervisor initial a guest check that has items crossed out or voided. Before initialing, the supervisor makes sure that the deleted items were not prepared by kitchen or bar staff.

Before food or beverage items are produced, servers must provide appropriate production staff with **requisition slips**. The server lists items on a requisition slip and also records his or her name (or staff member identification number) and the serial number of the corresponding guest check. Some operations use a **duplicate guest check system** for food orders. With this system, each guest check has at least two parts. The server turns in the duplicate copy to the kitchen and keeps the original copy for presentation to the guest. When the guest is ready to pay, the guest check is tallied. A calculator with a printer that produces a tape is sometimes used. The tape is stapled to the check for the guest's review of charges.

Requisition slips or duplicate checks are useful for routine guest-check audit functions. At the end of a meal period, the manager (or a designated staff member) can match requisition slips (or duplicate copies of guest checks) turned in to the kitchen with the corresponding guest checks for which revenue has been collected. This procedure identifies differences between what was produced and what was served. Routine audits of guest checks may also reveal mistakes made by servers in pricing items on guest checks or in calculating totals. These mistakes should be brought to the attention of the responsible staff members. By conducting routine audits of guest checks, management indicates to staff members its concern about effectively controlling the operation's revenue collection system.

Several other procedures apply to revenue control with a manual guest check system. Guest checks should be unique to the property. If guest checks are purchased from a local restaurant supply company, anyone—including a dishonest staff member—can buy them. In this situation, guest checks can be used in the operation with no record of who has them or from whom revenue is due. Therefore, it is best to order specially printed, hard-to-duplicate guest checks. Unused checks should be securely stored, not left unsecured in the manager's office or at the host stand.

Guest checks should be sequentially numbered and a record kept of which checks are given to which server. Beginning and ending serial numbers for all checks issued to each server should be listed on a guest check number log. Servers accepting the checks should sign the log to verify receiving the checks for which they will be held accountable.

All checks issued to each server must be accounted for at the end of a shift. Checks will be either used and turned in with revenue, unused and turned in as part of the server's closing duties, or kept in use and transferred to another server. All transfers of guest checks should be approved by a supervisor. Requisition slips or duplicate guest checks are helpful when a check is unaccounted for. If a requisition slip (or the duplicate guest check) corresponding to a missing guest check has been turned in to the kitchen, management knows that the missing guest check has been used, that items listed on it have been served, and that revenue is due from the server. According to property policy and in accordance with applicable wage and hour or other laws, penalties may be applied when checks are unaccounted for at the end of a server's shift.

Point-of-Sale Guest Check Systems

Some automated systems use preprinted, serially numbered guest checks like those used in manual guest check systems. Before entering an order, the server "opens" the guest check within the system by inputting his or her identification number and the paper guest check's serial number. Once the system has recognized the server and opened the electronic guest check, orders are entered and relayed to remote printers at food or beverage production areas. This eliminates the need for the requisition slips or duplicate paper checks used in manual guest check systems and also reduces the number of trips servers make to production areas—which gives servers more time to provide direct guest service. The same menu items (with their selling prices) are printed on the server's guest check.

Once a guest check has been opened, it becomes part of the system's **open check file**. For each opened guest check, the open check file may contain the following data:

- Terminal number where the guest check was opened
- Guest check serial number (if appropriate)
- Server identification number
- Time guest check was created
- Menu items ordered
- Selling prices of items ordered
- Applicable tax
- Total amount due

A server adds orders to the guest check at the terminal by first inputting the guest check's serial number and then entering the additional items.

There are many variations of this automated system. Some systems use guest checks with bar codes corresponding to the preprinted serial numbers. This eliminates the need for servers to input the guest check's serial number when opening a guest check or when adding items to guest checks already in use. When the guest check is placed in the guest check printer, the system reads the bar code and immediately accesses the appropriate file.

Receipt-printed check systems eliminate the traditional guest check altogether. These systems maintain only an electronic file for each open guest check. A narrow, receipt-like guest check may be printed at any time during service, but is usually not printed until after the meal when the server presents it to the guest for settlement. Since no paper forms are used during service, the table number often is the tracking identifier for the order. With some systems, seat numbers are used for tracking multiple checks per table. When presenting these checks to guests for settlement, the receipt-like guest checks can be inserted in high-quality paper, vinyl, or leather presentation jackets.

Some systems feature a receipt-like guest check that also serves as a credit card voucher. This reduces the time it takes servers to settle guest checks. Instead of presenting the guest check, collecting the guest's credit card, printing a credit card voucher, transferring information from the guest check to the voucher, and then presenting the voucher to the guest to sign, servers are able to present the guest check and the credit card voucher simultaneously.

POS technology simplifies guest check control functions and eliminates the need for many time-consuming manual audit procedures. Automated functions eliminate mistakes servers make in pricing items on guest checks or in calculating totals. When items must be voided, a supervisor (with a special identification number) accesses the system and deletes the items. Generally, automated systems produce a report that lists all guest checks with voided or returned items, the servers responsible, and the supervisors who voided the items. At any point during service, managers and supervisors can access the system and monitor the status of

Exhibit 8 Sample Server Check-Out Report

MRS

DEMONSTRATION

Server: **ANNA**

Date: **11/20**

In Time	Out Time	Total
12:36	15:23	02:47
15:25	15:26	00:01

Total Hours Worked: **02:48**

	Persons	Tables	Net	Tips
Lunch:	19	6	290.55	39.71
Dinner:	0	0	0.00	0.00
Total:	19	6	290.55	39.71

Tips on Credit Cards:	39.71
Credit Card Surcharge:	1.99
Net Total Tips:	37.72
Balance Due:	**37.72**

Source: Genlor Systems, Inc., Northport, New York.

any guest check. This check-tracking capability can help identify potential walk-outs, reduce server theft, and tighten guest check and revenue control.

The status of a guest check changes from open to closed when payment is received from the guest and is recorded in the system. Most automated systems produce an outstanding-checks report that lists all guest checks (by server) that have not been settled. These reports may list the guest check number, server identification number, time at which the guest check was opened, number of guests, table number, and guest check total. This makes it easier for managers to determine responsibility for unsettled guest checks. Exhibit 8 presents a sample server check-out report. Note that the report lists time in, time out, hours worked, number of guests served, tables attended, net sales, and the amount of tips to be paid to the server from guest charges during the shift.

Accepting Personal Checks

Some food and beverage operations allow guests to pay by personal check, while others have a strict policy against accepting personal checks. Although an operation has no obligation to accept personal checks, it cannot refuse to accept a check on the basis of a person's race, or sex, or other grounds that would constitute illegal discrimination.

Operations that accept personal checks should require proper identification. Many operations request at least two pieces of identification (such as a driver's license and a major credit card), one with a photograph. The guest's driver's license number, address, and telephone number should be recorded on the face of the check. Bank stamps and clearinghouse imprints will often appear on the back of the check.

Common guidelines that protect operations from accepting fraudulent personal checks include:

- Accept checks only for the amount of the purchase.
- Require that personal checks be made payable to the food and beverage operation, not to "Cash."
- Do not accept checks marked with "For Deposit Only," "For Collection Only," or similar terms.
- All checks should be legible and not have smudges, erasures, or other signs of tampering.
- Do not accept undated or postdated personal checks—that is, checks carrying no date or a future date instead of the current date.
- A guest should sign the check in the presence of a manager or designated staff member.
- Upon acceptance, personal checks should be marked with the operation's stamp "For Deposit Only."

Most food and beverage operations will not accept second- or third-party checks. A second-party check is one made out to the guest presenting the check. A third-party check is one made out to someone who has in turn signed the check over to the guest presenting it. Accepting such checks may create collection problems, especially if the writer of the check has registered a "stop payment" order on the check.

Some operations may choose to use a personal check guarantee service. When such a service is available, a manager or designated staff member telephones the service and provides data from the tendered check and the amount of the transaction. The check guarantee service, in turn, determines the check writer's credit history and either guarantees or refuses to support payment. Since these services charge a fee for each transaction, staff members should only accept checks that are written for the exact amount of the purchase. Otherwise, the operation is simply advancing cash to guests while paying a fee to provide the service.

Processing Credit Cards

Authorization and verification of credit cards are important revenue control functions. Food and beverage operations usually compile a set of steps for processing credit card transactions. In addition, credit card companies often require specific procedures in order to ensure payment. Exhibit 9 shows a portion of the Internet site of Visa International indicating the practical types of information provided to operations honoring their credit card. Local banks may also provide procedural

Exhibit 9 Tips from Credit Card Companies

VISA

Home | Products & Services | Offers & Promotions | Consumer Tips | For Businesses | Sponsorships & Events | New Technologies | About Visa

For Businesses

Becoming a Visa Merchant

Visa & Your Business

Why Prefer Visa?/Profit Calculator

Merchant Best Practices

Accepting Visa Purchasing Cards

Commercial Cards

Where to Use Visa Purchasing Cards

Small Business Site

New Technologies

Visa ePay

VisaPhone

Merchant Best Practices

The information on this page applies to businesses in the U.S.

Learn how to reduce administrative costs and increase productivity with these helpful tips for avoiding fraud and implementing best practices.

- Visa and the Year 2000 Challenge:
  What the Year 2000 means for Merchants and how you can be prepared.
- What to do when a customer presents a Visa card.
  An easy checklist of steps for merchants and associates to follow.
- How to recognize suspicious customer behavior.
  Tips to help you spot suspicious customers and avoid fraud.
- Making a "code 10" call.
  What to do if you are suspicious of the card or cardholder during a transaction.
- Case Studies
  Learn how other merchants have successfully reduced fraud.
- What to look for on the front of the Visa card.
  Guidelines for identifying counterfeit Visa cards.
- Reducing unnecessary key entry.
  Swiping cards through magnetic stripe readers can help you reduce fraud.
- Procedures for storage, retrieval, and audit of sales drafts.
  Find out about methods other merchants currently use.
- Merchant Education Program materials
  Important information about Visa policies, procedures, programs, and services.
- Visa Flag
  For Visa merchants: How to put the Visa flag on your Web site.

The Internet site of Visa International (http://www.visa.com) provides operations with practical information to guide credit card-processing procedures. (Courtesy of Visa International)

Exhibit 10 Suggestions for Resolving Credit Problems

When a credit card company refuses to authorize a transaction:

- Discuss the matter with the guest in private.
- Use care when describing the guest's unauthorized transaction (for example, do not call the guest's credit card "bad" or "worthless").
- Offer the use of a telephone to help resolve the matter with a credit card company representative.
- Allow the guest a chance to provide alternate, acceptable means of payment.

When a guest's personal check cannot be accepted:

- Explain the operation's check-cashing policy.
- Remain friendly and cooperative.
- Discuss alternative methods of payment with the guest.
- If local banks are open, direct the guest to a nearby branch, or extend the use of a telephone.

guidelines. It's often a good idea to have a legal review of the operation's credit card procedures to be sure of adherence to state and federal laws and to the specifications contained in credit card company contracts. Exhibit 10 provides some suggestions for resolving credit problems with guests. The following sections summarize basic guidelines for processing credit card transactions.

Expiration Date. When a guest presents a credit card, the staff member handling the transaction should immediately check the credit card's expiration date. If the date shows that the card has expired, the staff member should point this out to the guest and request an alternate method of payment. Since credit card companies are not required to honor transactions made with an expired card, accepting an expired card may lead to uncollectible charges.

Online Authorization. After checking a credit card's expiration date, the staff member should make sure the credit card isn't listed as stolen or otherwise invalid. Many operations validate credit cards through an online computer service accessed through a direct telephone connection. Once the connection is made, the required credit card and transaction data may be spoken, entered on a touch-tone key pad, or automatically captured through a magnetic strip reader. On the basis of the entered data, the credit card verification service consults an account database and generates either an **authorization code** or a **denial code** for the transaction. Online authorization services often charge a transaction-processing fee.

Cancellation Bulletins. In operations without online credit card authorization, the staff member should validate a credit card by checking the credit card company's current cancellation bulletin. Expired cancellation bulletins should be stored and filed in case a dispute eventually arises between a credit card company and the operation. The operation can refer to previous cancellation bulletins to prove that a credit card number was valid at the time the credit card was accepted for payment.

Invalid Card. Staff members should follow procedures established by the operation and by the credit card companies when a credit card appears to be invalid. The card may appear to be invalid because it has been tampered with or the signature on the credit card does not match the signature the guest writes on the voucher. Normally, it is appropriate for staff to politely request an alternate form of payment.

Imprinting the Voucher. Staff members imprint approved, valid credit cards onto credit card vouchers for the guest's signature. The imprinted voucher should be carefully checked to ensure that all card numbers are properly imprinted. If they are not legible, the first voucher should be destroyed and the procedure repeated, or the card numbers should be written in ink clearly on the hard copy of the voucher. Some operations require staff to circle the card's expiration date and initial the validation number on the imprinted voucher as proof that procedures have been followed. It's also wise to have the guest sign applicable guest checks as well as the credit card voucher.

Point-of-Sale Settlement Devices

POS technology offers several labor-saving settlement devices. A **magnetic strip reader** is an optional device that connects to a cashier terminal. These readers do not replace keyboards or touch-screens; they extend their capabilities. Magnetic strip readers are capable of collecting data stored on a magnetized film strip typically located on the back of a credit card or house account card. This enables a POS system to process credit card transactions. Some operations also distribute plastic, bar-coded identification cards to staff members who use them to log into the POS system. Managers may be issued specially encoded cards to access ongoing transactions and perform strictly managerial functions with POS system data.

Processing credit card transactions is simplified when a **power platform** is used to consolidate electronic communications between the operation and a credit card authorization center. A POS power platform connects all POS terminals to a single processor for settlement. This eliminates the need for individual telephone lines at each POS cashier terminal. Power platforms can capture credit card authorizations in three seconds or less. This fast data retrieval helps reduce the time, cost, and risk associated with credit card transactions.

Debit cards differ from credit cards in that the cardholder must deposit money in a personal account in order to establish value. The cardholder deposits money in advance of purchases through a debit card center. As purchases are made, the balance in the debit account is adjusted accordingly. For example, a cardholder who has deposted $300 to a debit card account has a value of $300 available for settling transactions. As the cardholder makes purchases, the money is electronically transferred from the guest's account to the account of the business where the purchase is made. A debit card is similar to an automatic-teller-machine (ATM) card in that the purchaser must have cash on account to complete a transaction successfully.

Restaurants may also accept ATM card payment through specially designed equipment at cashier stations. After the amount of payment is entered into an electronic cashier terminal, a display on the back of the terminal asks the guest to swipe the ATM card through a card reader. The guest then enters his or her personal identification number on a numeric keypad that is out of the cashier's sight. Usually within seconds, cash is transferred from the guest's checking account to the restaurant's bank account.

Revenue Collection

In food and beverage operations, revenue collection may be a duty assigned to individual servers, or it may be a function centralized at designated cashier stations. Whenever feasible, operations generally use cashiers because this ensures a **separation of duties**—a single staff member is not responsible for an entire series of transactions: order entry, delivery, collection, and reconciliation.

Staff members responsible for revenue collection are issued **cash banks** at the starts of their shifts. Generally, the staff member counts the opening bank in the presence of a manager. The cash bank should always contain the same amount of money and the minimum amount of each type of currency required for making change. In some operations, staff members sign a receipt form certifying that they received the cash bank and that they accept responsibility for it during their shifts.

Server Banking System

With a **server banking system,** servers (and bartenders) use their own banks of money to collect payments from guests and retain the collected revenue until they check out at the end of their shifts. In some operations, locking cash boxes are provided for each server to store collected revenue, credit card vouchers, and other sales materials.

After all checks are accounted for at the end of a shift, the amount of revenue due the operation is determined by tallying the totals from all guest checks assigned to each server. The tally is made by the manager (or cashier) in conjunction with the server. Totals from guest checks settled by credit card vouchers, personal checks, and house account charges are subtracted from the tally to arrive at the amount of cash to be collected from the server. The remaining cash represents the server's opening cash bank and any cash tips earned. After the actual revenue collected by the manager (or cashier) balances with the tally of totals from all guest checks assigned to the server, charged tips (as recorded on credit card or house account vouchers) are paid out to the server.

In nonautomated operations, these closing procedures can be very time-consuming. POS technology speeds up the process by producing a report at the end of a shift that automatically tallies the total revenue due from each server. These reports generally identify transactions opened by the server and itemizes each of them in terms of:

- Table number
- Number of covers
- Elapsed time from opening to closing of the transaction

Exhibit 11 Sample Daily Transactions Report

Date 8–30
Time 5:31 A.M. DAILY TRANSACTIONS

Guest Check	Tabl/ Covrs	Employee	ID	Time In	Time Out	Elapsed Time	Food	Bar	Wine	Guest Total	Tax	Tip	Settlement Method	Settlement Amount
11378	2–2	Jones	4	8:23	9:00	0:37	13.75	0.00	3.50	17.25	0.87	2.00	CASH	20.12
11379	2–1	Jones	4	8:25	9:00	0:35	2.35	0.00	0.00	2.35	0.12	0.00	COMP 1	2.47
													0004	
11380	3–3	Jones	4	8:32	9:01	0:29	13.15	0.00	5.50	18.65	0.93	0.00	CASH	9.58
													COMP 2	10.00
													0033	
11381	4–4	Jones	4	8:34	9:16	0:42	9.05	0.00	0.00	9.05	0.47	0.00	MC	9.52
11382	3–2	Jones	4	8:40	9:18	0:38	6.20	0.00	5.50	11.70	0.60	0.00	Cancelled	
11383	3–2	Jones	4	8:41	9:19	0:38	4.35	0.00	0.00	4.35	0.22	0.00	COMP 1	4.57
													0004	
11384	4–4	Jones	4	8:43	10:16	1:33	33.80	11.00	0.00	44.80	2.25	0.00	AMEXPRESS	47.05
11385	4–2	Jones	4	8:46	10:17	1:31	0.00	9.75	0.00	9.75	0.49	0.00	VISA	10.24
11386	4–5	Jones	4	8:51	10:17	1:26	0.00	18.50	0.00	18.50	0.91	0.00	MC	19.41
11387	8–2	Jones	4	8:54	10:18	1:24	14.65	2.50	0.00	17.15	0.85	0.00	COMP 1	18.00
													0004	
11388	4–3	Jones	4	9:23	10:17	0:54	4.70	3.00	0.00	7.70	0.39	1.00	CASH	9.09
11389	2–2	Jones	4	9:34	10:16	0:42	4.60	0.00	0.00	4.60	0.24	0.00	CASH	4.84
11398	3–2	Jones	4	12:09	12:10	0:01	11.35	0.00	0.00	11.35	0.57	0.00	CASH	11.92
11399	3–2	Jones	4	12:20	12:21	0:01	10.25	2.00	0.00	12.25	0.61	0.00	CASH	12.86
21615	3–2	Jones	4	11:39	11:41	0:02	13.15	0.00	0.00	13.15	0.65	0.00	CASH	13.80
21616	1–2	Jones	4	11:40	11:41	0:01	7.90	0.00	3.50	11.40	0.58	0.00	CASH	11.98
	Total cancelled			11.70										
	**** Totals						143.05	46.75	12.50	202.30	10.15	3.00		215.45

Source: American Business Computers, Akron, Ohio.

- Totals for food and beverage revenue
- Tax
- Tips due
- Settlement method

Exhibit 11 shows a sample daily transactions report that can be generated at any time during or after a shift. This type of report summarizes all major transactions by server and enables managers to trace and analyze revenue variances by guest check, server, time of day, food and beverage category, tips paid out, or settlement methods.

Cashier Banking System

With a **cashier banking system**, guests pay the cashier, the bartender, or the food or beverage server (who then pays the cashier or the bartender who has cashiering duties). Upon receiving a guest check for settlement, the cashier keys each item listed on the check into the register. The register tallies each item and imprints the total on the check for verification with the server's handwritten total. The cashier (or bartender) then retains the money and the accompanying guest checks. With most POS systems, the cashier does not to have to key each item from every guest check into the system. The cashier's terminal simply accesses the transaction number opened by the server, and the cashier closes it by collecting and recording the revenue.

At the end of a shift, each cashier completes a report that establishes the amount of revenue that should have been collected and compares this revenue standard with the amount of revenue actually collected. The revenue standard is the total of items such as:

- Food revenue—net system readings (subtracting the opening system reading at the start of the shift from the ending system reading at the close of the shift for this keyed item)
- Beverage revenue—net system readings
- Sales tax—net system readings
- Tips charged—tips that guests entered on credit card vouchers or house account drafts
- Guest collections—payments received from guests to be applied toward prior charges on house accounts
- Cash bank—the cashier's initial funds for making change

After the cash bank is restored to its original amount and types of currency (a certain number of pennies, nickels, dimes, quarters, one-dollar bills, five-dollar bills, and so on), the actual revenue collected is the total of the following items:

- Cash for deposit—cash, personal checks, and traveler's checks
- Credit card charges—Visa, MasterCard, American Express, Diners Club, and other charge cards.
- Purchases paid out—vouchers and receipts for incidentals paid from the cash drawer during the shift
- Tips paid out—payments for tips that guests entered on credit card vouchers or house account drafts
- Guest charges—charges made by guests on their house accounts

The total of cash funds and amounts represented on supporting documents should reconcile with the revenue standard, except for minor cash shortages or overages. Minor variances are generally due to errors in processing numerous cash transactions throughout the shift. Any significant variances should be investigated. Electronic POS systems can combine elements of cashier reports from several stations during the same shift. Exhibit 12 is a sample settlement methods report that indicates the amounts due (standard revenues) from four beverage cashier stations in the form of credit card vouchers, house account charges, and cash.

Protecting Cash after Collection

Revenue control procedures must address issues related to revenue collection, preparation of bank deposits, and the actual transportation of funds to the bank. All revenue collected should be deposited in the operation's bank account on a

Exhibit 12 Settlement Methods Report

Ring Off #22 —2:52 A.M. 1/06
Accumulators Cleared—8:00 A.M. 1/05

Settlement Methods	STATION 1 SALES	STATION 2 SALES	STATION 3 SALES	STATION 4 SALES	TOTAL SALES
Cash	1548.65	1560.20	1368.00	683.65	5160.50
Visa/MC	.00	10.75	.00	.00	10.75
Diners	179.70	.00	.00	.00	179.70
Amex	52.25	.00	96.60	24.25	173.10
Promo	.00	.00	.00	.00	.00
Company	.00	.00	.00	.00	.00
Discovery	.00	.00	.00	.00	.00
Direct Bill	.00	.00	.00	.00	.00
Total Settlements	1780.60	1570.95	1464.60	707.90	5524.05

Source: American Business Computers, Akron, Ohio.

daily basis. Some operations may make several daily deposits. Moreover, all revenue should be deposited intact. This means that bills should not be paid with cash from daily revenue; they should be paid by check. This policy makes it easier to trace the flow of revenue into the operation, on to the bank, into the proper account, and back out again through proper disbursement procedures in paying bills.

Separating duties is critical to protecting revenue collected. When possible, different staff members should collect revenue, audit and account for guest checks, and prepare the tallies of daily revenue. These staff members should not normally be involved in preparing bank deposits or paying bills. Specific practices that can help control revenue at the time of deposit include the following:

- Staff members should compare the amount of each bank deposit with records of daily revenue collected.
- Staff members who open mail should not make bank deposits. This reduces the possibility of staff members diverting revenue from checks received that should be deposited.
- All staff members who handle large sums of cash, assess bank deposits, and make cash disbursements should be bonded.
- The staff member who prepares a bank deposit should not be the staff member who actually makes the deposit—unless the owner/manager takes responsibility for these tasks.
- All personal checks should be marked "For Deposit Only," preferably at the time they are received. Local banks should be instructed to not issue cash for any personal checks made payable to the operation.

Two final rules are important for handling revenue receipts. First, the combination of the operation's safe should be changed periodically, and as few staff members as possible should know how to open the safe. Second, all cash-handling staff members should be required to take uninterrupted annual vacations. This way, another staff member can assume the duties and may uncover improper practices.

Key Terms

authorization code—A code generated by an online credit card verification service, indicating that the requested transaction has been approved.

cash bank—An amount of money to make change that is given to a staff member with cashiering duties at the start of each workshift.

cashier banking system—A revenue collection system in which all revenue is collected at cashier stations and accounted for by cashiers.

computerized time-clock system—Records time in and time out for staff members as they enter and leave the work area; when interfaced with an automated payroll system, relevant data can be transferred each day and the previous day's pay calculated for each staff member.

debit card—A plastic card similar in size to a credit card. The cardholder deposits money in advance of purchases through a debit card center; as purchases are made, the balance on the debit card falls.

denial code—A code generated by an online credit card verification service, indicating that the requested transaction has not been approved.

duplicate guest check system—A control system in which the server turns in a duplicate copy of the guest check to the kitchen and keeps the original check for presentation to the guest.

fixed labor—The minimum amount of labor required to operate a food service facility regardless of the volume of business.

job analysis—The process of determining the tasks, behaviors, and characteristics essential to a job.

labor master file—A file maintained by electronic point-of-sale systems containing one record for each staff member with data such as staff member name, staff member number, Social Security number, authorized job codes, and corresponding hourly wage rates.

labor standard—A time and productivity standard against which a staff member's actual work performance can be measured.

magnetic strip reader—An optional input device that connects to a point-of-sale system terminal and is capable of collecting data stored on a magnetized film strip that is typically located on the back of a credit card or house account card.

moving average method—A method of forecasting in which historical data over several time periods are used to calculate an average; as new data become available, they are used in calculating the average by adding the most recent time period and dropping the earliest time period. In this way, the calculated average is a "moving" one because it is continually updated to include only the most recent data for the specified number of time periods.

open check file—An electronic file maintained by automated point-of-sale systems that records information for each guest check used, such as terminal number where the guest check was opened, guest check serial number, server identification number, time guest check was opened, menu items ordered, prices of menu items ordered, applicable tax, and total amount due.

point-of-sale (POS) systems—A network of electronic registers or terminals capable of capturing data at point-of-sale locations, transferring data to other terminals, and integrating data for management reports.

power platform—Consolidates electronic communications between a hospitality establishment and a credit card authorization center; helps reduce the time, cost, and risk associated with credit card transactions.

requisition slips—Slips provided by servers to production staff before items are produced; the slips indicate items for preparation, the server's name or identification number, and the serial number of the corresponding guest check.

separation of duties—An element of internal control systems in which different staff members are assigned the different functions of accounting, custody of assets, and production; the purpose is to prevent and detect errors and theft.

server banking system—A revenue collection system by which servers (and bartenders) use their own banks of change to collect payments from guests and retain the collected revenue until they check out at the ends of their shifts.

staffing guide—A labor scheduling and control tool that outlines labor standards and tells managers the number of labor hours needed for each position according to the volume of business forecasted for any given meal period.

variable labor—Labor requirements that vary according to the volume of business activity; for example, as more guests are served or as more meals are produced, additional service or kitchen labor is needed.

weighted time series method—A forecasting method that places greater value on the most recent historical data when forecasting sales.

Review Questions

1. Why must managers consider quality requirements before developing labor standards?
2. How can managers use a position performance analysis to determine labor standards for each position and shift?
3. What are some factors managers must consider when constructing a staffing guide?
4. How is fixed labor different from variable labor?
5. How can managers evaluate a staffing guide in relation to budgeted goals?
6. How are requisition slips or duplicate guest checks useful in determining standard revenue for nonautomated food operations?
7. In what ways do electronic point-of-sale systems simplify guest check control functions?

8. What procedures should operations adopt to help ensure payment of credit card charges?
9. What elements distinguish a server banking system from a cashier banking system?
10. How is a daily cashier's report used to compare standard revenue and actual revenue collected?

Internet Sites

For more information, visit the following Internet sites. Remember that Internet addresses can change without notice.

Publications—Online and Printed

American Wine
http://www.2way.com:80/food/wine

Brew Magazine
http://RealBeer.com/brew/index.html

Bon Appetit
http://food.epicurious.com/b_ba/b00_home/ba.html

Cookbooks Online
http://www.cookbooks.com

CuisineNet Cafe
http://www.cuisinenet.com/cafe/index.html

Dietetics Online
http://www.dietetics.com

Electronic Gourmet Guide
http://www.foodwine.com

Food Network: Cyber Kitchen
http://www.foodtv.com

Food Magazine
http://www.penton.com/corp/mags/fm.html

Internet Food Channel
http://www.foodchannel.com

Lodging Hospitality
http://www.penton.com/corp/mags/lh.html

Lodging Online
http://www.ei-ahma.org/webs/lodging/index.html

Nation's Restaurant News Online
http://www.nrn.com

NutritiOnline
http://www.dietetics.com/news

On the Rail—News for Food Professionals
http://www.ontherail.com

Restaurant Hospitality
http://www.penton.com/corp/mags/rh.html

Restaurants and Institutions
http://www.rimag.com

Smart Wine Online
http://smartwine.com

Food Service Software Companies

Catering Connection
http://www.caterconnect.com

CaterMate Event Management Software
http://www.catermate.com

CaterWare Inc.
http://www.caterware.com

CLS Software
http://wwwmaisystems.com/html/cls.html

CMS Hospitality
http://www.cmshosp.com.au

Comtrex Systems Corporation
http://www.comtrex.com

Comus Restaurant Systems
http://www.comus.com

Eatec Corporation
http://www.eatec.com

Geac Computer Corporation Limited
http://www.geac.com

InfoGenesis
http://www.infogenesis.com

Instill Corporation
http://www.instill.com

Integrated Restaurant Software
http://www.rmstouch.com

Micros Systems, Inc.
http://www.micros.com

NCR Corporation
http://www.ncr.com

Newmarket Software Systems, Inc.
http://www.newsoft.com

Remanco International, Inc.
http://www.remanco.com

Restaurant Data Concepts
http://www.positouch.com

Sulcus Computer Corporation
http://www.sulcus.com

System Concepts, Inc.
http://www.foodtrak.com

Case Studies

Dom's Dilemma: Dealing with Staff Member Theft

Unfortunately for owners and managers, restaurants present plenty of opportunities for staff members to steal, in ways both large and small. Just a few examples can reveal the scope of the problem:

- Every Friday night at the Gourmet Eatery and Pub, a group of five men sit in the same five seats at the bar, tell stories, and drink for a couple of hours before going home. The head bartender makes sure their drinks are extra strong, and "Rusty's Regulars," as they are informally known, make sure that the head bartender's tips are extra generous.
- At Barnaby's Steakhouse, the assistant manager is closing on the first Sunday night of the month when he decides to take $100 worth of unsold gift certificates, scribble a signature on them, and put them in with the bank deposit. He then pockets $100. He knows that the restaurant only audits gift certificates at the end of the month, and he plans on giving his two-week notice tomorrow.
- At Tweedledee's Grill, a cook "accidentally" overcooks a steak during the lunch rush. "Hey, boss, can I take this home? It'd be a shame to waste it."
- At the White Knight Restaurant, servers maintain a cash bank during their shifts and "cash out" at shift's end. One day, after Michelle, a server, cashed out and left the restaurant, the manager goes into the computer system and voids off one of Michelle's $20 checks as a "complimentary meal," which

changes the end-of-day report. After manipulating the numbers in the computer, the manager pockets $20. Varying the day of the week, the shift, and the server, he has pocketed $10 to $20 a week in this way for almost a year now.

- Phil is a server at Richard's Bistro. He has become friendly with Mr. Ramos, a guest who comes in once or twice a week. A few months ago, Phil accidentally forgot to include Mr. Ramos's salad on his guest check and noticed that he got a larger tip. Since then, Phil has given Mr. Ramos either a free salad or a free dessert every time Mr. Ramos comes in, and Mr. Ramos has left a very large tip each time.

In most cases of income or product theft, restaurant managers know exactly what course of action to take with staff members. In some cases, however, the best way to handle a situation is not so clear cut.

• • •

All Dom could think as he watched Rebecca run out of his office Friday morning, crying, was: Not again. This can't be happening again so soon. Within one week, first Joshua, and now Rebecca—the last person he would suspect of stealing.

Dominick's is a 75-seat, fine-dining restaurant that Dom started five years ago. The first few years had been a struggle, but in the last year the restaurant had really caught on and Dom was beginning to hope that being the owner/operator of a small independent restaurant was not a sure road to bankruptcy and divorce after all. The long hours and hard work were paying off at last.

Even in the early, especially stressful days, Dom had always tried to make working at his restaurant as fun as possible. He wanted staff members to enjoy working at Dominick's and, partly due to his "we're all one big happy family" approach, many staff members had stayed with him for years—some had even been with him for the entire five years.

Losing staff members when they left voluntarily was bad enough; it was especially hard for Dom when he had to fire someone. Luckily, he hadn't had to fire that many people. In fact, not counting Joshua, it had been almost two years since he had fired anyone—that was one of the reasons why firing Joshua Monday night had been especially hard. But Dom had felt he had no choice.

Joshua was the son of Wendy Morris, one of Dom's best day cooks. Wendy had told Dom that Joshua needed a job, and Dom had hired him as a busperson. During Joshua's 60-day probationary period, there had been problems with his performance: he showed up late for work several times, he had broken quite a few dishes, and he wasn't friendly with the rest of the staff. As Helen, Dom's assistant manager, put it, "He has kind of a snotty, know-it-all attitude." Despite these problems, Dom kept Joshua on staff after his probation was up, giving him the benefit of the doubt because of Wendy. And then four nights ago—just two weeks after Joshua's probationary period was over—a server, Gail, had come up to Dom and said, "I think Joshua just stole some tips."

"You're kidding," Dom said. "Are you sure?"

"Well, the last time I checked table four to see if anyone wanted more coffee after their desserts, there was a lot of money in the middle of the table, but when I went back to pick it up after the guests left, it was gone. Sheila saw me looking around and came up to me and whispered that she saw Joshua stuff some money in his pocket while he was bussing the table."

"Sheila's sure about what she saw?"

"She seemed to be."

"Where is she now?"

"Last time I saw her, she was heading for the kitchen with a tray."

"Okay, I'll handle it."

Dom started off for the kitchen to find Sheila and confirm the story, but halfway there he saw Joshua loitering near the doorway to the staff breakroom, and something about Joshua's furtive reaction when he saw Dom coming down the hallway changed Dom's mind about the need to talk to Sheila.

"Hi, Joshua," Dom said. "Let's go to my office for a minute. I want to talk to you about something."

When they got to the office, Dom shut the door and got right to the point. "Someone just told me that some tips have disappeared. Do you know anything about that?"

Joshua said "No," but there was something guarded in his eyes and his cheeks flushed a sudden red.

"Are you sure?"

"Yes I'm sure. I didn't take anything."

Dom just looked at him and let the silence build.

Joshua blushed an even deeper red under Dom's gaze. Finally Joshua pulled some wadded bills from his pocket and threw them on Dom's desk.

"You took that money from Gail's table?"

Joshua nodded sullenly.

"Well, Joshua," Dom said, "stealing is a serious matter, so I think it's best that we end our relationship right now. I'll punch out for you—you can go on home."

"I don't care," Joshua said, "this job stunk anyway."

Dom let that pass. "I'm not going to tell your mother what happened, but I'm sure she's going to find out sooner or later, so I suggest you tell her before she hears it from someone else." Maybe having to break the news to Wendy would really drive this painful lesson home to Joshua.

"Can I go now?" Joshua snarled.

Dom nodded, and Joshua left without another word.

That was Monday night. During the next few days, everyone on staff but Wendy had come up to him and said he'd done the right thing—"that kid was just trouble waiting to happen" was how one staffer put it. But now, this morning, it had been Rebecca's turn to stand shame-faced in his office—Rebecca, who for five years had never given him even a moment's trouble and had long since become more friend than worker to him. Rebecca had been a hostess/cashier since opening day. In her late thirties with two children to support, she was the kind of staff member restaurant managers dream of: dependable, mature, hardworking. She always had a smile and a kind word for everyone. Not only was she nice to the restaurant's guests, she also went out of her way to be nice to the restaurant's staff. She remembered everyone's birthday with a card and was an adopted-mom figure to many of the teenagers on staff because she listened sympathetically to their dating troubles and their stories about shots at the buzzer that wouldn't fall at the end of basketball games. In short, she was a vital part of the Dominick's "family."

That's what made what Rebecca had done so hard to accept. After Dom had locked the restaurant's doors last night and was making up the bank deposit for the next day, he had counted down Rebecca's till over and over, but it always came up the same: $50.08 short. It was rare for any till in the restaurant to balance to the penny, but a shortfall of $50 definitely raised a red flag.

When Rebecca passed his office doorway that morning on her way to hang up her coat, Dom had called out to her to come see him when she had the chance. When she came in a few minutes later, she said good morning, but instead of her usual sunny smile, her eyes looked strained and she stood defensively in front of his desk instead of sitting down. Dom's heart sank, but he put a smile on his face and tried to sound matter of fact. "Something weird came up last night and I just wanted to talk to you about it. I couldn't get your till to balance—in fact it was fifty bucks short. Do you remember anything unusual about last night?"

There was a silence, then Rebecca's lower lip began to tremble and her eyes filled with tears. "I'm sorry," she said finally, so softly that Dom barely heard her. She cleared her throat and went on more strongly: "I took one of the fifties out of the drawer when no one was looking. I don't know why—I just did. Maybe it's because I've been under a lot of stress lately. My boyfriend just lost his job, my little one's sick and I've got to take her to the doctor, my tips have been down all week, and—I don't know—all of a sudden I just slipped it into my pocket. I'm really sorry," she said again, sniffing and wiping her eyes.

Dom pushed a box of tissues across his desk and she took one gratefully. "I don't know what to say," Dom said finally. "I'm sorry Samantha's sick, but—" his voice trailed off. Suddenly he thought of the time last year when his mother, who was in a wheelchair and couldn't get out much any more, had come to the restaurant with the rest of the family to celebrate her 80th birthday. Rebecca had fussed over her all evening, making her feel important and telling her how proud she should be of her son and the success he had made of Dominick's.

Dom came out of his thoughts to see Rebecca looking at him expectantly, waiting and scared. "I don't know what to say," he said again, and sighed. "I guess the best thing right now is for you to go home. We both need a chance to think about this." Dom stood up to signal Rebecca that the meeting was over. The gesture seemed uncomfortably formal, given their close relationship, but somehow appropriate under the present circumstances. "Go home and try not to be too upset, and when you come in tomorrow I'll have a decision for you."

"All right," Rebecca said. "I'm so sorry, I'll give the money back. I'd do anything if I could live last night over again."

Dom just smiled sadly and watched as Rebecca ducked her head and ran from the room. He didn't even see her go past on her way out after retrieving her coat—she must have left the restaurant the back way.

Dom was still at his desk an hour later when Helen stuck her head through the doorway. "I just can't believe the news about Rebecca," she said breathlessly.

Dom waived her to the chair across from his desk. "Who told you?" he asked.

"Tom saw her leave through the kitchen, crying and all upset, and called her when she got home. She told him the whole story."

"So everyone knows?"

"Yep. No one can believe it, though. Everybody's wondering what you're going to do. They think you should give her a second chance."

"Even Wendy?"

"Wendy's not here—she asked for the day off."

"Oh, right—I forgot."

Helen stood up to leave. "Rebecca's so good with guests, and you know how much everybody loves working with her—it would seem really strange not to have her around anymore. Are you going to let her go?"

Dom sighed. "I don't know. I told Rebecca I'd sleep on it. It'll be tough, but I'll have a decision for her when she comes in tomorrow."

Discussion Question

1. Should Dom fire Rebecca? Why or why not?

The following industry experts helped generate and develop this case: Christopher Kibit, C.S.C., Academic Team Leader, Hotel/Motel/Food Management & Tourism Programs, Lansing Community College, Lansing, Michigan; and Jack Nye, General Manager, Applebee's of Michigan, Applebee's International, Inc.

REVIEW QUIZ

When you feel you have covered all of the material in this chapter, answer these questions. Choose the *best* answer.

1. Jennifer, the new manager at the Crossroads Restaurant, completed an analysis of the operation and concluded that labor standards needed to be established for the service staff. Her first step in determining labor standards would be to:

   a. define the level of service quality for the operation.
   b. conduct performance analyses for service positions.
   c. adjust the staffing guide to raise productivity.
   d. align the staffing guide with budgeted labor costs.

2. Which of the following positions in a food and beverage operation is most likely to have a work schedule that varies in relation to changes in business volume?

   a. dining room supervisor
   b. server
   c. kitchen manager
   d. general manager

3. The Steak & Ale Restaurant uses the weighted time series method to forecast sales. Given the following data about dinners sold on Fridays, how many dinners would be forecasted for the upcoming Friday?

Previous Weeks	Dinners Sold	Weight Factor
1	85	5
2	80	4
3	75	3
4	65	2
5	70	1

   a. 70
   b. 73
   c. 78
   d. 82

REVIEW QUIZ *(continued)*

4. David, the new manager at the Knife & Fork Restaurant, compared the operation's current staffing guide with budgeted labor costs for the next several months. He concluded that if work schedules were prepared on the basis of the current staffing guide, the operation would end up significantly over budget. Which of the following would be the most reasonable action for David to take?

   a. lower quality requirements and lower productivity rates
   b. lower quality requirements and raise productivity rates
   c. raise quality requirements and lower productivity rates
   d. raise quality requirements and raise productivity rates

5. Food and beverage managers can identify differences between food items that were produced and items that were served during a specific meal period by matching requisition slips turned in to the kitchen with:

   a. sales forecasts.
   b. cashier totals.
   c. corresponding guest checks.
   d. storeroom issue reports.

Answer Key: 1-a-C1, 2-b-C3, 3-c-C4, 4-b-C5, 5-c-C6

Each question is linked to a competency. Competencies are listed on the first page of the chapter. An answer reading 3-b-C4 translates to:

3: the question number
b: the correct answer
C4: the competency number

Part II

Chapter 9 Outline

A Marketing Perspective
- Casual/Theme Markets
- Guest Feedback
- Menu Considerations: Food
- Menu Considerations: Beverages
- Value
- The Dining Environment, Supplies, and Equipment

Getting Ready for Service
- Training
- Dining Service Staff Positions

Delivering Service
- Taking Reservations
- Managing Waiting Guests
- Greeting and Seating Guests
- Presenting the Menu and Taking Beverage Orders
- Placing Beverage Orders at the Bar
- Serving Beverages
- Offering the Wine List and Serving Wine
- Taking Food Orders
- Placing and Picking Up Orders in the Kitchen
- Serving the Orders
- Presenting the Guest Check
- Serving Special Guests

After Service

Competencies

1. Describe casual/theme restaurants, including the following topics: markets; guest feedback; food and beverage trends; examples of ways casual/theme restaurants give value to guests; and environment, supply, and equipment issues.
2. Summarize some of the issues casual/theme restaurant managers face when getting their restaurants and staff members ready to serve guests, including training issues, and describe typical staff positions.
3. Describe characteristics of good service and summarize typical procedures staff members in casual/theme restaurants use when serving guests, from taking reservations to presenting the guest check; explain techniques servers can use to serve special guests; and describe the importance of planning and implementing service and product improvements.

9

Casual/Theme Restaurants

CASUAL/THEME RESTAURANTS are classified as full-service; that is, they offer table service and a variety of menu items. There are many types of **casual/theme restaurants,** most of which have moderate to moderately high guest-check averages. Their common denominators are informal dining environments (although there are differing degrees of informality) and the availability of alcoholic beverages in most cases (although there are some family-oriented casual/theme restaurants that do not serve alcohol). Themes range from homey to exotic. There are themes that seem to scream fun, fantasy, great food, and special drinks; themes that subtly promote enticing entrées and premium wines; themes designed to recall the pleasures of old-fashioned home cooking; and even themes that replicate a rain forest, complete with healthy choices on the menu and rainstorms every 20 minutes.

Many restaurants in the casual/theme segment are more than just places to eat and drink. They offer escape, fun, and convenience—the pleasure of not having to cook dinner and clean up the kitchen; a chance to be with friends; freedom from telephones, faxes, and e-mails after a hectic day at the office; a chance for a couple to have a meal and conversation without children in attendance; a place to celebrate a birthday or anniversary; a chance to meet new people; a chance to catch up on the news in the sports world; and more.

A Marketing Perspective

Competition in the casual/theme restaurant segment is fierce. Providing guest-driven service in such a competitive environment is not just a "should" but a "must." One of the few ways to build guest demand is to create and deliver guest service that differentiates a restaurant from the clutter of the competition.

Managers of casual/theme restaurants need to keep this marketing perspective in mind as they develop, implement, and evaluate plans that govern the service function. Managers must (1) know who their markets are, and (2) know what their markets want and expect.

This chapter first addresses market identification and market expectations. Later parts of the chapter focus on providing guest-driven service that meets or exceeds guests' expectations.

Casual/Theme Markets

There are casual/theme restaurants for virtually every market imaginable. There are restaurants that appeal to the twentysomethings, the thirtysomethings, and senior citizens. There are ethnic restaurants; restaurants that feature certain foods or certain food preparation methods; and restaurants that appeal to sports fans, theater-goers, video game buffs, romantics, health and fitness enthusiasts, and people who just enjoy good food in a comfortable setting.

Characteristics of Selected Markets. It would be impractical to attempt to describe every casual/theme market—there are local markets, visitor markets, single markets, family markets, and more. What follows are key characteristics of some of the major markets—Generation X, baby-boomers, influentials, and the affluent—and examples of what attracts them.(Keep in mind that there are many market overlaps; for example, an influential might also be a baby-boomer and might also be one of the affluent.)

Generation X. Generation X (also known as the "twentysomethings") is made up of smart, value-conscious consumers. They respond to restaurant concepts promoting excitement, entertainment, and group interaction.

Baby-boomers. Baby-boomers, those born sometime during the years 1946 to 1964, make up roughly one-third of the U.S. population. Baby-boomers have busy lifestyles and are likely to have dual-career families and hold white-collar positions as managers or professionals. If the past is an indicator of the future, as baby-boomers face age 50 and their peak earning years, the discretionary dollars they spend on food away from home should increase.

Baby-boomers respond well to target marketing. Compared to Generation X, they are easier to accommodate and satisfy. Baby-boomers are more likely to choose moderately priced restaurants over quick-service (fast-food) restaurants.

Influentials. "Influentials" is a market designation for those who are deemed leaders—people whose opinions on a variety of subjects are valued. If a restaurant can impress an influential by exceeding his or her expectations, the resulting positive word-of-mouth referrals could make the difference between profit or loss. By exceeding the expectations of influentials, a restaurant can connect with a large social network.

One of the most popular leisure activities of influentials is dining out, particularly on weekends. Influentials prefer full-service restaurants and report that they dine out often because it is fun. Influentials with children dine out to combine entertainment with family time. They value service and have little tolerance for poor service. Influentials also are more likely to enjoy food in moderation and practice a healthy lifestyle than the general public.

Influentials who are subcategorized as "intellectually curious" are lured by restaurants offering a combination of education and entertainment to create intrigue, excitement, and positive memories. To attract the "intellectually curious" market, some restaurants feature teaching chefs who offer cooking tips and classes. Other restaurants offer "theme dinners" during which guests can learn about the history of the unique menu items they are eating and how the ingredients were grown and prepared. If a special wine is part of the dinner, sometimes suppliers will co-sponsor the dinner and provide speakers who are knowledgeable about wines.

The affluent. The affluent market is composed of U.S. adults who earn $100,000 to $250,000 a year. The affluent can afford to sample and enjoy the best that money can buy.

The Rainforest Cafe restaurant chain bills itself as "A Wild Place to Shop and Eat." Each cafe re-creates a tropical rain forest, complete with live and robotic animals. Attached to the cafes are retail stores that sell rain-forest-themed merchandise from around the world, including bath and body products, toys, music, and an exclusive line of clothing. The chain's Internet site (http://www.rainforestcafe.com) carries over the rain forest theme, with a lush green background and colorful animals on almost every page. (Courtesy of RAINFOREST CAFE, Inc.)

In general, the affluent seek out exceptional service, and the quality of service is a big factor in whether they decide to return to a given restaurant. They like to be pampered and at the same time feel they are getting value for the dollars they spend. Fresh foods, regionally grown, are favorites of this market.

Guest Feedback

Casual/theme restaurants are constantly evolving to keep pace with the needs and expectations of guests. For that reason, managers and staff members of these restaurants must continually evaluate their products and services. To do so, they need to find out what their guests need and expect and then use that information. Guest feedback is only helpful if it is used properly.

Managers and staff members should seek guest comments on an ongoing basis. Guest comment cards, questionnaires, guest interviews, and other means can be used to determine guest needs and expectations and whether they are being met. One restaurant offers a free magazine subscription to those who complete and return its mailed questionnaire. Another restaurant phones guests two or three days after a private party to solicit feedback. One successful restaurant chain asks guests to complete "insight cards" and mail them back. When guests include positive comments on the cards, postcards are mailed to them, thanking them for their time. When negative comments are included, personal letters are sent that specifically address the comments and explain how the restaurant is going to deal with the problems raised.

Some restaurants use a **shopper's service** (also known as a "mystery shopper" service) to evaluate how guests' needs and expectations are being met. Shopper's services provide reports completed by anonymous "guests" (shoppers) who evaluate a restaurant's service from the guest's perspective. A sample shopper's service report form is shown in Appendix A. This form can be adapted as necessary to suit a specific restaurant.

Exhibit 1 is a sample shopper's service report form for evaluating wine service. It can be used in dining areas in conjunction with food service shopper forms. Note that Exhibit 1 refers to specific procedures; for example, the hypothetical restaurant that uses this form requires that red wine be poured so that glasses are no more than half full and white wine so that glasses are no more than three-fourths full. Exhibit 1 can be adapted as necessary to suit a specific restaurant's needs. Restaurants that use shopper services should use the reports as training tools, sharing them with all staff involved.

Menu Considerations: Food

Menus at casual/theme restaurants have evolved with the changing tastes of guests. Chicken, seafood, and salad entrées have become more popular. Based on the demand for healthier menu alternatives, vegetarian entrées are expected to continue improving in sales. Almost across the board, regardless of check average, beef entrées are being ordered less frequently by guests.

A major menu trend in casual/theme restaurants is the promotion of signature menu items. A **signature menu item** is one that guests perceive as special

Exhibit 1 Shopper's Report Form for Wine Service

	Strongly Agree				Strongly Disagree
A. The food server suggested a wine to complement the meal.	5	4	3	2	1
B. The wine was properly presented before opening.	5	4	3	2	1
C. The wine was opened properly (e.g., the server used a knife to cut the foil just below the bulge).	5	4	3	2	1
D. The glass selection was an excellent choice for the type of wine served.	5	4	3	2	1
E. The host was poured a sample of the wine.	5	4	3	2	1
F. The bottle was twisted at the completion of the pour.	5	4	3	2	1
G. The wine was filled to the proper glass level (e.g., no more than half full for red wine; three-fourths full for white).	5	4	3	2	1
H. The wine was served at an appropriate temperature (e.g., white wine chilled—50°F (10°C); red wine at cellar temperature—65°F (18°C).	5	4	3	2	1

I. Comments regarding your wine service: ______________________________

____

____

STANDARD POINT SCORE FOR WINE SERVICE 40 ACTUAL POINT SCORE ______

and closely associated with the restaurant promoting it. Outback Steakhouse's Bloomin' Onion appetizer is an example of a signature menu item. Signature menu items not only make the restaurant unique in the guests' minds, they also can help build repeat business and strong guest loyalty.

Premium menu items, as a category, are growing in popularity. Examples include premium baked products (freshly baked specialty breads, rolls, muffins, croissants), premium coffees (cappuccino, espresso, latte), innovative salsas and sauces with high-quality entrées, and seasonal or signature beers.

In keeping with the rising interest in local and regional cuisines, more "down-home" comfort foods—such American favorites as meat loaf, chicken-fried steak, and a variety of baked fruit cobblers—are being added to some casual/theme menus.

Many casual/theme restaurants are creating and featuring new sauces and condiments—particularly those restaurants featuring ethnic and regional cuisines. Examples include such entrée accompaniments as sweet-and-sour variations of teriyaki sauces, cranberry and cherry chutneys, Chardonnay artichoke salsa, and raspberry salsa—to name just a few.

Menu Considerations: Beverages

One of the most pressing menu considerations for managers of casual/theme restaurants is how to counter sagging beverage sales. Across the United States, restaurant guests are ordering fewer alcoholic beverages than they ordered in years past. Industry experts attribute the drop in alcoholic beverage sales to a number of circumstances:

- Baby-boomers are drinking less as they age.
- There is rising interest in fitness and health.
- Drunk-driving laws and penalties have been made tougher in almost every state.

Managers have come up with several strategies to offset the drop in alcoholic beverage sales. Creating good-tasting, visually appealing **signature drinks** is one strategy. Bob Chinn's Crab House in Wheeling, Illinois, promotes a signature mai tai with its seafood menu. The drink is served in a 22-ounce cup and guests get to take the logo-emblazoned cup home with them. The 8.0 (pronounced eight-oh) Restaurant in Houston, Texas, features vegetarian menu items and other menu choices prepared in healthy ways. To complement the food, 8.0 sells vodka infusion drinks in martini glasses. The vodka infusions are made of vodka blended with fruits, herbs, peppers, or spices.

Premium beverage options can also be promoted successfully. Premium wines by the glass (which are often available in **splits**—smaller bottles typically containing one to three glasses) are appealing to guests who want less than a full bottle of wine to accompany dinner. Red wines are particularly popular because of the health benefits they reportedly offer. With today's focus on quality—and in light of the fact that some guests order only one drink—premium brands make a great deal of sense. Beverage suppliers typically offer a wide range of promotional items (such as banners, table tents, and displays) to help restaurateurs sell these beverages.

And finally, brew pubs are helping to increase beer's popularity in the United States. Featuring on-premises brewing, some brew pubs offer signature menu items, others feature fine dining and upscale menus, and still others sell "pub-grub," casual menu foods such as burgers, nachos, ribs, and seafood. Some brew pubs stock over 100 choices of beers, domestic as well as imported, and specialty beers.

Beverage Selection. Beyond their concerns with lagging sales and developing strategies for offsetting the losses, restaurateurs need to make decisions about which types and brands of beer, wine, and liquor to offer.

Many casual/theme restaurants use three or more liquor classifications. The three commonly used classifications are house, call, and premium. **House brands** (or **well brands**) are served when the guest does not specify a particular brand of liquor when ordering a drink (a martini, for example); house brands are usually priced lower than call liquors. Likewise, house wines are served when the guest does not specify a label. **Call brands** are liquors that guests request (or "call") by brand name (a Beefeater martini, for example). **Premium brands** are costlier call brands requested by guests (an Absolut vodka martini, for example). In addition to premium liquors, there are premium beers and wines.

Attitudes of managers about house brands range from "Don't use anything you wouldn't be proud to display on the back bar," to "Use the least expensive; let people pay extra for premium brands." Many managers use neither the least nor the most expensive brands for their house brands; rather, they shop for value with an emphasis on what their guests desire.

It is generally not possible (nor, for that matter, desirable) to offer every available brand of liquor. A better approach is to stock call brands that guests most frequently request. If a specific brand is not available, most guests will order another. Obviously, if a number of guests frequently order an unavailable call brand, it should be added to the product list. Servers and bar staff can help managers identify which brands guests have been requesting.

Value

"Value" is the watchword for today's guests. The search for value is being led by increasingly sophisticated guests. Having experienced many dining-out occasions and a variety of dining concepts, guests are better educated in terms of what they want in food and beverage service. When they get what they want and expect relative to the price they pay, they perceive value.

Casual/theme restaurants need to emphasize and reinforce the value they offer. Value can be part of any number of promotions, including:

- Daily specials
- Gift certificates
- Seasonal specials and local or regional food tastings
- Senior-citizen discounts, often offered as part of early-bird dinner prices
- Complimentary samples of featured menu items
- Frequent-diner programs

The list can go on and on, as long as the promotions match what current and potential guests want and expect.

Several independent restaurants and table-service restaurant chains are promoting high-quality prepared foods to go. These restaurants are providing value by blending convenience and high quality for people on the go. Many people in the United States want high-quality elaborate foods at home, but they cannot or will not take the time to prepare them. In addition to traditional items such as chicken Kiev, lasagna, and chicken Marsala, unique items such as four-grain salads, veal entrées, and holiday specialties are being featured. The prepared-foods-to-go or home-replacement-meals concepts are driven largely by value. Restaurant-quality meals can be consumed at home where there are no service charges and consumers can dine as casually as they want. (See www.waiter.com for an example of how some restaurants are using the Web to market to guests who want to purchase prepared foods to go.)

Some people view brunch as a value option. Brunch today in casual/theme restaurants often differs from the unlimited buffets that were popular in the recent past, featuring instead an à la carte menu that includes at least a few light items. Some interesting brunch items are omelets made with herbs, cheeses, beans, chile peppers, and vegetables; pancakes and waffles topped with apples, bananas, kiwi, mangos, nectarines, peaches, or raspberries; French toast made from brioche, French bread, multigrain bread, raisin bread, or sourdough bread and flavored with almond extract, vanilla, or liqueurs; skillet eggs scrambled with a variety of cheeses and vegetables; and crepes filled with protein (chicken, lobster, or shrimp) or sweet fruit fillings. These unique brunch items add value by exceeding guests' expectations.

Hotel Examples of Value. Most hotel restaurants are included in the casual/theme segment because hotel food service has undergone a dramatic change in the past few years, becoming guest-driven rather than chef-driven and changing from formal, upscale dining rooms (often offering French cuisine) to more casual, informal dining areas that are priced to reflect increased value.

Some hotel food operations have re-engineered their kitchens and dining areas around *sous vide*—a low-temperature food preservation method in which foods are packaged in plastic bags or pouches that are then vacuum-sealed, cooked, chilled, and refrigerated until they are reheated in hot water for service. *Sous vide* offers restaurateurs a means of providing value to guests because this technique allows restaurants to offer a greater number of high-quality hot foods while employing fewer production staff members (which helps keep costs down). *Sous vide* also has applications for a hotel's banquet and catering departments.

Some hotels have alliances with restaurant companies; that is, business agreements that allow the restaurant companies to operate restaurants in the hotels (see Exhibit 2). Many of these alliances provide value for hotel guests by offering them a familiar place to eat and drink. For example, Hospitality Franchise Systems has formed alliances with Country Kitchen, Pizza Hut, and TGI Friday's; Loews Vanderbilt Plaza Hotel in Nashville, Tennessee, has Sfuzzi, an upscale Italian chain restaurant; and Budgetel Inns, Inc., has alliances with Applebee's Neighborhood Grill & Bar and Bob Evans Restaurants.

The Dining Environment, Supplies, and Equipment

Design and decor play a major role in shaping a casual/theme restaurant's ambiance—which is a fusion of design, decor, image, and service and is one of the most important factors in many guests' restaurant selection. By definition, design and decor are paramount in theme restaurants.

Whether subtle or eclectic, low-key or flashy, there are casual/theme restaurants for seemingly everyone's tastes. Some designs call for display kitchens and bakeries, some for furnishings reminiscent of neighborhood restaurants. Some casual/theme restaurants feature a nautical decor with a seafood theme; some, music of the '60s with a diner theme; and others, original artwork displayed with a gallery theme. Some restaurants spotlight sports memorabilia for an athletic theme, fresh pasta and garlic for an Italian theme, rustic furnishings for a steakhouse theme, and even tropical live and robotic animals for a rain forest theme.

Some casual/theme restaurants have gone so far as to offer virtual reality dining. Virtual reality (VR) is computer technology that can provide pseudo, lifelike experiences. A restaurant in Los Angeles, for example, blends decor and electronic

Exhibit 2 Examples of Hotel/Restaurant Alliances

Hotel Organization	Restaurant Organization
Best Western International	Pizza Hut
Budgetel Inns, Inc.	Applebee's Neighborhood Grill & Bar
	Bob Evans Restaurants
Cendant Hotel Division	Country Kitchen
	Pizza Hut
	TGI Friday's
Choice Hotels International	Metromedia Steakhouses Company
	Oh*la*la Coffee Company
	Pizza Hut
Country Inns	Country Kitchen
Embassy Suites	Pizza Hut
	Lettuce Entertain You Enterprises
Holiday Inn Crowne Plaza	McGuffey's Restaurants
La Quinta Inns	Denny's Restaurants
Loews Vanderbilt Plaza	Sfuzzi
Marriott Hotels & Resorts	Pizza Hut
Omni Ambassador East Hotel	Lettuce Entertain You Enterprises
Sholodge, Inc.	Shoney's Restaurants

Source: Adapted from "Linking Together," *Hotel & Motel Management* (May 9, 1994), pp. 14–15; Rajan Chaudhry, "Casual Dining Checks In," *Restaurants & Institutions* (November 1, 1993), pp. 18, 19, 22, 26, 30, 32; and James Scarpa, "Hotel Market Segment Report," *Restaurant Business* (January 20, 1993), pp. 108, 110, 114, 116.

simulations of submarine travel with a menu that features upscale soups and sub sandwiches.

The supplies and equipment that dining-area staff members need in order to fulfill their responsibilities are not the same in every casual/theme operation. There are differences based on markets, restaurant image and size, level of service, check average, location, and other factors. For example, some restaurants have service bars where servers can pick up their beverage orders; in others, servers may be required to go to the bar or lounge area. Casual/theme restaurants typically have assortments of beverage glassware, and servers need to know which glassware is used for which drinks. Tablecloths, cloth napkins, and full tableware service may be used in some of the more upscale theme restaurants, and servers may even need to learn special napkin-folding techniques.

For all casual/theme restaurants, it is imperative that supplies and equipment be clean and in good condition. Spotted, chipped glassware and tableware; bent flatware; messy condiment containers; and noisy, rusty, dented, or dirty pieces of equipment are simply not compatible with any dining atmosphere and do not exhibit a concern for sanitation. Health officials can close food service operations that are not sanitary.

Getting Ready for Service

Casual/theme independent restaurants and restaurant chains should develop their own service methods and procedures. Generally speaking, casual/theme restaurants use plate-service techniques with a casual approach based on their guests' desired levels of comfort. Whatever service methods and procedures a restaurant develops, they should be followed consistently. For instance, if the house rule is to have the ends of flatware handles an inch away from the table edge, staff members should set all of the tables in the restaurant this way. (While there is no universal standard that applies to flatware placement, flatware handles should always be set back from the table edge to some degree so that guests do not knock flatware off the table while being seated.) Similarly, whether the menu is already on the table when guests are seated or the host or server hands menus to guests after they are seated depends more on the rules of the house than on rules of etiquette. The point is that all of a casual/theme restaurant's service procedures should be consistently followed and enforced.

Another consideration in getting ready for service is quality standards. Based on guest requirements, a casual/theme restaurant's management team defines the quality standards that service staff members must meet as they get ready for service, actually serve guests, and perform a wide range of duties, including operating equipment, using income control procedures, placing and picking up food orders, and interacting with bar staff. Guests evaluate many factors other than food and beverages while in the dining room; therefore, managers and staff members must pay close attention to all details to ensure cleanliness and the compatibility of atmosphere and service with the quality of the products offered.

The restaurant's manager is ultimately responsible for all these details and for ensuring that the restaurant's standard operating procedures incorporate a concern for quality guest-driven service.

Training

Training for casual/theme restaurant service should focus on menu knowledge and sales skills as well as courtesy, consistency, efficiency, and teamwork.

Providing menu information to guests is one of the most important services servers perform. In order to sell menu items, servers must know the menu and the house policies and rules about what they can and cannot do (allowing substitutions, for example). In order to do their jobs properly, servers must:

- Be thoroughly familiar with the menu.
- Know how to pronounce the name of each menu item.
- Know the daily specials and the restaurant's signature items along with their prices.

- Know how every item is prepared, including ingredients. (Some guests must avoid certain ingredients because of food allergies or other health considerations.)
- Know how to describe every item properly. Truth-in-menu laws in many states prohibit misrepresenting menu items and ingredients. For example, servers should not try to pass margarine off as butter or describe frozen foods as fresh.
- Know portion sizes and what side dishes or garnishes are included.

At times, guests will ask servers to describe how an unfamiliar item tastes. Some restaurants provide tasting sessions for service staff so that servers can describe how an item tastes; the chef or a cook can attend these meetings to provide information about the item. Likewise, wine-tasting and beverage-tasting sessions can boost the staff's beverage sales skills. Bartenders and bar staff can provide information about specialty drinks.

Once servers know the menu, they will be able to use selling techniques that can increase not only guest satisfaction, but also the guest check, to the benefit of both the servers and the restaurant. (Since tips are usually based on the check total, a larger total generally means a larger tip.) **Suggestive selling** involves encouraging guests to order such extras as appetizers, cocktails, wine, desserts, and after-dinner drinks. **Upselling** means suggesting more expensive (and often better-quality) items than those that the guest first mentions. If a guest orders a scotch on the rocks, for example, the server might say, "Would you prefer a premium scotch such as Chivas Regal or Glenlivet?" Servers should be trained in suggestive selling and upselling on an ongoing basis to help the restaurant build revenues and promote guest satisfaction. Exhibit 3 gives additional selling tips.

Server training also should address timing and its effect on the **table-turn rate**—the average amount of time that a table is occupied. If a dining area seats 150 guests and staff members serve 300 guests during a specific shift, the table-turn rate is 2 (300 guests divided by 150 seats equals 2). In other words, each chair accommodated an average of two guests during the shift. Servers like to maximize table turns to enhance their tips (more people served in the same amount of time usually means more tips). Likewise, managers like the table-turn rate to be as high as possible for financial reasons. But as rates increase, it is important to ensure that the quality of service guests receive does not decrease. All other factors being equal, a high table-turn rate has a tendency to reduce levels of service. It is a balancing act to maximize both table turns and guest satisfaction. The timing of both production and service affects table turns. It is essential to time the entire dining experience so that guests do not feel rushed, yet the financial needs of the organization (dictated by table turns, in part) are met.

Servers in casual/theme restaurants should be trained to provide personalized service. For example, some restaurants use computers to record information about regular guests, including favorite food and beverages, preferred table in the dining area, and preferred server. During preshift lineup meetings, this information can be reviewed when these repeat guests have made a reservation. This personalized service helps the restaurant exceed guest expectations.

Exhibit 3 Tips for Effective Selling

Suggestive selling and upselling require tact and good judgment. If guests know exactly what they want, don't try to change their minds. However, you shouldn't hesitate to suggest additional items that will improve guests' meals. And learn to pick up on when guests want suggestions.

Suggestive selling might make you nervous. If so, it's probably because selling reminds you of a pushy salesperson you've known. Using suggestive selling and upselling techniques, however, is not being pushy. These techniques are part of providing good service.

The key to effective selling is knowing the menu. You should know all of the menu items your restaurant sells. When you are completely familiar with the menu and how each item is prepared, you can suggest dishes confidently and professionally.

Here are some tips for effective suggestive selling and upselling:

- Develop a "selling attitude."
- Be enthusiastic. It's easier to sell something you're excited about.
- Make food sound appetizing. Use words like "fresh," "popular," and "generous" when describing menu items.
- Ask questions. Find out if guests are really hungry or just want something light; whether they like chicken or beef; or if they feel like having something hot or cold.
- Suggest specific menu items. Don't simply ask: "Would you like soup with your meal?" Instead, point out: "A cold bowl of borscht would go nicely with your salad on a hot day like this."
- Suggest your favorites. Try as many menu items as you can, and tell guests you've tried them: "You'll like the Chicken Kiev. It's one of my favorites here." But be honest—don't say that something is your favorite when it isn't.
- Offer a choice: "Would you like a slice of our famous cheesecake or our homemade pecan pie for dessert?"
- Suggest the unusual. People dine out to get away from the routine fare they have at home. And most people don't know what they want to order when they arrive.
- Suggest foods and beverages that naturally go together—soups and sandwiches, bacon and eggs, steak and baked potatoes, coffee and dessert.
- Compliment guests' choices. Make guests feel good about their choices even if they don't order what you suggest.

Remember to always ask for the sale. After you suggest and describe an item, ask if the guest would like it. A good way to do this is to describe several items and ask which the guest would prefer: "A glass of cabernet sauvignon or the lighter merlot would go very well with your six-cheese lasagna. Which would you prefer?"

Source: Adapted from the "Restaurant Server Guide" in the *Hospitality Skills Training Series* (East Lansing, Mich.: Educational Institute of the American Hotel & Motel Association, 1995).

And finally, servers in casual/theme restaurants that serve alcohol need special training in how to serve alcoholic beverages responsibly. They should know the legal ramifications of serving alcohol to underage guests or to those who have had enough. (In states that have dram shop laws, servers and restaurateurs can be held liable for injury to a third person caused by an intoxicated restaurant guest.) Servers need to learn how to check identification to see that guests are of legal drinking age, and how to monitor guests' alcohol intake and handle alcohol-related problems.

Dining Service Staff Positions

Standard titles for dining service staff positions do not exist. For example, servers may be called *salespersons* or *waitpersons*, buspersons may be called *busers* or *food service attendants* or *assistants*, and the person in charge of the dining room may be called a *manager, host, captain, maître d'hôtel*, or some other title. Which titles are used depends on the restaurant's type of service and degree of informality, as well as management's preferences.

Likewise, the number of staff categories varies from restaurant to restaurant; in addition to those described in the following sections, there may be others, such as expediters and wine stewards, for example.

Bartenders and possibly cocktail servers and assistant bartenders will also be employed at many casual/theme restaurants. A head bartender typically supervises bar staff members and, depending on the restaurant's size, reports to the restaurant's general manager, beverage manager, or food and beverage director—not to the dining room manager. Even so, there is interaction between dining room and bar employees (just as there is between dining room and kitchen employees), and managers need to foster cooperation and team spirit among these staff members.

In the following sections we will discuss typical dining service staff positions in casual/theme restaurants—servers, buspersons, hosts, cashiers, and dining room managers—and the work staff members in these positions typically perform.

Server. In many casual/theme restaurants, servers perform the bulk of the food and beverage serving duties, assisted by buspersons. Servers typically present food and beverages to guests and perform a wide range of other tasks before, during, and after the service period. For example, in some restaurants, servers help with some food preparation—adding dressings to salads, portioning soups, and dishing up desserts from serving equipment located behind counters or in side stations. Servers are also usually responsible for a number of service-related but non-guest-contact tasks that are called **sidework**. Sidework typically includes making coffee, folding napkins, refilling condiment containers, end-of-shift activities, and other service-related responsibilities. Since servers can earn tips only when serving guests, they frequently view sidework with disfavor. However, these tasks are an extremely important part of a server's responsibilities.

The kind of service required in casual/theme restaurants suggests special concerns that managers must address as they select staff members. For example, servers must be able to work quickly yet carefully. They must be able to do several things during one trip through the dining area, such as carry food to one table, present a guest check to another, and remove used dishes from a third.

Servers must show genuine concern for guests' schedules. Servers working morning shifts may have to deal with guests who are easily irritated early in the day. A friendly "Good morning" accompanied by prompt, attentive service can really make a difference in a guest's attitude toward the server and the restaurant.

It is difficult to discuss the specific order-taking and food delivery duties of a server in a casual/theme restaurant because of the enormous variety of such restaurants. For example, in some casual/theme operations, the server takes the guests' orders but **runners** deliver them. This approach keeps servers in the dining room and in contact with guests, thus speeding up service. In other casual/theme restaurants, servers take guests' orders and give them to the production staff, but whichever server is available when the order is ready delivers it. This type of service is known as the "first-available-server" concept. In such cases, servers must be especially careful in writing order information on guest checks so that "who gets what" is clearly indicated for another server. In traditional operations, where servers are responsible for delivering the orders they have taken from guests, servers also have to be careful about clearly indicating to themselves "who gets what" so they will be able to provide smooth service.

Busperson. Typical duties of a busperson include stocking and replenishing supplies required in side stations. It is also common for buspersons to perform preopening duties such as setting tables, filling ice bins with ice, and moving tables.

During the service period, buspersons perform a wide array of tasks designed to help servers provide better service to guests. Such tasks include pouring water, refilling coffee and tea cups, taking bread and butter to the table, clearing tables, and even serving food and beverages during busy periods. If a restaurant offers tableside food preparation, buspersons may restock the food carts used for this purpose. Cleaning tables and chairs (including highchairs and booster chairs) and resetting tables with fresh linens, clean serviceware, and glasses are all jobs that buspersons often perform.

A busperson's closing responsibilities usually include cleaning and restocking side stations, cleaning and resetting dining area tables, emptying and cleaning food preparation carts, cleaning the coffee urn and the bread warmer, and returning soiled linens to the laundry.

Since buspersons typically have entry-level positions, it is important that managers take an active interest in them, show them the possibilities for career advancement, and provide them with training so that they can be ready to move to higher-paying and more responsible positions if they so desire.

Host. The person carrying out host responsibilities may be called a *host, greeter, receptionist, maître d'hôtel, captain,* or *dining room manager,* depending on the extent of his or her responsibilities. (Some restaurants use the term *hostess* for a female host, but *host* is acceptable for both men and women and is preferable for the purposes of this chapter.) In restaurants that also have a dining room manager, the host's responsibilities usually are limited to welcoming guests, providing menus, and performing other guest services such as confirming the number of guests in a party and leading guests to seats in the appropriate section of the restaurant. The host is sometimes responsible for inviting guests' comments on the food and service, and is usually responsible for thanking guests and inviting them to return as they are leaving.

Cashier. A cashier collects payments of guest checks from servers or guests, and is responsible for providing an accurate accounting of all transactions, collections, and disbursements. A cashier's responsibilities may overlap with those of a host. Cashiers who have guest-contact responsibilities should be friendly and courteous. Cashiers must follow income control procedures at all times.

Dining Room Manager. The manager in charge of dining room service has a wide variety of responsibilities and tasks (see Appendix B), which can differ from one operation to another. For example, in small restaurants, the dining room manager may perform the responsibilities of host and manage the entire restaurant as well as the dining room. In large restaurants, the dining room manager may have one or more hosts who report to him or her, and may in turn report to a general manager who manages the restaurant as a whole—in which case the dining room manager's responsibilities are more narrowly defined and consist mainly of managing the dining room and service staff.

Typically, dining room managers have had many years of training and experience and have worked their way up in the restaurant to assume this position. While some operations may not use the "manager" designation, they do employ individuals who are given managerial responsibilities designed to ensure that guests receive the proper quality of service.

Monitoring guests' expectations, ensuring their satisfaction, and encouraging repeat business are among the primary responsibilities of dining room managers today. These managers monitor guest expectations by soliciting guest feedback as well as feedback from staff members. One of the ways managers can meet guest requirements and ensure guest satisfaction is by enabling and motivating staff members to deliver the quality service that guests expect. Dining room managers can encourage repeat business in many ways. Some managers make a note of local residents' celebrations (birthdays, anniversaries, and similar events) held in the restaurant throughout the year. As the special event approaches the next year, they write to the guest who hosted the previous year's celebration to ask if the restaurant can again help make the occasion special. Or managers can send frequent guests a letter thanking them for their visits and enclose a card for a complimentary drink, dessert, or a "two meals for the price of one" discount.

Dining room managers have a number of preopening, operating, closing, and miscellaneous responsibilities that vary according to the restaurant. Before the dining room opens for guest service, managers inspect table settings, chairs, flowers and vase water, lamps and lampshades, tablecloths, napkins, place settings, glassware, condiment containers, candles, and any other tabletop items. They also check side stations to see that they are adequately stocked. Managers also look for safety problems such as loose tabletops and wobbly chairs or tables. They also might look for rough spots on furniture that could snag guests' clothing. Some

Welcome to T.G.I.Friday's Worldwide

Thanksgiving Leftover Recipe Ideas

The One Place in Cyberspace Where It's Always Friday... and the ONLY place to be when you can't be at your favorite Friday's®. (Dare we say it? You can even grab a byte here!)

FIND IT AT FRIDAY'S℠ | T.G.I.FASHION FRIDAY'S℠ | FREQUENT FRIDAY'S℠ | EAT, DRINK & BE MERRY | ABOUT FRIDAY'S®

Find It At Friday's® | T.G.I. Friday's Fashion℠ | Frequent Friday's℠ | Eat, Drink & Be Merry | About Friday's®

- **FIND IT AT FRIDAY'S®**
  Find out what we serve, and WHERE we serve it, all around the world...see what's coming to a Friday's® near you...even offer suggestions to our chefs! And check out these job opportunities.
- **FREQUENT FRIDAY'S℠**
  Free dining...trips...even cruises?! Move over, airlines: WE'LL show you how to treat loyal customers!
- **T.G.I.FRIDAY'S FASHION℠**
  We've got you covered! For the coolest shirts, jackets, packs, memorabilia, and more, take a scroll through our boutique.
- **EAT, DRINK & BE MERRY**
  The world's first on-line Happy Hour, complete with parties, contests, Friday's® mixers, drink specials, bar games, tricks, and a whole lot more.
- **ABOUT FRIDAY'S®**
  See how Friday's® started...and where we're headed. Plus, get a look at Italianni's℠ or the Front Row® Sports Grill, our newest restaurant sensations!

Designed by On-Line Design LTD.

Many casual/theme restaurants maintain Internet sites, which contain information that ranges from recipes and employment opportunities to company histories and restaurant locations. This site (http://www.tgifridays.com) is for TGI Friday's Worldwide. (Courtesy of T.G.I. Friday's)

dining room managers use a preopening checklist similar to the one shown in Appendix C.

Dining room managers may perform other miscellaneous tasks, such as checking that menus are in good order and are not dirty, worn, or torn. Since the menu represents the image, quality standards, and reputation of the restaurant and is something that every guest pays attention to, managers should frequently check the menus to make sure they are in good shape.

Supervising dining service staff members during the performance of their duties is a major responsibility of the dining room manager. Dining room managers make specific table assignments and conduct preopening meetings to inform the staff about daily specials, menu changes, and any potential difficulties. These managers should make certain that service flows smoothly, that ashtrays are kept empty, that water glasses are refilled, and, in general, that the desires of guests are anticipated and provided for. Dining room managers must know sanitation and safety procedures and ensure that staff members follow them.

Handling guest complaints and guest-related problems may be the dining room manager's responsibility, but more managers today empower staff members to take care of most of these matters and provide them with guidelines for doing so. For example, what should be done for a guest who complains about another guest's smoking? Enlightened managers empower servers to take care of this type of situation, typically suggesting that the best way to address it is to quietly move the guest who complains, not the guest who smokes.

After the dining room closes, dining room managers supervise staff members as they perform miscellaneous closing duties. They ensure that staff members properly set the tables for the next meal period, clean and fill all condiment containers, replace soiled tablecloths, and reset tabletops. Managers should also make sure that side stations and sidework areas are clean and restocked, and they should confirm that dining area tables are in the proper configuration for the next shift. Finally, dining room managers should ensure that supplies are properly secured and check such items as waste containers for smoldering cigarettes.

Delivering Service

The delivery of guest-driven service requires service staff members who are people-oriented and able to focus on helping guests enjoy their dining experience. Guests can recognize whether servers truly enjoy their work and whether their smiles are genuine. Guest expectations, almost without exception, include friendly, prompt, courteous service.

As noted earlier, another important factor in service delivery is consistency. Specific procedures for each casual/theme restaurant must be developed and all service staff members should be trained to use them consistently. Nothing is wrong with serving guests at tables one way and guests at booths another way, as long as all servers follow the same procedures and as long as the procedures are acceptable to the guests.

Some procedures that food and beverage servers might use from the time guests are seated until they depart from the dining area are explained in the following sections. Many casual/theme restaurants use some or all of these procedures, but there are many others as well. It would be impossible to discuss all of the variances that exist today. Our discussion begins with taking reservations, since, for casual/theme restaurants, this is often the initial guest-contact point.

Taking Reservations

Many restaurants take reservations to allow guests the chance to reserve seating at a specific time. A reservation system increases the manager's ability to pinpoint slow and busy times and plan for them. In addition, such a system can increase business, since many guests desire a formal commitment and guarantee about their dining arrangements and will visit only those restaurants that accept reservations. The use of reservations is a convenience and service to guests as well as a tool that helps staff members recognize guests by name, guarantee speed and quality of service, and promote production efficiency.

There are two basic types of reservation systems. One system offers seating at specific intervals during the meal period, such as seatings at 6:00 P.M. and 8:00 P.M. only. When this **interval reservations** system is used, at least 30 minutes must be allowed between serving periods to clean up, reset tables, and otherwise get ready for the next seating. Potential disadvantages to interval seating include crowd control problems when a large number of guests must be seated or allowed to leave the dining area at the same time, and food production problems when a large number of meals must be served simultaneously. Proper attention to these matters is critical to the success of interval seating reservation plans.

A second and more common type of reservation system is **staggered reservations**. This system staggers seating during the entire meal period; that is, reservations can be made for any time that tables are available (in other words, not yet reserved) during the meal period.

In order for a reservation system to work, the manager must be able to estimate the length of time it will take for guests to dine. For instance, because experienced managers know that large groups usually take longer to dine than small groups, they factor this into the reservation plan. The restaurant's environment and service style as well as the type of meal served are factors the manager should consider as well.

As the time required for meal consumption increases, taking reservations at specific intervals only may be more advantageous than staggered seating.

When restaurants offer buffet service, either type of reservation system is generally useful. However, if interval seating is used, staff members may require some time between seating periods in order to prepare the buffet for the next group of guests.

Reservation commitments affect production. For example, if three eight-top tables (an "eight-top table" is an industry term for a table that seats eight persons) are seated at the same time, there may be a rush of work in the kitchen 20 to 30 minutes later when servers place 24 entrée orders at approximately the same time. Reservation-takers may need to suggest staggered arrival times for large groups so that neither the large groups nor other guests in the dining area are inconvenienced.

Because of the need to gather information efficiently and courteously, only staff members trained and authorized to accept reservations should do so. Typically, reservation information is entered in a reservation book or computer software program, and specific tables are reserved by indicating directly on a seating chart the time of the reservation and the number of guests in the party.

Reservation-takers should obtain the following information from callers:

- The correct spelling of the name the reservation will be under
- The date and time of the reservation
- The number in the party
- Whether a smoking or no-smoking section is preferred
- Whether the guests want a table or a booth
- Special instructions
- The guest's phone number (or room number if the restaurant is in a hotel)

A special-information column in the reservation book or on the computer software spreadsheet can be used to record special instructions, such as the need for a certain type of cake, a wide aisle for a person who uses a wheelchair, or a special wine. If the person making the reservation asks to receive the check for the entire group at the end of the meal, the reservation-taker should make a note of the caller's request in the special-information column.

Some computerized reservation programs enable managers to keep very specific reservation information—such as the number of tables available, the number of guests to be seated, and the service staff needed—close at hand for several days in a row. Other computer programs provide detailed information only on the current dining period. Many programs indicate whether a specific table is in use, is being cleared and reset, or is ready to "sell." Such programs may also indicate, on a by-table basis, when tables are likely to be available. These aids are particularly helpful in large restaurants with several floors of dining space, or in other situations in which the manager or some other staff member would have to make several trips to the dining area to ensure that a table was ready for seating.

Handling Reservation Problems. What should be done when a guest with a reservation comes early or late, brings more or fewer guests than the reservation indicated, or does not wish to sit at the table that has been set aside for the group? Or what happens when a party arrives on time but the table isn't ready because the previous party is staying longer than the manager anticipated? Stated policies and procedures help staff members know what to do when these and similar problems associated with reservations come up. Common sense is also important. As problems arise, affected guests must be told the truth and offered appropriate alternatives; in other words, management must be prepared to find creative solutions so that guests are not frustrated.

Some restaurants offer an amenity, such as a drink or an appetizer, to guests inconvenienced by having to wait for their reserved table. This strategy may work well in some cases; in others, such as when guests have severe time limitations, it may not be adequate compensation for the inconvenience. Explaining to late-arriving guests that their table was held for 15 minutes past the reservation time but could be held no longer may be a good tactic if accompanied by management's promise to work the party into the dining area as soon as possible.

Managing Waiting Guests

Guests without reservations should be served on a first-come–first-served basis. When there is a waiting line, it is important that someone—the manager, receptionist, greeter, or another staff member—be at the door at all times to take the names of arriving guests and to call parties as tables become available. Names should be recorded on a waiting list. They should be printed very clearly along with the number of guests in the party. In some restaurants, the time of arrival is also noted.

As tables become available, guests should be paged. Some managers have the policy of paging a guest twice, two minutes apart. If, after two pages, the guest does not respond, the name is removed from the list and the next party of appropriate size is called. Some restaurants give waiting guests pocket electronic pagers to reduce noise and confusion.

Typically, the names of large groups are highlighted or listed separately so that they will not be overlooked. Generally, parties are called in the order in which they appear on the list, unless they include people who have disabilities, elderly persons, or families with small children requiring more immediate attention.

Policies about accepting tips from guests who want to reduce their waiting time should be developed and carefully followed. Generally speaking, staff members should never accept a gratuity before they render service; a tip before service is really a bribe. Guests typically do not like to wait for extended periods, and questions such as "We came in first—why were we not seated first?" are likely to arise if late-arriving guests without reservations tip the person greeting guests and are seated ahead of those who have been waiting.

It is critical that guests be given the best estimate of the length of waiting time when their names are placed on the waiting list. Staff members should tell the truth. If guests must wait for a long period of time, they should be informed of this so that they can decide whether they want to wait or go elsewhere. After guests are told about the waiting time, they can be referred to the lounge or other areas where their wait may be more enjoyable. If guests choose not to wait, they should be thanked for coming and invited to return on another occasion.

Greeting and Seating Guests

Someone must be available to greet guests at the front door of the dining area and answer the telephone at all times. Sometimes the dining room manager handles these responsibilities; in large restaurants they are often handled by a host, receptionist, or greeter. Since this person is often the first representative of the restaurant to come in face-to-face contact with guests, it is imperative that he or she make a good impression. (If guests should seat themselves, a sign indicating this should be located where they will easily see it.)

Guests should be greeted by name if possible. If the restaurant takes reservations, the person who is greeting and seating guests should know and refer to

Family Restaurants

Family restaurants are a large and important subcategory of casual/theme restaurants. As the name implies, family restaurants take extra care to appeal to guests with children.

While children often influence where families dine, obviously it is the parents who pay the bill. If parents sincerely believe that their children's as well as their own needs and expectations are being met, the payoff for the restaurant will be increased sales, repeat guests, positive word-of-mouth referrals, and a good image for the restaurant in the marketplace.

Although guests with children are the primary focus of family restaurants, there are other markets and submarkets as well—senior citizens, for example, who are drawn by a family restaurant's moderate prices. And, of course, each market may consist mostly of guests from the local area or guests who are traveling, depending on the restaurant's location and marketing thrust.

Many family restaurants offer a children's menu, either included on the regular menu or printed as a separate menu. Children's menus may or may not reflect the restaurant's regular menu. For example, a seafood restaurant's children's menu may offer such items as spaghetti, grilled cheese sandwiches, pizza, and hamburgers instead of seafood.

Comfort is critical for families, especially those with small children. Lighting plays an important role in family restaurants. Generally, bright lighting is preferable because children like it and it connotes cleanliness to many parents.

Some family restaurants are transforming empty banquet rooms and private dining rooms into places where children can eat and be entertained by staff members while parents enjoy their meal in the regular dining area. Separate areas with child-size furniture and children's reading materials and games also can occupy children while their parents finish their meals.

One feature is essential for family restaurants: diaper-changing stations, whether located in restrooms or some other area. Locating changing stations in both men's and women's restrooms indicates that the restaurant is in tune with the times. Changing stations, like highchairs, must be fitted with safety belts and cleaned regularly.

As is true in any service organization, managers of family restaurants set the tone for the style and quality of service delivered to guests. A family restaurant manager who directs a server to take care of "the table with the two rug-rats" does not set the right tone for guest-driven service to families.

Some food service professionals say that managers and staff members who are parents themselves provide family-friendly service better than those who are not parents, perhaps because they have first-hand knowledge of how children can behave when dining out. In any case, one of a manager's most important tasks in a family restaurant is to train staff members to be sensitive to the needs and expectations of guests with children. Servers especially must be trained to pay special attention to children, for it is often the server who makes or breaks a family-dining experience.

Tips for Serving Guests with Children

It is generally advisable to seat parents with young children—especially toddlers—in a section with other families with young children. The presence of others with

(continued)

(continued)

children usually eases the parents' nervousness about how their children will behave and whether they will negatively affect the dining experiences of others.

In some restaurants, after guests with children are seated, servers are instructed to greet the children first, kneeling down so they are speaking at the children's level. Forks, knives, and glasses can be dangerous in the hands of toddlers, so servers should remove these items soon after toddlers are seated. Some restaurants provide plastic cups with lids and straws for toddlers. Servers also must be sensitive to parental needs for assistance with booster chairs, highchairs, or cushions.

Since children have relatively short attention spans, it is important to quickly give them something that keeps them occupied and happy. Many restaurants present children with place mats and small packages of crayons to color figures and complete puzzles and mazes on the place mats. Some give children inexpensive toys or other giveaways. (Children who take these giveaways home may be reminded to ask parents for a return visit to the restaurant.) Many restaurants serve crackers, bread, or rolls immediately to keep children content. Restaurants might also provide children with a cup of ice to chew on while waiting for their meals. In any case, these distractions should be distributed as soon as children are seated.

Servers should request that the kitchen staff rush the orders of families with small children—especially the children's orders. (Families dining with children are generally not looking for a leisurely experience.) When serving families with infants, servers should be attentive to the need to heat formula bottles or jars of baby food. Some parents may want to share their food with small children rather than order from the children's menu.

Once service is completed, servers should clear plates quickly and deliver the check promptly. Parents may want to leave before their children get restless. And if the children have been active and boisterous, parents will want to leave quickly to avoid further disturbing other guests.

Servers and other staff members should offer departing parents a genuine thank-you and a reassuring comment about children being welcome. This helps reduce the anxiety that many parents feel about dining out with children and may convince them to return and to tell others about the restaurant.

guests by name and pronounce the name correctly. He or she might also identify regular guests: "Good evening, Mr. John, it's nice to see you again," or, "We have your usual table ready for you, Ms. Grace. Right this way." If the guest's name is known, it should be relayed to the server assigned to the table so that he or she can use the guest's name during the meal. Some casual/theme restaurants put place-setting tags, matchbooks, and other items imprinted with the guest's name on the table. Those that do so should make certain each guest's name is spelled correctly.

In contrast, some guests do not want their names announced, in which case their wishes should be respected. Well-known guests such as politicians, entertainers, and sports celebrities may well select restaurants in part because of their discretion when serving VIPs.

Staff members should be polite and use common sense at all times. For example, when they do not know the guest's name, they may address the guest as "Sir" or "Ma'am." If guests request a special table, they should get it if at all possible, and, of course, the table should be ready (clean tabletop, complete place settings, chairs free of crumbs) before they are taken to it.

While a guest's request for a certain table should be honored whenever possible, the manager often needs to balance server stations. For example, if a table of the appropriate size is available in several stations, a large party usually is given to the server with the least number of guests. However, managers in some restaurants feel that they should use a rotation plan so that each server has the opportunity to receive a fair share of tip income. Some restaurants do not use server stations; if seven food servers are on duty, each server gets every seventh party regardless of where the manager seats the group. This plan is used in some very famous, well-established restaurants with obvious success. Typically, however, a seating chart should be used to help even out server workloads, but it should be kept flexible to accommodate guests' requests.

After the guests have reached the appropriate table, they are often seated by giving women, the elderly, people with disabilities, or other special guests priority. If applicable, women are provided assistance with their coats. In some casual/theme restaurants, the staff member who seats guests may also remove extra place settings, present menus, fill water glasses, and perform other preliminary tasks before the server arrives. If it is the policy of the restaurant, this service staff member also tells guests the name of their server. Some restaurants require the person who seats guests to check back with them after a few minutes to ensure that the server assigned to the table has welcomed them.

Presenting the Menu and Taking Beverage Orders

If guests do not already have menus or if menus are not already on the table, the server presents them as he or she welcomes the guests. Making guests feel welcome is an important task for the server. Servers should smile and be tactful and friendly. In many restaurants, servers identify themselves by name even if they are wearing name tags.

In some casual/theme restaurants, food servers bring glasses of water on their first trip to the table, present the menu, then ask the guests if they would like to order drinks. They may also tell the guests about daily specials at this point, or they may wait until after drinks are served. Some restaurants have cocktail menus. Others use place mats, table tents, or similar devices to list beverage suggestions and specials. This is an ideal time for servers to use suggestive selling or upselling skills (see Exhibit 3). To avoid offending those who cannot or do not drink alcoholic beverages, servers should also suggest nonalcoholic drinks.

When taking beverage orders, servers should number guest checks so that they will know who ordered what, and note exact specifications from each guest—choice of garnish, whether the drink should be served with ice (on the rocks) or without ice (up or neat), and the specific call or premium brand if one is requested.

Placing Beverage Orders at the Bar

Procedures for obtaining drinks at the bar are frequently similar to procedures for ordering food in the kitchen. Servers write the beverage orders on the guest check, often using the back of it. Many systems require beverage servers to enter the order into a precheck register before giving the guest check to the bartender for drink preparation. An intermediate step may require the bartender to mark the guest check after preparing the drinks so that he or she will know if a server has failed to enter orders for second and third rounds into the precheck register. In some restaurants, servers place and pick up beverage orders at a service bar; in other restaurants, servers go to the lounge or public bar area to get drink orders.

Serving Beverages

Drinks should be carried on a cocktail tray, which the server should rest in one hand while serving with the other; the tray should never rest on the table (to avoid jostling guests, and in case the bottom of the tray is dirty). Drinks are typically served from the right. Servers should take care to serve exactly what guests order. For example, if a guest orders Maker's Mark and is served another bourbon without being told that Maker's Mark is not available, this could anger the guest if he or she finds out and might result in an ugly scene or even legal trouble.

Guests will need adequate time to enjoy their drinks and study their menus, so they should not be rushed.

Offering the Wine List and Serving Wine

Some casual/theme restaurants have wine lists on the table when guests are seated so that the lists are immediately available for those guests who wish to study them.

Selling wine is part of a server's job. While, generally speaking, light wines complement light foods and heavy wines complement heavy foods, most restaurateurs recognize that whatever the guest desires is appropriate for him or her. Therefore, while a server can make suggestions, the final decision is up to the guest. (Many restaurants develop wine lists with specific food recommendations or make wine suggestions on the food menu.) Servers should be trained not to react negatively to any wine orders that guests place.

Casual/theme restaurants generally have their own procedures for servers to follow while opening and serving bottles of wine. The following procedures are typical and can be adapted as necessary:

- Wrap the bottle in a linen napkin and present the bottle to the host (the guest who ordered the wine) so that he or she can see the label.
- Cut the foil below the top bulge on the bottle neck and peel the foil off.
- Wipe the cork and exposed glass rim with the napkin and twist the corkscrew into the cork until it is almost through the cork.
- Hook the lever on the bottle rim, draw the cork out, remove the cork from the corkscrew, and place the cork on the right side of the guest who ordered the wine.
- Wipe the bottle rim again.
- Offer a sample of the wine to the host. (Uncorked vintage red wines are often allowed to "rest" or "breathe" before they are poured.)

Red Lobster is a casual/theme restaurant chain featuring seafood. Its Internet site can be found at http://www.redlobster.com. (Courtesy of Red Lobster)

- After the host approves, fill the wine glasses of the other adult guests in the party. Frequently, wine service is counter-clockwise starting with the guest on the host's right. As a courtesy, many restaurants stipulate that female guests should be served first.
- Fill glasses according to the restaurant's standards; usually a "full" glass is no more than two-thirds full. (Guests who are wine connoisseurs may request the server to fill the glass no more than one-third full.)
- When wine remains in the bottle after pouring, bottles should be placed as follows: red wine to the right of the host's wine glass, with the label facing the host; white wine in an ice bucket or chilled holder to the host's right. The server refills glasses as needed.

Taking Food Orders

Unless one person orders for the party, it is traditional to begin with a woman and take orders clockwise. Servers should write the guest check in such a way that they will know "who gets what" when they serve the food or beverages. Many guests are annoyed if servers need to ask about the guests' selections at the time of service. Whenever possible, servers stand to the guest's left when taking orders. As servers take the orders, they should be certain to ask all necessary questions: "What type of salad dressing would you like?" "How would you like your steak cooked?" "What vegetable do you prefer?" "Would you like coffee now or later?" Servers should use upselling and suggestive selling techniques and answer questions about the menu as they arise.

Placing and Picking Up Orders in the Kitchen

Procedures for placing orders vary greatly among casual/theme restaurants. Some use a precheck register or an expediter. In others, servers simply call out orders. In still others, servers present guest checks to production personnel or use remote printing devices. It is important for servers to know and comply with the ordering systems established by management. Teamwork is critical to effective and efficient service.

Servers should follow procedures consistently in picking up orders. Before taking the food to the table, servers should check the written orders against the food and beverages on the serving tray to ensure that the order is correct. They should take the time to look at each plate and glass from the guest's perspective. Is the garnish attractive? Are there unsightly food spills on the rim of the plate that should be attended to? Does the food look tasty?

Servers must know how to carry a loaded tray. For safety's sake, the heaviest dishes and dishes containing liquids should be loaded toward the center of the tray. When trays are being loaded, hot dishes should be placed next to hot dishes, cold dishes next to cold dishes. When the tray is loaded properly, the server should bend from the knees, keeping his or her back straight and lifting the tray with the palm of the hand to shoulder height, using the other hand for balance. Experienced servers situate the heaviest side of the tray close to their bodies and make certain no items are likely to tip and spill.

There must be an established traffic pattern for service staff to follow. A server should announce "coming through" or "behind you" to alert others when he or she is going through a swinging door or is behind another staff member. When swinging doors are involved, they should be clearly marked "In" and "Out."

Serving the Orders

The restaurant's standard procedures determine how servers present food to guests. Typically, servers place their trays on food service stands, remove plate covers (if applicable), and then serve the guests. In some restaurants, service rules dictate that guests are served all food items from the left and beverages from the right. In others, guests are served everything from the right. In still others, especially those that have booths, the rule is "Serve with the least inconvenience to the guests."

Usually, children are served first, then women, then men. Entrée plates should be placed so that the main item is closest to the guest; for example, if a plate has a steak, some rice, and a vegetable on it, the plate is placed so the steak is closest to the guest. Any side dishes are usually placed to the left of the entrée plate.

Servers should check back with guests soon after delivering their orders. They should ask "Is everything to your satisfaction?" or a similar question and should ask if there is anything else the guests would like at this time. (Guests are more likely to appreciate this opportunity to comment if they are not in the process of taking a bite of food when asked these questions.)

When several courses are served, the dishes from one course should be cleared before the next course arrives; dishes are usually removed from the right. (This principle also applies to the service of drinks; if possible, the empty glassware should be removed—usually from the right—before the next round is served.) This method provides guests with more tabletop room, does not make them feel uncomfortable about eating too much, and puts dishes and glassware back into service more quickly.

Presenting the Guest Check

Timing the delivery of the guest check is important. Some guests may be in a hurry; others may linger over their meals. Whatever type of income collection system is used, the check should be totaled and ready when the guest desires it. Servers should accurately complete each guest check and double-check the figures. If guest-check totals must be hand-tallied, servers will find that a calculator with a printing tape is very helpful.

Some restaurants use a multiple guest-check system. With this plan, servers use separate guest checks for each round of drinks and each meal course. There are wall slot-racks or pigeonholes to hold all the guest checks for each table. When guests wish to leave, the server totals these individual guest checks and presents them to guests for payment.

There are two typical signals to guests that help them know how to pay the bill. Generally, if the guest check is presented on a plate or tray or in a folder, the server will collect the guest's payment and see that the guest gets proper change (or will handle the credit card transaction or charge the bill to the guest's room). Presenting the check without a plate or tray generally means that guests will pay at a cashier's stand. Many restaurants also clarify payment procedures for guests by printing them on the bill: "Please pay the cashier" or "Please pay the server." Clarification from the server is also helpful: "I can take your payment for you when you're ready" or "You may pay the cashier when you're ready." In all cases, servers should remember to thank the guests.

When presenting the check to a group, the server may already know who will pay the bill. A signal from the guest, an earlier conversation, or a specific request when the reservation was booked may have made this apparent. Servers undecided about who is responsible for the bill's payment often place the check in the center of the table.

The use of separate checks is also relatively common. While they create extra work for servers, many guests prefer them, and every restaurant should consider using them. Wise servers ask at the beginning of the meal whether the guests prefer individual checks.

When servers are responsible for taking guest payments, they should settle guest checks promptly and return the proper change, thanking the guest as they do so. If payment is by check or credit card, servers should follow the restaurant's procedures. Servers should not claim their tips until guests leave.

It goes without saying that the guests' last contact with the restaurant should be as pleasant as the first. The manager or some other representative of the restaurant should be on hand to say goodbye and cordially thank guests—by name, if their names are known—as they leave. Remembering and using a guest's name is a hallmark of personalized service.

Serving Special Guests

Before leaving this section on delivering service to guests, we should say a brief word about serving special guests. Although in one sense all guests are "special" and should be treated that way, servers sometimes find themselves serving guests who require out-of-the-ordinary attention. For example, staff members in family restaurants are trained to focus special efforts on children—one category of "special guests." What follows are other categories and considerations.

Guests with Special Diet Needs. Servers should know which menu items do not contain sodium and which items are available for vegetarians. Servers should know menu item ingredients in case guests have questions concerning food allergies. Servers should be able to suggest low-calorie menu items to those guests who request such information; however, low-calorie items should not be suggested unless a guest asks about them, lest the server anger a guest or hurt his or her feelings. People with special health concerns may need to speak to the manager or chef to ensure that their concerns are properly addressed.

Senior Citizens. Some older guests like light meals and tend to eat more slowly than other guests. They may prefer foods that are soft and bland rather than chewy and spicy. Some are on a limited budget. Servers should know which items senior guests might enjoy and, if asked, recommend them.

International Guests. Non-English–speaking guests should be spoken to slowly, not loudly. Servers should ask them if they have any special food preferences. Servers should try to put themselves in the guests' place and ask themselves, "How would I like to be treated if I were a visitor in another country?" Menus with pictures help communicate the identities of items.

Guests with Disabilities. Guests who have visual impairments should be welcomed in a normal tone of voice and asked whether they would like assistance, if they are not accompanied by guide dogs. (If a guest is accompanied by a guide dog, no one should attempt to feed, pet, or otherwise interact with the dog while it is "working.") If a guest who has a visual impairment desires assistance, the host should offer his or her arm and walk while informing the guest of steps, level changes, and crowded areas. Guests with visual impairments should be asked whether they prefer to receive a braille menu (if one is available) or to have the menu read. The host or server should use the positions of numbers on a clock to describe locations of glassware, food on plates, and other tabletop items.

When welcoming guests who have hearing impairments, it is important to remember not to shout at them. Rather, since many can read lips, the server should face them directly and speak slowly and distinctly. Alternatively, the server can offer a pad of paper and a pen so the guest can write requests.

Guests in wheelchairs should be asked if they would like assistance. These guests should be seated at tables with sufficient space to comfortably accommodate the wheelchairs.

After Service

This section serves as a reminder of the importance of controls and guest feedback in planning and implementing service and product improvements. Controls help casual/theme restaurants achieve their goals and protect their assets. Guest feedback helps managers maintain and enhance guest service. Taking guest comments into consideration when planning fosters guest-driven service.

Proper planning for food and beverage service is absolutely critical to the success of a casual/theme restaurant. Ongoing procedures to keep dining areas sanitary and in good order are necessary to maintain the restaurant's public image. And, of equal importance, human resources policies and procedures must help managers select, train, schedule, and retain staff members who are enthusiastic about creating and delivering excellent service to guests.

The planning involved in providing good food and beverage service never ends; it is ongoing and must have as its goal the continuous improvement of the products and services the restaurant provides.

Key Terms

call brand—A brand of liquor that guests request by brand name (a Beefeater martini, for example).

casual/theme restaurant—A segment of the full-service restaurant classification. There are many types of casual/theme restaurants, most of which serve alcoholic beverages and have moderate to moderately high guest-check averages and informal dining environments.

house brand—A brand of liquor a restaurant carries for use when guests order cocktails without specifying the use of any particular brand (a martini, for example); also called well brands, they are usually priced lower than call brands.

interval reservations—A reservations system that offers seating at specific intervals during the meal period, such as seatings at 6:00 P.M. and 8:00 P.M. only. This system typically requires at least 30 minutes between serving periods to clean up, reset tables, and otherwise get ready for the next seating.

premium brand—A costly call brand of liquor specified by guests when they order cocktails (an Absolut vodka martini, for example).

runner—A staff member who delivers guests' orders to the table, allowing servers to remain in the dining room and in contact with guests, thus speeding up service.

shopper's service—An agency that restaurants can employ to evaluate how guests' needs and expectations are being met. Shopper's services use shoppers (also called "mystery shoppers") who pose as guests in order to review a restaurant's service from the guest's perspective and complete evaluation reports.

sidework—Preparatory, service-related tasks such as making coffee, folding napkins, refilling condiment containers, restocking stations, and performing end-of-shift activities.

signature drink—A beverage that guests perceive as special and closely associated with the restaurant promoting it. Signature drinks help boost beverage sales.

signature menu item—A menu item that guests perceive as special and closely associated with the restaurant promoting it. Signature menu items help build repeat business and guest loyalty.

split—A small bottle of wine (usually a premium wine) typically containing one to three glasses.

staggered reservations—A reservations system that staggers seating during an entire meal period; that is, reservations can be made for any time that tables are available (not yet reserved) during the meal period.

suggestive selling—A technique by which servers can increase guest satisfaction and sales by encouraging guests to order such extras as appetizers, cocktails, wine, desserts, and after-dinner drinks.

table-turn rate—The average amount of time that a table is occupied. For example, if two separate parties are seated at the same table within a 120-minute period, the table-turn rate is one time per hour.

upselling—A technique by which servers can increase sales by suggesting more expensive (and often better-quality) items than those that the guest first mentions.

Review Questions

1. What are the characteristics of a casual/theme restaurant?
2. How do casual/theme restaurants solicit feedback on how successfully they are serving guests?
3. What is a house brand? call brand? premium brand?
4. In a casual/theme restaurant, what are the typical duties of a server? busperson? host? cashier? dining room manager?
5. What distinguishes an interval reservations system from a staggered reservations system?
6. What are some tips for managing waiting guests? greeting and seating guests?
7. What are some typical procedures servers use to take food and beverage orders, place them with appropriate production personnel, and serve ordered items to guests?
8. What are some techniques servers should keep in mind when serving special guests?

Internet Sites

For more information, visit the following Internet sites. Remember that Internet addresses can change without notice.

http://www.chi-chis.com

http://www.chilis.com

http://www.longjohnsilvers.com

http://www.outbacksteakhouse.com

http://www.perkinsrestaurants.com

http://www.pizzahut.com

http://www.pofolks.com

http://www.rainforestcafe.com

http://www.redlobster.com

http://www.tgifridays.com

http://www.waiter.com

References

Bartlett, Michael. "Industry Surges Ahead." *Restaurants & Institutions,* January 1, 1995.

Brennan, Denise M. "The Hotel Forum." *Restaurant Business,* July 1, 1992.

"Brew Pubs More Than a Passing Fad." *Future Food Trends,* No. 5, 1994.

Chaudhry, Rajan. "Casual Dining Checks In." *Restaurants & Institutions,* November 1, 1993.

Cook, Lou. "Mystery Shoppers." *Lodging*, April 1998.

"Edging Toward VR." *Future Food Trends,* No. 3, 1994.

George, Daniel P. "Boosting Check Averages." *F&B Management,* May/June 1993.

Hayes, Jack. "Battle Escalates Over Upscale Prepared Foods." *Nation's Restaurant News,* April 18, 1994.

Iwamuro, Renee. "The Baby-Boomers: Who They Are and How They Spend." *Restaurants USA,* October 1993.

"'Influentials' Drive Word of Mouth." *Restaurants USA,* February 1994.

Mann, Irma S. "Marketing to The Affluent: A Look at Their Expectations and Service Standards." *Cornell Quarterly,* October 1993.

"More and More Home Cooking!" and "International Concepts Emerge." *Future Food Trends,* No. 3, 1994.

Ortega, Bob. "Casual-Dining Stocks Plunge on Forecasts." *Wall Street Journal,* November 23, 1994.

Solomon, Jay. "Dazzling Brunches." *Restaurants USA,* December 1993.

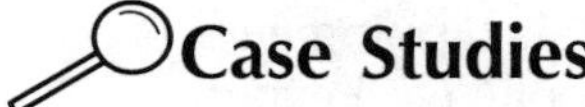

Case Studies

Terry Tackles Turnover

Fargo's is a casual-dining restaurant chain that was started just ten years ago. There are 70 units in the chain; each unit has 250 to 300 seats, with an average lunch check of $7 and an average dinner check of $13. Revenue per unit ranges from $2.5 to $3.1 million per year. Each unit employs about 35 to 40 servers, depending on the mix of full- and part-time staff members. Annual turnover per unit for the chain is from 80 percent on the low end to 160 percent on the high end. Until last year, the average turnover rate held steady at around 100 percent. However, when the chain grew from 50 to 70 units over the past 12 months, the average rate shot up to 138 percent, which raised a red flag for Terry Dickinson, the chain's new vice president of human resources.

When Terry was hired thirty days ago, one of his first goals was to come up with chain-wide selection tools that would help Fargo's managers choose wisely from among the many job applicants they interviewed. Fargo's is pursuing an aggressive growth strategy, with 20 more new units planned for next year and 10 to 15 planned for the next few years after that. Turnover will only get worse unless Terry can develop an effective selection guide.

Terry decided to meet with three unit managers representing different locales and turnover rates: Kate Pullum's unit, at 84 percent annual turnover, had one of the lowest turnover rates in the chain; Lisa Ragalado's turnover rate, at 125 percent, was about average; and Joe Eldrige's, at 156 percent, was one of the highest. Terry hoped to get an idea of how Fargo's managers, who so far had been left to their own devices, were actually selecting applicants. More importantly, Terry hoped these managers would help him come up with selection criteria that would be useful for managers throughout the chain.

Terry stood and began the meeting with one of his beloved sayings. "At the risk of sounding trite, I thought I'd start off with some 'words to live by' that a college professor of mine drummed into my head many years ago: 'Better hiring means less firing.' I've brought you together to help our company solve a chain-wide problem: high turnover—specifically, high turnover among our servers. Solving this problem will make your job and every manager's job at Fargo's easier in the long run. I don't have to tell you about all the headaches that high turnover causes—you experience it on the front lines every day." The managers around the table nodded and smiled ruefully. "Of course, this is also a financial issue," Terry went on. "Operating margins are dropping chain-wide, due in part to the high turnover.

"Kate, congratulations on having one of the lowest turnover rates in the company. You must be doing something right. Why don't you start us off and outline some of the things you look for in a job candidate." Terry sat down and picked up a pen to take notes.

"Well, I don't know that I have a secret formula or a magic wand," Kate began slowly. "Like most people, one thing I always look for in a job candidate is experience."

"That's nice if you have that luxury," Joe interjected, his fingers tapping nervously on the table. "But in my labor market, it's rare to find someone with experience. Heck, it's rare to find someone, period! Most of the time I end up taking anybody I can get."

Lisa smiled sympathetically. "The warm body syndrome."

Joe nodded. "Exactly."

"What kind of experience do you look for?" Terry asked.

"I look for 8 to 12 months of experience in a high-volume, full-service, chain restaurant," Kate said. "I used to take people with other types of experience—for example, if someone told me she worked in a small independent restaurant, I would take a chance on her. But I've found that those people usually can't adjust to the high-volume, high-pressure, fast pace of my restaurant. Either that, or they bring a lot of bad habits with them that are hard to break.

"Of course, hiring experienced people sometimes can cause problems, too," Kate continued. "You can run into the problem of someone who is *too* experienced. By that I mean they've worked for several restaurant chains and they know the system so well they can get around it when they want. For example, I've hired servers with a lot of experience who knew how to manipulate the ordering system and sneak free desserts to their regular guests to build up their tips. I'm especially careful with bartenders, because that's the easiest area for an unscrupulous staff member with some experience to rip you off. With bartenders I almost prefer to hire an 18- or 19-year-old college kid with no experience who doesn't know the control systems inside and out."

Lisa nodded in agreement. "I like to hire college students when I can, too, simply because they tend to be responsible and goal-oriented," she said. "That's the good news. The bad news is that the college in our town is small—just 2,000 students—and the students tend to belong to the same clubs and want to go to the same events. I constantly face the problem of half my staff wanting the same night off to go to the game, or the dance, or whatever. I've tried to combat that problem by spreading the students out throughout the restaurant—putting one in the host position, one in the kitchen, only one or two student servers on a particular shift—that kind of thing."

"Let's focus on the interview process itself," Terry said. "What do you do to make sure that an applicant is willing to work certain shifts, or won't leave right after you've spent months training them?"

"Yes, I'd be interested in some help with that," Joe said. "Time after time I've had people let me down that told me all the right things when I interviewed them. Just last week I had a guy quit on me after six months—nice guy, seemed mature, had some restaurant experience—and I had asked him all the right questions when I interviewed him: 'Are you willing to work at least two lunch shifts during the week?' 'Yes.' 'Are you willing to work Saturday nights?' 'Yes.' 'Do you plan on staying in the area for at least two years?' 'Yes.' 'Can you live on $300 a week?' 'Yes.' After I hired him it turns out he can only work one lunch shift a week, he can't work Saturday nights after the first month, and last Tuesday he tells me he's graduating and transferring to another school to get his master's degree."

Kate turned to Joe. "One thing I've learned about interviewing is to try not to ask too many yes-or-no questions. Instead of asking college-age applicants if they're going to be around for a year or two, I'll ask them to tell me where they are in their schooling. If they tell me 'I'm a freshman' or 'I'm starting my sophomore year,' I know that chances are they'll be around for a while. That's one hurdle that people have to jump before I get serious about hiring them—for me, they've got to be around for at least a year.

"Another hurdle is finding out what shifts they can work—but again, I don't ask yes-or-no questions. I'll say something like 'What hours are you available to work?' or 'What's your class schedule like next term?' Some people will literally show me their class schedules. That tells me whether they are available to work some lunch shifts for me. But if I had just asked them a yes-or-no question—'Are you willing to work a lunch shift?'—they might have said 'yes' just to get the job.

"Another hurdle," Kate continued, "is: 'What are your financial expectations?' I like to find out what the applicant is expecting in terms of take-home pay. With my restaurant's volume, the average server can expect to take home about $300 a week, so if a guy says, 'I can't work for less than $500 a week'—he's got kids, maybe, or a big car payment—that tells me he's not a good fit for my restaurant. On the other hand, if someone mumbles, 'Gee, I can get by on $100 a week'—that's not always a good situation either. That tells me this person probably isn't very ambitious or self-confident."

"One of my 'hurdles,' as you call them," Lisa smiled at Kate, "is: 'How *many* shifts can you work in a week?' Unless they say 'four or five,' at minimum, I tend to move on. And I've taken a hard line on lunch shifts, too. I don't have to tell you how hard it is to get people to work lunch shifts, especially experienced people, because you only need them for a couple of hours, the work is intense, and the tips don't compare to what they can make on a 6- or 8-hour dinner shift. But now I tell people flat out, 'You'll be a more attractive candidate if you can give me two lunch shifts a week.' In fact, I don't hire people anymore unless they can pull at least one lunch shift for me.

"I also look for clues as to how responsible an applicant is," Lisa went on. "Did they graduate from high school or did they drop out? Are they going to college now, or pursuing some other goal? Do they have any obligations that would encourage them to take their job seriously? If someone is buying a house, or has children, or is paying for college, he or she is less likely to quit for some frivolous reason."

"You can get that kind of information from an applicant by using the 'lantern principle' when you interview," Kate said. "Remember how the old-fashioned kerosene lanterns started out narrow at the top, then opened up where the flame was, then narrowed down again at the base?" Kate traced a lantern shape in the air with her hands. "When I interview, I start out with the narrow-scope, basic yes-or-no questions. 'Are you a student?' might be one of my first questions, and—depending on how desperate I am—I might end an interview with, 'Can you start tomorrow?'" Terry and the other managers laughed appreciatively. "But in the middle part of the interview I try to ask open-ended questions. Instead of asking someone, 'Are you ambitious?' or 'I'm looking for someone with a lot on the ball—are you that kind of person?'—because they're going to tell you what you want to hear, right?—I'll ask a question like, 'Where do you want to be in five years?' That gives people a chance to talk about themselves. If they tell me, 'I want to be lying on the beach without a care in the world,' that tells me maybe I'm not talking to a real go-getter. But if they say something like, 'In three years I'll have my teaching degree, so I hope I'll be teaching somewhere' or 'I'm a working mom, but what leisure time I have I devote to a local theater group and I hope to be the president of the group someday,' then I know maybe this person will be someone who can be counted on to take the initiative at my restaurant."

"Wow," Joe said to Kate, "I can't believe you spend so much time with applicants. I don't have time to have a long conversation with people—I'm usually so desperate I want to hire them on the spot and put them to work."

"Well, you learn a lot just by letting people talk," Kate said. "Sometimes it's not so much what they say as how they say it. So much of our business depends on communication—between server and cook, manager and host, server and bartender, staff member and guest—that it's important to pay attention to an applicant's communication style. For example, I once had someone interview for a server position who wouldn't stop talking! After I said hello I literally could hardly get a word in. That told me she would probably not let her guests get a word in, either, or would place an order in the kitchen and then spend ten minutes telling the cook how to prepare it."

"You also learn from the mistakes of others," Lisa added. "One of my restaurant-manager friends, a brilliant guy, used to hire college students just because they had a high grade-point average. 'Do they know anything about working in a restaurant?' I'd ask him. 'No, but they're smart,' he'd say. Most of the time they didn't work out, but he had to learn that lesson the hard way."

"Some managers only hire people who are like themselves," Kate agreed. "I used to work for a manager who was like your friend when it came to hiring, but just the reverse. He never went to college; he worked his way up from the bottom and took great pride in 'graduating from the school of hard knocks,' as he always put it. So he didn't want to hire college students."

Terry put his pen down with an air of satisfaction. "This has been a great learning experience for me," he said. "From what you've told me, I think I can generate five basic guidelines that all of Fargo's managers can use when hiring new staff members. They won't be anything fancy or complicated, but they'll hit key issues and be something that managers throughout the chain can benefit from. Thanks for meeting with me today."

Discussion Questions

1. What five basic guidelines can Terry pull from what the managers discussed that might be helpful to other Fargo's managers?
2. One of the things Kate talked about was the need to ask open-ended questions. How can you turn the following closed-ended questions into open-ended questions that can help you get more of the information you want?

   "Can you work Sundays?"

   "Can you work five shifts a week?"

   "Can you live on $300 a week?"

   "Do you think you will still be in this area a year from now?"

The following industry experts helped generate and develop this case: Timothy J. Pugh, Regional Manager, Damon's—The Place for Ribs (Steve Montanye Enterprises, East Lansing, Michigan); and Lawrence E. Ross, Assistant Professor, Florida Southern College, and owner of Sago Grill, Lakeland, Florida.

Appendix A

Shopper's Service Report

Name of Property (Dining Outlet) ______________________________
Address ______________________________
Date of Visitation ____________ Meal Period ____________ Time ____________
Manager/Supervisor on Duty ______________________________

ITEMS PURCHASED:

Beverages:

#	ITEM	PRICE
____	________	______
____	________	______
____	________	______
____	________	______
	TOTAL	______

Food:

#	ITEM	PRICE
____	________	______
____	________	______
____	________	______
____	________	______
	TOTAL	______

Total Price ____________

Please respond to each statement using the following scale:
5—Strongly Agree
4—Somewhat Agree
3—Neither Agree nor Disagree
2—Somewhat Disagree
1—Strongly Disagree
NA—The statement does not apply.
To Score: Total all points and compare the actual score with the Standard Point Score. (When statements are not applicable, change Standard Point Score correspondingly.)

TOTAL STANDARD POINT SCORE ______ TOTAL ACTUAL POINT SCORE ______

GREETING

A. You were greeted immediately upon entering the dining area.	5	4	3	2	1
B. The host/hostess moved away from the stand.	5	4	3	2	1
C. The host/hostess asked your name and/or made a friendly/gracious comment.	5	4	3	2	1

D. Comments regarding your greeting: ______________________________

____

____

STANDARD POINT SCORE FOR GREETING __15__ ACTUAL POINT SCORE ______

SEATING

A. You were asked whether you preferred to be seated in the nonsmoking or the smoking section.	5	4	3	2	1
B. When you were ready to be seated, you were immediately led to your table.	5	4	3	2	1
C. The host/hostess was attractively dressed.	5	4	3	2	1

(continued)

Appendix A *(continued)*

D.	The host/hostess was neat and clean.	5	4	3	2	1
E.	The selection of your table location showed good judgment.	5	4	3	2	1
F.	The chair/booth was comfortable. If uncomfortable, in what way? ______________________________	5	4	3	2	1
G.	The host/hostess distributed menus when you were seated.	5	4	3	2	1
H.	The host/hostess informed you of special or additional menu items.	5	4	3	2	1
I.	The host/hostess informed you of the name of your server(s).	5	4	3	2	1
J.	The host/hostess left with a pleasant message.	5	4	3	2	1
K.	The host/hostess seemed happy about his/her job and interested in you.	5	4	3	2	1

L. Comments regarding your seating: ______________________________

____

____

STANDARD POINT SCORE FOR SEATING 55 ACTUAL POINT SCORE __________

CLEANLINESS

A.	The dining area was clean.	5	4	3	2	1
B.	The table was clean and free of crumbs.	5	4	3	2	1
C.	The chair/booth was clean.	5	4	3	2	1
D.	Dirty dishes were completely cleared from the table as soon as they were empty.	5	4	3	2	1
E.	The flatware and dishes were clean.	5	4	3	2	1
F.	The glasses were clean.	5	4	3	2	1
G.	The carpet was clean.	5	4	3	2	1
H.	The restrooms were clean.	5	4	3	2	1
I.	Rank the overall cleanliness.	5	4	3	2	1

J. Comments regarding cleanliness: ______________________________

____

____

STANDARD POINT SCORE FOR CLEANLINESS 45 ACTUAL POINT SCORE __________

ATMOSPHERE

A.	The dining outlet was conducive to conversation.	5	4	3	2	1
B.	The lighting was appropriate. If not, what was wrong? ______________________________	5	4	3	2	1
C.	There was no noticeable kitchen noise.	5	4	3	2	1
D.	The background music was peaceful.	5	4	3	2	1
E.	The following were in agreement with the outlet's theme:					
	Decor	5	4	3	2	1
	Menu	5	4	3	2	1
	Uniforms	5	4	3	2	1
F.	The experience was what you expected.	5	4	3	2	1

Appendix A *(continued)*

G. Comments regarding atmosphere: ______________________________

____

____

STANDARD POINT SCORE FOR ATMOSPHERE 40 ACTUAL POINT SCORE ______

SERVICE

A. A server made contact with you within three minutes after you were seated.	5	4	3	2	1
B. The server provided water during his/her first contact.	5	4	3	2	1
C. The server had a pleasant greeting.	5	4	3	2	1
D. The server's hands and fingernails were clean.	5	4	3	2	1
E. The server's posture was good.	5	4	3	2	1
F. The server was cordial, smiled, and created a pleasant atmosphere.	5	4	3	2	1
G. The server was familiar with the menu items.	5	4	3	2	1
H. The server used suggestive selling and was courteous without being pushy.	5	4	3	2	1
I. The server could answer all your questions about the property.	5	4	3	2	1
J. The lady's order was taken first.	5	4	3	2	1
K. The server did not use his/her tray as a writing platform.	5	4	3	2	1
L. Beverage items were served promptly.	5	4	3	2	1
M. Food items were served promptly.	5	4	3	2	1
N. The timing between courses was appropriate.	5	4	3	2	1
O. The server knew which items to serve to each guest.	5	4	3	2	1
P. Beverages were served from the right.	5	4	3	2	1
Q. Food items were served from the left.	5	4	3	2	1
R. The server returned to the table within five minutes to provide additional assistance.	5	4	3	2	1
S. Water glasses were refilled promptly.	5	4	3	2	1
T. Empty dishes were removed promptly.	5	4	3	2	1
U. Dirty dishes were removed from the right.	5	4	3	2	1
V. Dirty ashtrays were properly removed (capped) and replaced.	5	4	3	2	1
W. It was not necessary to summon the server during the meal.	5	4	3	2	1
X. The server seemed to enjoy his/her job.	5	4	3	2	1
Y. The server did an excellent job.	5	4	3	2	1

Z. Comments regarding the service: ______________________________

____

____

____

____

____

STANDARD POINT SCORE FOR SERVICE 125 ACTUAL POINT SCORE ______

FOOD

(Please indicate suggestions to improve the quality of any item under "Additional comments.")

A. The food items corresponded with their menu descriptions.	5	4	3	2	1

(continued)

Appendix A *(continued)*

B. All items ordered were available.	5	4	3	2	1
C. The hot foods were served hot.	5	4	3	2	1
D. The cold foods were served cold.	5	4	3	2	1

APPETIZER (Name ____________________________)

E. The appetizer:

looked appetizing,	5	4	3	2	1
was fresh,	5	4	3	2	1
had excellent coloring,	5	4	3	2	1
had an excellent flavor, and	5	4	3	2	1
was seasoned well.	5	4	3	2	1

BREADSTICKS

F. The breadsticks:

were fresh and	5	4	3	2	1
were seasoned perfectly.	5	4	3	2	1

G. Additional comments regarding the appetizer or breadsticks: ____________________

____

____

____

____

SALAD (Name ____________________________)

H. The salad:

looked appetizing,	5	4	3	2	1
was neatly plated,	5	4	3	2	1
was appropriately portioned,	5	4	3	2	1
had excellent coloring,	5	4	3	2	1
was fresh,	5	4	3	2	1
had a dressing that complemented it, and	5	4	3	2	1
was of excellent quality.	5	4	3	2	1

I. Additional comments regarding the salad: ____________________

____

____

ENTREE (Name ____________________________)

J. The entree:

looked appetizing,	5	4	3	2	1
was neatly plated,	5	4	3	2	1
was appropriately portioned,	5	4	3	2	1
had excellent coloring,	5	4	3	2	1
was fresh,	5	4	3	2	1
was seasoned well,	5	4	3	2	1
had an excellent flavor, and	5	4	3	2	1
was of excellent quality.	5	4	3	2	1

K. Additional comments regarding the entree: ____________________

____

____

____

____

Appendix A *(continued)*

VEGETABLE (Name________________________________)

L. The vegetable:

was appropriately portioned,	5	4	3	2	1
had excellent coloring,	5	4	3	2	1
was fresh,	5	4	3	2	1
had the correct texture,	5	4	3	2	1
was seasoned well, and	5	4	3	2	1
had an excellent flavor.	5	4	3	2	1

M. Additional comments regarding the vegetable: ________________________________

____

STARCH (Name________________________________)

N. The starch item:

was appropriately portioned,	5	4	3	2	1
was fresh,	5	4	3	2	1
was seasoned well, and	5	4	3	2	1
had an excellent flavor.	5	4	3	2	1

O. Additional comments regarding the starch item: ________________________________

____

DESSERT (Name________________________________)

P. The dessert:

was appropriately portioned,	5	4	3	2	1
was fresh,	5	4	3	2	1
was served at the correct temperature, and	5	4	3	2	1
had an excellent flavor.	5	4	3	2	1

Q. Additional comments regarding the dessert: ________________________________

____

R. Each of the following items corresponded with its menu description:

Appetizer	5	4	3	2	1
Salad	5	4	3	2	1
Entree	5	4	3	2	1
Dessert	5	4	3	2	1

S. Additional comments regarding the overall food quality: ________________________________

____

____

____

____

STANDARD POINT SCORE FOR FOOD 220 ACTUAL POINT SCORE ______

MENU

A. The menu was clean and free from spots.	5	4	3	2	1
B. The menu fit the theme of the dining outlet.	5	4	3	2	1
C. The menu was well organized.	5	4	3	2	1
D. The menu was clearly written.	5	4	3	2	1
E. Descriptions were appetizing.	5	4	3	2	1

(continued)

Appendix A *(continued)*

F. The number of items available was appropriate.	5	4	3	2	1
G. Specials were available.	5	4	3	2	1
H. Vegetarian menu items were available.	5	4	3	2	1
I. The menu was an effective marketing tool.	5	4	3	2	1

J. Comments and changes you'd like to see regarding the menu: ____________________

____

____

____

STANDARD POINT SCORE FOR THE MENU 45 ACTUAL POINT SCORE ________

GUEST CHECK (BILL) HANDLING

A. The guest check arrived at the appropriate time.	5	4	3	2	1
B. The check was readable.	5	4	3	2	1
C. The check correctly reflected what had been served.	5	4	3	2	1
D. The check was correctly totaled.	5	4	3	2	1
E. The server informed you that he/she would return for your payment when you were ready.	5	4	3	2	1
F. The server said thank you after he/she received your payment.	5	4	3	2	1
G. The server took the payment directly to the cashier.	5	4	3	2	1
H. The server brought your change directly from the cashier.	5	4	3	2	1
I. You received the correct change.	5	4	3	2	1
J. You received the check stub.	5	4	3	2	1
K. The server invited you to return.	5	4	3	2	1

L. Please list restaurant check number ________ Total ________ Tip (if charged) ________

M. Comments regarding check handling: ____________________

____

____

STANDARD POINT SCORE FOR CHECK HANDLING 55 ACTUAL POINT SCORE ________

Appendix B

Typical Duties of a Dining Room Manager

OPENING DUTIES

Make sure the dining room temperature is comfortable.

Check the light level and all light bulbs. (Some operations have a policy that guests should be able to read a newspaper at the table. Other operations have discovered that guests wish for very subdued lighting.) Make sure lamp shades are straight.

Make sure pictures are straight and lighted.

Check table locations and room setup.

Inspect the dining room for cleanliness and safety. Check restrooms.

Communicate information regarding reservations (numbers and arrival times) to production personnel. (Put special emphasis on large parties.)

Check the schedule to confirm adequate staffing.

Gather as much information as possible about guests who are VIPs (Very Important Persons).

Check the menu items and the conditions of menus.

Make sure the music level is appropriate.

Check the sound system (if you use one).

Discuss special instructions with the staff.

Plan table arrangements according to group reservations.

Ensure that precheck and/or other registers and/or sales income control equipment are set for the beginning of the new dining period.

Make sure each food server is properly groomed.

Check each food server station's checklist to ensure that the dining room supplies are at proper inventory levels.

Meet with the service staff to discuss special guests, special menu items, daily specials, etc.

OPERATING DUTIES

Greet and seat guests.

Make recommendations and provide information about foods, wines, and spirits.

Ensure courteous and efficient service.

Make sure that the guests are satisfied, and follow up on any complaints.

Discreetly take care of intoxicated or hard-to-handle guests, or those who have disabilities. (It may be necessary to get assistance from another supervisor.)

Enforce procedures to detect fraudulent guests. (Also, ensure that dishonest service staff cannot steal from guests.)

(continued)

Appendix B *(continued)*

OPERATING DUTIES *(continued)*

Enforce safety regulations.

Relay any special instructions to the kitchen.

Maintain a pleasant atmosphere in the dining room.

Maintain the reservation book.

Take appropriate action in the case of an accident to guests or staff members.

Follow up on special requests.

Supervise food service.

CLOSING DUTIES

Inspect for fire hazards (especially look in waste containers and linen receptacles for lighted cigarettes).

Turn off lights and adjust the air conditioning to the proper level.

Lock all doors.

Leave written information concerning any items requiring correction and any other information that will help the dining room manager who opens the room for the next dining period.

Follow the procedures for processing cash and charge vouchers.

Report any maintenance problems.

Review the next day's schedule and menus if possible.

Be sure to communicate to the appropriate personnel any guest complaints or comments.

Close precheck and other registers; follow required closing procedures.

Inspect for safety and sanitation.

Turn in the required reports to the appropriate officials.

MISCELLANEOUS DUTIES

Conduct training sessions for dining service staff members.

Participate in food and beverage, safety, and other meetings.

Plan reservations. (This is a key element in efficient service flow.)

Review menu items for their sales popularity.

Interview prospective staff members.

Maintain staff-member time records.

Develop effective operating procedures for dining service with a special focus on periods of high business volume.

Prepare weekly work schedules according to forecasted guest demand.

Issue maintenance orders.

Adjust work assignments and schedules.

Appendix B *(continued)*

MISCELLANEOUS DUTIES *(continued)*

Authorize overtime, vacation time, and time off for dining room staff according to established practices.

Conduct accident/incident investigations and hold weekly training meetings, monthly safety meetings, and fire drills as required.

Implement and enforce safety regulations and house rules.

Coordinate cost control, purchasing, and maintenance duties with the assistant food and beverage director.

Order and requisition special-occasion cakes from the bake shop.

Prepare requisition sheet for operating supplies.

Observe and record staff member performance.

Make recommendations regarding staff member promotions.

Make complete dining room inspections at least weekly.

Source: Adapted from the *Dining Room Manual* of Hotel du Pont, Wilmington, Delaware.

Appendix C

Sample Preopening Checklist

	Required Quantities						
	M	T	W	TH	F	S	SU
1. Serving Supply Areas A. Prestock with all necessary service supplies							
tablecloths							
placemats							
napkins							
knives							
forks							
teaspoons							
soup spoons							
cocktail forks							
steak knives							
juice glasses							
water glasses							
coffee cups							
salad plates							
side dishes							
bread/butter plates							
dessert plates							
soup cups/bowls							
coffeepots							
water pitchers							
wine brackets/stands							
candles							
doilies							
bus tabs							
doggie bags							
sanitizing solution (to wipe tables)							
other:							
B. Prestock with food supplies:							
salt							

Appendix C *(continued)*

	M	T	W	TH	F	S	SU
pepper							
sugar							
sugar substitute							
steak sauce							
ketchup							
mustard							
Worcestershire sauce							
preserves							
butter							
cream							
milk							
sour cream							
crackers (saltine and/or oyster crackers							
decaffeinated coffee							
horseradish							
tea bags (variety of flavors)							
lemons							
filled ice bins							
other:							
2. Public Areas							
reception area clean							
foyer clean							
public restrooms clean							
entry clean							
exterior areas clean							
dining room areas clean							
other:							
3. Service Staff							
clean and proper uniforms worn							

(continued)

Appendix C *(continued)*

	M	T	W	TH	F	S	SU
preopening meeting held							
stations assigned							
daily specials reported							
run-outs reported							
out-of-stock items reported							
groups/reservations discussed							
guest checks dispensed							
other:							
4. Dining Room							
table decorations (flowers, candles, etc.)							
lighting							
regular and emergency exits							
air conditioning							
sound system							
no-smoking signs							
other:							
5. Service Stations							
tables steady							
tables set							
chairs clean							
napkins folded							
candles lit							
centerpieces fresh looking							
salt/pepper/etc. available							
ashtray/matches available							
table tents available							
table arranged for size of group reservation							
tray stand ready							

Appendix C *(continued)*

	M	T	W	TH	F	S	SU
other:							
6. Reception Stand							
reservation book							
menus (food/wine/beverage)							
pencils							
flashlights							
credit card authorization machines							
other:							

REVIEW QUIZ

When you feel you have covered all of the material in this chapter, answer these questions. Choose the *best* answer.

1. Which of the following statements about casual/theme restaurants is *false?*

   a. Casual/theme restaurants typically have informal dining environments.
   b. Alcoholic beverages are not served in most casual/theme restaurants.
   c. Casual/theme restaurants are classified as full-service restaurants.
   d. Guest-check averages range from moderate to moderately high in most casual/theme restaurants.

2. Liquors that guests request by name are called __________ brands.

   a. house
   b. well
   c. call
   d. premium

3. At the end of the meal, as she is clearing the dinner plates from the table, the server says the following to her guests: "We're known for our great Mile-High Sawdust Pie, featuring a delicious mixture of coconut and pecans, and our chef also takes pride in baking a real New York cheesecake, which we cover with fresh strawberries and lace with chocolate syrup. Can I bring anyone a piece of pie or cheesecake?" What the server is doing with these remarks is called:

   a. side work.
   b. upselling.
   c. selling premiums.
   d. suggestive selling.

4. Which of the following statements about wine service procedures is *true?*

   a. Once the server removes the cork from the bottle of wine, he or she should discreetly slip the cork in a pocket so the guest does not see it.
   b. Once the bottle of wine is open, the server should offer a sample of the wine to all of the male guests at the table.
   c. When filling the wine glasses of the guests, the server typically moves counter-clockwise around the table, starting with the guest on the host's right.
   d. Wine glasses should be filled to just below the rim.

REVIEW QUIZ *(continued)*

5. What is the typical order of service in a casual/theme restaurant?

   a. Children are served first, then women, then men.
   b. Women are served first, then children, then men.
   c. Men are served first, then women, then children.
   d. Women are served first, then men, then children.

Answer Key: 1-b-C1, 2-c-C1, 3-d-C2, 4-c-C3, 5-a-C3

Each question is linked to a competency. Competencies are listed on the first page of the chapter. An answer reading 3-b-C4 translates to:

3: the question number
b: the correct answer
C4: the competency number

Chapter 10 Outline

Selling Banquets and Catered Events
- Markets
- Sales Strategies
- The Offer

Booking and Planning Events
- The Function Book
- Contracts or Letters of Agreement
- Function Sheets

Getting Ready for Service
- Setting Up Function Rooms
- Scheduling Staff Members
- Preparing, Plating, and Storing Food

Delivering Service
- Food Service
- Beverage Service
- Protocol for Special Banquets and Catered Events

After Service
- Controls
- Guest Comments
- Using Feedback in Planning

Competencies

1. Describe how banquets and catered events are sold—through identifying markets, employing sales strategies to sell to prospective clients, and making offers.
2. Explain how banquets and catered events are booked and planned, and describe function books, contracts or letters of agreement, and function sheets.
3. Summarize how banquet and catering operations get ready to provide service to clients during an event, from setting up function rooms to scheduling staff members and preparing, plating, and storing food.
4. Describe different styles of food service; explain various beverage payment plans for banquet/catered event clients; list examples of protocol issues that banquet and catering staff members must be aware of; and describe "after service" issues for banquets and catered events, including controls, gathering guest comments, and using guest feedback in planning.

10

Banquets and Catered Events

PROFESSIONAL BANQUET AND CATERING MANAGERS know that having a first-class **banquet and catering operation** can enhance the overall image of their food service organizations within the community. For many guests, their first contact with a given food service operation occurs when they attend a banquet or catered event. If a guest's experience is positive, he or she may very well return to the operation with family and friends. Some banquet guests may also be the future organizers of similar functions for other groups. If these guests have already experienced a banquet that exceeded their expectations, they may simply return to the operation with their groups to experience the same kind of menu and service that delighted them previously.

A banquet and catering operation can be an independent business, part of a larger commercial or noncommercial food service operation, or a department within the food and beverage division of a lodging property. In all of these various forms, a well-run banquet and catering operation can generate substantial profits, for several reasons:

1. Banquets and catered events allow flexibility in pricing. Prime rib priced at $25 on a food service operation's restaurant menu may bring $38 on its banquet menu, for example. (Part of this increase is due to the cost of erecting and tearing down the banquet setup.)
2. Food costs for banquets and catered events are lower due to volume preparation and low food waste (because the number of guests is known).
3. Beverage costs can be controlled through pricing flexibility and volume purchasing.
4. Labor costs are lower. Since banquet servers can be supplemented by part-time workers on an as-needed basis, the regular banquet/catering service staff can be kept small. (The cost of restaurant staff members, in contrast, is largely fixed; restaurants must maintain a regular staff even during slow periods.)
5. Additional income can be generated from outside suppliers such as photographers, entertainers, bakeries, florists, and printers. Some banquet and catering operations work with preferred suppliers who pay them a commission for business generated from banquet clients.

In this chapter we will identify groups that typically book banquets or catered events and discuss strategies for selling to them. The process of booking and planning banquets and catered events will be the subject of the next section. We will then discuss getting ready for banquet or catering service, delivering service, and issues of concern after service.

Selling Banquets and Catered Events

Commercial food service operations face stiff competition for banquet and catering business in the United States—not only from each other, but from businesses outside the commercial sector. According to *Food Management* magazine's survey of onsite (noncommercial) food service operators, 87 percent of those responding said they offer catering services. Forty-one percent of these same managers have an onsite building or banquet rooms devoted to accommodating catered events. Supermarket chains and independent grocery stores have also entered the lucrative banquet/catering arena via new home-meal-replacement concepts.

Markets

Banquet and catering operations in commercial food service handle a wide variety of functions, including beverage service, snack service, special-event catering with a **buffet** or table service, and meal service delivered to guests off-premises. Other opportunities for banquet and catering operations include barbecues, conferences, hospitality suites, receptions, theme parties, wedding receptions, and sports banquets. Appendix A at the back of the chapter lists potential markets and some of the typical functions they plan. Banquet and catering managers should remember that each guest they serve is typically involved with many groups; a favorably impressed convention attendee might subsequently book social gatherings or business meetings with the operation, for example. The better the service and the more personal attention staff members give to guests, the more likely it is that guests will generate new business leads for the operation.

While there is countless variety in the types of banquets and catered events that are planned and executed, the markets for such events usually come from just three major sources: associations, corporate and business groups, and social groups.

Associations, or professional and special-interest groups, may include fewer than a hundred members to tens of thousands of members. These groups' annual meetings and other events may feature simultaneous meetings and a wide range of food and beverage functions, such as coffee breaks, hospitality suites, cocktail parties, and banquets.

Corporate and business groups are composed of business associates and number from a handful of people to many hundreds. These groups may require food and beverage service for meals and coffee breaks, and have the potential to produce high revenue for food service operations that offer banquet and catering services.

Social groups also can range from a handful of people to hundreds. Social groups' functions include private parties arranged by individuals for such family events as bar and bat mitzvahs, weddings, anniversaries, and graduations. Civic and political events, award or testimonial dinners, and fund-raising events are more examples of social-group events that often require banquet or catering services. Event planners for social groups are usually amateurs and may need extra help with planning their events.

The needs of associations and corporate groups are different from the needs of social groups. Associations and corporate groups normally require exhibit space and services, audiovisual equipment, office services, or other special equipment or services that social groups usually do not need. Managers of independent banquet and catering firms will feel market pressure to offer more than just food and beverage services if they target associations and corporate groups. Independent firms that cannot provide all of the services that these groups require sometimes partner with outside suppliers or hotels that can supply these services.

The regularity with which associations and corporate groups meet makes them prime prospects for a banquet and catering operation. Whether independent or part of a larger food service organization, a banquet and catering operation usually should book non-annual events only after it has booked all of the annual events it can, because of the long-term value of accounts that hold annual meetings. Almost all associations and corporate groups hold annual meetings, and many hold smaller, more sporadic meetings as well.

A large association usually books its annual national convention in a different city each year and often selects the city years in advance of the convention's date. Corporate meetings are held wherever it is most convenient, often near corporate headquarters or a field office. Training seminars, management meetings, and other corporate meetings often are not rotated among various locations. This lack of a geographic pattern opens the door for almost any banquet and catering operation, no matter what its location or size, to book corporate meetings business. Business from social groups typically comes from clients who live in the local area.

Association meeting planners usually plan conventions one or more years in advance. Corporate meetings have no particular "time cycle"; most corporate meetings are scheduled as needed and may occur at any time throughout the year. Lead time is far more variable for corporate meetings than for association meetings. The annual sales meetings of corporations are usually planned a year or more in advance, but training meetings and seminars may be set three to six months in advance, or with even less lead time if the meeting is called to deal with a crisis. Executive conferences and board meetings also may be called on short notice. Weddings, family reunions, award banquets, retirement parties, and other events sponsored by social groups are usually planned a year or less in advance.

Whether event planners are experienced professionals planning events for thousands, or brides-to-be or other individuals planning small-scale social events for the first time, event planners always prefer to deal with people who take the time to understand their needs. They also appreciate working with one representative of the banquet and catering operation from the beginning of negotiations to the end of their events—someone who both sells the operation's services to them and helps coordinate the actual event for them.

Sales Strategies

To be competitive, food service operations must aggressively sell their banquet and catering services. While detailed procedures for selling banquets are beyond

Washington State Convention & Trade Center

The Washington State Convention & Trade Center's award-winning food service caterer provides custom meals for every occasion. The Catering Sales Manager will meet with you during your initial site inspection visit and will assist you in planning your food & beverage functions. Our on-site state of the art kitchen and professional staff are prepared to meet the unique needs of your event.

Food service payment schedules are established as part of the Food & Beverage Contract. The food/beverage contract is negotiated for approval with ARAMARK. The final food and beverage guarantee is due 72 working hours prior to the date of the event, excluding weekends and holidays.

Contact the Catering Sales Manager to discuss contract and payment for all food and beverage needs and send us an e-mail to obtain menus and other information:

ARAMARK
c/o Washington State Convention & Trade Center
800 Convention Place
Seattle, WA 98101-2350
Phone: (206) 447-5087
Fax: (206) 447-5388

Home
Room Specifications ~ Calendar ~ Staff ~ Event Services
Food Services ~ Facility Overview ~ Local Map

The colorful photo on this Internet site (http://www.wsctc.com) gives potential clients an idea of the high-quality service and food presentation they can expect from the staff of the Washington State Convention and Trade Center. (Courtesy of DSC, Inc., and the Washington State Convention and Trade Center)

the scope of this chapter, the general principles are the same from operation to operation. Likewise, certain basic tasks must be performed regardless of who performs them. Depending on the type and size of the operation and the titles used, the person responsible for banquet and catering sales may be the general manager, the food and beverage director, the director of sales, a banquet and catering director, or a salesperson.

One of the most effective sales strategies for banquet and catering operations is building a tradition of service excellence. It is much easier to sell banquets to people who are aware of the operation's fine reputation—or better yet, to those people who have had previous excellent experiences at the operation—than to people who know nothing about the operation. An operation that has an unimpressive reputation, or that tries to sell banquet and catering services to prospective clients who have had problems with events catered by the operation in the past, has a difficult, if not impossible, sales job.

To sell banquets and catered events effectively, banquet and catering managers must segment the event market into groups and know what potential guests in those groups require, how the operation can best provide for those requirements, and how to negotiate a contract to provide the right products and services at the right price.

Prompt attention to prospects' inquiries about banquet/catering services demonstrates to prospects that the banquet and catering operation is efficient and has a concern for meeting the needs of clients and guests. This good first impression is something the operation can build on as it forms relationships with clients.

In addition to responding to inquiries, managers and salespeople in the banquet and catering area may also initiate contact with prospects, through telephone calls, direct mail letters, **sales blitzes** (personal visits to many prospects within a relatively small geographic area), or interaction with community organizations, convention centers, the local chamber of commerce, and tourist organizations. Whether salespeople or prospective guests make the initial contact, salespeople must convey to prospects that the food service operation is interested in their business.

If a client books a convention or large corporate group's meeting with the operation several years ahead and will require many diverse food and beverage products and services, the salesperson should try to attend that group's meeting the year previous to when the group will arrive at his or her operation. The salesperson's attendance at the convention or meeting will enable him or her to meet the client and learn details of the group's food and beverage needs. This approach could help ensure that the salesperson books all of the ancillary food and beverage functions connected with the event the following year.

Inexperienced planners of national conventions may base their budgets for next year's food and beverage functions on the previous year's costs—often with a small increase to cover inflation. This is a mistaken approach, because it overlooks such variables as differences in the cost of living for different geographic locations throughout the country. So that the planners of national conventions will not begin negotiations with unrealistic expectations, banquet/catering salespeople should contact them many months ahead of time, before the planners finalize their budgets.

Effective salespeople can sometimes find new clients by visiting competitors. Dropping in on the competition and looking at their bulletin boards and "reader boards" (the area below a hotel's outdoor sign that is devoted to spelling out temporary messages) are good ways for salespeople to learn about which groups are booking where. Then the salesperson can work on finding out who the event planners are for the groups and convincing them to book with his or her operation in the future.

To help generate sales from these and other prospects, a salesperson might offer **familiarization tours** or "fam" tours. These tours involve showing prospects the operation's banquet/catering facilities and function rooms, providing prospects with supplemental information to help them plan their events, providing complimentary food and beverage services, and providing complimentary lodging (if the banquet and catering operation is part of a hotel) as a sample of what the operation has to offer.

Many banquet and catering salespeople also use **presentation books** to help them sell clients on their operation. Presentation books illustrate the possible seating and table arrangements within banquet and meeting space, contain photographs of past events, and display options for table settings. Presentation books can showcase outstanding past events and provide useful ideas to clients. (Videos and slide shows depicting special events are also effective sales tools.)

Now let's take a closer look at the two elements of a banquet and catering operation's services that are of most importance to clients: the operation's function rooms and its menus.

Function Rooms. From the client's standpoint, choosing the right function room is very important, because it must comfortably accommodate the number of people expected, and its atmosphere must complement the event. The floor plans of function rooms can be very helpful to clients who need certain kinds of lighting, electrical outlets for equipment, or space that is free of pillars or other obstructions. (The floor plan for each function room can be included in an operation's presentation book.)

Association and corporate meeting planners sometimes want **breakout rooms** available near the main function room. Breakout rooms are small meeting rooms used when a large group session divides into smaller sessions for discussions and group work. Breakout rooms are especially suitable for training meetings or seminars.

In order to present clients with workable function room alternatives, salespeople and managers must know the capacities of all of the rooms for each kind of seating arrangement. Chair and table sizes should present no surprises when staff members set up function rooms in the way the salesperson has promised the client. While this may seem like a minor point, tables or chairs that are just a few inches larger than others can significantly reduce the number of guests that a room can accommodate. Every bit of space counts.

In addition, the following factors should be considered when a salesperson is helping a client decide on a particular function room:

1. Does the room have enough space to accommodate everything the client's event requires? In addition to a specific number of guests, it may be necessary to provide space for portable bars, buffet tables, entertainment bandstands, dance floors, and staging areas.

2. Does the event require guest seating? Function rooms can accommodate many more people for a stand-up reception than for a sit-down banquet. (A rule of thumb is ten square feet [.9 square meters] per person if guests sit, and nine square feet [.8 square meters] if they stand.) Similarly, the space requirements for theater-style and classroom-style seating differ significantly. Managers should develop charts that illustrate for clients the seating

arrangements and capacities of each function room under each setup. (Copies of these charts should also be given to the person in charge of setting up function rooms.) Exhibit 1 shows commonly used function room setups; Exhibit 2 shows a sample chart of seating capacities for various function rooms under various setups.

3. Are any events planned for the function room immediately before or after the event under consideration? For example, if staff members must break down a function room that held exhibits before they can set up for the next event, they will need much more time to prepare it for the next event than if the room had been set up for a theater-style meeting or a stand-up reception.
4. Are any events planned for the function room(s) next to the function room the client is thinking of booking? Noise from one room's meeting, setup, or cleanup/breakdown can disrupt a neighboring event that is happening simultaneously.
5. What occupancy limits are set for the room by municipal codes and ordinances? Fire or other safety codes might limit the number of people that may occupy a room.
6. Is the function room accessible to guests with disabilities? Rooms accessible only by stairs are undesirable; managers should use them only when no other appropriate space is available.

What should a salesperson do if a client wants to book a party of 20 into a room that can seat 50 guests? Obviously, if the client is booking the event a year in advance, the salesperson should make a serious effort to convince him or her of the benefits of a smaller room so that the salesperson can put the larger room to its optimal use with a future booking. However, if the client's party is only two weeks away and the room is available, the salesperson is more likely to fulfill the client's request, because the salesperson cannot easily sell the room within the next two weeks anyway.

Most operations set a minimum number of covers (meals served) for each banquet room, but if a client whose dinner doesn't meet the minimum requirement requests a large banquet room that will otherwise go unsold, the client will usually get it. Managers must consider heating, air conditioning, and other fixed costs when they establish minimum covers for their banquet rooms.

Most operations set **cutoff dates** for tentative reservations (or "holds") of rooms, dates by which clients must either confirm or cancel their tentative reservations. Managers often set cutoff dates for either two weeks after the hold was placed or 30 days before the date of the event. By doing so, they add urgency to the negotiations between the salesperson and the client, and they also guarantee that the operation will have some time to sell the space if the client decides to cancel.

While a room is on hold, the salesperson and the client are often involved in negotiations over prices and other variables concerning the event. The willingness of salespeople to make price and other concessions will depend on the extent to which they desire the business. As alluded to earlier, if a room will go unsold if the negotiations with a client fall through, the salesperson may offer an additional service or upgrade a menu without additional cost to close the deal. However, if there

Exhibit 1 Sample Meeting Room Setups

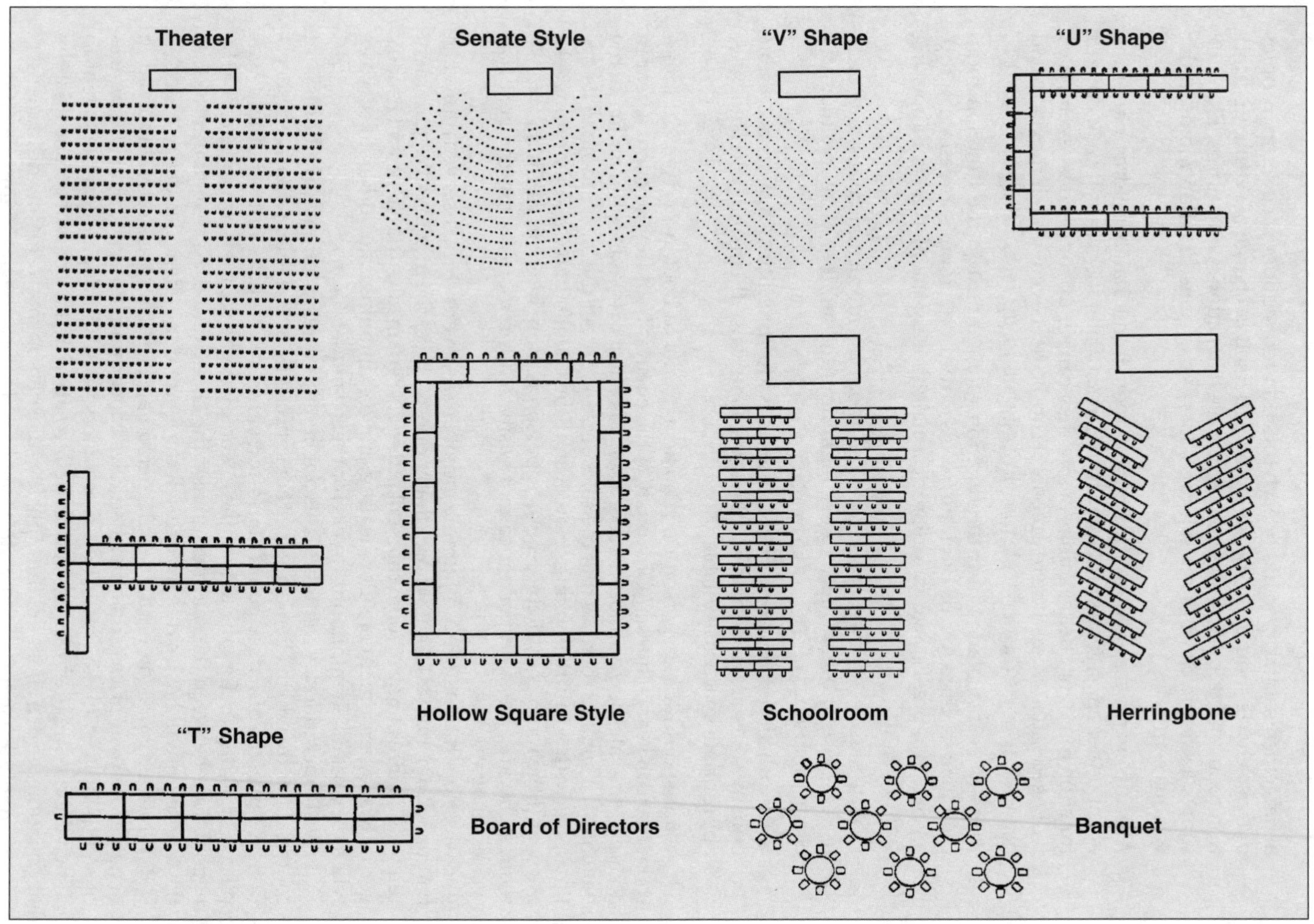

Source: Adapted from Convention Liaison Council, *The Convention Liaison Council Manual,* 6th ed. (Washington, D.C., 1994), pp. 81–91.

Exhibit 2 Sample Function Room Capacities and Dimensions

CAPACITIES AND DIMENSIONS*

ROOM	CAPACITIES								DIMENSIONS		
	THEATRE	SCHOOL ROOM	BANQUET	RECEPTION	U-SHAPE	HOLLOW SQUARE	EXHIBITS 8x10	EXHIBITS 10x10	SQUARE FEET	DIMENSIONS	CEILING HEIGHT
GRAND SALON	–	–	640	1,373	–	–	28	28	9,612	178'x54'	12'
GRAND BALLROOM	4,556	1,008	3,340	4,556	–	–	307	254	. 50,112	270'x150'	22'-16'
ADELPHI ROOM	1,896	1,008	1,020	1,929	–	–	85	74	13,500	150'x90'	22'-16'
BROADWAY ROOM	1,120	735	650	1,286	–	–	52	52	9,000	150'x60'	22'-16'
CAPITOL ROOM	1,120	735	660	1,286	–	–	52	52	9,000	150'x60'	22'-16'
RIALTO ROOM	1,120	735	600	1,286	–	–	52	52	9,000	150'x60'	22'-16'
RIALTO 1	150	84	120	264	52	65	–	–	1,850	45'x37'	22'-16'
RIALTO 2	150	84	120	264	52	65	–	–	1,850	45'x37'	22'-16'
RIALTO 3	150	84	120	264	52	65	–	–	1,850	45'x37'	22'-16'
RIALTO 4	150	84	120	264	52	65	–	–	1,850	45'x37'	22'-16'
REGISTRATION OFFICE	–	–	–	–	–	–	–	–	350	14'x25'	10'
GOLDWYN BALLROOM	5,000	3,400	3,400	5,200	–	–	291	237	44,600	180'x240'	10'-23'6"
GOLDWYN OFFICE	–	–	–	–	–	–	–	–	1,221	37'x33'	10'
GOLDWYN FOYER	–	–	–	–	–	–	–	–	1,232	22'x56'	12'
PALACE ROOM**	–	–	340	462	–	–	24	24	5,082	–	10'
PALACE 1	65	40	40	113	22	34	–	–	792	22'x36'	10'
PALACE 2	96	63	50	113	32	40	–	–	792	22'x36'	10'
PALACE 3	280	154	170	280	70	85	–	–	2,112	32'x66'	10'
PALACE 4	76	54	50	99	32	40	–	–	693	21'x33'	10'
PALACE 5	76	54	50	99	32	40	–	–	693	21'x33'	10'
PALACE 6	84	45	50	102	32	40	–	–	713	23'x31'	10'
PALACE 7	84	45	50	102	32	40	–	–	713	23'x31'	10'
DIRECTOR'S ROOM	Permanent Conference Table Seats 22								1,189	41'x29'	12'-10'
GROUP INFORMATION BOOTH	–	–	–	–	–	–	–	–	196	14'x14'	9'
ASSN. OFFICE 1, 2, 3, 4	–	–	–	–	–	–	–	–	108	9'x12'	9'
CELEBRITY ROOM	Permanent Seating for 1,499								2,640 Stage Dimensions Only	60'x44'	26'
ZIEGFELD ROOM	Permanent Seating for 1,096								5,016 Stage Dimensions Only	88'x57'	30'

Source: Bally's Casino Resort, Las Vegas, Nevada.

is a good chance that the salesperson can sell the space to someone else, obviously the salesperson is less likely to make concessions.

Menus. Most banquet and catering operations create standard banquet menus to help salespeople give prospective clients an indication of what is available within specific price ranges. Most clients find standard menus acceptable. However, some clients have special desires or needs—they might want an especially extravagant meal, for example, or might require kosher foods (see Appendix B for information on kosher service). Managers should decide in advance whether they will accommodate such requests. If managers are willing to let clients design their own menus, then salespeople must be knowledgeable enough about the operation to be able to point out to clients such details as the costs of the menu items they want and the projected effect their nonstandard menu will have on the speed of service. Therefore, allowing clients to customize menus or ask for special services may mean giving salespeople more training. In any case, salespeople should encourage clients to keep ease and speed of service in mind when choosing menu items for a custom menu, since all guests at most banquet or catered events should be served at about the same time.

Production concerns may limit options for customized menus. When a client requests melon balls, for example, the salesperson should point out how labor-intensive, and thus how expensive, their preparation will be. The salesperson might suggest using melon cubes or an entirely different option instead. Of course, before the salesperson makes any promises to a client, he or she should discuss the customized menu with the chef and others to ensure that it is practical from production, service, and financial standpoints.

If managers create a variety of tempting standard menus, clients are less likely to want to customize. When developing standard menus, managers should strive for a balance of colors, textures, shapes, and temperatures in addition to nutritional content. Today's clients tend to eat lighter and healthier, so items that are broiled, baked, or poached should be offered in addition to sautéed or fried dishes. Appetizers and desserts that are low in fat, cholesterol, and salt are also popular, but managers should watch out for the "food fads" trap; mesquite grilling, for example, died quickly in most areas of the United States. Instead, managers should investigate long-lasting trends in food and beverage preferences among the operation's target markets.

Managers and chefs at successful banquet and catering operations are always looking for new ideas for menus. There are many resources for menu ideas, including competitors' menus, suppliers, industry periodicals and other publications, and the Internet (see Exhibit 3).

When planning a standard menu, managers should select entrées first, then hot food accompaniments such as high-starch items and vegetables. The accompaniments' colors, textures, flavors, costs, and other factors must fit in with the entrées. After managers have selected hot foods, they should select salads. Finally, managers should choose desserts and beverages that complement the other food items.

When managers plan menus for banquets and catered events, they must take into consideration the resources available to the operation. Managers must recognize the following constraints as they plan menus:

- *Facility layout/design and equipment.* The operation must have the space and equipment to produce all of the items offered on the menus.
- *Available labor and skills.* Managers must have staff members with the skills required to produce and serve all of the items on the menu. If staff members do not have the skills to prepare certain menu items, managers must implement training programs, hire additional staff members, purchase pre-made or ready-prepared items, or reconsider including such items on the menu. (Often, banquet and catering managers employ part-time or temporary staff members to support full-time staff.)
- *Ingredients.* Before managers make final decisions about which menu items to include on banquet/catering menus, they should look at the standard recipes that production staff will use to prepare the menu items so they can make certain that all of the ingredients required by each recipe will be available during the life span of the menus. Managers should not choose menu items that require ingredients that are not always available, such as fresh seafood. If managers select items that require such seasonal ingredients as strawberries and asparagus, they must realize that they will have to pay premium prices for those ingredients during the off-season.

Exhibit 3 Sample Internet Source of Menu Ideas

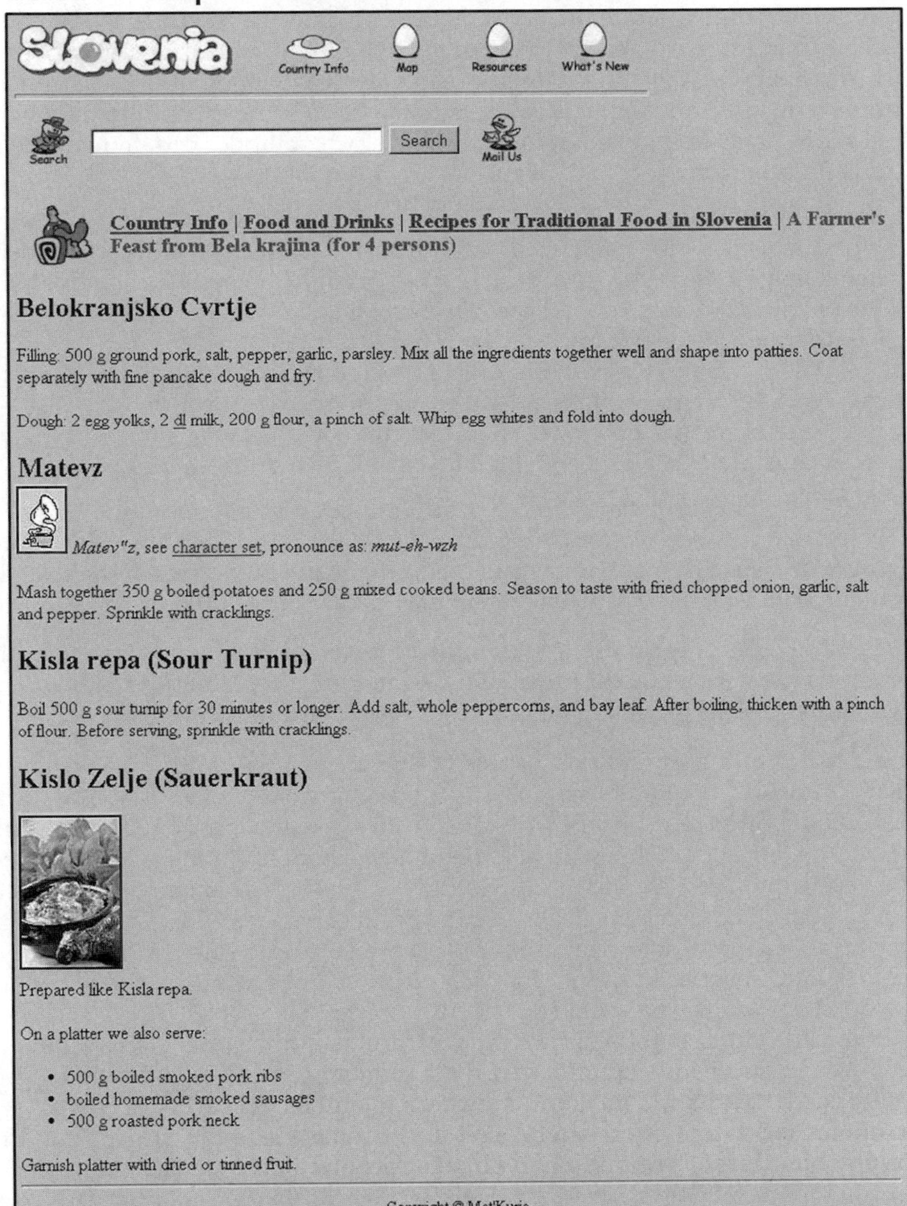

Slovenia

Country Info | Map | Resources | What's New

Search | Search | Mail Us

Country Info | Food and Drinks | Recipes for Traditional Food in Slovenia | A Farmer's Feast from Bela krajina (for 4 persons)

Belokranjsko Cvrtje

Filling: 500 g ground pork, salt, pepper, garlic, parsley. Mix all the ingredients together well and shape into patties. Coat separately with fine pancake dough and fry.

Dough: 2 egg yolks, 2 dl milk, 200 g flour, a pinch of salt. Whip egg whites and fold into dough.

Matevz

Matev"z, see character set, pronounce as: *mut-eh-wzh*

Mash together 350 g boiled potatoes and 250 g mixed cooked beans. Season to taste with fried chopped onion, garlic, salt and pepper. Sprinkle with cracklings.

Kisla repa (Sour Turnip)

Boil 500 g sour turnip for 30 minutes or longer. Add salt, whole peppercorns, and bay leaf. After boiling, thicken with a pinch of flour. Before serving, sprinkle with cracklings.

Kislo Zelje (Sauerkraut)

Prepared like Kisla repa.

On a platter we also serve:

- 500 g boiled smoked pork ribs
- boiled homemade smoked sausages
- 500 g roasted pork neck

Garnish platter with dried or tinned fruit.

Copyright © Mat'Kurja

The Internet is a marvelous source of ideas for theme events. This page (at http://www.ijs.si/slo/country/food/recipes/farmers-feast.html) offers recipes for a traditional Slovenian "Farmer's Feast from Bela Krajina." Users can click on the units in these recipes to access conversion tables; clicking on the phonograph icon allows a user to hear how a dish's name is pronounced. (Courtesy of Mat'Kurja, J. Stefan Institute, National Supercomputing Centre, Slovenia)

- *Quality levels.* Managers must know what level of quality their clients expect and how to incorporate quality requirements into the food items offered on the menu. If for any reason the operation cannot provide a certain proposed menu item with the desired degree of quality, managers should not include it on the menu. Staff members' skills and knowledge, the capabilities of the operation's food-holding equipment, and the availability of certain ingredients all affect the quality of food items.
- *Marketing implications.* Clients' preferences should be a primary concern when managers plan banquet and catering menus. Even though certain menu items may be especially practical to serve from the operation's standpoint, if the operation's clients do not care for them, managers should eliminate them from further consideration.

  Another marketing concern of menu planning deals with the meal period involved. Typically, breakfast and lunch menus focus on nutrition and fast service. Dinner menus, however, are designed to offer more leisurely dining because most dinner guests prefer a relaxed and festive experience.
- *Costs.* Food items that are expensive to produce and serve should be priced at levels that compensate for their high costs. Managers must know the costs of preparing specific menu items and their possible selling prices. If the cost of a menu item is excessive, management may decide not to offer it.

Most of these criteria also apply to menu items selected for inclusion on the operation's regular restaurant menus. However, these considerations are particularly important when planning menus for banquets or catered events.

Pricing. What prices should salespeople charge clients? Salespeople look to their managers for pricing guidelines. Unfortunately, many banquet and catering managers do not objectively consider the relationship between profit and price when they set up pricing guidelines. To help them arrive at appropriate prices, banquet and catering managers should create a budget or "profit plan" for the banquet and catering area. Once managers determine the profit they expect the banquet and catering area to generate, they can use the projected costs expressed in the budget to establish both a base selling price for each function and a standard against which they can measure financial performance.

Hypothetically, if the banquet and catering budget projected income of $1,000,000 and food costs of $250,000 for the year, managers could develop a simple base markup for food: banquet and catering food income ($1,000,000) divided by banquet and catering food costs ($250,000) equals a base markup of 4. In this example, managers or salespeople could sell functions for an average of 4 times the food costs, adjusting the pricing somewhat for each function according to what groups are willing to pay and what the competition charges. However, this is only an example; it is up to each operation to determine its own pricing system. Some managers may want to use a smaller markup to generate business during slow periods or a higher markup when they are busy, or (if the operation is part of a hotel) when the group under consideration shows low spending potential for the hotel's other revenue centers (such as guestrooms, lounges, and room service). Managers could use a menu markup factor to price both standard banquet menus and special menus developed for specific functions. Managers could also use similar procedures to price beverages.

In addition, managers can use budget information to monitor the financial performance of the banquet and catering area. Using figures from the previous example, managers can establish a standard (or target) food cost percentage as follows: budgeted food costs ($250,000) divided by budgeted banquet and catering income ($1,000,000) equals 25 percent. Managers can study monthly income statements knowing that the banquet and catering food percentage must be approximately 25 percent in order for the banquet and catering area to attain its budget goals.

Determining a menu's selling price is more difficult with buffets than with other service styles that allow the operation more control over guest selections. Some operations develop buffet pricing plans based on the anticipated number of guests for an event. For example, if an operation expects 200 guests at a buffet and it wants approximately $4,000 in revenue from the function, it might charge $20 per person for the buffet. Most food service operations allocate a specific percentage (usually 50 percent) of their buffet income to cover the buffet's food costs. Using this information, the menu planner can select food items for the buffet menu within the range of the operation's allowable costs. Other food service operations plan their buffet menus first, calculate their estimated costs, then set a selling price based on a markup factor. For example, if an operation felt that food costs should be 50 percent of the buffet income, the menu planner would first determine the per-person food costs of the buffet menu, then double that figure to determine the per-person selling price.

Of course, managers must consider other costs besides food costs when they are calculating prices. Labor is another big cost factor. Labor costs for a buffet include the cost of "runners" or other staff members that attend to the buffet throughout the meal period to keep it looking fresh and wholesome during service. Other buffet labor costs include staff time for setting the buffet up and breaking it down, and additional cleaning time required when some food preparation is done on the buffet line. Labor costs for table service are even higher than for buffet service.

The Offer

Once negotiations have reached the point where a salesperson makes an offer, the salesperson should draft a proposal letter for the client that summarizes the offer and includes preliminary prices. This written summary helps eliminate misunderstandings that could affect the success of the negotiations.

Salespeople must be very careful when negotiating with clients and writing up offers. The annual banquet business is very competitive. A cost difference of $2 or less per guest can make the difference between a client's choice of one banquet and catering operation over another. Some operations have lost the revenue from a dinner for 2,000 people over the price of a salad or side dish. When a banquet and catering operation loses a sale, managers or salespeople should record information about the loss, such as the estimated value of the event, the reasons for the loss, and the names of the client, the group, and the event. Careful study of information about lost business can help banquet and catering managers revise sales strategies to minimize future business losses.

Booking and Planning Events

Three documents play a primary role in booking and planning banquet and catering events: the **function book,** sometimes called the daily function room diary; the **contract** or **letter of agreement;** and the **function sheet,** which is sometimes called a banquet event order (BEO). Increasingly, these documents are computerized.

The Function Book

Managers and salespeople use the function book to determine if a certain room is available for a particular function at a particular time. The function book is also used to reserve a room after an event is sold so that no one else will commit the room for another function covering the same time period. The function book lists all of the operation's function space available for sale, and has a daily time log for each space to facilitate the recording of sold blocks of time. The function book's size and format depend on the size of the banquet and catering operation and the number of available function rooms. Some operations need less information in their function books than others, but entries typically include the group's name; the client's name, title, and phone number; the estimated attendance; the name of the event; and the type of event (for example, hospitality suite, lunch, or meeting). See Exhibit 4 for a sample screen from a computerized function book.

Typically, at operations without a computerized function book, one person is responsible for making entries into and otherwise maintaining the function book. This individual must notify banquet and catering managers and salespeople of any duplicate bookings or other conflicts concerning space in the book. Exhibit 5 is a sample **function room reservation form,** which is what a salesperson in an operation that uses a manual system would give the coordinator of the function book to tentatively or definitely reserve a room. At operations with computers, there is no need for a function book coordinator. Salespeople and managers can make entries into or consult the function book quickly and easily, since the book is computerized and accessible via their computer terminals. Because staff members can access the book instantaneously and simultaneously, there is less chance of selling the same room for the same time period to two different groups, and therefore less need for one-person oversight of entries.

Using a function book to accurately keep track of sold and unsold space is very important to the operation as well as to clients. Managers view function space as a potentially profitable commodity. Space that goes unsold represents lost income that can never be recuperated. That is why managers cannot afford to trust oral agreements with clients or make mistakes in making entries into the function book.

If negotiations are successful and a client decides to book with the operation, the function book coordinator (in operations with manual systems) or the salesperson (in operations with computerized systems) will officially enter the event into

Exhibit 4 Sample Computerized Function Book

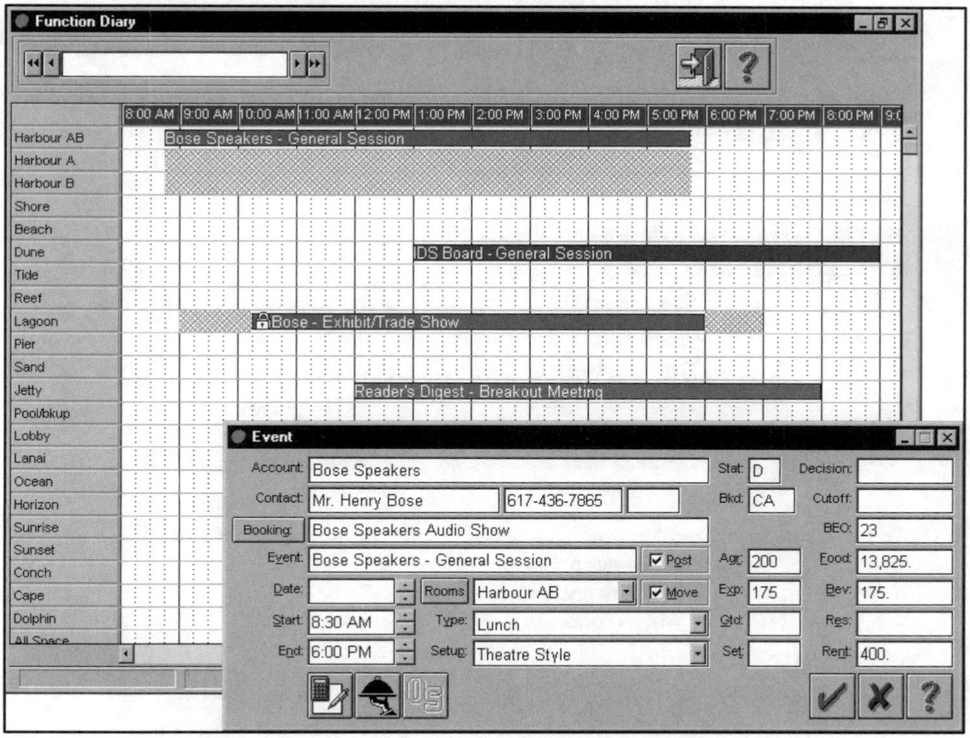

Source: Delphi 7/Newmarket Software Systems, Inc., Durham, New Hampshire.

the function book. A copy of the salesperson's proposal letter that the client has signed, a confirmation letter from the client, or a function room reservation form may serve as official authorization for the event. A confirmed reservation indicates to the salesperson that it is time to generate a contract or letter of agreement that outlines the client's and the operation's obligations.

Contracts or Letters of Agreement

As just mentioned, after the salesperson and client have agreed on terms, the salesperson should draw up a contract or letter of agreement. Every detail that the two parties have discussed and agreed upon should be covered in the contract.

It is important to estimate attendance figures at the time the contract is signed. However, if the event itself will be held months or even years later, the operation might not require an attendance estimate on the signing date. Some operations contact the client approximately two weeks before the event to get an update on the expected number of guests. Of course, if the event is large or requires special purchases, the operation will make this inquiry a month or more in advance of the function; operations may also contact the client for attendance updates more and more frequently as the date of the function approaches. In some cases (such as with

Exhibit 5 Sample Function Room Reservation Form

RMI

EXAMPLE

TIME: 2:35 P.M. SALES MANAGER: SS

DATE: 3/9/XX

CATERING INQUIRY

ORGANIZATION: Carter/Hale Wedding

ADDRESS: 1414 E. 14th St., Anywhere STATE: AZ ZIP: 81414

NAME: Mrs. Andrew Hale PHONE: 262-2626

TITLE: Mother of the Bride

BUSINESS POTENTIAL

TYPE OF FUNCTION: Wedding Reception TIME: 7 P.M.–12:30 A.M.

NO. OF PERSONS: 175 DATE: 8/22/XX

ALTERNATIVE DATE: None

GUEST ROOMS: 5 ROOM RATE: (current rack)

Have you ever used the Ramada Anywhere?
Where are/were functions held? No, but neighbor had her reception here last year

---

ACTION: X TENTATIVE BOOKING
____ DEFINITE BOOKING
____ FUTURE BOOKING

MENU ACTION:

TO BE MAILED: YES X NO ____ MENU: Wedding package

OTHER: ____

FOLLOW-UP BY: 3/18 HOLD SPACE UNTIL: 4/9

REPORT ON FOLLOW-UP—LOST DUE TO (check one)

SPACE RELEASE POLICY ____

PRICE ____ NO SPACE ____ SPACE NOT SATISFACTORY (reason below)

OTHER ____

NO EXPLANATION GIVEN ____

CHECK LIST

ENCLOSURES REQUIRED FOR LETTER(S) CHECKED-OFF:

BUSINESS CARD	X
CATERING MENU BROCHURE	X
MENU PRICE LIST ONLY	
LETTER	X
CREDIT APPLICATION	
RACK BROCHURE	
AIRPORT TRANSPORTATION BROCHURE	
A/V SHEET	
WEDDING INFORMATION	X

Catering Administration Manual

Source: James R. Abbey, *Hospitality Sales and Advertising,* Third Edition (Lansing, Mich.: Educational Institute of the American Hotel & Motel Association, 1998), p. 310.

conventions, which have optional attendance), ticket sales fluctuate so much from the original proposal that the group may need a larger or smaller room than was originally booked. On a date that is a certain number of days or weeks before the event and is specified in the contract (two days before the event for small-scale events is typical), the client must state the final number of attendees that are expected. This number is the **guarantee.**

A food service operation may apply a variance percentage to guarantees. For example, if the client guarantees an attendance of 240 guests, the operation might allow a 5 percent variance; since 5 percent of 240 is 12, the client would have to pay for at least 228 guests and at most 252, and the operation would prepare portions and set places for a maximum of 252 guests. Of course, if the menu is unusual or difficult to prepare, or if the estimated attendance is large, the variance percentage may be smaller. The larger the estimated attendance, the smaller the percentage of guests over the guarantee for which the operation should prepare. If an operation uses a 5 percent variance for an estimated attendance of 240, for example, it might prepare for only 3 percent over the guarantee for groups of 350 or more.

Unless the food service operation receives satisfactory credit references from the client, the contract often requires the client to pay a specific portion—as much as 100 percent—of the estimated cost of the function at least two weeks in advance of the event's date; clients usually pay any remaining balance within 30 days after the event. Food service operations generally reserve the right to cancel an event if the client has not established proper credit or made the required advance payment.

The contract must indicate the exact products and services that will be provided to the client's group. The food, beverages, labor, and other direct costs incurred to produce and serve the items required by the contract are included in the total price the operation charges for the event, as are rental charges (if any) for the function rooms. Some operations charge clients a room rental fee if the cost of the event does not exceed a specific amount; others require a room rental payment from clients whose events do not include dinner. Typically, the following services are included in room rental rates:

1. Setup labor for normal meetings (tables, chairs, tablecloths, ice water, and ashtrays)
2. Movement of large furniture in the room to other locations
3. Removal of carpets
4. Public address system and microphones
5. Easels, chart boards, movie screens, tables for projectors, and extension cords

The following services are often *not* included in room rental rates but are charged for separately:

1. Electrical layouts, plumbing, or other services for exhibits
2. Movie projectors, computers for PowerPoint presentations, VCRs, microphones, slide projectors, overhead projectors, and tape recorders (these items may be available from the operation for an additional charge, or the operation

might obtain them from an outside supplier and charge the client a fee that reflects a markup for the operation)

3. Table decorations
4. A dance floor
5. Service staff, including audiovisual, electrical, or other technicians

Once the contract is signed, the salesperson must generate a function sheet to inform the rest of the banquet and catering staff about the event.

Function Sheets

A function sheet lists all of the details that apply to the function—everything anyone at the food service operation might need to know about the function to prepare for it and provide service during it (see Exhibit 6 for a sample function sheet). The salesperson who books the event completes the function sheet, then makes as many copies of it as necessary to distribute to the banquet/catering office, the manager who will schedule staff for the event, the beverage department (which schedules staff and orders the necessary products), the accounting department (which prepares the billing), the convention service or floor manager (if the beverage and catering operation is part of a large hotel; the convention service or floor manager is the person in large hotels who arranges function room setups), the kitchen storeroom, the kitchen banquet staff, the kitchen's pantry area, the kitchen commissary, and the kitchen's bakeshop. Operations with computers may use software programs that make it easier to generate function sheets.

Coordination is critical to the success of any banquet or catered event. Typically, representatives from such areas as sales, accounting, and food and beverage will meet regularly to discuss the function sheets for upcoming banquets and catered events. The client may also be asked to attend these meetings. For very large and other special events, detailed planning begins months in advance. Some functions are annual events, so detailed planning that leads to a successful event can help secure repeat business the following year. (Managers should not assume that clients who choose their operation to host annual functions will stay with the operation forever. If their events are not serviced properly, clients will quickly take their business elsewhere.) Participants in event-planning meetings should study the function sheets closely to ensure that they clearly understand what is required for the event. This will help eliminate potential problems.

Getting Ready for Service

Getting ready for service for banquets and catered events includes setting up the function room(s); scheduling staff members; and preparing, plating, and storing banquet food.

Setting Up Function Rooms

The design and decor of function rooms, like the food and beverages that are served in them, can take many forms. A simple coffee break may be served in an

Exhibit 6 Sample Function Sheet

NOGA HILTON GENÈVE

BANQUETING DEPARTEMENT

Address

Name of the client:

INFORMATION BOARD

Date:

Master N°:

Telex:

Telephone:

Reservation N°:

Client:

Time	Type of Function	Rooms	N° Pers. guaranteed

MENU: .... Fr.

CONFERENCE SET UP .... Fr.

Room rental ....

Table set up ....

School / Cinema Style ....

Minerals ....

Writing pads / pencils ....

Flip chart ....

Head table .... pers. ....

Stage ....

Speaker desk ....

Welcome desk ....

LUNCH / DINNER

Table set up ....

Host table .... pers. ....

Candlesticks ....

Table numbers ....

Stage ....

Dance floor ....

ORCHESTRA by hotel ....

by client ....

Police authorization by hotel .... h. ....

by client .... h. ....

TECHNICAL EQUIPMENT

Video ....

Screen ....

Overhead projector ....

Film / Slide Projector ....

Large / small control center ....

Telephone ....

Microphone ....

Technician from .... to ....

COFFEE BREAK .... Fr.

....

....

Croissant .... Cake ....

BAR / APERITIF

Chips, peanuts, olives ....

International bar ....

Simple bar (without whisky, gin, wodka) ....

LUNCH / DINNER .... Fr.

Minerals ....

Wines ....

Liquors ....

Cigars ....

Drinks ....

MENUS

Simple print by our self ....

Double print by our self ....

Print by client ....

Title: ....

....

FLORAL DECORATIONS

Round and long terrine ....

Arrangement ....

Green plant ....

By the client ....

WARDROBE ROOM

Stander ....

.... personne(s) ....

NH 6206

IMPORTANT: SIGNATURE AND CONDITIONS ON THE REVERSE SIDE OF THIS PAGE

Courtesy of Noga Hilton Genève, Geneva, Switzerland

undecorated, themeless room, while an elaborate reception featuring foods from around the world may be served in a function room that has complex decorations to fit the theme. The type of function room chosen and how it is decorated are largely dictated by the needs and expectations of the client.

Frequently, managers come up with creative layouts for function rooms to help setup crews carry out instructions on the function sheet. Some clients have strong preferences about the layout of function rooms, and those might be expressed in unusual or creative layouts as well. Managers should carefully plan the location of such room elements as bars, food buffet stations, ice carvings, garden and tree decorations, and stages for speakers or entertainers. The location of these elements affects the guests' experiences in the room. The need for staff members to pay close attention to the details listed on the function sheet and illustrated on the layout is just as important for small events as it is for large, elaborate events.

Adequate space for display tables, guest tables, and other room elements (for example, stages and lecterns) is an important setup consideration for banquets and catered events. Crowded, hot rooms make for an unpleasant dining experience. Adequate space also allows for more efficient movement of inventory and people.

The client is usually responsible for reviewing any seating charts that the event may require. However, the manager can assist the client with that task and indicate the staff's preferences regarding seating arrangements.

As noted earlier, Exhibit 1 portrays several commonly used function room setups. Procedures for setting up function rooms vary according to the needs of the client and his or her group. The following is a partial list of activities and items that might be involved in setting up a function room:

1. Place runways, carpets, and pianos.
2. Place dinner tables, meeting tables, and head tables.
3. Place chairs, sofas, and other seats.
4. Place bars, buffets, and cake tables.
5. Place the registration, gift, and display tables.
6. Place the video/movie screen, projector table, projector, and extension cords.
7. Place chalkboards, easels, and any other display equipment.
8. Place microphones, lecterns, and flags.
9. Place linens, ashtrays, sugar bowls, salt and pepper shakers, and other tabletop items (see Exhibit 7 for one place-setting option).
10. Place cakes, candle holders, fountains, flowers, and decorations.
11. Place table numbers on each table, if necessary.

Because guests at banquets and catered events must be served quickly, service stations should be set up to allow for maximum staff efficiency. Equipment requirements vary with the type of function and the menu, but function-room service stations may have the following:

- Microwave ovens

Exhibit 7 Sample Place Setting

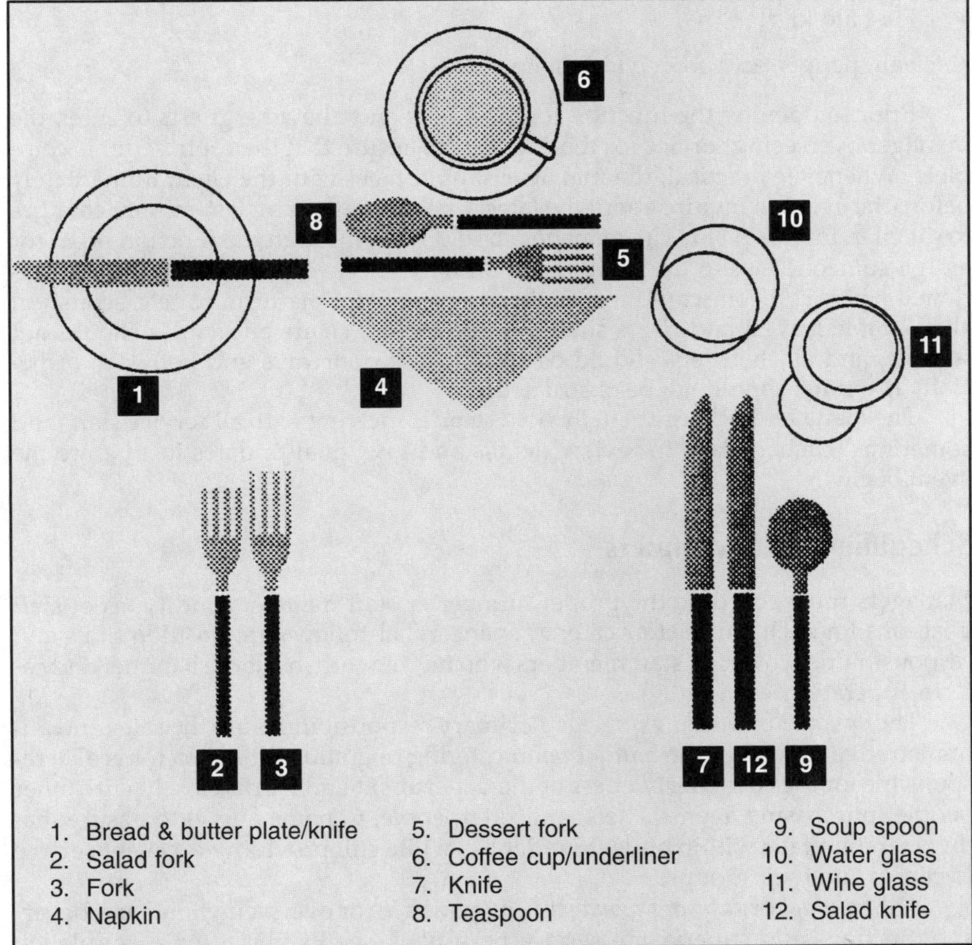

The banquet or catering manager will lay out a sample setting for service staff members to follow during setup. A typical place setting is shown here. Whatever setting is used, staff members must be consistent and pay attention to detail. Source: Adapted from the *Better Banquets: Basic Service Skills* video (East Lansing, Mich.: Educational Institute of the American Hotel & Motel Association, 1997).

- Flatware
- Glassware
- Water, coffee, and tea
- Cream, sugar, and stirrers
- Placemats and napery
- Candles, flowers, or other table decorations

- Matches or lighters
- First aid kits
- Salt, pepper, and other condiments

Prior to opening the function room's doors and allowing guests to enter, the manager overseeing service for the event must ensure that the room setup is complete. Whenever practical, the manager should meet with the client immediately before the event to inquire about the latest guest count or any last-minute changes to the plan for the event. The manager should walk through the function room (or assign someone else to do so) to make a safety check. No cords should be positioned where someone could trip on them; supports for platform panels, acoustical shells, table leaves, and risers should all be secure; chairs and tables should not wobble, and all their legs should be sturdy; and doorways and hallways (especially fire exits) should not be obstructed.

The manager in charge usually holds a brief meeting with all service staff (and sometimes kitchen staff) to review details and give final updates just before the event begins.

Scheduling Staff Members

Managers must schedule the proper number of staff members and types of staff positions for each banquet or catered event. What follows are position titles and responsibilities covering staff members who might work in a large banquet and catering operation.

The *banquet* or *catering director's* primary responsibilities are the sales and administrative aspects of the banquet and catering operation. The director is also responsible for the cost-effectiveness of the department and works closely with other people (purchasing agents, chefs, and salespeople, to name a few) to ensure that the operation falls within budget guidelines while still providing excellent service to clients and their groups.

The *banquet* or *catering manager* is responsible for overseeing food and beverage functions and supervising service personnel (see Exhibit 8 for a sample job description for a catering manager). He or she may be directly involved in setting up, cleaning up, and breaking down function rooms (at large convention hotels, however, setup duties are often handled by a convention service manager, head houseperson, or floor manager). Banquet or catering managers also schedule personnel, prepare payrolls, and work with the banquet or catering director on special functions.

Salespeople actively solicit business and follow up on written, telephone, and walk-in inquiries. Salespeople must know the proper procedures to follow to develop leads, process paperwork for an account, and follow up with clients after their functions. Knowledge of what types of business to book and when is also important. For example, hotel catering salespeople should avoid booking a social function such as a bridge tournament luncheon in the ballroom on a weekday. Such a booking could prevent someone from booking a four-day corporate meeting with rooms business and breakfast, lunch, and dinner business each of the four days.

Exhibit 8 Sample Job Description: Catering Manager

1. *Basic Function*

   To service all phases of group meeting or banquet functions; coordinate these activities on a daily basis; assist clients in program planning and menu selection; solicit local group catering business.

2. *General Responsibility*

   To maintain the services and reputation of Doubletree and act as a management representative to group clients.

3. *Specific Responsibilities*

   a. To maintain the function book and coordinate the booking of all meeting space with the sales department.

   b. To solicit local food and beverage functions.

   c. To coordinate with all group-meeting or banquet planners their specific group requirements with the services and facilities offered.

   d. To confirm all details relative to group functions with meeting or banquet planners.

   e. To distribute to the necessary inter-hotel departments detailed information relative to group activities.

   f. To supervise and coordinate all phases of catering, hiring, and training programs.

   g. To supervise and coordinate daily operation of meeting/banquet setups and service.

   h. To assist in menu planning, preparation, and pricing.

   i. To assist in referrals to the sales department and in booking group activities.

   j. To set up and maintain catering files.

   k. To be responsive to group requests or needs while in the hotel.

   l. To work toward achieving Annual Plan figures relating to the catering department (revenues, labor percentages, average checks, covers, etc.)

   m. To handle all scheduling and coverage for the servicing of catering functions.

4. *Organizational Relationship and Authority*

   Is directly responsible and accountable to the food and beverage manager. Responsible for coordination with kitchen, catering service personnel, and accounting.

This is the job description used for catering managers at Doubletree Hotels. (Courtesy of Doubletree, Inc.)

Clerical staff members maintain the paperwork generated by salespeople, handle routine inquiries, and follow up on accounts. In large properties, an administrative assistant may help the director with administrative duties or manage the banquet/catering office.

The *function book coordinator* (in operations that use a manual booking system) is the single person who makes entries into the function book and is responsible for ensuring their accuracy. (In operations that don't have this position, the banquet and catering director or manager is usually responsible for the function book.)

Service personnel serve food and beverages, set up function rooms, and maintain banquet areas and equipment. Service personnel include hosts or captains, food servers, buspersons, and housepersons or setup crews. During events, food servers and buspersons are either supervised directly by the banquet or catering manager or by a banquet host or captain. (Operations that can simultaneously host several groups are more likely to have mid-level supervisors such as hosts and captains.)

Based on the number of special functions scheduled each day, the banquet/catering director or manager must schedule staff members to set up and break down function rooms, as well as schedule service staff to perform all of the guest-contact service and related tasks involved in the events themselves.

The number of servers and other personnel that are scheduled for an event varies from operation to operation and from event to event. Among top private clubs, for example, the ratio seems to be one server for every 10 to 15 guests. A greater than usual number of servers and other personnel will also be needed for an event if a client asks for special services. **Synchronized service,** for example, requires the entire service staff to enter the function room through one set of doors to serve each course. In unison and using precise movements, servers place the courses in front of guests. Often wine service is also synchronized. Obviously, this style of banquet service requires a great deal of training, rehearsal, skill, and additional staff.

Training. The pressures inherent whenever food is served to guests are greater when large numbers of guests must be served in a relatively short period of time. Under these circumstances, mistakes can happen very easily if staff members are not well trained in service procedures.

Training staff members to be banquet servers requires that trainers have a fundamental knowledge of all service styles and skills that might be used at events that the operation hosts. Rehearsals in which service actions are repeated a number of times are often the best way to help servers internalize service styles and skills. Special styles of service as well as the details of the "script" (the function sheet) should be reviewed during practice sessions. Banquet servers at the Mirage Hotel in Las Vegas, Nevada, are required to participate in refresher training courses twice each year. The goal of training is to present consistent service styles to guests at banquets and catered events.

Banquet and catering service personnel also must be trained to realize that, as guest-contact staff members, they give guests first and last impressions of the operation. In successful banquet and catering operations, staff members follow the operation's service philosophy.

Some guests at banquet and catered events may have unique service needs. For example, international groups may have unique cultural customs that cannot be ignored. Business banquets are popular in Chinese culture; they end promptly after the host rises and gives a toast. Children from Asian countries such as Thailand and India should never be patted on the head—a common American way to show friendliness, but one that should be avoided in this instance—because in certain Asian countries the head is considered sacred and should never be touched. Even interpretations of facial expressions and hand gestures differ from culture to culture. Staff members who will serve guests at international functions should be trained to be sensitive to the guests' customs.

(Managers must be on their toes as well. In China, for example, someone named "Liang Cheng-wu" should be addressed as "Mr. Liang"; "Cheng-wu" is a compound of the man's first and middle names and it would be socially incorrect to use it. Some international clients may present a small gift to the banquet or catering manager, who should be prepared to give a modest gift in return.)

If the banquet and catering operation is part of a bigger food service operation, it is wise to cross-train dining area staff members in banquet and catering service procedures. Then, if a function room needs to be set up in a hurry, properly trained dining area staff members can help the banquet and catering staff.

Preparing, Plating, and Storing Food

Banquet and catering managers must be sensitive to the concerns of the chef and other personnel who prepare food for an event. Managers must never overlook the fact that the chef should be an integral member of the planning team. When the input of the chef and other food production staff members is used to develop menus for banquets and catered events, few, if any, production problems should arise when the staff prepares these menus.

Some banquet and catering operations that handle events with large numbers of guests use an automated assembly line to portion meals. More commonly, however, operations use a manual plating process. Exhibit 9 shows one arrangement of people, equipment, and supplies that can be used to plate and set up one kind of meal. As illustrated in Exhibit 9, one person carves and places roast beef slices on plates, then passes (slides) the plates along the table to a second staff member, who portions the green beans almandine. A third staff member portions the potatoes au gratin and slides the plates across the table to a fourth staff member, who places sauce on the meat. A fifth staff member puts covers on the plates and loads the plates onto a mobile cart. Using this system, five staff members can plate food for 300 people in approximately 45 minutes. (If the client wants the meal to be served in less time, a second plating line could be set up.) If the client had requested a plate garnish, the process would have required another staff member to provide it.

In banquet and catering service, time and temperature control for food is critical. It is virtually impossible to prepare hundreds of individual plates as service progresses. Therefore, foods are usually preplated for large banquets or catered events and then stored hot or cold in holding cabinets. Refrigerated mobile storage units must maintain internal product temperatures of 41°F (5°C) or less; mobile hot storage cabinets must maintain a minimum internal product temperature of 140°F

Exhibit 9 Possible Setup for Plating Banquet and Catered-Event Meals

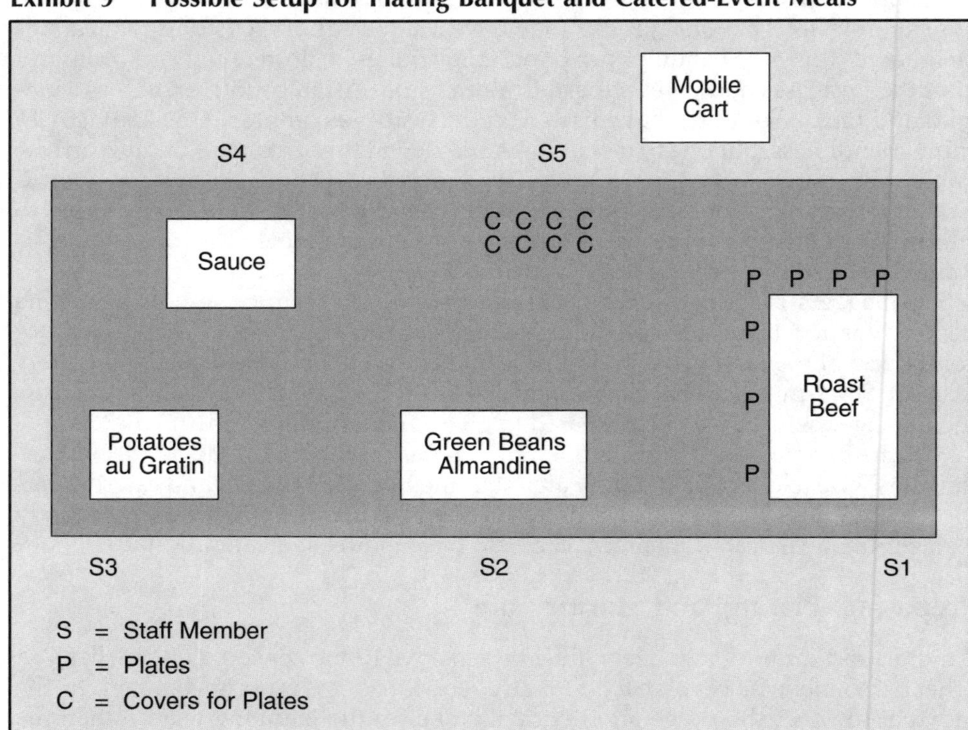

(60°C). This keeps held food out of the temperature danger zone (TDZ) of 41°F (5°C) to 140°F (60°C). (Because the TDZ may be defined slightly differently in various areas of the country, managers should check with local and state health authorities to make sure they are in compliance with all food safety codes.)

For holding cold products, ice is usually an acceptable means of maintaining chilled temperatures. However, food must not be directly exposed to ice or melted water; instead, it must be held in bowls or containers embedded in the ice.

Hot food can be kept hot in a number of ways. Chafing dishes powered by electricity or canned heat are usually used to hold hot foods on a buffet table. Large roasts, hams, and turkeys that are to be carved in the function room should be displayed under infrared heat lamps. Sneeze guards or other equipment to prevent contamination of displayed food may be required by local or regional health regulations.

Outdoor service presents unique holding challenges. Food must be protected from dust and other contaminates, so staff members may need to use special coverings for food and beverage products to protect them between production and service. Outdoor food preparation involves other holding problems as well (such as maintaining foods at proper temperatures). It is a good idea to check with state or local authorities for laws governing the outdoor cooking and serving of food before planning such functions.

Delivering Service

Because of all the planning and other preparatory work that goes into every banquet or catered event, you might think that a banquet or catering manager would only need to supervise staff members from a distance during the event itself. In reality, last-minute issues and challenges often occupy the manager throughout an event. Because challenges arise, the manager in charge should either be present at the event or easy to reach, both by staff members and the client. The following are examples of challenges that managers and staff members may face just before or during an event:

- Supply shortages
- Staff members who phone in sick or become ill during the event
- The arrival of an unexpectedly large number of extra guests
- Equipment malfunctions
- Guests who need assistance to operate equipment
- Conflicts between staff members
- Large or dangerous spills
- Injuries, choking, and other medical emergencies
- Angry guests
- Inebriated guests
- Speakers or entertainers who show up late or not at all
- Power outages
- Fire alarms
- Natural disasters

Wise managers have contingency plans in place for the most common challenges.

Food Service

If a client wants table service at his or her event, it is usually one of four common types:

- **Plate** or American service—A service style in which fully cooked menu items are individually portioned, plated, and garnished in the kitchen, then carried to each guest directly.
- **Family-style** or English service—A service style in which servers take food on large platters or in large bowls from the kitchen and deliver it to guest tables; guests at each table then pass the food around their table, serving themselves.
- **Cart** or French service—An elaborate service style in which menu items are prepared on a cart beside guest tables by specially trained staff members.

- **Platter** or Russian service—A service style that requires servers to take platters of fully cooked food to tables, present the food for the guests' approval, then plate the food from the platters at tableside and serve it to the guests.

In the United States, the guests at most banquets featuring table service are served using the plate service style. With plate service, a server's main responsibility is to deliver the plated courses to the guests as quickly and efficiently as possible. In contrast, the Opryland Hotel in Nashville, Tennessee, likes to offer family-style service as an option for banquets and catered events. One Easter, for example, the hotel's banquet operation staged "Easter in Song and Story," including a Passion play and a banquet. The hotel reported that guests liked the family-style service because it was interactive and guests could select as much of an item as they wanted.

Sometimes a client prefers buffet service rather than table service. By attractively arranging a seemingly endless array of food, a food service operation can delight guests who enjoy being able to choose whatever they like in the quantities they prefer. Buffet service also provides staff members with the opportunity to create food displays and showpieces. Ice carvings, tallow (fat) sculptures, flowers, fruit, or other decorations often enhance a buffet's presentation. Buffets may also offer novelty foods chosen to fit the theme of the buffet (e.g., Rocky Mountain oysters for a Western theme).

Chef Josef in Agawam, Massachusetts, uses **action stations** instead of a traditional buffet food display. These action stations feature international cuisine choices such as Cajun, Chinese, Italian, Mexican, or Western; a chef at each station prepares guests' selections to order. For example, the Italian station features angel hair pasta with sun-dried tomatoes and pine nuts, fettuccine à la scampi, pesto pasta, and seafood and vegetable pasta primavera. The Mexican station gives guests choices of fajitas prepared to order and a variety of burritos, nachos, and tacos.

Sometimes events feature a combination of table service and a buffet—the appetizers are displayed in a buffet during the cocktail hour and the rest of the meal is provided via table service, for example, or servers deliver beverages, bread and butter, and desserts directly to guest tables but the guests help themselves to main-course items from a buffet.

Whether the food is served through table service, a buffet, or a combination of the two, managers in the banquet and catering area must see to it that service personnel follow the operation's rules for serving food properly and graciously. A list of basic service rules for banquets or catered events that feature plate service can be found in Exhibit 10. Service rules vary from operation to operation, but all are founded on the basic principle that guests should be given an enjoyable service experience and inconvenienced as little as possible.

Beverage Service

Managers must carefully plan procedures for providing beverage service to guests at banquets and catered events. Just as lounges and bars must do, banquet and catering operations must observe liquor laws. Age limits and legal hours for

Exhibit 10 General Service Rules for Banquet and Catered-Event Service

1. All servers must carry a napkin or side towel at all times.
2. All food must enter the room on a tray with a cart unless otherwise specified.
3. All liquids (hot or cold) must be on trays with spouts facing inward.
4. When placing plates in front of guests, servers must place them so that the operation's logo is at the top.
5. Used plates, glasses, and flatware must leave on properly stacked trays.
6. Leftover foods must be placed on a tray and set under the cart.
7. Servers should always pick up glasses by the base, flatware by the handle, and plates by the rim.
8. Serve all plated food from the right. Serve anything that is actually passed by the guests from the left.
9. Serve all beverages from the right.
10. Serve the head table first.
11. Serve ladies first.
12. Clear all dishes and glasses from the right.
13. Do not stack dishes or scrape plates in front of guests.
14. Place appetizers on the tables before service begins, unless they are hot items that must be served after the guests are seated.
15. Set salads on tables unless they are served as a separate course.
16. Clear the empty appetizer plates.
17. Serve the main course.
18. Serve coffee and/or wine.
19. Serve more water if needed.
20. Change ashtrays if needed.
21. Clear entrée plates, bread and butter plates, butter, melba toast, rolls, salt and pepper, and any flatware not needed for dessert.
22. Serve the dessert.
23. Serve more coffee if needed.
24. Clear dessert plates and any empty wine glasses and coffee cups. Remove napkins. If a meeting follows food and beverage service, leave water glasses and partially filled coffee cups on the table.

beverage service are among the most important beverage laws that affect banquet and catering operations. In some localities, laws may require clients to obtain permits to serve alcoholic beverages to private groups in function rooms during certain hours. If this is the case, banquet/catering managers or salespeople must make this known to clients and tell them how to obtain the special approvals or permits. In addition, managers may need to curtail the service of alcoholic beverages on election days in some states.

The banquet and catering operation is responsible for preventing underage drinking in its function rooms; the operation's managers cannot delegate this responsibility to clients. Because of this, it is wise for a banquet or catering manager to closely monitor beverage service when underage guests attend an event.

Many operations use one or a combination of the following popular beverage plans to provide beverage service at banquets or catered events.

Cash Bar. At a **cash bar,** guests pay cash to the bartender or purchase tickets from a cashier to pay for drinks prepared by the bartender. With a ticket system, the cashier may be issued numbered tickets of various colors, which represent different drink prices. Guests pay the cashier for the drinks they want and are given tickets of the appropriate colors that they can present to the bartender. The banquet/catering manager or salesperson generally specifies the drink prices in the contract; the prices can be the same as or different from normal selling prices. Frequently, managers or salespeople will reduce beverage prices from the normal lounge rates in order to attract group business.

Host Bar: Charge by the Drink. A **host bar** that charges the host by the drink uses a system to keep track of the number of each type of drink served (through tickets turned over to the bartender by guests, transactions recorded by a point-of-sale system, or marks on a tally sheet). Guests do not pay anything. Managers will frequently reduce the prices of the drinks from the normal charges in order to obtain the host's business.

Host Bar: Charge by the Bottle. This plan involves charging for beverages consumed on the basis of the number of bottles used or opened. The difference between the number of bottles of each type of liquor, beer, or wine in the beginning inventory and ending inventory at the function room's portable bar represents the number of bottles used. An agreed-upon price for each bottle opened is assessed to the host (who is, in effect, purchasing the beverages that remain in open bottles but were not consumed by guests).

Host Bar: Charge by the Hour. This pricing plan charges hosts a fixed beverage fee per person per hour. This plan involves estimating the number of drinks guests will consume each hour. While estimates are not easy to make that will apply to all groups (health- or weight-conscious groups will probably consume less than fraternities, for example), a rule of thumb used by some banquet and catering managers is three drinks per person during the first hour, two the second, and one-and-a-half the third. Managers who want to price drinks for special events on a per-person, per-hour basis can use this formula to estimate the number of drinks each person will consume during the event. They must then multiply the number of drinks per person by an established drink charge to arrive at the hourly drink charge per person. As managers use the hourly charge system, they should maintain their own statistics on consumption; these statistics can assist them in more accurately setting hourly charges for future events.

Wine Service. When banquets or catered events involve wine service, service staff may circulate with bottles of several wines (red and white, dry and semi-dry) so that they can offer guests a choice. Of course, these staff members must be trained to serve wine properly. (So that staff members will be knowledgeable about the wines they serve, managers should tell them about the wines during the briefing prior to the event.) Other operations set up a portable bar in a nearby area so that bartenders can prepare glasses of wine (and other drinks) as needed.

Wines that should be chilled before service might be handled in one of the following ways:

- The bottles might be moved to refrigerators in the banquet serving kitchens close to the time of service.
- The bottles might be maintained for small groups using ice in totes or other containers.
- The bottles might be chilled in remote walk-ins and quickly transported to the banquet site when they are needed.

Portable beverage service equipment makes the tasks of providing beverages at banquets and catered events much easier. Most portable equipment is on wheels; it can be stored in remote areas and wheeled to the point of use as needed.

Protocol for Special Banquets and Catered Events

Every banquet or catered event is special to the guests who attend it, and banquet and catering staff members must always be courteous and exercise common sense to make the guests' experiences as enjoyable as possible. However, there are some "special" banquets and catered events in which staff members must also understand **protocol**—the formal rules of etiquette used for ceremonies of state, military functions, and other special events.

While the details of protocol are beyond the scope of this chapter, banquet and catering managers should be aware that there are rules that dictate the proper way to do things when very special guests are served. Managers and service personnel who will come in direct contact with special guests must understand and be able to practice protocol. The following examples illustrate the types of issues that can come up.

At formal events, the seat of honor at the head table is to the right of the host. The second seat of honor is to the left of the host. If another seat of honor is required, it is the second seat on the right of the host. The rest of the seats at the head table should be allocated according to the rank or prominence of the guests. These guests should be assigned seats by alternating from the right to the left of the host out from the center of the head table (see Exhibit 11).

Flag display is also important in protocol. In the United States, for example, at a cocktail party, a standing gathering, or an event with theater seating for which flags must be positioned before the guests arrive, the U.S. flag is placed on the left side of the front of the room, as viewed from the dining area. If a five-place arched flag stand is used, the U.S. flag takes the center (highest) position. Other flags are placed to the left and right of the U.S. flag in order of importance: the second most important flag is placed in the hole immediately to the left of the U.S. flag, from the audience's perspective; the third most important flag goes immediately to the right

Exhibit 11 Protocol for Seating Guests at the Head Table

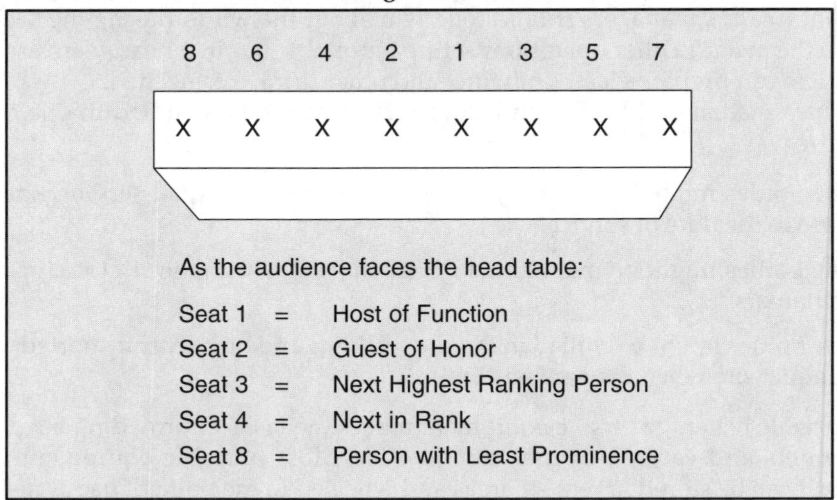

of the U.S. flag; and the next most important flag goes in the hole furthest to the left, leaving the hole furthest to the right for the least important flag.

When flags are used behind a podium, the national colors are placed on the physical right of the speaker as he or she addresses the audience. When displayed behind the speaker's platform without a pole, the flag must be flat against its display surface and must have its longest dimension parallel to the floor, directly behind and slightly above the podium.

Staff members should never use the flag of any country as a table cover, drape, rosette, or any other type of decoration. To decorate with bunting that has the national colors of the United States (red, white, and blue), staff members should place the color blue uppermost, then white, and finally red as the lowest of the three colors.

After Service

After the completion of food and beverage service at an event, the manager in charge must perform several after-service tasks. One such task is supervising staff members to ensure that they complete their clean-up and breakdown duties properly. Exhibit 12 is a checklist for many of these required tasks. Staff members must clean up the function room(s) and break down temporary structures (such as a dance floor or stage). Managers must evaluate how well the operation handled the banquet or catered event. The experience gained from each event can help with the planning of other events.

During the cleanup and breakdown of the function room(s), control efforts must occur to ensure that both the client and the operation attain the goals established for the event. Guest comments must also be sought to provide guest input into continuous quality improvement.

Exhibit 12 Checklist for Post-Event Managerial Duties

Banquet/Catered Event

- ☐ Clear all tables of china, glass, flatware, and ashtrays.
- ☐ Remove all linens.
- ☐ Straighten legs on all tables.
- ☐ Rearrange all chairs around tables neatly.
- ☐ Store salt and pepper shakers, sugar bowls, ashtrays, water pitchers, and other tabletop items.
- ☐ Clear all remaining carts and lock them.
- ☐ Remove candles and any melted wax from candelabras and return to storage.
- ☐ Pour several pitchers of water into garbage cans in kitchen to prevent possible fire hazard.
- ☐ Check out with supervisor on duty.

Banquet/Catered Event Supervisor

- ☐ Supervise the banquet/catered event service staff.
- ☐ Turn off public address system.
- ☐ Collect microphones and cords and return to proper storage area(s).
- ☐ Collect projectors and other audiovisual equipment and return to storage.
- ☐ Search area for valuable items left behind.
- ☐ Check cloakroom and restroom areas.
- ☐ Secure any items found and turn them in to the Lost and Found the following day.
- ☐ Inspect for fire hazards.
- ☐ Turn off lights.
- ☐ Lock all doors. (If a band is moving out, remain until the move is completed).
- ☐ Leave written information regarding any maintenance problems or items helpful to the supervisor who will open the room the next day.
- ☐ Leave written information on the manager's desk regarding any guest complaints or serious staff-member relations problems.
- ☐ Lock, secure, and turn off lights and air conditioning units in all other function rooms.

Controls

Managers must establish systems of control for the food and beverages served in banquets and catered events.

Food Controls. Payments may or may not be collected from clients at the time of the banquet or catered event; the contract for each event specifies the payment terms that the operation and the client agreed upon. However, when the banquet actually occurs, the operation must count the number of guests served to determine if payment is due for guests served in excess of the original estimate.

How do managers determine how many guests were served? If a buffet is planned in which no one can go back for seconds and therefore guests only use one plate, managers can take a plate count. The number of plates on the buffet line at the beginning of service plus any plates that were put on the line during service minus the number of plates on the buffet line at the end of service equals the number of guests served.

At buffets where guests go through the line more than once or at table service events, the manager must personally count the number of guests served. Typically, the manager takes a count that he or she confirms through separate counts taken by other supervisors in charge of specific function room areas or through counts of meals served by individual food servers. Another way to take a count is to count the number of empty seats and subtract that number from the total number of chairs set up; this gives the manager the number of guests served. In some operations, the guests receive tickets from their host that they turn in either as they enter the function room or after they are seated.

At stand-up receptions, a representative of the operation might be stationed at the entrance of the reception area to count guests as they arrive. To avoid re-counting guests who leave and return, a ticket system could be used; the count of guests served would then be based on the number of tickets turned in.

At coffee breaks and similar functions, the price charged to the client usually is based on the volume of products used to set up the event, such as gallons of coffee or dozens of pastries. If, however, a coffee break's price is determined by the number of people served, a manager should count the number of guests seated in the meeting immediately before the start of coffee service.

The responsibility for determining the number of guests served, no matter what type of service or counting method is used, rests with the manager in charge of the event. Having more than one count performed is a good way to ensure accuracy. It is often a good idea to involve the client in the process of counting guests or supplies, too. Managers try to avoid disagreements over counts, and when the client monitors or is otherwise involved in determining the count, he or she is less likely to dispute it later.

Beverage Controls. Revenue control for beverages is just as important in managing cash bars at banquets and catered events as it is in managing dining and lounge areas. In some respects, however, managers can simplify the control procedures, since fewer kinds of alcoholic beverages are generally available at banquets and catered events. For example, if only two types of wine (house and call) are available, management can easily reconcile the amount of alcohol sold with the amount of income collected.

The amount of alcoholic beverages issued to a portable bar (both initially and during service) can be recorded on a form similar to the one in Exhibit 13. (Managers should remember to count partial bottles as whole bottles in the "Net Use" column on the far right if the payment plan is "charge by the bottle.") By conducting a beginning and an ending inventory, the amount of each product actually used can be determined. In a by-the-drink payment plan, the amount of income that the servers should have generated from a particular product can be determined by converting the figure in the farthest right column of Exhibit 13—"Net Use"—into

Exhibit 13 Portable Bar Setup Sheet

Function Order Number *1007-F* Number of People *25*

Name *Anne Helmstead* Date *5/2/XX*

Room *Blue* Time *5:00-6:00 P.M.*

Number of Bottles or Drinks

Name of Item	Size	Setup	Add'l.	Add'l.	Add'l.	Total	Returns			
							Full	Empty	Partial	Net Use
House Scotch	liter	*5*	*3*	*1*	*1*	*10*	*1*	*8*	*.5*	*8.5*
House Bourbon	liter	*3*	*1*			*4*	*1*	*3*	*0*	*3.0*
Call Scotch	liter									
Call Gin	liter									
Vodka	liter									

standard portion sizes and then converting that into the number of drinks sold (Exhibit 14 illustrates this process). The form works reasonably well when the same price for all drinks of one type (house or call) is charged. However, if different prices are charged for drinks that are of the same type but that have different amounts of spirits (e.g., a double), the average number of ounces of liquor per drink must first be calculated. The calculation must also be adjusted when different drinks have different amounts of the same ingredient. For example, a martini that contains two ounces of house gin might be sold for $5, while a gin and tonic that contains one-and-a-half ounces of house gin might be sold for $4.

You can see the difficulty in assessing standard income per bottle that arises in complex cases. Many managers resolve the problem by tracking drink sales, ounces used, and income generated in order to arrive at average rates that they can easily include in the calculation in Exhibit 14. The same process is used to reconcile the amount of beverage sold with the income generated by all other types of beverages listed on the setup sheet in Exhibit 13.

Guest Comments

After major functions, the client usually meets with the operation's managers to give feedback and to settle accounts as much as possible. After small functions, the

Exhibit 14 Sample Calculation of Potential Income

For Scotch:

8.5 liter bottles (Net amount used)	×	33.8 oz. per liter (Ounces/Bottle)	=	287.3 (Total oz. used)
287 (rounded) (Total ounces used)	÷	1.5 oz (Average portion size)	=	191.33 (number of drinks sold)
191 (rounded) (number of drinks sold)	×	$4.00 (Average sales price)	=	$764.00 (Potential income)

Typically, bartenders pour (measure) liquor on the basis of ounces; however, they purchase liquor bottles in metric units. Managers can calculate potential income from sales of a particular beverage as follows:

1. Calculate the number of ounces actually used. (In Exhibit 13, you will note that 8.5 one-liter bottles of scotch were used at the banquet. Since each liter contains 33.8 ounces, approximately 287 ounces of scotch were actually used.)
2. Determine the approximate number of drinks sold. (Divide the total ounces used by the portion size: 287 oz. ÷ 1.5 oz = approximately 191 drinks sold.)
3. Estimate the potential income. (Multiply the number of drinks sold by the selling price: 191 drinks × $4.00 selling price = $764).

review process may be more modest: the manager in charge may give the client an evaluation sheet and ask him or her to fill it out and return it. A telephone call to the client a day or two after the event provides the manager with an opportunity to thank the client and ask for additional feedback. This reinforces for the client the operation's commitment to guest service. It also helps communicate to clients that their future business is desired.

Using Feedback in Planning

Planning is a critical activity for banquets and catered events, and feedback about past events can help managers plan future events. Regardless of whether an operation holds a review meeting with the client after an event, managers should hold such a meeting with all staff members who were involved in providing service during the event. These meetings are particularly helpful when mistakes that guests noticed occurred. Such mistakes may happen again if managers do not take the time to review them and discuss possible solutions. Managers and staff should relay to each other any comments from guests or the client. This exchange should lead to action plans to correct problems that were mentioned most often by guests. Continuous quality improvement is the key to the development of a profitable and guest-pleasing banquet and catering operation.

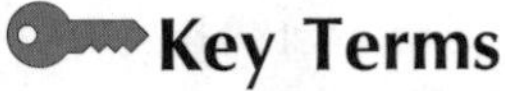

Key Terms

banquet and catering operation—An operation that sells and plans food and beverage functions for meetings and special events. As a hotel department, a department within the food and beverage division that arranges and plans food and beverage functions for (a) conventions and smaller functions, and (b) local events booked by the sales department.

breakout rooms—Small meeting rooms used when large group sessions divide into smaller ones for discussion and group work.

buffet—A typically large assortment of foods attractively arranged for self-service by guests.

cart service—A table service style in which specially trained staff members prepare menu items beside the guests' tables using a cart; the food is prepared and plated on the cart, then served to the guest. Also called French service.

cash bar—A beverage setup for a banquet or some other special event in which each guest pays for each drink as it is ordered. Also known as a C.O.D. bar or an à la carte bar.

contract—A document listing the services, space requirements, and products that the food service operation promises to provide the client and the client promises to pay for at an agreed-upon price; it becomes binding when it is signed by both parties. Sometimes called a letter of agreement.

cutoff date—The designated date when the client must either book or release the function room(s) being tentatively held for him or her.

familiarization ("fam") tour—A reduced-rate or complimentary trip or tour, designed to acquaint potential clients with the food service operation's products and services.

family-style service—A table service style in which servers take food on large platters or in large bowls from the kitchen and deliver it to guest tables; the guests at each table then pass the food around their table, serving themselves. Also called English service.

function book—The master control of all function space, broken down by function room and time of day.

function room reservation form—A form a salesperson submits to the function book coordinator to reserve or determine the availability of a certain function room for a certain event at a certain time. These forms are used at properties with manual booking systems.

function sheet—A document that includes all of the details about a function's requirements. Also called a banquet event order (BEO).

guarantee—Prior to an event, the figure the client gives the food service operation for the number of persons to be served. Payment is made on the basis of the guaranteed number or the total number actually served, whichever is greater.

host bar—A function-room bar setup where drinks are prepaid by the host. The price, agreed upon ahead of time, may be determined by the drink, by the bottle, or by the hour.

plate service—A table service style in which fully cooked menu items are individually produced, portioned, plated, and garnished in the kitchen, then carried to each guest directly. Also called American service.

platter service—A table service style in which servers carry platters of fully cooked food to the dining room and present them to guests for approval. Servers then set hot plates in front of each guest and place food from the platters onto the plates. Also called Russian service.

presentation book—A book of pictures, diagrams, menus, and other promotional materials that salespeople use to sell their operation's products and services to clients.

protocol—Sets of formal guidelines or rules for the conduct of business, dining, and entertaining.

sales blitz—A concentrated campaign of personal sales calls to prospects in a selected geographic area.

synchronized service—A type of service in which servers enter the function room through one set of doors to serve each course; they serve all of the tables in unison, using precise movements.

Review Questions

1. What should catering salespeople know about associations and corporate groups to effectively sell banquets and catered events to them?
2. What are the major records, documents, and forms used to book and plan banquets and catered events, and how is each used?
3. What are the types of table service that are commonly used in banquets and catered events?
4. What factors should banquet and catering managers keep in mind when developing standard menus?
5. What positions are typically found in a large banquet and catering operation?
6. What kinds of skills and knowledge do service personnel need to provide service during banquets and catered events?
7. What are some common beverage service payment options for banquets and catered events, and how do they work?
8. How do banquet and catering managers obtain and use feedback to improve operations?

Internet Sites

For more information, visit the following Internet sites. Remember that Internet addresses can change without notice.

CaterWare Inc.
http://www.caterware.com

The Catering Connection
http://www.caterconnect.com

Chef's Store
http://www.chefstore.com

Convene
http://www.pcma.org/pub_convene.htm

Cuisine
http://www.cuisine.com

CuisineNet
http://www.cuisinenet.com

Delphi/NewMarket Software
http://www.newsoft.com

Food Net
http://www.foodnet.com

Food Network
http://www.foodtv.com

Foodwine
http://www.foodwine.com

Hilton Hotels
http://www.hilton.com

Hyatt Hotels and Resorts
http://www.hyatt.com

Internet Food Channel
http://www.foodchannel.com

Marriott International
http://www.marriott.com

Meeting News
http://www.meetingnews.com

Meeting Professionals International (MPI)
http://www.mpiweb.org

Meetings and Conventions
http://www.meetings-conventions.com

Professional Convention Management Association (PCMA)
http://www.pcma.org

Sheraton Hotels
http://www.sheraton.com

Successful Meetings
http://www.successmtgs.com

Virtual Vineyards
http://www.virtualvin.com

Westin Hotels
http://www.westin.com

References

Abbey, James R. *Hospitality Sales and Advertising,* Third Edition. Lansing, Mich.: Educational Institute of the American Hotel & Motel Association, 1998.

Astroff, Milton T., and James R. Abbey. *Convention Management and Service,* Fifth Edition. Lansing, Mich.: Educational Institute of the American Hotel & Motel Association; and Cranbury, N.J.: Waterbury Press, 1998.

Buss, Dale. "Melting Pot of Gold." *Restaurant Business,* December 10, 1993.

Depew, Virginia, ed. *The Social List of Washington, D.C.* Kensington, Md.: Jean Shaw Murray, 1980.

Gee, Chuck Y. *International Hotels Development and Management.* East Lansing, Mich.: Educational Institute of the American Hotel & Motel Association, 1994.

Hertneky, Paul B. "If They Won't Come To You ..." *Restaurant Hospitality,* June 1992.

Lee, Gretchen. "Puttin' on the Ritz." *Club Management,* May–June 1993.

Liberson, Judy. "The Great Taste of Coffee Profits." *Lodging,* June 1997.

McCaffree, Mary Jane, and Pauline Innis. *Protocol: The Complete Handbook of Diplomatic, Official, and Social Usage.* Englewood Cliffs, N.J.: Prentice-Hall, 1977.

National Restaurant Association. "1994 Foodservice Industry Forecast." *Restaurants USA,* December 1993.

Ninemeier, Jack D. *Planning and Control for Food and Beverage Operations,* Fourth Edition. Lansing, Mich.: Educational Institute of the American Hotel & Motel Association, 1998.

Post, Elizabeth. *Emily Post's Etiquette.* New York: Funk and Wagnalls, 1969.

Rowe, Megan. "Volume Feeding à la Vegas." *Lodging Hospitality,* April 1991.

Ruggles, Ron. "Catering to the Off-Premise Request." *Nation's Restaurant News,* November 29, 1993.

Straus, Karen. "Catering to Every Whim." *Restaurants & Institutions,* November 25, 1992.

Straus, Karen. "Dial-A-Breakfast." *Restaurants & Institutions,* June 15, 1993.

Sullivan, Jim. "Great Holiday Service Jingles Cash Register Bells." *Nation's Restaurant News,* November 15, 1993.

Sullivan, William A. "Software Power." *Lodging,* July 1998.

"What You Report … About the Business of Catering." *Food Management,* May 1994.

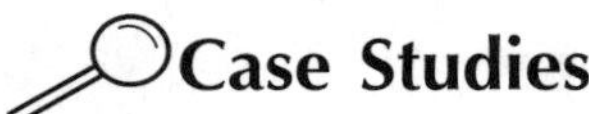

Case Studies

Banquet Gone Bad

It was a beautiful Saturday morning at the club. In his office, Foster Neuman moved reluctantly from the window, sat down at his desk, and pulled out the banquet event orders (BEOs) for the weekend. His meeting with the general manager, Susan Truscott, was in ten minutes and he wanted to make sure he was familiar with all the details of the weekend's events.

Foster had been hired as banquet manager for the High Hills University Club two weeks earlier. He spent his first week reading the employee manual and reviewing club policies. The second week had been spent meeting staff members and learning where things were kept in the club. This weekend, Susan was going to work with him on each banquet, training him in the club's policies and procedures for banquets.

Just as Foster finished scanning the first BEO, his phone rang. "University Club, Foster Neuman speaking. How can I help you?"

"Hello, Foster, this is Susan."

"Susan, hello! Where are you? I can barely hear you through all the background noise."

"I'm at the airport. My father is in the hospital, and I'm taking the next flight to London so I can be with him. You'll have to take care of the banquets this weekend by yourself. But don't worry, it shouldn't be too bad. It's just a baby shower this afternoon, the Woodstone wedding this evening, and a poker tournament tomorrow afternoon. The wedding is a big one, but Mrs. Woodstone is a long-time member of the club and is very supportive of our entire staff."

"No problem, Susan, don't worry about a thing. I'll have everything under control. I hope everything goes well with your father. We'll be thinking about you."

"Great, Foster, I knew I could count on you. If you need anything, you have a very talented staff to help you. Good luck," Susan said as she hung up.

Foster smiled as he replaced the receiver. He'd left his previous position because there were few challenges; this weekend was just the sort of opportunity he needed to prove his talent. He picked up the BEO for the wedding and had just begun studying it when his phone rang again. "University Club, Foster Neuman speaking. How can I help you?"

"Good morning, Mr. Neuman, this is Mrs. Woodstone. Cindy at the switchboard said I should talk to you about the wedding tonight."

"Yes, ma'am, I'm the new banquet manager. Ms. Truscott was called out of town at the last minute. What can I do for you?"

"I'm afraid that, with all of the wedding preparations, my daughter's been a little absent-minded. She forgot to give me 28 names of people who told her they'd be coming to the reception tonight."

Foster scanned the BEO quickly. Two days ago, Mrs. Woodstone had guaranteed the reception for 300 people. Cornish hens were being served, and Foster was fairly certain that exact orders had been placed for the meal. At any rate, there wouldn't be enough for a 10 percent increase. Valetta, a long-time, experienced banquet captain, walked into Foster's office and smiled at him as she moved past his desk and pulled one of the banquet order binders off his bookshelf.

"I'm sorry, Mrs. Woodstone," Foster said, "but it says here that on Thursday you confirmed the reception at 300 guests, and the club requires a 48-hour notice for changing the guest count and other major items on an event order." Valetta looked at Foster in surprise. "We have that rule because it gives the club the best chance to prepare properly and give members what they want and expect."

"What I want, Mr. Neuman," Mrs. Woodstone replied icily, "is for my daughter's reception to be perfect. That means that we're not going to call her friends and tell them they can't come. I know this club's staff is capable of serving an extra 28 people. Surely it's not a big deal to add them now. You have all day to prepare."

"I'm sorry, but rules are rules," Foster said. Valetta began waving frantically at him to get his attention. "Could you hold for just a moment, Mrs. Woodstone?" Foster asked as he hit the hold button. "What is it, Valetta?"

"Mr. Neuman, you can't say 'no' to Mrs. Woodstone!" She glanced at her watch. "It's only a little after eight. Tell her we'll find a way to fit in the extra people. Just make sure you tell the chef about it."

Foster narrowed his eyes. He didn't like having a banquet captain telling him how to do his job, but he supposed she knew the members better than he did. "Thank you, Valetta, I'll tell her. Now, do you need anything else?" Valetta shook her head. "Then please leave so I can finish this phone conversation uninterrupted."

Valetta frowned and left his office. Foster punched the hold button again. "Mrs. Woodstone, thank you for waiting. I've just spoken with my staff and told them that we must do our best to accommodate you. Is there anything else we can do for you?"

Foster and Mrs. Woodstone reviewed the remaining details of the banquet. When they hung up, Foster basked in Mrs. Woodstone's profuse gratitude. He then began putting together a diagram for the evening's setup. Foster had noticed that very few BEOs had seating diagrams with them; that was one thing he planned on changing as the new banquet manager. He quickly sketched out where all the tables would go to fit 328 people in the ballroom.

He then went in search of Valetta. He found her pulling deep-purple table skirting and tablecloths from storage. "Hello, Valetta. What an awful color!"

Valetta gave him a half-smile. "It's the wedding's color. Unusual for summer, but if the bride wants it, it's what we'll do."

"No accounting for taste," Foster said. "I've diagramed how the tables need to be set up tonight. Please pass this along to your setup staff."

"Yes, sir," Valetta replied. "Have you spoken with Chef Cohen about the additional guests yet?"

"No, but I will. I'll be in my office later if you need me." Foster went to the kitchen and poked his head in the door. He didn't see Chef Cohen, and decided he could return later to talk to him. In the meantime, he was going to go meet a friend for lunch downtown.

Several hours later, Foster returned to the club and went to the ballroom to see how the setup was progressing. He glanced at the tables, frowned, and reached into his shirt pocket and pulled out a copy of the diagram he had sketched earlier. He was dismayed to see that the table setup didn't match his diagram. He spotted Valetta at the far end of the ballroom and hurried over for an explanation.

"What's the meaning of this?" Foster demanded, indicating the tables with a sweep of his hand.

"I beg your pardon?" Valetta responded. "We're setting up for tonight's wedding."

"You're not following the diagram I gave you. Why not?"

"Oh, that," Valetta shook her head. "You weren't around when I looked for you to talk about it. If we set it up your way, it would be too cramped. What we have to do in this room is—"

"Are you the banquet manager?" Foster interrupted. "It's not your job to decide how to set these tables up. I know what I'm doing. Tear down these tables and set them up according to the diagram I gave you." Foster briefly wondered if Valetta was trying to sabotage him, make him look bad just because he was the new guy. Maybe she'd applied for his job and hadn't gotten it. He made up his mind to lay down the law with her from now on, so she wouldn't get him into trouble.

Valetta had been standing with pursed lips, but now she spoke up again: "I've helped set up banquets at this club for 15 years. I know what this room is capable of. Your way doesn't work."

"Listen, you do it my way, or you're fired."

"Oh yeah? Well, let me save you the trouble," she retorted. "I quit! And when Ms. Truscott gets back, I'll tell her exactly how you've behaved."

"Oh, going to run and tattle to Mommy like a five-year-old?" Foster said, his voice rising angrily. "This isn't kindergarten anymore, missy. We have a job to do, and if you're not going to do it right, we don't need you here."

Valetta's face flushed with anger. She jerked her apron and name tag off, flung them toward a table, and stalked out without another word.

Oblivious to the growing number of banquet staff members who had stopped working and gathered around to listen to his tirade, Foster shouted at Valetta's back: "And don't bother coming back! And you!" he barked at a nearby staff member. "Follow little miss 'I'm-too-good-to-do-as-I'm-told' and make sure she doesn't steal anything on her way out!"

The staff member stared at him incredulously for a moment, then ran for the door. Foster was too angry to hear her call out, "Mom, wait!" He had already turned to the remaining staff members, all of whom were staring at him, uncertain what to do. "Who's worked here the longest?" Foster asked.

Pierre stepped forward. "I haven't been here as long as Valetta, but I've been here over ten years."

"Well, hopefully you're not as rigid as her, either. Here's the way these tables are supposed to be set up." Foster shoved his diagram into Pierre's hands. "Take care of it and do it right. This banquet's too important to screw up." With that, Foster stormed out of the ballroom. On the way back to his office, he remembered that he still hadn't gotten in touch with Chef Cohen about the extra wedding guests. Oh well, he thought, wedding counts never match the guarantee anyway. It won't be a problem.

By the time the wedding guests began to arrive, Foster had calmed down and was again looking forward to the banquet. He walked down to the club's lobby when he saw the limousines pull up with the bridal party. He stood at the top of the stairs as the door attendant opened the door for the guests. Foster quickly spotted Mrs. Woodstone (he had looked up her photo in the club's files so that he'd know what she looked like). He approached her with a smile and introduced himself to her and her husband. He then escorted them to the ballroom and pointed out the head table.

Mrs. Woodstone told him she was thrilled with the decorations and especially appreciated him making the arrangements for their extra guests. "The next time I see her, I'll be sure to tell Susan what a wonderful job you're doing," she said as she left him to join the receiving line.

Foster smiled and headed for the kitchen. He complimented one of the banquet servers on the plate presentation as she passed by, then joined the service line in the kitchen, where the chef and other staff members were frantically plating orders. Foster had only been helping for a few minutes when one of the servers rushed over to him. "Mr. Neuman, we have a problem. The tables are so crammed together we can't get between them to serve the drinks. And the groom is complaining because his aunt's wheelchair can't make it to her table. Could you come talk to them?"

Foster hurried out to reassure the groom and help find a place for the groom's aunt. In the meantime, another server came into the kitchen looking for Foster. Not finding him, she hurried over to Chef Cohen. "Chef, there aren't enough tables for the guests. There are a bunch of people without seats."

Chef Cohen, bent over the serving line, put a hand to his back and straightened up slowly. His face turned red and there was an angry look in his eye. Those who recognized the warning signs of his notorious temper quickly found somewhere else in the kitchen that they desperately needed to be. "That fool of a banquet manager!" the chef snorted. "He doesn't have a clue about what he's doing! I'll have to take care of it myself or it'll never get done right. You!" Cohen pointed at a cowering server. "Go get me a head count of how many people don't have seats. Linda!" He turned to another server. "You have half a brain. Take Phil and Tom and go set up another table on the dance floor. We may need more than one, but get started now and we'll let you know if we need more. I'll send Sonya out with some additional place settings in a few minutes."

The staff members scurried to do the chef's bidding. Chef Cohen turned to his assistant and shook his head. "For Foster's sake, I hope he just forgot a table and there aren't that many extra guests. Because if there are, they'll have to go hungry. I only made 12 extra servings."

Meanwhile, Mrs. Woodstone joined Foster and the groom, who were having a tense conversation in the corner. The groom was telling Foster exactly what he thought about the table setup, and Foster was working to keep the defensive edge out of his voice. Foster turned to Mrs. Woodstone with a smile, hoping she had come over to defend him and take her new son-in-law back to the wedding festivities. His smile faded as he saw the anger in her eyes. "Mr. Foster, what's the meaning of that!" She pointed a trembling finger toward the dance floor, where three aproned staff members had set up a table and were putting a bright yellow tablecloth on it.

"Um, I'll be happy to find out for you," he stammered.

"Well, let me inform you of what your staff members have told me. They said that there weren't enough seats for everyone, so they're having to set up extra tables. And those atrocious yellow tablecloths are the only clean linen you have available to put on them! My husband is telling *everyone*—" Mrs. Woodstone paused to catch her breath, her voice heaving with emotion—"that my daughter's wedding reception"—another pause for breath—"is starting to look like an L.A. Laker's awards banquet!" She closed her eyes at the horror of it all, then managed to collect herself. "I called you this morning and told you we would have extra people. We even had six no-shows and you *still* seem to be utterly incapable of responding appropriately to the simplest of needs. I hope you have a good explanation for this!"

Discussion Questions

1. What did Foster do wrong?
2. What should Foster do now?
3. How did Susan's actions contribute to the failure of the event? What should she do now to make things right?

The following industry experts helped generate and develop this case: David Brown, CCM, General Manager, The Heritage Club, Mason, Ohio; and Sara J. Shaughnessy, Clubhouse Manager, Somerset Country Club, Mendota Heights, Minnesota.

Banquet Ballyhoo at the Brunswick

The annual member's meeting and banquet at the Brunswick Club was only three days away, and dining room manager Alex King was a little worried. He had just hired five new servers, but he wasn't completely convinced they could handle the job. The selection process had been dismal: the applicants with experience didn't want to work for the hourly wage the club was offering, and the five applicants who would accept $7 an hour had less-than-stellar work histories. But he had been forced to hire all five of these latter applicants, despite his misgivings. One had been fired from a previous job, one had only quick-service restaurant experience, and another seemed to move from job to job. Still, warm bodies were better than no bodies at all, he figured.

Alex was swamped with the final preparations for the banquet and was counting on his experienced servers to give the new staff members enough of an orientation to get them through this first big affair. Then he could take the time to train them thoroughly. For now, he planned to quickly review the employee manual with the new servers, go over some basic club procedures, and have them shadow the veteran servers during the lunch and dinner shifts between now and the banquet. It was only two days. Alex crossed his fingers and hoped for the best.

On Saturday evening, the dining room gleamed with crystal and candlelight. Alex strode through the room, straightening a centerpiece here, pushing in a chair there. At the back of the dining room he found the club's senior servers—Charlotte, Margie, and Alfred—giving the five new servers some final instructions. Wait, there were only four new servers.

"Where's Tammy?" asked Alex. He turned as the young woman rushed in, hair billowing around her shoulders. As she brushed her hair out of her face, her bright red fingernails caught Alex's eye. When he explained that her hair would need to be pulled back and that bold nail polish was *not* part of the server's uniform, she said sullenly, "No one told me." "Well, you've been told now," he replied. Alex hoped this incident wouldn't set the tone for the evening.

For a while, things seemed to progress without a hitch. Then Alex spotted Miranda, another new server, pop a canapé into her mouth as she mingled among the club members with her tray. I hope nobody else saw that, he thought, scanning the faces of nearby members. Then he saw Phil, the bartender, apologizing as he handed over a drink to Mr. Finley, who was obviously perturbed. Alex hurried over to see if he could help.

Phil explained that Mr. Finley was the fourth member who had complained about a botched drink order. "Didn't anyone tell these new kids how to place drink orders?" he asked. "Mr. Finley only drinks Dewar's scotch, but I didn't know it was his order and made the drink with our house scotch. If I'd known we had so many new servers, I would've given them a crash course in member service and bar procedures. They sure need it."

Kevin, another of the new servers, approached the bar. Phil pointed him out as the server who had messed up the drink orders. When Alex asked Kevin why he didn't specify the brand of liquor the member had requested, Kevin looked amazed. "Scotch is scotch, right?" he shrugged. Phil groaned and rolled his eyes.

Alex turned from the bar just in time to see a disaster—Tammy and Miranda colliding with full trays of salad. After a stunned silence, the young women began giggling as they grabbed for the scattered plates. Two busboys came over to help them get the mess cleaned up. Charlotte and Margie had witnessed the disaster and, veterans that they were, had hurried back to the kitchen to get more salads so that the club members seated at Tammy and Miranda's tables wouldn't go hungry.

The beleaguered dining room manager continued to "put out fires" throughout the evening. He brought the board president and his wife a new bottle of merlot when they pointed out to him that their server, Kelsey, had brought their first bottle in an ice bucket. "When we asked about the wine, she told us there was red and white—and she called me 'sweetie,'" the president harrumphed. At the muffled sounds of arguing from the kitchen, Alex excused himself from the president's table and entered the kitchen, where he found the chef shouting at Alfred.

"What's the problem here?" asked Alex, surprised that two veteran staff members would be arguing where members might hear them.

The chef was upset because entrées hadn't been picked up and delivered to tables. Alfred was upset because he was working as fast as he could—serving his tables *and* Kevin's tables.

"Where's Kevin?" asked Alex. His question was answered by a furious Charlotte, who explained that she was scrambling to cover for two other new servers—Kelsey and Dakota. "They're all outside having a cigarette break!" she fumed. "It's not fair—we're having to do all the work. Don't they know what kind of service we give at the Brunswick Club?"

"Well, they've been shadowing you for the past two days. Didn't you tell them that our members expect superb service?" Alex retorted. "Don't they know better than to take a break now?"

"That's right, blame me!" Charlotte exclaimed. "I've tried to teach those kids, but I can't make a silk purse out of a sow's ear, not in two days. That Dakota thinks every meal ought to come with fries and a prize, and the rest of them aren't much better. It's not my job to turn burger-flippers into club servers. Come to think of it, it's *your* job!"

Alex knew she was right. As he headed outside to haul in the smoking servers, he caught sight of the general manager headed his way. He knew the look on her face. Looks like I'd better make some time in my schedule for a meeting tomorrow. A long meeting, he thought ruefully.

Discussion Questions

1. What did the new servers do wrong at the members' banquet?
2. What five training topics should Alex have covered with the new servers in the two days before the banquet?
3. What should Alex acknowledge as his mistakes when he meets with the general manager?
4. What steps should Alex take after the meeting?

The following industry experts helped generate and develop this case: David Brown, CCM, General Manager, The Heritage Club, Mason, Ohio; and Sara J. Shaughnessy, Clubhouse Manager, Somerset Country Club, Mendota Heights, Minnesota.

Appendix A

Potential Banquet and Catering Markets

Markets/Submarkets	Lead Source	Possible Functions
Hospitals		
Auxiliary	Public Relations or Administrative Office	Luncheon fashion shows, evening fund-raisers, art auctions, etc.
Medical Staff	Medical Staff Secretary	Quarterly or annual dinners/ dances, graduation dinners (interns)
Volunteer Functions	Director of Volunteers	Lunches
Staff Recreation Club	Personnel Office	Holiday parties, seasonal parties, dinners/dances
Staff Awards Dinner	Personnel Office	Usually midweek dinners
Credit Union	President of Credit Union	Annual dinner/dance or meeting
Colleges & Universities		
Alumni	Alumni Office, University Affairs Office, or individual schools	Recruiting parties, annual dinner/dance, class reunions, fund-raisers, alumni functions related to athletic events
Sororities and Fraternities	Panhellenic or Inter-Fraternity Council or social chairperson of each sorority or fraternity University Affairs Office	Founders day luncheons, formal installations, dinner/dances
Ceremonial Events	University Affairs Office	Groundbreaking, dedication events
Athletics	Athletic Department, Business Manager, Athletic Director	Awards dinner/alumni events
Department Functions (e.g., Math or English department)	Department Head	Dinner meetings
Graduation Parties	Affairs Office for graduating classes/schools	Weeknight & weekend dinner functions
Faculty & Staff Functions	Faculty Club President, Personnel or Business Office	Dinners
High School		
Proms	School Office for names of class officers	Friday night dinners

Appendix A *(continued)*

Markets/Submarkets	Lead Source	Possible Functions
Reunions (past years) 10 year, 25 year, etc.	School Office	Weekend dinner/dance
Athletic Dinners	Athletic Office	Annual banquets
Faculty Events	Faculty Club President	Annual banquet
Churches/Synagogues		
Anniversary Events	Pastor's Office, Rabbi's Office, Church or Temple Business Manager	Annual dinner, usually weeknights
Women's Council or Auxiliary	Church Office	Fashion show luncheon
Choir	Musical Director or Church Office	Annual dinner
Budget/Finance Committee	Church Office	Dinner meetings
Banks		
Staff Member Clubs (25/50 yr.)	Personnel Office	Midweek dinners, holiday parties
Stockholders Meeting	Administrative Office	Annual meeting, various meal functions
Friends of the Bank	Corporate Development Office	Dinners/meetings
Local Corporations		
Long-Term Staff Member Clubs	Personnel Office	Dinners & dinner/dance
Retirement Dinners	Personnel Office	Weekday dinners
Credit Unions	Credit Union Office	Annual meeting or dinner/dances
Staff Member Groups	Personnel Office	Holiday parties
Charitable Groups, Service Clubs & Miscellaneous Organizations		
Charitable Groups (e.g., American Heart Assn., Cerebral Palsy)	Chamber of Commerce, Public Library	Fund-raising banquets
Men's Club, Women's Assn. (e.g., Rotary, Lions, etc.)	Chamber of Commerce	Midweek luncheons, evening functions

(continued)

Appendix A *(continued)*

Markets/Submarkets	Lead Source	Possible Functions
Professional Associations		
State/Local Bar Assn., Medical Assn., Home-builders Assn., etc.	Chamber of Commerce, Public Library	Monthly luncheon or dinner meetings, annual dinner/dance
Miscellaneous Markets		
Weddings	Newspapers	Receptions & dinners, rehearsal dinners
Bowling Leagues	Secretary of League, Manager of Bowling Alley	Weeknight awards dinner (low budget)
Political Organizations	Local Party Chairperson	Dinners
Major Department Stores (Long-Term Staff Member Clubs, Store Anniversaries)	Personnel Office	Midweek/weekend dinner functions, holiday parties
Cultural/Musical Organizations (Opera, Ballet Society, etc.)	Chamber of Commerce	Weekend evening dinners
Local Youth Sports Groups (e.g., Little League, Adult Softball Leagues)	Little League Regional Headquarters (for names of local groups): County, City or Town Recreation Department (has names of all leagues)	Awards dinner (low budget)

Courtesy of Resorts International Hotel and Casino, Atlantic City, New Jersey

Appendix B

Preparing for Kosher Service

Many hotel food and beverage operations enjoy extensive kosher catering and banquet operations. Other facilities could expand into this market if they knew more about kosher laws and how they apply to menu planning and other aspects of food and beverage operations. The following questions and answers provide background information on this subject.

What is the definition of kosher? Kosher is a term that means "fit or proper"; it applies to foods that meet the specifications and requirements established by Jewish dietary laws. These laws are extremely rigid, do not permit deviation, and mandate many aspects of the purchase, preparation, and service of food.

What meat, fish, or poultry are edible by kosher law? Meat from those animals that have split hooves and chew their cud may be eaten. Pigs have split hooves but do not chew their cud; that is why pork is not eaten. (Some people erroneously believe that health reasons prohibit the consumption of pork; this is not correct.) Specifically, those animals that may be eaten are cattle, sheep, goats, and deer (Leviticus 11:10). Only fish that swim and have easily removable scales and fins may be eaten. Shellfish and mollusks are forbidden, which eliminates lobster, shrimp, crab, clams, oysters, and mussels from the menu. Only domestic birds such as chicken, duck, goose, turkey, and Cornish hen can be eaten. Neither birds of prey, nor scavenger birds, nor those used in the hunt are permitted. Only specific portions of permitted animals and food may be consumed. There are, for example, certain nerves, veins, and fats that cannot be eaten and must be removed before eating.

Are there restrictions on eating certain fruits and vegetables? No. There is no prohibition against anything that grows on the land. All fruits, vegetables, and edible grasses (e.g., oats, wheat) are permitted by kosher law.

What rituals are involved in the preparation of kosher food? The rituals of preparation basically apply to the slaughter of animals and how they must be treated immediately after slaughter, *before* being prepared for eating. Meat for any kosher food production must be slaughtered and "kashered" by an authorized "shocket." Meat and poultry are "kashered" by the following process: within 72 hours of slaughter, the meat or poultry must be soaked in cold water for one-half hour in vessels kept specifically for soaking purposes. The meat is then rinsed with cold water, sprinkled with coarse (kosher) salt, and placed upon a grooved board that is tilted to allow the blood to flow from the meat. The meat must then remain on the board for one hour, at which time it is again washed and finally readied for use. Meat may not be frozen for future use unless it is first kashered. Only meat from

(continued)

Appendix B *(continued)*

the forequarters may be eaten. The hindquarters may be used *only* if certain textured fat and all veins have first been removed. (Unfortunately, the process of removing those veins and fat is entirely too labor-intensive to make it commercially feasible.) After meat is prepared according to this procedure, it may be ground, frozen, or processed in any desired manner.

Are there any exemptions to this rule? Yes. Meat used for broiling need not be kashered *if* it is used within 72 hours of slaughter. Livers need not be kashered and may be frozen for preparation later. However, when livers are ready to be processed, they must be completely thawed, washed, sliced, broiled, sprinkled with salt while broiling, rinsed, and prepared for eating.

Are there other regulations governing kosher food? Yes. All meat and meat products may not be cooked with any dairy product or dairy derivatives. For instance, you cannot serve chicken à la king or creamed chipped beef at a kosher function. Dairy food may not be served at a meal where meat is being used. For example, butter may not be served at a steak dinner. In addition, coffee may not be served with cream; however, a nondairy substitute may be used. The pots and pans in which meats have been cooked and the dishes upon which they are served may only be used for meat products. The same is true of pots, pans, and dishes used for dairy food preparation and service. If these utensils are used incorrectly, they must be discarded. Drinking glassware need not be changed as service moves from meat to dairy products; however, glass dishes used for service of hot food require a separation of meat and dairy items.

Do fish have to be kashered? No. Fish may be used in its entirety and requires no salting after cleaning. Fish dishes may be combined with dairy foods, but must not be combined with meat dishes. Fish may, however, be eaten separately at a meat meal as an appetizer (separate forks should be set).

Do vegetables require special handling or ritual? Vegetables and fruits may be combined with either dairy or meat dishes. If the vegetables are used with meat dishes, they must be cooked in pots and pans used for meat service. All fruits and vegetables, including vegetable oils, and all cereals and derivatives (as well as eggs) are called "parve."

What is meant by milchik and fleshik? "Milchik" refers to milk-containing foods, including milk, milk derivatives, and any product that contains milk in any proportion. "Fleshik" refers to meat products and includes any item containing meat, its byproducts, or derivatives.

Is there a term used to denote forbidden foods? Yes. "Trefe" is used to denote all forbidden foods.

Do these rules apply all year? Are there times when they may be relaxed or modified? These rules are never relaxed. They become even more stringent during the eight days of Passover. During Passover, for instance, unleavened bread is the only bread that may be eaten. Also, the separate

Appendix B *(continued)*

cooking and serving of meat and dairy products is done with special pots, pans, and china set aside for use only during Passover. Specific utensils are also used only for Passover and are stored for the remainder of the year.

What are the rules for the preparation of kosher foods? Since it is not possible to mix meat and milk, separate sets of utensils become necessary. Most kosher caterers prepare only meat dinners and eliminate the need to maintain two sets of utensils. Some hotels with extensive kosher business maintain two separate kitchens, one for the preparation of meat and one for dairy products, and use color codes to distinguish the utensils used in each unit.

Kosher regulations prohibit the cooking of kosher food in nonkosher equipment; similarly, kosher food cannot be served in nonkosher serving utensils. (The reason is that hot food can absorb traces of nonkosher food from a nonkosher dish even if the utensil is clean.) Therefore, utensils used in hot food preparation and subsequent service must be used for kosher purposes only.

In contrast, since cold foods do not absorb food traces from utensils used to handle them, solids that contain kosher ingredients can be eaten from nonkosher dishes.

Utensils, equipment, and flatware can be made kosher even if they were previously used for handling nonkosher items. Techniques include immersing them in boiling water, passing them through a flame, or putting them into the soil. However, these techniques must be performed with a mashgiach (a trained supervisor) or rabbi in attendance.

Utensils made of porcelain, enamel, and earthenware cannot be made kosher, since they are porous and absorbent. Solid flatware made of a single metal piece can be made kosher; items made with a plastic or bone handle or with uncleanable crevices or grooves cannot.

Is supervision required during preparation, service, and cleanup? Since some kosher laws are very technical and complex, the supervision of a mashgiach is required. The food service operation offering kosher food must ensure that all aspects of the function are in accordance with kosher dietary laws.

What are alternatives for kosher catering in a hotel? Hotels make various provisions for kosher catering. For example, as previously mentioned, some hotels maintain separate kosher kitchens in which hotel personnel prepare the food. In contrast, others contract with an external kosher caterer who does catering exclusively for kosher functions at the property. Still other hotels rent their kitchen facilities to one or more kosher caterers. The subcontracting of facilities for kosher events is frequently justifiable due to the extensive amount of thorough cleaning required to render utensils and equipment items kosher.

(continued)

Appendix B *(continued)*

Sometimes kosher food is ordered only as needed for a specific function; no separate storage areas for meat are then required. In contrast, dry products can be stored in a central storeroom as long as they do not come into direct contact with nonkosher products.

Exactly how is kosher food preparation undertaken? Under the supervision of a mashgiach, the kitchen area must be thoroughly cleaned and then koshered. Ovens and stoves can be koshered by sterilizing the interior surfaces with a propane torch. Or, salt can be spread inside an oven that is then heated to its highest temperature for 30 minutes.

Hotels with extensive kosher business frequently purchase dishes especially for this business. Since solid flatware made of one metal piece can be koshered, it is not usually necessary to purchase separate flatware for kosher functions. However, since items to be koshered cannot be used for 24 hours prior to the koshering process, a larger supply of silverware may be needed. The koshering process for flatware involves immersing it in a pot of boiling water, removing it, and then rinsing it in cold water.

Sometimes the hotel supplies kosher caterers with all the necessary equipment; in other instances, caterers provide their own utensils. It is necessary to mark all utensils with an identifying feature when the caterer and the hotel mix equipment so that each business can identify its own utensils.

Dishwashing machines can be made kosher; the soaps used should be of vegetable or chemical origin. All areas in the immediate vicinity of the kosher preparation, even if they are not used by the kosher caterer, must be covered with paper or aluminum foil. Exact procedures may vary with the particular equipment and should be done only by rabbinic authority and under the careful supervision of a mashgiach.

Should a contract be used when an external caterer uses the hotel's facility? Yes. Typically a formal agreement is necessary to ensure that misunderstandings do not arise. Frequently, revenues are split according to an agreed upon formula between the hotel and the caterer. In addition, the hotel includes the costs of the foods it provides. A hotel may, for example, prepare such parve foods as melons and fruit cups, raw vegetables, salads, and coffee. Typically, the hotel is responsible for liquor service, but—because of restrictions placed upon wine—wine service is frequently the caterer's responsibility.

The hotel should charge for the space used, the dishwashing costs, and the labor expenses. Most often, service personnel are provided by the hotel; members of the kitchen staff are provided by the kosher caterer.

The menu is conceived jointly by the caterer and the hotel. While menus are starting to reflect a trend toward lighter and more healthful foods, traditional products are still very popular. Typically the hotel will establish the selling price of the kosher event. Occasionally the caterer will bill the client and reimburse the hotel for the prearranged costs; however, it is

Appendix B *(continued)*

generally more advantageous for the hotel to contract with the caterer, add its costs and profit margin, then bill the client directly.

How can kosher functions be classified? There are two basic types of kosher functions: commercial activities, such as fund-raising events and awards programs, and social or family functions, such as weddings and bar and bat mitzvahs.

Is the kosher catering business seasonal? Generally, kosher catering is not seasonal, but that depends in part on the scheduling of community activities. Usually there are no catered kosher functions during Jewish holidays or during brief periods that are designated as times of mourning. Cooking is prohibited on the Jewish Sabbath (from sunset on Friday until after sunset on Saturday). Therefore, most kosher functions are not routinely scheduled for Saturday evenings during the summer months, since the Sabbath ends late in the evening.

What conditions are necessary for the success of a kosher catered event? In order for kosher catering to be successful, all individuals participating in the catered affair must be aware of their specific responsibilities. Trust is also important. Clients trust the caterer to provide the kosher meals that have been arranged. Likewise, the caterer trusts that the mashgiach and the hotel will provide necessary services.

Source: Some of this material was adapted from Marianna Desser, "Kosher Catering: How and Why," *Cornell Quarterly*, Vol. 20, No. 2, pp. 83–91.

Task Breakdowns: Banquet Service

The procedures presented in this section are for illustrative purposes only and should not be construed as recommendations or standards. While these procedures are typical, readers should keep in mind that each food service facility has its own procedures, equipment specifications, and safety policies.

BANQUET SERVER: Follow Banquet Event Orders and Change Orders

Materials needed: *Banquet event orders (BEOs) and change orders (if any).*

STEPS	HOW-TO'S
1. Review banquet event orders for functions that you will serve.	❑ Note the following information: • The room the function will be held in • The number of guests expected • Table setup specifications (including the sizes, types, and colors of tablecloths and table skirts) • The menu for the function (including beverages, number of courses, and dessert) • The time guests will arrive • The time food should be plated (put on plates) • The time to serve each course • The type of function • Special requests ❑ Always make sure the BEOs are in order, with the first function of your work shift at the front.
2. Review change order for changes that will affect service or room setup.	

BANQUET SERVER: Take and Serve Beverage Orders

Materials needed: *A guest check, a pen, a service tray or beverage tray, clean linen napkins, beverages, beverage napkins, and a tray jack.*

STEPS	HOW-TO'S
1. Take beverage orders.	❑ The function's host will have selected the beverages when booking the function. The beverage choices will be listed on the banquet event order. If a guest asks for a beverage not included on the BEO, know whether there is an extra charge, and tell the guest what the charge is. ❑ Tell guests which beverages are available. ❑ Ask if guests would like to order beverages. ❑ Write orders on the guest check according to how guests are seated. ❑ Assign a number to each chair at a table. Chair #1 is typically the one closest to the door or other landmark in the room. All banquet servers should use the same reference point. ❑ Write the order for the guest in chair #1 on the first line of the guest check. ❑ Write the order for the guest in chair #2 on the second line of the guest check, and so forth. ❑ Take orders from women first, then men. For instance, if the guest in chair #2 is the only woman at the table, take her order first and write it on the second line of the guest check. ❑ Continue to take orders clockwise around the table. ❑ Use standard drink abbreviations. ❑ Listen carefully to each order. Repeat the order and any special requests. Find out the guest's preference for service, such as "on the rocks" or "straight up."

BANQUET SERVER: Take and Serve Beverage Orders

(continued)

STEPS	HOW-TO'S
	❑ Check the IDs of guests who order alcohol if they look underage.
2. Place beverages on a cork-lined tray.	❑ Line the tray with a clean linen napkin to improve the look of the tray and to absorb spills and moisture. You'll likely use service trays—not beverage trays—to serve drinks at banquets. ❑ Center glasses so the tray is well-balanced. Put heavy or tall glasses in the center of the tray. ❑ Place a stack of beverage napkins on the tray.
3. Carry the tray to function room and place it on a tray jack near your guests.	
4. Serve beverages.	❑ Serve each beverage from the guest's right with your right hand. ❑ Place a beverage napkin on the table in front of each guest. ❑ If the beverage napkins at your property have a logo, place the napkins so that the logo faces the guest. ❑ Handle glasses by their stem, base, or handle. Place each glass on the center of each beverage napkin. ❑ Follow your guest check to serve the correct beverage to each guest. Do not ask who ordered which drink. ❑ If pouring a beverage from a pitcher or bottle, pour into the glass or cup without picking it up. ❑ When pouring, use a folded linen napkin as a splash guard to protect guests.

BANQUET SERVER: Serve Each Course at Sit-Down Banquets

Materials needed: *Service trays, tray jacks, condiments, and ashtrays.*

STEPS	HOW-TO'S
1. Prepare the table for each course before serving it.	❑ Clear any empty plates or glasses from the guest's right with your right hand. Always ask guests if they are finished. ❑ Never stack dirty plates in front of guests. Pick them up separately and stack them away from guests. ❑ Bring all condiments and accompaniments to the table before serving the order. ❑ Only bring full—not partially full—condiment bottles to guests. ❑ If you will be serving an item that guests will share, bring a plate for each guest.
2. Pick up each course.	❑ The banquet manager or captain will signal when to serve each course. ❑ You will typically serve courses in the following order: • Appetizers • Soup • Salads • Entrees • Dessert • Cordials • Coffee ❑ Check the order before you take it out of the kitchen: • Does the food look fresh and appealing? • Have all preparation instructions been followed? • Is the presentation garnished? • Have all special requests been met? • Is the plate clean? • Is hot food hot and cold food cold?

BANQUET SERVER: Serve Each Course at Sit-Down Banquets *(continued)*

STEPS	HOW-TO'S
	❑ Ask the cook to make any corrections necessary to meet the operation's high standards. ❑ Notify your supervisor immediately of any problem in the food preparation so that he or she can speak to the guests and correct the situation. ❑ If you are having trouble meeting guest needs, ask your supervisor or another server for help until you can catch up. ❑ Don't let the guests suffer because you're busy. ❑ Thank the kitchen staff for their cooperation.
3. Deliver each course.	❑ Carry loaded service trays to tray jacks in the function rooms. ❑ Serve the children first, women next, then men, and the host last. ❑ Serve food from the guest's left side with your left hand whenever possible. Don't reach in front of guests. ❑ Place the plate with the first course on top of the base plate, if a base plate is included in the table setting. ❑ Place the entree plate so that the main item is closest to the guest. ❑ Place side dishes to the left of the entree plate. ❑ If a guest asks for something extra, deliver it as quickly as possible so that the meal does not get cold. ❑ Ask if guests would like you to bring or do anything else for them at this time. ❑ Remove empty beverage glasses and exchange ashtrays as needed.

BANQUET SERVER: *Maintain Buffets*

Materials needed: *Pitchers of water, cans of gel-type fuel, matches, pitchers of ice, dishes, serving utensils, and food-safe cleaning cloth.*

STEPS	HOW-TO'S
1. Keep hot items hot.	❑ If there is less than one quarter of an inch of water in the liners of hot chafing dishes, use a pitcher of water to refill the liners. ❑ If the chafing dishes are heated by canned, gel-type fuel, make sure the cans stay lit, and replace them when they become empty. ❑ Replace the lids on serving dishes when guests are not in the buffet line.
2. Keep cold items cold.	❑ Use pitchers to add ice to the buffet as needed to keep the containers holding cold items surrounded by ice. ❑ Remove ice that gets into the food containers, and replace any items that become waterlogged.
3. Refill food.	❑ When a container is less than one-quarter full, get a full container from the kitchen. ❑ Remove the old container and replace it with the full one. Do not combine food from the old and new containers. ❑ Bring the old container to the kitchen and give it to the appropriate person.
4. Maintain serviceware.	❑ Restock dishes when there are fewer than ten dishes in a stack. Never let a stack get below five dishes. ❑ Make sure each container has an appropriate serving utensil. ❑ Return serving utensils to the correct containers. ❑ Replace utensils that fall on the floor with clean utensils from the kitchen.
5. Use a damp, food-safe cleaning cloth to wipe spills on the buffet table.	

BANQUET SERVER: Set Up and Maintain Hors d' Oeuvres for Receptions

Materials needed: *A banquet event order (BEO), change orders (if any), tables, tablecloths, table skirts, flounces, food or flower displays, equipment for hot and cold food, ice, water, cans of gel-type fuel, bread-and-butter plates, matches, beverage napkins, cocktail forks or picks, knives, small plates, linen roll-ups, and serving utensils.*

STEPS	HOW-TO'S
1. Place tablecloths on tables.	
2. Skirt and flounce tables.	
3. Decorate tables with food or flower displays as specified by your supervisor or the banquet event order (BEO).	
4. Set up equipment for hot and cold food.	❑ Make sure all equipment is clean and polished. Return soiled equipment to the dish room. ❑ Set up ice beds for cold items. (The steps to set up ice beds vary among properties.) ❑ Set up chafing dishes or electric warmers for hot items. ❑ Make sure there is enough water in the liners of chafing dishes to prevent scorching equipment and burning food. ❑ If the chafing dishes are heated by canned, gel-type fuel, place one can on a bread-and-butter plate under a half-size chafer and two cans under a full-size chafer. Light the cans of fuel 10 minutes before putting the food in the chafing dishes.
5. Put silverware and napkins on the table.	❑ Arrange stacks of beverage napkins on the table. ❑ Place cocktail forks or picks, knives, and small plates on the table. ❑ Place linen roll-ups on the table if they are requested on the BEO.

(continued)

BANQUET SERVER: Set Up and Maintain Hors d' Oeuvres for Receptions *(continued)*

STEPS	HOW-TO'S
6. Bring food from the kitchen 10 to 15 minutes before the guests are expected.	❑ Place cold food containers on the beds of ice. ❑ Place hot food in the chafing dishes. ❑ Place the appropriate serving utensils in the serving dishes.
7. Maintain the hors d'oeuvres table.	

BANQUET SERVER: Provide Service for Cocktail Receptions

Materials needed: *Beverage trays, linen napkins, beverage napkins, food and beverages, and a cleaning cloth.*

STEPS	HOW-TO'S
1. Prepare trays.	❑ Only use trays that are clean (and polished if necessary). ❑ You typically will use a 12-inch beverage tray to serve cocktails and hors d' oeuvres at cocktail receptions. Sometimes silver or glass trays are used. ❑ Line trays with linen napkins. ❑ Place a stack of beverage napkins on each tray. ❑ Place food or beverages on the trays. Center items so each tray is balanced.
2. Serve beverages to reception guests.	❑ At large cocktail receptions, the banquet event order may specify that servers will pass trays of food and trays of the most popular beverages to speed service. ❑ Balance a tray of beverages on your fingertips and hold it in front of your chest. Do not try to hold beverage trays above your shoulder. ❑ Approach guests and offer them a beverage from your tray. ❑ Pick up a beverage napkin and beverage and hand them to the guest with your free hand. If guests try to remove a beverage from your tray, politely ask them to let you serve them so you don't upset the balance of your tray. ❑ Refill your tray as needed. ❑ As you return to the bar to refill your tray, collect empty glasses and place them on your tray.

(continued)

BANQUET SERVER: Provide Service for Cocktail Receptions *(continued)*

STEPS	HOW-TO'S
	❑ Place dirty glasses in the dirty glass racks in the service bar. ❑ Wipe spills from your tray and from tables using a clean, damp cloth.
3. Serve food to reception guests.	❑ Carry a tray of food on your fingertips above your shoulder. Move among the guests, and offer the food. ❑ Lower the tray and present it at chest level to the guests. Try to avoid interrupting conversations. Usually if you approach a group, they will pause to pick up a food item. ❑ Refill your tray as needed. ❑ As you return to the kitchen or other area to refill your tray, place empty plates on the tray and bring them to the dish room. ❑ Wipe spills from your tray and from tables using a clean, damp cloth.
4. Suggest courtesy transportation or a taxi to guests who have had too much to drink.	

Source: Adapted from the "Banquet Server Guide" in the *Hospitality Skills Training Series* (East Lansing, Mich.: Educational Institute of the American Hotel & Motel Association, 1995).

REVIEW QUIZ

When you feel you have covered all of the material in this chapter, answer these questions. Choose the *best* answer.

1. Tracey is a catering salesperson who wants to check the availability of a certain function room for a certain time. The item Tracey needs to check is the:

   a. function book.
   b. function sheet.
   c. function room reservation form.
   d. contract or letter of agreement.

2. The budget for a certain catering firm calls for food costs that are 25 percent of food revenue. To price a banquet using the simple markup method, a manager at this firm should set the price at:

   a. the level of food costs.
   b. twice the level of food costs.
   c. three times the level of food costs.
   d. four times the level of food costs.

3. Which of the following positions of a large hotel's banquet and catering department would typically be responsible for recording entries into the function book, if the property had no computers?

   a. banquet captain
   b. reservationist
   c. function book coordinator
   d. banquet server

4. Beatrice is attending a wedding reception; she orders a drink at the portable bar set up in the ballroom and is told by the bartender that she must pay him for her drink. The host of the wedding reception has set up which type of beverage payment plan with the banquet and catering operation?

   a. host bar with a charge by the drink
   b. cash bar
   c. host bar with a charge by the bottle
   d. host bar with a charge by the hour

REVIEW QUIZ *(continued)*

5. For coffee breaks, banquet and catering operations typically charge clients according to the:

   a. amount of coffee consumed.
   b. duration of the break.
   c. number of people served.
   d. volume of beverages or the number of food items used to set up the event.

Answer Key: 1-a-C1, 2-d-C1, 3-c-C3, 4-b-C4, 5-d-C4

Each question is linked to a competency. Competencies are listed on the first page of the chapter. An answer reading 3-b-C4 translates to:

3: the question number
b: the correct answer
C4: the competency number

Chapter 11 Outline

Competencies

1. Describe typical markets for room service and techniques for reaching these markets, summarize considerations for planning and creating room service menus, and describe room service variations and alternatives.
2. Explain considerations for preparing for room service, including organization, typical duties of room service staff members, forecasting and staffing, facility design, inventory and equipment management, and preparations for service shifts.
3. Describe typical procedures for taking, routing, preparing, delivering, cleaning up after, and following up on room service orders; and explain how room service provides wine service and special amenities.
4. Summarize room service income control procedures, ways to gather guest comments, and typical guest complaints about room service; and describe the use of feedback in planning.

11

Room Service

MANY LODGING PROPERTIES provide their guests with the opportunity to order and enjoy food and beverages in the privacy of their own guestrooms or suites. Some guests enjoy **room service** as a way of adding a special touch to a special occasion. Others see it as a status symbol, and still others appreciate it simply for its convenience.

In this chapter we will take a look at room service issues, including markets, marketing, menus, and room service variations and alternatives. We will then discuss the room service cycle: getting ready for service, delivering service, and attending to various responsibilities after the service has been delivered.

Room Service Issues

Many people, when they see a room service menu for the first time, are surprised at the relatively high prices. Even more surprising is the fact that few room service operations make a significant profit. Why, then, is room service offered? One reason is that guests at many properties desire room service. In a guest survey by *Lodging Hospitality*, room service breakfast was found to be the number one guestroom amenity for which respondents were willing to pay extra, out of a list that included video movies, Internet access, an in-room microwave oven, and in-room coffee. Professional hospitality managers have guest satisfaction as their goal. These managers know that when room service is well managed, it can give their property a competitive edge, enhance guest satisfaction, and enhance the property's public image.

From the perspective of guests, the key elements of well-managed room service include the following:

- Prompt and courteous responses when guests call to place orders
- Correctly filled orders
- Efficient and quick delivery of orders to guestrooms
- Tact and courtesy from staff members who deliver and serve orders
- Staff members who strictly adhere to rules of safety when using equipment that involves liquid fuels or open flames
- Hot and cold foods and beverages that are at the correct temperatures when they are served
- The prompt removal of trays and other equipment when guests have finished their meals or snacks

Room service should be designed to meet the needs of guests, but it should also be designed with the property's human and material resources in mind. Managers should consider the extra resources required before implementing a new room service program: new facilities might have to be built, new equipment purchased, and additional staff members hired. Some properties add a surcharge to room service menu items to cover some or all of these costs, although the industry trend is toward pricing room service menus at the same levels as dining room menus. For example, Wyndham Hotels and Resorts has eliminated room service surcharges and views room service as if it were simply another restaurant in the hotel.

Twenty-four-hour room service is much easier when one or more of the hotel's restaurants are also open around the clock; room service generally costs much more than it brings in if a separate production facility must be maintained for it. For this reason, room service at some lodging properties ends whenever the restaurant closes for the night. Some properties use separate production facilities for room service and transfer the production responsibilities from the room service kitchen to a restaurant or coffee shop kitchen only during slow times.

Increasingly, because of the growing number of alliances between hotel companies and chain or independent restaurants, hotel food and beverage departments that have not traditionally offered room service have added it to the amenities they offer, but they have their affiliated restaurants provide it. For example, a Holiday Inn hotel with a TGI Friday's restaurant may provide its room service via the restaurant. This kind of arrangement gives the hotel the cost-effectiveness of quantity cooking that most stand-alone room service operations cannot achieve.

Some hotels do a large volume of **hospitality suite** business, offering food and beverage service for small group meetings, corporate meetings, organizations entertaining guests during conventions, and other occasions. These properties are able to increase the productivity of their room service operations by placing the responsibility for hospitality suites with room service rather than with the banquet or catering department. Room service then provides all food and beverage service in any hotel room, including suites, for any number of guests. Since food and beverage sales in hospitality suites usually produce a profit, they can help offset losses accrued from offering traditional room service.

Markets

Few guests rely on room service for the majority of their meals. Exhibit 1 shows that most hotel guests eat in one of the hotel's restaurants or make other arrangements for meals rather than use room service. It also shows that room service is most popular with both business and pleasure travelers at breakfast.

Limited-service properties rarely offer room service. In contrast, luxury hotels that cater to executive business travelers, convention groups, and the upscale leisure market generally feel it is necessary to offer 24-hour room service. Guests who are traveling on birthdays, anniversaries, or holidays may be more willing to consider ordering room service. When targeting these kinds of markets, managers may want to protect the novelty or prestige factor of room service by keeping room

Exhibit 1 Where Hotel Guests Eat

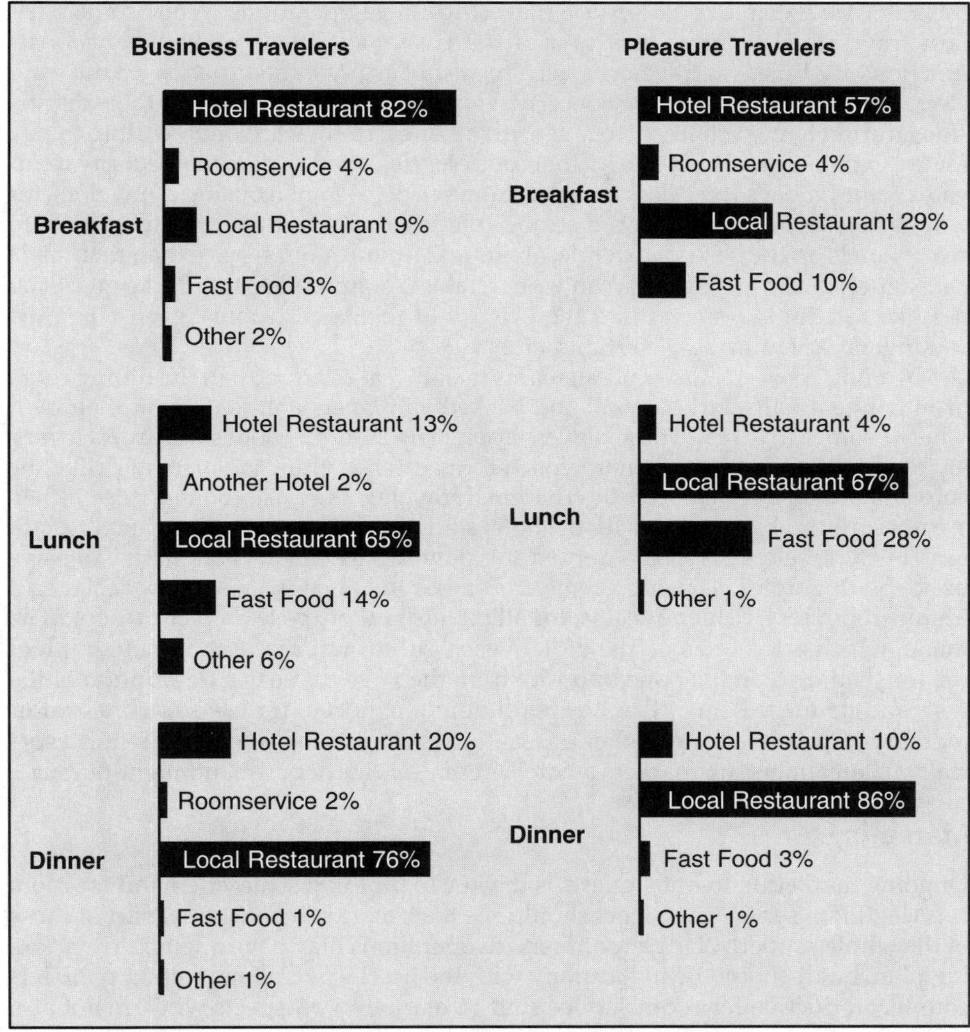

Source: Carlo Wolff, "Roomservice Blues," *Lodging Hospitality,* December 1992, pp. 55–56.

service menu prices higher than dining room prices and offering items that enhance the special image of room service, such as escargot.

On the other hand, managers may attempt to position room service as an amenity that can be enjoyed as much for its functional merits as its symbolic merits. Its functional merits include the privacy of eating in the guestroom, solitude for those who prefer to eat alone, security, and the convenience of not having to leave the guestroom for a meal. If managers position room service this way, they should keep menu prices low and choose menu items that are nutritious and attractive but inexpensive and easy to prepare.

Whichever route managers choose for positioning room service, business travelers are a viable room service market for most operations. While some business travelers view room service as a status symbol, others appreciate it for its functionality. Business travelers typically are not as price conscious as leisure travelers, but they are often more concerned about saving time. Some of their discussions during a meal concern very sensitive issues, so they are often willing to pay for the extra privacy and security that room service affords. Personal security motivates some business travelers to order room service. Women business travelers, for whom personal security plays a strong role in hotel selection, are more likely to select hotels on the basis of extended-hour or 24-hour room service than their male colleagues. (Security concerns can work against room service, too. Some guests do not like to admit strangers into the privacy of their guestrooms, even when the "strangers" are room service staff members.)

Among sports teams, football teams usually eat as a group in the dining room or in banquet halls, but baseball and basketball players are usually on their own when it comes to meals. These players appreciate 24-hour room service and a variety of menu options. Many motorcoach tours cater to older travelers who like the convenience of room service. International travelers may use room service if they are not comfortable enough with the hotel staff's language to dine in a hotel restaurant. Such travelers especially appreciate room service menus that make extensive use of photographs. (The management of the Grand Hyatt in New York designed a unique room service menu that is, for all intents and purposes, a picture book. The menu, which is left open on the desk in each guestroom, features a photograph of the finished dish on the page opposite from the page that has a description of the dish and its ingredients.) Families with young children, travelers with visual or mobility impairments, and other guests for whom leaving the guestroom is especially inconvenient are markets a hotel's room service department might pursue.

Marketing

Ongoing marketing to hotel guests is the key to building steady demand for room service. Room service managers should see their marketing efforts as part of those of the whole property. Large room service operations may have a separate marketing plan, but it should be in harmony with the hotel's overall marketing plan. It is counterproductive for room service staff to market to prospects who are not also being targeted by the property's other revenue centers.

A lodging property's salespeople should have access to information about the kinds of service and menus the room service operation offers. Most often this communication takes place through the property's **fact book**—a book salespeople use to familiarize themselves with and remind themselves about the property's products and services. The room service department's hours of operation and menu(s) should be included in this important publication. Room service managers should check regularly to ensure that telephone salespeople, front desk agents, and all other guest-contact staff members have the same information about room service and that their information is complete, accurate, and up-to-date.

The external aspect of room service marketing involves using room service as an attraction to help convince prospects to choose the property for a stay. To this end, the property can entice prospects through both rack and convention brochures. In these brochures, properties should not merely mention room service; they should use photographs, testimonials, abbreviated menus, or examples of the kind of room service prospects can expect to receive. A property's video brochures, video magazines, CD-ROMs, faxes, and Internet site can all be used to promote room service as well.

Once prospects become guests, they may forget some of the amenities that first attracted them to the property. Some of the biggest obstacles to room service success are unawareness that it is offered and ignorance of the kinds of menu items and services offered and their prices. **Internal selling,** especially cross-selling, can help overcome both of these obstacles. Staff members who practice internal selling create awareness of room service by regularly reminding guests that room service is available. A short segment on the property's guest-services television channel or fliers placed in strategic spots throughout the hotel can tell guests about room service specials and menu items.

Hotel operators must know the number for room service if they are to be good internal sellers of this amenity. In properties that operate room service out of a room service kitchen during busy hours and out of other production facilities at slower times, the operator should know which room service telephone number to give guests at any given time: it could be the room service department's order-taker's number during busy periods, the "theme" dining-room cashier's number when the dining room is open, or the family-dining restaurant operator's number during still other periods.

Cross-selling involves staff members or advertisements in one hotel area promoting the products or services of another revenue center in the hotel. For example, a room service staff member might remind a guest that the gift shop has souvenirs or personal hygiene items for sale, or a front desk representative might encourage a registering guest to try the property's room service. In the area of advertising, tent cards promoting room service that are placed on tables near the swimming pool are also examples of cross-selling.

Personal cross-selling can take place as part of routine interactions with guests such as the following:

- Taking guest orders for wake-up calls, for cribs or extra blankets, and other services
- Making wake-up calls
- Checking in or checking out

In the case of a front desk representative making a wake-up call, the representative, rather than simply saying, "Hello, it's seven o'clock" might say, "Good morning, Ms. Ricker. It's seven o'clock. Would you like room service to bring you a fresh pot of coffee and a Danish?" Cross-selling keeps room service in the forefront of guests' minds and also helps keep it in the minds of staff members.

Room service managers should advertise room service with prominently displayed menus, posters, fliers, and tent cards. Just as with any in-house advertising, managers should choose locations that receive a lot of traffic. Elevators, lobbies, and stairways are usually high-traffic areas in hotels. In-house promotions can tie room service revenues to other revenues. Managers may choose to offer a discount on one room service order for guests who stay at the property for three days or more, for example. A sample of room service could be built into familiarization ("fam") packages that the property offers to meeting planners or travel intermediaries.

Menus

Menu design is closely related to room service marketing in that both should match the operation's products and services with guest needs and expectations. The following sections discuss considerations for planning and designing a room service menu.

Menu Planning. Menu planning for room service should take place at the same time the marketing plan for room service is created, because menu items must meet profitability criteria as well as quality criteria. Too many room service managers set themselves up for failure when they plan menus that cannot fulfill budgetary goals. Room service menus must also reflect the positioning of the property and appeal to its target markets. As mentioned earlier, managers should consider the property's needs as well as the needs of guests when planning a room service menu. The people who can best represent these two perspectives should be involved in the menu-planning process: the room service manager, the food and beverage manager, the chef, and possibly the director of sales.

Room service menus generally offer more expensive food items and frequently provide less variety than dining room menus. Often, managers build a room service menu with items from the operation's restaurant menu(s) that can maintain their quality during transportation to guestrooms. In other instances, managers must plan special room service menus featuring items not found on the restaurant menu(s). Some properties use both their dining room and coffee shop menus as sources for the room service menu, then add fast-service items.

Regardless of the approach used, managers must be sure that the items on the room service menu will meet guest and property quality requirements. Such items as french fries may become soggy, cold, or otherwise suffer a loss of quality if they are held for long time periods between production and subsequent service in guestrooms. Likewise, egg soufflés are a poor choice for most room service menus. Other items, such as a chicken breast in a wine sauce, tournedos, or beef sauté à la Deutsch could require tableside preparation that room service attendants may not be able to perform.

More and more properties are limiting their room service menus to only those items they can prepare and deliver best. Some properties have seen increased profitability by using specialty kitchens that offer a single item, such as pizza, fried chicken, burgers, or sandwiches. Room service managers might also focus on a single meal, such as breakfast (35 percent of the breakfast business at some upscale properties is generated by room service).

For most room service operations, breakfast is the easiest meal to sell and the most difficult to deliver properly. Many breakfast combinations that feature eggs simply do not maintain product temperatures during transportation. It is also

The Room Service Depot markets room service equipment online at http://www.valflo.com/roomservice.html. (Courtesy of Room Service Depot)

difficult to deliver toast to guestrooms at proper temperatures. A limited breakfast menu that lists only menu items that will survive the trip from the kitchen to the guestroom may be a good alternative to an extensive menu. Specialty pastries, for example, may be offered instead of toast; scrambled eggs may be preferable to eggs Benedict, because hollandaise sauce is highly perishable.

During the week, breakfasts are usually served through room service for business travelers. Additionally, business meetings in function rooms may include breakfast. In general, these breakfasts are light and quick, since these are two features that business guests most often request. For example, the Omni Hotel in Houston, Texas, has introduced a "Simply Healthy" breakfast featuring freshly squeezed juice, fresh in-season fruits, vanilla bean yogurt made on the premises, granola, and a selection of "healthy" muffins such as carrot-raisin bran and seven-grain. The "Simply Healthy" breakfast is a popular room service choice, since it provides convenience and value (a healthy breakfast alternative) for guests.

Many properties use **menu engineering** to select and monitor the success of restaurant menu items; room service managers should consider applying menu engineering to the room service menu as well. Menu engineering involves analyzing both the demand and the profit contribution margin for each item on the menu, then adjusting prices and adding or subtracting menu items as necessary.

In summary, managers should consider the following factors when planning a room service menu:

- What are the requirements and preferences of the hotel's target markets?
- What types of food and beverages should we offer?
- How many menu items should we offer?

- How long does it take to prepare each menu item? (Complicated menu items or items that for other reasons take a long time to prepare are not suitable for the room service menus of most properties.)
- Will each menu item be reasonably popular?
- Can the quality of each menu item survive the transport to the guestrooms farthest from the room service department's food preparation areas?
- Can we make a reasonable profit on each menu item? That is, are guests willing to pay the price we must charge to cover the costs of purchasing and preparing the menu item, plus a reasonable markup?

Menu Design and Presentation. A room service menu's design and presentation should reflect the property's positioning and the requirements and preferences of its target markets. Guests should be able to easily understand the information on the menu and easily find what they're looking for. Because guests should be able to easily locate the telephone number for room service, for example, this number should be in a conspicuous location on the room service menu. Of course, the menu itself should be placed in the guestroom so that guests can easily find it.

In hotels that cater to international guests, room service menus are frequently written in several languages. This feature is important, since guests who are alone in their rooms do not have service staff available to help them, as the guests in public dining areas do. As mentioned earlier, to help international guests, some room service menus include many pictures. Some hotels offer special menus in braille (in domestic as well as international versions) for guests with visual impairments. (Hotels who serve a lot of international guests also employ multilingual room service operators.)

Designing menus in a way that highlights the products with the highest contribution margins (food income minus food and labor costs) is just as important to room service as it is to any other food and beverage outlet. Uniquely designed room service menus can influence guest purchases in much the same way that restaurant menus do. Menu designers should first determine which menu items they most want to sell (such as those items with the highest contribution margin) then provide good descriptions of those items and use boxes, pictures, or other techniques to focus attention on them. For most properties, all items available through room service should be included on their room service menus. However, some room service departments at upscale properties sometimes include a notice on their menus that invites guests to inquire about unlisted items.

In addition to menus, some properties put tent cards on the dresser, television, nightstand, or other pieces of furniture to promote room service as well as other food and beverage services. Some properties offer a nightly turndown service in which housekeepers prepare the guest's bed, tidy up the room, provide additional linens if necessary, and place a flower, candy, or a cheerful note on the guest's pillow; housekeepers may also place a breakfast **doorknob menu** on the guest's pillow. Other properties may always have a breakfast doorknob menu available in every guestroom for guests to complete and hang on the doorknobs outside their rooms. Staff members then pick up these menus during the early-morning hours. Guests indicate on the menu not only which items they want, but the approximate times at which they would like their breakfasts to be served as well. (Some flexibility, such as one-half hour, should be built into the delivery time, since the time that a guest prefers could be a very busy period for the room service staff.) A doorknob menu expedites room service, since guests can place orders and room service staff can prepare and deliver them without involving the order-taker during the breakfast rush.

Variations and Alternatives

Room service is undergoing dramatic changes at some properties. Because it is a costly amenity in a time when labor is short and maintenance and overhead costs are high, some hotels are opting for lower-cost alternatives. To avoid the risks and costs of providing room service themselves, many economy and all-suite hotels have added food to guestroom minibars, placed combination microwave-oven-and-refrigerator units in guestrooms, added pizza delivery service, or outsourced room service to nearby quick-service or casual/theme restaurants. Other properties feature delicatessens where guests can pick up their favorite foods and prepare them in their rooms.

Many properties are giving guests an alternative to paper room service menus by offering room service via **video ordering.** Guests can turn on the televisions in their guestrooms, select the room service option from a menu of hotel services, and order food and beverages using their television's remote control. Managers must make video ordering an easy process if they expect guests to use this option, however. One guest commented on the complexity of one property's video ordering service by saying, "Only a computer nerd can use it." Video ordering has the potential to reduce mistakes in room service orders, but it must be guest-friendly.

The Sheraton New York Hotel in New York City augments its regular room service menu with a supplemental room service menu. This menu lists popular menu items from three neighborhood ethnic restaurants: China Regency, New York's Stage Deli, and San Leone. Overall, there are about 100 menu items from which to choose. Menu prices are the same as guests would pay if they actually went to these neighborhood restaurants (there is also a nominal delivery charge). The supplemental menu has the same delivery promise that is printed on the regular room service menu: "If the order is not delivered in 30 minutes or less, the order is free." This creative strategy gives guests a wider selection, builds strategic alliances with neighborhood restaurants, and can enhance the guest's stay significantly.

The Mirage Hotel in Las Vegas, Nevada, has eight elevators assigned to the room service department. Two of the elevators are designed to deliver one of three kinds of breakfasts in ten minutes or less. Guests in the hotel's suites receive extra attention. As soon as they order breakfast, a first service of coffee, Danish, juice, and a newspaper is delivered immediately; breakfast follows shortly thereafter. Throughout the hotel, a 20-minute-delivery guarantee for room service is stressed. Behind the scenes, the actual goal is 15 minutes or less.

Holiday Inn Express limited-service hotels give guests a free continental breakfast to complement their in-room coffee makers. Another hotel chain presents guests with complimentary continental breakfasts in plastic bags that are hung on the guestrooms' outside door handles; the breakfast consists of a four-ounce container of orange juice and a wrapped muffin or sweet roll. This limited type of room service adds value for guests, particularly those traveling with children.

Finally, some properties are offering room service options that have nothing to do with food and beverages. For example, the Four Seasons Hotel in London offers in-room tailoring services by the master tailors of Saville Row. Several hotels in the Detroit area, including The Ritz-Carlton and River Place Inn, have entered into agreements with a local company called "Hotel Doctor" that sends doctors on "house calls" direct to hotel guestrooms. The company averages about 100 calls per week; doctors arrive at the hotels complete with white hospital jacket, dress shirt and tie, photo identification, and black bag, and treat everything from common colds to serious ailments.

Other non-food room service options offered at upscale hotels and resorts include the following:

- Beauty services such as hairstyling and manicures
- Psychological consultations (in addition to traditional therapists for people, some hotels even offer "pet therapists," who will counsel owners of travel-traumatized pets)
- Yoga sessions
- Fitness training
- Massages
- Acupuncture treatments

Getting Ready for Room Service

Getting ready for room service includes attending to staffing requirements as well as gathering the inventory and equipment necessary to provide excellent room service. Room service managers must give careful thought to staffing. A limited-service property may have ten or fewer room service staff members, while full-service properties may have large room service departments. The inventory and equipment required for room service ranges from simple trays for delivering continental breakfasts, to the carts, candles, special tablecloths and napkins, and other items involved in serving an elaborate candlelight dinner.

Staff member knowledge of the room service menu will enhance a guest's enjoyment of the property in general and room service in particular. At the very least, all room service staff members should know the following:

- Proper pronunciation of the names of menu items
- Menu specials of the day
- Signature or featured menu items
- Room service menu items that are in or out of season
- Ingredients and preparation methods

- Prices
- Alcoholic and other beverages that are available and that go well with certain menu items

Room service staff members must also be prepared to suggest items that may be prepared and delivered quickly to guests who are in a hurry, and menu items that are not on the menu but may be prepared for a guest who is on a special diet.

Staffing Requirements

Managers of a new room service department or a department that is reorganizing need to decide how to allocate their staff members. What tasks need to be performed, which position should perform which tasks, and what are the standards by which performance should be measured for each position are just some of the questions managers must ask themselves. The answers to these and other questions affect the hiring, training, and evaluation of staff members.

To answer these questions, managers should first create a task list for each position (see Exhibit 2 for a sample task list for the room service attendant position). The tasks on task lists are arranged roughly in the order in which they should be performed. Tasks are not described in depth on a task list; detailed descriptions of how to do the tasks appear in separate job breakdowns for each task on the list (see Exhibit 3 for a sample job breakdown). A job breakdown supplies all the information and instructions a staff member needs to perform the task being described. To figure out what training a staff member needs, room service managers can complete a training needs evaluation form similar to the one shown in the chapter appendix. Finally, managers should construct a training schedule to plan their training (see Exhibit 4 for an excerpt from a sample training schedule).

While titles and duties vary from property to property, most of the duties listed under the position descriptions that follow must be performed at every property that offers room service.

Room Service Manager. The **room service manager** has a large number of management responsibilities, ranging from planning and executing the department's operation to enforcing its rules. He or she is responsible for organizing the room service staff and often selects, orients, trains, and schedules staff members. Handling problems with food and beverage orders and delivery, controlling costs, and ensuring that staff members collect all sales income due the operation are additional duties.

When guests plan hospitality suites and if room service is responsible for these functions, the room service manager becomes an important member of the hospitality-suite planning team. Furthermore, the room service manager must handle complaints from guests, staff members, and others; ensure that room service equipment is properly maintained; and order equipment and supplies. Room service is labor-intensive, so supervisory duties form a significant part of the room service manager's work.

Assistant Room Service Manager. In large properties that have an **assistant room service manager**, this individual performs some of the tasks that would otherwise

Exhibit 2 Sample Task List: Room Service Attendant

1. Perform beginning-of-shift duties.
2. Preset room service trays and carts.
3. Process express breakfast orders.
4. Deliver VIP amenities.
5. Use point-of-sale (POS) equipment.
6. Take and record room service orders.
7. Handle special room service requests.
8. Place the room service order.
9. Perform pantry prep for room service orders.
10. Prepare coffee.
11. Prepare hot tea.
12. Prepare hot chocolate.
13. Prepare iced tea.
14. Set up bottled wine or champagne for service.
15. Assemble the beverage order and food condiments.
16. Pick up the room service order.
17. Deliver the room service order.
18. Serve the room service order.
19. Serve coffee or hot tea.
20. Check guest IDs.
21. Open and serve wine or champagne.
22. Present and settle the guest check.
23. Retrieve trays and carts.
24. Close out the guest check.
25. Follow up with guests.
26. Respond to dissatisfied guests.
27. Clear and reset trays and carts.
28. Handle soiled room service linens.
29. Set up portable bars in suites or guestrooms.
30. Set up and serve small group dinners and receptions.
31. Set up and serve small buffet banquets.
32. Set up and serve coffee breaks.
33. Maintain room service side stations.
34. Pick up and restock room service supplies.
35. Perform closing shift duties.
36. Make the shift deposit and collect due-backs.
37. Use the room service logbook.

Source: Adapted from the "Room Service Attendant Guide" in the *Hospitality Skills Training Series* (East Lansing, Mich.: Educational Institute of the American Hotel & Motel Association, 1995).

be the responsibility of the room service manager. Frequently, the assistant room service manager supervises staff members, undertakes many of the daily or routine decision-making tasks associated with special functions, solves operational problems, and completes departmental records and reports.

Room Service Captain. During a specific shift, the **room service captain** is in charge of the department's order-takers, room service attendants, and buspersons. Captains help the assistant room service manager ensure that staff members follow all operating procedures and maintain performance standards. They also issue guest checks, ensure that room service supply areas are adequately stocked, and personally supervise functions in hospitality suites. When VIPs order room service, the captains themselves may prepare and deliver the orders to these guests.

Room service captains may also expedite room service when special problems arise, such as an unexpectedly busy period. Rescheduling or reassigning room service attendants is an example of how they could expedite room service. Captains

Exhibit 3 Sample Job Breakdown

Place the Room Service Order

STEPS	HOW-TO'S
1. Turn in the food order to the kitchen	❑ At some properties, room service attendants hand-carry orders to the kitchen. Other properties use point-of-sale equipment that automatically transmits orders to the kitchen.
2. Let the cook or expediter know about any guest request.	❑ Guest requests may include the degree of doneness for eggs and steaks, a fat-free preparation, extra sauce, etc.
3. Place beverage orders.	❑ When food orders are almost ready, place the beverage orders with the bar. ❑ Do not place bar orders too early—the ice will melt and water-down the drinks. ❑ Timing room service drink orders is important. Food must stay at the correct temperature, and the ice in beverages must not melt and water-down the drinks.

This is the job breakdown for Task 8 on the task list shown in Exhibit 2. Source: Adapted from the "Room Service Attendant Guide" in the *Hospitality Skills Training Series* (East Lansing, Mich.: Educational Institute of the American Hotel & Motel Association, 1995).

may make inspection rounds to ensure that buspersons remove room service equipment and dishes promptly from guestrooms and hallway floors. The captain may also check incoming orders to ensure that order-takers are taking them in a timely fashion and that room service attendants are delivering them quickly. When room service attendants are preparing to leave the kitchen area, captains may serve as checkers to confirm that orders are correct. Properties with heavy room service demand (such as resorts) may assign a captain to a room service area or pantry on each floor. Overall, captains help ensure that the room service operation runs smoothly.

Room Service Order-Taker. The **room service order-taker** or room service operator is a critical guest-contact position. An order-taker's shift begins when he or she takes possession of numbered guest checks; learns about any problems, substitutions, or other concerns related to the menu; and ensures that room service

Exhibit 4 Excerpt of a Sample Training Schedule

Day 1:

Department Orientation

Knowledge for All Staff Members:

- Quality Guest Service
- Bloodborne Pathogens
- Personal Appearance
- Emergency Situations
- Lost and Found
- Recycling Procedures
- Safe Work Habits
- Manager on Duty
- Your Property's Fact Sheet
- Staff Member Policies
- The Americans with Disabilities Act

The Task List for room service attendants

Day 2:

Review Day 1 (Plan additional training time, if necessary)

Knowledge for All Front-of-House Food and Beverage Staff Members:

- Telephone Courtesy
- Safety and Security
- Alcoholic Beverage Terms
- House Brands and Call Brands
- Liquor Brands and Categories
- Beverage Prices

Knowledge for Room Service Attendants:

- What Is a Room Service Attendant?
- Working as a Team With Co-Workers and Other Departments
- Key Control
- Property Floor Plan
- Par Stock System
- Room Service Equipment Terms
- VIPs

The Job Breakdowns for Tasks 1–4:

Task 1 Perform Beginning-of-Shift Duties
Task 2 Preset Room Service Trays and Carts
Task 3 Process Express Breakfast Orders
Task 4 Deliver VIP Amenities

Source: Adapted from the "Room Service Attendant Guide" in the *Hospitality Skills Training Series* (East Lansing, Mich.: Educational Institute of the American Hotel & Motel Association, 1995).

attendants are on duty as assigned. As guests place room service orders, the order-taker must record their orders on the guest checks according to hotel procedures, see that the orders get to food production areas, and, in many properties, enter the check into a precheck register or another data machine. A room service order-taker may also serve as a food checker to confirm that orders that are about to be removed from the production area match the items listed on their corresponding guest checks.

The order-taker's role during initial contacts with guests is much like that of a food or beverage server with dining room guests; that is why suggestive selling and knowing the menu are among this staff member's responsibilities. The order-taker is really a salesperson rather than someone who simply takes orders.

Room Service Attendants. Room service attendants accept orders from production areas, ensure that all items listed on the guest check are on the food tray or cart, permit the order-taker or captain to double-check the order if procedures require it, deliver orders to designated guestrooms, and serve guests in their guestrooms. They may also perform station setup and breakdown tasks in the room service area and do the work of buspersons during busy shifts. Procedures for delivering room service orders will be discussed in more detail later in the chapter.

It is absolutely essential for room service attendants to be thoroughly familiar with the property's layout and the location of each guestroom and suite. Time lost while an attendant looks for a guestroom affects not only the quality of that guest's service, but also the service of subsequent guests who will receive their orders later than expected. The quality of food deteriorates as the length of time between production and service increases during transportation.

In lodging properties that are spread over many areas and buildings (many resorts fit this description, for example), room service attendants often deliver orders in motorized vehicles such as golf carts. Room service managers at resorts must often meet the needs of very demanding guests and should ask for input from room service attendants to help them develop creative methods to ensure that those needs are met.

In general, room service attendants function like food and beverage servers; they not only serve food and beverages to guests, but also ensure that the guests are completely satisfied with the items and the service.

Buspersons. Buspersons may help set up room service stations in food production areas, assemble items for an order, deliver small orders, pick up room service equipment and dishes from guestrooms and hallways, take used serviceware to dishwashing areas, clean room service tables and trays, and perform miscellaneous tasks that increase the efficiency of room service attendants. Buspersons may help set up hospitality suites by placing tablecloths on tables and delivering serviceware and food and beverage supplies to the suites.

Forecasting and Staff Member Scheduling

Room service managers must plan carefully when scheduling staff members. Unfortunately, this task is not easy, because it is difficult to assess all of the factors that have an impact on room service demand. Some of these factors include

(1) occupancy levels (experienced room service managers can estimate from the house count the approximate number of guests who will desire room service); (2) the number of guests who are traveling on an expense account; (3) the number of convention and business groups in-house (front desk and catering department staff can help room service managers forecast how many people will require room service based on the estimated attendance of organized meal functions); and (4) the number of guests whose room rates include a continental breakfast, a fruit basket, or similar in-room amenities (obviously there will be a direct correlation between these guest counts and room service needs).

Some lodging properties transfer service staff back and forth between dining areas and the room service department as volume fluctuates in these areas. When this system is used, all service staff members must be well trained in all of the service procedures that apply to each area. Properties that do not use this system have a much greater need to accurately forecast the volume of business anticipated for room service, since slow service is likely to result if the estimates for room service staff are inaccurate and not enough staff members are scheduled. (And if too many room service staff members are scheduled, labor costs are unnecessarily high.) Room service business that is arranged in advance (such as cocktails and appetizers in hospitality suites or small group dining in guestrooms) is not as difficult to staff. The schedule planner will need to study the applicable **function sheets** that provide detailed information about room service staff needs in those areas.

Facility Design

Room service production and order-assembly areas must be designed to use space efficiently and facilitate the prompt delivery of room service orders to guestrooms. It may be worthwhile for managers to conduct a motion study on room service food and beverage preparation procedures and examine room service areas (or hire a consultant to do so) to see how design improvements could improve service speed.

Guestrooms in which guests consume room service orders must also be designed for efficiency. In some properties, all of the items needed for room service, including a mobile dining table, are rolled into the guestroom when the order is delivered. Designers must make certain that the chairs already present in the guestroom are compatible in design (particularly in height and width) with room service tables. At some properties, room service orders are delivered on trays to guestrooms. In this case, there must be a comfortable eating surface in the guestroom, such as a table or desk.

Inventory and Equipment

Room service varies greatly from one lodging property to the next, but there are some inventory and equipment items that almost all use.

Carts are used to transport food to guestrooms and hospitality suites. These carts may be equipped with electrically heated hot boxes or canned, jellied alcohol fuels that are lit by the room service attendant. Some properties use a two-piece pellet system. Room service staff members place a preheated pellet in a base and put the plate in or on the base; they place a second hot pellet on the cover.

A wide variety of equipment and supplies should be available in appropriate quantities in room service areas. Storing equipment close to where it will first be used can improve transportation time. While some small room service departments may require only a cart, shelving units, or one or two shelves on a wall to store their supplies, larger departments require more storage space. Setting par stock levels and keeping a log of supplies and equipment will help room service managers know when more items need to be ordered. In some properties, inventory maintenance for room service may be handled by housekeeping or the food and beverage department. Equipment repair should be coordinated with the property's maintenance and engineering department.

The number of room service orders will differ by day and by shift. For example, if a lodging property caters primarily to business travelers, its weekday occupancy rates and room service breakfast volumes will be higher than those on weekends. Therefore, the property will require a different quantity of room service equipment and supply items at different times. The checklist shown in Exhibit 5 allows for variations between busy and slow shifts.

Preparations for Service Shifts

In well-run room service departments, room service attendants have completed preparation work during slow times or prior to the beginning of a service shift so they have only a minimum number of these tasks to perform during peak business hours. For example, they will have preset room service carts or trays (they make certain the cart or tray is clean; they place a placemat, tablecloth, or other covering on it; and they set it properly with tableware, napkins, and appropriate condiments). Preset carts and trays are generally stored in out-of-the-way aisle areas where room service attendants can conveniently obtain them. To ensure that attendants have an adequate number of items at the beginning of their shifts, some managers use a checklist similar to the one in Exhibit 5.

Before room service attendants begin work, they should be briefed about any special functions occurring at the property, the amount of forecasted business, any unavailable menu items, specials of the day, a list of VIPs and groups of people staying at the hotel, and any other information that will enable them to provide superior service to guests. Order-takers should be well-informed about menu item ingredients and production techniques so they can answer guest questions.

Delivering Room Service

Now that you understand the roles of the various positions associated with room service, it's time to consider how room service actually operates. What follows is an overview of room service procedures, first for food and beverage orders, then for wine service and special room service amenities. (Sample job or task breakdowns for typical tasks performed by room service personnel are included at the end of the chapter.)

Exhibit 5 Checklist of Room Service Equipment and Supplies

Items	Amount Required			
	Day/Shift	Day/Shift	Day/Shift	Day/Shift
	Weekday (A.M.)	Weekend (A.M.)	Weekday (P.M.)	Weekend (P.M.)
Service Trays				
Tables				
Tablecloths				
Cloth Napkins				
Paper Napkins				
Bread Baskets				
Placemats				
Coffee Cups				
Saucers				
Juice Glasses				

Procedures

Room service procedures involve taking the room service order, routing the order, preparing the order, delivering the order, and clean-up and follow-up.

Taking the Order. Order-takers should follow the specific procedures developed by their lodging property as they take orders from guests. Order-takers should answer all telephone calls promptly and offer an apology if the phone rings for a long period of time. Many properties require the telephone to be answered promptly within three rings.

The order-taker should identify him- or herself and indicate that the caller has reached room service. The order-taker should use a cheerful voice to convey a spirit of hospitality. Caller identification systems that identify guests' names for order-takers enable them to provide personalized service. Most guests are impressed when an order-taker uses their names when the guests haven't identified themselves yet. Some computerized systems create guest lists that can be printed at the front desk and taken to the room service department; other systems display the guest's name and room number when the phone rings. Order-takers should ask for the guest's name and guestroom number immediately if they are not already available. If the order-taker is reading a guest's name on a caller-identification-system screen and is unsure how to pronounce it, he or she should politely ask the guest for the proper pronunciation. It is important to pronounce a guest's name correctly.

Order-takers in automated room service operations can input orders at point-of-sale (POS) systems. They typically use the same type of POS system used by catering or other food and beverage departments at the property. Lodging properties without POS systems use manual guest check systems; as the guest recites the order, the order-taker fills out a paper guest check with a pen or pencil (see Exhibit 6). Frequently, duplicate guest checks are used. Guest checks are usually prenumbered and assigned to specific order-takers; all guest checks must be accounted for at the end of each order-taker's shift. When order-takers use manual systems, it is very important that they write legibly, since production staff, service personnel, the guest, and in some cases a cashier all may need to read the check. Order-takers should also use standard menu abbreviations to help prevent misunderstandings.

Order-takers should include all details about the order on the guest check, such as how the guests wish their eggs to be prepared, or what type of salad dressings they prefer. Guests may make special requests about how a menu item should be prepared, such as without oil, salt, or sugar. They may also request a different type of side dish. Good communication systems allow special requests to be accurately and completely transmitted from the order-taker to production staff members.

The order should be repeated to the guest to confirm its accuracy. Order-takers should also give callers an estimate of the delivery time, particularly during rush periods, when several orders may be in line for preparation and delivery. Some guests may be in a hurry and will not want to wait for a room service order. If it later becomes clear that it will be impossible to deliver room service orders within the originally estimated time, the order-taker should call the guests and let them know when to expect delivery.

Order-takers can sell by suggestion. The same procedures that servers use in the dining room apply here. **Suggestive selling** gives guests the opportunity to order something extra. This helps guests enjoy the best that the property has to offer, helps the property receive higher revenues, and helps room service staff earn more tips. Everyone wins. Guests may forget to order beverages, appetizers, or desserts if order-takers do not specifically ask about these kinds of items. Informing guests about specials, describing item preparation and presentation, suggesting high-contribution-margin items, and asking **open-ended questions** (as opposed to closed-ended questions, to which guests can answer "yes" or "no") or **forced-choice questions** such as "Which of our two excellent desserts would you

Exhibit 6 Sample Guest Check

❶ *Cutler*

Holiday Inn®

Room Service

Table	Guest ❸
	1
Server	**Room Number**
Ed	*330* ❷
Date	**Check Number**

	Item		Price
❽	*7.30*	*8.15* ❾	
❹ 1	*Zoe/BAC*		*3.95*
2			
3			
4			
5			
6			
7			
8			
❺ 9	*Lg OJ*		*1.05*
10	*Cof*		*.75*
11			
12			
13			
14			*5.75* ❼
		Tax	*.29*
		Sub Total	
		Tip	
		Total	

❻ *Charge*

Signature________________ Room No. *330*

Address______________________________

❶ Ask for guest's name and write on check.

❷ Ask for the room number and write on check.

❸ Ask the guest how many settings they would like.

❹ Request and write the entrée using standard abbreviations. Ask for and write details (i.e., rare, medium, well for steaks, choice of salad dressing, etc.).

❺ Upsell side orders, larger portions, desserts, and beverages. Advise guest of any "specials."

❻ Ask if the order will be cash or charged to the room. Check the prepaid list to verify the guest has charging privileges. If not, write "prepay" on the check so the server knows to collect cash.

❼ Price the items, total the check, and tell the guest the amount.

❽ Tell the guest the time and write it on the check.

❾ Advise the guest of the approximate time of delivery.

Note: When separate bar checks are used, transfer the total of the bar check to the front of the food check. As a reminder to include bar totals, write the word "BAR" on the food check when taking the bar order.

Source: *Room Service* (Memphis, Tennessee: Holiday Inns, Inc.—U.S. Hotel Operations, 1981), p. 20.

like, Mr. Marshall?" are all techniques that can increase room service sales. Good order-takers learn to gauge how well callers know what they want. Suggestive-selling techniques should not be used on guests who seem to know exactly what they want, since they might become annoyed. When the order-taking process is completed, order-takers should always thank the guest.

Some properties use a voice mail or tape-recorded message system for room service; the guest phones the room service number and places the order without talking to a staff member. Other properties use this system only during very slow periods when an order-taker is not on duty. For example, during slow periods a room service attendant may serve as the order-taker as well; a taped message could then be used when the attendant is away from the station, delivering an order. The impersonal service and the possibility of confusion about the guest's exact needs are two potential disadvantages to this system. The room service manager must ensure that the advantages of faster service and reduced operating (labor) costs offset these potential problems before using a voice mail or other message system.

Telephone etiquette may be a matter of common sense to some room service staff members; nevertheless, all staff should receive initial as well as refresher training on the rules of telephone etiquette. Room service attendants, though they typically spend much less time on the phone with guests than order-takers, should be familiar with telephone etiquette so that when they do phone guests, answer guests' calls, or substitute for order-takers, they are prepared. Whoever answers the phone should stop talking with others before picking up the receiver. Because guests should not have to hear unnecessary noise and background conversations, and to help ensure accurate order-taking, nearby staff members should not converse among themselves while another staff member is speaking to a guest on the phone.

Putting callers on hold the right way is a part of good telephone etiquette. When two phone calls are coming in or when a phone call comes in while the order-taker is on the line with another guest, the order-taker should put guests on hold using the following procedures:

- Ask Caller #1 if you may put him or her on hold to answer another line.
- Ask Caller #2 to please hold while you complete another order.
- Return to Caller #1, apologize for the delay, and finish taking the first order.
- Return to Caller #2, apologize for the delay, and take the order.
- If you think Caller #2 will be on hold for too long, or if a third call is received, apologize to Caller #2 and offer to call back for the order. Take the guests' orders as soon as possible.
- Anytime you must interrupt the conversation, explain the reason to the guest.

Exhibit 7 summarizes telephone etiquette guidelines and order-taking procedures for room service personnel.

Routing the Order. After the order-taker receives a guest's order, he or she must route it to the appropriate food or beverage production area. There are several methods of doing so:

1. The order-taker may carry the guest check to the production area by hand. This system may work well when a separate room service kitchen and service

Exhibit 7 Telephone Etiquette and Order-Taking Procedures

1. Answer the telephone promptly—within three rings when possible.
2. Identify yourself and your department with a friendly greeting. For example, a property may specify that from 7:00 A.M. to noon an order-taker named Carla should say, "Room Service, Carla speaking, good morning"; from noon to 6:00 P.M., "Room Service, Carla speaking, good afternoon"; from 6:00 P.M. to 9:00 P.M., "Room Service, Carla speaking, good evening"; and from 9:00 P.M. to closing, "Room Service, Carla speaking, may I help you?"
3. Politely ask for the guest's name and room number (if the room service department doesn't use a caller identification system or receive guest lists from the front desk).
4. Use the caller's name whenever possible, being certain that it is pronounced correctly. Ask the caller how to pronounce his or her name if necessary.
5. Use a cheerful voice throughout the conversation.
6. Obtain a complete order by asking the guest about appetizers, entrées, desserts, beverages, and special preparation instructions.
7. Use suggestive selling to encourage guests to order something extra and help them make sure that they remember all they want to order. If it is clear that the guest knows exactly what he or she wants, make fewer suggestions or none at all.
8. To help eliminate errors, repeat the order the guest has placed.
9. State the approximate time that the guest can expect the order to be delivered. State a range of time, depending on the amount of business that room service is currently handling. If the guest has ordered items that require extra preparation time or that are usually prepared at tableside, inform the guest about this to confirm that the order will be ready when the guest wants it.
10. Thank the guest for calling. Allow the guest to hang up the phone first.

Source: Adapted from the video *Room Service* (East Lansing, Mich.: Educational Institute of the American Hotel & Motel Association, 1989).

bar are located close to the order-taker's telephone stand or when the order-taker is a cashier or receptionist in the dining room.

2. The order-taker may give the guest check to a room service attendant, who then takes it to the production area.
3. The order-taker may use a precheck register or POS system with a remote printer. With this equipment, the order-taker automatically transmits the order to production staff members as he or she enters the information into the precheck register or POS system. This technology can dramatically expedite the order-taker's job and speed service.

Order-takers using a manual system must then enter information from the guest check onto a **room service order form** (see Exhibit 8). Properties use this form to record information about each order, such as the room number, the guest's

Exhibit 8 Room Service Order Form

Date: ____________________						
Room #	Guest Name	Time Order	Delivery Time	Order	Tray	Cart

Courtesy of Hotel du Pont, Wilmington, Delaware

name, and the time the order was placed. The order-taker must also make an entry on the **room service control form** (see Exhibit 9), which keeps track of all guest checks. It indicates the person responsible for delivering the order, the time required to prepare the order, and the total amount of cash and charge sales generated by room service. A POS system can automatically generate reports covering the information recorded on both of these forms, since the system can maintain all of the information related to each order.

Procedures for transmitting room service orders to production personnel become more complicated when order-takers must give copies of orders to two kinds of production stations (those at which hot food is produced and those at which cold food is produced) as well as to the service bar. One operation solves this problem by using a five-part order ticket. The order-taker writes the entire order on this ticket; one copy goes to the cashier, another goes to the hot food station, a third goes to the cold food station, a fourth goes to the service bar, and the fifth copy goes to the room service attendant so that he or she can put the order together on a tray or service cart. Automation would drastically improve service in room service operations at which orders are prepared in several different areas.

Preparing the Order. Room service attendants should be aware of the orders being prepared by production staff so they can do any additional setup work. For example, attendants may prepare or portion salads and desserts while production staff members prepare other parts of the order. If necessary, attendants should cover these salads and desserts with plastic wrap or store them in protective

Exhibit 9 Room Service Control Form

Food & Beverage Department
Room Service Control

❶ Day________ Date________ Cashier________ Shift________

LOCATION ❷

Guest Name	Server	Order taken ❺ A.M./P.M.
Check No. ❸	Amount $ ❹	Tray out A.M./P.M. ❻
Room No.	No. Served ( ) paid ❽ ( ) charge	Tray in A.M./P.M. ❼
Guest Name	Server	Order taken A.M./P.M.
Check No.	Amount $	Tray out A.M./P.M.
Room No.	No. Served ( ) paid ( ) charge	Tray in A.M./P.M.
Guest Name	Server	Order taken A.M./P.M.

❶ Complete the heading at the beginning of the shift.

❷ Write the guest's name and room number. This information should be checked with the front desk to verify:

- The guests are registered
- The correct room number
- The guest's credit standing

❸ Write the guest check number and obtain the server's signature. This signals a change of responsibility from the order taker to the server for the proper use of guest check.

❹ Write the dollar amount of the order and the number of guests served.

❺ Record the time the order was taken.

❻ Record the time the tray is taken out for delivery.

❼ Record the time of day the tray is returned to the kitchen.

❽ Record the form of payment (cash or charge).

NOTE: Charged tips should be recorded on a tip tally form.

Source: *Room Service* (Memphis, Tennessee: Holiday Inns, Inc.—U.S. Hotel Operations, 1981), p. 30.

containers to help maintain quality. Room service attendants could also obtain beverages, typically from a service bar located close to the room service area. Attendants must give the bartender a copy of the room service order indicating the beverages they need.

In properties with a central beverage storeroom, a manager issues full bottles of alcoholic and other beverages from the central storeroom to the room service beverage storage area. The manager can use a standard issue requisition and then transfer the costs of issued beverages to the room service department. If guests request full bottles from room service, room service attendants at some hotels may obtain bottles from the room service beverage storeroom. Room service managers must always have controls in place to keep track of beverage inventory, supply accounting information, and protect inventory from theft or quality deterioration.

When food orders are ready, the room service attendants pick them up, cover them with lids or some other insulated material, and present them to the order-taker, food checker, or another designated staff member for inspection. At some properties, room service attendants put caps or covers on cups to prevent spills. The entire cart or serving tray should be covered with a washable cloth or disposable clear plastic cover. The food and beverages are now ready for one final inspection and then rapid delivery to the guest.

Why is each order checked so thoroughly before it is delivered? A frequent guest complaint is that condiments or other items are missing from room service orders. Because guestrooms can be a long way from the kitchen, an error found by a guest takes more time to correct and creates more problems than it would if the error had been discovered in or near the kitchen by a staff member.

During the final inspection, room service attendants should look for the following:

- Does the order match the guest check? Is anything missing? Has everything been prepared as the guest requested?
- Are all of the appropriate condiments, sauces, side dishes, flatware, and beverages where they should be? These items should be double-checked to be sure nothing has been forgotten.
- Does the food look appetizing? If you were the guest, would you be pleased with the presentation of the order?
- Does the attendant have all the equipment (tray stands, special tables, serving utensils, matches or a lighter, and heating or cooling devices) needed to serve this order?

Delivering the Order. It is imperative that room service attendants deliver orders as quickly as possible. The fastest route to the guestroom should be used; attendants and other room service staff members must know the layout of the property extremely well. Hot food should still be hot, and cold food should still be cold when it gets to the guest. Time and temperature are the most important elements in room service delivery, because as product holding times increase, so does the likelihood of contamination and loss of quality. Some properties offer **split service,** which means that room service attendants deliver courses separately. Split service helps maintain food quality and safety; each course can be portioned and served when it is ready, eliminating short-term holding in the kitchen. The disadvantage of split service is that it takes more staff to deliver courses separately, and therefore is more costly.

Some lodging properties use **dumbwaiters** (small service elevators) to expedite order delivery. Using dumbwaiters to move products between floors may work well when continental breakfasts (coffee, juice, and rolls) are offered to all guests or when standard breakfasts are offered to VIPs and guests in guestroom suites. Some properties designate one or more freight or passenger elevators for room service use during busy periods. **Flying kitchens**—well-equipped elevators that enable service staff to prepare a limited number of menu items as they move between floors—are sometimes installed. A room service attendant could be assigned to one or more floors during peak business periods; after the carts are transported to each floor, the assigned attendant could deliver the orders. From time to time, managers should brainstorm ways to keep service timely with room service staff.

Room service managers should develop procedures for delivering room service orders. For example, all room service staff members should know that when entering or exiting elevators with a room service cart, the cart should be pulled rather than pushed. Why? Pulling gives the staff member more control over the cart and there is less chance that a guest or another staff member will bump into it. Other procedures might include delivering orders approximately in the sequence in which they were received, using a uniform greeting and method of alerting guests that their orders have arrived (for example, a light knock followed by the statement "Room Service with your order"), greeting the guest warmly, and verifying the guest's name and room number when the guest opens the door. At some lodging properties, room service attendants ask guests for permission to enter their guestrooms, then ask them where they prefer their orders to be placed—on a table, left on the cart, or elsewhere. Hot foods should be left in warmers for the guest's self-service unless he or she indicates otherwise. If the order requires tableside preparation, attendants may be required to tell guests how long the order will take to prepare and to ask if they may begin the preparation.

Normally, room service attendants ask guests to sign a copy of the guest check to verify that they received the order. It is a good idea to give the guest the guest check and a pen before setting up the order. This will eliminate an awkward time lag while the guest reviews and signs the check. Usually, the guest's signature is sufficient; however, cash payments are required in certain circumstances, such as when the guest has no guest folio set up with the front desk.

The room service attendant should use discretion in the guest's room. It is critical to respect the guest's privacy and not disturb any of the guest's personal items. If it is absolutely necessary to move items to serve the order, the attendant should politely ask the guest for permission to do so. The attendant should offer to pour beverages for the guest. When serving food on the room service cart, the attendant should check the supporting braces of the cart extensions to be certain that they are secure and will not collapse. If the room service cart has a heating element, it should be extinguished by the attendant according to the property's procedures. Guests should be cautioned about handling plates that are hot.

Before leaving, room service attendants should offer additional assistance to the guest and remind the guest about cart or tray pickup procedures. Attendants may give the guest a number to dial for additional service or to request tray pickup; this information might also be provided on a courtesy card left on the tray or cart. The attendant should always thank the guest and wish him or her an enjoyable meal.

Clean-Up and Follow-Up. Properties should have a system in place for removing used room service trays and carts quickly. On their way back to the room service area after delivering an order, room service attendants should pick up any carts or trays left in hotel corridors. Coordination and effective communication between housekeeping personnel and the room service staff are essential. Housekeepers could phone room service staff to remove room service equipment from guestrooms, or housekeepers could move used room service items to a central location, or (as just mentioned) a card left on the tray or cart could ask guests to phone room service or the housekeeping department when they wish room service equipment to be removed.

If time permits, order-takers or other room service staff members should phone guests after their orders are delivered to ask them how they are enjoying the meal and to offer additional assistance. Many guests appreciate this extra service.

Providing Wine Service and Special Amenities

Guests may order table or sparkling bottled wines from room service; therefore, room service attendants should know the proper ways to uncork them. Room service attendants may also be responsible for delivering fruit baskets, cheese trays, and other special amenities for guests; therefore, management should develop standard procedures for preparing, arranging, and delivering these items. In addition, if special amenities require cloth napkins, flatware, or plates, the attendants must ensure that those supplies accompany the orders. A form like the one shown in Exhibit 10 can be used whenever a hotel executive or a friend, relative, or business associate orders a special room service amenity for a guest. Often, these amenities are a good source of revenue for the room service department. (When a hotel executive provides a special amenity for a guest, he or she should credit room service for at least the cost of the item. The executive can charge the item to a sales promotion account.)

Frequently, a welcome card accompanies special room service amenities, and the room service attendant is often responsible for ensuring that it is in place. Managers design or write welcome cards simply to welcome a guest and to wish him or her a pleasant stay. This special touch can be instrumental in gaining the favor of a VIP. In cosmopolitan hotels, welcome cards may be available in many languages. Room attendants must make sure the guest receives a card in his or her language.

Guests frequently order bar setups through room service. Typical items in a bar setup are alcoholic beverages, cocktail napkins, stir sticks, glasses, a pitcher of water, a bucket of ice, and appropriate garnishes. In addition to alcoholic beverages, the guest requesting a bar setup may order mixers such as tonic water, club soda, or bottled water. Depending on the guestroom's location, attendants may bring ice to the guestroom from the room service area or from an ice machine that is close to the guestroom.

Exhibit 10 Order Form for Special Room Service Amenities

NR: 1555

Special Room Service Order

For Mr./Mrs.: ______________________ **Room:** __________

Delivery Date: ______________ **Cost Code:** __________

From: ☐ __________ ☐ __________

☐ __________ ☐ __________

☐ __________

☐ **$XX.XX** **Large deluxe fruit tray with one bottle of wine**
(Selection of fruits and chocolate, presented on a silver tray including one bottle of wine white or red)

☐ **$XX.XX** **Large deluxe fruit tray**
(Selections of fruit and chocolate, presented on a silver tray)

☐ **$XX.XX** **Small fruit mirror with cheese and 1/2 bottle of wine**
(Selection of fruit, cheese, and chocolate presented on a small mirror with 1/2 bottle of wine)

☐ **$XX.XX** **Small fruit mirror with cheese and chocolate**
(Selection of fruit, cheese, and chocolate presented on a small mirror)

☐ **$XX.XX** **Fruit arrangement in a wicker basket**
(Assorted fruits in a basket)

☐ **$XX.XX** **Presentation of chocolate cups with 2 small liquor bottles**
(Presented on a blue plate with chocolate cups and flowers)

☐ $______ Champagne Domestic __________ Import __________

Name: ______________________ Total Cost: $__________

Courtesy of Hotel du Pont, Wilmington, Delaware

Some properties offer executive coffee service. Guests who are staying on special VIP floors, specific guests identified by management, guests paying the full rate for expensive rooms, and others may receive this extra room service amenity. This complimentary morning coffee service may consist of juice, pastries, hot beverages, and a morning newspaper. Special order forms for executive coffee service typically supply the information that room service staff members need to provide this amenity.

After Room Service

After room service has been delivered, issues important to managers include income control procedures, guest comments, and funneling feedback about room service into planning activities.

Income Control Procedures

While many of the income control procedures used in the room service department mirror those used in public dining areas, some are unique to room service operations. Control procedures to collect payment for all orders served through room service begin at the time order-takers write orders on guest checks or enter orders into a POS system. In manual systems, order-takers enter information about an order and the amount of income it will generate on the room service control form (see Exhibit 9). After service, attendants return copies of guest checks that guests have signed to the order-taker. The order-taker then enters information about the payment (cash or charge) into a log. At the end of the shift or at another time designated by management, order-takers must carry the room service control form and the signed guest check copies to the front desk for posting into **guest folios**. Hotels increasingly are using POS systems rather than manual systems in their room service departments. When room service uses POS equipment, charged sale information is electronically transferred to the guest folio at the front desk.

Because most guests wish to have their room service charges billed to their guestroom accounts, procedures to accommodate these requests should be developed. Sometimes, however, charges are not possible. For example, a guest may have paid for the room in advance with cash, or guests may have reached or exceeded their lines of credit. The front office should regularly report guests who are on a cash basis to the room service department so that order-takers can note the need for cash payments on the guest checks of these guests. In addition, order-takers should inform these guests that the room service attendant will require cash when he or she delivers their orders. Some properties provide room service attendants with a credit card imprinter and appropriate supplies in anticipation of guests who wish to use their credit cards. Policies and procedures regarding the acceptance of credit cards and checks must comply with those developed by the lodging property for use in other property areas.

Guest Comments

Guest complaints about room service span a wide range of topics (see Exhibit 11). High prices are the main reason that guests do not use room service. Guests may resist tipping staff members because of perceived high menu charges; some hotels add an automatic gratuity percentage to room service charges for that reason. In general, business travelers are not as price conscious as pleasure travelers, most likely because their room service charges are often paid by their companies.

Some guests focus on the quality of the food and beverages served or the quality of the service rather than price. Guests dislike slow service. They often expect their meals to arrive no more than 20 minutes after they order. Some properties'

Exhibit 11 Why Guests Do Not Use Room Service

Reason	Percentage
High Prices	33
Slow Service	12
Don't Like Eating Alone	12
Food Not Hot/Cold	11
Limited Hours	9
Inadequate Menu	8
Insufficient Variety	7
Other	6
Mixed-Up Orders	1
Rude Staff	1

Source: Carlo Wolff, "Roomservice Blues," *Lodging Hospitality,* December 1992, pp. 55–56.

room service order-takers cannot speak the native language well, so communicating with guests can be difficult. Even without the language barrier, guests who use room service often complain that the items that were delivered were not what they ordered, were delivered at improper temperatures, or were presented poorly. Many guests complain about dirty dishes left in hotel hallways from room service deliveries.

Guests sometimes complain that there is not enough variety on room service menus. Today's guests often expect a selection of fresh fruits and the option to design their own meals to suit their preferences or dietary restrictions. Clearly, guest expectations of room service today are high, and it is worthwhile for room service managers to familiarize themselves with the expectations of their property's target markets.

Managers may obtain guest comments by asking them in person or recording comments that guests made to service staff. They may also ask guests to complete comment forms that cover all areas of their hotel stay. Room service should be included on this form as a way to obtain additional feedback for planning.

Another strategy for obtaining detailed, timely guest feedback is to have the room service manager regularly phone a sampling of guests who have used room service. Specific details about menus, staff member service styles, and the overall room service experience can be obtained if the right questions are asked. As an incentive, managers could offer a slight reduction in the hotel's guestroom rate to guests who provide this valuable feedback.

Using Feedback in Planning

Information obtained during and after room service can be a valuable source of feedback for room service planners. Room service menus must continue to evolve based on the needs and expectations of guests. Guests today are generally in search of higher quality menu items, served in smaller quantities, at affordable prices. These three criteria translate to value for guests.

Lodging Hospitality's survey about room service (see Exhibit 11) can help provide an example of how managers can use guest feedback to improve room service. If all of the guests who responded to the survey were staying at the same property (they were *not* in reality; they were a random sampling of frequent travelers, as identified by Penton Publishing), how could managers at the property improve the room service to make it more guest-driven? First, the managers should consider reducing room service menu prices, since that was the top complaint. Next, the managers should evaluate how room service is delivered at the property, because slow service and food not at its proper temperature are two major reasons related to service that guests cited for not using the property's room service. (Mixed-up orders and rude staff, although not cited very often, are other service-related problems that can be looked into.) To alleviate these service-related problems, the managers should make sure room service staff members are properly trained and have the inventory and equipment it takes to deliver quality food and beverages to guests. Managers can't do anything about the fact that some guests don't like eating alone, but they can look into doing something about the limited room service hours and insufficient variety on the room service menu, and do more investigating to find out why guests think the menu is "inadequate." Of course, managers must keep budget constraints in mind as they think about making improvements to room service.

In a guest-driven room service operation, the needs and expectations of guests come first. Room service staff must be trained to embrace the philosophy that when they deliver a room service order, they are really bringing the dining room to the guest's room. By respecting the guest's privacy and providing prompt and attentive service, room service staff members can delight guests. Positive room service experiences can help give guests a good impression of the property, enhance the property's reputation, and increase revenues for all of the property's revenue centers.

Key Terms

assistant room service manager—An assistant to the room service manager who assumes some of the responsibilities that would otherwise be the room service manager's, such as supervising staff, making daily or routine operational management decisions, and completing records and reports.

busperson—A staff member who helps set up room service stations in the kitchen, assembles items for an order, delivers small orders, picks up room service equipment and tableware from rooms and hallways, takes used serviceware to dishwashing areas, cleans room service tables and trays, and otherwise supports room service attendants.

cross-selling—In internal selling, a sales technique in which hotel staff members working in one hotel area suggest that guests take advantage of the products and services of other hotel areas. Cross-selling can also be accomplished with advertising media.

doorknob menu—A type of room service menu that guests use to select what they want to eat and the time they want it delivered; they then hang the menu outside the guestroom door on the doorknob. Later, staff members collect the menus so that the orders can be prepared and sent to the rooms at the indicated times.

dumbwaiters—Small service elevators that can be used to deliver room service orders.

fact book—A book salespeople and others at a lodging property use to familiarize themselves with and remind themselves about their property's products and services.

flying kitchen—A well-equipped elevator that enables room service staff members to produce a limited number of menu items as they move between floors.

forced-choice question—A question that seeks to limit the respondent to choosing from the alternatives presented by the questioner.

function sheet—A document that gives a detailed breakdown of items, people, and tasks needed to prepare for, provide service during, and clean up after a special event. Also called a banquet event order (BEO).

guest folio—A file (electronic or paper) containing all of a guest's charges during the guest's stay at a lodging property.

hospitality suite—A guestroom, suite of guestrooms, function room, or parlor that guests use for entertaining (for example, by throwing a cocktail party).

internal selling—Specific sales activities of staff members used in conjunction with an internal merchandising program to promote additional sales and guest satisfaction once guests have arrived at the establishment.

menu engineering—A menu management technique that analyzes the profitability and popularity of menu items.

open-ended question—A question that cannot be answered with a "yes" or "no."

room service—The department within a lodging property's food and beverage division that is responsible for delivering food and beverages to guests in their guestrooms. May also be responsible for producing the food and beverages.

room service attendant—A staff member who accepts orders from the kitchen, ensures that all items listed on the guest check are on the food tray or table, permits the order-taker to double-check the order if procedures require it, delivers orders to designated guestrooms, and serves guests in their rooms. May also take orders from guests, return carts, trays, and dirty dishes to the room service area, and perform other duties to help the department run smoothly and deliver quality service to guests.

room service captain—A staff member who oversees order-takers, room service attendants, and buspersons for a particular area or shift. Room service captains typically report to the room service manager or assistant room service manager.

room service control form—An accounting form that keeps track of guest checks and indicates the person responsible for delivering each order, the time required to prepare each order, and the total amount of cash and charge sales generated by room service.

room service manager—The head of the room service department, responsible for organizing, selecting, orienting, training, and scheduling room service staff; handling problems with food and beverage orders and delivery, controlling costs, and ensuring revenue collection; and monitoring department operations. Reports to the lodging operation's food and beverage director or assistant director.

room service order form—A form used to record information about each room service order, such as the room number, the guest's name, and the time the order was placed.

room service order-taker—A staff member who answers guest phone calls for room service, takes guest orders, fills out logbooks and accounting forms, and acts as an intermediary between guests and room service staff members.

split service—A room service delivery method in which staff members deliver courses separately. Split service helps maintain food quality because each course can be portioned and served when it is ready, eliminating short-term holding in the kitchen.

suggestive selling—The practice of influencing a guest's purchase decision through the use of sales phrases.

video ordering—A means of ordering room service through the guestroom television, usually with the television's remote control.

Review Questions

1. From the guest's perspective, what are the key elements of a well-managed room service department?
2. What should managers keep in mind when planning and designing room service menus?
3. What are the responsibilities of typical room service positions?
4. How do room service staff members usually prepare for an individual service period?
5. How do room service staff members take orders, route them, prepare them, deliver them, and clean up after they have been delivered?
6. What is room service's role in providing wine service and special room service amenities?
7. What income control procedures are used in room service?
8. What are typical guest comments and complaints about room service? How can this feedback be used in planning?

Internet Sites

For more information, visit the following Internet sites. Remember that Internet addresses can change without notice.

American Culinary Federation
http://www.acfchefs.org

CaterWare Inc.
http://www.caterware.com

The Catering Connection
http://www.caterconnect.com

Chef's Store
http://www.chefstore.com

CuisineNet
http://www.cuisinenet.com

Delphi/NewMarket Software
http://www.newsoft.com

Food Net
http://www.foodnet.com

Food Network
http://www.foodtv.com

Foodwine
http://www.foodwine.com

Internet Food Channel
http://www.foodchannel.com

Myriad Restaurant Group
http://www.cuisine.com

Resorts Online
http://www.resortsonline.com

Room Service Depot
http://www.valflo.com/roomservice.html

Virtual Vineyards
http://www.virtualvin.com

References

Achorn, Edward C. "Food Fight: The Free Breakfast War." *Lodging,* December 1990.

"Dial for Luxury." *U.S. News & World Report,* January 26, 1998.

Flint, Jerry. "Room Service." *Forbes,* April 29, 1991.

"Ideas." *Innkeeping World,* September 1994.

Report to the Nation: Trends in Travel and Hospitality. Washington, D.C.: Public Affairs Group, 1997.

Rowe, Megan. "Volume Feeding à la Vegas." *Lodging Hospitality,* April 1991.

———. Rowe, Megan. "What It's Worth." *Lodging Hospitality,* December 1997.

Scarpa, James. "Hotel Market Segment Report." *Restaurant Business,* January 20, 1993.

Straus, Karen. "Dial-A-Breakfast." *Restaurants & Institutions,* June 15, 1993.

Wolff, Carlo. "Roomservice Blues." *Lodging Hospitality,* December 1992.

Appendix

Sample Training Needs Evaluation Form for Room Service Attendants

How well are your current staff members performing? Use this form to observe and rate their work.

Part I: Job Knowledge

Rate the staff member's knowledge of each of the following topics:	Well Below Standard	Slightly Below Standard	At Standard	Above Standard
Knowledge for All Staff Members				
Quality Guest Service				
Bloodborne Pathogens				
Personal Appearance				
Emergency Situations				
Lost and Found				
Recycling Procedures				
Safe Work Habits				
Manager on Duty				
Your Property's Fact Sheet				
Staff Member Policies				
The Americans with Disabilities Act				
Knowledge for All Front-of-House Food and Beverage Staff Members				
Telephone Courtesy				
Safety and Security				
Kitchen Safety				
Alcoholic Beverage Terms				
House Brands and Call Brands				
Liquor Brands and Categories				
Standard Drink Abbreviations				
U.S. Alcoholic Beverage Laws				
Responsible Alcohol Service Procedures				
OSHA Regulations				

(continued)

Rate the staff member's knowledge of each of the following topics:	Well Below Standard	Slightly Below Standard	At Standard	Above Standard
Knowledge for All Front-of-House Food and Beverage Staff Members *(continued)*				
Beverage Prices				
Restaurant Menus				
Basic Food Preparation Terms and Timing				
Correct Plate Presentation and Garnishes				
The Restaurant Reservation System				
Tipping Policies				
Heimlich Maneuver and First Aid				
Sanitation				
Health Department Regulations				
Point-of-Sale Equipment				
Community Services				
Knowledge for Room Service Attendants				
What Is a Room Service Attendant?				
Working as a Team With Co-Workers and Other Departments				
Superior Performance Standards				
Key Control				
Property Floor Plan				
Special Guest Situations				
Guestroom Safety				
Suggestive Selling				
Room Service Equipment Terms				
Glassware Types and Use				
China				
Silverware				
Linens and Napkin Folding				
Standard Drink Ingredients and Garnishes				

Rate the staff member's knowledge of each of the following tasks:	**Well Below Standard**	**Slightly Below Standard**	**At Standard**	**Above Standard**
Knowledge for Room Service Attendants *(continued)*				
Standard Tray and Cart Setups				
Standard Portable Bar Setup				
Standard Place-Setting Arrangement for Small Group Dinners				
Standard Setup for Small Receptions and Buffets				
Standard Setup for Coffee Breaks				
Par Stock System				
VIPs				
Part II: Job Skills				
Rate the staff member's skills in performing each of the following tasks:				
Perform Beginning-of-Shift Duties				
Present Room Service Trays and Carts				
Process Express Breakfast Orders				
Deliver VIP Amenities				
Use the Point-of-Sale Equipment				
Take and Record Room Service Orders				
Handle Special Room Service Requests				
Place the Room Service Order				
Perform Pantry Prep for Room Service Orders				
Prepare Coffee				
Prepare Hot Tea				
Prepare Hot Chocolate				
Prepare Iced Tea				
Set Up Bottled Wine or Champagne for Service				
Assemble the Beverage Order and Food Condiments				

(continued)

Rate the staff member's skills in performing each of the following tasks:	**Well Below Standard**	**Slightly Below Standard**	**At Standard**	**Above Standard**
Rate the staff member's skills in performing each of the following tasks: *(continued)*				
Pick Up the Room Service Order				
Deliver the Room Service Order				
Serve the Room Service Order				
Serve Coffee or Hot Tea				
Check IDs				
Open and Serve Wine or Champagne				
Present and Settle the Guest Check				
Retrieve Trays and Carts				
Close Out the Guest Check				
Follow Up with Guests				
Respond to Dissatisfied Guests				
Clear and Reset Trays and Carts				
Handle Soiled Room Service Linens				
Set Up Portable Bars in Suites or Guestrooms				
Set Up and Serve Small Group Dinners and Receptions				
Set Up and Serve Small Buffet Banquets				
Set Up and Serve Coffee Breaks				
Maintain Room Service Side Stations				
Pick Up and Restock Room Service Supplies				
Perform Closing Shift Duties				
Make Shift Deposit and Collect Due-Backs				
Use the Room Service Logbook				

Source: Adapted from the "Room Service Attendant Guide" in the *Hospitality Skills Training Series* (East Lansing, Mich.: Educational Institute of the American Hotel & Motel Association, 1995), pp. 15–17.

Task Breakdowns: Room Service

The procedures presented in this section are for illustrative purposes only and should not be construed as recommendations or standards. While these procedures are typical, readers should keep in mind that each food service facility has its own procedures, equipment specifications, and safety policies.

Preset Room Service Trays and Carts

Materials needed: *Room service trays and carts, tray and cart setup charts, lemon wedges, a brush, cleaning cloths, sanitizing solution, tablecloths, hot boxes, and canned, gel-type fuel.*

STEPS	HOW-TO'S
1. Ask your supervisor for the tray and cart setup charts for each meal.	
2. Clean service trays.	❑ Wash trays in the dish room. ❑ If the trays are cork-lined, rub the cork with lemon wedges to remove odors. Then let the trays stand for a few minutes before washing. ❑ Spray trays with hot water to remove food residue. ❑ If the trays are cork-lined, use a brush to scrub the cork. Then rinse the trays. ❑ Spray the trays with an approved sanitizing solution. Then stack them upside-down at right angles to allow them to air-dry.
3. Clean room service carts.	❑ Remove all equipment and supplies from the carts. ❑ Use a clean cloth and a sanitizing solution to wipe the carts, including the shelves, legs, and wheels. ❑ Polish the carts with a clean, dry cloth. ❑ Replace equipment and supplies. ❑ Report any squeaky wheels to maintenance staff members or stewards immediately, so they can fix the carts quickly.
4. Place tablecloths neatly over room service carts.	
5. Organize and preset trays and carts before the meal period begins.	❑ Make sure you have the number of carts and trays requested on the tray and cart setup charts.

Preset Room Service Trays and Carts *(continued)*

STEPS	HOW-TO'S
	❑ Items you may place on a tray or cart include salt, pepper, ketchup, mustard, mayonnaise, sugar, and artificial sweetener. ❑ Make sure each item is clean before placing it on a tray or cart. ❑ Wipe containers with a clean cloth if necessary. ❑ Follow the tray and cart setup charts to place items on trays and carts. ❑ Spread the weight of the items evenly across the tray. Place heavy items in the center and lighter items around the edges.
6. Replace cans of gel-type fuel in hot boxes.	❑ Carefully open the hot box door. ❑ Remove the empty can. ❑ Place a new can in the box. Never place a new can in a hot box containing a can that is in use. ❑ Close the hot box door. ❑ Wash your hands right away. Canned, gel-type fuel is poisonous.
7. Position preset trays and carts where they won't be in the way.	

Take and Record Room Service Orders

Materials needed: *Guest checks, a pen, point-of-sale equipment, room service menus, the cash-only list, a telephone, and a time-date stamp.*

STEPS	HOW-TO'S
1. Greet callers warmly.	❑ Pick up the telephone within three rings. ❑ Identify your department and introduce yourself by name. ❑ Ask how you may help. For example: "Thank you for calling room service. This is Marla, your room service attendant. How may I help you?"
2. Use good telephone etiquette.	
3. Ask the guests for their names and room numbers.	❑ Always use the guest's last name with a courtesy title during the conversation: "Good morning, Ms. Mars." ❑ Even if your computerized telephone system displays the guest's name and room number, confirm that you are talking to the registered guest. ❑ Neatly write the guest's name and room number on the guest check. (With automated point-of-sale equipment, the system will record room numbers on the check).
4. Determine whether guests have approved credit accounts at the front desk.	❑ As soon as you have the guest's name and room number, check the cash-only list to see if the guest's name is on that list. ❑ If the guest's name and room number are on the list, politely explain that the guest will have to pay for the order when it is delivered. ❑ If the guest's name and room number are not on the cash-only list, take the order without discussing payment.

Take and Record Room Service Orders *(continued)*

STEPS	HOW-TO'S
5. Use suggestive selling.	❑ Suggest appetizers, soups, salads, specials, profitable entrees, desserts, wine, and other features. Suggest premium-brand alcoholic beverages. ❑ Recommend specific items to enhance the meal. For instance, say, "Would you like stuffed mushrooms or shrimp cocktail to begin your meal?" ❑ Describe the daily specials. Always give the prices of specials. Your descriptions help guests "see" the items, and the guests may be more likely to order items they can picture. ❑ Describe the ingredients and preparation in an appealing way.
6. Take orders.	❑ Pay attention to orders, and know the menu thoroughly. ❑ Ask questions to find out the guest's choices or preferences for service, such as how he or she would like an item cooked or prepared (medium rare, "on-the-rocks," etc.). Ask the guest for his or her choice of salad dressings and for any special requests such as fat-free preparation, etc. ❑ Write down all information clearly. Highlight special requests. ❑ Ask how many guests will be eating and write the number on the guest check. You (or another room service attendant) will set up trays or carts based on these numbers. ❑ Record the time the order was taken on the check, or stamp the check with a time-date stamp. ❑ Be prepared to suggest one or two appropriate wines or champagnes.

(continued)

Take and Record Room Service Orders *(continued)*

STEPS	HOW-TO'S
7. Help guests select a wine.	❑ In general, white wines go best with white meats and seafood, and red wines go best with red meats and game. Rose, blush, and sparkling wines go with any type of food. ❑ White wine is served chilled, and red wine is served at room temperature (about 68°F or 20°C). ❑ Guests are never wrong in their selection of wines, regardless of the general rules. ❑ Answer any specific questions about the wines or champagnes at your property. ❑ Never argue with a guest over the selection of a wine or the pronunciation of a name. ❑ Allow the guest to make his or her own selection. Always support the guest's preference.
8. Politely read the order back to guests and repeat all details.	
9. Tell guests how long delivery will take.	
10. Thank guests for the order.	
11. Tell guests what the total charges will be, including tax and the service charge or automatic tip.	
12. Combine bar and room service checks.	❑ If your property uses separate bar checks for room service orders, transfer the bar check totals to the front of room service checks. This will allow you to present one check to guests.

Perform Pantry Prep for Room Service Orders

Materials needed: *A guest check, a service tray or room service cart, foil, foodservice film, lids, napkins, straws, an ice bucket, ice, and an ice compote.*

STEPS	HOW-TO'S
1. Set up a service tray or room service cart so the order can be delivered as soon as the food is ready.	❑ Set up the tray or cart according to the items listed on the guest check. Double-check every detail. ❑ Make sure all china, glasses, and silverware are clean and free from chips, cracks, water spots, and food residue. ❑ Throw away chipped or cracked china or glasses. Return soiled or spotted items to the dish room. ❑ Handle china, glasses, and silverware by the edges, and do not touch anywhere food or a guest's mouth will touch. ❑ Arrange items attractively on the tray or cart.
2. Prepare beverages, salads, crackers or bread and butter, and desserts.	❑ Cover dishes with foil, foodservice film, or lids. ❑ If the order includes food for children, include straws and extra paper napkins.
3. Get an ice bucket.	❑ If bottled beer or wine is to be served, pick up a filled ice bucket. ❑ If ice buckets were not prepared during opening sidework, fill a clean bucket two-thirds full with ice and pour enough water to cover the ice. ❑ Put a clean linen napkin through the ring of the bucket and drape it over the top of the bucket.
4. Set up an ice compote.	❑ Rest dishes filled with items that need to be kept cold in a bed of ice to keep the items from melting during delivery.

Assemble the Beverage Order and Food Condiments

Materials needed: *Beverages, glasses, food condiments, an ice scoop, ice, beverage containers, teapots, underliners, cream, lemon wedges, hot chocolate garnishes, a cleaning cloth, foodservice film or lids for glasses, and a service tray or room service cart.*

STEPS	HOW-TO'S
1. Preheat containers that will be used to carry hot beverages to the guestroom.	❑ Fill each container with hot water from the drip coffee maker and allow it to stand for three to five minutes. ❑ Preheating ensures that a cool container won't cool the hot beverage while you're delivering it. You will preheat teapots when you prepare hot tea.
2. Pour cold beverages without ice into the correct glass when the hot food is nearly ready.	
3. Pour hot drinks into preheated containers.	❑ Hot drinks include coffee, hot tea, and hot chocolate. ❑ Empty the water from the preheated container. ❑ Immediately fill the container with the hot drink. ❑ Make sure coffee is fresh. Never serve coffee that is more than 30 minutes old.
4. Pour drinks with ice.	❑ If glasses were previously filled with ice, drain off any water from melted ice before adding the beverages. ❑ If the glasses were not filled with ice, use a clean ice scoop to fill each glass. Then add the beverage.
5. Place beverages on a service tray or room service cart.	❑ Place preheated containers of hot chocolate and coffee on the tray or cart. ❑ Place teapots full of hot tea on underliners and place them on the tray or cart. Wide-based teapots may not need underliners.

Assemble the Beverage Order and Food Condiments

(continued)

STEPS	HOW-TO'S
	❑ Place cold beverages on the tray or cart.
6. Cover all glasses with foodservice film or lids to prevent spills.	
7. Place cream, lemon wedges, hot chocolate garnishes, and other appropriate items for beverage service on the tray or cart.	
8. Place the appropriate food condiments on the tray or cart.	❑ Make sure condiment containers are full and free from food residue. ❑ Wipe containers with a clean cloth if necessary.

Pick Up the Room Service Order

Materials needed: *Foodservice film or lids for glasses, a service tray or room service cart, aluminum foil or plate lids, a hot box, and canned, gel-type fuel.*

STEPS	HOW-TO'S
1. Pick up the beverage order from the bar.	❑ Check that the order is complete. ❑ Check that the drinks have been prepared correctly. ❑ Check that the drinks have been garnished correctly. ❑ If there is a problem with the beverage order, work with the bartender to resolve the problem right away. ❑ Cover all glasses with foodservice film or lids to prevent spills. The steps to place beverages on a service tray or room service cart vary among properties.
2. Pick up the food order as soon as it is ready.	❑ The steps to pick up food orders from the kitchen varies among properties.
3. Check the food order.	❑ Make sure the order includes all entrees and side dishes. ❑ Check the food before you take it out of the kitchen. • Does it look fresh and appealing? • Have all preparation instructions been followed? • Is the presentation garnished correctly? • Have all special requests been met? • Is the plate clean? • Is the hot food hot and the cold food cold? ❑ If the food does not meet your property's standards, bring it to the attention of the cook or your supervisor. Do not deliver substandard food to guests. Thank the kitchen staff for their cooperation.

Pick Up the Room Service Order *(continued)*

STEPS	HOW-TO'S
	❑ Immediately notify your supervisor of any problems with the food preparation so he or she can speak to the guests and help correct the situation.
4. Place cold food on the tray or cart.	
5. Cover hot food with aluminum foil or plate lids.	
6. Place hot food in a hot box.	❑ Light the canned, gel-type fuel in the hot box if this type of fuel is used. Gel-type fuel is poisonous. Proper safety precautions should be taken when handling it. ❑ Wash your hands immediately. ❑ Place the hot box on a room service cart, then place covered plates in the hot box.

Deliver the Room Service Order

Materials needed: *A service tray or room service cart with a complete order.*

STEPS	HOW-TO'S
1. Double-check the order to make sure nothing is missing, damaged, or soiled.	❑ Check everything carefully before leaving the kitchen to save unnecessary return trips to pick up items that were missed. ❑ Check the following: • Serviceware • Linens (napkins and tablecloth as appropriate) • Condiments • Bread and butter • Cold food (salad, cold appetizers, etc.) • Hot food • Garnishes • Hot beverages • Cold beverages • Beer or wine • Cocktails • Guest check in a check folder • Pen • Corkscrew (if needed) • Ice bucket (if needed) • Matches • Extra napkin for cleaning up spills
2. Lift and carry the room service tray.	❑ Lift the tray carefully, using your legs for leverage. ❑ Bend at the knees to pick up the tray. Pull the tray with one hand onto the palm of your other hand. ❑ Balance the tray on your palm or fingertips at shoulder height. ❑ Use your free hand to steady the tray as you stand. ❑ Keep your back straight as you stand.

Deliver the Room Service Order *(continued)*

STEPS	HOW-TO'S
	❑ Watch where you are going. Be aware of opening doors and wet spots on the floor. ❑ Use correct entrance and exit doors and pass to the left of people walking toward you. ❑ Say "behind you" to let people know when you are behind them and to avoid a collision.
3. Carefully move room service carts.	❑ Ease carts over uneven surfaces, such as where carpets meet tile floors. ❑ Pull carts into and out of elevators. This allows you to see where you are going. ❑ Avoid running into walls, guests, or co-workers. ❑ Do not push more than one cart at a time.
4. Go directly to the guestroom.	❑ Know where the guestroom is before you leave for the delivery. Know the best way to get to the guestroom. ❑ Use stairwells, service elevators, and halls to speed delivery time. Avoid congested areas such as public elevators, lobbies, function areas, and restaurant entrances. ❑ Do not stop along the way. The food will get cold, the drinks will be watered down by melting ice, and the guest will grow impatient.
5. Enter the guestroom.	❑ Knock firmly three times with your knuckles and announce "room service." Do not use a key or any other hard object to knock on the door. ❑ If there is no answer, knock and announce again. The guest may be in the shower or the bathroom.

(continued)

Deliver the Room Service Order (continued)

STEPS	HOW-TO'S
	❑ If the guest still does not answer, check the room number. If the room number is correct, call the room service department and tell your supervisor about the situation. ❑ When the guest opens the door, greet the guest by name in the form of a question, to verify that you have the right room: "Mr. Johnson?" ❑ As soon as the guest acknowledges that you are at the right room, follow up with a greeting, such as: "Good morning. I have your breakfast." ❑ If you are at the wrong room, apologize for disturbing the guest, and go to the correct room or call your supervisor right away. ❑ Do not enter the room until the guest acknowledges you and invites you in. Remember that the guestroom is the guest's "home away from home." Just as you wouldn't barge into someone's home, you don't want to enter the guestroom unless you're invited.

Serve the Room Service Order

Materials needed: *A guest check and a service tray or room service cart with a complete order.*

STEPS	HOW-TO'S
1. Set up the order in the guestroom.	❑ Offer to place the order on the table, desk, or credenza, whichever the guest prefers. ❑ If using a room service cart, fold out the wings of the table and spread out the tablecloth. ❑ Place the linen napkins and silverware on the table
2. Serve food.	❑ Remove the hot food from the hot box or service tray and place it on the table. ❑ Place entree plate so that the main item is closest to the guest. ❑ Place side dishes to the left of the entree plate. ❑ Remove the foil or plate covers from the hot foods. ❑ Place condiments within the guest's reach, but out of his or her way.
3. Serve beverages.	❑ Place beverages, beverage napkins, glasses, mugs, cups, and saucers to the right of the entree plate. ❑ Handle glasses, mugs, and cups by their stems, bases, or handles. ❑ Remove foodservice film or lids from glasses. ❑ If wine or champagne is included, offer to open and serve it.
4. Place cream, sugar, spoons, and other appropriate items on the table.	
5. Present and settle the guest check.	

(continued)

Serve the Room Service Order *(continued)*

STEPS	HOW-TO'S
6. Ask if the guest would like you to bring or do anything else at this time.	
7. Ask the guest to call the room service department for any further service and when he or she is ready for the tray or cart to be picked up.	
8. Thank the guest for the room service order.	

Retrieve Trays and Carts

STEPS	HOW-TO'S
1. Go to the guestroom.	❑ Before you leave to retrieve a service tray or room service cart, know where the guestroom is located, and know the best way to get to the guestroom. You will pick up trays or carts when a guest calls you to retrieve them and whenever you see trays or carts in guestroom corridors. ❑ Use stairwells, service elevators, and halls to speed delivery time. Avoid congested areas such as public elevators, lobbies, function areas, and restaurant entrances. ❑ Trays and carts in guestrooms and corridors are hazards. A guest could trip over these items. Also, soiled dishes and equipment in corridors are unsightly and indicate a poorly run room service department.
2. Enter the guestroom.	❑ Knock firmly three times with your knuckles and announce "room service." Do not use a key or any other hard object to knock on the door. ❑ If no one answers, knock and announce again. The guest may be in the shower or the bathroom. ❑ If the guest still does not answer, check the room number. If the room number is correct, call the room service department and tell your supervisor about the situation. ❑ When the guest opens the door, greet the guest by name in the form of a question, to verify that you have the right room: "Ms. Martin?" ❑ If you are at the wrong room, apologize for disturbing the guest, and go to the correct room or call your supervisor right away. ❑ If you are at the right room, let the guest know that you are there to pick up the tray or cart.

(continued)

Retrieve Trays and Carts (*continued*)

STEPS	HOW-TO'S
	❑ Do not enter the room until the guest acknowledges you and invites you in. Remember that the guestroom is the guest's "home away from home." Just as you would not barge into someone's private home, you don't want to enter the guestroom unless you're invited.
3. Retrieve a room service tray.	❑ Place serviceware, glasses, used linens, and trash on the tray. ❑ Bend at the knees to pick up the tray. Pull the tray with one hand onto the palm of the other hand. ❑ Balance the tray on your palm or fingertips at shoulder height. Use your free hand to steady the tray as you stand.
4. Retrieve a room service cart.	❑ Secure soiled items inside and in the center of the cart and fold down the leaves of the cart. ❑ Pull—don't push—the cart into the hallway.
5. Thank the guest and leave the room.	
6. Retrieve trays and carts whenever you see them in guestroom corridors. If your hands are full, note where the trays and other carts are and go back for them as soon as you can.	
7. Return to the room service area quickly.	❑ Use stairwells and service elevators. ❑ Be careful and watch where you are going when carrying a tray or moving a cart.

REVIEW QUIZ

When you feel you have covered all of the material in this chapter, answer these questions. Choose the *best* answer.

1. According to a survey by *Lodging Hospitality,* the number one hotel guest-room amenity for which respondents were willing to pay extra was:

   a. Internet access.
   b. an in-room microwave oven.
   c. video movies.
   d. room service breakfast.

2. Valerie's room service department has been receiving very few orders. Valerie thinks the reason for this is that the menu does not appeal to guests' tastes. The first step she should take when analyzing the menu is to:

   a. gather and analyze guest feedback to determine their preferences.
   b. lower prices to match those of the hotel's restaurant menu.
   c. translate the menu into another language.
   d. put more pictures in the menu.

3. The room service department in which David works serves different courses of a guest's order at different times. This type of room service is called:

   a. menu engineering.
   b. dumbwaiter service.
   c. split service.
   d. the "flying kitchen" technique.

4. More and more properties are using point-of-sale (POS) systems in all aspects of their food and beverage service. For which of the following stages of room service does the use of a POS system usually save the most time?

   a. taking the order
   b. routing the order
   c. preparing the order
   d. delivering the order

REVIEW QUIZ *(continued)*

5. Bernice, a room service attendant, must inform a guest that he must pay for his room service order in cash. All of the following are situations in which hotels typically require guests to pay for room service with cash *except:*

   a. when guests exceed their credit limits.
   b. when guests pay for their stays in advance with cash.
   c. when guests pay for their stays with credit.
   d. when guests reach their credit limits.

Answer Key: 1-d-C1, 2-a-C1, 3-c-C3, 4-b-C3, 5-c-C4

Each question is linked to a competency. Competencies are listed on the first page of the chapter. An answer reading 3-b-C4 translates to:

3: the question number
b: the correct answer
C4: the competency number

Chapter 12 Outline

Major Market Segments of the On-Site Food Service Industry
- Self-Operated and Contract Management Options
- Branded Food Options

Business and Industry Food Service
- Reducing Subsidies from Host Organizations

Health Care Food Service
- Reinventing the Cafeteria
- Tray Service—Hospitality Style

College and University Food Service
- Flexible Meal Plans
- Serving Policies
- Menu Planning
- Encouraging Healthy Food Choices
- Smart Card and Debit Card Technology

Competencies

1. List major market segments of the on-site food service industry and the types of organizations within them; list contract management companies and distinguish self-operated food service facilities from those operated by contract management companies; summarize the advantages of including branded foods and food outlets in on-site food service operations; describe the business and industry food service segment; and explain how on-site food service operations can reduce the subsidies they receive from their host organizations.

2. Describe health care food service and summarize issues important to this segment of the on-site food service industry, including commercialization, reinventing the cafeteria, and improving tray service to patients; and describe the college and university food service segment, including issues ranging from scramble systems and flexible meal plans to menu planning and smart/debit card technology.

12

On-Site Food Service Operations

MANAGING FOOD AND BEVERAGE SERVICES within larger host organizations has changed dramatically over the past decade. On-site food service operations used to be characterized as "institutional" or "noncommercial," but these terms carried negative connotations. "Institutional" suggested regimented menus and impersonal service; "noncommercial" implied inefficient operations that survived only through subsidies from the host organization. Overall, on-site food service operations were depicted as somehow substandard or second-rate when compared to freestanding, profit-oriented food service operations.

Today's on-site food service operations can be as varied, innovative, and successful as any restaurant or catering company. From menu planning and service delivery to cost control systems and the design of facilities, on-site food service operations have implemented concepts, processes, and practices that have truly modernized this segment of the food service industry.

This chapter describes the types of services offered by on-site food service operations. These services range from self-service vending facilities in staff member dining areas to upscale service in executive dining rooms. Depending on the needs of the host organization, on-site operations may include traditional forms of food service such as table service, banquet service, and even room service. The focus of this chapter, however, is on the unique service features of on-site operations: dining areas featuring multiple food stations, food courts offering a mix of signature and branded food items, convenience stores with packaged carry-out items, and mobile cart services offering such items as hot dogs, pizza, and gourmet coffees.

The chapter also explores the challenges of managing food service operations in three of the major on-site markets—business and industry, health care, and college and university. An appendix at the end of the chapter presents sample job descriptions of line-level, supervisory, and managerial positions associated with on-site food service operations.

Major Market Segments of the On-Site Food Service Industry

An **on-site food service operation** is part of a larger **host organization** whose primary business is not that of providing food and beverage services. Some of the major market segments for on-site food service operations are:

- Business and industry
- Health care
- College and university
- School
- Military
- Correctional institution
- Sports and entertainment facility
- Transportation

The business and industry segment includes manufacturing and industrial plants, commercial centers, office complexes, financial institutions, and government agencies. The health care segment includes hospitals and eldercare facilities specializing in extended care and assisted living. Post-secondary educational institutions make up the college and university segment; on-campus food service operations and activities include food service for catered events and conference centers, dining halls, and food courts. The school segment covers day care centers as well as elementary and secondary schools. Sports and entertainment facilities include stadiums, convention centers, recreational facilities, and park systems. Airports, inflight catering, trains, and cruise ships are within the transportation segment.

While the types of organizations within these segments have very different primary functions, on-site food and beverage services play important supportive roles in fulfilling their overall missions. For example, in the business and industry segment, organizations often approach food services as an investment. As a return on this investment, on-site food service operations are expected to help achieve organizational goals. The Society for Foodservice Management (SFM) surveyed managers at host organizations in the business and industry segment on the importance of ten characteristics (or attributes) commonly associated with on-site food service. As indicated in Exhibit 1, the three most important attributes were the added convenience to the staff members of the host organizations, the positive impact on staff member morale, and the potential for increased staff member productivity.

Important characteristics in relation to food services for correctional institutions differ tremendously from those identified for the business and industry segment. Correctional institutions operate under many regulatory restrictions and other rules. For example, the American Correctional Association upholds the U.S. Recommended Daily Allowance (RDA) standards and insists that on-site food service operations in correctional facilities meet or exceed these standards while, at the same time, containing costs and offering the greatest amount of control and security possible. Exhibit 2 details the features and benefits of the program offered by ARAMARK Correctional Services. The list of benefits could easily serve as a list of attributes that correctional institutions expect from their on-site food service operations.

Clearly, the priorities of on-site food service operations change as the nature of the host organization changes. Sophisticated dietary and nutritional programs are

Exhibit 1 The Importance of On-Site Food Service to Responding Organizations

The Importance of Onsite Foodservice to Responding Organizations

Senior or middle management positions (i.e., senior vice president or vice president) of the client organizations were asked to rate the overall importance and the importance of 10 specific attributes of onsite foodservice to their organizations, using a 5-point scale (1 = very unimportant to 5 = very important). When asked how they would rate the overall importance of onsite foodservice to their organizations, the average rating was 4.32. Thus, overall, senior management perceived onsite foodservice to be important to their organizations. The following table ranks the average ratings on each of the 10 importance attributes.

	Importance Attribute	# of Respondents	Average Rating
1.	Convenience	147	4.43
2.	Employee morale	148	4.41
3.	Productivity	148	4.22
4.	Multi-purpose facility	148	3.74
5.	Employee networking	148	3.69
6.	Recruitment/retention	148	3.67
7.	Less entertaining costs	147	3.53
8.	Employee health	148	3.52
9.	Employee benefit	146	3.28
10.	More revenue potential	147	2.58

For more information about the business and industry segment of on-site food services, access other areas of the Society of Foodservice Management's Internet site at http://www.sfm-online.org.

critical features of a health care organization's primary mission to care for patients. However, on-site health care food service operations are also expected to attract and cater to the needs and tastes of staff and visitors by offering low-cost, nutritious meals in a variety of food service formats. Similarly, the primary function of colleges and universities is to educate students. An on-site food service operation in a college or university residence hall contributes to its school's mission by providing meals to students living and studying in the residence hall. However, these on-site operations are also expected to contribute to the learning environment by offering flexible meal plans and dining options that meet the needs of students with irregular class and study schedules.

Exhibit 2 Important Features of On-Site Food Service to Correctional Institutions

FOOD SERVICE PROGRAMS THAT GIVE YOU GREATER CONTROL

We begin by touring your facility and meeting with your management team. The end result is a food service program that is customized to suit your facility's specific needs. You'll find our streamlined operations improve quality and reduce costs. We insure quality and control by:

1. *Containing cost.*
   Our bids guarantee the costs of meals for a specific period of time.
2. *Increasing efficiency.*
   Our computerized recipe and menu management system reduces waste. Accurate meal accounting prevents the ordering of excess meals.
3. *Improving food quality.*
   Our registered dietitians plan and certify the nutritional value of the basic menu cycle, while our food service directors determine the acceptability of meals for their local inmate populations.
4. *Meeting applicable standards.*
   We meet or exceed all of the mandatory local and state standards.
5. *Preparing for contingencies.*
   Our comprehensive plans account for such situations as loss of power or water, lockdowns, natural disasters, and other unexpected emergencies.
6. *Staffing our team with qualified managers.*
   All of our managers have previous experience in correctional food service.
7. *Satisfying staff and inmate tastes.*
   Our recipes are modified to reflect local tastes and specific needs of the facility.

For more information about the food service needs of correctional institutions, access other areas of ARAMARK's Correctional Services Internet site at http://www.aramark correctional.com.

Self-Operated and Contract Management Options

Self-operated food services are on-site operations whose managers and staff members are employed by the larger organization within which the food service operation resides. Host organizations can also outsource their food service operations to **contract management companies.** Some host organizations have both types of food service operations. For example, a large university might outsource its vending operations and the operation of a food court to a contract management company, but retain other food services as self-operated departments.

While self-operated on-site food service operations can be very successful, the market share captured by contract management companies has grown over the past decade as more and more businesses have adopted strategies to outsource functions that do not directly relate to their core business functions. Exhibit 3 shows the market share of contract management companies within some segments of the on-site food service market. Some contract management companies have become appealing outsource alternatives by offering a wide range of services such as

Exhibit 3 Market Share of Contract Management Companies

Segment	% Penetration
Airlines	90%
B&I	82.5%
Colleges	60%
Hospitals	40%
Nursing Homes	17.5%
Corrections	4.5%
Primary/Secondary Schools	10%
Recreation	40%

Source: *Nation's Restaurant News,* February 24, 1997, p. 56. For information updates, check the magazine's Internet site at http://www.nrn.com.

laundry, housekeeping, and facilities management in addition to their food and beverage services.

There are scores of contract management companies throughout the United States, including:

- HDS Services
- ARAMARK Managed Services
- Sodexho Marriott Services
- The Compass Group
- Bon Appétit Management Company
- Service America
- Gardner Merchant Food Services

Exhibit 4 explains the structure of The Compass Group and also illustrates how contract management companies operate in many segments of the on-site food service market.

Exhibit 4 Market Segments Served by The Compass Group

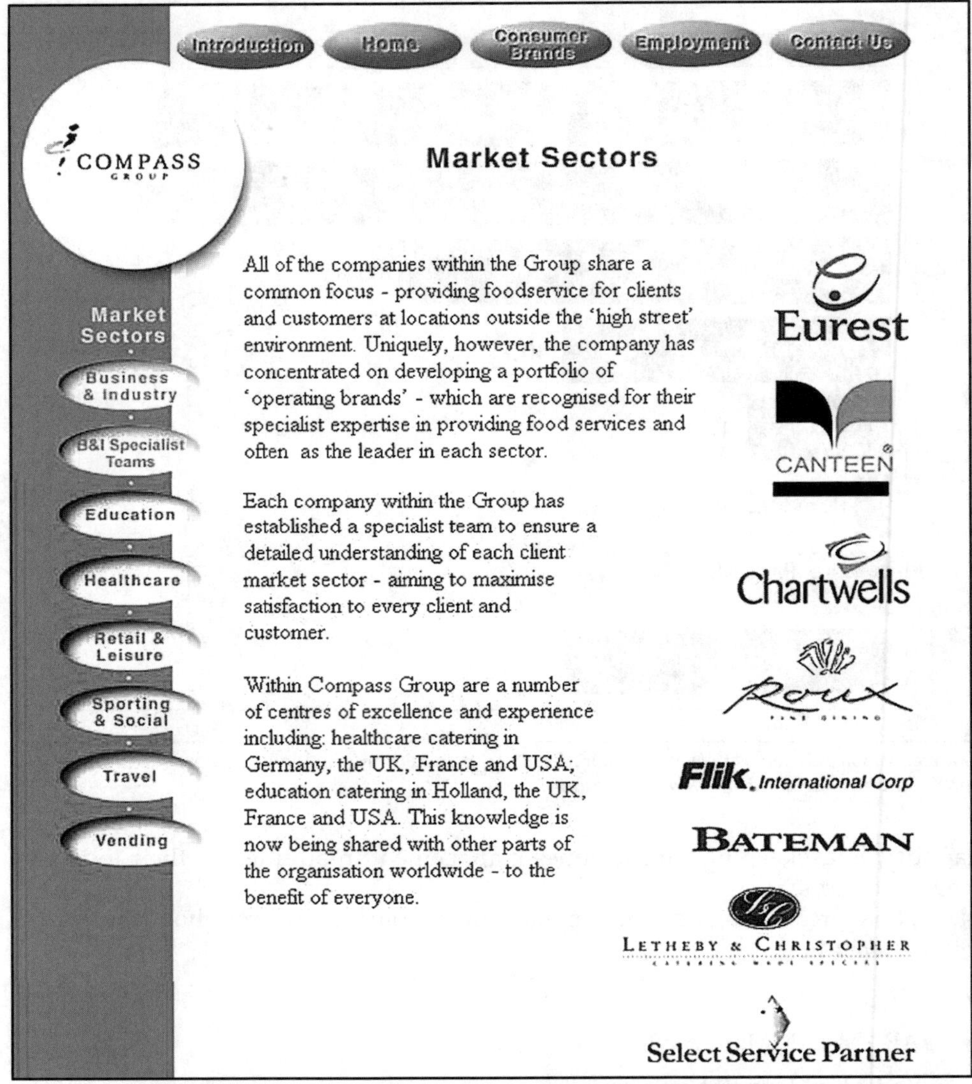

For more information about The Compass Group, access other areas of the company's Internet site at http://www.compass-group.com.

In addition to operating on-site food service facilities, a contract management company may operate different types of commercial, freestanding food service units. This breadth of experience enables contract management companies to create synergies that are beyond the scope of many self-operated on-site food service operations. By cross-training on-site food service managers at commercial operations, a contract management company can create a culture of guest-driven service that builds guest loyalty and repeat business for the company's on-site operations. New menu items, new design and decor concepts, and creative service styles can be developed, tested, and refined in the commercial sector before being implemented at on-site operations. Also, company-wide professional development and training programs bring managers from different on-site market segments and managers from commercial operations together for a regular exchange of best practices, successful promotions, suggestions, and operating strategies.

Self-operated on-site food service operations obtain financial, technical, and managerial benefits through membership in various nonprofit associations. These associations help self-operated food service programs achieve economies of scale similar to those attained by large contract management companies. Members of these associations may benefit from volume purchasing, professional development programs, and peer-networking opportunities. The Society for Foodservice Management (SFM) is a professional association of individuals employed in or providing services to the on-site food service industry. SFM provides support and education for the continuous improvement of on-site food service professionals in this rapidly changing industry. As indicated in Exhibit 5, the National Society for Healthcare Foodservice Management (HFM) serves the interests of self-operated food service facilities in the health care industry. Exhibit 6 describes how the National Association of College and University Food Services (NACUFS) addresses the needs of self-operated food service departments in this segment of the on-site market.

Branded Food Options

In many segments of the on-site food service market, both self-operated and contract-managed operations have linked with national chain restaurants and offer branded food options. By blending popular national brands and name-brand food products with their own menu offerings, on-site food service operations can create more choices for their guests and capitalize on the consistent quality and service guests associate with branded foods. This can increase overall guest traffic in on-site food courts and other service areas featuring branded outlets and may increase food revenues in nonbranded outlets as well.

ARAMARK and other large contract management companies are able to "bundle" their own signature brands (see Exhibit 7) with those of nationally recognized restaurant chains. For example, The Compass Group operates franchised brands such as Pizza Hut, KFC, Burger King, and TGI Friday's, and also offers its own in-house brands such as Upper Crust, Caffé Ritazza, Not Just Donuts, and Franks Deli. The Wood Company partners with Board Walk Fries, Burger King, Colombo Frozen Yogurt, Dunkin' Donuts, China Jump, Healthy Choice, Richfield's Yogurt, Taco Bell, and Chick-fil-A, while offering its own signature brands, such as C.C. Cinnamon's, Jupiter's Grille, and Mesa Jake's.

Business and Industry Food Service

Business and industry is the largest segment of the on-site food service market. The guest mix is primarily the workers, supervisors, middle managers, and top executives employed by the host organization and, secondarily, visitors to the

Exhibit 5 The National Society for Healthcare Foodservice Management

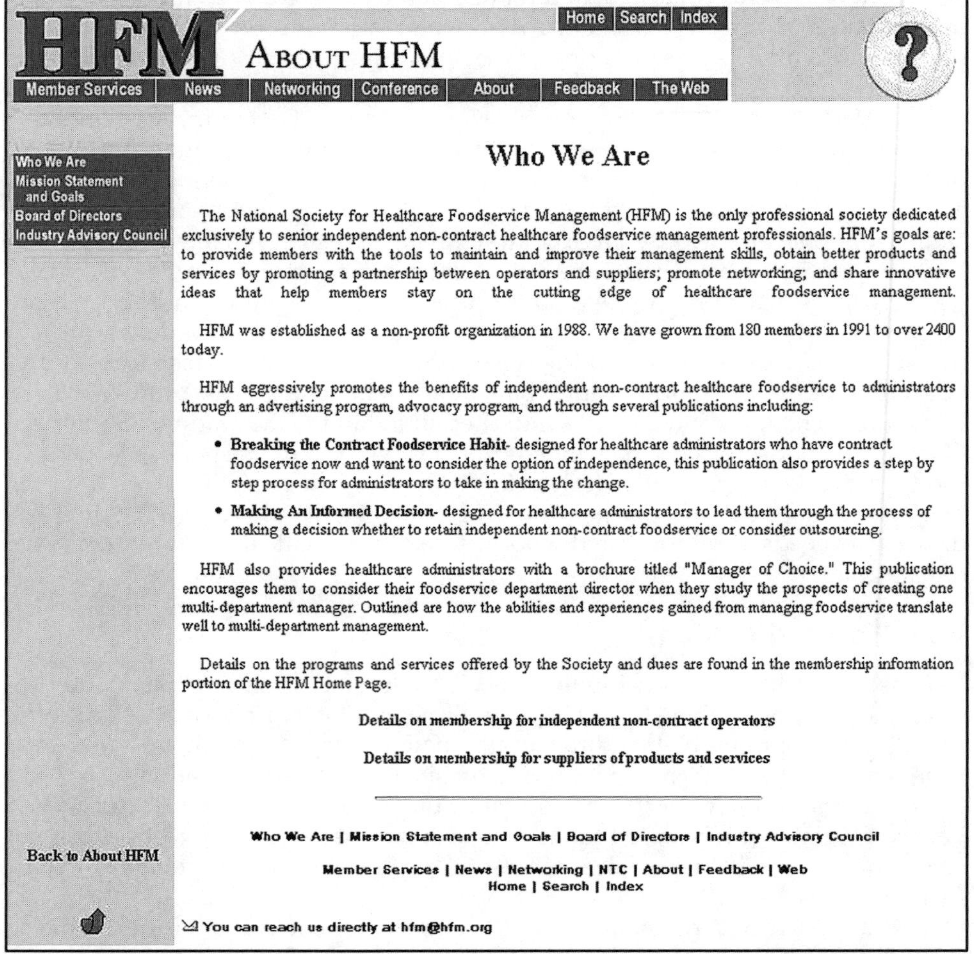

HFM ABOUT HFM

Home | Search | Index

Member Services | News | Networking | Conference | About | Feedback | The Web

Who We Are
Mission Statement and Goals
Board of Directors
Industry Advisory Council

Who We Are

The National Society for Healthcare Foodservice Management (HFM) is the only professional society dedicated exclusively to senior independent non-contract healthcare foodservice management professionals. HFM's goals are: to provide members with the tools to maintain and improve their management skills, obtain better products and services by promoting a partnership between operators and suppliers; promote networking; and share innovative ideas that help members stay on the cutting edge of healthcare foodservice management.

HFM was established as a non-profit organization in 1988. We have grown from 180 members in 1991 to over 2400 today.

HFM aggressively promotes the benefits of independent non-contract healthcare foodservice to administrators through an advertising program, advocacy program, and through several publications including:

- **Breaking the Contract Foodservice Habit**- designed for healthcare administrators who have contract foodservice now and want to consider the option of independence, this publication also provides a step by step process for administrators to take in making the change.
- **Making An Informed Decision**- designed for healthcare administrators to lead them through the process of making a decision whether to retain independent non-contract foodservice or consider outsourcing.

HFM also provides healthcare administrators with a brochure titled "Manager of Choice." This publication encourages them to consider their foodservice department director when they study the prospects of creating one multi-department manager. Outlined are how the abilities and experiences gained from managing foodservice translate well to multi-department management.

Details on the programs and services offered by the Society and dues are found in the membership information portion of the HFM Home Page.

Details on membership for independent non-contract operators

Details on membership for suppliers of products and services

Back to About HFM

Who We Are | Mission Statement and Goals | Board of Directors | Industry Advisory Council

Member Services | News | Networking | NTC | About | Feedback | Web
Home | Search | Index

You can reach us directly at hfm@hfm.org

For more information about member services, access other areas of HFM's Internet site at http://www.hfm.org.

organization who may include shareholders, customers, and vendors. As shown in Exhibit 3, over 80 percent of this market segment is served by contract management companies. An important contributing factor to the dominance of contracted food service operations is the widespread practice of large companies to outsource "non-core" or peripheral business functions. However, there are several large companies that still retain a number of self-operated food service facilities, including:

- Motorola Corporation (Schaumburg, Illinois) with 45 food service outlets
- Ford Motor Company (Dearborn, Michigan) with 30 outlets
- 3M Corporation (St. Paul, Minnesota) with 17 outlets

Exhibit 6 The National Association of College and University Food Services

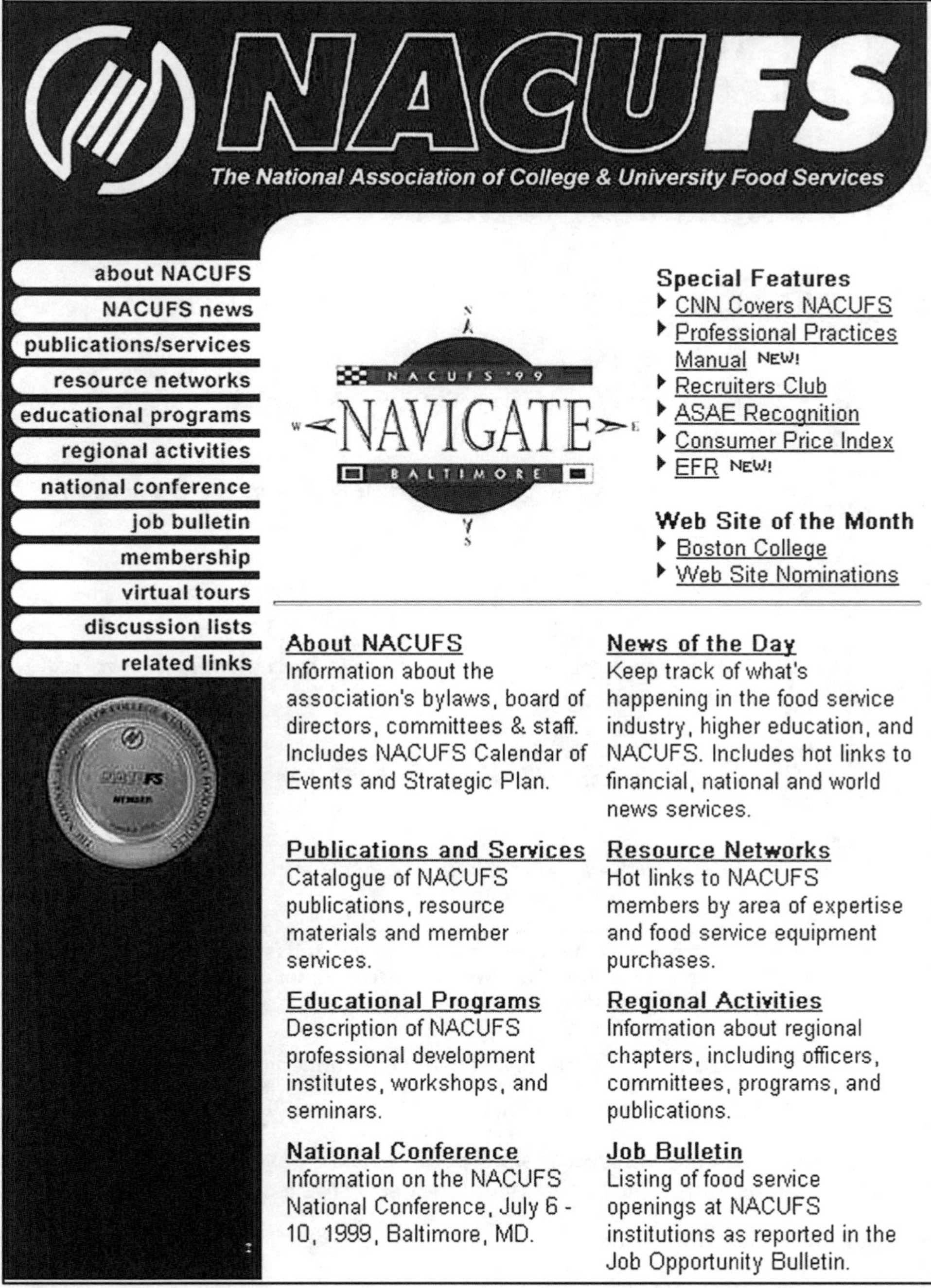

For more information about member services, access other areas of NACUFS's Internet site at http://www.nacufs.org.

Exhibit 7 Signature Brands Offered by HDS Services

HDS Signature Programs

Fast Breaks - HDS' rapid, convenient meal take out service

MMMuffins - A tasty selection of fresh baked muffins

Prime Grind - a fresh-brewed and whole bean gourmet coffee program

On Display - HDS' "fresh to order" cooking concept

Target Your Heart - a comprehensive heart-healthy meals and nutrition education program

Mrs. T's Cookies - offering a daily variety of fresh-baked, gourmet cookies

Bakery Fresh - an array of fresh-baked "old world" breads and rolls

HDS Services is a large contract management company that has its own line of signature brands. For more information about HDS Services, access other areas of the company's Internet site at http://www.hdsservices.com.

- Aetna Life & Casualty Company (Hartford, Connecticut) with 9 outlets
- Procter & Gamble Company (Cincinnati, Ohio) with 9 outlets

Whether contract-managed or self-operated, the types of on-site food services for organizations within the business and industry segment generally include:

- Staff member dining areas
- Executive dining rooms
- Banquet facilities

- Vending services
- Mobile cart services
- Concession stores
- Concession vehicles

Regional and national branded food options are prevalent in many staff member dining areas. These options may be offered through individual mobile cart service or as kiosks within an open-area food court. As mentioned earlier, a contract management company will often mix and match its own signature brands with nationally recognized brands to meet the needs of the particular guest mix of the host organization. Branded food outlets (especially quick-service outlets such as Taco Bell) have a distinctive draw within this market segment because they are perceived as offering consistent quality.

Factors in the overall business environment of host organizations significantly affect their on-site food service operations. The most significant environmental factors are international expansion, increased automation, and consolidation through mergers and acquisitions. All three factors contribute to the downsizing of organizations and reduce the potential guest base for on-site food services. As organizations reduce their workforces, they are inclined to also review the amounts by which they subsidize the cost of providing on-site food services.

Reducing Subsidies from Host Organizations

In the past, while some host organizations expected their on-site food service operations to at least break even, many organizations subsidized costs in an attempt to offer their staffs the lowest possible prices. Today, most of these organizations want to minimize (or eliminate) these subsidies.

There are two fundamental ways by which a host organization can subsidize its on-site food service operation. One is to subsidize the operation's overhead—the fixed costs of doing business. This entails covering all, or part, of the operation's administrative expenses and fixed costs such as energy, housekeeping, and maintenance. The other way is to subsidize the costs associated with daily operations. This entails picking up that portion of expenses that cannot be covered by revenues generated by the on-site food service operation. Operational expenses include food, labor, serviceware, merchandising, insurance, and office supply expenses.

Reducing overhead subsidies can be difficult. However, if a host organization allocates fixed costs on the basis of square footage, the on-site food service operation can reduce its overhead subsidies by decreasing its space. On-site operations can reduce the square footage they need by capitalizing on new equipment and technology made available through partnering with chain restaurants or through contracting with management companies. Changing service delivery systems can also impact overhead costs. For example, providing more take-out or "grab-and-go" meals and increasing mobile cart services could decrease the amount of space the operation needs for sit-down dining areas.

On-site food service managers can also reduce the host organization's subsidies to their operations by generating more revenue. However, if meals are currently priced below costs, increasing participation levels at on-site food service outlets will certainly increase total revenue but will also increase the total net loss for operations and, thereby, increase the subsidy needed from the host organization. Or, to put it another way, doing more business at a loss will only increase the magnitude of the loss. If participation rates stay constant, raising prices will increase revenue, decrease net operational losses, and reduce the operation's subsidy. However, if the majority of the guest mix is price-sensitive, raising prices could lower participation levels and perhaps even reduce the total amount of revenue. If so, increasing prices would, in effect, backfire and only serve to increase, rather than decrease, the subsidy needed from the host organization.

Price increases must be carefully considered in relation to guests' perceptions of value. In general, price increases are met with resistance from guests unless the perceived value is increased at the same time. One way to accomplish this is to raise prices while bundling items into combination packages or "value" meals. However, any strategy that involves increasing prices must be consistent with the host organization's objectives and overall strategies in providing on-site food service.

Some on-site food service operations reduce host-organization subsidies by actively pursuing new sources of revenue. For example, one on-site food service operation implemented a "Conferences After 5" program. After regular business hours, the operation's facilities and services were offered to local businesses, associations, and other outside organizations for meetings and catered events.

Subsidies for on-site food service operations also might be reduced through greater cost-control efforts. For example, it might be possible to lower food costs by lowering the quality of ingredients or by decreasing portion sizes. Again, guests' perceptions of value must be considered, because lowering quality without lowering prices may also lower participation rates. This would reduce overall revenue and end up costing the host organization more in subsidies. It might be possible to lower food costs by reducing the number of menu items offered. However, this is always a double-edged sword. Too little variety may decrease participation because guests become bored with the same menu items. However, too much variety may increase waste and cause food costs to rise. Generally, a combination of actions works best—for example, eliminating menu items that are high in cost, low in price, and low in popularity while, at the same time, adding menu items that are low in cost, reasonably priced, and at least as popular as the items taken off the menu. Depending on the guest mix, it might be possible to add more "upscale" menu items that can be priced higher but would still be perceived as a value to the target guests.

Reducing labor costs can be achieved by offering more self-service options and increasing vending services. In most cases, instead of completely eliminating a service, it is better to substitute a lower-cost alternative. For example, prepackaged food items might be substituted for cooked-to-order menu items. Or, centralized coffee and snack areas could be substituted for transport systems used to deliver similar food items throughout the organization.

Health Care Food Service

Health care organizations can be divided into several subsegments, including hospitals, psychiatric facilities, rehabilitation centers (sometimes referred to as "convalescent centers"), and eldercare facilities specializing in extended care and assisted living (sometimes referred to as "nursing homes"). The guest mix for on-site food service operations within these organizations varies. Guests include patients or residents, staff members (including administrators, technicians, maintenance and cleaning personnel, and therapists as well as doctors and nurses), visitors (including family members and friends of patients or residents), and members of the community (in cases where health care organizations cater events for local community groups).

The changing business environment of the health care industry is characterized by declining patient admissions and shorter patient stays, as well as by consolidations, acquisitions, and mergers of hospitals and other heath care organizations. The changing business conditions within health care organizations have prompted changes in the management of their on-site food service operations, affecting areas such as the selection of the type of menu (cyclical or restaurant style), food production systems (cook-chill, cook-freeze, or conventional), service delivery procedures, and cost-control systems.

The dominant trend emerging from these changes in the business environment is a distinct move toward the "commercialization" of food service operations in the health care industry. While some attribute this shift to the increased use of contract management companies and the influx of management teams experienced in the freestanding, profit-oriented sectors of the food service industry, others point to the changing needs and expectations of health care's guest mix as the primary stimulus for change.

Further evidence of this commercialization surfaces in a position paper, "Management of Health Care Food and Nutrition Services," developed by the American Dietetic Association and distributed over its Internet site (http://www.eatright.org). The paper emphasizes the need for creativity, innovation, and flexibility in managing on-site food service operations in the health care industry and identifies competencies for directors of such operations. What is noteworthy about the following competencies is that, for the most part, they apply equally well to managers of commercial food service operations:

- Manage change and transitions.
- Identify the appropriate medical nutrition-therapy services required by patients and ensure the competency of the service providers.
- Develop menus and food services that exceed guest expectations.
- Identify, develop, and evaluate new business opportunities.
- Lead teams of culturally diverse staff members.
- Incorporate new information technologies that support department activities.
- Ensure service of safe food to guests through hazard analysis techniques.

- Analyze and improve production and service processes through the application of appropriate operations-management and quantitative-business-analysis techniques.
- Measure guest satisfaction, accurately interpret the data, and make appropriate operational changes.
- Lead in a constantly changing environment.

The trend toward commercialization manifests itself as a movement to greater cost control and more personalized guest service. The sections on health care food service that follow show how the dual focus of the commercialization trend impacts everything from the design and decor of health care food service facilities to menu development, food production processes, and service delivery systems.

Reinventing the Cafeteria

In the past, the only type of food service center open to health care patients, staff members, and visitors was a cafeteria that was functional and efficient, but cold and uninviting in its design and decor. Typically, guests walked along a terrazzo floor, selected food items from a straight-line, stainless-steel serving counter, took their trays to metal-framed tables with plastic laminate tops, sat in tubular metal chairs with vinyl backs and seats, and "enjoyed" their meals surrounded by bland, sparsely decorated tile walls.

Today, health care cafeterias have undergone a name change and a face-lift. "Dining center," "dining area," and even "restaurant" are replacing the term "cafeteria." Health care food service operations are now designed and decorated to appeal to the operation's guest mix, reflect the image or theme of the health care organization or local community, and allow for the flexibility and mobility needed to coordinate changing menu items and featured cuisines.

The reinvented health care cafeteria has become an open dining area with multiple food stations that increase choices for guests. Some food stations feature colored square tiles complemented with brass-trimmed wooden tray-slides. Stations may include entrée and vegetable stations; salad, dessert, and beverage bars; and soup, delicatessen, grill, and pasta stations. Some health care organizations set food stations at angles in their dining areas to promote visual appeal as well as to help merchandise food in retail display cases. Mobile carts are also used in dining and other areas. These carts may feature popcorn, specialty coffees, cookies, or other snacks.

A hospital in New Mexico coordinates its cuisine with a Southwestern theme throughout the dining area. Floors are a combination of tile and carpeting in warm shades of peach to complement the colors of the walls. The dining area uses natural lighting and indirect cove lighting to lend accents to decorative areas around the ceiling. Dining area furniture is blond pinewood. Tabletops are turquoise in color, and sculptures are displayed along the walls in glass-enclosed niches.

One children's hospital has its dining area constructed with tray-slides and countertops set at heights appropriate for children; they also meet requirements of the Americans with Disabilities Act for guests in wheelchairs. The dining area includes many food stations and has an entrance decorated with wall murals picturing children in various ethnic costumes. White ceramic-tile walls are highlighted with primary colors and soft pastels. Food stations include "Dilly of a Deli," "Pizza Perfectto," and "The Cookery." Multicolored support arms, reminiscent of a Tinker Toy set, are used to hold sneeze guards at food stations. In the dining area, complementary shades of red, blue, yellow, teal, orange, and white are used. Chairs and tables are of various colors; even the china pattern is colorful.

Mobile, interchangeable food station equipment can help health care food service operations easily accommodate changes in menus. Some health care organizations devote one or two food stations to new menu items or different international cuisines every week. Menus are also changing to offer guests lighter, healthier menu items. In general, menu changes follow trends found in the commercial sector of the food service industry.

Tray Service—Hospitality Style

The traditional form of food service for patients in health care organizations is termed **tray service**. With tray service, a printed menu is sent to each patient the day before service. Patients circle the items they want to order for the following day. The marked menus are delivered to the kitchen. The next day, individual trays of food are assembled along tray lines in the kitchen area. The process is similar to that used by restaurants, hotels, and clubs in preparing to serve large banquet functions. Once assembled, the trays are grouped by floors or units, placed in carts, and transported to delivery points. Staff from the dietary department or from the nursing area deliver the trays to individual patients in their rooms.

While the traditional tray service system is a well-organized work process, it is a difficult system to integrate with other processes involving patients and often fails to meet patients' needs. For example, while food production areas enjoy the luxury of a 24-hour time delay from order to delivery of patient meals, the dynamics of daily patient care such as early discharges, room transfers, diet changes, and medical tests can disrupt the food delivery system, increase costs through greater waste, and create patient dissatisfaction with late meals or with meals that they received on time but did not order.

Some health care organizations have improved their tray-service systems by decreasing the time lag from order to delivery and personalizing both points of service (ordering and delivery) with host programs borrowed from the commercial operations of hotels and restaurants. Host programs vary among health care organizations, but all focus on improving patient service. For example, in one type of program, the work traditionally performed by a tray passer and a nutrition technician is performed by the host. Hosts meet with patients each morning to help them select meal items for that day's lunch and dinner and for the next day's breakfast. Patients enjoy the opportunity to interact with hosts, who are often knowledgeable about nutrition and are able to compare patients' selections with their dietary restrictions and requirements. Hosts may actually deliver meal trays or follow tray delivery with "courtesy carts" that enable them to serve condiments, juices, desserts, or other items that patients wanted but did not receive on their trays. Trained in guest service and hospitality skills, hosts are generally empowered to help with patient requests and to respond immediately to most problems or complaints relating to food service. The result is lower costs with less waste and increased patient satisfaction through greater personalized service.

Some hospital on-site food service operations find creative ways to involve the hospital chef in personalizing service to patients. For example, at one hospital, the chef visits a selected floor one evening each week, plates meals for patients in their rooms (visiting family members receive complimentary meals), and educates patients and visitors on culinary issues and cooking techniques related to nutrition and healthy food choices. The hospitality of the visiting chef often improves patient and visitor satisfaction with the hospital's food service program. Exhibit 8 shows how the Methodist Health Care System involves its chef in personalizing a culinary educational service to guests through a "Chef's Corner" Web page on its Internet site.

College and University Food Service

The design and decor of on-site food service outlets in colleges and universities has also moved away from traditional cafeteria-style service to more modern service concepts adapted from commercial operations. The narrow, single-file, stainless-steel tray line has given way to kiosks, mobile carts, convenience stores, and open-area food courts with as many as 14 food stations.

A college or university food court may simulate a mall, marketplace, or plaza and generally consists of "storefront" food outlets that may include delicatessen, bakery, grill, and gourmet coffee concepts as well as nationally branded outlets such as Burger King, Chick-fil-A, and Panda Express. The addition of branded outlets in college and university food courts was made possible when national restaurant chains redesigned their traditional store units to make them smaller, reduce startup and operating costs, and take advantage of efficiencies brought about by new technology. Continuing advances have led some large universities to install several small food courts throughout their campuses. These operations are designed as separate kiosks along a counter, with service staff shifting as needed between kiosks; the entire system can be served by a single cashier.

In college or university dining areas that feature a **scramble system**, students do not wait for portions to be plated by staff members behind a serving line. Instead, they go directly to the food stations of their choice. These stations might include display cooking stations offering international food items; self-serve pasta stations; pizza, grill, and wok stations; and traditional salad bars, beverage stations, and dessert stations. Flexible designs and mobile food stations that can be reconfigured as menu offerings change maximize choice and convenience for students.

The design and decor of college and university dining areas have changed from the traditional rows of tables set in military style to a variety of seating options, with the dining area's decor matching the featured cuisines. For example, one university sets tables with red-and-white-checkered cloths and candles in empty wine bottles to give the dining area an Italian motif; this change in decor matched menu changes that included adding anchovies, olives, and grated cheeses to the salad bar and Italian dessert items to the dessert station. Some colleges and

Exhibit 8 Using the Internet to Personalize Service

Health Watch

Methodist Health Care System

Food and Nutrition Services

Chef's Corner

Winter / Spring, 1998

Welcome!

Let me share a chef's secret with you.....there is nothing new in cooking. While food writers, restaurant critics, food and wine enthusiasts, and even I may wax poetic about a great new restaurant, a fabulous chef (I write about one in each issue), an innovative cuisine or the hottest trends in food, it has all been done before in one form or another. A steak is still medium at 140 degrees, soft eggs take 4 minutes, water boils at 212°F .

We roast, grill, sauté, fry, blanch, bake, steam, braise. We slice, chop, mince, dice, julienne. Deglaze, reduce, puree, knead, fold. Proteins coagulate, sugars caramelize. Cooking, at a fundamental level, is very much a science and a craft. We, as chefs and cooks, may apply unique interpretations, combine ingredients in unusual ways, develop artistic presentations, but basic truisms always apply. Great ingredients, properly prepared, yield great food. The art of cooking requires a solid foundation in the fundamentals...the science.

I strongly encourage those of you with an interest in food and cooking to go beyond following a recipe to exploring the "whys" and "hows". Become comfortable with technique and you will be a better cook.

Among the books that immediately spring to mind are *La Methode* and *La Technique*, the two classics from Jacques Pepin, a great French chef and living legend. The great chefs in modern history were all French, Pierre-François de la Varenne, Jean-Anthelme Brillat-Savarin, Marie-Antoine Carême, Georges Auguste Escoffier, Ferdinand Point. And while I utilize and encourage the fusion of ingredients and techniques from a variety of

Here we are at the Winter season and comfort foods sound good. Don't they? Steak and potatoes. Spaghetti and meatballs. Red beans and rice. I hear the dietitians screaming, "What about the vegetables?" We'll cook some of those, too.

Thanks for reading my column.

For more information about the food services offered by the Methodist Health Care System, access other areas of the company's Internet site at http://www.methodisthealth.com.

Exhibit 9 Student Meal Plans and Prices at Brown University

Plan:	Annual:	Semester I:	Semester II:	Per Meal:	Points:
20	$2,622	$1,311	$1,311	$4.32	100 each semester
14	$2,468	$1,234	$1,234	$5.57	75 each semester
10	$2,240	$1,120	$1,120	$6.85	50 each semester
7	$2,044	$1,022	$1,022	$8.70	35 each semester
5	$1,098	$549	$549	$6.54	none

Kosher/Halal Plans:

Plan:	Annual:	Semester I:	Semester II:	Per Meal:	Points:
20	$3,122	$1,561	$1,561	$5.14	100 each semester
14	$2,968	$1,484	$1,484	$6.70	75 each semester

Prices per meal for those paying cash or using FlexPlus Points:

Breakfast	Lunch	Brunch	Dinner
$6.00	$8.55	$8.55	$9.95

Brown University's Internet site (http://www.brown.edu) offers more detailed information about food services offered to its students.

universities have implemented a sports-grill dining concept, with high bar-style tables and stools arranged near large-screen television sets mounted on the walls.

Flexible Meal Plans

In the past, board plans offered by many colleges and universities were designed to fit the needs of their on-site food service operations rather than the needs of students. Students were assigned to specific campus dining halls, and meal transfers to other food and beverage outlets on campus were discouraged by inconvenient, bureaucratic procedures. Also, all students housed in residence halls generally paid the same board fee for the same number of breakfasts, lunches, and dinners—regardless of how many meals they wanted or actually consumed. This "one-plan-fits-all" approach has given way to flexible meal plans that address the needs of students whose lifestyles and academic responsibilities may conflict with rigidly scheduled meal periods.

While meal plans vary among colleges and universities, many have elements similar to the meal plans offered by Brown University in Providence, Rhode Island. The meal plans shown in Exhibit 9 are defined by the total meals per week (20, 14, 10, 7, or 5). The annual fee for each plan is shown, as well as semester breakdowns and the average price per meal. The 20-meal plan includes 3 meals each day, Monday through Saturday, and 2 meals on Sunday. Meals not used on a given day are not carried over to the next day. The 14-, 10-, and 7-meal plans set a number of meals per week, not per day, and meals not used in a given week are not carried over to the next week. The 5-meal plan applies only to breakfasts and lunches, not dinners or snacks. The Kosher and Halal meal plans serve Jewish and Muslim students who wish to follow the dietary laws of their faiths. Generally, these special dietary needs are met at a designated dining hall on campus.

In response to the demanding class and study schedules of students, many colleges and universities have implemented express breakfast bars, "grab-and-go" meals, and sack lunches and dinners at their residence halls. At some institutions, students phone a day in advance to order a prepared take-out meal; at others, students simply pack their own meals at designated self-service lines at food outlets.

Focusing food services on the needs of students and making the services more flexible have enabled many colleges and universities to increase their overall food revenues by marketing special meal plans to off-campus students. As shown in Exhibit 10, Colorado State University's residence hall food services department has developed an Internet site targeting students living off campus.

Serving Policies

Most college and university meal plans have "all-you-can-eat" policies for food served at dining halls. Lunches and dinners usually include a selection of three to four entrées, with access to dessert bars, salad bars, and fresh fruit baskets. When service is cafeteria style, students can enter the serving line as often as they like. When using a dining hall meal credit at a snack bar or branded food court, students are generally limited to a specific dollar value for the meal items they select. At some colleges and universities, serving policies are explained on their housing or food services Internet sites.

Menu Planning

The differences in menu planning between on-site college and university food service operations and freestanding commercial restaurants emerge from the different needs and expectations of their guests. A loyal, repeat guest may dine at a freestanding restaurant as many as four or five times over a 30-day period. At each visit, the guest expects the same basic menu offerings. Daily specials are welcome, but the basic menu is a strong part of the attraction the restaurant has for the repeat guest. In contrast, a student with a full meal plan might dine at the residence hall more than 60 times a month. The last thing the student wants are the same basic menu offerings, over and over again. This is why many on-site food service operations at colleges and universities use cycle menus.

A **cycle menu** changes every day for a certain number of days, then repeats the cycle. Cycle menus vary; many are designed for 6-, 5-, or 4-week periods (the trend is toward shorter menu cycles). The frequency of menu changes challenges on-site college and university food service operations to develop a number of ways to communicate each day's menu to guests. Colleges and universities generally post menus near the entrances to campus dining halls. Some food service

Exhibit 10 Marketing Off-Campus Student Meal Plans

Off-Campus Student Meal Plans

Meal plans for students not living in residence halls.

Students Make Your Lives Easier!

Colorado State Residence Hall Food Services can provide you with easy, convenient and nutritional meal plans. Start enjoying "Great Deals In Meals."

"No shopping, cooking, or clean up"

Unlimited servings are available on most entrees. Beverages, salads, specialty bars, and desserts are all unlimited. All this makes residence hall dining the best value you can find. *Plus, you can choose to eat in any residence hall dining center for each meal.*

Enjoy a variety of special events throughout the semester - banquets, theme nights, brunches, ice cream socials are all included in the price of any meal plan. Also available are "branded concepts" featuring Stone Willy's Pizza Shoppe, Pasta al' Strada, Light & Lean Bar, and The Grill.

Students can sign up anytime during the semester and charges will be prorated from the starting date of the student's meal services. Meal Plans can be charged to your Student Account.

Convenience

- For each meal, students can choose the most convenient dining hall at that time.
- Meal hours are scheduled to accommodate students' needs and are structured around most class schedules.
- Time conflicts with meal schedules are no problem - Just fix your own sack lunch and/or dinner, at breakfast time, through the sack meals bar or use the convenient "Grab 'n Go" at any meal.
- Save up to 20 hours out of your busy week because you will not be using the time for planning and preparing meals.
- Eliminate roommate hassles about what food to buy, how to divide it up, or who has to clean the kitchen.
- Don't worry about what to cook or where to eat, plus have more free time for fun activities.
- Also there are 20 Shared Interest Living Programs where students live with others sharing the same major or having common interests. These halls are fun places to eat with your fellow classmates or those having similar interests.

Colorado State University's Internet site (http://lamar.colostate.edu) offers more detailed information about food services offered to its students.

programs put their entire cycle menu on a Web page through the school's Internet site. Others provide a "dial-a-menu" service, enabling students to learn about the day's menu offerings by dialing a telephone number and listening to a recorded message.

Web pages and email through the college's or university's computer network are fast becoming popular ways for directors of food service operations to communicate directly with students. Directors can use these new communication channels to explain to students the cost-based pricing system of meal plans, gather feedback to improve service, and monitor students' acceptance of newly introduced menu items.

Encouraging Healthy Food Choices

Most colleges and universities offer meatless options on their cycle menus; many offer vegetarian menu choices at every meal period. Vegetarian options are becoming popular in the college and university environment, where learning new things and sampling new experiences are embraced and encouraged.

Healthy food trends in colleges and universities extend beyond vegetarian menu choices. Reduced-calorie and reduced-fat menu options are often available at each meal. Many campus food service operations promote healthy choices on their menus and educate students on the basics of nutrition. Food guide pyramids, such as the one shown in Exhibit 11, appear on the Web sites of many college and university food service operations. Managers of the food service program at Stanford University distribute booklets to students that feature explanations of the basic nutritional guidelines of the American Dietetic Association and the American Heart Association. The university also displays nutritional analyses on cards in front of items in dining-area food stations.

Smart Card and Debit Card Technology

Technological advances such as the **smart card** enable colleges and universities to manage the flexibility of their multiple meal plans. The computer chip embedded within a smart card can store large amounts of data. This enables colleges and universities to exercise control over a wide range of activities and transactions such as accessing buildings, tracking meal plan credits, and processing cashless purchases. Smart card technology not only improves services but also offers a new level of safety and convenience for students and the entire campus community.

The smart card at Brown University (shown in Exhibit 12) also functions as a **debit card**. Debit cards differ from credit cards in that the cardholder must establish value by depositing money in a personal account managed by a debit card center. At Brown University, students may deposit up to $2,000 into a declining balance account and use the card to make food purchases at any of the university's food service outlets. Up to $20 a day can be transferred from the debit card balance to the card's vending stripe. The vending stripe is used to pay for the use of on-campus vending machines, laundry machines, photocopy machines, and other point-of-sale services. The cash value of the vending stripe is limited to a maximum of $50 because if the card is lost, stolen, or damaged, the cash value is lost and is not refundable. Given the card's convenience and incredible number of uses, a maximum risk factor of $50 seems reasonable in exchange for the safety and security of cashless purchases.

While commercial food service operations have been cautious and slow in accepting smart card and debit card technology, colleges and universities have generally embraced it and are pioneering its possibilities. A smart-card system proposed at Pennsylvania State University will allow students to load their

Exhibit 11 Educating Students on Nutrition Basics

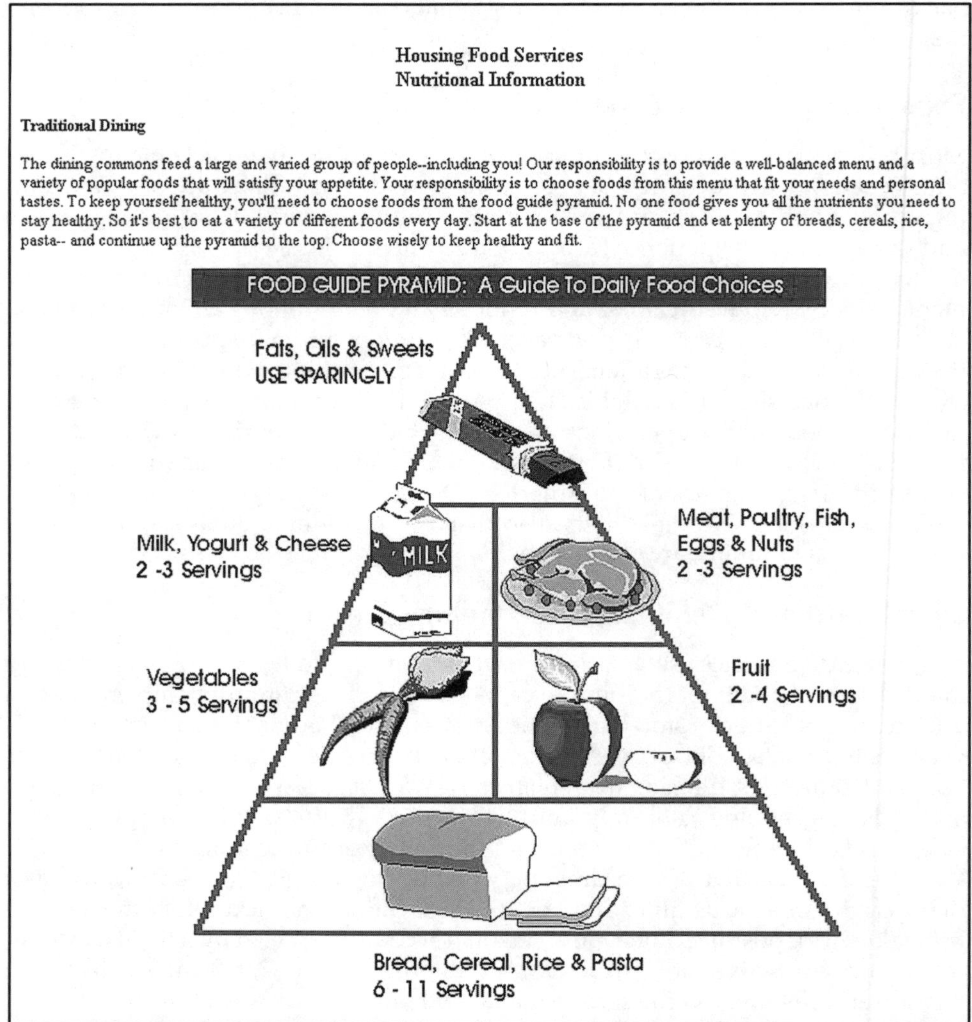

Housing Food Services
Nutritional Information

Traditional Dining

The dining commons feed a large and varied group of people--including you! Our responsibility is to provide a well-balanced menu and a variety of popular foods that will satisfy your appetite. Your responsibility is to choose foods from this menu that fit your needs and personal tastes. To keep yourself healthy, you'll need to choose foods from the food guide pyramid. No one food gives you all the nutrients you need to stay healthy. So it's best to eat a variety of different foods every day. Start at the base of the pyramid and eat plenty of breads, cereals, rice, pasta-- and continue up the pyramid to the top. Choose wisely to keep healthy and fit.

Ohio State University's Internet site (http://www-foodservice.rdh.ohio-state.edu) uses the food guide pyramid to educate students on the benefits of a well-balanced diet and encourages them to make healthy choices.

student identification cards with funds from any financial institution they choose. This eliminates the need for students to set up a debit account through the school and enables them to use automated teller machines (ATMs) to transfer funds from checking accounts at their own banks to the embedded computer chip on their university identification cards. The cards can be used in lieu of cash or checks to make purchases at on-campus and some off-campus retailers, as well as at campus vending machines, coin-operated laundries, and food service outlets.

Exhibit 12 Smart Card Technology

The information on the front of the Brown Card includes: name, photograph, ID and ISO numbers and barcode.

The barcode provides identification for admittance to and use of Brown University Libraries and also for charge account transactions at the Brown Bookstore.

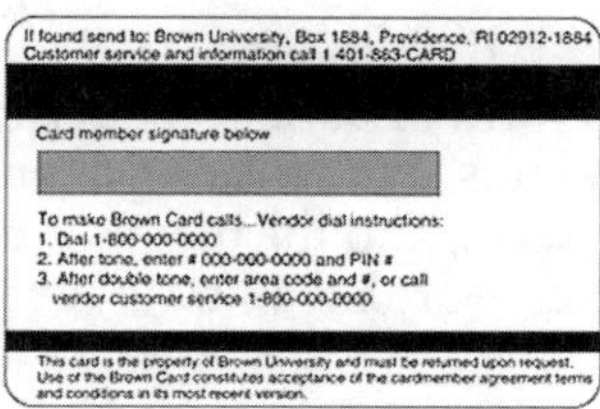

The information on the back of the Brown Card includes: signature line (sign immediately), a wide magnetic access stripe, a thin magnetic vending stripe, and also AT&T long distance calling card option information.

The wide access stripe allows users access to restricted buildings (e.g., residence hall, labs, parking, etc.), to University Food Services (UFS) meal plans, Flex-Plus, and the declining balance account for food purchases at UFS dining halls and purchases at the Brown Bookstore and Computer Store.

The thin vending stripe is used for campus vending, laundry machines, snack machines, BEU machines, and self-serve copier purchases at Brown's libraries and copy centers.

The AT&T long distance calling feature is provided as a user option.

For more information about how the smart card is used at Brown University, access the school's Internet site at http://www.brown.edu.

Key Terms

contract management company—An independent food service company contracted to manage on-site food services (and possibly other services) within a host organization.

cycle menu—A menu that changes every day for a certain number of days, then repeats the cycle.

debit card—Plastic and similar in size to a credit card, a debit card requires the cardholder to deposit money at a debit card center in advance of purchases; as purchases are made, the balance on the debit card falls.

host organization—A business or other organization that operates, or hires a contract management company to operate, an on-site food service facility for use by staff members, managers, visitors, and others.

on-site food service operations—Food service facilities that operate within larger host organizations whose primary businesses are not that of providing food and beverage services.

scramble system—An open food service area with multiple food stations that presents an alternative to the single-file serving line of traditional cafeteria service. Also called a scramble servery system or scatter system.

self-operated food services—On-site food service operations whose managers and staff members are employed by the host organization.

smart card—Plastic and similar in size to a credit card, a smart card contains a computer chip capable of storing and transferring large amounts of data. Smart cards are used to control a wide range of activities and transactions, from accessing buildings to processing cashless purchases.

tray service—The traditional form of patient food service in health care organizations. Typically, a printed menu is sent to each patient the day before service; patients indicate the items they want, and the menus are returned to the kitchen. The next day, staff members assemble orders on trays, group the trays by floor or unit, and deliver them to patients.

Review Questions

1. What are the major market segments of the on-site food service industry?
2. How do self-operated on-site food service facilities differ from on-site operations run by contract management companies?
3. How can on-site food service operations in the business and industry segment reduce the subsidies they receive from their host organizations?
4. How are health care on-site food service operations becoming more like commercial food service operations?
5. How are some health care organizations changing the tray service they provide to patients?
6. What are some examples of flexible meal plans that colleges and universities are providing to students?
7. What are smart cards? debit cards?

Internet Sites

For more information, visit the following Internet sites. Remember that Internet addresses can change without notice.

Associations

American Dietetic Association
http://www.eatright.org

American School Food Service Association (ASFSA)
http://www.asfsa.org

National Association of College and University Food Services (NACUFS)
http://www.nacufs.org

National Society for Healthcare Foodservice Management (HFM)
http://www.hfm.org

Society for Foodservice Management (SFM)
http://www.sfm-online.org

Contract Management Companies

ARAMARK Managed Services
http://www.aramark.com

Bon Appétit Management Company
http://www.bamco.com

Compass Group
http://www.compass-group.com

HDS Services
http://www.hdsservices.com

Sodexho Marriott Services
http://sodexhomarriott.com

The Wood Company
http://www.woodco.com

Health Care Food Service

Boone Hospital Center
http://www.boone.org/cafeteria.html

Children's Hospital Boston
http://web1.tch.harvard.edu/services/resources/food.html

Hospitality & Tourism Global Forum
http://www.mcb.co.uk/htgf

Methodist Health Care System
http://www.methodisthealth.com/health/nutrition/food

College and University Food Service

California Polytechnic State University
http://www.fdn.calpoly.edu/dining/

Michigan State University
http://www.hfs.msu.edu/food

Purdue University
http://www.adpc.purdue.edu/HFS/

Stanford University
http://www-leland.stanford.edu/dept/hds/dining

Texas Tech University
http://www.texastech.edu/housing/

University of Delaware
http://www.udel.edu/dining

The University of Houston
http://www.uh.edu/admin/housing/dining

University of Notre Dame
http://www.nd.edu/~ndfood

Appendix

Model Job Descriptions for Selected Positions in On-Site Food Service Operations

The job descriptions presented in this section are for illustrative purposes only and should not be construed as recommendations or standards. While these job descriptions are typical, readers should keep in mind that each food service facility has its own procedures and ways of dividing up job responsibilities.

JOB DESCRIPTION

POSITION TITLE: **COUNTER PERSON**

REPORTS TO: **Counter Supervisor**

POSITION SUMMARY: Performs a variety of duties relating to cafeteria-style service including greeting and serving customers, cold food preparation, stocking counters and steam table, and maintaining sanitation standards. Responsible customer service is a major component of this position.

DUTIES AND RESPONSIBILITIES:

1. Stocks counters, display refrigerators, salad bar, and steam table neatly, accurately, and timely as per menu.
2. Checks to insure that all display foods are merchandised attractively as per standards.
3. Displays food under appropriate hot or cold conditions as per standards.
4. Completes cold food preparation assignment neatly, accurately, and timely.
5. Handles cold food items appropriately during preparation.
6. Maintains appropriate portion control and merchandising standards when preparing cold food items.
7. Maintains proper food handling, safety and sanitation standards while preparing food, serving food, and clean-up.
8. Keeps display equipment clean and free of debris during meal service, as assigned.
9. Cleans tables and chairs, as assigned, by the start of each meal period. Arranges same as per diagram. Always checks for salt, pepper, and napkins, and stocks accordingly.
10. Cleans up spills during meal service immediately.
11. Cleans equipment, as assigned, thoroughly and timely.
12. Keeps floor in work or service area clean and free of debris.
13. Cleans work station thoroughly before leaving area for other assignment.
14. Greets customers courteously.
15. Handles customers swiftly. Does not allow for back-ups or snags in cafeteria line.
16. Consistently exhibits the ability to keep up with peak cafeteria hours and does so calmly, accurately, and efficiently.
17. Serves appropriate portion sizes as per standards.
18. Exhibits a cheerful and helpful manner when dealing with customers.
19. Demonstrates a complete understanding of daily menu items and explains same to customers accurately.
20. Serves food neatly and attractively as per standards.
21. Informs cook in a timely manner when food quantities are low.

(continued)

COUNTER PERSON *(continued)*

22. Maintains professional appearance at all times, clean and well-groomed as per standards.
23. Demonstrates complete understanding of department policies and procedures.
24. Exhibits outstanding attendance and punctuality and takes corrective action to prevent recurring absences.
25. Displays a positive and enthusiastic approach to all assignments.
26. Develops a positive working relationship with department and organization staff and avoids conflict.
27. Relays relevant comments received from customers directly to supervisor.
28. Views, as required, safety and risk management films and reviews fire safety and disaster plans.
29. Completes shift work, as assigned, timely and thoroughly in accordance with department standards.

PREREQUISITES:

Education: High school diploma or equivalent.

Experience: Demonstrated ability to understand and implement written and verbal instructions.

Physical: Position requires bending, standing, and walking the entire work day. Must be able to lift full pans, not to exceed 25 pounds. Light cleaning duties such as wiping tables and small equipment, sweeping and refilling stock. Must be able to speak clearly and listen attentively to guests and other staff members.

JOB DESCRIPTION

POSITION TITLE: COUNTER SERVER

REPORTS TO: Shift Manager

POSITION SUMMARY: Responsible for providing quick and efficient service to customers. Greets customers, takes their food and beverage orders, rings orders into register, and prepares and serves hot and cold drinks. Assemble food and beverage orders, checks them for completeness and accuracy and packages orders for on-premise or take-out. Collects payment from guest and makes change. Maintains cleanliness of counters and floors at all times.

DUTIES AND RESPONSIBILITIES:

1. Checks supplies in counter area and restocks items to ensure a sufficient supply throughout the shift.
2. Wipes off front counter with cleaning solution and a clean cloth. Keeps counter and floor clean at all times.
3. Greets customers and takes their orders. May give orders to cook or punch keys of register which records the order and computes the amount of the bill.
4. Serves drinks from dispensing machines or makes and serves hot drinks from water heat or coffee maker. Puts lid on drinks and places on tray with liner or in take-out container.
5. Picks up food items from serving bar or storage area. Places items on tray or in take-out containers. Checks orders to ensure that guest is receiving a complete and correct order.
6. Informs kitchen staff of shortages or special requests.
7. Collects payment from guest and makes change.

PREREQUISITES:

Education: Some high school. Must be able to perform simple mathematical calculations. Must be able to speak, read, write, and understand the primary language(s) used by guests who typically visit the work location.

Experience: Previous foodservice experience not required.

Physical: Must be able to stand and quickly walk for periods of up to four (4) hours in length and have the ability to bend and lift up to 10 pounds frequently. Must be able to speak clearly and listen attentively to guests and other staff members.

JOB DESCRIPTION

POSITION TITLE: COUNTER SUPERVISOR

REPORTS TO: Manager

POSITION SUMMARY: The Counter Supervisor directly supervises the daily operation of a specified unit and insures that daily schedules of activity and established quality standards are maintained. This includes the coordination of the individual and collective efforts of assigned staff.

DUTIES AND RESPONSIBILITIES:

1. Demonstrates complete understanding of departmental requirements and interprets their intent accurately to staff members.
2. Monitors daily performance of staff and ensures compliance with established timetables.
3. Monitors quality of products and services produced by staff and insures compliance with established standards.
4. Monitors sanitation and food-handling practices of assigned unit and insures staff compliance with established standards.
5. Routinely inspects areas of assigned responsibility and reports all substandard safety, security, or equipment conditions to Manager as observed by Manager.
6. Consistently monitors standards and makes recommendations for change as observed by Manager.
7. Supervises staff in a consistently fair and firm manner. Maintains steady productivity through close observation. Provides direction when necessary.
8. Schedules staff for assigned unit within daily F.T.E. allocation and projected workload.
9. Adjusts daily schedule and shifts personnel to complete essential duties when the need arises.
10. Coordinates work of staff to promote efficiency of operations
11. Consistently recommends actions necessary for staff discipline, terminations, promotions, etc.
12. Trains staff, as assigned, and assists with orientation of new staff members in a timely and efficient manner.
13. Schedules staff member time off so as not to interfere with heavy workload periods.
14. Monitors staff member attendance and notices all absence patterns and brings to the attention of management all relevant findings.
15. Monitors customer traffic and makes appropriate adjustments to decrease waiting time.
16. Monitors customer buying trends and makes relevant recommendations for product additions and deletions.
17. Accurately inventories supplies daily and requisitions items needed to meet par levels.

COUNTER SUPERVISOR *(continued)*

18. Ensures that supplies are utilized properly and cost-effectively as per standards.
19. Reports changes in menus or items substitutions to Managers.
20. Insures that all food and supplies are stored and/or maintained under proper conditions as per standards.
21. Monitors food and supply quality and makes relevant recommendations for product utilization.
22. Inspects all unit storage facilities each day so that proper temperatures and conditions are maintained, food is covered, labeled, and dated.
23. Completes counter supervisor reports in an accurate and timely manner.
24. Completes staff member appraisals in a timely fashion.
25. Keeps immediate supervisor informed of all relevant information including any diversions from normal activity, any substandard condition, personnel matters, etc.
26. Meets routinely with assigned staff to relay relevant information and encourage suggestions for service and/or quality improvements.
27. Works effectively and efficiently with other department supervisors and consistently demonstrates the ability to solve problems at this level.
28. Analyzes relevant data to make informed decisions compatible with department philosophy.
29. Treats staff with courtesy, respect, and empathy and displays good listening skills.
30. Displays team-building skills and always handles all assignments with a positive and enthusiastic attitude.
31. Maintains professional appearance as per standards.

PREREQUISITES:

Education: High school diploma or equivalent.

Experience: A minimum of two years as a counter server or equivalent position.

Physical: Position requires walking and giving direction most of the working day. May be required to push heavy food carts. May be required to lift trays of food or food items weighing up to 30 pounds.

JOB DESCRIPTION

POSITION TITLE: DIETITIAN

REPORTS TO: Administrator/Director of Dietary Department

POSITION SUMMARY: Provides consultation, guidance, direction, and support to Dietary Department Head in planning in the areas of clinical nutrition and food-service management. Provides information to promote quality food service and resident/patient nutritional care.

DUTIES AND RESPONSIBILITIES:

1. Participates in nutritional assessments, resident care conferences, discharge planning, and diet consultation.
2. Assists in determining policies for therapeutic nutrition and implementing nutritional care.
3. Assists Director in developing dietary policies and procedures.
4. May assist Director with budget development.
5. Assists Director in promoting work efficiency.
6. May assist in planning, remodeling, or new kitchen development.
7. May assist in new equipment selection and purchase.
8. Assists Director in promoting cost control in the department.
9. Assists Director in developing needed forms, schedules, checklists, and quality assurance forms to meet department objectives.
10. Assists Director in menu development and writing therapeutic diets.
11. Assists Director in development of standardized recipes and food preparation procedures to obtain quality food production.
12. Assists Director in developing a quality assurance program.
13. Evaluates audit findings and makes recommendations for change as appropriate.
14. Ensures that the department adheres to current regulations.

PREREQUISITES:

Education: College graduate in foods and nutrition or related field. Must be able to speak, read, write, and understand the primary language(s) of the work location. Must be sufficiently ambulatory and dexterous to move directly between and among the various areas of the kitchen and storage facilities, and to visit with patients, clients throughout the facility. Must be a registered dietitian.

Experience: Must have sound knowledge of the operations of a dietary department. Must understand LTC/hospital regulations. Minimum three years experience in LTC/hospital setting.

Physical: Some lifting of food cases and other forms of packaging may be required on occasion.

JOB DESCRIPTION

POSITION TITLE: DIRECTOR OF DIETARY DEPARTMENT

REPORTS TO: Administrator

POSITION SUMMARY: Provides overall management of the Dietary Department to ensure quality food and nutritional services to clients.

DUTIES AND RESPONSIBILITIES:

1. Responsible for overseeing purchasing, production, and service of food in a timely manner.
2. Responsible for departmental policy formulation and adherence and for procedure development.
3. Purchases supplies and equipment.
4. Directs the receipt, storage, and distribution of food products.
5. Responsible for establishing and maintaining departmental budget.
6. Maintains records to meet the needs of the department.
7. Hires, orients, trains, evaluates, disciplines, and terminates dietary department employees.
8. Develops and maintains work schedules.
9. Participates in department head meetings and other facility meetings as required.
10. Maintains security in the department.
11. Ensures that department is in compliance with all applicable federal and state regulations.
12. Coordinates dietary services with all other departments.
13. Maintains appropriate records of dietary staff members.
14. Orders food and supplies for the department.
15. Maintains inventory.
16. Monitors food preparation to ensure quality.
17. Maintains standardized recipe file and ensures guidelines are followed.
18. Develops menus with the assistance of the dietitian(s).
19. Ensures that food tray assembly is accurate.
20. Monitors entire therapeutic nutrition system to ensure optimum nutrition is obtained for all clients.
21. May interview new patient admissions. Charts in the medical record.
22. Attends client care conferences.
23. Processes diet orders to ensure the physician's directions are being carried through.
24. Periodically audits diet orders for accuracy.

(continued)

DIRECTOR OF DIETARY DEPARTMENT *(continued)*

25. May monitor food intake of residents. Addresses problems with dietitian and/or nursing services.
26. Monitors sanitation/safety standards in the department.
27. Complies with facility policies.
28. Conducts in-service training classes.
29. Conducts periodic dietary staff meetings.
30. Works to meet the goals of the facility with enthusiasm and a spirit of cooperation.

PREREQUISITES:

Education: Completion of a dietary manager training program required. Must be able to speak, read, write, and understand the primary language(s) of the work location. CDM preferred.

Experience: Must have good understanding of dietary management, quality food production, and therapeutic nutrition. Must possess leadership attributes coupled with administrative skills as demonstrated in prior positions.

Physical: Must be in good physical and mental health due to the multiple demands associated with the position.

JOB DESCRIPTION

POSITION TITLE: DIRECTOR, DINING SERVICES

REPORTS TO: Executive Director, Campus Hospitality Services

POSITION SUMMARY: Directs the foodservice operations and related activities that include multiple fine dining locations, the campus club, a snack bar, and catering.

DUTIES AND RESPONSIBILITIES:

1. Manages and directs the departmental staff consisting of both student and part-time workers.
2. Establishes policies and objective for Dining Services. Informs and discusses with managers and staff any changes in policy.
3. Responsible for staff and labor relations including the training and development of all staff members.
4. Collaborates with the Business Manager in determining the correct pricing of the daily bill of fare and board rates for meal contracts.
5. Plans and administers the Dining Service budgets.
6. Oversees the facilities maintenance and new construction programs.
7. Approves all expenditures for equipment.
8. Reviews all monthly, quarterly, and annual operating statements for each Dining Service unit with the Business Manager.
9. Formulates, administers, and oversees the planning of all capital projects.
10. Develops and implements all marketing programs.
11. Acts as a liaison with all student organizations.
12. Meets with student customers on a daily basis.
13. Meets with the union president every other week.
14. Acts as a hearing officer of all second-level union grievances.
15. Considers recommendations of the Labor/Management and Health/Safety committees.
16. Participates directly in union negotiations.
17. Schedules management staff to ensure proper coverage during downtimes and at catering functions.
18. Directs the proper implementation of in-house catering in all dining service units.
19. Responsible for the final pricing of all catering functions.
20. Formulates and implements any policy that affects the student worker program via the student General Manager and professional Unit Manager.
21. Ensures compliance with environmental laws including recycling, garbage disposal, and source reduction.

(continued)

DIRECTOR, DINING SERVICES *(continued)*

22. Conducts weekly management meetings.
23. Attends seminars and actively participates in professional organizations.

PREREQUISITES:

Education: Bachelor's degree from a hotel and restaurant school or a degree in business administration desired. Must be able to speak, read, write, and understand the primary language(s) of the work location.

Experience: Five years' experience in a large, multi-unit diversified university dining service operation, embracing budget/financial planning, production, marketing, purchasing, catering, and staff supervision responsibilities. A working knowledge of computer systems, construction projects, and collective bargaining agreements is required.

Physical: Must be able to maintain a rigorous 50- to 70-hour workweek. Some travel involved. On location, must be able to traverse a large campus area pursuant to daily and weekly supervisory responsibilities.

JOB DESCRIPTION

POSITION TITLE: FOODSERVICE DIRECTOR (HEALTH CARE)

REPORTS TO: Administrator/CEO

POSITION SUMMARY: Directs the delivery of professional food services which will be a material factor in producing cost-effective, positive financial and customer satisfaction results and a positive public image.

DUTIES AND RESPONSIBILITIES:

1. In conjunction with supervisory staff, develops systems and procedures for each departmental operation.
2. Investigates new methodology in health care and commercial foodservice delivery.
3. Maintains productivity data.
4. Makes regular reports on operations to organizational superior with recommendations for improvements as appropriate.
5. Jointly with superior and with input from staff, develops annual budgets for several cost centers, including coffee shop, cafeteria, patient services, and vending.
6. Analyzes and monitors cost and revenue budgets on an ongoing basis.
7. Makes necessary operational adjustments throughout the year to assure conformance with policy, procedures, and practices.
8. Keeps assistant and supervisors informed about budget performance. Solicits suggestions.
9. Investigates and recommends methodological and labor improvements to contain/reduce costs and increase income.
10. Interviews vendors, reviews bids, authorizes and monitors numerous supply and services contracts.
11. Helps determine specifications for and amounts of supplies and equipment needed for operations. Approves requisitions.
12. Appropriately utilizes expertise of others in the hospital such as Human Resources, Business Office.
13. Maintains records as required by hospital and outside agencies.
14. As requested, participates in planning for improvements in systems, services, physical facilities, new programs, cost containment, increasing revenue, etc.
15. Develops short- and long-range plans for the department, utilizes various resources such as internal research, hospital, and outside area.
16. Prepares written goals and objectives for entire department. Translates these into action plans for self and subordinate managers.
17. Prepares statistical forecasts for food and labor costs, catering sales and scheduling, etc.

(continued)

FOODSERVICE DIRECTOR (HEALTH CARE) *(continued)*

18. On an ongoing basis, evaluates departmental and subordinate performance against established standards, goals, and objectives.
19. Develops and/or uses a variety of measurements to determine performance effectiveness, from statistics to input from the department and the company.
20. Directs the work of the entire department, through intermediate supervisors.
21. Interviews, selects, counsels, appraises performance, disciplines, and recommends salary and other personnel actions.
22. Prepares and oversees maintenance of confidential personnel records.
23. Seeks assistance to improve staffing/productivity, morale, and other aspects of staff member relations as appropriate from others in the company.
24. Assures that job descriptions and performance standards for each subordinate position are always current, complete, and properly utilized.
25. Supervises departmental education activities, including initial orientation and skills training for staff, students, and volunteers.
26. Assures that regular departmental meetings for entire staff are held to communicate plans, programs, and policies; to teach; to resolve problems; and to seek suggestions for improvements.
27. With individual subordinate supervisors, identifies development needs and counsels on personal development plans.
28. Makes recommendations to and works with company educators in design/support of programs.
29. Except as limited by policy, serves as spokesperson on departmental matters to community groups, vendors, government and health care agencies, and the press.
30. Represents the department in handling important inquiries or complaints from the public or refers these to others such as department assistants.
31. Develops brochures and other written materials about the department for public use.
32. Directs, plans, and coordinates food services for parties, banquets, socials, seminar meals, fundraisers, etc.
33. Coordinates services with those offered by other departments.
34. Participates in interdisciplinary task forces, in department head meetings, and similar joint activities.
35. Confers with other department heads regarding technical and administrative problems of nutrition services.
36. Deals with serious complaints from other departments. Clarifies issues, negotiates agreements.
37. Provides technical guidance and administrative direction over menu planning and the preparation and service of all food.

FOODSERVICE DIRECTOR (HEALTH CARE) *(continued)*

38. In health care situations: Reviews regular diet manuals as to costs and suitability. Standardizes recipes for menu requirements. Reviews therapeutic menus to ascertain conformance to prescription.
39. Makes frequent inspections of all work, storage, serving, and administrative areas to determine that regulations and directions governing handling and storing of supplies and equipment, methods of sanitation, maintenance of records, compilation of reports, and adherence standards are followed.
40. Reviews records and reports regarding costs of raw food; computation of daily food costs; inventory of equipment, food, and supplies; types of storage facilities available; patient and cafeteria menus; cafeteria sales reports and pricing; and various staff member time and cost records.
41. Oversees the selling, planning, pricing, and coordinating of all catering.
42. Visits customers and discusses and solves problems.

PREREQUISITES:

Education: Bachelor's degree in foodservice management, food & nutrition, business management, or related degree desired.

Experience: A minimum of 5 years in the hospitality industry in increasingly responsible foodservice supervisory positions.

Physical: Subject to wet floors, temperature extremes, and excessive noise. Position frequently involves long hours and widely diverse duties. Must be able to bend, stoop, and perform extensive walking. Must be able to move quickly to the different areas of the facility as demands require.

REVIEW QUIZ

When you feel you have covered all of the material in this chapter, answer these questions. Choose the *best* answer.

1. The business and industry segment of the on-site food service industry includes:

   a. manufacturing and industrial plants, office complexes, financial institutions, and government agencies.
   b. day care centers as well as elementary and secondary schools.
   c. sports stadiums, convention centers, recreational facilities, and park systems.
   d. a and c.

2. Contract management companies have captured more than _________ percent of the business and industry food service market.

   a. 25
   b. 48
   c. 75
   d. 80

3. On-site food service operations in the business and industry segment can reduce the subsidies they receive from their host organizations by:

   a. increasing the size of their dining areas.
   b. pursuing new sources of revenue outside their host organizations.
   c. offering fewer self-service options to guests.
   d. dramatically increasing the number of menu items they offer guests.

4. With a traditional hospital tray system, most patients:

   a. have no choice in what they eat.
   b. place their order with a nurse or orderly just before the meal is served.
   c. circle menu items on a printed menu, turn in the menus, and receive the items the next day.
   d. must eat in the hospital cafeteria.

REVIEW QUIZ *(continued)*

5. Many college and university food service operations put "food guide pyramids" on their Internet sites to:

   a. advertise their products and services.
   b. encourage students to think about nutrition when making choices about what to eat.
   c. communicate each day's cycle-menu choices to students; some operations publish their entire cycle menu on the pyramid.
   d. allow students to vote on which items they prefer to see on the menus of residence hall dining areas.

Answer Key: 1-a-C1, 2-d-C1, 3-b-C1, 4-c-C2, 5-b-C2

Each question is linked to a competency. Competencies are listed on the first page of the chapter. An answer reading 3-b-C4 translates to:

3: the question number
b: the correct answer
C4: the competency number

Index

A

B

C

G

H

I

J–L

M